Sociology

Readings

Eleventh Edition

Sara Miller McCune founded SAGE Publishing in 1965 to support the dissemination of usable knowledge and educate a global community. SAGE publishes more than 1,000 journals and over 800 new books each year, spanning a wide range of subject areas. Our growing selection of library products includes archives, data, case studies, and video. SAGE remains majority owned by our founder and after her lifetime will become owned by a charitable trust that secures the company's continued independence.

Los Angeles | London | New Delhi | Singapore | Washington DC | Melbourne

Sociology

Exploring the Architecture of Everyday Life

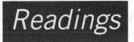

Readings

Eleventh Edition

Editors

David M. Newman
DePauw University

Jodi O'Brien
Seattle University

Michelle Robertson
St. Edward's University

Los Angeles | London | New Delhi
Singapore | Washington DC | Melbourne

FOR INFORMATION:

SAGE Publications, Inc.
2455 Teller Road
Thousand Oaks, California 91320
E-mail: order@sagepub.com

SAGE Publications Ltd.
1 Oliver's Yard
55 City Road
London EC1Y 1SP
United Kingdom

SAGE Publications India Pvt. Ltd.
B 1/I 1 Mohan Cooperative Industrial Area
Mathura Road, New Delhi 110 044
India

SAGE Publications Asia-Pacific Pte. Ltd.
18 Cross Street #10-10/11/12
China Square Central
Singapore 048423

Printed in the United States of America

Library of Congress Cataloging-in-Publication Data

Names: Newman, David M., editor. | O'Brien, Jodi, editor. | Robertson, Michelle, editor.

Title: Sociology, exploring the architecture of everyday life : readings / editors, David M. Newman, DePauw University, Jodi O'Brien, Seattle University, Michelle Robertson, St. Edward's University.

Description: Eleventh edition. | Thousand Oaks, California : SAGE, [2019] | Includes bibliographical references.

Identifiers: LCCN 2018030608 | ISBN 9781506350219 (pbk. : alk. paper)

Subjects: LCSH: Sociology.

Classification: LCC HM586 .S64 2019 | DDC 301—dc23 LC record available at https://lccn.loc.gov/2018030608

This book is printed on acid-free paper.

Acquisitions Editor: Jeff Lasser
Editorial Assistant: Tiara Beatty
Production Editor: Jane Martinez
Copy Editor: Lynne Curry
Typesetter: Hurix Digital
Proofreader: Dennis Webb
Cover Designer: Candice Harman
Marketing Manager: Kara Kindstrom

18 19 20 21 22 10 9 8 7 6 5 4 3 2 1

Contents

Preface

One of the greatest challenges we face as teachers of sociology is getting our students to see the relevance of the course material to their own lives and to fully appreciate its connection to the larger society. We teach our students to see that sociology is all around us. It's in our families, our careers, our media, our jobs, our classrooms, our goals, our interests, our desires, and even our minds. Sociology can be found at the neighborhood pub, in conversation with the clerk at 7-Eleven, on a date, and in the highest offices of government. It's with us when we're alone and when we're in a group of people. Sociology focuses on questions of global significance as well as private concerns. For instance, sociologists study how some countries create and maintain dominance over others and also why we find some people more attractive than others. Sociology is an invitation to understand yourself within the context of your historical and cultural circumstances.

We have compiled this collection of short articles, chapters, and excerpts with the intent of providing comprehensive examples of the power of sociology for helping us to make sense of our lives and our times. The readings are organized in a format that demonstrates

- the uniqueness of the sociological perspective

- tools of sociological analysis

- the significance of different cultures in a global world

- social factors that influence identity development and self-management

- social rules about family, relationships, and belonging

- the influence of social institutions and organizations on everyday life

- the significance of socioeconomic class, gender, and racial/ethnic backgrounds in everyday life

- the significance of social demographics, such as aging populations and migration, and

- the power of social groups and social change.

In general, our intent is to demonstrate the significance of sociology in everyday life and to show that what seems obvious is often not so obvious when subjected to rigorous sociological analysis. The metaphor of "architecture" used in the title for this reader illustrates the sociological idea that as social beings, we are constantly building and rebuilding our own social environment. The sociological promise is that if we understand these processes and how they affect us, we will be able to make more informed choices about how to live our lives and engage in our communities.

As in the first ten editions of the reader, the selections in this edition are intended to be vivid, provocative, and eye-opening examples of the practice of sociology. The readings represent a variety of styles. Some use common or everyday experiences and phenomena (such as drug use, employment, athletic performance, religious devotion, eating, and the balance of work and family) to illustrate the relationship between the individual and society. Others focus on important social issues or problems (transgender visibility, race relations, poverty, educational inequalities, sexuality, immigration, incarceration, or global economics) or on specific historical events (massacres during war, drug scares, and social movements). Some were written quite recently; others are sociological classics. In addition to accurately representing the sociological perspective and providing rigorous coverage of the discipline, we hope the selections are thought provoking, generate lots of discussion, and are enjoyable to read.

Several of the readings in this edition are new, and all are based on research studies that were written in the past few years. Our aim is to offer more selections drawn from recent social research. We are confident that you will find them timely and relevant and will come away with a sense of being immersed in the most significant details of contemporary sociology.

To help you get the most out of these selections, we've written brief introductions that provide the sociological context for each chapter. We also have included reflection points that can be used for comparing and contrasting the readings in each chapter and across chapters. For those of you who are also reading the accompanying textbook, these introductions will furnish a quick link between the readings and information in the textbook. We have also included in these introductions brief instructions on what to look for when you read the selections in a given chapter. After each reading, you will find a set of discussion questions to ponder. Many of these questions ask you to apply a specific author's conclusions to some contemporary issue in society or to your own life experiences. It is our hope that these questions will generate a lot of classroom debate and help you see the sociological merit of the readings.

A website established for this eleventh edition includes assessment questions for each reading and lecture notes. The instructor site can be accessed via the SAGE website at www.sagepub.com.

Books like these are enormous projects. We would like to thank our editorial assistants, Annamarie DeGennaro and Jennifer Hamann, as well as Jeff Lasser, Tiara Beatty, Jane Martinez, Lynne Curry, and the rest of the staff at SAGE for their expert advice and assistance in putting this reader together. It's always a pleasure to work with this very professional group. We're also grateful to Hortencia Jimenez (Hartnell College), Steve McGlamery (Radford University), and Marta Rodriguez-Galan (St. John Fisher College) for providing detailed reviews and suggestions. Enjoy!

David M. Newman
Department of Sociology/Anthropology
DePauw University
Greencastle, IN 46135
E-mail: dnewman@depauw.edu

Jodi O'Brien
Department of Sociology
Seattle University
Seattle, WA 98122
E-mail: jobrien@seattleu.edu

Michelle Robertson
Sociology Program
St. Edward's University
Austin, TX 78704-6489
E-mail: michelr@stedwards.edu

About the Editors

David M. Newman (PhD, University of Washington) is Professor of Sociology at DePauw University. In addition to the introductory course, he teaches courses in research methods, family, social psychology, deviance, and mental illness. He has won teaching awards at both the University of Washington and DePauw University. His other written work includes *Identities and Inequalities: Exploring the Intersections of Race, Class, Gender, and Sexuality* (2012) and *Families: A Sociological Perspective* (2008).

Jodi O'Brien (PhD, University of Washington) is Professor of Sociology at Seattle University. She teaches courses in social psychology, social differences and inequalities, gender, and sexuality and religion. She writes and lectures on the cultural politics of transgressive identities and communities. Her other books include *Everyday Inequalities* (Basil Blackwell), *Social Prisms: Reflections on Everyday Myths and Paradoxes* (Pine Forge Press), and *The Production of Reality: Essays and Readings on Social Interaction*, Sixth Edition (Pine Forge Press).

Michelle Robertson (PhD, Washington State University) is Associate Professor of Sociology at St. Edward's University. In addition to the introductory course, she teaches courses in research, statistics, theory, sport, masculinities, family, and social inequality. She won a teaching award at Washington State University and does research on classroom incivility.

The Individual and Society

CHAPTER 1

Taking a New Look at a Familiar World

The primary claim of sociology is that our everyday feelings, thoughts, and actions are the product of a complex interplay between massive social forces and personal characteristics. We can't understand the relationship between individuals and their societies without understanding the connection between them. As C. Wright Mills discusses in the introductory article, the "sociological imagination" is the ability to see the impact of social forces on our private lives. When we develop a sociological imagination, we gain an awareness that our lives unfold at the intersection of personal biography and social history. The sociological imagination encourages us to move beyond individualistic explanations of human experiences to an understanding of the mutual influence between individuals and society. So, rather than study what goes on within people, sociologists study what goes on between and among people, as individuals, groups, organizations, or entire societies. Sociology teaches us to look beyond individual personalities and focus instead on the influence of social phenomena in shaping our ideas of who we are and what we think we can do.

Sociologist Lisa McIntyre applies the sociological imagination to one of the first cases she observed while studying public defenders in the city of Chicago. In the case of Hernando Washington, she discovered the importance of understanding the "social milieu" in which Washington's case unfolded. While not excusing the horrific crimes Washington committed, McIntyre shows us how using our sociological imagination can help us understand his actions and the larger forces at work that have shaped his life up to that point in time. As she notes, sociology helps us to explain and predict human behavior, which can lead to recommendations and policies that might create positive change in the social milieu of these individuals and the communities they live in.

The influence of social institutions on our personal lives is often felt most forcefully when we are compelled to obey the commands of someone who is in a position of institutional authority. The social institution with the most explicit hierarchy of authority is the military. In "The My Lai Massacre: A Military Crime of Obedience," Herbert Kelman and V. Lee Hamilton describe a specific example of a crime in which the individuals involved attempted to deny responsibility for their actions by claiming that they were following the orders of a military officer who had the legitimate right to command them. This incident occurred in the midst of the Vietnam War. Arguably, people do things under such trying conditions that they wouldn't ordinarily do, even—as in this case—kill defenseless people. Kelman and Hamilton make a key sociological point by showing that these soldiers were not necessarily psychological misfits who were especially mean or violent. Instead, the researchers argue, they were ordinary people caught up in tense circumstances that made obeying the brutal commands of an authority seem like the normal and morally acceptable thing to do.

Something to Consider as You Read

As you read these selections, consider the effects of social context and situation on behavior. Even though it might appear extreme, how might the behavior of these soldiers or the university students be similar to other examples of social influence? Consider occasions in which you have done something publicly that you didn't feel right about personally. How do you explain your behavior? How might a sociologist explain your behavior? What does the sociological perspective tell you about the importance of understanding the complexity of individual outcomes in society?

The Sociological Imagination

C. WRIGHT MILLS

(1959)

"The individual can . . . know his own chances in life only by becoming aware of those of all individuals in his circumstances."

Nowadays men often feel that their private lives are a series of traps. They sense that within their everyday worlds, they cannot overcome their troubles, and in this feeling, they are often quite correct: What ordinary men are directly aware of and what they try to do are bounded by the private orbits in which they live; their visions and their powers are limited to the close-up scenes of job, family, neighborhood; in other milieux, they move vicariously and remain spectators. And the more aware they become, however vaguely, of ambitions and of threats which transcend their immediate locales, the more trapped they seem to feel.

Underlying this sense of being trapped are seemingly impersonal changes in the very structure of continent-wide societies. The facts of contemporary history are also facts about the success and the failure of individual men and women. When a society is industrialized, a peasant becomes a worker; a feudal lord is liquidated or becomes a businessman. When classes rise or fall, a man is employed or unemployed; when the rate of investment goes up or down, a man takes new heart or goes broke. When wars happen, an insurance salesman becomes a rocket launcher; a store clerk, a radar man; a wife lives alone; a child grows up without a father. Neither the life of an individual nor the history of a society can be understood without understanding both.

Yet men do not usually define the troubles they endure in terms of historical change and institutional contradiction. The well-being they enjoy, they do not usually impute to the big ups and downs of the societies in which they live. Seldom aware of the intricate connection between the patterns of their own lives and the course of world history, ordinary men do not usually know what this connection means for the kinds of men they are becoming and for the kinds of history-making in which they might take part. They do not possess the quality of mind essential to grasp the interplay of man and society, of biography and history, of self and world. They cannot cope with their personal troubles in such ways as to control the structural transformations that usually lie behind them.

Surely it is no wonder. In what period have so many men been so totally exposed at so fast a pace to such earthquakes of change? That Americans have not known such catastrophic changes as have the men and women of other societies is due to historical facts that are now quickly becoming "merely history." The history that now affects every man is world history. Within this scene and this period, in the course of a single generation, one-sixth of mankind is transformed from all that is feudal and backward into all that is modern, advanced, and fearful. Political colonies are freed, new and less visible forms of imperialism installed. Revolutions occur; men feel the intimate grip of new kinds of authority. Totalitarian societies rise and are smashed to bits—or succeed fabulously. After two centuries of ascendancy, capitalism is shown up as only one way to make society into an industrial apparatus. After two centuries of hope, even formal democracy is restricted to a quite small portion of mankind. Everywhere in the underdeveloped world, ancient ways of life are broken up and vague expectations become urgent demands. Everywhere in the overdeveloped world, the means of authority and of violence become total in scope and bureaucratic in form. Humanity itself now lies before us, the supernation at either pole concentrating its most coordinated and massive efforts upon the preparation of World War Three.

The very shaping of history now outpaces the ability of men to orient themselves in accordance with cherished values. And which values? Even when they do not panic, men often sense that older ways of feeling and thinking have collapsed and that newer beginnings are ambiguous to the point of moral stasis. Is it any wonder that ordinary men feel they cannot cope with the larger worlds with which they are so suddenly confronted? That they cannot understand the meaning of their epoch for their own lives?

That—in defense of selfhood—they become morally insensible, trying to remain altogether private men? Is it any wonder that they come to be possessed by a sense of the trap?

It is not only information that they need—in this Age of Fact, information often dominates their attention and overwhelms their capacities to assimilate it. It is not only the skills of reason that they need—although their struggles to acquire these often exhaust their limited moral energy.

What they need, and what they feel they need, is a quality of mind that will help them to use information and to develop reason in order to achieve lucid summations of what is going on in the world and of what may be happening within themselves. It is this quality, I am going to contend, that journalists and scholars, artists and publics, scientists and editors are coming to expect of what may be called the sociological imagination.

The sociological imagination enables its possessor to understand the larger historical scene in terms of its meaning for the inner life and the external career of a variety of individuals. It enables him to take into account how individuals, in the welter of their daily experience, often become falsely conscious of their social positions. Within that welter, the framework of modern society is sought, and within that framework the psychologies of a variety of men and women are formulated. By such means the personal uneasiness of individuals is focused upon explicit troubles and the indifference of publics is transformed into involvement with public issues.

The first fruit of this imagination—and the first lesson of the social science that embodies it—is the idea that the individual can understand his own experience and gauge his own fate only by locating himself within his period, that he can know his own chances in life only by becoming aware of those of all individuals in his circumstances. In many ways, it is a terrible lesson; in many ways, a magnificent one. We do not know the limits of man's capacities for supreme effort or willing degradation, for agony or glee, for pleasurable brutality or the sweetness of reason. But in our time, we have come to know that the limits of "human nature" are frighteningly broad. We have come to know that every individual lives, from one generation to the next, in some society; that he lives out a biography, and that he lives it out within some historical sequence. By the fact of his living he contributes, however minutely, to the shaping of this society and to the course of its history, even as he is made by society and by its historical push and shove.

The sociological imagination enables us to grasp history and biography and the relations between the two within society. That is its task and its promise. To recognize this task and this promise is the mark of the classic social analyst. It is characteristic of Herbert Spencer—turgid, polysyllabic, comprehensive; of E. A. Ross—graceful, muckraking, upright; of Auguste Comte and Emile Durkheim; of the intricate and subtle Karl Mannheim. It is the quality of all that is intellectually excellent in Karl Marx; it is the clue to Thorstein Veblen's brilliant and ironic insight, to Joseph Schumpeter's many-sided constructions of reality; it is the basis of the psychological sweep of W. E. H. Lecky no less than of the profundity and clarity of Max Weber. And it is the signal of what is best in contemporary studies of man and society.

No social study that does not come back to the problems of biography, of history, and of their intersections within a society has completed its intellectual journey. Whatever the specific problems of the classic social analysts, however limited or however broad the features of social reality they have examined, those who have been imaginatively aware of the promise of their work have consistently asked three sorts of questions:

1. What is the structure of this particular society as a whole? What are its essential components, and how are they related to one another? How does it differ from other varieties of social order? Within it, what is the meaning of any particular feature for its continuance and for its change?

2. Where does this society stand in human history? What are the mechanics by which it is changing? What is its place within and its meaning for the development of humanity as a whole? How does any particular feature we are examining affect, and how is it affected by, the historical period in which it moves? And this period—what are its essential features? How does it differ from other periods? What are its characteristic ways of history making?

3. What varieties of men and women now prevail in this society and in this period? And what varieties are coming to prevail?

In what ways are they selected and formed, liberated and repressed, made sensitive and blunted? What kinds of "human nature" are revealed in the conduct and character we observe in this society in this period? And what is the meaning for "human nature" of each and every feature of the society we are examining?

Whether the point of interest is a great power state or a minor literary mood, a family, a prison, a creed—these are the kinds of questions the best social analysts have asked. They are the intellectual pivots of classic studies of man in society—and they are the questions inevitably raised by any mind possessing the sociological imagination. For that imagination is the capacity to shift from one perspective to another—from the political to the psychological; from examination of a single family to comparative assessment of the national budgets of the world; from the theological school to the military establishment; from considerations of an oil industry to studies of contemporary poetry. It is the capacity to range from the most impersonal and remote transformations to the most intimate features of the human self—and to see the relations between the two. Back of its use there is always the urge to know the social and historical meaning of the individual in the society and in the period in which he has his quality and his being.

That, in brief, is why it is by means of the sociological imagination that men now hope to grasp what is going on in the world, and to understand what is happening in themselves as minute points of the intersections of biography and history within society. In large part, contemporary man's self-conscious view of himself as at least an outsider, if not a permanent stranger, rests upon an absorbed realization of social relativity and of the transformative power of history. The sociological imagination is the most fruitful form of this self-consciousness. By its use men whose mentalities have swept only a series of limited orbits often come to feel as if suddenly awakened in a house with which they had only supposed themselves to be familiar. Correctly or incorrectly, they often come to feel that they can now provide themselves with adequate summations, cohesive assessments, comprehensive orientations. Older decisions that once appeared sound now seem to them products of a mind unaccountably dense. Their capacity

for astonishment is made lively again. They acquire a new way of thinking, they experience a transvaluation of values: in a word, by their reflection and by their sensibility, they realize the cultural meaning of the social sciences.

Perhaps the most fruitful distinction with which the sociological imagination works is between "the personal troubles of milieu" and "the public issues of social structure." This distinction is an essential tool of the sociological imagination and a feature of all classic work in social science.

Troubles occur within the character of the individual and within the range of his immediate relations with others; they have to do with his self and with those limited areas of social life of which he is directly and personally aware. Accordingly, the statement and the resolution of troubles properly lie within the individual as a biographical entity and within the scope of his immediate milieu—the social setting that is directly open to his personal experience and to some extent his willful activity. A trouble is a private matter: values cherished by an individual are felt by him to be threatened.

Issues have to do with matters that transcend these local environments of the individual and the range of his inner life. They have to do with the organization of many such milieux into the institutions of an historical society as a whole, with the ways in which various milieux overlap and interpenetrate to form the larger structure of social and historical life. An issue is a public matter: some value cherished by the publics is felt to be threatened. Often there is a debate about what that value really is and about what it is that really threatens it. This debate is often without focus if only because it is the very nature of an issue, unlike even widespread trouble, that it cannot very well be defined in terms of the immediate and everyday environments of ordinary men. An issue, in fact, often involves a crisis in institutional arrangements, and often too it involves what Marxists call "contradictions" or "antagonisms."

In these terms, consider unemployment. When, in a city of 100,000, only one man is unemployed, that is his personal trouble, and for its relief we properly look to the character of the man, his skills, and his immediate opportunities. But when in a nation of 50 million employees, 15 million men are unemployed, that is an issue, and we may not hope to find its solution within the range of opportunities open to any one individual. The very structure of opportunities has collapsed. Both the correct statement of the problem and the range of possible solutions require us to consider the economic and political institutions of the society, and not merely the personal situation and character of a scatter of individuals.

Consider war. The personal problem of war, when it occurs, may be how to survive it or how to die in it with honor; how to make money out of it; how to climb into the higher safety of the military apparatus; or how to contribute to the war's termination. In short, according to one's values, to find a set of milieux and within it to survive the war or make one's death in it meaningful. But the structural issues of war have to do with its causes; with what types of men it throws up into command; with its effects upon economic and political, family, and religious institutions, with the unorganized irresponsibility of a world of nation-states.

Consider marriage. Inside a marriage a man and a woman may experience personal troubles, but when the divorce rate during the first four years of marriage is 250 out of every 1,000 attempts, this is an indication of a structural issue having to do with the institutions of marriage and the family and other institutions that bear upon them.

Or consider the metropolis—the horrible, beautiful, ugly, magnificent sprawl of the great city. For many upper-class people, the personal solution to "the problem of the city" is to have an apartment with private garage under it in the heart of the city, and forty miles out, a house by Henry Hill, garden by Garrett Eckbo, on a hundred acres of private land. In these two controlled environments—with a small staff at each end and a private helicopter connection—most people could solve many of the problems of personal milieux caused by the facts of the city. But all this, however splendid, does not solve the public issues that the structural fact of the city poses. What should be done with this wonderful monstrosity? Break it all up into scattered units, combining residence and work? Refurbish it as it stands? Or, after evacuation, dynamite it and build new cities according to new plans in new places? What should those plans be? And who is to decide and to accomplish whatever choice is made? These are structural issues; to confront them and to solve them requires us to consider political and economic issues that affect innumerable milieux.

Insofar as an economy is so arranged that slumps occur, the problem of unemployment becomes incapable of personal solution. Insofar as war is inherent in the nation-state system and in the uneven industrialization of the world, the ordinary individual in his restricted milieu will be powerless—with or without psychiatric aid—to solve the troubles this system or lack of system imposes upon him. Insofar as the family as an institution turns women into darling little slaves and men into their chief providers and unweaned dependents, the problem of a satisfactory marriage remains incapable of purely private solution. Insofar as the overdeveloped megalopolis and the overdeveloped automobile are built-in features of the overdeveloped society, the issues of urban living will not be solved by personal ingenuity and private wealth.

What we experience in various and specific milieux, I have noted, is often caused by structural changes. Accordingly, to understand the changes of many personal milieux we are required to look beyond them. And the number and variety of such structural changes increase as the institutions within which we live become more embracing and more intricately connected with one another. To be aware of the idea of social structure and to use it with sensibility is to be capable of tracing such linkages among a great variety of milieux. To be able to do that is to possess the sociological imagination. . . .

THINKING ABOUT THE READING

Consider the political, economic, familial, and cultural circumstances into which you were born. Make a list of some of these circumstances and also some of the major historical events that have occurred in your lifetime. How do you think these historical and social circumstances may have affected your personal "biography"? Can you think of ways in which your actions have influenced the course of other people's lives? Identify some famous people and consider how the intersection of "history and biography" led them to their particular position. How might the outcome have differed if some of the circumstances in their lives were different?

The My Lai Massacre

A Military Crime of Obedience

HERBERT KELMAN AND
V. LEE HAMILTON

(1989)

March 16, 1968, was a busy day in U.S. history. Stateside, Robert F. Kennedy announced his presidential candidacy, challenging a sitting president from his own party—in part out of opposition to an undeclared and disastrous war. In Vietnam, the war continued. In many ways, March 16 may have been a typical day in that war. We will probably never know. But we do know that on that day a typical company went on a mission—which may or may not have been typical—to a village called Son (or Song) My. Most of what is remembered from that mission occurred in the subhamlet known to Americans as My Lai 4.

The My Lai massacre was investigated and charges were brought in 1969 and 1970. Trials and disciplinary actions lasted into 1971. Entire books have been written about the army's year-long cover-up of the massacre (for example, Hersh, 1972), and the cover-up was a major focus of the army's own investigation of the incident. Our central concern here is the massacre itself—a crime of obedience—and public reactions to such crimes, rather than the lengths to which many went to deny the event. Therefore, this account concentrates on one day: March 16, 1968.

Many verbal testimonials to the horrors that occurred at My Lai were available. More unusual was the fact that an army photographer, Ronald Haeberle, was assigned the task of documenting the anticipated military engagement at My Lai—and documented a massacre instead. Later, as the story of the massacre emerged, his photographs were widely distributed and seared the public conscience. What might have been dismissed as unreal or exaggerated was depicted in photographs of demonstrable authenticity. The dominant image appeared on the cover of *Life*: piles of bodies jumbled together in a ditch along a trail—the dead all apparently unarmed. All were Oriental, and all appeared to be children, women, or old men. Clearly there had been a mass execution, one whose image would not quickly fade.

So many bodies (over twenty in the cover photo alone) are hard to imagine as the handiwork of one killer. These were not. They were the product of what we call a crime of obedience. Crimes of obedience begin with orders. But orders are often vague and rarely survive with any clarity the transition from one authority down a chain of subordinates to the ultimate actors. The operation at Son My was no exception.

"Charlie" Company, Company C, under Lt. Col. Frank Barker's command, arrived in Vietnam in December 1967. As the army's investigative unit, directed by Lt. Gen. William R. Peers, characterized the personnel, they "contained no significant deviation from the average" for the time. Seymour S. Hersh (1970) described the "average" more explicitly: "Most of the men in Charlie Company had volunteered for the draft; only a few had gone to college for even one year. Nearly half were black, with a few Mexican-Americans. Most were eighteen to twenty-two years old. The favorite reading matter of Charlie Company, like that of other line infantry units in Vietnam, was comic books" (p. 18). The action at My Lai, like that throughout Vietnam, was fought by a cross-section of those Americans who either believed in the war or lacked the social resources to avoid participating in it. Charlie Company was indeed average for that time, that place, and that war.

Two key figures in Charlie Company were more unusual. The company's commander, Capt. Ernest Medina, was an upwardly mobile Mexican-American who wanted to make the army his career, although he feared that he might never advance beyond captain because of his lack of formal education. His eagerness had earned him a nickname among his men: "Mad Dog Medina." One of his admirers was the platoon leader Second Lt. William L. Calley, Jr., an undistinguished, five-foot-three-inch junior-college dropout who had failed four of the seven courses in which he had enrolled his first year. Many viewed him as one of those "instant officers" made possible only by the army's then-desperate need for manpower. Whatever the cause, he was an insecure leader whose frequent claim was "I'm the boss." His nickname among some of the troops was "Surfside 5½," a reference to the swashbuckling heroes of a popular television show, "Surfside 6."

The Son My operation was planned by Lieutenant Colonel Barker and his staff as a search-and-destroy mission with the objective of rooting out the Forty-eighth Viet Cong Battalion from their base area of Son My village. Apparently, no written orders were ever issued. Barker's superior, Col. Oran Henderson, arrived at the staging point the day before. Among the issues he reviewed with the assembled officers were some of the weaknesses of prior operations by their units, including their failure to be appropriately aggressive in pursuit of the enemy. Later briefings by Lieutenant Colonel Barker and his staff asserted that no one except Viet Cong was expected to be in the village after 7 A.M. on the following day. The "innocent" would all be at the market. Those present at the briefings gave conflicting accounts of Barker's exact orders, but he conveyed at least a strong suggestion that the Son My area was to be obliterated. As the army's inquiry reported: "While there is some conflict in the testimony as to whether LTC Barker ordered the destruction of houses, dwellings, livestock, and other foodstuffs in the Song My area, the preponderance of the evidence indicates that such destruction was implied, if not specifically directed, by his orders of 15 March" (Peers Report, in Goldstein et al., 1976, p. 94).

Evidence that Barker ordered the killing of civilians is even more murky. What does seem clear, however, is that—having asserted that civilians would be away at the market—he did not specify what was to be done with any who might nevertheless be found on the scene. The Peers Report therefore considered it "reasonable to conclude that LTC Barker's minimal or nonexistent instructions concerning the handling of noncombatants created the potential for grave misunderstandings as to his intentions and for interpretation of his orders as authority to fire, without restriction, on all persons found in target area" (Goldstein et al., 1976, p. 95). Since Barker was killed in action in June 1968, his own formal version of the truth was never available.

Charlie Company's Captain Medina was briefed for the operation by Barker and his staff. He then transmitted the already vague orders to his own men. Charlie Company was spoiling for a fight, having been totally frustrated during its months in Vietnam—first by waiting for battles that never came, then by incompetent forays led by inexperienced commanders, and finally by mines and booby traps. In fact, the emotion-laden funeral of a sergeant killed by a booby trap was held on March 15, the day before My Lai. Captain Medina gave the orders for the next day's action at the close of that funeral. Many were in a mood for revenge.

It is again unclear what was ordered. Although all participants were alive by the time of the trials for the massacre, they were either on trial or probably felt under threat of trial. Memories are often flawed and self-serving at such times. It is apparent that Medina relayed to the men at least some of Barker's general message—to expect Viet Cong resistance, to burn, and to kill livestock. It is not clear that he ordered the slaughter of the inhabitants, but some of the men who heard him thought he had. One of those who claimed to have heard such orders was Lt. William Calley.

As March 16 dawned, much was expected of the operation by those who had set it into motion. Therefore, a full complement of "brass" was present in helicopters overhead, including Barker, Colonel Henderson, and their superior, Major General Koster (who went on to become commandant of West Point before the story of My Lai broke). On the ground, the troops were to carry with them one reporter and one photographer to immortalize the anticipated battle.

The action for Company C began at 7:30 as their first wave of helicopters touched down near the sub-hamlet of My Lai 4. By 7:47 all of Company C was present and set to fight. But instead of the Viet Cong Forty-eighth Battalion, My Lai was filled with the old men, women, and children who were supposed to have gone to market. By this time, in their version of the war, and with whatever orders they thought they had heard, the men from Company C were nevertheless ready to find Viet Cong everywhere. By nightfall, the official tally was 128 VC killed and three weapons captured, although later, unofficial body counts ran as high as 500. The operation at Son My was over. And by nightfall, as Hersh reported: "the Viet Cong were back in My Lai 4, helping the survivors bury the dead. It took five days. Most of the funeral speeches were made by the Communist guerrillas. Nguyen Bat was not a Communist at the time of the massacre, but the incident changed his mind. 'After the shooting,' he said, 'all the villagers became Communists'" (1970, p. 74). To this day, the memory of the massacre is kept alive by markers and plaques designating the spots where groups of villagers were killed, by a large statue, and by the My Lai Museum, established in 1975 (Williams, 1985).

But what could have happened to leave American troops reporting a victory over Viet Cong when in fact they had killed hundreds of noncombatants? It is not hard to explain the report of victory; that is the essence of a cover-up. It is harder to understand how the killings came to be committed in the first place, making a cover-up necessary.

Mass Executions and the Defense of Superior Orders

Some of the atrocities on March 16, 1968, were evidently unofficial, spontaneous acts: rapes, tortures, killings. For example, Hersh (1970) describes Charlie Company's Second Platoon as entering "My Lai 4 with guns blazing" (p. 50); more graphically, Lieutenant "Brooks and his men in the second platoon to the north had begun to systematically ransack the hamlet and slaughter the people, kill the livestock, and destroy the crops. Men poured rifle and machine-gun fire into huts without knowing—or seemingly caring—who was inside" (pp. 49–50).

Some atrocities toward the end of the action were part of an almost casual "mopping-up," much of which was the responsibility of Lieutenant LaCross's Third Platoon of Charlie Company. The Peers Report states: "The entire 3rd Platoon then began moving into the western edge of My Lai (4), for the mop-up operation. . . .The squad . . . began to burn the houses in the southwestern portion of the hamlet" (Goldstein et al., 1976, p. 133). They became mingled with other platoons during a series of rapes and killings of survivors for which it was impossible to fix responsibility. Certainly, to a Vietnamese all GIs would by this point look alike: "Nineteen-year-old Nguyen Thi Ngoc Tuyet watched a baby trying to open her slain mother's blouse to nurse. A soldier shot the infant while it was struggling with the blouse, and then slashed it with his bayonet." Tuyet also said she saw another baby hacked to death by GIs wielding their bayonets. "Le Tong, a twenty-eight-year-old rice farmer, reported seeing one woman raped after GIs killed her children. Nguyen Khoa, a thirty-seven-year-old peasant, told of a thirteen-year-old girl who was raped before being killed. GIs then attacked Khoa's wife, tearing off her clothes. Before they could rape her, however, Khoa said, their six-year-old son, riddled with bullets, fell and saturated her with blood. The GIs left her alone" (Hersh, 1970, p. 72). All of Company C was implicated in a pattern of death and destruction throughout the hamlet, much of which seemingly lacked rhyme or reason.

But a substantial amount of the killing was organized and traceable to one authority: the First Platoon's Lt. William Calley. Calley was originally charged with 109 killings, almost all of them mass executions at the trail and other locations. He stood trial for 102 of these killings, was convicted of 22 in 1971, and at first received a life sentence. Though others—both superior and subordinate to Calley—were brought to trial, he was the only one convicted for the My Lai crimes. Thus, the only actions of My Lai for which anyone was ever convicted were mass executions, ordered and committed. We suspect that there are commonsense reasons why this one type of killing was singled out. In the midst of rapidly moving events with people running about, an execution of stationary targets is literally a still life that stands out and whose participants are clearly visible. It can be proven that specific people committed specific deeds. An execution, in contrast to the shooting of someone on the run, is also more likely to meet the legal definition of an act resulting from intent—with malice aforethought. Moreover, American military law specifically forbids the killing of unarmed civilians or military prisoners, as does the Geneva Convention between nations. Thus, common sense, legal standards, and explicit doctrine all made such actions the likeliest target for prosecution.

When Lieutenant Calley was charged under military law it was for violation of the Uniform Code of Military Justice (UCMJ) Article 118 (murder). This article is similar to civilian codes in that it provides for conviction if an accused:

without justification or excuse, unlawfully kills a human being, when he—

1. has a premeditated design to kill;

2. intends to kill or inflict great bodily harm;

3. is engaged in an act which is inherently dangerous to others and evinces a wanton disregard of human life; or

4. is engaged in the perpetration or attempted perpetration of burglary, sodomy, rape, robbery, or aggravated arson. (Goldstein et al., 1976, p. 507)

For a soldier, one legal justification for killing is warfare; but warfare is subject to many legal limits and restrictions, including, of course, the inadmissibility of killing unarmed noncombatants or prisoners whom one has disarmed. The pictures of the trail victims at My Lai certainly portrayed one or the other of these. Such an action would be illegal under military law; ordering another to commit such an action would be illegal; and following such an order would be illegal.

But following an order may provide a second and pivotal justification for an act that would be murder when committed by a civilian. American military law assumes that the subordinate is inclined to follow orders, as that is the normal obligation of the role. Hence, legally, obedient subordinates are protected from unreasonable expectations regarding their capacity to evaluate those orders:

An order requiring the performance of a military duty may be inferred to be legal. An act performed manifestly beyond the scope of authority, or pursuant to an order that a man of ordinary sense and understanding would know to be illegal, or in a wanton manner in the discharge of a lawful duty, is not excusable. (Par. 216, Subpar. *d*, Manual for Courts Martial, United States, 1969 Rev.)

Thus, what *may* be excusable is the good-faith carrying out of an order, as long as that order appears to the ordinary soldier to be a legal one. In military law, invoking superior orders moves the question from one of the action's consequences—the body count—to one of evaluating the actor's motives and good sense.

In sum, if anyone is to be brought to justice for a massacre, common sense and legal codes decree that the most appropriate targets are those who make themselves executioners. This is the kind of target the government selected in prosecuting Lieutenant

Calley with the greatest fervor. And in a military context, the most promising way in which one can redefine one's undeniable deeds into acceptability is to invoke superior orders. This is what Calley did in attempting to avoid conviction. Since the core legal issues involved points of mass execution—the ditches and trail where America's image of My Lai was formed—we review these events in greater detail.

The day's quiet beginning has already been noted. Troops landed and swept unopposed into the village. The three weapons eventually reported as the haul from the operation were picked up from three apparent Viet Cong who fled the village when the troops arrived and were pursued and killed by helicopter gunships. Obviously, the Viet Cong did frequent the area. But it appears that by about 8:00 A.M. no one who met the troops was aggressive, and no one was armed. By the laws of war Charlie Company had no argument with such people.

As they moved into the village, the soldiers began to gather its inhabitants together. Shortly after 8:00 A.M. Lieutenant Calley told Pfc. Paul Meadlo that "you know what to do with" a group of villagers Meadlo was guarding. Estimates of the numbers in the group ranged as high as eighty women, children, and old men, and Meadlo's own estimate under oath was thirty to fifty people. As Meadlo later testified, Calley returned after ten or fifteen minutes: "He [Calley] said, 'How come they're not dead?' I said, 'I didn't know we were supposed to kill them.' He said, 'I want them dead.' He backed off twenty or thirty feet and started shooting into the people—the Viet Cong—shooting automatic. He was beside me. He burned four or five magazines. I burned off a few, about three. I helped shoot 'em" (Hammer, 1971, p. 155). Meadlo himself and others testified that Meadlo cried as he fired; others reported him later to be sobbing and "all broke up." It would appear that to Lieutenant Calley's subordinates something was unusual, and stressful, in these orders.

At the trial, the first specification in the murder charge against Calley was for this incident; he was accused of premeditated murder of "an unknown number, not less than 30, Oriental human beings, males and females of various ages, whose names are unknown, occupants of the village of My Lai 4, by means of shooting them with a rifle" (Goldstein et al., 1976, p. 497).

Among the helicopters flying reconnaissance above Son My was that of CWO Hugh Thompson.

By 9:00 or soon after, Thompson had noticed some horrifying events from his perch. As he spotted wounded civilians, he sent down smoke markers so that soldiers on the ground could treat them. They killed them instead. He reported to headquarters, trying to persuade someone to stop what was going on. Barker, hearing the message, called down to Captain Medina. Medina, in turn, later claimed to have told Calley that it was "enough for today." But it was not yet enough.

At Calley's orders, his men began gathering the remaining villagers—roughly seventy-five individuals, mostly women and children—and herding them toward a drainage ditch. Accompanied by three or four enlisted men, Lieutenant Calley executed several batches of civilians who had been gathered into ditches. Some of the details of the process were entered into testimony in such accounts as Pfc. Dennis Conti's: "A lot of them, the people, were trying to get up and mostly they was just screaming and pretty bad shot up. . . .I seen a woman tried to get up. I seen Lieutenant Calley fire. He hit the side of her head and blew it off" (Hammer, 1971, p. 125).

Testimony by other soldiers presented the shooting's aftermath. Specialist Four Charles Hall, asked by Prosecutor Aubrey Daniel how he knew the people in the ditch were dead, said: "There was blood coming from them. They were just scattered all over the ground in the ditch, some in piles and some scattered out 20, 25 meters perhaps up the ditch. . . .They were very old people, very young children, and mothers. . . .There was blood all over them" (Goldstein et al., 1976, pp. 501–502). And Pfc. Gregory Olsen corroborated the general picture of the victims: "They were—the majority were women and children, some babies. I distinctly remember one middle-aged Vietnamese male dressed in white right at my feet as I crossed. None of the bodies were mangled in any way. There was blood. Some appeared to be dead, others followed me with their eyes as I walked across the ditch" (Goldstein et al., 1976, p. 502).

The second specification in the murder charge stated that Calley did "with premeditation, murder an unknown number of Oriental human beings, not less than seventy, males and females of various ages, whose names are unknown, occupants of the village of My Lai 4, by means of shooting them with a rifle" (Goldstein et al., 1976, p. 497). Calley was also charged with and tried for shootings of individuals (an old man and a child); these charges were clearly supplemental to the main issue at trial—the mass killings and how they came about.

It is noteworthy that during these executions more than one enlisted man avoided carrying out Calley's orders, and more than one, by sworn oath, directly refused to obey them. For example, Pfc. James Joseph Dursi testified, when asked if he fired when Lieutenant Calley ordered him to: "No I just stood there. Meadlo turned to me after a couple of minutes and said 'Shoot! Why don't you shoot! Why don't you fire!' He was crying and yelling. I said, 'I can't! I won't!' And the people were screaming and crying and yelling. They kept firing for a couple of minutes, mostly automatic and semi-automatic" (Hammer, 1971, p. 143). . . .

Disobedience of Lieutenant Calley's own orders to kill represented a serious legal and moral threat to a defense *based* on superior orders, such as Calley was attempting. This defense had to assert that the orders seemed reasonable enough to carry out; that they appeared to be legal orders. Even if the orders in question were not legal, the defense had to assert that an ordinary individual could not and should not be expected to see the distinction. In short, if what happened was "business as usual," even though it might be bad business, then the defendant stood a chance of acquittal. But under direct command from "Surfside 5½," some ordinary enlisted men managed to refuse, to avoid, or at least to stop doing what they were ordered to do. As "reasonable men" of "ordinary sense and understanding," they had apparently found something awry that morning; and it would have been hard for an officer to plead successfully that he was more ordinary than his men in his capacity to evaluate the reasonableness of orders.

Even those who obeyed Calley's orders showed great stress. For example, Meadlo eventually began to argue and cry directly in front of Calley. Pfc. Herbert Carter shot himself in the foot, possibly because he could no longer take what he was doing. We were not destined to hear a sworn version of the incident, since neither side at the Calley trial called him to testify.

The most unusual instance of resistance to authority came from the skies. CWO Hugh Thompson, who had protested the apparent carnage of civilians, was Calley's inferior in rank but was not in his line of command. He was also watching the ditch from his helicopter and noticed some people moving after the first round of slaughter—chiefly children who had been shielded by their mothers' bodies. Landing to rescue the wounded, he also found some villagers hiding in a nearby bunker. Protecting the Vietnamese with his own body, Thompson ordered his men to train their guns on the Americans and to open fire if the Americans fired on the Vietnamese. He then radioed for additional rescue helicopters and stood between the Vietnamese and the Americans under Calley's command until the Vietnamese could be evacuated. He later returned to the ditch to unearth a child buried, unharmed, beneath layers of bodies. In October 1969, Thompson was awarded the Distinguished Flying Cross for heroism at My Lai, specifically (albeit inaccurately) for the rescue of children hiding in a bunker "between Viet Cong forces and advancing friendly forces" and for the rescue of a wounded child "caught in the intense cross-fire" (Hersh, 1970, p. 119). Four months earlier, at the Pentagon, Thompson had identified Calley as having been at the ditch.

By about 10:00 A.M., the massacre was winding down. The remaining actions consisted largely of isolated rapes and killings, "clean-up" shootings of the wounded, and the destruction of the village by fire. We have already seen some examples of these more indiscriminate and possibly less premeditated acts. By the 11:00 A.M. lunch break, when the exhausted men of Company C were relaxing, two young girls wandered back from a hiding place only to be invited to share lunch. This surrealist touch illustrates the extent to which the soldiers' action had become dissociated from its meaning. An hour earlier, some of these men were making sure that not even a child would escape the executioner's bullet. But now the job was done and it was time for lunch—and in this new context it seemed only natural to ask the children who had managed to escape execution to join them. The massacre had ended. It remained only for the Viet Cong to reap the political rewards among the survivors in hiding.

The army command in the area knew that something had gone wrong. Direct commanders, including Lieutenant Colonel Barker, had firsthand reports, such as Thompson's complaints. Others had such odd bits of evidence as the claim of 128 Viet Cong dead with a booty of only three weapons. But the cover-up of My Lai began at once. The operation was reported as a victory over a stronghold of the Viet Cong Forty-eighth. . . .

William Calley was not the only man tried for the event at My Lai. The actions of over thirty soldiers and civilians were scrutinized by investigators; over half of these had to face charges or disciplinary action of some sort. Targets of investigation included Captain Medina, who was tried, and various higher-ups, including General Koster. But Lieutenant Calley was the only person convicted, the only person to serve time.

The core of Lieutenant Calley's defense was superior orders. What this meant to him—in contrast to what it meant to the judge and jury—can be gleaned from his responses to a series of questions from his defense attorney, George Latimer, in which Calley sketched out his understanding of the laws of war and the actions that constitute doing one's duty within those laws:

Latimer: Did you receive any training which had to do with the obedience to orders?

Calley: Yes, sir.

Latimer: . . . what were you informed [were] the principles involved in that field?

Calley: That all orders were to be assumed legal, that the soldier's job was to carry out any order given him to the best of his ability.

Latimer: . . . what might occur if you disobeyed an order by a senior officer?

Calley: You could be court-martialed for refusing an order and refusing an order in the face of the enemy, you could be sent to death, sir.

Latimer: [I am asking] whether you were required in any way, shape or form to make a determination of the legality or illegality of an order?

Calley: No, sir. I was never told that I had the choice, sir.

Latimer: If you had a doubt about the order, what were you supposed to do?

Calley: . . . I was supposed to carry the order out and then come back and make my complaint. (Hammer, 1971, pp. 240–241)

Lieutenant Calley steadfastly maintained that his actions within My Lai had constituted, in his mind, carrying out orders from Captain Medina. Both his own actions and the orders he gave to others (such as the instruction to Meadlo to "waste 'em") were entirely in response to superior orders. He denied any intent to kill individuals and any but the most passing awareness of distinctions among the individuals: "I was ordered to go in there and destroy the enemy. That was my job on that day. That was the mission I was given. I did not sit down and think in terms of men, women, and children. They were all classified the same, and that was the classification that we dealt with, just as enemy soldiers." When Latimer asked if in his own opinion Calley had acted "rightly and according to your understanding of your directions and orders," Calley replied, "I felt then and I still do that I acted as I was directed, and I carried out the orders that I was given, and I do not feel wrong in doing so, sir" (Hammer, 1971, p. 257).

His court-martial did not accept Calley's defense of superior orders and clearly did not share his interpretation of his duty. The jury evidently reasoned that, even if there had been orders to destroy everything in sight and to "waste the Vietnamese," any reasonable person would have realized that such orders were illegal and should have refused to carry them out. The defense of superior orders under such conditions is inadmissible under international and military law. The U.S. Army's *Law of Land Warfare* (Dept. of the Army, 1956), for example, states that "the fact that the law of war has been violated pursuant to an order of a superior authority, whether military or civil, does not deprive the act in question of its character of a war crime, nor does it constitute a defense in the trial of an accused individual, unless he did not know and could not reasonably have been expected to know that the act was unlawful" and that "members of the armed forces are bound to obey only lawful orders" (in Falk et al., 1971, pp. 71–72).

The disagreement between Calley and the court-martial seems to have revolved around the definition of the responsibilities of a subordinate to obey, on the one hand, and to evaluate, on the other. This tension . . . can best be captured via the charge to the jury in the Calley court-martial, made by the trial judge, Col. Reid Kennedy. The forty-one pages of the charge include the following:

> Both combatants captured by and noncombatants detained by the opposing force . . . have the right to be treated as prisoners. . . . Summary execution of detainees or prisoners is forbidden by law. . . . I therefore instruct you . . . that if unresisting human beings were killed at My Lai (4) while within the effective custody and control of our military forces, their deaths cannot be considered justified. . . . Thus if you find that Lieutenant Calley received an order directing him to kill unresisting Vietnamese within his control or within the control of his troops, *that order would be an illegal order.*

A determination that an order is illegal does not, of itself, assign criminal responsibility to the person following the order for acts done in compliance with it. Soldiers are taught to follow orders, and special attention is given to obedience of orders on the battlefield. Military effectiveness depends on obedience to orders. On the other hand, the obedience of a soldier is not the obedience of an automaton. A soldier is a reasoning agent, obliged to respond, not as a machine, but as a person. The law takes these factors into account in assessing criminal responsibility for acts done in compliance with illegal orders.

> The acts of a subordinate done in compliance with an unlawful order given him by his superior are excused and impose no criminal liability upon him unless the superior's order is one which a man of *ordinary sense and understanding* would, under the circumstances, know to be unlawful, or if the order in question is actually known to the accused to be unlawful. (Goldstein et al., 1976, pp. 525–526; emphasis added)

By this definition, subordinates take part in a balancing act, one tipped toward obedience but tempered by "ordinary sense and understanding."

A jury of combat veterans proceeded to convict William Calley of the premeditated murder of no less than twenty-two human beings. (The army, realizing some unfortunate connotations in referring to the victims as "Oriental human beings," eventually referred to them as "human beings.") Regarding the first specification in the murder charge, the bodies on the trail, [Calley] was convicted of premeditated murder of not less than one person. (Medical testimony had been able to pinpoint only one person whose wounds as revealed in Haeberle's photos were sure to be immediately fatal.) Regarding the second specification, the bodies in the ditch, Calley was convicted of the premeditated murder of not less than twenty human beings. Regarding additional specifications that he had killed an old man and a child, Calley was convicted of premeditated murder in the first case and of assault with intent to commit murder in the second.

Lieutenant Calley was initially sentenced to life imprisonment. That sentence was reduced: first to twenty years, eventually to ten (the latter by Secretary of Defense Callaway in 1974). Calley served three years before being released on bond. The time was spent under house arrest in his apartment, where he was able to receive visits from his girlfriend. He was granted parole on September 10, 1975.

Sanctioned Massacres

The slaughter at My Lai is an instance of a class of violent acts that can be described as sanctioned massacres (Kelman, 1973): acts of indiscriminate, ruthless, and often systematic mass violence, carried out by military or paramilitary personnel while engaged in officially sanctioned campaigns, the victims of which are defenseless and unresisting civilians, including old men, women, and children. Sanctioned massacres have occurred throughout history. Within American history, My Lai had its precursors in the Philippine war around the turn of the century (Schirmer, 1971) and in the massacres of American Indians. Elsewhere in the world, one recalls the Nazis' "final solution" for European Jews, the massacres and deportations of Armenians by Turks, the liquidation of the kulaks and the great purges in the Soviet Union, and more recently the massacres in Indonesia and Bangladesh, in Biafra and Burundi, in South Africa and Mozambique, in Cambodia and Afghanistan, in Syria and Lebanon. . . .

The occurrence of sanctioned massacres cannot be adequately explained by the existence of psychological forces—whether these be characterological dispositions to engage in murderous violence or profound hostility against the target—so powerful that they must find expression in violent acts unhampered by moral restraints. Instead, the major instigators for this class of violence derive from the policy process. The question that really calls for psychological analysis is why so many people are willing to formulate, participate in, and condone policies that call for the mass killings of defenseless civilians. Thus, it is more instructive to look not at the motives for violence but at the conditions under which the usual moral inhibitions against violence become weakened. Three social processes that tend to create such conditions can be identified: authorization, routinization, and dehumanization. Through authorization, the situation becomes so defined that the individual is absolved of the responsibility to make personal moral choices. Through routinization, the action becomes so organized that there is no opportunity for raising moral questions. Through dehumanization, the actors' attitudes toward the target and toward themselves become so structured that it is neither necessary nor possible for them to view the relationship in moral terms.

Authorization

Sanctioned massacres by definition occur in the context of an authority situation, a situation in which, at least for many of the participants, the moral principles that generally govern human relationships do not apply. Thus, when acts of violence are explicitly ordered, implicitly encouraged, tacitly approved, or at least permitted by legitimate authorities, people's readiness to commit or condone them is enhanced. That such acts are authorized seems to carry automatic justification for them. Behaviorally, authorization obviates the necessity of making judgments or choices. Not only do normal moral principles become inoperative, but—particularly when the actions are explicitly ordered—a different kind of morality, linked to the duty to obey superior orders, tends to take over.

In an authority situation, individuals characteristically feel obligated to obey the orders of the authorities, whether or not these correspond with their personal preferences. They see themselves as having no choice as long as they accept the legitimacy of the orders and of the authorities who give them. Individuals differ considerably in the degree to which—and the conditions under which—they are prepared to challenge the legitimacy of an order on the grounds that the order itself is illegal, or that those giving it have overstepped their authority, or that it stems from a policy that violates fundamental societal values. Regardless of such individual differences, however, the basic structure of a situation of legitimate authority requires subordinates to respond in terms of their role obligations rather than their personal preferences; they can openly disobey only by challenging the legitimacy of the authority. Often people obey without question even though the behavior they engage in may entail great personal sacrifice or great harm to others.

An important corollary of the basic structure of the authority situation is that actors often do not see themselves as personally responsible for the consequences of their actions. Again, there are individual differences, depending on actors' capacity and readiness to evaluate the legitimacy of orders received. Insofar as they see themselves as having had no choice in their actions, however, they do not feel personally responsible for them. They were not personal agents, but merely extensions of the authority. Thus, when their actions cause harm to others, they can feel relatively free of guilt. A similar mechanism operates when a person engages in antisocial behavior that was not ordered by the authorities but was tacitly encouraged and approved by them—even if only by making it clear that such behavior will not be punished. In this situation, behavior that was formerly illegitimate is legitimized by the authorities' acquiescence.

In the My Lai massacre, it is likely that the structure of the authority situation contributed to the massive violence in both ways—that is, by conveying the message that acts of violence against Vietnamese villagers were *required,* as well as the message that such acts, even if not ordered, were *permitted* by the authorities in charge. The actions at My Lai represented, at least in some respects, responses to explicit or implicit orders. Lieutenant Calley indicated, by orders and by example, that he wanted large numbers of villagers killed. Whether Calley himself had been ordered by his superiors to "waste" the whole area, as he claimed, remains a matter of controversy. Even if we assume, however, that he was not explicitly ordered to wipe out the village, he had reason to believe that such actions were expected by his superior officers. Indeed, the very nature of the war

conveyed this expectation. The principal measure of military success was the "body count"—the number of enemy soldiers killed—and any Vietnamese killed by the U.S. military was commonly defined as a "Viet Cong." Thus, it was not totally bizarre for Calley to believe that what he was doing at My Lai was to increase his body count, as any good officer was expected to do.

Even to the extent that the actions at My Lai occurred spontaneously, without reference to superior orders, those committing them had reason to assume that such actions might be tacitly approved of by the military authorities. Not only had they failed to punish such acts in most cases, but the very strategies and tactics that the authorities consistently devised were based on the proposition that the civilian population of South Vietnam—whether "hostile" or "friendly"—was expendable. Such policies as search-and-destroy missions, the establishment of free-shooting zones, the use of antipersonnel weapons, the bombing of entire villages if they were suspected of harboring guerrillas, the forced migration of masses of the rural population, and the defoliation of vast forest areas helped legitimize acts of massive violence of the kind occurring at My Lai.

Some of the actions at My Lai suggest an orientation to authority based on unquestioning obedience to superior orders, no matter how destructive the actions these orders call for. Such obedience is specifically fostered in the course of military training and reinforced by the structure of the military authority situation. It also reflects, however, an ideological orientation that may be more widespread in the general population. . . .

Routinization

Authorization processes create a situation in which people become involved in an action without considering its implications and without really making a decision. Once they have taken the initial step, they are in a new psychological and social situation in which the pressures to continue are powerful. As Lewin (1947) has pointed out, many forces that might originally have kept people out of a situation reverse direction once they have made a commitment (once they have gone through the "gate region") and now serve to keep them in the situation. For example, concern about the criminal nature of an action, which might originally have inhibited a person from becoming involved, may now lead to deeper involvement in efforts to justify the action and to avoid negative consequences.

Despite these forces, however, given the nature of the actions involved in sanctioned massacres, one might still expect moral scruples to intervene; but the likelihood of moral resistance is greatly reduced by transforming the action into routine, mechanical, highly programmed operations. Routinization fulfills two functions. First, it reduces the necessity of making decisions, thus minimizing the occasions in which moral questions may arise. Second, it makes it easier to avoid the implications of the action, since the actor focuses on the details of the job rather than on its meaning. The latter effect is more readily achieved among those who participate in sanctioned massacres from a distance—from their desks or even from the cockpits of their bombers.

Routinization operates both at the level of the individual actor and at the organizational level. Individual job performance is broken down into a series of discrete steps, most of them carried out in automatic, regularized fashion. It becomes easy to forget the nature of the product that emerges from this process. When Lieutenant Calley said of My Lai that it was "no great deal," he probably implied that it was all in a day's work. Organizationally, the task is divided among different offices, each of which has responsibility for a small portion of it. This arrangement diffuses responsibility and limits the amount and scope of decision making that is necessary. There is no expectation that the moral implications will be considered at any of these points, nor is there any opportunity to do so. The organizational processes also help further legitimize the actions of each participant. By proceeding in routine fashion—processing papers, exchanging memos, diligently carrying out their assigned tasks—the different units mutually reinforce each other in the view that what is going on must be perfectly normal, correct, and legitimate. The shared illusion that they are engaged in a legitimate enterprise helps the participants assimilate their activities to other purposes, such as the efficiency of their performance, the productivity of their unit, or the cohesiveness of their group (see Janis, 1972).

Normalization of atrocities is more difficult to the extent that there are constant reminders of the true meaning of the enterprise. Bureaucratic inventiveness in the use of language helps to cover up such meaning. For example, the SS had a set of *Sprachregelungen,* or "language rules," to govern descriptions of their extermination program. As Arendt (1964) points out, the term *language rule* in itself was "a code name; it meant what in ordinary language would be called a lie" (p. 85). The code names for killing and liquidation were "final solution," "evacuation," and "special treatment." The war in Indochina produced its own set of euphemisms, such as "protective reaction," "pacification," and "forced-draft urbanization and modernization." The use of euphemisms allows participants in sanctioned massacres to differentiate their actions from ordinary killing and destruction and thus to avoid confronting their true meaning.

Dehumanization

Authorization processes override standard moral considerations; routinization processes reduce the likelihood that such considerations will arise. Still, the inhibitions against murdering one's fellow human beings are generally so strong that the victims must also be stripped of their human status if they are to be subjected to systematic killing. Insofar as they are dehumanized, the usual principles of morality no longer apply to them.

Sanctioned massacres become possible to the extent that the victims are deprived in the perpetrators' eyes of the two qualities essential to being perceived as fully human and included in the moral compact that governs human relationships: *identity*—standing as independent, distinctive individuals, capable of making choices and entitled to live their own lives—and *community*—fellow membership in an interconnected network of individuals who care for each other and respect each other's individuality and rights (Kelman, 1973; see also Bakan, 1966, for a related distinction between "agency" and "communion"). Thus, when a group of people is defined entirely in terms of a category to which they belong, and when this category is excluded from the human family, moral restraints against killing them are more readily overcome.

Dehumanization of the enemy is a common phenomenon in any war situation. Sanctioned massacres, however, presuppose a more extreme degree of dehumanization, insofar as the killing is not in direct response to the target's threats or provocations. It is not what they have done that marks such victims for death but who they are—the category to which they happen to belong. They are the victims of policies that regard their systematic destruction as a desirable end or an acceptable means. Such extreme dehumanization becomes possible when the target group can readily be identified as a separate category of people who have historically been stigmatized and excluded by the victimizers; often the victims belong to a distinct racial, religious, ethnic, or political group regarded as inferior or sinister. The traditions, the habits, the images, and the vocabularies for dehumanizing such groups are already well established and can be drawn upon when the groups are selected for massacre. Labels help deprive the victims of identity and community, as in the epithet "gooks" that was commonly used to refer to Vietnamese and other Indochinese peoples.

The dynamics of the massacre process itself further increase the participants' tendency to dehumanize their victims. Those who participate as part of the bureaucratic apparatus increasingly come to see their victims as bodies to be counted and entered into their reports, as faceless figures that will determine their productivity rates and promotions. Those who participate in the massacre directly—in the field, as it were—are reinforced in their perception of the victims as less than human by observing their very victimization. The only way they can justify what is being done to these people—both by others and by themselves—and the only way they can extract some degree of meaning out of the absurd events in which they find themselves participating (see Lifton, 1971, 1973) is by coming to believe that the victims are subhuman and deserve to be rooted out. And thus the process of dehumanization feeds on itself.

REFERENCES

Arendt, H. (1964). *Eichmann in Jerusalem: A report on the banality of evil.* New York: Viking Press.

Bakan, D. (1966). *The duality of human existence.* Chicago: Rand McNally.

Department of the Army. (1956). *The law of land warfare* (Field Manual, No. 27-10). Washington, DC: U.S. Government Printing Office.

Falk, R. A., Kolko, G., & Lifton, R. J. (Eds.). (1971). *Crimes of war.* New York: Vintage Books.

French, P. (Ed.). (1972). *Individual and collective responsibility: The massacre at My Lai.* Cambridge, MA: Schenkman.

Goldstein, J., Marshall, B., & Schwartz, J. (Eds.). (1976). *The My Lai massacre and its cover- up: Beyond the reach of law?* (The Peers Report with a supplement and introductory essay on the limits of law). New York: Free Press.

Hammer, R. (1971). *The court-martial of Lt. Calley.* New York: Coward, McCann, & Geoghegan.

Hersh, S. (1970). *My Lai 4: A report on the massacre and its aftermath.* New York: Vintage Books.

_____. (1972). *Cover-up.* New York: Random House.

Janis, I. L. (1972). *Victims of groupthink: A psychological study of foreign-policy decisions and fiascoes.* Boston: Houghton Mifflin.

Kelman, H. C. (1973). Violence without moral restraint: Reflections on the dehumanization of victims and victimizers. *Journal of Social Issues,* 29(4), 25–61.

Lewin, K. (1947). Group decision and social change. In T. M. Newcomb & E. L. Hartley (Eds.), *Readings in social psychology.* New York: Holt.

Lifton, R. J. (1971). Existential evil. In N. Sanford, C. Comstock, & Associates, *Sanctions for evil: Sources of social destructiveness.* San Francisco: Jossey-Bass.

_____. (1973). *Home from the war—Vietnam veterans: Neither victims nor executioners.* New York: Simon & Schuster.

Manual for courts martial, United States (Rev. ed.). (1969). Washington, DC: U.S. Government Printing Office.

Schirmer, D. B. (1971, April 24). *My Lai was not the first time.* New Republic, pp. 18–21.

Williams, B. (1985, April 14–15). "I will never forgive," says My Lai survivor. *Jordan Times* (Amman), p. 4.

THINKING ABOUT THE READING

According to Kelman and Hamilton, social processes can create conditions under which usual restraints against violence are weakened. What social processes were in evidence during the My Lai massacre? The incident they describe provides us with an uncomfortable picture of human nature. Do you think most people would have reacted the way the soldiers at My Lai did? Are we all potential massacrers? Does the phenomenon of obedience to authority go beyond the tightly structured environment of the military? Can you think of incidents in your own life when you've done something—perhaps harmed or humiliated another person—because of the powerful influence of others? How might Kelman and Hamilton explain the actions of the individuals who carried out the hijackings and attacks of September 11, 2001, or of the American soldiers who abused Iraqi prisoners in their custody?

Hernando Washington

LISA J. MCINTYRE

(1998)

One of the things that sets sociologists apart from ordinary people is their concern for the social. In their professional lives, sociologists tend to ignore individual cases and focus on aggregates or groups. For example, Émile Durkheim studied suicide in order to discover what factors contributed to fluctuations in the overall rates of suicide; he had no interest in what might lead particular individuals to take their lives.

Professional sociologists study *social* facts simply because these are interesting (at least to us). But to the layperson trying to live life in society, social facts may seem irrelevant. Why a society's crime rate goes up and down seems much less intriguing than why *my* house was robbed, or why *I* was mugged on the street. Likewise, the social forces that propel the unemployment rate are not nearly as interesting as the matter of why I am having a difficult time finding a job.

As C. Wright Mills pointed out, however, having a sociological imagination allows us to make connections between individuals and the societies in which they live. And, for the student of sociology, the acquisition of this imagination brings with it an enhanced ability to make sense of the behavior of individuals. Recall what Mills stressed as the "first fruit" of the sociological imagination: "the idea that the individual can understand his own experience and gauge his own fate only by locating himself within his period." It was in this sense that Stephanie Coontz brought to bear the sociological concept of "situated social power" to help her understand her own relationships with her teaching assistants, as well as the personal troubles of the woman whose husband did not appreciate her heroic housework.

From the viewpoint of the professional sociologist, the following reading may seem out of place in a sociology reader, because its focus is on an individual and how he responded to his immediate social milieu. But I have included it for the benefit of nonsociologists; written in 1999, it provides an example of how having an understanding of the impact of the social milieu can help us to understand the all-too-frequently unintelligible behaviors of individuals in our environment.

To get a PhD, one has to write something called a dissertation. It's essentially a research paper, and sometimes a very long research paper. Mine, for example, ended up being two hundred plus pages. I wrote my dissertation on public defenders—those attorneys who are paid by the state to defend people who are accused of crimes but can't afford to hire their own lawyer. The basic question was this: How can these attorneys defend individuals they know are guilty of crimes, especially if they are terrible crimes? Ultimately, I arrived at my answer by looking not just at the private consciences of the public defenders but also at what Mills would have called their social milieux or surroundings.

I met a number of murderers in the course of my research, but Hernando was my first one; and in part because he was my first, he left a large impression on me. But this crime also made a big impression on me because it seemed so bizarre. It never should have happened the way it did. But you can judge for yourself. I will tell you the story as I learned it.

Warning; The first time I heard this story, I remember being shocked. I remember, in fact, feeling nauseous. It's not because anyone showed me terrible pictures of the crime scene; it's just because the whole thing seemed so awful. And it *seemed* so awful because it *was* awful. That led me to wonder. Should I share this story with college students? Possibly, no one is (or should be) worldly enough to hear about this sort of thing.

The Case

This story takes place in Chicago. The major player in the story is a man named Hernando Washington. At various times, his nicknames included the Reverend and the Deacon, because he was president of the youth choir. His other nickname was Prince, because he was so charming and good-looking.

Before I get to the story, let me tell you a bit about the neighborhood in which Hernando lived, or as Mills would put it, *his social milieu*. It was on the South Side of Chicago. In a song from the 1970s, Jim Croce called the South Side of Chicago "the baddest part of town." That was an astute observation. It is the baddest part of town; chances are, if you lived on the South Side, you'd never be able to get a cab driver to take you home at night; some cabs won't even venture there in the daytime.

The police refer to a murder that involves a man and woman on the South Side as a "South Side divorce." A great deal of its reputation involves the fact that the South Side of Chicago is heavily populated by people who are poor—mostly African Americans. Perhaps that's why the police tend to disrespect the people who live there. The police often call murders that involve African American killers and victims as "63rd Street misdemeanors." Police also take much longer to respond to calls on the South Side. The clear message to the people who live there is that they really aren't a part of the community that the Chicago police are pledged to "serve and to protect." This, I think, is an important fact.

On April 1, 1978, Hernando "Prince" Washington was arrested and charged with robbery, aggravated kidnapping, rape, and murder. His victim, 29-year-old Sarah Gould, was the wife of a physician and the mother of a small child. Sarah Gould had the great misfortune to be one of the 787 people in Chicago and one of the 20,432 people in the United States who were murdered that year.

When I say that Sarah had the "great misfortune" to be murdered, I mean that. Statistically, she should not have been a murder victim. Nationally, the murder rate for white women in 1978 was 2.8 per 100,000 population. For white men, it was 9.0; for black women, 12.8; and for black men, 58.1. Not only was Sarah white, but she was killed by a stranger. And in 1978, most murder victims were killed by people they knew—friends, lovers, family members, acquaintances, or neighbors. Of all the recorded acts of criminal violence—batteries, assaults, murders—in 1978, less than a third were committed by strangers. This was especially true for women: When the violent act was committed by a stranger, the victim was typically male.

Finally, Sarah Gould was white while Hernando was black. This was one of the more unusual aspects of the case. Most violence, and certainly most murders, involve persons of the same race.

So, the odds were really against Sarah Gould being murdered—however you want to look at it.

That year, April 1, April Fool's Day, fell on a Saturday. The story actually begins two days earlier. That Thursday afternoon, Hernando went out to do his sister Leah a favor. She had just bought a car, a used two-year-old Oldsmobile Cutlass, and the dealer had called the day before to tell her it was ready to be picked up. Hernando offered to do this for her, partly because he wanted to drive the car. His sister, who is ten years older than Hernando, said that would be fine as long as Hernando came to pick her up when she was done with work. Leah worked at the post office and got off work ten minutes before midnight.

Hernando picked up the car, but of course he didn't drive it straight home. Instead, he cruised around his South Side neighborhood for a while. However, he didn't see any of his friends, so he decided to cruise up to the north part of the city.

For Sarah Gould, that was a fatal decision.

Hernando later said he didn't have any particular plan, but eventually he admitted that just maybe, in the back of his mind, he thought he might rob someone. But it was nothing definite. He would simply drive around and see what happened,

Once up north, he drove to Northwestern University's hospital parking lot. He got out of his car and sat on the steps of a nearby building.

Robbery and Abduction

Around 7:30 P.M., Hernando saw a woman getting out of a reddish-orange VW Rabbit. *He* approached her, gun in hand, and demanded her money. Sarah gave him $25, explaining that it was all the money she had, but he grabbed her by the arm, dragged her back to his car, and shoved her inside.

Later, when asked why he did that, he told his lawyers that he'd noticed a bunch of people walking toward them and he didn't want them to know that he had just robbed this woman. He said he was afraid that she'd scream or run or something.

Once Hernando got Sarah into the car, he was still afraid that she'd somehow make trouble, so he ordered her to take off her slacks and underpants. He threw her clothing underneath her car and then drove off.

In his confession to the police, Hernando had this to say:

She was real excited, you know, asking me not to hurt her and I was constantly telling her I wouldn't hurt her, that all I want is money. She was sitting in the front seat alongside of me. We drove off, and she asked me, "What are you going to do to me?" *and* I told her that I would take her away from the area, so I would have a chance, you know, to get away without being caught.

He kept assuring her that he would not hurt her.

The Phone Call

After Hernando drove around for several hours, Sarah said that he should let her go because her husband and son would be getting worried about her. He considered this for a while and then asked her if she'd like to call home. He stopped at a gas station that was closed for the evening, but it had a phone booth.

Sarah's husband, who was indeed worried about her, later told police that she had said something to the effect that she was okay. He asked her, "When are you coming home?" There was a pause, and then he could hear Sarah asking someone when she'd be home. In the background, he heard a male voice saying "an hour." He then asked, "Where are you?" She asked, "Where are we?" Her husband heard the answer: "You'll be home in an hour, bitch, come on."

After the phone call, Hernando told police,

I turned from the phone, going around the car and at this time, when I, you know, walked around to my car, she broke and ran. I was running after her. I asked her, I said, "Why are you acting like that? I have not hurt you, I told you I will let you go, I just want to make it as safe for me as you want it safe for yourself."

Then, as it was approaching midnight, Hernando pulled the car into a dark alley. He explained to Sarah that he had to go pick someone up and that she couldn't stay in the front seat of the car while he did this. Perhaps for a moment Sarah thought he was going to let her go, but instead, he forced her into the trunk telling her that if she was quiet, everything would be okay.

At exactly 11:50 P.M., Hernando was where he was supposed to be—in the car in front of the main post office. His sister Leah came out and got into the front seat with him. As he drove her home, they talked about the sorts of things that you would expect a brother and sister to talk about—mostly about the new car.

When they got home, Hernando waited in the car until Leah was inside the house. He had always been very concerned about her safety.

A few years earlier, Leah had been raped on her way home from work. Two men grabbed her, dragged her into an alley, stripped off her clothes, and raped her repeatedly. Afterwards, she crawled out of the alley and was relieved to see a police car there. The two officers looked at her, a black woman with her face bleeding and her clothes torn up, and said "Get home by yourself, bitch." Maybe they didn't want her to mess up the back of their patrol car.

Usually, Hernando met his sister after work—but that night he'd had a bike accident and was running late.

Indeed, Hernando's family had not had a great deal of luck when it came to dealing with the police. A few years earlier, Hernando's brother James had been at a party when he was shot by one of the neighborhood guys. Some of James's friends took him to the emergency room, but they were afraid to stay with him because gunshot wounds tend to attract attention. They left him in the emergency room, where he bled to death before the medical staff got to him. "Everyone knew" who had shot Hernando's brother, but for some reason the police didn't take him into custody. It was at that point that Hernando bought his first gun.

Then Hernando drove a few blocks away, stopped, and let Sarah out of the trunk. She reminded him of his promise to let her go, but he said they'd have to go back and get her clothes, because he didn't want to let her go until she was fully dressed again., He drove back to the hospital parking lot, but her clothes were gone; by now, the police had them.

When Sarah had driven into that parking lot earlier in the evening, she was on her way to a Lamaze class she was supposed to teach that night. Eventually, her students became worried about her, called her husband, and found out that she wasn't home. And, of course, he thought she was in class. Next, the class notified hospital security, which investigated and found Sarah's car in the parking lot. When they saw her keys in the ignition and her pants and underpants under the car, the security officers were naturally concerned. They called her husband, who immediately called the police to file a missing person's report.

Finding the clothes missing from under the car scared Hernando. Sarah told him that it didn't matter, that she could go home without them—she was covered enough, she said, by her long raincoat. But he was adamant that he wasn't going to let her go until he'd found her something to wear or, as he put it, until she was "decent" again. He said, "I've got to think of somewhere to get you some clothes."

The Rape

By now, it was well past midnight. Hernando thought it was much too late to go to a friend's house and borrow some clothes, so instead, he drove them back down to the South Side. On the way, he stopped and bought a pint of rum, leaving Sarah alone in the car for a moment. Then, he drove to a motel, got out of the car (again leaving Sarah in the front seat alone), registered for a room—in his name. He later told police, "I let her wash up. First, she was kind of skeptical. I guess she was frightened. I kept reassuring her that I would not do anything to her. After a while, she went into the bathroom and washed up." Then, he told police, they both went to sleep.

But that was a lie. What really happened next, as Hernando admitted to his attorneys, was that he raped Sarah.

The next morning, Hernando left Sarah alone in the room while he checked out. After they left the motel, he stopped the car and put her back into the trunk. Then he drove to his parents' house to get a change of clothing for himself.

A few blocks later, Hernando let Sarah out of the trunk. Then he drove to a northwestern suburb where he had an appointment. On the way, he again stopped in an alley and forced her into the trunk while he "took care of some business."

What was this urgent appointment? Hernando's "appointment" was in one of the felony trial courtrooms in Cook County, Illinois. At the time all of this was going on, Hernando was out on bail. A year

earlier, Hernando had been arrested on charges of rape and aggravated kidnapping. His parents had taken out a loan, paid his bail, and hired him a private lawyer, who told Hernando that he would probably beat the rap and not to worry.

In any case, that Friday, March 31, was the scheduled trial date for the year-old rape case. When the case was called, however, the prosecutor requested a continuance, which the judge granted. Feeling good, Hernando walked out of the courtroom a relatively free man; he even offered his lawyer's assistant a ride back downtown.

When Hernando got back to his car, he saw a couple of people standing near it, seemingly talking to his trunk. Hernando told them to get lost and sped away. But one of the people got Hernando's license plate number and called it in to the police. The dispatcher who took the call about a "woman in the trunk" relayed the message to the detective division; someone placed it on a detective's desk.

Unfortunately, that particular detective had taken off—unannounced—for the weekend, and so no one found the message until the next morning. By then, it was too late. Sarah was dead.

Hernando let Sarah out of the trunk and told her he was disappointed that she'd tried to get help. After all, hadn't he told her that he wasn't going to hurt her and that he would let her go as soon as she got some clothes?

Hernando drove around for a while, and then, as he later told his lawyers, he noticed how dirty her raincoat was. Once again, he told Sarah that he just had to find some decent clothes for her. And once again, she protested that it really wasn't necessary, that she could get home without being fully dressed. Instead, Hernando went to the home of an old girlfriend to borrow some clothes. But he ended up not getting any clothes, claiming that he just didn't quite know how to ask and that her boyfriend was home and he didn't want the boyfriend to hear.

So, he released Sarah from the trunk and drove around some more.

As evening approached, Hernando put Sarah back into the trunk of the car and went to meet some friends at a bar. Actually, they ended up going to several bars. He was, he said, getting pretty tired, but he liked being with his friends. And he was "reluctant" to go back to his car because he knew he'd have to deal with this problem. Finally, well after midnight, he returned to the car.

At this point, as they were listening to Hernando tell his story, one of his attorneys asked him, "If you were beginning to be uncomfortable about your situation, why didn't you just let her go, then and there?"

Hernando said, "Because the neighborhood I was in wasn't a safe neighborhood for a white woman to be alone in."

Instead of letting her go, he took Sarah to another motel and again raped her. Details about the rape are sketchy because Hernando was a "little shy," as he put it, when it came to talking about "sex." And that's how he referred to the rapes—as sex.

The Murder

Early the next morning, Hernando checked out of the motel, drove around for about an hour, and then came to a decision: Clothing or no clothing, it was time to let Sarah go. He parked the car on a residential street, gave her some change, and told her to get on the bus. He said he told her, "All you got to do is walk straight down the street there and get on the bus. Go straight home."

And Sarah, as Hernando always emphasized when he got to this part of the story, Sarah Gould *promised* him that she would get on the bus and go straight home. And, of course, she *promised* not to tell the police.

Hernando let Sarah out of the car, and as he drove away, she was walking toward the bus stop. But, as soon as he was out of sight, she changed her course, walked up to a house, and rang the doorbell.

The house belonged to a Chicago firefighter, who was getting ready for work. He opened the door and saw Sarah—messy, dirty, bruised, and distraught. She told him that she needed help; he told her that he would call the police and that she should stay right there on the porch. Then he closed the door and went to phone the police.

Meanwhile, Hernando had begun to wonder whether Sarah had kept her promise and gotten on the bus. So, he doubled back to where he had left her. He saw Sarah standing on the porch of that house; he saw the firefighter talking to her; he saw the firefighter close the door.

As Hernando recounted it, he felt betrayed—she had broken her promise to him. He parked and got

out of the car. He said that he called out to her. In Hernando's words, here's what happened next:

> I called to her and she came down. I took her by the arm and around the corner to the alley.
>
> I said, "What are you doing? All you had to do was get on the bus. You promised that you would get on the bus."
>
> She protested that I was hurting her, that I was going to kill her.
>
> I said, "No. All you had to do was get on the bus!"
>
> She screamed, "You are going to kill me!"
>
> I said, "No, you said you was going to get on the bus. All you had to do was to get on the bus. Stop screaming. I'm not going to hurt you."
>
> She said, "You are going to kill me."
>
> I said, "I am not going to kill you, shut up, stop screaming."
>
> She said, "You are going to kill me. You are going to kill me."
>
> I said, "I am not going to kill you."
>
> She said, "You are going to kill me. I know you are going to kill me."
>
> So, I shot her. Then I shot her again. She fell. I looked at her, then I broke and ran to my car.

The Chicago firefighter kept his promise and called the police, but they were too late to save Sarah. Around one of her wrists was a cloth stamped with Hernando's father's name. When the police asked the firefighter why he didn't let Sarah into his home, he said that when he saw how beat up she was and saw a black man out on the street calling to her, he assumed it was a domestic dispute and didn't want to get in the middle of it.

Shortly thereafter, the police found Hernando at his parents' home, washing the trunk of his car. At first, he denied everything. Then, when police confronted him with the fact that witnesses had said he had a woman in the trunk of his car, he said it was a prostitute. He varied his story every time the police introduced more information. The police were gentle with him; they read him his Miranda rights, they offered him food and drink. But they confused him with their questions, and it didn't take too long for

Hernando to confess to having robbed, kidnapped, and murdered Sarah.

But when police asked Hernando to sign the confession, he refused, saying that it might make his attorney mad. It didn't matter. That attorney didn't really want to have anything to do with Hernando the murderer, and besides, his parents had no money left to pay him.

Before his trial, his new attorneys—public defenders—persuaded him that his only chance to beat the death penalty was to plead guilty. This was one of those cases that defense attorneys in Chicago, not without a certain amount of irony, call a "dead bang loser case"—one in which "the state has everything but a videotape of the crime." At first, Hernando didn't want to plead guilty; he didn't want his parents to know that he was guilty. But ultimately, in hopes of saving his own life, he did plead guilty.

It didn't work. In January 1980, Hernando was sentenced to death. Finally, on March 25, 1995, after his appeals were exhausted, Hernando was executed by lethal injection.

Hernando's lawyers spent a lot of time trying to find some explanation for what happened. Maybe if they could have understood what had been going on in his mind, it would have helped to save his life. But Hernando couldn't really say. What he kept saying, in essence, was, "What is the big deal? Why is everyone so upset with me?" It was not that, in his mind, Hernando did not understand that robbery, kidnapping, rape, and murder are against the law. The fact that he at first denied doing them helped to prove that. So, Hernando was not legally insane—in the sense that he didn't know right from wrong. It was simply that he could not understand why everyone was so worked up about what he had done.

This is difficult for most of us to understand. Why would someone be surprised at getting into really serious trouble for robbing, kidnapping, raping, and murdering another human being? At first, I could not make any sense of Hernando's confusion on this point. But eventually, as my horror receded, I was able to bring a more sociological perspective to bear on the whole subject. In other words, I had to call upon my sociological imagination—I had to look for the general in the particular.

Let me begin my explanation with an analogy. Last semester, in my introductory class, two students decided to turn in the same paper. They weren't in the same section, so I guess they thought they could get away with it. Unfortunately for them, in my department the professors discuss the papers because we want to be sure that we are all grading consistently. We noticed that the two students had submitted the same paper, so we called them in and said, "Hey, you cheated. And, as it says in the syllabus, if you cheat, you flunk."

At first, in each case, the students denied the accusation. However, when confronted with positive proof (copies of the papers with their names on them), they admitted what they had done. But, they said, our reaction was way out of line. Yes, they had read in the syllabus that getting caught cheating meant flunking the course. But flunking was simply *too much* punishment. In one case, flunking meant more than getting an F; it meant losing scholarship and loan money.

Hernando's reaction was much the same: "Okay, I did this, but you shouldn't punish me; certainly, you shouldn't punish me this much."

You may be thinking that my analogy isn't really appropriate, that there is no way to compare students who cheat with people who murder And, of course, I would not compare the behaviors. What I am comparing is how the individuals thought about their acts and especially their reactions to the punishment.

Both the murder and the cheating were done in hopes of not getting caught; and in neither case did the perpetrators plan on getting caught. Furthermore, when they were caught, each thought the punishment was way out of proportion to the crime. In the case of the students, they argued that the consequences were much too severe, that cheating on a paper wasn't that bad and that losing a scholarship is unfair. In part, too, I think the students were shocked to find that we actually were going to flunk them. I suspect that to the degree they thought about it in advance, they expected *to* be given another chance, or to receive some lesser punishment. It's possible that they knew of other students who had been caught but not punished for cheating. In any case, their view was that punishment was unfair.

Hernando's reaction was much the same. He acted as if he thought that people were simply too worked up over his deeds. Being sentenced to death was just not acceptable to him. Like our students, he showed no real remorse for what he had done. He was only sorry that he had been caught and had to deal with the consequences.

Again, I suspect that some of you won't like my analogy. Perhaps you can understand why the students might feel that the punishment for cheating was too harsh. But you might wonder how Hernando could think that he should not be given the more serious punishment for what he'd done wrong.

This is where having a sociological imagination becomes helpful. The students felt abused because they did not see cheating as such a horrendous crime. After all, cheating happened all the time, and in any case, it was only a class paper.

The same kind of logic can be used to explain Hernando's reaction. Recall that Hernando had grown up on Chicago's South Side, where, when a husband killed his wife, it was jokingly referred to by police as a "South Side divorce." That sort of attitude from officials teaches people that life is not very valuable. And, as I mentioned previously, Hernando had learned some more personal, and painful, lessons about the low value placed on life. When his sister was raped, the police would not help her; they would not even give her a ride home. Also, when his brother was murdered, no one moved to identify the killer, much less to arrest him.

What I did not stress was the degree to which Hernando himself had committed violent acts against others. I did mention that he was out on bail on a rape and kidnapping charge, but in addition to that, he had raped at least three other women. No charges were brought in any of those cases—perhaps because they were not reported, for his victims knew there would be little point. *Those* victims also lived on the South Side.

What about the one charge he did have against him? Hernando's parents had mortgaged their home to get him a private lawyer, who told him he would beat the rape charge. Again, Hernando got the same message: His acts had no consequences. As a result of his life experiences, Hernando had learned that human life doesn't count for too much and that it's okay to take what you want. That's why he was so surprised that he was in so much trouble.

Let's look at what two psychiatrists had to say about Hernando.

He appeared to mask any signs of strong emotions and states that "this is typical for me." He gave an example of—if he were upset about something and it pertained mostly to himself, he wouldn't reveal it to anyone. He would give the impression that he didn't have any feelings, and that he does not reveal his real emotions. . . . He shows a recall of dates and times not in synchrony with reality—this, together with his difficulty with complex problem solving and concept formation—shows impairment, possibly indicative of minimal brain dysfunction. . . .

The evaluation of this man indicates that he is suffering from a borderline personality disorder with episodic deterioration in reality testing and thought processes with episodic psychotic thinking. There is the impression of someone who may be seen as withdrawn or aloof, with a superficial intellectual achievement in the use of language which masks a lowered intellectual achievement. There is also the indication of minimal brain damage, which combined with his psychological profile, would indicate that at times of stress (as existed prior to the commission of the alleged offense) he lacks the ability to plan and to comprehend the consequences of action.

He has at best a fragile purchase on reality. He feels overwhelmed by external stimulation and must constantly narrow his perceptual field in order to manage it. These overwhelmed feelings include those of inferiority and paranoia. While he generally stays close to the normal bounds of reality, he does occasionally lapse into abnormal perception and thinking. His capacity to recover from such lapses is the major reason for forgoing a diagnosis of schizophrenia. In general, his thinking and perception are idiosyncratic. He often does not see what others see. The mode of this distortion is to experience and understand the world in ways that are egocentric and sociopathic. . . . [The results of projective tests] present a picture of a highly impoverished internal world where fantasy finds imagination [and is] often enacted according to the most basic laws of "kill or be killed," or "eat or be eaten."

Note that this second psychiatrist stressed his expert opinion that *Hernando did not have much of a grasp of reality.* The psychiatrist made that judgment because Hernando persisted in seeing the world as a jungle in which the rule is to kill or be killed.

If this psychiatrist had possessed a sociological imagination, he might have realized that Hernando actually had an uncannily accurate grasp of reality.

The understanding of his world as one in which the most basic law was kill or be killed was no delusion or misunderstanding; that was the way things worked on the South Side of Chicago. The very structure of social life in that part of the city meant that people were vulnerable: without help from the police, they had only themselves to fall back on.

But Hernando, too, lacked a sociological imagination—the ability to see beyond his own immediate social milieu, to understand that there are different rules for different people in places like Chicago. On the South Side, where the population is mostly poor and mostly African American, people don't have much power to call on "the establishment" to help them, so life is like a jungle. But on the North Side, things are different. When Hernando drove his sister's car to the North Side of Chicago, he made a fatal error because he drove into a part of the world where life does have value.

On the face of it, we seemingly can never understand what Hernando did. However, it is easier to understand if we use our sociological imagination (as Mills told us to do) and look past Hernando to his social milieu or environment. Then, things begin to make sense.

Don't get me wrong! I'm not saying that we should excuse Hernando for what he did because of the harsh environment in which he grew up. That's not the point. And certainly, that's not the *sociological* point. The goal of sociology is to understand and make predictable people's behavior, to explain what can lead people to act as they do.

What's the benefit of this sort of sociological thinking? What if it were your job to help prevent such crimes? Wouldn't you want to understand how the social environment affects people so that you could, if possible, make changes in that environment? Wouldn't you want to have a sociological imagination?

THINKING ABOUT THE READING

Lisa McIntyre claims that sociologists view people's behavior through the lens of the social milieu in which they live. What are some of the factors that shaped Hernando Washington's social milieu? How do these help us to understand his crimes? Consider other examples of individuals who might be unemployed, stuck in traffic, or experiencing the breakup of an intimate relationship, and discuss what larger forces may have impacted their individual experiences. Finally, what larger forces have shaped your social milieu?

CHAPTER 2

Seeing and Thinking Sociologically

Where is society located? This is an intriguing question. Society shapes our behavior and beliefs through social institutions such as religion, law, education, economics, and family. At the same time, we shape society through our interactions with one another and our participation in social institutions. In this way, we can say that society exists as an objective entity that transcends us. But it is also a construction that is created, reaffirmed, and altered through everyday interactions and behavior. Humans are social beings. We constantly look to others to help define and interpret the situations in which we find ourselves. Other people can influence what we see, feel, think, and do. But it's not just other people who influence us. We also live in a *society,* which consists of socially recognizable combinations of individuals (e.g., relationships, groups, and organizations) as well as the products of human action (statuses, roles, culture, and institutions). When we behave, we do so in a social context that consists of a combination of institutional arrangements, cultural influences, and interpersonal expectations. Thus, our behavior in any given situation is our own, but the reasons we do what we do are rooted in these more complex social factors.

In "The (Mis)Education of Monica and Karen," Hamilton and Armstrong explore how some institutions of higher learning are structured to serve well-funded and academically accomplished out-of-state students to the detriment of modestly funded and less academically prepared in-state students. These authors identify how the social and academic structures of these types of universities negatively impact students who do not have the resources to navigate through them. This article shows that educational achievement and outcomes are not solely determined by individuals, but organizationally produced. They suggest that universities need to rethink their approaches in order to serve the needs of all students, by providing more diverse pathways to achievement, and better academic and financial resources.

This social structure provides us with a sense of order in our daily lives. But sometimes that order breaks down. In "Culture of Fear," Barry Glassner shows us how the news media function to *create* a culture that the public takes for granted. He focuses, in particular, on the emotion of fear in U.S. society. We constantly hear horror stories about such urgent social problems as deadly diseases, violent strangers, and out-of-control teens. But Glassner points out that the terrified public concern over certain issues is often inflated by the media and largely unwarranted. Ironically, when we live in a culture of fear, our most serious problems often go ignored.

In the third reading for this chapter, "The Social Context of Hoarding Behavior," Shaeffer delves into the important social context of hoarding and how we can view it as much more than just a psychological disorder. She notes it is embedded in a larger economic, cultural, and historic context that constructs our attitudes towards objects. Practices like consumerism, interior design, collecting, and waste disposal demonstrate the social and economic expectations of our cultural context and the lifestyle these expectations promote in contemporary western society. Moving beyond the medical model allows us to understand that we all, to some degree, practice the behaviors associated with hoarding due to the powerful influence of our historical and cultural roots.

Something to Consider as You Read

When reading the selections in this section, consider how larger structures shape the social context we live in. What rules do educational and economic structures follow in their practices, how are these rules created, and what is their impact? What rules do media journalists use in deciding whether a story is interesting? What role might politics play in decisions of both science and the media about what topics to focus on? What rules do medical institutions use to define medical disorders? On the other hand, in what way might other spheres of social life like cultural and economic systems impact how these various structures operate? In the end, how do such decisions shape our perception of important social problems?

The (Mis)Education of Monica and Karen

LAURA HAMILTON AND ELIZABETH A. ARMSTRONG

(2012)

Monica grew up in a small, struggling Midwestern community, population 3,000, that was once a booming factory town. She was from a working-class family, and paid for most of her education at Midwest U, a "moderately selective" residential university, herself. She worked two jobs, sometimes over 40 hours a week, to afford in-state tuition. Going out-of-state, or to a pricey private school, was simply out of the question without a large scholarship. Attending MU was even a stretch; one year there cost as much as four years at the regional campus near her hometown.

Karen grew up in the same small town as Monica, but in a solidly middle-class family. Her college-educated parents could afford to provide more financial assistance. But even though MU was only three hours away, her father "wasn't too thrilled" about her going so far from home. He had attended a small religious school that was only 10 minutes away.

Neither Karen nor Monica was academically well prepared for college. Both had good, but not stellar, grades and passable SAT scores, which made admission to a more selective school unlikely. Given the lower cost, ease of admission, and opportunity to commute from home, they might have started at the regional campus. However, MU offered, as Monica's mother put it, a chance to "go away and experience college life." Karen refused to look at any other school because she wanted to leave home. As she noted, "I really don't think I'm a small town girl." Monica's family was betting on MU as the best place for her to launch her dream career as a doctor.

Karen and Monica's stories offer us a glimpse into the college experiences of average, in-state students at large, mid-tier public universities. Though they struggled to gain entrance to the flagship campus, they soon found that the structure of social and academic life there served them poorly—and had deleterious effects.

The Great Mismatch

Most four-year residential colleges and universities in the United States are designed to serve well-funded students, who have minimal (if any) caretaking responsibilities, and who attend college full-time after they graduate from high school. Yet only a minority of individuals who pursue post-secondary education in the United States fit this profile. There is a great gap between what the vast majority of Americans need and what four-year institutions offer them.

This mismatch is acutely visible at Midwest U, where Karen and Monica started their college careers. Almost half of those attending four-year colleges find themselves at schools like this one. Students from modest backgrounds who have above average, but not exceptional, academic profiles attend state flagship universities because they believe such schools offer a surefire route to economic security.

Public universities were founded to enable mobility, especially among in-state populations of students—which contributes to their legitimacy in the eyes of the public. In an era of declining state funding, schools like Midwest U have raised tuition and recruited more out-of-state students. They especially covet academically accomplished, ambitious children of affluent families.

As sociologist Mitchell Stevens describes in *Creating a Class,* elite institutions also pursue such students. While observing a small, private school, Stevens overheard an admissions officer describe an ideal applicant: "He's got great SATs [and] he's free [not requiring any financial aid] . . . . He helps us in every way that's quantifiable." Once private colleges skim off affluent, high-performing students, large, middle-tier, public universities are left to compete for the tuition dollars of less studious students from wealthy families.

How, we wondered, do in-state students fare in this context? To find out, for over five years we followed a dormitory floor of female students through their college careers and into the workforce, conducted an ethnography of the floor, and interviewed the women and their parents. What we found is that schools like MU only serve a segment of their student body well—affluent, socially-oriented, and out-of-state students—to the detriment of typical in-state students like Karen and Monica.

"I'm Supposed to Get Drunk"

Monica and Karen approached the housing application process with little information, and were unprepared for what they encountered when they were assigned to a room in a "party dorm." At MU, over a third of the freshman class is housed in such dorms. Though minimal partying took actually place in the heavily policed residence halls, many residents partied off-site, typically at fraternities, returning in the wee hours drunk and loud. Affluent students—both in and out-of-state—often requested rooms in party dorms, based on the recommendations of their similarly social siblings and friends.

Party dorms are a pipeline to the Greek system, which dominates campus life. Less than 20 percent of the student body at MU is involved in a fraternity or sorority, but these predominately white organizations enjoy a great deal of power. They own space in central campus areas, across from academic buildings and sports arenas. They monopolize the social life of first-year students, offering underage drinkers massive, free supplies of alcohol, with virtual legal impunity. They even enjoy special ties to administrators, with officers sitting on a special advisory board to the dean of students.

Over 40 percent of Monica and Karen's floor joined sororities their first year. The pressure to rush was so intense that one roommate pair who opted out posted a disclaimer on their door, asking people to stop bugging them about it. The entire campus—including academic functions—often revolved around the schedule of Greek life. When a math test for a large, required class conflicted with women's rush, rather than excusing a group of women from a few rush events, the test itself was rescheduled.

Monica, like most economically disadvantaged students, chose not to rush a sorority, discouraged by the mandatory $60 t-shirt, as well as by the costly membership fees. Karen, who was middle class, had just enough funds to make rushing possible. However, she came to realize that Greek houses implicitly screened for social class. She pulled out her boots—practical rain boots that pegged her as a small town, in-state girl instead of an affluent, out-of-state student with money and the right taste in clothing. They were a "dead give-away," she said. She soon dropped out of rush.

Like all but a few students on the 53-person floor, Monica and Karen chose to participate in the party scene. Neither drank much in high school. Nor did they arrive armed with shot glasses or party-themed posters, as some students did. They partied because, as a woman from a similar background put it, "I'm supposed to get drunk every weekend. I'm supposed to go to parties every weekend." With little party experience, and few contacts in the Greek system, Monica and Karen were easy targets for fraternity men's sexual disrespect. Heavy alcohol consumption helped to put them at ease in otherwise uncomfortable situations. "I pretty much became an alcoholic," said Monica. "I was craving alcohol all the time."

Their forced attempts to participate in the party scene showed how poorly it suited their needs. "I tried so hard to fit in with what everybody else was doing here," Monica explained. "I think one morning I just woke up and realized that this isn't me at all; I don't like the way I am right now." She felt it forced her to become more immature. "Growing up to me isn't going out and getting smashed and sleeping around," she lamented. Partying is particularly costly for students of lesser means, who need to grow up sooner, cannot afford to be financially irresponsible, and need the credentials and skills that college offers.

Academic Struggles and "Exotic" Majors

Partying also takes its toll on academic performance, and Monica's poor grades quickly squelched her pre-med dreams. Karen, who hoped to become a teacher, also found it hard to keep up. "I did really bad in that math class, the first elementary ed math class," one of three that were required. Rather than retake the class, Karen changed her major to one that was popular among affluent, socially oriented students on the floor: sports broadcasting.

She explained, "I'm from a really small town and it's just all I ever really knew was jobs that were around me, and most of those are teachers." A woman on her floor was majoring in sports broadcasting, which she had never considered. "I would have never thought about that. And so, I saw hers, and I was like that's something that I really like. One of my interests is sports, watching them, playing them," she reasoned. "I could be a sportscaster on ESPN if I really wanted to."

Karen's experience shows the seductive appeal of certain "easy majors." These are occupational and professional programs that are often housed in their own schools and colleges. They are associated with a higher overall GPA and, as sociologists Richard Arum and Josipa Roksa report in *Academically Adrift*, lower levels of learning than majors in the more challenging sciences and humanities housed in colleges of arts and sciences.

In many easy majors, career success also depends on personal characteristics (such as appearance, personality, and aesthetic taste) that are developed outside of the classroom—often prior to entering college. Socially oriented students flock to fields like communications, fashion, tourism, recreation, fitness, and numerous "business-lite" options, which are often linked to sports or the arts, rather than the competitive business school. About a third of the student body majored in business, management, marketing, communications, journalism, and related subfields.

Karen's switch to sports broadcasting gave her more time to socialize. But education is a more practical major that translates directly into a career; hiring rests largely on the credential. In contrast, success in sports broadcasting is dependent on class-based characteristics—such as family social ties to industry insiders. Several of Karen's wealthier peers secured plum internships in big cities because their parents made phone calls for them; Karen could not even land an unpaid internship with the Triple-A baseball team located 25 minutes from her house.

No one Karen encountered on campus helped her to assess the practicality of a career in this field. Her parents were frustrated that she had been persuaded not to graduate with a recognizable marketable skill. As her mother explained, "She gets down there and you start hearing all these exotic sounding majors, which half I'm not sure quite what jobs they're going to end up with." Her mother was frustrated that Karen "went to see the advisor to make plans for her sophomore year, and they're going, 'Well, what's your passion?'" Her mother was not impressed. "How many people do their passion? To me, that's more what you do for a hobby . . . . I mean most people, that's not what their job is."

Halfway through college, when Karen realized she could not get an internship, much less a job, in sports broadcasting, her parents told her to switch back to education. The switch was costly: it was going to take her two more years to complete. As her mother complained, "When you're going through the orientation . . . they're going, 'oh, most people change their major five times.' And they make it sound like it's no big deal. But yeah, they're making big bucks by kids changing."

Leaving Midwest U Behind

Monica left MU after her first year. "I was afraid if I continued down there that I would just go crazy and either not finish school, or get myself in trouble," she explained. "And I just didn't want to do that. "She immediately enrolled in a beauty school near her home. Dissatisfied with the income she earned as a hairstylist, she later entered a community college to complete an associate degree in nursing. She paid for her nursing classes as she studied, but had 10,000 dollars in student loan debt from her time at MU. Still, her debt burden was substantially smaller than if she had stayed there; some of her MU peers had amassed over 50,000 dollars in loans by graduation.

Because her GPA was too low to return to elementary education at MU, Karen transferred to a regional college during her fourth year. Since the classes she took for sports broadcasting did not fulfill any requirements, it took her six years to graduate. Karen's parents, who reported that they spent the first 10 years of their married life paying off their own loans, took out loans to cover most of the cost, and anticipated spending even longer to finance their daughter's education.

Monica and Karen were not the only ones on their dormitory floor to leave MU. Nine other in-state women, the majority of whom were from working-class backgrounds, did as well. The only out-of-state student who transferred left for a higher-ranked institution. While we were concerned that the in-state leavers, most of whom were moving down the ladder of prestige to regional campuses, would suffer, they actually did better than in-state women from less privileged families who stayed at MU. Their GPAs improved, they selected majors with a more direct payoff, and they were happier overall.

The institutions to which women moved played a large role in this transformation. As one leaver described the regional campus to which she transferred, it "doesn't have any fraternities or sororities. It only has, like, 10 buildings." But, she said, "I just really love it." One of the things she loved was that nobody cared about partying. "They're there just to graduate and get through." It prioritized the needs of a different type of student: "Kids who have lower social economic status, who work for their school."

Without the social pressures of MU, it was possible to, as Karen put it, "get away from going out all the time, and refocus on what my goal was for this part of my life." Few majors like sports broadcasting and fashion merchandising were available, reducing the possible ways to go astray academically. Those who attended regional or community colleges trained to become accountants, teachers, social workers, nurses, or other health professionals. At the conclusion of our study, they had better employment prospects than those from similar backgrounds who stayed at MU.

The Importance of Institutional Context

It is tempting to assume that academic success is determined, in large part, by what students bring with them—different ability levels, resources, and orientations to college life. But Monica and Karen's stories demonstrate that what students get out of college is also organizationally produced. Students who were far more academically gifted than Monica or Karen sometimes floundered at MU, while others who were considerably less motivated breezed through college. The best predictor of success was whether there was a good fit between a given student's resources and agendas, and the structure of the university.

Monica and Karen's struggles at MU can be attributed, in part, to the dominance of a "party pathway" at that institution. These organizational arrangements—a robust, university-supported Greek system, and an array of easy majors—are designed to attract and serve affluent, socially oriented students. The party pathway is not a hard sell; the idea that college is about fun and partying is celebrated in popular culture and actively promoted by leisure and alcohol industries. The problem is that this pathway often appeals to students for whom it is ill suited.

Regardless of what they might want, students from different class backgrounds require different things. What Monica and Karen needed was a "mobility pathway." When resources are limited, mistakes—whether a semester of grades lost to partying, or courses that do not count toward a credential—can be very costly. Monica and Karen needed every course to move them toward a degree that would translate directly into a job.

They also needed more financial aid than they received—grants, not loans—and much better advising. A skilled advisor who understood Karen's background and her abilities might have helped her realize that changing majors was a bad idea. But while most public universities provide such advising support for disadvantaged students, these programs are often small, and admit only the best and brightest of the disadvantaged—not run-of-the-mill students like Monica and Karen.

Monica, Karen (and others like them) did not find a mobility pathway at MU. Since university resources are finite, catering to one population of students often comes at a cost to others, especially if their needs are at odds with one another. When a party pathway is the most accessible avenue through a university, it is easy to stumble upon, hard to avoid, and it crowds out other pathways.

As Monica and Karen's stories suggest, students are not necessarily better served by attending the most selective college they can get into. The structure of the pathways available at a given school greatly influences success. When selecting a college or university, families should consider much more than institutional selectivity. They should also assess whether the school fits the particular student's needs.

Students and parents with limited financial resources should look for schools with high retention rates among minority and first-generation students, where there are large and accessible student services for these populations. Visible Greek systems and reputations as party schools, in contrast, should be red flags.

Families should investigate what majors are available, whether they require prerequisites, and, to the extent it is possible, what additional investments are required to translate a particular major into a job. Are internships required? Will the school link the student to job opportunities, or are families expected to do so on their own? These are some questions they should ask.

Collectively, the priorities of public universities and other higher education institutions that support "party pathways" should be challenged. Reducing the number of easy majors, pulling university support from the Greek system, and expanding academic advising for less privileged students would help. At federal and state levels, greater commitment to the funding of higher education is necessary. If public universities are forced to rely on tuition and donations for funding, they will continue to appeal to those who can pay full freight. Without these changes, the mismatch between what universities offer and what most postsecondary students need is likely to continue.

THINKING ABOUT THE READING

Institutions of higher education provide opportunities to achieve social mobility. Ironically, according to Hamilton and Armstrong, universities like MU seem to do quite the opposite, in some cases. Indeed, the authors suggest that institutions like MU are structured to serve one specific population of students. What is that population? Using your sociological imagination, what organizational structures at MU shaped the decisions of students and their opportunity for academic achievement and success following graduation? What would the organizational structures look like that could have helped Monica and Karen achieve success? Furthermore, what social forces beyond the university impacted the structures of MU and the experiences of all students on campus? How, if at all, do you see some of the themes in this article reflected in your institution and campus life?

Culture of Fear

BARRY GLASSNER

(1999)

Why are so many fears in the air, and so many of them unfounded? Why, as crime rates plunged throughout the 1990s, did two-thirds of Americans believe they were soaring? How did it come about that by mid-decade 62 percent of us described ourselves as "truly desperate" about crime—almost twice as many as in the late 1980s, when crime rates were higher? Why, on a survey in 1997, when the crime rate had already fallen for a half dozen consecutive years, did more than half of us disagree with the statement "This country is finally beginning to make some progress in solving the crime problem"?[1]

In the late 1990s the number of drug users had decreased by half compared to a decade earlier; almost two-thirds of high school seniors had never used any illegal drugs, even marijuana. So why did a majority of adults rank drug abuse as the greatest danger to America's youth? Why did nine out of ten believe the drug problem is out of control, and only one in six believe the country was making progress?[2]

Give us a happy ending and we write a new disaster story. In the late 1990s the unemployment rate was below 5 percent for the first time in a quarter century. People who had been pounding the pavement for years could finally get work. Yet pundits warned of imminent economic disaster. They predicted inflation would take off, just as they had a few years earlier—also erroneously—when the unemployment rate dipped below 6 percent.[3]

We compound our worries beyond all reason. Life expectancy in the United States has doubled during the twentieth century. We are better able to cure and control diseases than any other civilization in history. Yet we hear that phenomenal numbers of us are dreadfully ill. In 1996 Bob Garfield, a magazine writer, reviewed articles about serious diseases published over the course of a year in the *Washington Post,* the *New York Times,* and *USA Today*. He learned that, in addition to 59 million Americans with heart disease, 53 million with migraines, 25 million with osteoporosis, 16 million with obesity, and 3 million with cancer, many Americans suffer from more obscure ailments such as temporomandibular joint disorders (10 million) and brain injuries (2 million).

Adding up the estimates, Garfield determined that 543 million Americans are seriously sick—a shocking number in a nation of 266 million inhabitants. "Either as a society we are doomed, or someone is seriously double-dipping," he suggested.[4]

Garfield appears to have underestimated one category of patients: for psychiatric ailments his figure was 53 million. Yet when Jim Windolf, an editor of the *New York Observer,* collated estimates for maladies ranging from borderline personality disorder (10 million) and sex addiction (11 million) to less well-known conditions such as restless leg syndrome (12 million) he came up with a figure of 152 million. "But give the experts a little time," he advised. "With another new quantifiable disorder or two, everybody in the country will be officially nuts."[5]

Indeed, Windolf omitted from his estimates new-fashioned afflictions that have yet to make it into the *Diagnostic and Statistical Manual of Mental Disorders* of the American Psychiatric Association: ailments such as road rage, which afflicts more than half of Americans, according to a psychologist's testimony before a congressional hearing in 1997.[6]

The scope of our health fears seems limitless. Besides worrying disproportionately about legitimate ailments and prematurely about would-be diseases, we continue to fret over already refuted dangers. Some still worry, for instance, about "flesh-eating bacteria," "a bug first rammed into our consciousness in 1994 when the U.S. news media picked up on a screamer headline in a British tabloid, "Killer Bug Ate My Face." The bacteria, depicted as more brutal than anything seen in modern times, was said to be spreading faster than the pack of photographers outside the home of its latest victim. In point of fact, however, we were not "terribly vulnerable" to these "superbugs," nor were they "medicine's worst nightmares," as voices in the media warned.

Group A strep, a cyclical strain that has been around for ages, had been dormant for half a century or more before making a comeback. The British pseudoepidemic had resulted in a total of about a dozen deaths in the previous year. Medical experts roundly rebutted the scares by noting that of 20 to 30 million strep infections each year in the United States fewer than 1 in 1,000 involve serious strep A complications, and only 500 to 1,500 people suffer the flesh-eating syndrome, whose proper name is necrotizing fasciitis. Still the fear persisted. Years after the initial scare, horrifying news stories continued to appear, complete with grotesque pictures of victims. A United Press International story in 1998 typical of the genre told of a child in Texas who died of the "deadly strain" of bacteria that the reporter warned "can spread at a rate of up to one inch per hour."[7]

Killer Kids

When we are not worrying about deadly diseases, we worry about homicidal strangers. Every few months for the past several years it seems we discover a new category of people to fear: government thugs in Waco, sadistic cops on Los Angeles freeways and in Brooklyn police stations, and mass-murdering youths in small towns all over the country. A single anomalous event can provide us with multiple groups of people to fear. After the 1995 explosion at the federal building in Oklahoma City, first we panicked about Arabs. "Knowing that the car bomb indicates Middle Eastern terrorists at work, it's safe to assume that their goal is to promote free-floating fear and a measure of anarchy, thereby disrupting American life," a New York Post editorial asserted. "Whatever we are doing to destroy Mideast terrorism, the chief terrorist threat against Americans, has not been working," wrote A. M. Rosenthal in the New York Times.[8]

When it turned out that the bombers were young white guys from middle America, two more groups instantly became spooky: right-wing radio talk show hosts who criticize the government—depicted by President Bill Clinton as "purveyors of hatred and division"—and members of militias. No group of disgruntled men was too ragtag not to warrant big, prophetic news stories.[9]

We have managed to convince ourselves that just about every young American male is a potential mass murderer—a remarkable achievement, considering the steep downward trend in youth crime throughout the 1990s. Faced year after year with comforting statistics, we either ignore them—adult Americans estimate that people under eighteen commit about half of all violent crimes when the actual number is 13 percent—or recast them as "The Lull

Before the Storm" (Newsweek headline). "We know we've got about six years to turn this juvenile crime thing around or our country is going to be living with chaos," Bill Clinton asserted in 1997, even while acknowledging that the youth violent crime rate had fallen 9.2 percent the previous year.[10]

The more things improve the more pessimistic we become. Violence-related deaths at the nation's schools dropped to a record low during the 1996–97 academic year (19 deaths out of 54 million children), and only one in ten public schools reported any serious crime. Yet Time and U.S. News & World Report both ran headlines in 1996 referring to "Teenage Time Bombs." In a nation of "Children Without Souls" (another Time headline that year), "America's beleaguered cities are about to be victimized by a paradigm shattering wave of ultraviolent, morally vacuous young people some call 'the superpredators,'" William Bennett, the former Secretary of Education, and John DiIulio, a criminologist, forecast in a book published in 1996.[11]

Instead of the arrival of superpredators, violence by urban youths continued to decline. So we went looking elsewhere for proof that heinous behavior by young people was "becoming increasingly more commonplace in America" (CNN). After a sixteen-year-old in Pearl, Mississippi, and a fourteen-year-old in West Paducah, Kentucky, went on shooting sprees in late 1997, killing five of their classmates and wounding twelve others, these isolated incidents were taken as evidence of "an epidemic of seemingly depraved adolescent murderers" (Geraldo Rivera). Three months later in March 1998 all sense of proportion vanished after two boys ages eleven and thirteen killed four students and a teacher in Jonesboro, Arkansas. No longer, we learned in Time, was it "unusual for kids to get back at the world with live ammunition." When a child psychologist on NBC's "Today" show advised parents to reassure their children that shootings at schools are rare, reporter Ann Curry corrected him. "But this is the fourth case since October," she said.[12]

Over the next couple of months young people failed to accommodate the trend hawkers. None committed mass murder. Fear of killer kids remained very much in the air nonetheless. In stories on topics such as school safety and childhood trauma, reporters recapitulated the gory details of the killings. And the news media made a point of reporting every incident in which a child was caught at school with a gun or making a death threat. In May, when a fifteen-year-old in Springfield, Oregon, did open fire in a cafeteria filled with students, killing two and wounding twenty-three others, the event felt like a continuation of a "disturbing trend" (*New York Times*). The day after the shooting, on National Public Radio's "All Things Considered," the criminologist Vincent Schiraldi tried to explain that the recent string of incidents did not constitute a trend, that youth homicide rates had declined by 30 percent in recent years, and more than three times as many people were killed by lightning than by violence at schools. But the show's host, Robert Siegel, interrupted him. "You're saying these are just anomalous events?" he asked, audibly peeved. The criminologist reiterated that *anomalous* is precisely the right word to describe the events, and he called it "a grave mistake" to imagine otherwise.

Yet given what had happened in Mississippi, Kentucky, Arkansas, and Oregon, could anyone doubt that today's youths are "more likely to pull a gun than make a fist," as Katie Couric declared on the "Today" show?[13]

Roosevelt Was Wrong

We had better learn to doubt our inflated fears before they destroy us. Valid fears have their place; they cue us to danger. False and overdrawn fears only cause hardship.

Even concerns about real dangers, when blown out of proportion, do demonstrable harm. Take the fear of cancer. Many Americans overestimate the prevalence of the disease, underestimate the odds of surviving it, and put themselves at greater risk as a result. Women in their forties believe they have a 1 in 10 chance of dying from breast cancer, a Dartmouth study found. Their real lifetime odds are more like 1 in 250. Women's heightened perception of risk, rather than motivating them to get checkups or seek treatment, can have the opposite effect. A study of daughters of women with breast cancer found an inverse correlation between fear and prevention: the greater a daughter's fear of the disease the less frequent her breast self-examination. Studies of the general population—both men and women—find that large numbers of people who believe they have symptoms of cancer delay going to a doctor, often for several months. When asked why, they report they are terrified about the pain and financial ruin cancer can cause as well as poor prospects for a cure. The irony of course is that early treatment can prevent precisely those horrors they most fear.[14]

Still more ironic, if harder to measure, are the adverse consequences of public panics. Exaggerated perceptions of the risks of cancer at least produce beneficial by-products, such as bountiful funding for research and treatment of this leading cause of death. When it comes to large-scale panics, however, it is difficult to see how potential victims benefit from the frenzy. Did panics a few years ago over sexual assaults on children by preschool teachers and priests leave children better off? Or did they prompt teachers and clergy to maintain excessive distance from children in their care, as social scientists and journalists who have studied the panics suggest? How well can care givers do their jobs when regulatory agencies, teachers' unions, and archdioceses explicitly prohibit them from any physical contact with children, even kindhearted hugs?[15]

Was it a good thing for children and parents that male day care providers left the profession for fear of being falsely accused of sex crimes? In an article in the *Journal of American Culture*, sociologist Mary DeYoung has argued that day care was "refeminized" as a result of the panics. "Once again, and in the time-honored and very familiar tradition of the family, the primary responsibility for the care and socialization of young children was placed on the shoulders of low-paid women," she contends.[16]

We all pay one of the costs of panics: Huge sums of money go to waste. Hysteria over the ritual abuse of children costs billions of dollars in police investigations, trials, and imprisonments. Men and women went to jail for years "on the basis of some of the most fantastic claims ever presented to an American jury," as Dorothy Rabinowitz of the *Wall Street Journal* demonstrated in a series of investigative articles for which she became a Pulitzer Prize finalist in 1996. Across the nation expensive surveillance programs were implemented to protect children from fiends who reside primarily in the imaginations of adults.[17]

The price tag for our panic about overall crime has grown so monumental that even law-and-order zealots find it hard to defend. The criminal justice system costs Americans close to $100 billion a year, most of which goes to police and prisons. In California, we spend more on jails than on higher education. Yet increases in the number of police and prison cells do not correlate consistently with reductions in the number of serious crimes committed. Criminologists who study reductions in homicide rates, for instance, find little difference between cities that substantially expand their police forces and prison capacity and others that do not.[18]

The turnabout in domestic public spending over the past quarter century, from child welfare and antipoverty programs to incarceration, did not even produce reductions in *fear* of crime. Increasing the number of cops and jails arguably has the opposite effect: It suggests that the crime problem is all the more out of control.[19]

Panic-driven public spending generates over the long term a pathology akin to one found in drug addicts. The more money and attention we fritter away on our compulsions, the less we have available for our real needs, which consequently grow larger. While fortunes are being spent to protect children from dangers that few ever encounter, approximately 11 million children lack health insurance, 12 million are malnourished, and rates of illiteracy are increasing.[20]

I do not contend, as did President Roosevelt in 1933, that "the only thing we have to fear is fear itself." My point is that we often fear the wrong things. In the 1990s middle-income and poorer Americans should have worried about unemployment insurance, which covered a smaller share of workers than twenty years earlier. Many of us have had friends or family out of work during economic downturns or as a result of corporate restructuring. Living in a nation with one of the largest income gaps of any industrialized country, where the bottom 40 percent of the population is worse off financially than their counterparts two decades earlier, we might also have worried about income inequality. Or poverty. During the mid- and late 1990s 5 million elderly Americans had no food in their homes, more than 20 million people used emergency food programs each year, and one in five children lived in poverty—more than a quarter million of them homeless. All told, a larger proportion of Americans were poor than three decades earlier.[21]

One of the paradoxes of a culture of fear is that serious problems remain widely ignored even though they give rise to precisely the dangers that the populace most abhors. Poverty, for example, correlates strongly with child abuse, crime, and drug abuse. Income inequality is also associated with adverse outcomes for society as a whole. The larger the gap between rich and poor in a society,

the higher its overall death rates from heart disease, cancer, and murder. Some social scientists argue that extreme inequality also threatens political stability in a nation such as the United States, where we think of ourselves not as "haves and have nots" but as "haves and will haves." "Unlike the citizens of most other nations, Americans have always been united less by a shared past than by the shared dreams of a better future. If we lose that common future," the Brandeis University economist Robert Reich has suggested, "we lose the glue that holds our nation together."[22] . . .

Two Easy Explanations

In the following discussion I will try to answer two questions: Why are Americans so fearful lately, and why are our fears so often misplaced? To both questions the same two-word answer is commonly given. . . . [One] popular explanation blames the news media. We have so many fears, many of them off-base, the argument goes, because the media bombard us with sensationalistic stories designed to increase ratings. This explanation, sometimes called the media-effects theory . . . contains sizable kernels of truth. When researchers from Emory University computed the levels of coverage of various health dangers in popular magazines and newspapers they discovered an inverse relationship: much less space was devoted to several of the major causes of death than to some uncommon causes. The leading cause of death, heart disease, received approximately the same amount of coverage as the eleventh-ranked cause of death, homicide. They found a similar inverse relationship in coverage of risk factors associated with serious illness and death. The lowest-ranking risk factor, drug use, received nearly as much attention as the second-ranked risk factor, diet and exercise.[23]

Disproportionate coverage in the news media plainly has effects on readers and viewers. When Esther Madriz, a professor at Hunter College, interviewed women in New York City about their fears of crime they frequently responded with the phrase "I saw it in the news." The interviewees identified the news media as both the source of their fears and the reason they believed those fears were valid. Asked in a national poll why they believe the country has a serious crime problem, 76 percent of people cited stories they had seen in the media. Only 22 percent cited personal experience.[24]

When professors Robert Blendon and John Young of Harvard analyzed forty-seven surveys about drug abuse conducted between 1978 and 1997, they too discovered that the news media, rather than personal experience, provide Americans with their predominant fears. Eight out of ten adults say that drug abuse has never caused problems in their family, and the vast majority report relatively little direct experience with problems related to drug abuse. Widespread concern about drug problems emanates, Blendon and Young determined, from scares in the news media, television in particular.[25]

Television news programs survive on scares. On local newscasts, where producers live by the dictum "if it bleeds, it leads," drug, crime, and disaster stories make up most of the news portion of the broadcasts. Evening newscasts on the major networks are somewhat less bloody, but between 1990 and 1998, when the nation's murder rate declined by 20 percent, the number of murder stories on network newscasts increased 600 percent (*not* counting stories about O.J. Simpson).[26]

After the dinnertime newscasts, the networks broadcast newsmagazines, whose guiding principle seems to be that no danger is too small to magnify into a national nightmare. Some of the risks reported by such programs would be merely laughable were they not hyped with so much fanfare: "Don't miss *Dateline* tonight or YOU could be the next victim!" Competing for ratings with drama programs and movies during prime-time evening hours, newsmagazines feature story lines that would make a writer for "Homicide" or "ER" wince.[27]

"It can happen in a flash. Fire breaks out on the operating table. The patient is surrounded by flames," Barbara Walters exclaimed on ABC's "20/20" in 1998. The problem— oxygen from a face mask ignited by a surgical instrument—occurs "more often than you might think," she cautioned in her introduction, even though reporter Arnold Diaz would note later, during the actual report, that out of 27 million surgeries each year the situation arises only about a hundred times. No matter, Diaz effectively nullified the reassuring numbers as soon as they left his mouth. To those who "may say it's too small a risk to worry about" he presented distraught victims: a woman with permanent scars on her face and a man whose son had died.[28]

The gambit is common. Producers of TV newsmagazines routinely let emotional accounts trump objective information. In 1994 medical authorities attempted to cut short the brouhaha over flesh-eating bacteria by publicizing the fact that an American is fifty-five times more likely to be struck by lightning than die of the suddenly celebrated microbe. Yet TV journalists brushed this fact aside with remarks like, "whatever the statistics, it's devastating to the victims" (Catherine Crier on "20/20"), accompanied by stomach-turning videos of disfigured patients.[29]

Sheryl Stolberg, then a medical writer for the *Los Angeles Times,* put her finger on what makes the TV newsmagazines so cavalier: "Killer germs are perfect for prime time," she wrote. "They are invisible, uncontrollable, and, in the case of Group A strep, can invade the body in an unnervingly simple manner, through a cut or scrape." Whereas print journalists only described in words the actions of "billions of bacteria" spreading "like underground fires" throughout a person's body, TV newsmagazines made use of special effects to depict graphically how these "merciless killers" do their damage.[30]

In Praise of Journalists

Any analysis of the culture of fear that ignored the news media would be patently incomplete, and of the several institutions most culpable for creating and sustaining scares, the news media are arguably first among equals. They are also the most promising candidates for positive change. Yet by the same token critiques such as Stolberg's presage a crucial shortcoming in arguments that blame the media. Reporters not only spread fears, they also debunk them and criticize one another for spooking the public. A wide array of groups, including businesses, advocacy organizations, religious sects, and political parties, promote and profit from scares. News organizations are distinguished from other fear-mongering groups because they sometimes bite the scare that feeds them.

A group that raises money for research into a particular disease is not likely to negate concerns about that disease. A company that sells alarm systems is not about to call attention to the fact that crime is down. News organizations, on the other hand, periodically allay the very fears they arouse to lure audiences. Some newspapers that ran stories about child murderers, rather than treat every incident as evidence of a shocking trend, affirmed the opposite. After the schoolyard shooting in Kentucky, the *New York Times* ran a sidebar alongside its feature story with the headline "Despite Recent Carnage, School Violence Is Not on Rise." Following the Jonesboro killings they ran a similar piece, this time on a recently released study showing the rarity of violent crimes in schools.[31]

Several major newspapers parted from the pack in other ways. *USA Today* and the *Washington Post,* for instance, made sure their readers knew that what should worry them is the availability of guns. *USA Today* ran news stories explaining that easy access to guns in homes accounted for increases in the number of juvenile arrests for homicide in rural areas during the 1990s. While other news outlets were respectfully quoting the mother of the thirteen-year-old Jonesboro shooter, who said she did not regret having encouraged her son to learn to fire a gun ("it's like anything else, there's some people that can drink a beer and not become an alcoholic"), *USA Today* ran an op-ed piece proposing legal parameters for gun ownership akin to those for the use of alcohol and motor vehicles. And the paper published its own editorial in support of laws that require gun owners to lock their guns or keep them in locked containers. Adopted at that time by only fifteen states, the laws had reduced the number of deaths among children in those states by 23 percent.[32]

The *Washington Post,* meanwhile, published an excellent investigative piece by reporter Sharon Walsh showing that guns increasingly were being marketed to teenagers and children. Quoting advertisements and statistics from gun manufacturers and the National Rifle Association, Walsh revealed that by 1998 the primary market for guns—white males—had been saturated and an effort to market to women had failed. Having come to see children as its future, the gun industry has taken to running ads like the one Walsh found in a Smith & Wesson catalog: "Seems like only yesterday that your father brought you here for the first time," reads the copy beside a photo of a child aiming a handgun, his father by his side. "Those sure were the good times—just you, dad and his Smith & Wesson." [33]

As a social scientist, I am impressed and somewhat embarrassed to find that journalists, more often than media scholars, identify the jugglery involved in making small hazards appear huge and huge hazards disappear from sight. Take, for example, the scare several years ago over the Ebola virus. Another

Washington Post reporter, John Schwartz, identified a key bit of hocus-pocus used to sell that scare. Schwartz called it "the Cuisinart Effect," because it involves the mashing together of images and story lines from fiction and reality. A report by *Dateline NBC* on death in Zaire, for instance, interspersed clips from *Outbreak,* a movie whose plot involves a lethal virus that threatens to kill the entire U.S. population. Alternating between Dustin Hoffman's character exclaiming, "We can't stop it"! and real-life science writer Laurie Garrett, author of *The Coming Plague,* proclaiming that "HIV is not an aberration . . . it's part of a trend," *Dateline*'s report gave the impression that swarms of epidemics were on their way.[34]

Another great journalist-debunker, Malcolm Gladwell, noted that the book that had inspired *Outbreak,* Richard Preston's *The Hot Zone,* itself was written "in self-conscious imitation of a sci-fi thriller." In the real-world incident that occasioned *The Hot Zone,* monkeys infected in Zaire with a strain of Ebola virus were quarantined at a government facility in Reston, Virginia. The strain turned out not to be lethal in humans, but neither Preston in his book nor the screenwriters for *Outbreak* nor TV producers who sampled from the movie let that anticlimax interfere with the scare value of their stories. Preston speculates about an airborne strain of Ebola being carried by travelers from African airports to European, Asian, and American cities. In *Outbreak* hundreds of people die from such an airborne strain before a cure is miraculously discovered in the nick of time to save humanity. In truth, Gladwell points out in a piece in *The New Republic,* an Ebola strain that is both virulent to humans and airborne is unlikely to emerge and would mutate rapidly if it did, becoming far less potent before it had a chance to infect large numbers of people on a single continent, much less throughout the globe. "It is one of the ironies of the analysis of alarmists such as Preston that they are all too willing to point out the limitations of human beings, but they neglect to point out the limitations of microscopic life forms," Gladwell notes.[35]

Such disproofs of disease scares appear rather frequently in general-interest magazines and newspapers, including in publications where one might not expect to find them. The *Wall Street Journal,* for instance, while primarily a business publication and itself a retailer of fears about governmental regulators, labor unions, and other corporate-preferred hobgoblins, has done much to demolish medical myths. Among my personal favorites is an article published in 1996 titled "Fright by the Numbers," in which reporter Cynthia Crossen rebuts a cover story in *Time* magazine on prostate cancer. One in five men will get the disease, *Time* thundered. "That's scary. But it's also a lifetime risk—the accumulated risk over some 80 years of life," Crossen responds. A forty-year-old's chance of coming down with (not dying of) prostate cancer in the next ten years is 1 in 1,000, she goes on to report. His odds rise to 1 in 100 over twenty years. Even by the time he's seventy, he has only a 1 in 20 chance of *any* kind of cancer, including prostate.[36]

In the same article Crossen counters other alarmist claims as well, such as the much-repeated pronouncement that one in three Americans is obese. The number actually refers to how many are overweight, a less serious condition. Fewer are *obese* (a term that is less than objective itself), variously defined as 20 to 40 percent above ideal body weight as determined by current standards.[37]

Morality and Marketing

To blame the media is to oversimplify the complex role that journalists play as both proponents and doubters of popular fears. . . . Why do news organizations and their audiences find themselves drawn to one hazard rather than another?

Mary Douglas, the eminent anthropologist who devoted much of her career to studying how people interpret risk, pointed out that every society has an almost infinite quantity of potential dangers from which to choose. Societies differ both in the types of dangers they select and the number. Dangers get selected for special emphasis, Douglas showed, either because they offend the basic moral principles of the society or because they enable criticism of disliked groups and institutions. In *Risk and Culture,* a book she wrote with Aaron Wildavsky, the authors give an example from fourteenth-century Europe. Impure water had been a health danger long before that time, but only after it became convenient to accuse Jews of poisoning the wells did people become preoccupied with it.

Or take a more recent institutional example. In the first half of the 1990s U.S. cities spent at least $10 billion to purge asbestos from public schools, even though removing asbestos from buildings posed a greater health hazard than leaving it in place. At a time when about one-third of the nation's schools were in need of extensive repairs, the money might have been spent to renovate dilapidated buildings. But hazards posed by seeping asbestos are morally repugnant. A product that was supposed to protect children from fires might be giving them cancer. By directing our worries and dollars at asbestos we express outrage at technology and industry run afoul.[38]

From a psychological point of view extreme fear and outrage are often projections. Consider, for example, the panic over violence against children. By failing to provide adequate education, nutrition, housing, parenting, medical services, and child care over the past couple of decades we have done the nation's children immense harm. Yet we project our guilt onto a cavalcade of bogey people—pedophile preschool teachers, preteen mass murderers, and homicidal au pairs, to name only a few.[39]

When Debbie Nathan, a journalist, and Michael Snedeker, an attorney, researched the evidence behind publicized reports in the 1980s and early 1990s of children being ritually raped and tortured, they learned that although seven out of ten Americans believed that satanic cults were committing these atrocities, few of the incidents had actually occurred. At the outset of each ritual-abuse case the children involved claimed they had not been molested. They later changed their tunes at the urging of parents and law enforcement authorities. The ghastly tales of abuse, it turns out, typically came from the parents themselves, usually the mothers, who had convinced themselves they were true. Nathan and Snedeker suggest that some of the mothers had been abused themselves and projected those horrors, which they had trouble facing directly, onto their children. Other mothers, who had not been victimized in those ways, used the figure of ritually abused children as a medium of protest against male dominance more generally. Allegations of children being raped allowed conventional wives and mothers to speak out against men and masculinity without having to fear they would seem unfeminine. "The larger culture," Nathan and Snedeker note, "still required that women's complaints about inequality and sexual violence be communicated through the innocent, mortified voice of the child."

Diverse groups used the ritual-abuse scares to diverse ends. Well-known feminists such as Gloria Steinem and Catharine MacKinnon took up the cause, depicting ritually abused children as living proof of the ravages of patriarchy and the need for fundamental social reform.[40]

This was far from the only time feminist spokeswomen have mongered fears about sinister breeds of men who exist in nowhere near the high numbers they allege. Another example occurred a few years ago when teen pregnancy was much in the news. Feminists helped popularize the frightful but erroneous statistic that two out of three teen mothers had been seduced and abandoned by adult men. The true figure is more like one in ten, but some feminists continued to cultivate the scare well after the bogus stat had been definitively debunked.[41] . . .

Final Thoughts

The short answer to why Americans harbor so many misbegotten fears is that immense power and money await those who tap into our moral insecurities and supply us with symbolic substitutes. . . .

[Other tactics include] (1) Statements of alarm by newscasters; (2) glorification of wannabe experts are two telltale tricks of the fear mongers' trade; (3) the use of poignant anecdotes in place of scientific evidence; (4) the christening of isolated incidents as trends; and (5) depletions of entire categories of people as innately dangerous.

If journalists would curtail such practices, there would be fewer anxious and misinformed Americans.

Ultimately, though, neither the ploys that narrators use nor what Cantril termed "the sheer dramatic excellence" of their presentations fully accounts for why people in 1938 swallowed a tall tale about martians taking over New Jersey or why people today buy into tales about perverts taking over cyberspace, unionizing employees taking over workplaces, heroin dealers taking over middle-class suburbs, and so forth.[42] . . .

Fear mongers have knocked the optimism out of us by stuffing us full of negative presumptions about our fellow citizens and social institutions. But the United States is a wealthy nation. We have the resources to feed, house, educate, insure, and disarm our communities if we resolve to do so.

There should be no mystery about where much of the money and labor can be found—in the culture of fear itself. We waste tens of billions of dollars and person-hours every year on largely mythical hazards like road rage, on prison cells occupied by people who pose little or no danger to others, on programs designed to protect young people from dangers that few of them ever face, on compensation for victims of metaphorical illnesses, and on technology to make airline travel—which is already safer than other means of transportation—safer still.

We can choose to redirect some of those funds to combat serious dangers that threaten large numbers of people. At election time we can choose candidates that proffer programs rather than scares.[43]

Or we can go on believing in martian invaders.

NOTES

1. Crime data here and throughout are from reports of the Bureau of Justice Statistics unless otherwise noted. Fear of crime: Esther Madriz, *Nothing Bad Happens to Good Girls* (Berkeley: University of California Press, 1997), ch. 1; Richard Morin, "As Crime Rate Falls, Fears Persist," *Washington Post* National Edition, 16 June 1997, p. 35; David Whitman, "Believing the Good News," *U.S. News & World Report*, 5 January 1998, pp. 45–46.

2. Eva Bertram, Morris Blachman et al., *Drug War Politics* (Berkeley: University of California Press, 1996), p. 10; Mike Males, *Scapegoat Generation* (Monroe, ME: Common Courage Press, 1996), ch. 6; Karen Peterson, "Survey: Teen Drug Use Declines," *USA Today*, 19 June 1998, p. A6; Robert Blendon and John Young, "The Public and the War on Illicit Drugs," *Journal of the American Medical Association* 279 (18 March 1998): 827–32. In presenting these statistics and others I am aware of a seeming paradox: I criticize the abuse of statistics by fearmongering politicians, journalists, and others but hand down precise-sounding numbers myself. Yet to eschew all estimates because some are used inappropriately or do not withstand scrutiny would be as foolhardy as ignoring all medical advice because some doctors are quacks. Readers can be assured I have interrogated the statistics presented here as factual. As notes throughout the book make clear, I have tried to

rely on research that appears in peer-reviewed scholarly journals. Where this was not possible or sufficient, I traced numbers back to their sources, investigated the research methodology utilized to produce them, or conducted searches of the popular and scientific literature for critical commentaries and conflicting findings.

3. Bob Herbert, "Bogeyman Economics," *New York Times,* 4 April 1997, p. A15; Doug Henwood, "Alarming Drop in Unemployment," *Extra,* September 1994, pp. 16–17; Christopher Shea, "Low Inflation and Low Unemployment Spur Economists to Debate 'Natural Rate' Theory," *Chronicle of Higher Education,* 24 October 1997, p. A13.

4. Bob Garfield, "Maladies by the Millions," *USA Today,* 16 December 1996, p. A15.

5. Jim Windolf, "A Nation of Nuts," *Wall Street Journal,* 22 October 1997, p. A22.

6. Andrew Ferguson, "Road Rage," *Time,* 12 January 1998, pp. 64–68; Joe Sharkey, "You're Not Bad, You're Sick. It's in the Book," *New York Times,* 28 September 1997, pp. Nl, 5.

7. Malcolm Dean, "Flesh-eating Bugs Scare," *Lancet* 343 (4 June 1994): 1418; "Flesh-eating Bacteria," *Science* 264 (17 June 1994): 1665; David Brown, "The Flesh-eating Bug," *Washington Post* National Edition, 19 December 1994, p. 34; Sarah Richardson, "Tabloid Strep," *Discover* (January 1995): 71; Liz Hunt, "What's Bugging Us," *The Independent,* 28 May 1994, p. 25; Lisa Seachrist, "The Once and Future Scourge," *Science News* 148 (7 October 1995): 234–35. Quotes are from Bernard Dixon, "A Rampant Non-epidemic," *British Medical Journal* 308 (11 June 1994): 1576–77; and Michael Lemonick and Leon Jaroff, "The Killers All Around," *Time,* 12 September 1994, pp. 62–69. More recent coverage: "Strep A Involved in Baby's Death," UPI, 27 February 1998; see also, e.g., Steve Carney, "Miracle Mom," *Los Angeles Times,* 4 March 1998, p. A6; KTLA, "News at Ten," 28 March 1998.

8. Jim Naureckas, "The Jihad That Wasn't," *Extra,* July 1995, pp. 6–10, 20 (contains quotes). See also Edward Said, "A Devil Theory of Islam," *Nation,* 12 August 1996, pp. 28–32.

9. Lewis Lapham, "Seen but Not Heard," *Harper's,* July 1995, pp. 29–36 (contains Clinton quote). See also Robin Wright and Ronald Ostrow, "Illusion of Immunity Is Shattered," *Los Angeles Times,* 20 April 1995, pp. Al, 18; Jack Germond and Jules Witcover, "Making the Angry White Males Angrier," column syndicated by Tribune Media Services, May 1995; and articles by James Bennet and Michael Janofsky in the *New York Times,* May 1995.

10. Tom Morganthau, "The Lull Before the Storm?" *Newsweek,* 4 December 1995, pp. 40–42; Mike Males, "Wild in Deceit," *Extra,* March 1996, pp. 7–9; *Progressive,* July 1997, p. 9 (contains Clinton quote); Robin Templeton, "First, We Kill All the 11-Year-Olds," *Salon,* 27 May 1998.

11. Statistics from "Violence and Discipline Problems in U.S. Public Schools: 1996–97," National Center on Education Statistics, U.S. Department of Education, Washington, DC, March 1998; CNN, "Early Prime," 2 December 1997; and Tamar Lewin, "Despite Recent Carnage, School Violence Is Not on Rise," *New York Times,* 3 December 1997, p. A14. Headlines: *Time,* 15 January 1996; *U.S. News & World Report,* 25 March 1996; Margaret Carlson, "Children Without Souls," *Time,* 2 December 1996, p. 70. William J. Bennett, John J. Dilulio, and John Walters, *Body Count* (New York: Simon & Schuster, 1996).

12. CNN, "Talkback Live," 2 December 1997; CNN, "The Geraldo Rivera Show," 11 December 1997; Richard Lacayo, "Toward the Root of Evil," *Time,* 6 April 1998, pp. 38–39; NBC, "Today," 25 March 1998. See.also Rick Bragg, "Forgiveness, After 3 Die in Shootings in Kentucky," *New York Times,* 3 December 1997, p. A14; Maureen Downey, "Kids and Violence," 28 March 1998, *Atlanta Journal and Constitution,* p. A12.

13. Jocelyn Stewart, "Schools Learn to Take Threats More Seriously," *Los Angeles Times,* 2 May 1998, pp. Al, 17; "Kindergarten Student Faces Gun Charges," *New York Times,* 11 May 1998, p. A11; Rick Bragg, "Jonesboro Dazed by Its Darkest Day" and "Past Victims Relive Pain as Tragedy Is Repeated," *New York Times,* 18 April 1998, p. A7, and idem, 25 May 1998, p. A8. Remaining quotes

are from Tamar Lewin, "More Victims and Less Sense in Shootings," *New York Times,* 22 May 1998, p. A20; NPR, "All Things Considered," 22 May 1998; NBC, "Today," 25 March 1998. See also Mike Males, "Who's Really Killing Our Schoolkids," *Los Angeles Times,* 31 May 1998, pp. M1, 3; Michael Sniffen, "Youth Crime Fell in 1997, Reno Says," Associated Press, 20 November 1998.

14. Overestimation of breast cancer: William C. Black et al., "Perceptions of Breast Cancer Risk and Screening Effectiveness in Women Younger Than 50," *Journal of the National Cancer Institute* 87 (1995): 720–31; B. Smith et al., "Perception of Breast Cancer Risk Among Women in Breast and Family History of Breast Cancer," *Surgery* 120 (1996): 297–303. Fear and avoidance: Steven Berman and Abraham Wandersman, "Fear of Cancer and Knowledge of Cancer," *Social Science and Medicine* 31 (1990): 81–90; S. Benedict et al., "Breast Cancer Detection by Daughters of Women with Breast Cancer," *Cancer Practice* 5 (1997): 213–19; M. Muir et al., "Health Promotion and Early Detection of Cancer in Older Adults," *Cancer Oncology Nursing Journal* 7 (1997): 82–89. For a conflicting finding see Kevin McCaul et al., "Breast Cancer Worry and Screening," *Health Psychology* 15 (1996): 430–33.

15. Philip Jenkins, *Pedophiles and Priests* (New York: Oxford University Press, 1996), see esp. ch. 10; Debbie Nathan and Michael Snedeker, *Satan's Silence* (New York: Basic Books, 1995), see esp. ch. 6; Jeffrey Victor, "The Danger of Moral Panics," *Skeptic* 3 (1995): 44–51. See also Noelle Oxenhandler, "The Eros of Parenthood," *Family Therapy Networker* (May 1996): 17–19.

16. Mary DeYoung, "The Devil Goes to Day Care," *Journal of American Culture* 20 (1997): 19–25.

17. Dorothy Rabinowitz, "A Darkness in Massachusetts," *Wall Street Journal,* 30 January 1995, p. A20 (contains quote); "Back in Wenatchee" (unsigned editorial), *Wall Street Journal,* 20 June 1996, p. A18; Dorothy Rabinowitz, "Justice in Massachusetts," *Wall Street Journal,* 13 May 1997, p. A19. See also Nathan and Snedeker, *Satan's Silence;* James Beaver, "The Myth of Repressed Memory," *Journal of Criminal Law and Criminology* 86 (1996): 596–607; Kathryn Lyon,

Witch Hunt (New York: Avon, 1998); Pam Belluck, "'Memory' Therapy Leads to a Lawsuit and Big Settlement," *New York Times,* 6 November 1997, pp. A1, 10.

18. Elliott Currie, *Crime and Punishment in America* (New York: Metropolitan, 1998); Tony Pate et al., *Reducing Fear of Crime in Houston and Newark* (Washington, DC: Police Foundation, 1986); Steven Donziger, *The Real War on Crime* (New York: HarperCollins, 1996); Christina Johns, *Power, Ideology and the War on Drugs* (New York: Praeger, 1992); John Irwin et al., "Fanning the Flames of Fear," *Crime and Delinquency* 44 (1998): 32–48.

19. Steven Donziger, "Fear, Crime and Punishment in the U.S.," *Tikkun* 12 (1996): 24–27, 77.

20. Peter Budetti, "Health Insurance for Children," *New England Journal of Medicine* 338 (1998): 541–42; Eileen Smith, "Drugs Top Adult Fears for Kids' Well-being," *USA Today,* 9 December 1997, p. D1. Literacy statistic: Adult Literacy Service.

21. "The State of America's Children," report by the Children's Defense Fund, Washington, DC, March 1998; "Blocks to Their Future," report by the National Law Center on Homelessness and Poverty, Washington, DC, September 1997; reports released in 1998 from the National Center for Children in Poverty, Columbia University, New York; Douglas Massey, "The Age of Extremes," *Demography* 33 (1996): 395–412; Notes Trudy Lieberman, "Hunger in America," *Nation,* 30 March 1998, pp. 11–16; David Lynch, "Rich Poor World," *USA Today,* 20 September 1996, p. B1; Richard Wolf, "Good Economy Hasn't Helped the Poor," *USA Today,* 10 March 1998, p. A3; Robert Reich, "Broken Faith," *Nation,* 16 February 1998, pp. 11–17.

22. Inequality and mortality studies: Bruce Kennedy et al., "Income Distribution and Mortality," *British Medical Journal* 312 (1996): 1004–7; Ichiro Kawachi and Bruce Kennedy, "The Relationship of Income Inequality to Mortality," *Social Science and Medicine* 45 (1997): 1121–27. See also Barbara Chasin, *Inequality and Violence in the United States* (Atlantic Highlands, NJ: Humanities Press, 1997). Political stability: John Sloan, "The Reagan Presidency, Growing Inequality, and the American Dream," *Policy Studies Journal* 25

(1997): 371–86 (contains Reich quotes and "will haves" phrase). On both topics see also Philippe Bourgois, *In Search of Respect: Selling Crack in El Barrio* (Cambridge: Cambridge University Press, 1996); William J. Wilson, *When Work Disappears* (New York, Knopf, 1996); Richard Gelles, "Family Violence," *Annual Review of Sociology* 11 (1985): 347–67; Sheldon Danziger and Peter Gottschalk, *America Unequal* (Cambridge, MA: Harvard University Press, 1995); Claude Fischer et al., *Inequality by Design* (Princeton, NJ: Princeton University Press, 1996).

23. Karen Frost, Erica Frank et al., "Relative Risk in the News Media," *American Journal of Public Health* 87 (1997): 842–45. Media-effects theory: Nancy Signorielli and Michael Morgan, eds., *Cultivation Analysis* (Newbury Park, CA: Sage, 1990); Jennings Bryant and Dolf Zillman, eds., *Media Effects* (Hillsdale, NJ: Erlbaum, 1994); Ronald Jacobs, "Producing the News, Producing the Crisis," *Media, Culture and Society* 18 (1996): 373–97.

24. Madriz, *Nothing Bad Happens to Good Girls,* see esp. pp. 111–14; David Whitman and Margaret Loftus, "Things Are Getting Better? Who Knew," *U.S. News & World Report,* 16 December 1996, pp. 30–32.

25. Blendon and Young, "War on Illicit Drugs." See also Ted Chiricos et al., "Crime, News and Fear of Crime," *Social Problems* 44 (1997): 342–57.

26. Steven Stark, "Local News: The Biggest Scandal on TV," *Washington Monthly* (June 1997): 38–41; Barbara Bliss Osborn, "If It Bleeds, It Leads," *Extra,* September–October 1994, p. 15; Jenkins, *Pedophiles and Priests,* pp. 68–71; "It's Murder," *USA Today,* 20 April 1998, p. D2; Lawrence Grossman, "Does Local TV News Need a National Nanny?" *Columbia Journalism Review* (May 1998): 33.

27. Regarding fearmongering by newsmagazines, see also Elizabeth Jensen et al., "Consumer Alert," *Brill's Content* (October 1998): 130–47.

28. ABC, "20/20," 16 March 1998.

29. Thomas Maugh, "Killer Bacteria a Rarity," *Los Angeles Times,* 3 December 1994, p. A29; Ed Siegel, "Roll Over, Ed Murrow," *Boston Globe,* 21 August 1994, p. 14. Crier quote from ABC's "20/20," 24 June 1994.

30. Sheryl Stolberg, "'Killer Bug' Perfect for Prime Time," *Los Angeles Times,* 15 June 1994, pp. A1, 30–31. Quotes from Brown, "Flesh-eating Bug"; and Michael Lemonick and Leon Jaroff, "The Killers All Around," *Time,* 12 September 1994, pp. 62–69.

31. Lewin, "More Victims and Less Sense"; Tamar Lewin, "Study Finds No Big Rise in Public-School Crimes," *New York Times,* 25 March 1998, p. A18.

32. "Licensing Can Protect," *USA Today,* 7 April 1998, p. A11; Jonathan Kellerman, "Few Surprises When It Comes to Violence," *USA Today,* 27 March 1998, p. A13; Gary Fields, "Juvenile Homicide Arrest Rate on Rise in Rural USA," *USA Today,* 26 March 1998, p. A11; Karen Peterson and Glenn O'Neal, "Society More Violent, So Are Its Children," *USA Today,* 25 March 1998, p. A3; Scott Bowles, "Armed, Alienated and Adolescent," *USA Today,* 26 March 1998, p. A9. Similar suggestions about guns appear in Jonathan Alter, "Harnessing the Hysteria," *Newsweek,* 6 April 1998, p. 27.

33. Sharon Walsh, "Gun Sellers Look to Future— Children," *Washington Post,* 28 March 1998, pp. A1, 2.

34. John Schwartz, "An Outbreak of Medical Myths," *Washington Post* National Edition, 22 May 1995, p. 38.

35. Richard Preston, *The Hot Zone* (New York: Random House, 1994); Malcolm Gladwell, "The Plague Year," *New Republic,* 17 July 1995, p. 40.

36. Erik Larson, "A False Crisis: How Workplace Violence Became a Hot Issue," *Wall Street Journal,* 13 October 1994, pp. A1, 8; Cynthia Crossen, "Fright By the Numbers," *Wall Street Journal,* 11 April 1996, pp. B1, 8. See also G. Pascal Zachary, "Junk History," *Wall Street Journal,* 19 September 1997, pp. A1, 6.

37. On variable definitions of obesity see also Werner Cahnman, "The Stigma of Obesity," *Sociological Quarterly* 9 (1968): 283–99; Susan Bordo, *Unbearable Weight* (Berkeley: University of California Press, 1993); Joan Chrisler, "Politics and Women's Weight," *Feminism and Psychology* 6 (1996): 181–84.

38. Mary Douglas and Aaron Wildavsky, *Risk and Culture* (Berkeley: University of California Press, 1982), see esp. pp. 6–9; Mary Douglas, *Risk and Blame* (London: Routledge, 1992). See also Mary

Douglas, *Purity and Danger* (New York: Praeger, 1966). Asbestos and schools: Peter Cary, "The Asbestos Panic Attack," *U.S. News & World Report,* 20 February 1995, pp. 61–64; Children's Defense Fund, "State of America's Children."

39. See Marina Warner, "Peroxide Mug-shot," *London Review of Books,* 1 January 1998, pp. 10–11.

40. Nathan and Snedeker, *Satan's Silence* (quote from p. 240). See also David Bromley, "Satanism: The New Cult Scare," in James Richardson et al., eds., *The Satanism Scare* (Hawthorne, NY: Aldine de Gruyter, 1991), pp. 49–71.

41. Of girls ages fifteen to seventeen who gave birth, fewer than one in ten were unmarried and had been made pregnant by men at least five years older. See Steven Holmes, "It's Awful, It's Terrible, It's . . . Never Mind," *New York Times,* 6 July 1997, p. E3.

42. CNN, "Crossfire," 27 August 1995 (contains Huffington quote); Ruth Conniff, "Warning: Feminism Is Hazardous to Your Health," *Progressive,* April 1997, pp. 33–36 (contains Sommers quote). See also Susan Faludi, *Backlash* (New York: Crown, 1991); Deborah Rhode, "Media Images, Feminist Issues," *Signs* 20 (1995): 685–710; Paula Span, "Did Feminists Forget the Most Crucial Issues?" *Los Angeles Times,* 28 November 1996, p. E8.

43. See Katha Pollitt, "Subject to Debate," *Nation,* 26 December 1994, p. 788, and idem, 20 November 1995, p. 600.

THINKING ABOUT THE READING

Glassner originally wrote this piece over a decade ago. What are some contemporary examples of cultural fears that he might include if he were writing this today? How do you determine if the fear is a cultural myth or something that should be taken seriously as a social problem? According to Glassner, how are these cultural myths created, and why are we so inclined to believe in them? Do you think a culture less organized by the medium of television would be more or less likely to support such myths?

The Social Context of Hoarding

MEGAN SHAEFFER

(2017)

In 2013, hoarding was listed as its own discrete disorder in the *Diagnostic and Statistical Manual of Mental Disorders 5* (*DSM-5*). The move to medicalize hoarding serves as a prompt for sociologists to examine social cues that underlie hoarding behavior.

My aim is to understand how each hoarding behavior—acquisition, clutter, and retention of objects—has been vigorously promoted in the United States culture and consequently has become embedded in our collective conscience. The social framework of this set of behaviors can be used in further research to understand how and why the confluence of these three socially acceptable behaviors in excess can lead to a diagnosis of a socially marginalizing disorder: hoarding.

I suggest that hoarding behaviors should be viewed as normal activities within a contemporary socioeconomic context. I do not propose that hoarding is unproblematic or not a real psychological disorder, simply that hoarding behaviors are neither unusual nor relegated only to those with the disorder. The view that hoarding behaviors are a deviation from the norm underlies much of the current research into hoarding as it has undergone the process of medicalization.

Hoarders experience significant distress or impairment in their health, relationships, and activities because of their extreme acquisition, clutter, and discard behaviors.

Hoarding can take a toll on social relationships as well. Family members or friends may be forced to use external interventions such as Family Services or the American Society for the Prevention of Cruelty to Animals (ASPCA) to remove children, the elderly, or pets from unsafe or unsanitary conditions within a hoarder's home (Tolin et al., 2008, p. 205). Legal interventions or threats of eviction are often the catalyst for the quick cleanups featured in hoarding television shows such as The Learning Channel's [TLC's] *Hoarding: Buried Alive* or Arts & Entertainment's (A&E) *Hoarders*. In the short 2009 film, *My Mother's Garden,* documentarian Cynthia Lester captures the process of cleaning out her mother's home after the city demands the property be cleaned. Throughout the film Lester describes how hoarding affected her relationship with her mother as she recounts painful childhood memories that are common for many children of hoarders, including the shame she felt about her home and her increasing frustration at her mother's dumpster-diving tendencies (Lester, 2009). Lester, like many children of hoarders, left home as a teenager and limited contact with her mother until the hoarding became a legal issue requiring intervention. Similar stories can be found on websites for hoarders and their loved ones such as *Squalor Survivors* and *Children of Hoarders*.

The Social Context of Objects

How can sociology help us bring together the medicalized view of hoarding and what we know about our social relationships with objects? Through the medicalization of hoarding behaviors, we may lose some perspective on the way that broader social and cultural forces influence the way hoarders and non-hoarders alike perceive, use, and experience objects. Medicalization shifts attention from the social context as we see behavioral problems and pathologies on an individual level and "ignore the possibility that the behavior is not an illness but an adaptation to a social situation" (Conrad & Schneider, 1992, p. 250).

In a case that mirrors hoarding in many ways, Hemler notes that research on compulsive buying in the 1980s began to focus on the qualitative, rather than quantitative, difference between "normal" and "abnormal" shopping tendencies (2013, p. 142). Compulsive buying moved from a social sphere with potential social solutions into a sphere where psychological interventions would be required, and soon diagnostic criteria for compulsive buying emerged in psychological literature (Hemler, 2013, p. 142-145). Similarly, hoarding is now diagnosed and treated within the realm of psychology. Examining hoarding from a sociological perspective is important because, as Hemler points out in discussing compulsive buying, it can shed light on a vital factor that contributes to seemingly pathological behaviors: social setting (2013, p. 154).

Humans live in a world of material culture in which objects are imbued with meaning and used actively. An object in and of itself may be inanimate, but the social meaning(s) and value(s) attributed to it make it part of a dynamic cultural discourse. Special events are commemorated and social relationships are affirmed through the giving of objects on birthdays, holidays, and other important occasions (Pearce, 1998, p. 106). In passing heirlooms from generation to generation, we identify ourselves with our ancestors in the past as well as our successors in the future. The objects we own signal our identities to others and become physical manifestations of memory and sentiment. Objects can be markers of status, tokens of emotion, or symbols of obligation. Possession of objects can mean prestige and wealth while a lack of material goods can mean social degradation and relative poverty. The things we acquire and keep are important to us, whether we are hoarders or not. How and why we acquire things, how we construct our things meaningfully in the spaces we occupy, and why we keep things—these behaviors are socially rooted in a historic context.

In the extreme case of the hoarder, objects may be viewed as an extension of the self, which must be cared for as one would care for their own body. Frost et al. (1995, p. 902) found that hoarders elevated their material possessions to human-like status and thus felt a sense of responsibility to keep their objects safe, undamaged, and free from harm. Protecting objects from harm, such as being touched or moved by family members or friends, became a way of protecting the self from harm. Cases of hoarding show us how feelings of connection and servitude to objects can alienate the hoarder from family and friends, isolating them within a world of material culture.

Acquisition

Histories of consumerism show us that during the 19th century in industrializing nations, such as the United States and England, material culture was emphasized as never before and people of all social classes, particularly the emerging middle class, were affected by this emphasis. The history of consumerism provides

a social context for understanding attitudes toward the acquisition of objects. Here, the literature shows that shopping and consumption are part of the social fabric of modern identity.

Shopping provides a good illustration of the way that attitudes toward material goods were changing. During the later 19th century, shopping moved from being a practical endeavor to a leisure activity, allowing one to socialize at the same time one purchased goods. Extravagant luxury department stores like Wanamaker's in Philadelphia, Marshall Field's in Chicago, and R.H. Macy & Co. in New York opened in the latter half of the 19th century. John Wanamaker's store, which opened in 1877, featured parlors, retiring rooms, 129 counters, and 1,400 stools for his shoppers. Department stores were more than places to simply purchase goods: they had become luxury service centers with reading rooms, coat checks, and telegraph offices, all amenities designed to make a long visit appealing. Though they carried a wide range of goods, the main emphasis in these new kinds of stores was on household goods, which "transformed shopping from a wifely duty into a mechanism by which women refined their tastes and expanded their visions of the good life. The department store facilitated a woman's transition from a homemaker to a consumer."

At the other end of the spectrum, five- and tens emerged to accommodate the lower classes and the working poor by operating as chains with a centralized office purchasing the merchandise to sell in bulk, allowing them to keep prices low. Stores like Woolworth's (which began in 1879 in Lancaster, Pennsylvania) and Kresge's (which began in 1899 in Detroit) gave these groups the opportunity to raise their quality of life, at least in terms of material culture. Economically, immigrants and ethnic minorities might be part of the lowest classes, but low-cost goods allowed them to improve their social standing through their material culture. In rural America, mail-order catalogues like Montgomery Ward and Sears, Roebuck and Company allowed those far from urban centers to enjoy the shopping experience.

Through shopping, material culture could be used by all classes to harness social prestige via prevailing trends of fashion. As Simmel noted, fashion is a means by which people express themselves and create social ties at the same time (Simmel, 2003, p. 245). Those who consider themselves at the forefront of fashion are adhering to a set of rules that mark them as members of a given class. As Simmel notes, fashionable people may feel they are pioneering new trends, but in truth they do not step far outside the bounds of their social group (1957, p.549). Though dressing fashionably is often viewed as a way of showing individuality, Simmel believed that the adoption of fashionable clothing, mannerisms, or objects is a way of garnering both the approval and the envy of one's social class (Simmel, 2003, p. 245). Through production of objects of fashion such as clothing, economic and industrial growth had (and still have) intimate ties to social identity and relationships.

Fashion, then, plays an important part in group relations and affects economic demand as people begin acquiring more than is necessary to fulfill their basic physical needs. The increasing desire for objects among all classes becomes socially and morally acceptable.

Perhaps the most important vehicle for creating desire for objects while simultaneously giving them socially constructed meanings was advertising. The first advertising agency in the United States was N.W. Ayer & Son in Philadelphia in 1869, and others soon followed to take advantage of the proliferation of print media being distributed at the time.

Advertisements were a way of showing consumers how products could offer them a better life and better social standing as well. Through advertising, an object could be linked to appealing social traits, which helped increase its monetary worth and desirability. Veblen observed that conspicuous consumption in the United States played an important role in people's lives in terms of their status and identity. According to Veblen, objects have manifest and latent functions, both of which motivate people to acquire them. (Berger, 2009, p. 70-71) In the late 1800s, for example, advertisements for bicycles featured young, middle-class men and women enjoying these vehicles. Businesses like Sears, Roebuck and Company emphasized that bicycles were a fashionable status symbol, "in short, pushing an object 'everybody else has' or should want" (Bronner, 1989, p. 35). The manifest function of a bicycle or automobile in the late 1800s was that it provided transportation that was faster and easier than the horse-drawn carriage. Objects also enhance one's sense of self and signal inclusion in a certain social class, which can be as important as the object's manifest function. The social function of a bicycle in the late 1800s was

that it showed one's membership in a more fashionable, forward-thinking kind of middle class. It also allowed for independent mobility and increased social integration in both towns and the countryside (Bronner, 1989, p. 32–36). Advertisements helped to establish the link between objects, brands, and personal identity, a link that strongly influences what we buy today.

The drive to acquire goods has been socially encouraged, and the very act of acquisition was made into a pastime to be enjoyed. Shopping, buying, displaying, and taking pride in the ownership of goods are activities that virtually all members of U.S. society take part in and have been doing so since the later 1800s. Continuous acquisition of objects not just necessary for sustaining life but for creating a social identity, for entertainment, and for day-to-day modern living has become part of our social and economic reality.

Clutter

Clutter is arguably the most recognizable hoarding behavior, made even more identifiable with recent television, magazine, and newspaper articles showing the hoarder's environment. In the criteria for hoarding disorder in the DSM-5, clutter is defined as "extensive accumulation of possessions in the home or workplace (such that the intended use of these spaces is no longer possible)" (Mataix-Cols et al., 2010). Though the term clutter suggests disorder and disorganization of objects within a space, here, I discuss the intersection of person, objects, and space within the home. In creating a home space, a person acquires objects and brings them into a personal sphere and arranges those objects, either consciously or unconsciously, within that sphere. In doing so, a person asserts control over their environment and over the meaning of both the space and the objects. Literature examining the history of living spaces and the organization of objects within them can give us insight as to the connection between our identities and our homes.

As the United States transformed from an agricultural to an industrial society in the mid- to late 1800s, the middle-class home underwent a transformation of its own. Home ownership was viewed as a symbol of American virtues such as hard work, economy, and self-discipline (Blaszczyk, 2009, p. 31).

The form and content of the home showed social position and acted as an indicator of moral character. Nowhere was this more evident than in the parlor, a room in which physical space served as a symbol of status. The parlor was separated out from the rest of the home and reserved solely for receiving guests or other special occasions. Its very existence showed that a homeowner could afford to set aside precious interior space for this single-purpose, rarely used room. Proper furnishings, particularly those in the parlor, were important because the arrangement of the home had the power to enlighten its occupants. Glimpses into the homes of the famous (provided by magazines and newspapers) encouraged homeowners to see expensive furnishings as markers of social merit; many were inspired to outfit their own parlors with less expensive imitations.

By the early 1900s, the Victorian parlor was being replaced by the living room of the American bungalow, a home style that was widely popular from the late 1800s through the 1950s. The interior of the bungalow was decorated more simply and tended to emphasize uniquely American decorating trends such as the Arts and Crafts Movement and Colonial Revivalism. Though simpler decorating reflected a general move away from the overcrowded Victorian parlor, it should not be mistaken for uninterest in interior design. Homes could be individualized through the use of asbestos, vinyl, or rubber floor and wall products, which gave people a wide variety of decorative options for their homes. With so many choices available to them, homeowners could easily personalize their living spaces to their own tastes.

Here is the intersection of the attitude toward the home and the objects within it: What we have within our homes speaks to who we are as individuals and members of society. In modern American society, we view the home as an extension of ourselves; our class, our status, our intellect, and our personal taste are made manifest in our dwelling places. Objects become material representations of what humans perceive as the inner reality of self and influence how they present that self in the world. The objects we use to delineate the space in our homes are a way of constructing identity. Given the social connection that exists between our objects, our homes, and ourselves, if hoarders view their objects as a part of themselves, can we really assert that this is an unusual attitude? The clutter that overwhelms the living space of the hoarder may seem disjointed and incomprehensible on its face, but perhaps we can understand it as an attempt to express identity through control over objects and space. The extremity of clutter in the hoarder's home may, at least in part, signal a desire to express multiple facets of one's character in many ways.

We can see where personality and home decor can be linked, but how does this translate directly into object ownership and the phenomenon of clutter? Here, it is worthwhile to mention literature tracing the history of collecting. Throughout the 1900s, collecting became a popular form of structured personal activity away from, but in many ways mirroring, the workplace. People had more time and money to spend on recreational pursuits, but idleness was discouraged. Collecting (along with activities such as making handicrafts, taking classes, joining sport clubs, or hiking) facilitated the maintenance of a strong work ethic and was viewed as a constructive use of time, making it a guilt-free way to spend one's leisure time.

During the 1930s, books and articles such as the *Care and Feeding of Hobby Horses* (1934), *The Challenge of Leisure* (1934), "Time Out! The Psychology of a Hobby" (1938); and *Fun with a Hobby* (1938) sought to define and categorize hobbies, signaling their widespread popularity in the United States (Gelber, 1991, p. 744). Hobbies such as collecting were not only viewed as a way to combat idleness but also loneliness, depression, nervous disorders, and a host of other medical or psychological problems. Hobbies became important among older Americans as the concept of retirement emerged as a legitimate stage of later life. Retirees, upon leaving the working world, could keep mind and body active through the adoption of a hobby. Here, then, is a link between consumerism, maintaining objects in the home, and health: not only was collecting an important economic activity, it was good for the body and mind. Collecting is an activity that has been socially constructed as an overall good and healthy way to spend one's time.

Discarding

The failure to throw away or clean out is what makes the other behaviors associated with hoarding so socially problematic: if people can adequately thin out their belongings on a regular basis, acquisition and clutter become much more manageable and much less noticeable. The inability to discard objects is what causes the most mental anguish for the hoarder, whose attachment to seemingly useless items may confuse or anger friends and loved ones. Difficulty discarding, or retention, might seem like the absence of action, but I will examine it here as both action and inaction. On one hand, it is the avoidance of the action of discarding; on the other, it is the act of saving, storing, and curating one's belongings.

The failure to discard objects creates a blockage in the normal, expected cycle of use of many things. In our economic system, objects have a limited life cycle, or so conventional wisdom suggests. The adoption of fashion is representative of a focus of one's consciousness on the present and the "fleeting and fluctuating elements of life," thus the struggle to maintain fashion requires constant reassessment of material culture (Simmel, 2003, p. 238). If we are socially encouraged to cycle through goods in an attempt to remain fashionable, how is the retention of objects also socially encouraged? In looking at literature on discarding and disposal, we can see that these acts are equally socially motivated.

Social motivation is involved in the creation and treatment of household waste and the process of discarding or reusing objects. Disposal is a key part of the consumption process, one that goes beyond the process of ceasing to use and throwing away an object as the final act in our relationship to that object. We may be throwing away more things, but we are keeping more things at the same time. Lucas describes this as the dilemma between the competing moral systems of thrift and hygiene: Disposability carries the virtue of hygiene, but retaining objects carries the virtues of thrift and economy (Lucas, 2002, p. 6).

Aside from thrift and economy, another virtue that is exemplified by retention of objects is environmentalism. Environmentalism is exemplified through the reusing rather than the disposing of objects as people are encouraged to "reduce, reuse, and recycle" in order to limit waste production. Reuse of cardboard boxes, plastic food containers, wrapping paper, and other items is very common and may even be practiced more often than recycling.

Sometimes objects that would otherwise be classified as waste and thrown away make it into "twilight zones" within the home. Twilight zones are out-of-sight between places like sheds, attics, cellar racks, top shelves, or junk drawers, which can accumulate items

without invading on the aesthetic or function of the rest of the house. Objects that have no clear reuse purpose may make their way into twilight zones, where they wait indefinitely until a need for them arises. The people storing the items may also not have a completely clear idea why they are keeping something; they may just be keeping it because they view it as potentially useful. "Reasons for consigning packaging to a twilight zone seem to range from a conscious desire to be thrifty and to minimize waste to the inertia that can overtake possessions that for no clear reasons are not got rid of but are stored" (Fisher & Shipton, 2010, p. 108). Physical twilight zones may also help us create mental ones. By moving an object into a new place, we are mentally moving it along in the disposal practice and dealing with the chore of getting rid of waste without actually getting rid of it.

An examination of the ways in which people practice disposal is important for understanding the behavior associated with the retention of objects. The above shows that throwing a thing away is not a simple process, and that there are viable alternatives that individuals use to keep objects from becoming waste. Reusing, recycling, and saving are all viewed in a positive light in the present day, as these actions represent the virtues of eco-consciousness, thrift, efficiency, and economy. Certainly, the reasoning explored here that keeps objects from leaving the home can be seen in hoarders, who may view their collections as monuments of their own environmentalism or frugality and who may fear that simply discarding an item is a show of wastefulness. They may view many things as occupying a twilight zone, waiting for the right moment for reuse.

Conclusion and Future Directions

Throughout this paper, I have examined an interplay of social forces that have created a cultural atmosphere in which hoarding behaviors have arisen. The acquisition of goods through shopping was transformed in the mid to late 1800s from a solely economic necessity into a social practice in which anyone could participate. The acquisition of goods was and still is promoted as a normal and even healthy activity. Creating a sense of home and self through the accumulation and display of objects has also been discussed.

The mass production of goods and new consumption habits fostered from the mid-1800s allowed homeowners access to a wide variety of goods that could be used to represent their character and middle or upper-class standards. Hobbies such as collecting objects became intensely popular among all social classes in the United States in the early 1900s. Social ties could be made and maintained through collecting, and it was viewed as a physically and mentally healthy pastime. Here, we can see how not just acquiring but keeping objects, a key component to creating the household clutter associated with hoarding, has been encouraged as a socially acceptable practice. Finally, hoarding is characterized by the inability of hoarders to part with their objects. The life cycle of an object does not necessarily end in disposal: It may be reused, recycled, given away, or saved with the possibility of future use in a new context. Hoarders and nonhoarders alike may feel that their decision to save items rather than throw them away shows their thrift, economy, or environmental awareness.

When not in extreme excess, all of the behaviors explored here—acquisition, clutter, and failure to throw things out—are behaviors in which all people in modern society engage to some degree. The behaviors associated with hoarding have been historically developed and are actively encouraged in contemporary western society.

Sociologists of mental health and sociologists of culture can contribute to a wider understanding of hoarding and hoarding behaviors by looking at the factors outside the medical model that influence hoarding behavior and the orientation of the hoarder toward their objects. Regardless of any individual psychopathology that may trigger the desire to accumulate and keep a large number of objects, people in the United States live in a social world in which the behaviors associated with hoarding have been historically developed and are actively encouraged in day-to-day living. The push to buy new goods is ingrained in our economic system. Identity, home, and memory are concepts that are tied to the objects we keep, arrange, and display. Our ideas about thrift, efficiency, and resourcefulness shape the way we treat objects once we have used them. What we view to be appropriate for recycling, reusing, saving, or throwing away is culturally influenced, and may be as much a social act as shopping or collecting.

REFERENCES

Belk, R. W. (1995). *Collecting in a consumer society*. New York, NY: Routledge.

Berger, A. A. (2009). *What objects mean: An introduction to material culture*. Walnut Creek, CA: Left Coast Press.

Blaszczyk, R. L. (2009). *American consumer society, 1865–2005: From Hearth to HDTV*. Wheeling, IL: Harlan Davidson, Inc.

Bronner, S. J. (1989). "Reading Consumer Culture." In S. J. Bronner (Ed.). *Consuming visions: Accumulation and display of goods in America, 1880–1920* (pp. 13–53). New York, NY: Norton.

Cohen, L. A. (1984). "Embellishing a Life of Labor: An Interpretation of the Material Culture of American Working-Class Homes, 1885–1915." In *American material culture: The shape of things around us* (pp. 158–181). Bowling Green, OH: Bowling Green State University Popular Press.

Cohen, N. E. (2002). *America's marketplace: The history of shopping centers*. Lyme, CT: Greenwich Publishing Group.

Conrad, P., and J. Schneider (1992). *Deviance and medicalization: From badness to sickness*. Philadelphia, PA: Temple University Press.

Dant, T. (1999). *Material culture in the social world: Values, activities, lifestyles*. Philadelphia, PA: Open University Press.

Durkheim, E. (1951). *Suicide: A study in sociology*. Glencoe, IL: Free Press.

Fisher, T., and J. Shipton (2010). *Designing for re-use: The life of consumer packaging*. Sterling, VA: Earthscan.

Flanders, J. (2015). *The making of home: The 500-year story of how our houses became our homes*. New York, NY: St. Martin's Press.

Foucault, M. (1965). *Madness and civilization*. New York: Random House.

Frost, R. O., and T. Hartl (1996). "A cognitive-behavioral model of compulsive hoarding." *Behaviour Research and Therapy*, 34(4): 341–350.

Frost, R. O., and G. Steketee (1998). "Hoarding: Clinical Aspects and Treatment Strategies." In M. A. Jenike, L. Baer, & W. E. Minichiello (Eds.), *Obsessive compulsive disorders: Practical management* (pp. 533–554). St. Louis, MO: Mosby.

Frost, R. O, T. L. Hartl, R. Christian, and N. Williams (1995). "The value of possessions in compulsive hoarding: Patterns of use and attachment." *Behaviour Research and Therapy*, 33(8): 897–902.

Gelber, S. (1991). "A job you can't lose: Work and hobbies in the great depression." *Journal of Social History,* 24(4): 741–766.

Gelber, S. (1992). "Free market metaphor: The historical dynamics of stamp collecting." *Comparative Studies in Society and History,* 34(4): 742–769.

Gregson, N., A. Metcalfe, and L. Crewe (2007a). "Identity, mobility, and the throwaway society." *Environment and Planning D: Society and Space,* 25(4): 682–700.

Gregson, N., A. Metcalfe, and L. Crewe (2007b). "Moving things along: The conduits and practices of divestment in consumption." *Transactions of the Institute of British Geographers*, 32(2): 187–200.

Halttunen, K. (1989). "From Parlor to Living Room: Domestic Space, Interior Decoration, and the Culture of Personality." In S. J. Bronner (Ed.), *Consuming visions: Accumulation and display of goods in America, 1880–1920* (pp.157–189). New York, NY: Norton.

Heinze, A. (1989). "From Scarcity to Abundance: The Immigrant as Consumer." In L. B. Glickman (Ed.), *Consumer society in American history: A reader* (pp. 190–206). Ithaca, NY: Cornell University Press.

Hemler, J. (2013). "The Medicalization of Compulsive Shipping: A Disorder in the Making?" In M. Dellwing & M. Harbusch (Eds.), *Krankheitskonstruktionen und Krankheitstreiberei*, (pp. 133–161). Weisbaden, Germany: Springer.

Hetherington, K. (2004). "Secondhandedness: Consumption, disposal, and absent practice." *Environment and Planning D: Society and Space*, 22 (1): 157–173.

James, W. (1890). *The principles of psychology* (Vol. 1). New York, NY: Henry Holt and Company.

Klaffke, P. (2003). *Spree: A cultural history of shopping.* Vancouver, B.C.: Arsenal Pulp Press.

Lears, J. (1989). "Beyond Veblen: Rethinking Consumer Culture in America." In S. J. Bronner (Ed.), *Consuming visions: Accumulation and display of goods in America, 1880–1920* (pp. 73–97). New York, NY: Norton.

Lester, C. (2009). *My mother's garden:* A film. Retrieved 2/20/2013 (www.MyMothersGardenMovie.com).

Lucas, G. (2002). "Disposability and dispossession in the twentieth century." *Journal of Material Culture*, 7(1): 5–22.

Maier, T. (2004). "On phenomenology and classification of hoarding: A review." *Acta Psychiatrica Scandinavica*, 110 (5): 323–337.

Marx, K. (1964). In T. B. Bottomore & M. Rubel (Eds.), translated by T.B. Bottomore. *Karl Marx: Selected writings in sociology and social philosophy.* New York, NY: McGraw–Hill Book Company.

Mataix-Cols, D., R. O. Frost, A. Pertusa, L. A. Clark, S. Saxena. J. F. Leckman, . . .D. J. Stein, H. Matsunaga, S. Wilhelm (2010). "Hoarding disorder: A new diagnosis for DSM-V?" *Depression and Anxiety*, 27 (6): 556–572.

McDannell, C. (1992). "Parlor Piety: The Home as Sacred Space in Protestant America." In J. H. Foy & T. J. Schlereth (Eds.), *American home life, 1880–1930: A social history of spaces and services*, (pp. 162–189). Knoxville, TN: The University of Tennessee Press.

Muroff, J., G. Steketee, J. Himle, and R. O. Frost (2010). "Delivery of internet treatment for compulsive hoarding (D.I.T.C.H.)." *Behaviour Research and Therapy,* 48(1): 79–85.

Paquet, L. B. (2003). *The urge to splurge: A social history of shopping.* Toronto, ON: ECW Press.

Pearce. S. (1998). *Collecting in contemporary practice.* London, UK: Sage Publications.

Pogosian, L. (2010). "Treatment of compulsive hoarding: A case study." *The Einstein Journal of Biology and Medicine.* 25(26): 8–11.

Rosenhan, D. L. (1973). "On being sane in insane places." *Science*, 179(4070): 250–258.

Saxena, S., and K. M. Maidment (2004). "Treatment of compulsive hoarding." *Journal of Clinical Psychology: In Session*, 60(11): 1143–1154.

Scheff, T. (1974). "The labeling theory of mental illness." *American Sociological Review* 39: 444–452.

Schlereth, T. J. (1989). "Country Stores, County Fairs, and Mail Order Catalogues: Consumption in Rural America." In S. J. Bronner (Ed.), *Consuming visions: Accumulation and display of goods in America, 1880-1920* (pp. 339–375). New York, NY: W. W. Norton.`

Simmel, G. (1957). "Fashion." *American Journal of Sociology*, 62(6): 541–558.

Simmel, G. (2003). "The Philosophy of Fashion." In D. B. Clarke, M. A. Doel, & K. M. L. Housiaux (Eds.), *The consumption reader* (pp. 238–245). New York, NY: Routledge.

Szasz, T. (1960). "The myth of mental illness." *American Psychologist*, 15:113–118.

Timpano, K. R., J. D. Buckner, J. A. Richey, D. L. Murphy, and N. B. Schmidt (2009). "Exploration of anxiety sensitivity and distress tolerance as vulnerability factors for hoarding behaviors." *Depression and Anxiety*: 26(4): 343–353.

Tolin, D. F., R. O. Frost, and G. Steketee (2008). *Buried in treasures: Help for compulsive acquiring, saving, and hoarding.* New York, (NY): Oxford University Press.

Veblen, T. (1912). *The theory of the leisure class: An economic study of institutions.* New York, NY: The Macmillan Company.

THINKING ABOUT THE READING

According to Shaeffer, hoarding is a social problem, but one with more than just a medical outlook to it. Indeed, is it a socially acceptable practice as the author suggests? Reflect on the objects in your possession and your disposal practices. What meaning do you attach to these objects and what practices do you follow in terms of disposal, reuse, recycling, and donations? What economic and cultural forces impact these definitions and practices? Furthermore, what does it mean that this social problem has entered the media and entertainment sphere in the form of reality television (*Hoarders*)?

The Construction of Self and Society

CHAPTER 3

Building Reality
The Social Construction of Knowledge

Sociologists often talk about reality as a social construction. What they mean is that truth and knowledge are discovered, communicated, reinforced, and changed by members of society. Truth doesn't just fall from the sky and hit us on the head. What is considered truth or knowledge is specific to a given culture. All cultures have specific rules for determining what counts as good and right and true. As social beings, we respond to our interpretations and definitions of situations, not to the situations themselves. We learn from our cultural environment what sorts of ideas and interpretations are reasonable and expected. Thus, we make sense of situations and events in our lives by applying culturally shared definitions and interpretations. In this way, we distinguish fact from fantasy, truth from fiction, myth from reality. This process of interpretation or "meaning making" is tied to interpersonal interaction, group membership, culture, history, power, economics, and politics.

Discovering patterns and determining useful knowledge are the goals of any academic discipline. The purpose of an academic field such as sociology is to provide the public with useful and relevant information about how society works. This task is typically accomplished through systematic social research—experiments, field research, unobtrusive observation, and surveys. But gathering trustworthy data can be difficult. People sometimes lie or have difficulty recalling past events in their lives. Sometimes the simple fact of observing people's behavior changes that behavior. Sometimes the information needed to answer questions about important, controversial issues is hard to obtain without raising ethical issues or encountering challenges from institutional gatekeepers in the field.

Moreover, sometimes the characteristics and phenomena we're interested in understanding are difficult to observe and measure. Unlike other disciplines in, say, the natural sciences, sociologists deal with concepts that can't be seen or touched. In "Concepts, Indicators, and Reality," Earl Babbie gives us a brief introduction to some of the problems researchers face when they try to transform important but abstract concepts into *indicators* (things that researchers can systematically quantify so they can generate statistical information). In so doing, he shows us that although sociologists provide us with useful empirical findings about the world in which we live, an understanding of the measurement difficulties they face will provide us with the critical eye of an informed consumer as we go about digesting research information.

Valerie Jenness shows us how even the most well-planned research can take a detour. When researchers are willing to veer from strict positivist traditions and allow the research process to lead them in unexpected directions, exciting sociological questions and research can develop along the way. Despite challenges in identifying her population, and unexpected data gathering moments, the adjustments made to the data collection approach and her intellectual curiosity led to exciting discoveries. In what started as a policy related research project on where to house transgender prisoners, Jenness shares how the gender and sexuality order in prisons presented methodological confounds that informed the original policy driven purpose of her research and ultimately led to valuable insight on larger sociological questions.

How do you tell the difference between pseudoscience and true science? In the discipline of sociology, it is of the utmost importance to have scientific studies drive our understanding of the social world, especially when policy decisions about critical social and political issues are hanging in the balance. In "Critical Scientific Thinking," Peter Nardi emphasizes the importance of separating real scientific research from pseudoscience. In a media-driven world that constructs and communicates meaning and dances around topics like "alternative facts," having competent and informed citizens is paramount to critical decision making on issues ranging from health decisions to the political process.

Something to Consider as You Read

Babbie's comments remind us that even scientists must make decisions about how to interpret information. Thus, scientists, working within academic communities, define truth and knowledge in their measures and interpretations. This knowledge is often significant and useful, but we need to remember that it is the construction of a group of people following particular rules, not something that is just "out there." And while the research process can be downright messy at times, it offers valuable contributions to understanding and making decisions in the social world. As you read these selections, think about the kind of information you would need or would want that might convince you to question some truth that you have always taken for granted. Also, consider the way these readings show how knowledge from official sources, such as reputable news organizations or government, can heavily influence the research process and social understanding.

Concepts, Indicators, and Reality

EARL BABBIE

(1986)

Measurement is one of the fundamental aspects of social research. When we describe science as logical/empirical, we mean that scientific conclusions should (1) make sense and (2) correspond to what we can observe. It is the second of these characteristics I want to explore in this essay.

Suppose we are interested in learning whether education really reduces prejudice. To do that, we must be able to measure both prejudice and education. Once we've distinguished prejudiced people from unprejudiced people and educated people from uneducated people, we'll be in a position to find out whether the two variables are related.

Social scientific measurement operates in accordance with the following implicit model:

- Prejudice exists as a *variable*: some people are more prejudiced than others.

- There are numerous *indicators* of prejudice.

- None of the indicators provides a perfect reflection of prejudice as it "really" is, but they can point to it at least approximately.

- We should try to find better and better indicators of prejudice—indicators that come ever closer to the "real thing."

This model applies to all of the variables social scientists study. Take a minute to look through the following list of variables commonly examined in social research.

Arms race	Tolerance
Religiosity	Fascism
Urbanism	Parochialism
TV watching	Maturity
Susceptibility	Solidarity
Stereotyping	Instability
Anti-Semitism	Education

Voting	Liberalism
Dissonance	Authoritarianism
Pessimism	Race
Anxiety	Happiness
Revolution	Powerlessness
Alienation	Mobility
Social class	Consistency
Age	Delinquency
Self-esteem	Compassion
Idealism	Democracy
Prestige	Influence

Even if you've never taken a course in social science, many of these terms are at least somewhat familiar to you. Social scientists study things that are of general interest to everyone. The nuclear arms race affects us all, for example, and it is a special concern for many of us. Differences in *religiosity* (some of us are more religious than others) are also of special interest to some people. As our country has evolved from small towns to large cities, we've all thought and talked more about *urbanism* —the good and bad associated with city life. Similar interests can be identified for all of the other terms.

My point is that you've probably thought about many of the variables mentioned in the list. Those you are familiar with undoubtedly have the quality of reality for you: that is, you know they exist. Religiosity, for example, is real. Regardless of whether you're in favor of it, opposed to it, or don't care much one way or the other, you at least know that religiosity exists. Or does it?

This is a particularly interesting question for me, since my first book, *To Comfort and to Challenge* (with Charles Glock and Benjamin Ringer), was about this subject. In particular, we wanted to know why some people were more religious than others (the sources of religiosity) and what impact differences in religiosity had on other aspects of life (the consequences of religiosity). Looking for the sources and consequences of a particular variable is a conventional social scientific undertaking; the first step is to develop a measure of that variable. We had to develop methods for distinguishing religious people, nonreligious people, and those somewhere in between.

The question we faced was, if religiosity is real, how do we know that? How do we distinguish religious people from nonreligious people? For most contemporary Americans, a number of answers come readily to mind. Religious people go to church, for example. They believe in the tenets of their faith. They pray. They read religious materials, such as the Bible, and they participate in religious organizations.

Not all religious people do all of these things, of course, and a great deal depends on their particular religious affiliation, if any. Christians believe in the divinity of Jesus; Jews do not. Moslems believe Mohammed's teachings are sacred; Jews and Christians do not. Some signs of religiosity are to be found in seemingly secular realms. Orthodox Jews, for example, refrain from eating pork; Seventh-Day Adventists don't drink alcohol.

In our study, we were interested in religiosity among a very specific group: Episcopal church members in America. To simplify our present discussion, let's look at that much narrower question: How can you distinguish religious from nonreligious Episcopalians in America?

As I've indicated above, we are likely to say that religious people attend church, whereas nonreligious people do not. Thus, if we know someone who attends church every week, we're likely to think of that person as religious; indeed, religious people joke about church members who only attend services on Easter and at Christmas. The latter are presumed to be less religious.

Of course, we are speaking rather casually here, so let's see whether church attendance would be an adequate measure of religiosity for Episcopalians and other mainstream American Christians. Would you be willing to equate religiosity with church attendance? That is, would you be willing to call religious everyone who attended church every week, let's say, and call nonreligious everyone who did not?

I suspect that you would not consider equating church attendance with religiosity a wise policy. For example, consider a political figure who attends church every Sunday, sits in the front pew, puts a large contribution in the collection plate with a flourish, and by all other evidence seems only interested in being known as a religious person for the political advantage that may entail. Let's add that the politician in question regularly lies and cheats, exhibits no Christian compassion toward others, and ridicules religion in private. You'd probably consider it inappropriate to classify that person as religious.

Now imagine someone confined to a hospital bed, who spends every waking minute reading in the Bible, leading other patients in prayer, raising money for missionary work abroad—but never going to church. Probably this would fit your image of a religious person.

These deviant cases illustrate that, while church attendance is somehow related to religiosity, it is not a sufficient indicator in and of itself. So how can we distinguish religious from nonreligious people?

Prayer is a possibility. Presumably, people who pray a lot are more religious than those who don't. But wouldn't it matter what they prayed for? Suppose they were only praying for money. How about the Moslem extremist praying daily for the extermination of the Jews? How about the athlete praying for an opponent to be hit by a truck? Like church attendance, prayer seems to have something to do with religiosity, but we can't simply equate the two.

We might consider religious beliefs. Among Christians, for example, it would seem to make sense that a person who believes in God is more religious than one who does not. However, this would require that we consider the person who says, "I'll believe anything they say just as long as I don't rot in Hell" more religious than, say, a concerned theologian who completes a lifetime of concentrated and devoted study of humbly concluding that who or what God is cannot be known with certainty. We'd probably decide that this was a misclassification.

Without attempting to exhaust all the possible indicators of religiosity, I hope it's clear that we would never find a single measure that will satisfy us as tapping the real essence of religiosity. In recognition of this, social researchers use a combination of indicators to create a *composite measure*—an index or a scale—of variables such as religiosity. Such a measure might include all of the indicators discussed so far: church attendance, prayer, and beliefs.

While composite measures are usually a good idea, they do not really solve the dilemma I've laid out. With a little thought, we could certainly imagine circumstances in which a "truly" religious person nonetheless didn't attend church, pray, or believe, and we could likewise imagine a nonreligious person who did all of those things. In either event, we would have demonstrated the imperfection of the composite measure.

Recognition of this often leads people to conclude that variables like religiosity are simply beyond empirical measurement. This conclusion is true and false and even worse.

The conclusion is false in that we can make any measurement we want. For example, we can ask people if they attend church regularly and call that a measure of religiosity just as easily as Yankee Doodle called the feather in his hat macaroni. In our case, moreover, most people would say that what we've measured is by no means irrelevant to religiosity.

The conclusion is true in that no empirical measurement—single or composite—will satisfy all of us as having captured the essence of religiousness. Since that can never happen, we can never satisfactorily measure religiosity.

The situation is worse than either of these comments suggests in that the reason we can't measure religiosity is that it doesn't exist! Religiosity isn't real. Neither is prejudice, love, alienation, or any of those other variables. Let's see why.

There's a very old puzzle I'm sure you're familiar with: when a tree falls in the forest, does it make a sound if no one is there to hear it? High school and college students have struggled with that one for centuries. There's no doubt that the unobserved falling tree will still crash through the branches of its neighbors, snap its own limbs into pieces, and slam against the ground. But would it make a sound?

If you've given this any thought before, you've probably come to the conclusion that the puzzle rests on the ambiguity of the word *sound*. Where does sound occur? In this example, does it occur in the falling tree, in the air, or in the ear of the beholder? We can be reasonably certain that the falling tree generates turbulent waves in the air; if those waves in the air strike your ear, you will experience something we call *hearing*. We say you've heard a sound. But do the waves in the air per se qualify as sound?

The answer to this central question is necessarily arbitrary. We can have it be whichever way we want. The truth is that (1) a tree fell; (2) it created waves in the air; and (3) if the waves reached someone's ear, they would cause an experience for that person. Humans created the idea of *sound* in the context of that whole process. Whenever waves in the air cause an experience by way of our ears, we use the term *sound* to identify that experience. We're usually not too precise about where the sound happens: in the tree, in the air, or in our ears.

Our imprecise use of the term *sound* produces the apparent dilemma. So, what's the truth? What's really the case? Does it make a sound or not? The truth is that (1) a tree fell; (2) it created waves in the air; and (3) if the waves reached someone's ear, they would cause an experience for that person. That's it. That's the final and ultimate truth of the matter.

I've belabored this point, because it sets the stage for understanding a critical issue in social research—one that often confuses students. To move in the direction of that issue, let's shift from sound to sight for a moment. Here's a new puzzle for you: Are the tree's leaves green if no one is there to see them? Take a minute to think about that, and then continue reading.

Here's how I'd answer the question. The tree's leaves have a certain physical and chemical composition that affects the reflection of light rays off of them; specifically, they only reflect the green portion of the light spectrum. When rays from that portion of the light spectrum hit our eyes, they create an experience we call the color green.

"But are the leaves green if no one sees them?" you may ask. The answer to that is whatever we want it to be, since we haven't specified where the color green exists: in the physical/chemical composition of the leaf, in the light rays reflected from the leaf, or in our eyes.

While we are free to specify what we mean by the color green in this sense, nothing we do can change the ultimate truth, the ultimate reality of the matter. The truth is that (1) the leaves have a certain physical and chemical composition; (2) they reflect only a portion of the light spectrum; and (3) that portion of the light spectrum causes an experience if it hits our eyes. That's the ultimate truth of the universe in this matter.

By the same token, the truth about religiosity is that (1) some people go to church more than others; (2) some pray more than others; (3) some believe more than others; and so forth. This is observably the case.

At some point, our ancestors noticed that the things we're discussing were not completely independent of one another. People who went to church seemed to pray more, on the whole, than people who didn't go to church. Moreover, those who went to church and prayed seemed to believe more of the church's teachings than did those who neither went to church nor prayed. The observation of relationships such as these led them to conclude literally that "there is more here than meets the eye." The term *religiosity* was created to represent the *concept* that all the concrete observables seemed to have in common. People gradually came to believe that the concepts were real and the "indicators" only pale reflections.

We can never find a "true" measure of religiosity, prejudice, alienation, love, compassion, or any other such concepts, since none of them exists except in our minds. Concepts are "figments of our imaginations." I do not mean to suggest that concepts are useless or should be dispensed with. Life as we know it depends on the creation and use of concepts, and science would be impossible without them. Still, we should recognize that they are fictitious, then we can trade them in for more useful ones whenever appropriate.

THINKING ABOUT THE READING

Define the following terms: *poverty, happiness, academic effort, love.* Now consider what indicators you would use to determine people's levels of each of these concepts. The indicator must be something that will allow you to clearly determine whether or not someone is in a particular state (e.g., poor or not poor; happy or not happy; in love or not in love). For example, you might decide that blushing in the presence of someone is one indicator of being in love or that the number of hours a person spends studying for a test is an indicator of academic effort. What's wrong with simply asking people if they're poor, if they're in love, if they're happy, or if they work hard? Consider the connection between how a concept is defined and how it can be measured. Is it possible that sociology sometimes uses concepts that seem meaningless because they are easier to "see" and measure?

A "Soft Mixed Methods" Approach to Studying Transgender Prisoners

VALERIE JENNESS

(2010)

In the summer of 2007, Alexis Giraldo, a transgender parolee who served over two years in California prisons, sued the California Department of Corrections and Rehabilitation (CDCR) and individual prison staff members who allegedly allowed her to be serially raped by her male cellmates while in Folsom State Prison. After successfully navigating a complex and exhausting extra-legal and legal complaint process, Giraldo, a young Puerto Rican transgender woman—a biological male who identifies and presents as female—had her day in court. During the two week trial in San Francisco Superior Court, the plaintiff and her attorney communicated to the jury, the witnesses in the courtroom, and the press how she was placed in a men's prison without regard for the obvious risk of sexual assault from the male prisoners she was housed with; endured daily beatings and brutal sexual assaults by her cellmate; begged for help from prison staff and was told to "be tough and strong"; reported the injuries to doctors and therapists; and officially documented her situation and experiences.

In turn, the State's attorneys representing the CDCR contested these claims. They argued that Giraldo's allegations were unsubstantiated and discredited him as a disgruntled parolee with a history of manipulative and deceitful behavior. They explained that inmates with male genitalia are, of course, housed in men's prisons; and they emphasized the plaintiff's request to be placed in the housing assignment where the alleged sexual assaults occurred and subsequent refusal to transfer to alternative housing when given multiple opportunities to do so. They pointed to the consensual nature of his sexual liaisons with other inmates, including the alleged rapist, and to his failure to clearly and unequivocally inform CDCR staff of sexual assaults at the time they occurred. They claimed he had financial motivations for filing suit. They argued that he is a convicted felon who, by virtue of his previous convictions, has demonstrated he is capable of—and well rehearsed at—engaging in fraudulent endeavors in the obvious pursuit of self-interest.

Both sides in this high profile legal dispute emphasized that the plaintiff is a gendered subject, but they differed—in fact, they were diametrically opposed—in their assessment of the plaintiff's gender and attendant standing as a legal subject: the plaintiff's attorney maintained that Giraldo is, for all intents and purposes, a female and should be understood as such, while the State's attorney maintained that Giraldo is, for all intents and purposes, a male and should be understood as such. The jury charged with wading through these claims and counterclaims considered the evidence, including a report on which I was the lead author (Jenness et al. 2007). They assessed the credibility of the parties participating in the trial and rendered a verdict. Without explicitly taking sides in the gender dispute that characterized this case, the jury found in favor of the CDCR on the alleged civil charges. To quote one legal observer, the CDCR "dodged a bullet."

This case raises a series of policy and scholarly questions related to transgender prisoners in men's prisons; and it reveals a complicated picture of the nexus between sex, gender, sexuality, and corrections. On the policy side, what are the causes, contours, and prevalence of sexual assault for transgender inmates in men's prisons in California? How do transgender inmates in prisons for adult men perceive and navigate the risks they face in prison? What "best practices" can prison officials embrace to ensure they meet their responsibility to house transgender prisoners in safe, secure, humane, and constitutional carceral environments? On the more academic side, the Giraldo case raises a broader set of questions about what it means to be transgender in prison and what that, in turn, can teach us about gender, inequality, marginalization, intergroup and domestic violence, and the workings of prison culture.

With these questions in mind, in 2008 I conducted in-prison research on "the girls among men," (as transgender prisoners have often described themselves to me), in California's prisons for adult men. In this essay, I present my study as what I am calling "a soft mixed methods approach" to policy research that ultimately served to address basic research questions as well. By qualifying the term "mixed methods" with the term "soft," I do not mean to reify the image of quantitative research as "hard" and qualitative research as "soft" (and I certainly do not mean to do so in the context of talking about transgender lives!). Instead, in this article I describe both the official protocol and the unexpected contingencies that shaped data collection, with a particular focus on gender and sexuality as methodological confounds that, surprisingly and productively, ultimately served to shed insight into basic sociological questions about the social organization of sex, sexuality, and gender in the context of prisons. . .

This study was not designed as an ethnography and it does not, strictly speaking, qualify as an ethnography; however, it necessarily included an ethnographic component as a result of being in many prisons, among many prisoners, and engaged with many CDCR personnel. As the research unfolded across twenty-eight prisons in California, qualitative data purposely collected in face-to-face interviews with over three hundred transgender prisoners and ethnographic data serendipitously collected in the field site emerged as valuable sources of information, especially in terms of revealing the contours of gender and sexuality in prisons for men. The qualitative interview data and the ethnographic information shed considerable insight into the basic policy question—where best to house transgender inmates if keeping them safe is the primary goal . . .

Setting the Stage: Making the Case for Policy Research and "Getting in" Prisons in the Golden State

[Researchers face] many challenges as they struggle to gain access to spheres of social life that are routinely off limits and render invisible marginal populations. This is especially problematic when it comes to studying criminal justice–related issues and conducting research in prisons. In the case of this research, meeting these objectives is even more challenging by virtue of treating the largest correctional system in the western world—often referred to as a dysfunctional organization—as a field site; when the topic to be studied inside prisons is sexual assault; and when the population to be studied is transgender inmates in men's prisons—a group with special vulnerabilities and, in some cases, considerable motivation to remain "unknown."

Capitalizing on an Historic Moment and the Need for Policy Research

My study of transgender prisoners in California prisons for men was commissioned by the CDCR shortly after they were presented with my previous in-prison research on sexual assault, which revealed that transgender inmates are considerably more likely to be sexually assaulted in prison than their non-transgender counterparts (Jenness et al. 2007; Jenness, Maxson, et al. 2010). This central finding, coupled with the increasing visibility of transgender inmates in prisons and the high profile Giraldo case, raised questions about the well-being of transgender prisoners while in the care of state officials. Questions about the well-being of transgender prisoners in the care of the CDCR were, for a variety of reasons, defined as "pressing" by an array of stakeholders both within and outside of the CDCR.

In this context, the CDCR funded my study of transgender prisoners in their prisons in order to help them address a very specific set of policy questions with which they were grappling: Where is it best to house transgender inmates—in general populations, segregated populations, or sensitive needs populations, for example—in order to minimize sexual assault and other forms of victimization? Related, are transgender inmates in prisons for men safer from sexual assault in housing units with other transgender inmates or in housing units among non-transgender inmates? With these interrelated policy questions in mind, my study, the first systematic empirical study of transgender inmates, was primarily designed to collect quantifiable self-report data from transgender prisoners, official demographic data on transgender prisoners, and official data on the housing environments in which transgender prisoners reside in state prisons for men to discern where best to house them and who best to house them with.

Getting in the Golden State's Prisons in the Age of Mass Incarceration

With a policy concern front and center and the full support of the CDCR, I was fortunate to gain access to California prisons and the transgender prisons housed therein; securing access to prisoners and approval to do in-prison research is currently at odds with larger trends in in-prison research. Despite the unprecedented growth of the correctional population in the U.S., especially the massive increases in incarceration rates since the early 1970s, there has been a discernable decline in scholarly attention to life inside prison walls. In "The Curious Eclipse of Prison Ethnography in the Age of Mass Incarceration," Wacquant (2002, 386-87) argued that researchers need to get "inside and around penal facilities to carry out intensive, close-up observation of the myriad relations they contain and support." With this in mind, the good news is that I got "inside" California prisons. The bad news is that I did not get in to do a "close up observational study" of the type Wacquant would appreciate. Rather, I embraced the opportunity to collect official data and self-report data on currently incarcerated transgender prisoners as an opportunity to also collect qualitative, ethnographic data on transgender inmates. In other words, the former can be seen as a catalyst for the latter.

. . .The State of California currently has the largest corrections agency in the nation. When field data collection began, there were approximately 160,000 adult prisoners incarcerated in thirty-three prisons in California spanning 745 miles from the southern-most prison to the northernmost prison. Despite the rising rate at which females are being incarcerated in California, well over 90 percent of California inmates are housed in thirty prisons for men, including nine reception centers for adult men. This was my sprawling research site.

Not surprisingly, there is a wealth of statistical data on the California prison population. However, when I began this study, there were no data available on transgender inmates in California prisons. From the point of view of those charged with managing prisons, transgender inmates are a visible population because they are often thought of as the source of in-prison disorder and attendant management problems; likewise, from the point of view of those who contest the management of prisons, transgender prisoners are a visible population because others target them for victimization and rights violations. However, from the point of view of systematic, empirical social science data, they are—or more accurately, were—what Tewksbury and Potter (2005) dubbed "a forgotten group" of prisoners.

Identifying, Accessing, and Understanding Transgender Prisoners

Plans for data collection for this project began with a consequential fact: transgender prisoners are an undecipherable population in the CDCR's official databases. Because the CDCR does not officially track inmates by gender status in its sex-segregated prison system in the way that it keeps track of sex, race/ethnicity, age, height and weight, and so on, prison officials could not attest to how many transgender inmates were in the system and where they were located within California's sprawling prison system. Likewise, prior to the first article that derives from this work (Sexton, Jenness, and Sumner 2010), no one could provide a demographic profile of transgender inmates in California prisons for men and how they compare to their non-transgender counterparts on standard indicators such as race/ethnicity, prison term start date, mental health status, verified gang membership, classification score, custody level, current sentence length, time remaining on sentence, commitment offense, sex offender registration, age of first arrest in California, and so on.

What I did know at the outset of the study is that, true to the sex-segregated nature of California prisons, transgender inmates assigned male at birth were housed in men's prisons and transgender inmates assigned female at birth were housed in women's prisons. A taken-for-granted gender binary resulted in routine automatic placement along these lines— so routine, in fact, that it made news when, shortly after data collection, officials transferred a prisoner who was born male but identifiable as transgender to a women's prison in California (Collins 2008). Also before data collection began, I was told that the CDCR has historically concentrated transgender inmates in three prisons for adult men. This proved to be true, even as I discovered over the course of the research that another prison also housed a disproportionate number of transgender inmates. The result is a prison system that simultaneously segregates and concentrates some transgender inmates and, at the same time, desegregates and isolates other transgender inmates in prisons for men . . .

It is within this context that identifying all transgender inmates in prisons for men in California presented a considerable challenge. Rather than sample transgender inmates from a single prison or a subgroup of prisons, the study design included attempting to contact every transgender prisoner in a California prison at the time of the data collection. Therefore, I worked collaboratively with CDCR officials to identify and make face-to-face contact with all transgender inmates in California prisons for men, including reception centers and excluding camps. My goal was to arrive at a credible estimate of how many transgender inmates are housed in California prisons for men and invite each and every one of them to participate in the study . . .

Quite unexpectedly, however, the process whereby I attempted to identify, access, and interview all transgender inmates in California prisons resulted in a series of ethnographic moments with experts, my fellow researchers, and prisoners that simultaneously muddied the methodological waters and generated empirical findings that ultimately proved as informative as the data collected according to protocol. As I describe in the following, determining who is and is not transgender and, related, how transgender is understood in the context of prison life, is tricky business. In large part, this is because gender and sexuality are tricky business replete with ambiguities and contradictions—the very things that can derail a research project anchored in categorical understandings of the social world built around the establishment and reification of social boundaries that define categories of people. This is especially complicated when so-called "gender normals" interact with transgender people (Schilt and Westbrook 2009).

Consulting with Experts to Define and Operationalize "Transgender Inmate"

Before data collection commenced, I secured advice from consultants about how best to identify, label, and address transgender prisoners in a respectful and, from the point of view of data collection, fruitful manner. The consultants on this project included a person with a master's degree in the social sciences who identifies as female but for many years was recognizable as male and lived as a man, a transgender advocate for transgender inmates, an academic who has studied sexual politics and nonnormative sexual identities for decades, and a few of

my colleagues at the University of California, Irvine. In retrospect, it is not surprising that my concerted effort to arrive at the "one right way" to signify the target population—to the research team, to the CDCR, and to the "human subjects"—failed to produce consensus among the consultants.

However, it did produce insightful commentary. For example, a consultant I hired because of her background in the social sciences and because I thought she was transgender (she was born physically recognizable as a male and underwent surgery as an adult to become physically recognizable as a female) suggested that the research team use phrases such as "others like you," "women like you," or "those presenting as female" when addressing the target population. She encouraged me to avoid using the term "transgender" with transgender inmates . . .

In contrast, other experts encouraged me to use the term transgender because it is, they argued, well equipped to capture a range of identities. As one well-known transgender activist in the Bay Area who has considerable experience working with transgender prisoners said to me: "Just use transgender, they'll get it." When I explained that I wanted to be sensitive about language and labels and questioned the degree to which the "target population" would feel comfortable with the term transgender above and beyond just getting it, he said:

> Val, the cutting-edge term is gender variant, but I wouldn't use this term. It's too academic. These folks in prison do not have the room, space and luxury to think about distinctions between those who wish to be seen as transgender, those who wish to be seen as women, and those who just wish to be seen. They don't care about identity politics like you think.

. . . From his point of view, my concern with getting language "right" was misguided—what he called "a waste of time and energy"—and in some ways beside the point for a group of people who want to be seen and heard but others often ignore. As I later learned, he was right. The girls in men's prisons would be happy to talk with me and other interviewers on the research team under conditions of confidentiality. Indeed, 95 percent of the transgender inmates with whom we made contact consented to be interviewed and completed a usable interview.

Taking competing expert advice as well as my own positivistic training seriously, I was convinced that collecting reliable and valid (categorical) data required developing criteria by which transgender inmates could be discerned. Given that there is very little consensus on how best to define the term transgender and that "transgender" is often used as an umbrella term for a plethora of identities and practices, I decided to focus data collection on those inmates who: (1) self-identify as transgender (or something analogous); (2) present as female, transgender, or feminine in prison or outside of prison; (3) have received any kind of medical treatment (physical or mental) for something related to how they present themselves or think about themselves in terms of gender, including taking hormones to initiate and sustain the development of secondary sex characteristics to enhance femininity; or (4) participate in groups for transgender inmates. Meeting any one of these criteria would qualify an inmate for inclusion in this study. By deploying these criteria, I hoped to bypass larger debates about who is and is not transgender and, instead, rely on a comprehensive understanding that would maximize inclusion without diluting the target population beyond recognition. In short, my intention was to move from questions of policy to comprehension of prisoners.

Also prior to commencing data collection, I was convinced that collecting reliable and valid data required ensuring that those participating in the study as human subjects needed to be oriented to what we—the researchers—mean by "transgender" at the beginning of every interview. Failing to do so, I thought, would surely lead to problematic data. Thus, at the beginning of interviews with transgender inmates, interviewers said the following: "Knowing that different people use different terms for things, I want to clarify that, during this interview, when I talk about transgender inmates, I am referring to those inmates who identify or present as female in men's prisons." This, then, was the (presumably) agreed upon understanding of "transgender" used during the interviews. With definitions and operationalizations in hand, I confidently set about working with the CDCR to find the target population. This is the "prisoners" part of the main title of this article.

Working with CDCR Administrators to Identify Transgender Inmates in CDCR Prisons

For CDCR personnel, evaluating various definitions and attendant understandings of "transgender" was decidedly unproblematic. With very rare exception, they had considerable agreement on labels and how they signify types of inmates and enjoin multiple features of inmates' status characteristics. More often than not, however, their native knowledge collided head-on with the definition and operationalization described previously. Fortunately, the collision was sociologically telling insofar as it revealed the social organization of gender and sexuality as contested terrain.

Before data collection commenced, I presented an overview of the research plans to wardens and other CDCR officials in attendance at a wardens' meeting in Santa Barbara, California, on February 5, 2008. During and after this presentation, I solicited the assistance of the wardens to identify all transgender inmates in their respective facilities. After delineating the four-pronged criteria by which I hoped to identify transgender inmates in California prisons, as described previously, the first warden to ask a question said: "So you want our homosexuals?" Sincerely delivered, this question came off as reasonable and attentive as he was genuinely trying to ensure he understood who should and should not be on the list produced at his prison. At this moment, it became clear to me that, for this group of professionals, who have considerably more experience with the target population than I or anyone on my research team, "transgender" and "homosexual" are conflated social types in a perceptual scheme that sees very little distinction between the two. Recognizing this "misunderstanding," I politely responded: "Well, some transgender inmates might be homosexual, but some might not; and, in any event, we want to select transgender inmates, not homosexual inmates." I then went over the four-pronged criteria again, emphasizing that we are selecting transgender inmates quite apart from whether they are homosexual. My review of the criteria for including study participants, in turn, evoked a few blank stares and an ensuing discussion about the difference. It was a discussion that, I am convinced, did not lead to much shared understanding despite our—theirs and my—best efforts . . .

[M]y research team and I proceeded to head into the field to collect data. As we did, there was considerable sifting and predictable attendant loss of cases as we moved from the total number of names provided on all the lists (n = 751) to the number of inmates we actually saw face-to-face at a prison (n = 505) to the number of inmates who actually met our eligibility requirements to participate in the study (n = 332) to the number of inmates who consented to an interview (n = 316) and the number of inmates who successfully completed a usable interview (n = 315). The largest loss of potential cases as we went from the names on the master list to actually seeing the person at the prison is due to a variety of factors, including inmates paroling, dying, or being transferred to another prison after we received our list and before we arrived at the prison; inmates being unwilling to come out of their cell; inmates being unavailable as a result of an urgent medical or psychiatric appointment; and inmates—believe it or not—being "lost" in the prison and, thus, unavailable for an interview.

The gap between the number of transgender inmates on the original list at any given prison and the number of inmates who successfully completed an interview varies immensely across prisons . . . Most telling for my purposes here, many inmates on the list provided by the prison officials did not qualify for our study because, as they would tell us once face-to-face in an interview room, "I'm just gay," "I'm not a girl," and "You're barking up the wrong tree here."

This kind of misidentification often created an awkward moment as the interviewer had to explain there was, no doubt, a clerical error, apologize for making an inappropriate assumption, and assure the person that, of course, no one thinks of him as anything other than what he is. In some cases, this was no big deal and in other cases, interviewers had to do more interactional work to respond to the awkward moment and engage in interactional repair work . . .

Working with CDCR Personnel in the Field

. . . As the research team traveled to twenty-eight prisons to interview over 300 transgender inmates, I spent hundreds of hours with prison officials in prisons. This included countless hours meeting with wardens and their administrative delegates "on-site," being escorted in and out of prisons and housing units within prisons by staff, and simply "hanging out" with officers and inmates alike as I waited for interviewees to be escorted to confidential interview rooms. Countless serendipitous ethnographic observations gathered during this "non-interview" time associated with the research revealed that CDCR staff routinely referred to transgender inmates in men's prisons by using masculine generic pronouns and/ or by using their male names rather than adhering to transgender inmates' preference to be referred to with feminine generic pronouns and/or by using their female names.

The practice of ordaining transgender inmates in prisons for men as men was particularly vivid when I was walking across a prison yard with two other interviewers and the lieutenant with whom we had been working for days. A Cuban transgender inmate described by an officer on site as "very flamboyant" was sauntering across the yard with her CDCR-issued blue shirt tied at the waist such that it appeared like a female blouse, rubbing her butt, and announcing to anyone within earshot that she had just had a hormone shot. She made it clear the shot was both painful and welcome. As other inmates made note of her visibility on the yard and directed her way what could be perceived as playful or rude comments—for example, "Hey, aren't you looking fine, I'd like a piece of that . . . "—the lieutenant amicably and matter-of-factly told the transgender inmate to stop drawing attention to herself. He said: "Okay, Mr. Hernandez, that's enough." She smiled and quickly retorted: "That's Ms. Hernandez." The officer called her Mr. again and she corrected him again. This exchange happened three times, with Ms. Hernandez and the lieutenant finally just walking off in different directions—her toward the center of the yard and us inside a programming building. Once inside, I respectfully asked the lieutenant if that kind of exchange is typical and he said "Yes, but we try to keep it to a minimum." I then asked: "Why not just call her Ms. Hernandez? What does it cost you?" He respectfully explained that Mr. Hernandez is in a male prison, he's a male, and policy requires foregoing the use of aliases. He went on to explain that the use of aliases constitutes a threat to security. What made this particularly telling to me was that this lieutenant proved to be one of my favorite officers to work with in the field because he helped us get our work done in an efficient and effective manner and because, in the process, he struck me as a

CDCR official who genuinely respects the transgender inmates and truly cares about their welfare. In my field notes, I wrote "helpful and nice guy.". . .

Debriefing with Fellow Researchers

Almost without fail, interviewers followed each day of data collection with some "debriefing," usually in the car on the way home or back to the hotel. These debriefing sessions are as revealing as the "after the interview" moment described by Warren et al. (2003) insofar as they provide a window into how we—the researchers—related to, and indeed managed, gender in the field. Predictably, this debriefing was sometimes humorous and sometimes shocking.

For example, I had to laugh when an interviewer reported that a transgender inmate mistook her for being pregnant. When the interviewer informed the inmate that she was not pregnant, the inmate apologized for her rudeness by saying, "Oh, I'm such a cunt!" What a thing for a transgender inmate in a men's prison to say about herself. I found myself thinking: "Well, that's an awful thing to call yourself." But, I also thought: "What does calling yourself a cunt mean in a context in which having female body parts, especially breasts and vaginas, is desperately desired and creatively pursued as a necessity for the Self (with a capital S)?" It occurred to me that maybe a transgender inmate calling herself a cunt has meaning I do not understand, and, in any event, I now like to think of it as a playful, positive, multifaceted comment—a comment defined more by context than cliché . . .

As data collection unfolded, I could not predict what the new case would be, but debriefing always generated a provocative case to be shared and a venue for challenging our individual and collective views of the transgender population. Although I occasionally cringed when I sensed the debriefing session could be read as "gossipy" or we could (wrongly, I think) be accused of treating the transgender inmates like a "zoo exhibit" more than an oral "case study comparison" (to use the official words of social science), I looked forward to debriefing at the end of a long day of interviewing. During debriefing sessions, I occasionally thought that someone should study us, with an eye toward trying to make sense of how we do gender, make attributions related to our human subjects, and otherwise reveal the social fabric in which we were—and are—inevitably and inextricably entangled.

Most notably for my purposes here, what was not predictable to me was when we, members of the interview team, "slipped" and, in the process of debriefing among ourselves, referenced a transgender inmate in our study by using a masculine generic pronoun. We all did it more than once. The "slip" usually took the form of saying something like, "Well, he said . . .," "His situation included . . .," "The guy I interviewed . . .," "I told him . . .," and so on. These slips occurred despite our commitment to enact the interview training that dictated referring to the transgender inmates as they would like to be referred to (i.e., as transgender or female) and despite a genuine desire to be respectful of their self-designations and gendered identities. Sometimes these slips were followed by immediate self-correction, such as "uh, I mean her . . .," or "I mean she . . .," but sometimes they went unmarked . . .

[Another] example occurs outside the parameters of an interview and involves a moment of engagement with an inmate who does not self-identify as transgender but was nonetheless happy to explain "prison types" to me while we were both waiting in a hallway. While I was standing in a hallway waiting for officers to escort another inmate to the building in which I was conducting interviews, a Latino inmate who appeared to be in his mid 20s was sitting on a bench waiting to be escorted back to his housing unit when he initiated a discussion. He began by revealing to me that he knew why I was waiting in the hallway, indicating that I was "the professor in charge of the research by the university" as opposed to one of the other interviewers. Because he had been escorted to an interview room but was not interviewed, he rightly surmised that we were there to interview some inmates and not others. He volunteered to me that he is not transgender and is not on hormones, but that he is a "gay boy from [name of his home town]." I seized the moment to ask him the difference between being a gay boy and being transgender, and he gladly described the difference between three (easily confused) types of inmates:

> Gay boys are men who have feminine characteristics. They don't want to be girls. They are more like pretty boys, but they are boys. Transgenders want to be the girls. They want hormones, they want boobs to look like girls. They tend to think they were born to be girls and they are always bottoms. I don't

want boobs, no way; and, I'm not always a bottom, but I like that. Homosexual men are just masculine men—they don't want and they don't have feminine characteristics. They are men men—like the Village People, you know that group?

I answered "yes" and asked "what about sexually?" He replied: "You wouldn't know they were homosexual, they are almost always tops, but you'll find about 25 percent go both ways. Have you heard about gunslingers?" I said: "I've heard of them." Thereafter he explained: "The gay boys and the tgs are all in one group, we get along, we're like community. We have to stick together in here." According to him, getting along was made easier insofar as the CDCR personnel can't tell them apart. When I commented that his eyebrows were shaped in the same way many transgender inmates do their eyebrows, he gleefully replied: "Oh, thank you, I try to keep them looking good." Throughout this study, I came to learn that carefully plucked eyebrows designed to reveal high—some would say exaggerated—arches is a key signifier of something important related to gender presentation, gender identity, sexual orientation, and sexual attraction—a recognizable marker of femininity. Their own sense of self along these lines complicates any picture of transgender prisoners as a homogeneous group. . .

[Transgender inmates] membership in an array of social categories is complicated by their location in prison and by the larger sex/gender system in which they reside and to which they respond. The complexity of social categorization became particularly clear toward the end of data collection when, I presumed, data collection had become routine and I was beginning to think "saturation" had been reached. In one of the final prisons in which I collected data, I was taken to a visiting room to do interviews, and as I approached the visiting room, I saw what appeared to be all the transgender inmates—I would estimate about thirty inmates—standing in a very unorganized single file line waiting for us (I was with two other interviewers). The transgender inmates were talking, giggling, calling out to us, and otherwise enjoying being out of "lockdown" (the officer informed me that they had been on "lockdown" status for months). As I approached the (pseudo) line of transgender inmates to explain why we were there and how I hoped we could proceed, an inmate

toward the end of the line yelled, "We've got lesbians!" I assumed this was a comment about me or us—the interviewers—directed to the other transgender inmates in the makeshift single file line. The two interviewers who were with me receded into the background as I ignored the comment, and I stepped forward to introduce myself to the entire group, explain who we were and why we were there, and ask for their cooperation. Slightly altered, the comment—"the lesbians are here"— was delivered again. And, again I ignored it. Later that day, toward the end of a very long day of non-stop interviewing, the person I was interviewing responded to a question about involvement in "marriage-like relationships" by recalling her earlier comments—"we've got lesbians." She answered "no" to my specific question, and then she went further to explain: "But we do have some lesbians here. I thought you'd want to talk with them. I tried to get them to the front of the line." At that moment, I learned she was not referencing me or any other member of the research team when she yelled, "We've got lesbians." Rather, she was trying to put forth the most interesting cases for us to interview. Later, during debriefing, another interviewer confirmed that she had interviewed two transgender inmates, each of whom confirmed they were part of a couple with another transgender inmate. At this point, my stereotype defied reality.

Moments like this one, including the debriefing that followed it, required that we complicate the picture of transgender inmates in men's prisons. In this case, it resulted in recognizing the presence of lesbian transgender inmates in prisons for men as an anomalous configuration. More broadly, the ethnographic information presented throughout the article, coupled with the self-report data presented earlier, ensured that transgender inmates in prisons for men do not easily fit into any one social recognizable category. This is the "people" part of the main title.

Discussion

. . . Although the research described in this article was first and foremost driven by policy questions and an attendant commitment to quantitative data collection, I was able to gain an invaluable ethnographic sense of the context in which transgender prisoners live and to which they respond. This type of engagement in the field routinely served to complicate the questions asked, the empirical portrayal of transgender inmates, and the sociological sensemaking surrounding both the policy and basic concerns that undergird this work. Indeed, it is difficult for me to make sense of this diverse population without the ethnographic engagement that, at times, only punctuated the work. Fortunately, this punctuation served to make the project messy by revealing the uncontested gender order that underpins prison life as well as the lived experience of gender and sexuality that contextualizes and thus permeates the lives of transgender inmates in prisons for men.

Ironically, messy is often something both researchers and transgender prisoners strive to avoid. Researchers strive to avoid it, or at least mitigate it, in the name of rigor, reliability, and validity. Transgender prisoners report a desire to avoid "messy" situations because they inevitably lead to undesirable outcomes. For them, "messy" is a term used to refer to "drama" (usually born of gossip or competition for the attention of men) or conflict between other transgender inmates and/or the men in prison (Sumner 2009, 180). For me, in this case of this research, a messy terrain served as a catalyst for a more nuanced sociological understanding of the social organization of gender and sexuality in California prisons. To use Goffman's (1963) term, the "primal sociological scenes" described in this article provided the windows through which the identities, desires, and performativity of transgender prisoners were rendered sociologically sensible—or at least more sensible. This, in turn, facilitated more thorough thinking about the policy question—where to house them to keep them safe in light of the social organization of sex, sexuality, and gender in prisons—while also stimulating an analysis of the situational complexity of gender.

Thinking about it this way harkens back to O'Brien's (2008) recently published presidential address to the Pacific Sociological Association. She reminds us that social life is messy, and as a result the practice of sociology is filled with tension, contradiction, conflict, and ambiguity. She reminds us that the impact and resonance of sociological knowledge are enhanced when we open ourselves to the tensions and contradictions we observe and experience in our work as sociologists. My own experiences in the field and with the "messiness" and complexity of social life ultimately point to the importance of methodological flexibility that allows ethnography to seep into even the most non-ethnographic studies and be utilized for analytic purposes when addressing policy questions. Therefore, I argue for the value of adopting what I call a "soft mixed methods" approach when doing non-ethnographic work designed to inform policy. To do so stimulates sociological imagination and, as I argue in this article, can ultimately provide answers to policy questions that might otherwise go unaddressed empirically.

REFERENCES

Collins, C. (2008, December 6). "Transgender inmate faces complaint: woman who was man in Chowchilla prison for rape." *The Fresno Bee*.

Goffman, E. 1963. *Stigma: Notes on the management of a spoiled identity*. New York: The Free Press.

Jenness, V., C. L. Maxson, K. N. Matsuda, and J. M. Sumner. (2007). *Violence in California correctional facilities: An empirical examination of sexual assault*. Report to the California Department of Corrections and Rehabilitation. Irvine, CA: University of California, Irvine.

Jenness, V., C. L. Maxson, J. M. Sumner, and K. N. Matsuda. (2010). "Accomplishing the difficult, but not impossible: Collecting self-report data on inmate-on-inmate sexual assault in prison." *Criminal Justice Policy Review*, 21 (1): 3–30.

Jenness, V., L. Sexton, and J. M. Sumner. (2010). *Transgender inmates in California's prisons: An empirical study of a vulnerable population*. Report to be submitted to the California Department of Corrections and Rehabilitation. Irvine, CA: University of California, Irvine.

Mazzei, J., and E. E. O'Brien. (2009). "You got it, so when do you flaunt it?: Building rapport, intersectionality, and the strategic deployment of gender in the field." *Journal of Contemporary Ethnography*, 38 (3): 358–383.

O'Brien, J. (2008). "Sociology as an epistemology of contradiction." *Sociological Perspectives,* 52: 5–22.

Schilt, K., and L. Westbrook. (2009). "Doing gender, doing heteronormativity: 'Gender normals,' transgender people, and the social maintenance of heterosexuality." *Gender & Society,* 23 (4): 440–464.

Sexton, L., V. Jenness, and J. M. Sumner. (2010). "Where the margins meet: A demographic assessment of transgender inmates in men's prisons." *Justice Quarterly,* 27, 835–866.

Sumner, J. M. (2009). "Keeping house: Understanding the transgender inmate code of conduct through prison policies, environments, and culture." PhD Diss., University of California, Irvine.

Tewksbury, R., and R. Potter. (2005). "Transgender prisoners—A forgotten group." In *Managing special populations in jails and prisons,* ed. S. Stojkovic, 15-1–15-14. New York: Civic Research Institute.

Wacquant, L. (2002). "The curious eclipse of prison ethnography in the age of mass incarceration." *Ethnography,* 3 (4): 371–397.

Warren, C. A. B., T. Barnes-Brus, H. Burgess, L. Wiebold-Lippisch, J. Hackney, G. Harkness, V. Kennedy, R. Dingwall, P. C. Rosenblatt, A. Ryen, and R. Shay. (2003). "After the interview." *Qualitative Sociology,* 26(1): 93–110.

THINKING ABOUT THE READING

How would you approach the study of a marginal population who is often rendered invisible? What challenges specific to that group do you think you would encounter along the way? Is it possible for researchers who are not members of a population to gain an accurate understanding of the culture and lived experiences of these individuals? Why is it important to embrace the messiness of research, including the tension, contradiction, conflict, and ambiguity? How can this "messy" practice illuminate new and exciting discoveries from our social world?

Scientific Thinking

PETER NARDI

(2018)

Here's a story about unroasted (green) coffee beans and weight reduction. In 2012, TV personality Dr. Mehmet Oz exclaimed: "Green Coffee Bean Extract: The Fat Burner That Works!" Based on the idea that these green coffee beans contain chlorogenic acid, which acts as an antioxidant to reduce blood sugar levels and possibly lead to weight loss, Dr. Oz touted a study that was eventually retracted from an open-access journal (Vinson, Burnham, and Nagendran, 2012). This study had the appearance of scientific methodology but on closer inspection turned out to be based on poorly designed pseudoscience methods.

Only 16 subjects from India between the ages of 22 and 46 who exhibited preobesity (as measured by BMI, the body mass index) participated in the study. They were divided randomly into three groups, each of which varied in the sequence of taking capsules for 22 weeks containing either green coffee bean extract with chlorogenic acid or a placebo. One group ($n = 6$) began with a high-dose/low-dose/placebo sequence; another group ($n = 4$) followed a low-dose/placebo/high-dose sequence; and the third group ($n = 6$) had a placebo/high-dose/low-dose sequence. Results indicated that all three groups had lost weight at the end of the trial period. The authors, however, said that the subjects lost more weight during the weeks when they were taking the green coffee extract, even though they still lost weight during the placebo period.

What critical thinking questions would you ask to get at the integrity of this research? The three comparison groups were so small in size, it's difficult to know if weight loss was due to the coffee extract or to simply engaging in daily diet monitoring. BMI is also not the best method for monitoring weight loss. Furthermore, despite the claim that it was a randomized double-blind study, there was no separate control group with placebo; each group was its own control group. For these design flaws and other ethical reasons, the paper was eventually retracted.

It is not unusual in today's social media world to hear about the curative powers of various foods, the incredible health benefits of certain vitamins, and the wonders of some new, secret, gluten-free diet plan. Questionable studies and sensational advertising touting all sorts of secret ingredients for weight, hair, or memory loss are widely available. Along with claims of paranormal occurrences, near-death experiences, UFO appearances, urban-legend truths, and conspiracy-theory beliefs, the media reports and personal stories many of us post and pass along can justifiably be called, at best, only entertainment and, at worst, pseudoscientific thinking.

We need to look more closely at the methodologies propping up these anecdotes, miraculous cures, and questionable surveys. Distinguishing quality scientific research from pseudoscience is essential, especially when the reports are focused on social and political issues impacting our daily lives, such as climate change, school curricula, gun control, and public health, to name a few.

Scientific Methods

Many scientific research designs are available, and all depend on certain characteristics that distinguish them from nonscientific approaches. There is no one scientific method; it's about how science is practiced and adopted for different disciplines, research questions, and ethical standards. Scientific research can be designed for several purposes, including

- *explore* a new topic as a preliminary step for a more in-depth study,

- *describe* social behavior and opinions,

- *explain* social phenomena and cause-and-effect relationships,

- *predict* future behavior and opinions once they have been described and explained.

Each of these goals requires a methodology suited to achieving the particular purpose of the research. Critical thinking involves identifying the main goals of the project and evaluating the relationship between those research goals and the scientific elements needed to carry them out successfully. Several key principles characterize scientific methods, not all of which apply to all research designs. And in actual practice, science is an iterative process, sometimes of trial and error, unexpected findings, and serendipity, and often not following the linear pattern presented in standard definitions of science. The critical thinker needs to ask which of the following elements are relevant for determining whether what is reported in the media or published reports is scientific:

- Systematic design,

- Testable hypotheses,

- Reliable and valid measurements or observations,

- Replication,

- Control of alternative explanations,

- Random probability sampling for some research,

- For experiments: double-blind control groups, randomization,

- and placebos.

Let's discuss these characteristics of a scientific method and how you can use them to critically evaluate reports of research and distinguish scientific studies from pseudoscientific claims. We begin with a study that illustrates not only the scientific process but also the way it evolved when two researchers read a book that struck them as needing some scientific verification.

Let the following example serve as a guide to how you can use critical thinking and apply the elements of a scientific methodology when reading research in scholarly publications or the popular media.

In 2014, law professors Amy Chua and Jed Rubenfeld published *The Triple Package: How Three Unlikely Traits Explain the Rise and Fall of Cultural Groups in America*. The authors focused their book on why certain groups (for example, Chinese, Jews, and Nigerians) achieve higher socioeconomic status in life than other groups. Their argument emphasized three traits: impulse control, personal insecurity, and a sense of group superiority. Individuals from cultural groups that socialize their children with these traits tend to be more successful in terms of higher education and income (socioeconomic status). The implication of their theoretical idea is that the interaction of the three traits leading to success is not limited to the specific groups Chua and Rubenfeld discuss; the theory should also be applicable to any individuals raised with these personality and social characteristics.

Needless to say, the media had a field day with this thesis, generating much publicity for the book as well as controversy about child-rearing practices, cultural influences, and "model minorities" issues. *At first glance, with just this very brief summary, what do your critical thinking tools alert you to about the book's ideas? What methods would you use to deduce some hypotheses and carry out a research project to evaluate them?*

Many critics of the book noticed this dependence on stories about cultural differences and child-rearing patterns rather than any kind of systematic data collection. They also called attention to the problematic ways that the three traits had not been clearly and consistently defined. Are rules of rabbinic law, resisting temptation, and self-subordination considered "impulse control"? What exactly is a sense of group superiority? Is it the same as ethnocentrism? And what are feelings of inferiority? Maybe low self-esteem or cultural persecution? How do you assess "success in life"? *Instead of using anecdotes, how would you measure these characteristics with some reliability and validity?*

Driven to do something about a fascinating research question concerning what makes some people more successful than others, the psychology professors Joshua Hart and Christopher Chabris (2016) decided to use Chua and Rubenfeld's theory to conduct a scientific study and critically evaluate the relationship among these three traits and success. The methods that Hart and Chabris use in their published research illustrate the scientific method and show clearly how critical thinking works in guiding them to go beyond anecdotes. In so doing, they demonstrate the crucial differences between pseudoscience and scientific methodology.

Systematic Design

A scientific project may begin with some casual observations, from ideas that pop into your head or from questions that come to mind when reading studies and media reports, as it did for Hart and Chabris with the Triple Package model espoused by

Chua and Rubenfeld. Yet, what makes a research plan scientific is the development of some *systematic* methods to investigate those observations, informal ideas, and unanswered questions. Scientific research requires an organized plan or design demonstrating that it is not based on anecdotal and informal methodology. The components of the research plan should be specifically detailed enough for others to replicate the research.

In their published article, Hart and Chabris detailed their methodology for two studies they conducted testing the Triple Package ideas, including how they obtained their representative cross-sectional samples ($n = 430$ for Study One, and $n = 828$ for Study Two), measured the concepts, and statistically analyzed the data. For example, "Participants completed surveys of personality traits first, cognitive ability variables second, 'success' variables third, and demographic variables last." This is not a haphazard, discursive study without a plan. For a qualitative or quantitative study to be scientific, it needs to be explicit about what it will be doing and how any changes in the research design are decided upon as the study moves along.

Testable Hypotheses

Fundamental to most scientific research is a set of research questions or hypotheses that predict some outcomes. A hypothesis is a proposed explanation of the relationships among variables based logically on prior research, observation, and sometimes intuition. For qualitative research, questions guide the study plan, even if not stated in hypothetical language. Hypotheses must be testable and refutable (sometimes called *falsifiable)*: that is, they must be about phenomena that can be measured, tested experimentally, or observed, not something that is supernatural or paranormal. And they must allow the possibility of being shown to be false because, technically, science does not prove; it only fails to disprove. As Goode (2012) argues, paranormal statements "are very *rarely* falsifiable," and "scientific thinking . . . is *usually* falsifiable."

Returning to the Triple Package idea, Hart and Chabris (2016: 217) state Chua and Rubenfeld's book's hypothesis as "group superiority combined with insecurity leads to 'drive,' which is ineffectual without 'grit,' or the determination to persevere in the face of obstacles; grit is purportedly derived from

a combination of superiority and impulse control. In turn, the combination of drive and grit create success." They fault the book for basing its argument on "evidence that consists mostly of anecdotes . . . or simple descriptive statistics," and state that the original book has "imprecise definitions of constructs," which fail to specify whether the three traits are additive or multiplicatively interactive.

In other words, the original book presents a hypothesis but does not specify how to operationalize the concepts or collect evidence systematically. Therefore, it does not have some key characteristics of a scientific study; rather the book's premise provides the opportunity for conducting a proper scientific study.

Reliable and Valid Measurements

What makes scientific research systematic involves providing details about how concepts are measured or observed in a study. It's not clear in the Triple Package study what exactly is meant, for example, by a belief in a group's superiority, let alone how it may be observed or assessed. *How would you measure it if you were designing this research?* Hart and Chabris decided to use a published 22-item Revised Ethnocentrism Scale to measure the concept in their attempt to be more scientific. Note that using this scale was a choice made by the researchers and was not spelled out by the original Triple Package theory. Someone else could do a similar test of the theory by deciding to measure a sense of group exceptionalism in another way. Selecting a method of measurement is called *operationalizing* the variables.

Hart and Chabris similarly spelled out their measures for insecurity and impulse control, using various scales and multiple indicators of these traits. Given that their goal was to explain success (which can be defined in numerous ways), Hart and Chabris chose Chua and Rubenfeld's definition, which emphasizes income, status, and prestige, and created a composite measure as well as ones for each of those elements: "We asked participants to report their annual income (in increments of $20,000, up to $80,000, and then in increments of $40,000 to 'greater than $200,000'), and their highest level of education (seven options, from 'Grade school or less' to 'Graduate/professional degree)." *In what other ways could you measure these concepts and variables?*

More important, Hart and Chabris provide data on the reliability of the scales used in their study. For example, the Revised Ethnocentrism Scale has a very high (0.93) reliability coefficient, indicating that it is consistently measuring ethnocentrism. When reviewing research, be alert to indicators that the tools used to operationalize the concepts and variables of the study are reliable and valid.

Replication

Even with reliable and valid findings, research remains *tentative:* that is, it is open to further investigation. Recall that research does not prove hypotheses directly but fails to disprove them. Data analysis is also based on probability, rather than 100 percent certainty. Additional evidence is often required to secure the original findings, build on them, modify them, or even correct them when information is uncovered that falsifies them.

Tentativeness also provides a way of distinguishing science from pseudoscience. According to Timmer (2006):

> Many forms of pseudoscience, such as creationism, strive to squeeze data into support of a pre-ordained and invariant conclusion. Others, such as belief in UFO abductions, persist despite extensive counterevidence. In light of this, one potential way to gain a sense of how scientific a concept is would be to ask one of its proponents what pieces of data would cause them to modify or discard their favored model.

Finding data to modify or discard a theory occurs through seeking replication. See it as a type of reliability: consistency of results across multiple research studies. Replication requires following the methods described in a research project and either altering small elements (for example, does a study get similar or different results with a sample of non-college students in comparison with an original study's college students?) or reproducing a study a second time with the exact same measurements and sampling.

Many times, researchers attempt to replicate their study before announcing or publishing their results in order to guarantee some reliability in their findings. A critical thinker asks this question about replication: *When you read about the latest food that is supposed to be good or bad for you, is there any indication that the findings have been replicated, or is this the one-and-only study that says coffee, or blueberries, or kale will add years to your longevity?*

Hart and Chabris replicated their research before publication. They repeated their own study with a sample size twice that of the original: "Study 2 followed the same procedure as Study I, but with some measures omitted to minimize the demands on participants while still conceptually replicating Study 1". Study 2's results duplicated the findings of Study 1 and found that the Triple Package hypotheses of Chua and Rubenfeld could not be supported:

> Across two studies with sizable samples of U.S. adults (N = 1,258), we found that achievement of awards, education, and income was predicted by the educational attainment of individuals' parents (a proxy for socioeconomic status) and individuals' own cognitive ability as estimated by brief verbal and math tests. However, we found scant support for a 'Triple Package' hypothesis that a group superiority complex (i.e., ethnocentrism), personal insecurity (operationalized in four different ways), and impulse control interact to predict exceptional achievement.

Control of Alternative Explanations

As discussed in chapter 5, correlations require several conditions before causation can be declared, including ruling out alternative explanations. Critically evaluating media reports and scientific studies involves raising questions about other possible reasons for the findings. The use of control groups in classic experimental research designs is the primary scientific method for investigating alternative explanations for this type of study. Qualitative research, on the other hand, can include observations and interviews about other plausible factors in order to address alternative explanations. However, for some studies (such as cross-sectional surveys) evaluating the role of other explanations can be accomplished through data analysis techniques by statistically controlling for specific variables.

This is what Hart and Chabris did by collecting data on parents' educational attainment to control for socioeconomic status (SES) when their subjects were growing up. They also introduced a cognitive ability measurement (a composite of mathematical and reading test scores), since that is typically related to success. And, as they discovered, parental SES and cognitive ability were statistically stronger predictors of success than the three variables posited in the Chua and Rosenfeld book.

By including alternative explanations, researchers can discover stronger relationships, nullify other findings, and begin to explain causality. Pseudoscience, however, rarely controls for additional variables that may be related to the outcomes under scrutiny. *What would be some alternative explanations of UFO abductions or Bigfoot sightings?*

Experiments and Placebo Control Groups

Experiments involve conditions in which the researcher can manipulate the conditions to test out the effects of independent variables on some dependent or outcome variables. Seeking to explain relationships and establish causation, experiments require:

- a treatment/experimental group (that receives the independent variables),

- a control group (that either does not get the treatment or else receives a placebo version),

- random assignment of subjects to the control and treatment groups,

- measures both before and after the treatment or placebo,

- no knowledge by either the subjects or the researchers as to which participants are in the treatment or the control group (known as double-blind procedure).

We've mentioned placebos several times already. A *placebo* (Latin for "I will please") is a substance or procedure given to a *control group* to compare with an equivalent *treatment group* receiving the real intervention or pill. In medical research, the look-alike placebo is often a sugar pill that does not have any real effect on the condition being studied, allowing comparisons to be made between the actual medicine and the fake one. For other kinds of research, a control group can simply be the absence of some treatment or, when using a placebo, some benign equivalent treatment.

It's fairly common for about a third of people in a placebo control group to report positive changes or lessening of symptoms. Some patients even when told outright that they had received a fake or placebo treatment continue to report positive outcomes. Occasionally, recipients of a placebo claim negative side-effects (the *nocebo* effect), such as headaches or nausea. In a study from New Zealand, for example, university students who were told they were drinking vodka and tonic, but were really sipping a tonic-only placebo, acted drunk, demonstrated worse eyewitness accounts, and were more easily swayed by misleading information. Similarly, many people in a placebo group reported gastrointestinal problems when participating in a study of gluten sensitivity even after consuming gluten-free food.

Now consider this research design about the efficacy of acupuncture in relieving pain after a wisdom tooth extraction: One hundred and twenty patients were randomly assigned to one of three groups: an experimental group consisting of those receiving real acupuncture and two placebo groups. One placebo group ($n = 40$) received four fake acupuncture needle insertion sensations and one very shallow insertion, whereas the other placebo group ($n = 40$) received four very shallow insertions and one insertion sensation. The experimental group ($n = 40$) received true acupuncture needle insertions in the same locations as the placebo groups but with the greater depth required by traditional Chinese practice. All subjects' eyes were covered to avoid seeing the real or fake needle insertions. *With just this limited information, how would you evaluate the research methods so far?*

Results showed no significant differences in the average scores on a pain scale experienced between the acupuncture treatment group and the two placebo control groups. To replicate the research, a modified follow-up study using one placebo group ($n = 120$) instead of two and a larger acupuncture group ($n = 60$) confirmed similar findings: "There was no difference between real and fake acupuncture with respect to the average amount of pain experienced". In addition, the researchers discovered that patients who thought they were receiving real acupuncture—regardless of whether they were in the actual or fake acupuncture groups—reported experiencing significantly less dental pain. *What does this suggest about placebos?*

Although this brief summary of the study does not provide more in-depth findings and other research design elements, the point is to demonstrate what to look for when critically thinking about research and the basic components of a scientific methodology. *What makes this study a scientific one, rather than the anecdotal writings or pseudo-science studies found in many public media about the efficacy of acupuncture to relieve pain?*

Other Scientific Methods

Not all quality scientific research fits the randomized double-blind placebo control (RDBPC) design model of interventional experiments. Although that may be what many label the gold standard when testing new products, medicines, diets, and related health issues, it is often not possible to assign people randomly into groups or even to provide placebo treatments. Yet these research designs could still represent scientific thinking.

Some research may begin with a current baseline survey and follow subjects who periodically complete follow-up questionnaires over time. This longitudinal design is a *cohort prospective* methodology and is best represented by the Nurses' Health Study (NHS). Originally developed in 1976 to investigate the long-term heart disease and cancer outcomes of contraceptive use and smoking, the NHS recruited female nurses to complete detailed surveys every two years. Almost 90 percent of the nurses continued to answer questions about diet, nutrition, and lifestyle issues in the follow-up surveys, making this prospective research one of the most successful and important longitudinal projects on women's health. (See Nurses Health Study, 2016, for a complete description of the methodology.)

Yet, it's important to keep in mind what Heather Gilligan (2015) wrote about nutritional science methodologies and the conflicting advice on which foods are good for us and which ones to avoid:

> Many nutritional studies are observational studies, including massive ones like the Nurses' Health Study. Researchers like [Harvard nutritionist Walter] Willett try to suss out how changes in diet affect health by looking at associations between what people report they eat and how long they live. When many observational studies reach the same conclusions, Willett says, there is enough evidence to support dietary recommendations. Even though they only show correlation, not cause and effect, observational studies direct what we eat. Apart from their inability to determine cause and effect, there's another problem with observational studies: The data they're based on—surveys where people report what they ate the day (or week) before—are notoriously unreliable. Researchers have long known that people (even nurses) misreport, intentionally and unintentionally, what they eat. Scientists politely call this "recall bias."

Science is not some fixed method with a one-size-fits-all approach. What's important for the critical thinker is to ask the questions about the data collection methodologies, the scientific elements of the research, and whether the conclusions drawn are limited and relevant to the research questions asked. To understand what makes reports and claims scientific is to understand the differences from pseudoscience, anecdotes, and opinions, and not simply see the research as following a rigid checklist of objective techniques.

REFERENCES

Chua, Amy and Jed Rubenfeld. 2015. *The Triple Package: How Unlikely Traits Explain the Rise and Fall of Cultural Groups in America*. New York: Penguin.

Gilligan, Heather Triado. 2015 [April 12]. "The Science Behind Dietary Recommendations Isn't as Conclusive as You Think. *Slate*.

Goode, Eric. 2012. *The Culture of Fear*. New York: Basic Books.

Hart, Joshua and Christopher F. Chabris. 2016. Does A "Triple Package" of Traits Predict Success? *Personality and Individual Differences*, 94, 216–222.

Nurses Health Study. [Brigham and Women's Hospital and Harvard T.H. Chan School of Public Health.] 2016. "About: History."

Timmer, John. 2006 [Oct.13]. "Scientists on Science: Tentativeness." *Ars Technica*.

Vinson, Joe, Bryan Burnham, and Mysore Nagendran. 2012. "Randomized, Double-Blind, Placebo-Controlled, Linear Dose, Crossover Study to Evaluate the Efficacy and Safety of Green Coffee Bean Extract in Overweight Subjects." *Diabetes, Metabolic Syndrome and Obesity*, 5:21–27.

THINKING ABOUT THE READING

After reading Nardi's article, what would you say makes a study scientific? Was this how you viewed scientific evidence prior to reading this article? What are the potential risks of accepting the conclusions from pseudoscience? Are anecdotes and opinions always dangerous to consider? Why or why not? Consider your academic field of study. How might not only understanding proper scientific knowledge but also developing the skills to conduct your own research benefit you in your education and future profession?

CHAPTER
4

Building Order
Culture and History

Culture provides members of a society with a common bond and a set of shared rules and beliefs for making sense of the world in similar ways. Shared cultural knowledge makes it possible for people to live together in a society. Sociologists refer to shared cultural expectations as social norms. Norms are the rules and standards that govern all social encounters and the mechanisms that provide order in our day-to-day lives. Shared norms make it possible to know what to expect from others and what others can expect from us. When norms are violated, we are reminded of the boundaries of social behavior. These violations lead us to notice otherwise taken-for-granted rules about what is considered right and wrong.

When we examine the social influences on our behavior, things that were once familiar and taken for granted suddenly become unfamiliar and curious. During the course of our lives, we are rarely forced to examine *why* we do the common things we do; we just do them. But, if we take a step back and examine our common customs and behaviors, they begin to look as strange as the "mystical" rituals of some far-off, exotic land. It is for this reason that Horace Miner's article "Body Ritual Among the Nacirema" has become a classic in sociology and anthropology. As you read this selection, consider the process of using the sociological imagination to understand your own life and the lives of others. When you think about other cultures, how can you be sure that your perceptions, as an outsider, are not as bizarre as Miner's perspective on the Nacirema? When done well, sociological research helps us to understand different points of view and different cultural contexts from the perspective of insiders.

What are the vehicles for where we learn our norms and rules of behavior? In sociology, the family is often referred to as the primary socializing agent. In "Country Masculinity," Matthew Desmond introduces us to the culture of wildland firefighters in Elk River. This mostly male fire crew was initiated into firefighting culture early on, usually from previous generations of male family members who were part of this rural, masculine, and blue-collar culture. As you read this selection, consider the traditions that led these country boys to embrace this culture and the skills they brought with them to it. How did they use this culture to make sense of their world and the external one beyond the flames?

Sometimes more formalized norms can lead to key changes in an existing culture. In "From Hippie to Hip: Street Vending in Vancouver, Canada," Amy Hanser compares the food cart and truck culture of the 1970s to the more contemporary one of the 2010s. She discovers how informality, a once fundamental characteristic of street vending, was obscured in the formalization and regulation of the culture. As you read this selection, consider how the larger social and political context can shape a culture like street vending and, in some cases, may contribute to a process that excludes certain individuals from the culture.

Something to Consider as You Read

How do cultural practices provide social order? Where is this order located? In our minds? In our interactions with others? Think about what happens to your own sense of order when you become immersed in a different culture. What are some of the challenges you might face in trying to maintain your own cultural beliefs and practices while living in a completely different culture? Are some cultural practices easier to export than others? Why? As you read and compare these selections, think about why some cultures consider their ways to be better and more "real" than others. Do you think this ethnocentrism is a hallmark of all cultures or just some? How does the public display of cultural values and the environment it's done in impact the sanctions or absence of sanctions to these actions? As processes of globalization increase, what are the consequences for local cultures?

Body Ritual among the Nacirema

HORACE MINER

(1956)

The anthropologist has become so familiar with the diversity of ways in which different peoples behave in similar situations that he is not apt to be surprised by even the most exotic customs. In fact, if all of the logically possible combinations of behavior have not been found somewhere in the world, he is apt to suspect that they must be present in some yet undescribed tribe. This point has, in fact, been expressed with respect to clan organization by Murdock (1949, p. 71). In this light, the magical beliefs and practices of the Nacirema present such unusual aspects that it seems desirable to describe them as an example of the extremes to which human behavior can go.

Professor Linton first brought the ritual of the Nacirema to the attention of anthropologists twenty years ago (1936, p. 326), but the culture of this people is still very poorly understood. They are a North American group living in the territory between the Canadian Cree, the Yaqui and Tarahumara of Mexico, and the Carib and Arawak of the Antilles. Little is known of their origin, although tradition states that they came from the east. According to Nacirema mythology, their nation was originated by a culture hero, Notgnihsaw, who is otherwise known for two great feats of strength—the throwing of a piece of wampum across the river Pa-To-Mac and the chopping down of a cherry tree in which the Spirit of Truth resided.

Nacirema culture is characterized by a highly developed market economy which has evolved in a rich natural habitat. While much of the people's time is devoted to economic pursuits, a large part of the fruits of these labors and a considerable portion of the day are spent in ritual activity. The focus of this activity is the human body, the appearance and health of which loom as a dominant concern in the ethos of the people. While such a concern is certainly not unusual, its ceremonial aspects and associated philosophy are unique.

The fundamental belief underlying the whole system appears to be that the human body is ugly and that its natural tendency is to debility and disease. Incarcerated in such a body, man's only hope is to avert these characteristics through the use of the powerful influences of ritual and ceremony. Every household has one or more shrines devoted to this purpose. The more powerful individuals in this society have several shrines in their houses and, in fact, the opulence of a house is often referred to in terms of the number of such ritual centers it possesses. Most houses are of wattle and daub construction, but the shrine rooms of the more wealthy are walled with stone. Poorer families imitate the rich by applying pottery plaques to their shrine walls.

While each family has at least one such shrine, the rituals associated with it are not family ceremonies but are private and secret. The rites are normally only discussed with children, and then only during the period when they are being initiated into these mysteries. I was able, however, to establish sufficient rapport with the natives to examine these shrines and to have the rituals described to me.

The focal point of the shrine is a box or chest which is built into the wall. In this chest are kept the many charms and magical potions without which no native believes he could live. These preparations are secured from a variety of specialized practitioners. The most powerful of these are the medicine men, whose assistance must be rewarded with substantial gifts. However, the medicine men do not provide the curative potions for their clients, but decide what the ingredients should be and then write them down in an ancient and secret language. This writing is understood only by the medicine men and by the herbalists who, for another gift, provide the required charm.

The charm is not disposed of after it has served its purpose, but is placed in the charm-box of the household shrine. As these magical materials are specific for certain ills, and the real or imagined maladies of the people are many, the charm-box is usually full to overflowing. The magical packets are so numerous that people forget what their purposes were and fear to use them again. While the natives are very vague on this point, we can only assume that the idea in retaining all the old magical materials is that their presence in the charm-box, before which the body rituals are conducted, will in some way protect the worshipper.

Beneath the charm-box is a small font. Each day every member of the family, in succession, enters the shrine room, bows his head before the charm-box, mingles different sorts of holy water in the font, and proceeds with a brief rite of ablution. The holy waters are secured from the Water Temple of the community, where the priests conduct elaborate ceremonies to make the liquid ritually pure.

In the hierarchy of magical practitioners, and below the medicine men in prestige, are specialists whose designation is best translated "holy-mouth-men." The Nacirema have an almost pathological horror of and fascination with the mouth, the condition of which is believed to have a supernatural influence on all social relationships. Were it not for the rituals of the mouth, they believe that their teeth would fall out, their gums bleed, their jaws shrink, their friends desert them, and their lovers reject them. They also believe that a strong relationship exists between oral and moral characteristics. For example, there is a ritual ablution of the mouth for children which is supposed to improve their moral fiber.

The daily body ritual performed by everyone includes a mouth-rite. Despite the fact that these people are so punctilious about care of the mouth, this rite involves a practice which strikes the uninitiated stranger as revolting. It was reported to me that the ritual consists of inserting a small bundle of hog hairs into the mouth, along with certain magical powders, and then moving the bundle in a highly formalized series of gestures.

In addition to the private mouth-rite, the people seek out a holy-mouth-man once or twice a year. These practitioners have an impressive set of paraphernalia, consisting of a variety of augers, awls, probes, and prods. The use of these objects in the exorcism of the evils of the mouth involves almost unbelievable ritual torture of the client. The holy-mouth-man opens the client's mouth and, using the above-mentioned tools, enlarges any holes which decay may have created in the teeth. Magical materials are put into these holes. If there are no naturally occurring holes in the teeth, large sections of one or more teeth are gouged out so that the supernatural substance can be applied. In the client's view, the purpose of these ministrations is to arrest decay and to draw friends. The extremely sacred and traditional character of the rite is evident in the fact that the natives return to the holy-mouth-man year after year, despite the fact that their teeth continue to decay.

It is to be hoped that, when a thorough study of the Nacirema is made, there will be careful inquiry into the personality structure of these people. One has but to watch the gleam in the eye of a holy-mouth-man, as he jabs an awl into an exposed nerve, to suspect that a certain amount of sadism is involved. If this can be established, a very interesting pattern emerges, for most of the population shows definite masochistic tendencies. It was to these that Professor Linton referred in discussing a distinctive part of the daily body ritual which is performed only by men. This part of the rite involves scraping and lacerating the surface of the face with a sharp instrument. Special women's rites are performed only four times during each lunar month, but what they lack in frequency is made up in barbarity. As part of this ceremony, women bake their heads in small ovens for about an hour. The theoretically interesting point is that what seems to be a preponderantly masochistic people have developed sadistic specialists.

The medicine men have an imposing temple, or *latipso*, in every community of any size. The more elaborate ceremonies required to treat very sick patients can only be performed at this temple. These ceremonies involve not only the thaumaturge but a permanent group of vestal maidens who move sedately about the temple chambers in distinctive costume and headdress.

The *latipso* ceremonies are so harsh that it is phenomenal that a fair proportion of the really sick natives who enter the temple ever recover. Small children whose indoctrination is still incomplete have been known to resist attempts to take them to the temple because "that is where you go to die." Despite this fact, sick adults are not only willing but eager to undergo the protracted ritual purification, if they can afford to do so. No matter how ill the supplicant or how grave the emergency, the guardians of many temples will not admit a client if he cannot give a rich gift to the custodian. Even after one has gained admission and survived the ceremonies, the guardians will not permit the neophyte to leave until he makes still another gift.

The supplicant entering the temple is first stripped of all his or her clothes. In everyday life the Nacirema avoids exposure of his body and its natural functions. Bathing and excretory acts are performed only in the secrecy of the household shrine, where they are ritualized as part of the body-rites. Psychological shock results from the fact that body secrecy is suddenly lost upon entry into the *latipso*. A man, whose own wife has never seen him in an excretory act, suddenly finds himself naked and assisted by a vestal maiden while he performs his natural functions into a sacred vessel. This sort of ceremonial treatment is necessitated by the fact that the excreta are used by a diviner to ascertain the course and nature of the client's sickness. Female clients, on the other hand, find their naked bodies are subjected to the scrutiny, manipulation, and prodding of the medicine men.

Few supplicants in the temple are well enough to do anything but lie on their hard beds. The daily ceremonies, like the rites of the holy-mouth-men, involve discomfort and torture. With ritual precision, the vestals awaken their miserable charges each dawn and roll them about on their beds of pain while performing ablutions, in the formal movements of which the maidens are highly trained. At other times they insert magic wands in the supplicant's mouth or force him to eat substances which are supposed to be healing. From time to time the medicine men come to their clients and jab magically treated needles into their flesh. The fact that these temple ceremonies may not cure, and may even kill the neophyte, in no way decreases the people's faith in the medicine men.

There remains one other kind of practitioner, known as a "listener." This witch-doctor has the power to exorcise the devils that lodge in the heads of people who have been bewitched. The Nacirema believe that parents bewitch their own children. Mothers are particularly suspected of putting a curse on children while teaching them the secret body rituals. The counter-magic of the witch-doctor is unusual in its lack of ritual. The patient simply tells the "listener" all his troubles and fears, beginning with the earliest difficulties he can remember. The memory displayed by the Nacirema in these exorcism sessions is truly remarkable. It is not uncommon for the patient to bemoan the rejection he felt upon being weaned as a babe, and a few individuals even see their troubles going back to the traumatic effects of their own birth.

In conclusion, mention must be made of certain practices which have their base in native esthetics but which depend upon the pervasive aversion to the natural body and its functions. There are ritual fasts to make fat people thin and ceremonial feasts to make thin people fat. Still other rites are used to make women's breasts larger if they are small, and smaller if they are large. General dissatisfaction with breast shape is symbolized in the fact that the ideal form is virtually outside the range of human variation. A few women afflicted with almost inhuman hypermammary development are so idolized that they make a handsome living by simply going from village to village and permitting the natives to stare at them for a fee.

Reference has already been made to the fact that excretory functions are ritualized, routinized, and relegated to secrecy. Natural reproductive functions are similarly distorted. Intercourse is taboo as a topic and scheduled as an act. Efforts are made to avoid pregnancy by the use of magical materials or by limiting intercourse to certain phases of the moon. Conception is actually very infrequent. When pregnant, women dress so as to hide their condition. Parturition takes place in secret, without friends or relatives to assist, and the majority of women do not nurse their infants.

Our review of the ritual life of the Nacirema has certainly shown them to be a magic-ridden people. It is hard to understand how they have managed to exist so long under the burdens which they have imposed upon themselves. But even such exotic customs as these take on real meaning when they are viewed with the insight provided by Malinowski when he wrote (1948, p. 70):

> Looking from far and above, from our high places of safety in the developed civilization, it is easy to see all the crudity and irrelevance of magic. But without its power and guidance early man could not have mastered his practical difficulties as he has done, nor could man have advanced to the higher stages of civilization.

REFERENCES

Linton, R. (1936). *The study of man.* New York: Appleton-Century.

Malinowski, B. (1948). *Magic, science, and religion.* Glencoe, IL: Free Press.

Murdock, G. P. (1949). *Social structure.* New York: Macmillan.

THINKING ABOUT THE READING

What do you think of this culture? Do their ways seem very foreign, or are there some things that seem familiar? This article was written more than 50 years ago and, of course, much has changed since then. How might you update this description of the Nacirema to account for current values and rituals? Imagine you are an anthropologist from a culture completely unfamiliar with Western traditions. Using your own life as a starting point, think of common patterns of work, leisure, learning, intimacy, eating, sleeping, and so forth. Are there some customs that distinguish your group (religious, racial, ethnic, friendship, etc.) from others? See if you can find the reasons why these customs exist, which customs serve an obvious purpose (e.g., health), and which might seem arbitrary and silly to an outside observer.

Country Masculinity

MATTHEW DESMOND

(2007)

"It just builds up in you," he says.

"What? "What do you mean?" I ask, squinting.

"Just being in the forest, it's, it's—" Nicholas Masayesva pauses and rubs his thin black mustache in a contemplative rhythm. He starts again. "It's just being Hopi, it's being close to nature. The joy of it. It's hard work, and we all have to have money now. And most of it is not much money, but the joy of being here. Working with your comrades. But it's not for everybody, fighting fire. You have to learn to like it, to love it. And I guess that I'm one of those guys who like it, or love it. So I guess it just builds up in you or something. . . . I guess it's hard to explain how you really feel about something like that."

Nicholas is a spiritual man. The forty-year-old Hopi prays at dawn and regularly travels back to the Second Mesa Reservation to participate in dances and ceremonies. He inherits his beliefs and practices from his father, who taught him Hopi folklore, medicine, and language. He also inherits the tradition of fighting fire.

> "My dad was a firefighter. My dad and his dad," Nicholas tells me with a tincture of pride in his voice. "And my great-grandfather, he was one too. My uncles . . . I guess their blood was in me."

Nicholas began fighting fire at age eighteen to prove to his parents that he could do something more than get drunk and high. He quit high school three months before graduation and started working odd jobs on the Hopi reservation before selling drugs. When he decided to clean up his act, he applied for a job through the "all-Indian" job corps center called Kicking Horse, located in Montana. Nicholas requested a position in forestry and was hired onto a helitack squad.

Wildland firefighting did not seem so strange and alien to Nicholas, since his father, grandfather, and great-grandfather had all chased smoke. It came naturally to him. It was in his blood. Since that day he joined the helitack crew, he has returned season after season for twenty-two years.

What kinds of people find their way to firefighting units? What do they have in common? Where do they come from, and what do they bring with them? Are they young, as Nicholas was? Are they the sons of sons of sons of firefighters, like him? This chapter describes the circumstances that led my crewmembers to wildland firefighting, and more important, it focuses on the dispositions and skills they brought with them.

Family Traditions and Hometown Connections

Through small-town social connections, most crewmembers were recruited to the Forest Service informally over dinner conversations or chance meetings at the local supermarket. In this way these crewmembers do not differ from most blue-collar workers (or professional, technical, or managerial workers, for that matter) who predominantly use personal contacts to find and land jobs. However, a handful of crewmembers found out about potential positions in wildland firefighting through personal contacts but applied for these positions when Rex Thurman formally recruited them during their senior year at Atwater High School. Diego Alvarado was one such crewmember.

Diego is a twenty-year-old self-described Chicano who spends his free time fixing up old cars. His father, a high-spirited man with thick, wavy gray-and-black hair and a burly cowboy-style mustache that trails below his chin, is a letter carrier for the Post Office. His mother, a short middle-aged woman who wears round wire-framed glasses and two necklaces with three *medallas* displaying the Lady of Guadalupe and two saints, is a teacher's aide at an elementary school. In the off-season, Diego works as a cook at La Hacienda, his family's Mexican restaurant in Atwater. Good-humored and sharply intelligent, Diego, I believe, would have excelled in college (majoring, he tells me, in archaeology) could his family have afforded it. But instead of being recruited to college, he was recruited to the Forest Service.

"When I went to high school," Diego recalls, "they had us fill out this form that tells you what to do with college and scholarships. Well, I just filled out that I was interested in forestry and outdoors work, and one day I got a call from Mrs. Ingersol [the guidance counselor], that there was a man looking for recruits for firefighting. And *lo and behold* it was Rex Thurman at the high school!"

Diego laughs to himself and continues. "Thurman was sittin' there. He didn't have a beard. He was clean-shaven. And he had, uh, J.J., George, me, and that was it. Just us four. . . . From what Mrs. Ingersol was telling me, as long as I'm working in the Forest Service they'll pay for college, I said, shit, that's a good deal. . . . And I knew Thomas Hernandez [a retired supervisor from Elk River]. Yeah, his wife was my teacher, and I've known her forever. And I just met Thomas a couple years beforehand. I met him out here. So, Mrs. Hernandez was telling me that Thomas could help me out getting a job. . . . Fuck, the next thing you know I fuckin' get a call, a letter in the mail saying I should buy three-hundred-dollar boots and all this shit. And 'engine crew.' I said, shit, engine crew will be nice and easy. . . . It wasn't as easy as I thought."

In the urban fire sector, especially in East Coast cities such as New York and Boston, many firefighting genealogies can be traced back to the 1800s.[1] In a similar way, most of my crewmembers knew firefighting long before they entered its ranks. Their fathers and friends had dug line before them, and because they were embedded in networks of firefighters, they did not find the profession alien. Most crewmembers were recruited either informally through interpersonal network ties or formally through high school presentations by Thurman.

Backcountry Boys

Crewmembers vary in racial composition, age, religion, interests, and what they do after the season ends. But all are bound together by their rural upbringing. In fact, every wildland firefighter I have ever met comes from rural America. Norman Maclean, while writing about smokejumpers, encountered the same trend: "So basically they had to be young, tough, and in one way or another from the back country."[2]

Raised in small towns with populations under 10,000, most of my crewmembers have known each other since kindergarten, played on the football team together, and are familiar with each other's families.

Allen, Nicholas, and Scott were raised on the Hopi reservation. Most are not proud of their hometown per se; rather, they take pride in being from a small town in general, as opposed to a big city. My crewmembers are country boys, and the culture of the country—that "small town way of life" thought to be distinctly different from urban modes of existence—greatly influences how they perceive themselves and what "being a man" means.

Many of my crewmembers are deeply familiar with the woods they protect. They know where the best fishing spots are and where to find wild turkey at the right season. They know the different types of vegetation, where to gather the best firewood for winter, and the hundreds of miles of dirt roads, mapped and uncharted, running like tributaries through millions of acres of the Wannokee Forest, the site of Elk River. This knowledge is important to them. It provides a *sense* of place, comfort, and ownership, and it lets them know where they belong.

"I've always liked being in the woods," Diego reflects. "I would come here since I was little, camping, hunting, fishing. I've been here forever." Most of the men at Elk River feel the same way. Their family albums are filled with photos of small boys hoisting stringers of fish or dressed in Mossy Oak camouflage, smiling for the camera next to a freshly killed buck. Many have been going hunting with their fathers for as long as they can remember, and they are possessed by the sport.

To my crewmembers, the fact that they can earn a paycheck while "playing in the woods" seems like a too beautiful con. This is why most of them pick up odd jobs in the off-season that allow them to work outside, like construction work or furring, and why most fantasize about securing a full-time position with the Forest Service. As self-described "outdoor people," my crewmembers fervently reject any type of indoor work, regularly symbolized by the dull, predictable, sanitary desk. "I guess I've always been an outdoors person," remarks Nicholas. "You know, I've never been like an indoor type of guy, a desk or something," Making a living indoors, under the hum of fluorescent lights, in front of the bluish glow of computer monitors, is thought to be a terrible way to live. Although they would enjoy a larger salary, they view the cubicle, computer, and necktie that accompany white-collar professions as too large a sacrifice. The desk represents the world of paperwork, sycophants, and middle-class managerial masculinity. The forest represents freedom, wilderness, and working-class masculinity.

The rejection of indoor work, the denial of the desk, reinforces a major distinction in the minds of the men of Elk River. This distinction between "outdoor" and "indoor" people, between "the country" and "the city," functions as their primary symbolic binary.

The division between the country and the city is not created at Elk River; it is reproduced and reinforced there. Crewmembers bring this polarized scheme to the fire station. As we saw, most of my crewmembers come from working-class rural America, and they bring with them specific masculine dispositions structured by their working-class and country backgrounds. In other words, they come to Elk River with *a country-masculine habitus*. The country-masculine habitus guides the firefighters' thoughts, tastes, and practices. It serves as their fundamental sense of self, guides how they understand the world around them, influences how they codify sameness and difference, and determines who does and does not belong at Elk River.

Country Competence

George is from Atwater and in his third season at Elk River. A large cross, tattooed in blue with magnificent detail, draped with a banner that reads (a bit ironically), "Only the Strong Survive," covers George's sun-spotted white left shoulder; on his right shoulder "GEORGE" is tattooed in large letters, encased in a jagged border and surrounded by green and blue stars; and in the center of his back, directly between his shoulder blades, is a hand-sized Maltese cross, filled in by the Stars and Stripes and surrounded by orange and yellow flames that reach up to the bottom of his neck. A bit of a daydreamer, George earned the nickname "Space Case" from his crewmembers, "S.C." for short. George turned twenty-one in June, and the crew made sure to migrate to Atwater to give him a bibulous welcome into the ranks of legal drinkers. He stumbled out of the bar grinning from ear to ear—but then George always seems to have a smile on his face.

On a hot Friday afternoon George drove the chase truck, an F-150 painted in Forest Service green, down a dirt road congested with weekend campers eager to secure the best spots. I watched from the passenger seat as cars zoomed past at dangerous speeds. As we rounded a corner, a teal two-door hatchback, whose driver had let the car drift too far toward the outside of the road, jerked back onto the right side and sped past.

"Fuckin' valley rats," George grumbled as he guided the truck slowly along.

A "valley rat" is a city boy. "Valley" is a reference to Phoenix, the metropolis of Arizona, where over a million people find refuge in a low desert valley. "Rat," however, is another matter.

"So, why do you call them 'rats,' George? What's a valley rat?" I asked.

He glanced at me from behind the steering wheel with a puzzled look. George often looked puzzled. He turned his eyes back to the road and contemplated his answer. Staring at his freckled face shaded beneath a faded blue baseball cap, I waited as George meditated on his phrase by repeating quietly, "Valley rat? Val-ley rat? What would I say is a valley rat?"

He settled on an answer: "Someone who's not been around, around here. I would say a valley rat is someone who has been in a big city for most of their life. They don't really, they, they have *an idea* of what happens in small towns, but they don't *really* know how things work."

"So, George, would it be an insult if I called you a valley rat or a city-boy?" I asked, smiling.

He returned my smile, looked at me out of the corner of his eye, and replied. "It wouldn't be an insult. I'd just think you didn't know what the hell you're talking about."

Valley rats could not distinguish poison oak from wild sumac. They are ignorant of all things wild. The men at Elk River, by contrast, see themselves as possessing a specific body of knowledge—a country competence, a woodsy *techne*—that makes them country boys and the lack of which makes other men city boys.

Country masculinity is practiced and displayed primarily through country competence. At Elk River, crewmembers' practical knowledge of the woods, their embodied outdoorsmanship—the way a hand grips an ax, the way a foot mounts a trail—is directly bound up with their core sense of self, their masculinity and identity, for that which is "'learned by body' is not something that one has, like knowledge that can be brandished, but something that one is." This means that an attack on one's outdoorsmanship translates into a direct attack on one's masculinity. This is why Bryan did not take it lightly when he heard that George thought he could run a chain saw better than him.

It happened on a lazy Wednesday morning. Most of the crew had gathered in the shop, carefully avoiding the gaze of the supervisors. Crewmembers spread out through the large warehouse-like room lined with tools, a freestanding drill, a long wooden countertop, and a cherry picker used to pull engine blocks. Conversation was slow. Donald fidgeted with a metal rod on an anvil, and most of us milled around and watched him, since there was nothing else to watch. George propped himself against the concrete wall and drifted off to sleep, but his nap did not last long, because minutes later Bryan stomped into the shop, marched straight up to George, stopping inches from his face, and in a confrontational voice barked, "You think you can run a saw better than me?"

Everyone in the shop turned to watch. Bryan's loud voice signaled the beginning of an altercation both in tone and in subject. He was talking about a chain saw, a crucial tool used in wildland firefighting. Because of its mass, violence, and ability to harm, only the strongest, most skilled, and most experienced firefighters wield a saw. Thus, sawyering skills signal much more than the ability to drop a full-grown oak; they represent a skilled firefighter— more, a competent and mature country man. Bryan had advanced a serious response to a serious challenge supposedly advanced by George.

George blinked. He blinked again. He stared silently up at the large man in front of him. George was at once confused, startled awake, and a bit scared. He slowly peeled his body away from the wall and stuttered, "Wh-what?"

Immediately Bryan snapped back, "Someone told me you were saying you could run a saw better than me. Is that true, *George?*"

Bryan's shoulders rolled to the front, his arms ready at his sides; balanced over his legs, he pushed his torso toward George. Bryan was not kidding around. A casual observer taking in the scene from a distance might have guessed that George had made an uncouth remark about Bryan's sister. But the remark in question was about a chain saw.

"Uh, uh, no. No. I never said anything like that," George denied.

The room remained silent. Crewmembers stared at the immobile Bryan to see if he was satisfied by George's refutation.

"Are you *sure* George?' Cause somebody told me that you said that." Bryan wanted to hear George deny it again.

"Yeah. I mean, I don't know who told you that, but I didn't say nothin' about that."

"Well, *do* you think you can run a saw better than me, George?"

George thought about the question before answering. "No. Not *better,*"

"Are you sure?"

"Yeah."

After a few seconds Bryan turned away and marched stone-faced out of the shop, "That's what I thought, *George.*"

A week later the crew responded to a one-acre fire called the Alligator Juniper fire. I was assigned the task of spotting the sawyer; Bryan made sure to grab the chain saw first. I hoisted an army green bag full of chain-saw equipment such as hatchets and wedges onto my back, and we went to work. We policed the fire in search of trees with the potential to topple and came upon a medium-sized (B-class) pine seared most of the way up, which, we thought, needed to be dropped.

Bryan stood in the ashes and began to cut into the trunk while I looked on to make sure the tree was stable and would fall in the direction we wanted. He maneuvered the saw in and out of the trunk by making two front slices to form a pie cut a quarter of the way into the wood followed by a perfectly straight back cut. "Wood chips flew out from behind the saw in a light brown cloud to the familiar high-pitched whine of the chain ferociously whipping around the bar. When the pie cut began to close in on itself and the tree started to bend, Bryan pulled the saw out and stepped back, staring up at the falling trunk. The pie cut narrowed, and the tree tipped to the slow cracking of breaking wood. It hit the blistered ground with a *slam* and stirred up a cloud of ash. The cut was picture perfect, and Bryan knew it. He shut off the saw with a flick of *his* thumb and, turning to me. bragged, "And

George thought he could run a saw better than me. I said, 'George. I've been running a saw since I was thirteen!'"

Just as working-class men tend to judge the measure of a man through a value system that prizes attainable attributes (breadwinning, a hard work ethic, integrity) over ones perceived as unattainable (wealth, education, a powerful career), county boys define masculinity through standards of country competence. The men at Elk River value their "human capital," country competence, over economic capital and city competence. This is why, although Hutchinson might *own* some land, Clarence and my crewmembers *know* the land, and as such they believe they have more rights to the Wannokee Forest than some millionaire developer. They, country boys, belong at Elk River, and they feel it belongs to them.

Knowledge of the country is a practical and specific type of knowledge. If one can gut an elk, string a catfish line, reload .45 bullets, fell a juniper with a twelve-pound chain saw, or throw a rig into four-low, and climb a rocky hill, then one exhibits country competence. This knowledge not only binds crewmembers together (as Kris observes, "I'm not concerned with the similarities between their backgrounds, you know, where they're from, or their race or their ethnicity. I'm looking at the similarities of, like, their knowledge that pertains to the forest. I'm looking at their similarities for the love for the forest or why they are even out here."), it also allows them to adapt to the rigors of wildland firefighting as well as to the organizational common sense of the U.S. Forest Service with quickness and aptness.

Do you know how to tie a slipknot? Do you know the difference between four-low and four-high? Can you drive an ATV? Can you weld? Do you know what poison ivy looks like? Do you know how to pick up a snake? Can you hike fast without wasting your energy? Have you ever slept in the woods without a tent? Do you know what a cotter pin is? Most of my crewmembers could answer yes to more questions like these than Vince could; that is, whereas most of them came to Elk River with a refined and well-developed set of country-masculine skills, Vince had fewer resources to draw on. Most crewmembers adapted to the everyday practices of wildland firefighting—from digging line to repairing vehicles—more easily than he did. Thus, although it seems strange that Vince was not well adjusted to the world of wildland firefighting after seven years' experience, we might now say that he had *only* seven years' experience, whereas other crewmembers, regardless of the number of summers they had been employed by the Forest Service, had lifetimes.

NOTES

1. Mark Tebeau, Eating Smoke: Fire in Urban America, 1800–1950 (Baltimore: Johns Hopkins University Press, 2003); Terry Golway, So Others Might Live: A History of New York's Bravest, The FDNY from 1700 to the Present (New York: Basic Books, 2002).

2. Maclean, Young Men and Fire, 26.

THINKING ABOUT THE READING

According to Desmond, what is country masculinity? What are the social norms and values of this identity and what happens when they are transgressed? How does this culture and its masculine habitus help us to better understand and explain interactions and relations within it, as well as beyond it? In what way did this culture build their sense of collective identity?

From Hippie to Hip-Hop

Street Vending in Vancouver, BC

AMY HANSER

(2017)

In the late summer of 1974, two Vancouver alder-men made an inspection tour of street vending on Granville Street, one of the city's major downtown shopping streets. They were not happy with what they found. "That's ridiculous," Jack Volrich, one of the aldermen, was quoted as saying of a homemade brown-and-yellow-striped wooden kiosk. "It looks like an oversized outhouse" (*Vancouver Sun,* Aug. 31, 1974). Other vending setups, involving portable tables, were deemed "completely inappropriate" by city officials (*Vancouver Sun,* Aug. 31, 1974).

By contrast, decades later, Vancouver city coun-cilor Heather Deal described the city's new food carts, first welcomed downtown in 2010, as "like public art . . . it makes the streets a more exciting, vibrant place to be" (*Province* [Vancouver], Apr. 30, 2012). Serving foods described as "delectable" and "tastebud-boggling," the shiny new carts and trucks generated enormous excitement. In the words of Vancouver Mayor Gregor Robertson, "We've got a world-class city, and people want a world-class street food scene to match" (*Province,* July 11, 2010). Or as Peter Waal, a Vancouverite who directs the Food Network Canada show *Eat St.,* said of food carts, "It's more like a party. It's more like a backyard barbecue" (Mar. 2, 2012).

What distinguishes the "outhouse" from the "party" on the street? Both the hippie vendors of the 1970s and the hip new food vendors of the 2010s were enmeshed in important instances of new stan-dards or rules related to street vending being debated and decided upon in Vancouver. However, the con-trast between the two time periods illustrates a pair of contradictory impulses shaping regulation of com-mercial activity on city streets. First, there is a pro-cess of *formalization* (the imposition of new rules, standards, and regulations) that seeks to tame the informality and "messiness" of street vending. In Vancouver, what I call *hippie vending* of the 1970s was viewed as disorderly, aesthetically unacceptable, and in violation of standards of fair competition. Therefore, the city enacted a new bylaw regime to impose a set of formal rules and standards that effec-tively regulated most of the unruly vendors out of existence.

By the 2010s, however, a second, contradictory impulse had appeared: a seeming embrace of the vitality, spontaneity, and creativity associated with informality. Changing cultural values that embrace the informal—changes that themselves have roots in the 1960s and 1970s—produced new ideas about city streets and now identify street vending, in the form of food trucks and carts, as "hip." The result in Vancouver has been a city-led effort to introduce new forms of food vending to the city. However, this seeming embrace of the informal has neverthe-less unfolded through the formal procedures that characterize much of how city governance operates (Valverde 2012), and as such food carts and trucks represent a highly regulated form of street vending. In fact, the vitality associated with vending—in Van-couver, at least—is acceptable precisely because it has been reintroduced in a highly formalized, regu-lated form. This may, perhaps, be the essence of the difference between the *hippie* and the *hip:* True infor-mality and marginality have been replaced with a gloss of the informal.

Background

Numerous scholars—sociologists as well as geogra-phers, urban planners, historians, and others—have documented and described urban sidewalks as sites of contention and negotiation, and in cities around the world street commerce has a long but often contested history. Historically, conflicts over street and sidewalk commerce have revolved around notions of what pur-poses sidewalk space is supposed to serve and what city neighborhoods are supposed to look like.

Over the years, the urban sidewalk has come to be perceived as primarily a space through which pedestrian traffic should flow smoothly and has been shaped by efforts to "specialize" urban space through municipal zoning laws (Benson 2006). Recent growth of street vending in cities like New York City and Los Angeles, usually dated to the 1980s and the arrival of particular immigrant groups in each city, has resulted in more restrictive municipal regulation for street vending, as well as efforts by neighborhood business associations to assert a "view of sidewalks as a landscaped strip."

By contrast, advocates for street vendors present "a multipurpose vision for the sidewalks" or characterize it as a "sustaining habitat" (Duneier 1999) for economic survival. Sidewalks and street vending are represented as spaces where and means by which marginalized people—recent immigrants, homeless men, and the poor—can eke out a living, though often under the threat of harassment from police or other city authorities (Stoller 2002; Duneier 1999; Devlin 2011) and in the face of social stigmas against working on the street (Estrada and Hondagneu-Sotelo 2011).

Governance of city streets and sidewalks is a prime example of what urban scholars have called *police powers,* a form of state regulation in the name of public good (Foucault 2009). In most North American cities, vending is largely banned, and when it is allowed vendors are usually limited to a specific range of products (artwork or handicrafts, for example, or certain types of food) and specific locations that reflect the sense that public sidewalks and streets should be preserved for more legitimate uses, primarily circulation.

In recent years there has been a resurgence of street commerce in the form of gourmet food carts and trucks, this time sanctioned and in some cases even promoted by municipal governments. Propelled in part by broad public interest in food trends, cities across North America have embraced new forms of street food. The contrast between the continued restrictions on more traditional forms of street vending and the welcome extended to new, trendy food trucks raises important questions about access and equity in public spaces.

This trend reflects the importance of hierarchies of consumption to the regulation of space in contemporary North American cities. As Zukin (2010) notes, as cities have become important sites for consumption and as city governments have become invested in cultural strategies for urban (re)development, consumer tastes and cultural power increasingly shape how urban space is used and by whom.

She argues that this new cultural politics of urban space mobilizes the "gentrifier's aesthetic appreciation of urban authenticity" (18), how in the context of gentrification in one Washington, D.C., neighborhood, the concept of *diversity* changes over time such that it becomes a depoliticized commodity for individual lifestyle consumption as opposed to a term representing social justice and equity goals.

Why has the street, and street food, become a site for elite aesthetics and tastes to demand expression? What has made formerly problematic forms of street commerce quite literally palatable? The perceived authenticity of ethnic street foods (Zukin 2010), a "democratizing" trend among elite consumers embracing lowbrow foods (Johnston and Baumann 2010), and the perception of high-end street food as creative (Martin 2014) all partially explain the phenomenon. Each of these trends can also be linked to a larger set of cultural trends that have seen an embrace of certain elements of the informality associated with the rebellious and countercultural 1960s and 1970s.

The contrast between how street vending was characterized and addressed in Vancouver in the 1970s and how it is understood today illustrates a consistent discomfort with the messiness and informality associated with street vending across time. The experience of Vancouver's hippie vendors in the 1970s specifically illustrates how a proliferation of street vending in the city's downtown provided the context in which what Valverde (2012) terms "the law of the street corner"—in this case, regulations for vending—was elaborated and formalized, ultimately to the disadvantage of vendors. Today, that discomfort with street vending has been transformed into a desire to recapture the vitality associated with informality as an antidote to urban blandness.

Hippie Vendors, Hippie Wares: 1970S in Vancouver

Concerns about racialized immigrant populations; police concerns with unobstructed circulation, hygiene, and informal economic activity; and the imposition of elite visions of urban aesthetics can be found in the history of street vending in Vancouver. In the 1910s, the Vancouver city government reacted to fears about Chinese merchants operating beyond the monitored bounds of Chinatown by taxing mobile Chinese vegetable peddlers out of existence (Anderson 1991, 118). In 1968, popcorn vendors along a beachfront road were threatened with expulsion after they were accused of creating traffic congestion (*Province,* July 9, 1968), and in the late 1970s the city cracked down on farmers selling produce from roadside locations because they were perceived as a threat to public health, blocked traffic, and used "unacceptable" weighing devices such as bathroom scales (Report to Council, Standing Committee on Transportation, June 28, 1979, p. 4).

It was in fact in the 1970s that regulations on street vending underwent considerable scrutiny and revision, resulting in a set of changes prompted by a proliferation of hippie vendors in several key downtown locations. At the time, peddling was legal on city sidewalks, though licensed peddlers were required to spend no more than ten minutes in one place. Despite these restrictions, de facto street markets had developed in downtown Vancouver, especially in the historic Gastown neighborhood and along parts of Granville Street, a central boulevard that was simultaneously a key retail and transit location but also dubbed Canada's "roughest main drag." The vendors themselves were a varied group: one newspaper story describes local artisans; an American without legal immigrant status; and eleven-year-old Danny McGinnis, selling totem poles with his "license pinned to his lapel" (*Vancouver Sun,* July 28, 1973). Images of the vendors published in news reports portray long-haired men and women selling goods that reflect a hippie aesthetic: beaded jewelry, handcrafted leather goods, pottery, flowing skirts and dresses, and an abundance of candles.

By the summer of 1973, the volume of vendors generated complaints from local shop owners concerned about unfair competition and congestion. The city's license inspector, Milt Harrell, was quoted as saying that vendors were "taking over the sidewalk. . . selling everything from candles to racks of clothing" (*Vancouver Sun,* July 28, 1973), prompting the city to review and revise its regulations for street vending. Although vendors argued that they acted as "a real tourist attraction. . . People like the atmosphere we give the city, especially Gastown" (*Vancouver Sun,* July 28, 1973), a spokesman for a group of retailers accused the vendors of selling "shlock" on a "here today-gone tomorrow" basis (*Vancouver Sun,* Mar. 1, 1974) and called street peddlers "ugly things" (*Province,* Mar. 1, 1974).

Such complaints from retail store owners, coupled with vendors' dissatisfaction with the ten-minute rule and general difficulties in policing concentrations of vendors in certain downtown neighborhoods, led the city to spend more than a year consulting with local merchants, various city departments (engineering, social planning, law), and to a lesser extent with vendors themselves in order to draft a new street vending bylaw.

Although the new bylaw easily passed a city council vote, it was not without controversy. Bill Friedel, a representative for a group of vendors on Granville Street who feared they would be blocked from selling downtown, complained about the lack of consultation with street vendors (*Vancouver Sun,* Jan. 30, 1974), and at a city development committee meeting he argued that vending downtown represented a "lifestyle unique to very few cities in Canada" for artists and craftspeople selling their wares (*Vancouver Sun,* Jan. 18, 1974). Alderman Darlene Marzari, usually allied with the mayor, walked out of the council meeting in protest, arguing that the bylaw was a result of pressure from Granville Street merchants and that the city council was "flagrantly protecting one group over the other" (*Vancouver Sun,* June 12, 1974). Another city council member, Henry Rankin, viewed the new bylaw as overreaching in its level of detail, suggesting that the new rules would result in a Granville Mall where "every vendor will be told where to stand and every dog will be told where to urinate" (*Vancouver Sun,* June 12, 1974).

In fact, one of the most important changes introduced by the new bylaw was that it did indeed tell every vendor where to stand.

Ultimately, the unruly aesthetics of Vancouver's hippie street vendors—what Alderman Harry Rankin described as "the inherent crappiness of big boxes up and down the street" (*Province,* Oct. 25, 1974)—could not be left to chance. In response to concerns about the appearance of vendors' stands and carts, the city retained an architect to produce a series of approved vending cart designs, all of which were to be removed from downtown sidewalks at the end of each day. These designs were imposed upon Granville street.

For the vendors who received a fixed location, bought a kiosk, and went through the trouble of hauling their new kiosk to and from their vending site every day, they had effectively lost one of the key elements that initially lent much appeal to their vending—and perhaps the larger lifestyle associated with it: They had lost their "scene" (Woo, Rennie, and Poyntz 2015). In fact, the scene associated with hippie street vendors was not one city hall sought to support, and was in many ways the real point of conflict around beautification and gentrification efforts at the time.

Food Carts: Street Vending Becomes Hip

In the spring of 2008, one of Vancouver's city councilors, Heather Deal, read an article about New York City's Green Carts program in the *New York Times* and the effort to increase access to fresh fruits and vegetables in disadvantaged urban neighborhoods through the introduction of city-subsidized mobile grocery carts. Deal, inspired by a good idea, thought it would be great for Vancouver to do something similar, so she wrote and forwarded a motion to city council that called for the city to expand street food offerings. The motion called for work on a report to explore expanding the range of foods sold and the areas in the city where food vending was allowed, as well as possibilities for "increasing access to affordable, nutritious food in low-income communities" through street vending (City Council Minutes, Mar. 13, 2008, pp. 3-4). As Deal later told me in an interview (Jan. 19, 2012), "no one could come up with a reason not to like it," and the motion passed unanimously.

By the time concrete efforts began to expand street food in Vancouver, the plan quickly shifted from *green carts* (which would require subsidies from the city) to food carts and trucks selling "culturally diverse" and often gourmet offerings.

Why would the city government go to all this effort to reintroduce street food vending? The hippie vendors of the 1970s, who had not even sold food products with potential public health concerns, had long since disappeared under the weight of city regulations and changing social and economic times. Part of the story is most certainly the cultural currency of food, particularly as food connoisseurship has been broadly popularized (Johnston and Baumann 2010; Hanser and Hyde 2014). But another key factor is a renewed interest in the virtues of informality, what David Ley has characterized as the "expressive" or "romantic" tendency in urban planning and design,

an ideological position that emphasizes aesthetics and experience over the function and efficiency valued by the "instrumental" tendencies of rational modernism. Ley portrays these competing, and counter, ideologies being written upon urban landscapes like the swinging of a pendulum. In a similar vein, contemporary food carts and trucks were believed to offer an expressive antidote to the anonymity, corporate dominance (i.e., food chains), and blandness of downtown spaces, promising to inject a dose of the spontaneity, creativity, and vitality associated with informality into the relatively rigid, regulated spaces of an urban downtown.

This embrace of informality was expressed in a variety of ways: From the outset, reports and documents generated by city staff characterized food vending on city streets as "an effective means" to "enliven the public realm, promote neighborhood vitality. . . [and] improve sense of place" (Administrative Report to Standing Committee of City Services and Budgets, Jan. 7, 2011). Interviews with Councilor Deal and city staff also revealed an orientation toward city streets that emphasized the virtues of informality and, in contrast to the 1970s, now valued them. For example, when I asked Councilor Deal why the new food carts were good, she described her commitment to "vibrant streets" and noted how the "jumbled form" of food carts helps "animate" a public realm that has become too sterile (Jan. 19, 2012).

Support within city hall for food vending was more than matched by enthusiasm in the local media. Before even the first round of new vending licenses had been issued, newspaper articles profiled aspiring food vendors inspired by the lively street markets of Asia or Latin America (*Vancouver Sun,* May 3, 2010). A letter to a local paper called on city hall to "liven up the place a little and give us some variety" (*Vancouver Courier,* Apr. 30, 2010), and an opinion piece in the *Vancouver Sun* observed that opening the streets to more street foods is "a political move even the most hardened civic cynic can get behind"(*Vancouver Sun,* May 29, 2010)

In fact, the process for bringing this breath of fresh air to dull downtown sidewalks was carefully regulated and in some ways became even more so over time. This was particularly true of the evolution of the system for issuing new food. In June 2010, the City of Vancouver announced a call for applications for seventeen downtown food vending locations to be awarded by lottery, the procedure that had been used to distribute licenses to the existing hot dog vendors for many years. New applicants were required to "offer menu items *other than* hot dogs and pre-packaged, non-perishable food like soft drinks, chips, candy bars, granola and nuts" ("Request for Applications," 2010; emphasis in original).

Excitement over the prospect of new, trendy forms of street food resulted in an explosion of interest, and some eight hundred lottery entries for the seventeen initial locations. The result seemed chaotic—many winners of the lottery announced at the beginning of July were not ready to start operations at the end of the month, whereas other entrepreneurs who had already secured trucks and designed menus were left without vending locations. Some lottery winners appeared to have no intention of ever setting up their own business, instead renting their vending locations to other vendors for a profit. There were many expressions of dissatisfaction in the local media, both with the wait and with the seeming unfairness and randomness of the lottery system (e.g., *Vancouver Courier,* July 14, 2010).

In part as a response to these criticisms, the next two iterations of licensing involved increasingly elaborate application processes. After the city council voted in January 2011 to expand the street food vending pilot program, city staff called for applications for fifteen additional downtown vending locations. This time, however, applications had to include a business plan, a proposed menu that conformed to minimum nutritional standards developed by the regional health authority, and a waste management plan, and applicants were evaluated on these elements as well as "readiness, experience, qualifications. . . menu diversity, innovation, [and] use of local/ organic/fair trade food" (Administrative Report to Standing Committee of City Services and Budgets, Jan. 7, 2011). Ultimately, fifty applications were short-listed for a panel of judges made up of local chefs, food bloggers, nutritionists, and ordinary community members; in April 2011, nineteen new food carts and trucks were approved by the city.

The new, more elaborate process was not without controversy, however. Two members of the judging panel quit, presumably because they were unhappy with how nutritional value expectations and emphasis on "organic and fair-trade menu choices" were emphasized in the selection process (*Globe and Mail* [Toronto], Mar. 31, 20ll). There were other complaints about the city acting as "nutrition police" (*Vancouver Courier,* Jan. 19, 2011), and an article in the *Vancouver Sun* acknowledged that the new selection process disadvantaged some applicants, especially longtime, immigrant hot dog vendors with language limitations (*Vancouver Sun*, June 25, 2011).

A third round of permitting unfolded in early 2012, and yet another step was added to the selection process: City staff decided to add a taste test judged by a panel of community members—essentially a cooking competition—to determine who would receive permits for twelve new vending locations. Recognizing the complexity of the application process, the city also offered an information session and a business plan resource guide to assist potential applicants in navigating an application that required food safety certification; a food safety plan; plans for a vending unit; evidence that the unit was already or could be operational within a short time; a tentative rental agreement for a commissary kitchen; a pitch about why the new business would be "offering something unique to Vancouver and the Street Food Vending Programme"; a waste management plan and any special sustainability practices that would be adopted; a menu plan accompanied by a chart for applicants to highlight homemade, unprocessed, organic, and fair-trade ingredients; a nutritional "write-up"; information about future suppliers/producers of ingredients; and a business plan completed with an executive summary, a market research section, a marketing strategy, and a financial plan (City of Vancouver 2013).

From the original fifty-nine applications, twenty-five were short-listed to compete in a February taste competition held at a local community college, producing dishes that one judge described as "gloriously tasty and often thrillingly unexpected" (*Vancouver Sun*, Feb. 25, 2012) in a fast-paced but carefully coordinated atmosphere that one participant likened to "a reality TV program." Although some were critical of the latest iteration of permitting—one letter written to a local newspaper called the taste test "a colossal waste of money" (*Vancouver Courier,* Jan. 20, 2012)—the announcement of the new vendors in April 2012 was greeted with excitement. As one newspaper headline exclaimed, "City Gets Hooked on Street Food." The article went on to quote Vancouver's mayor dubbing the vendors "the ambassadors of the streets" (*Province*, Apr. 3, 2012).

By the beginning of 2014, the city had expanded the number of stationary food vendors to 110 from the 61 carts, mostly selling hot dogs, that had been operating just four years earlier. Roaming vendors operating outside of the downtown area, unknown on city streets prior to 2010, numbered almost fifty. Indeed, unlike the imposition of order on unruly sidewalk use in 1974, the introduction of street food vending in Vancouver in the 2010s saw the careful, iterative development of a program that conformed with food safety requirements, engineering guidelines for sidewalk use, and the nutritional, aesthetic, and culinary standards of an "expert" panel, and it was meant to promote, rather than impede, street vending.

Conclusion

The language that celebrates the food cart or food truck often locates its virtues in its informality: the excitement of eating with your hands, chance encounters in line, friendly and direct interactions with those preparing the food, and, of course, the unexpectedly delicious food delivered by an unconventional form of food service. These vendors break up the monotony of the downtown grid of streets and sidewalks that primarily service the flow of cars and pedestrians, instead making the city street a destination in itself and returning urban vitality to a space people believe was once central to public life.

The differential reception of Vancouver's hippie vendors in the 1970s and its hip food cart and truck vendors of the 2010s reveals how the desire to embrace the energy and vitality associated with informality—a fundamental element of 1970s counterculture—can seemingly only occur through the codifying and formalizing mechanisms of city governance.

The virtues of the informal—creativity, spontaneity, vitality, and perhaps even authenticity—have come to be associated with a particular form of street vending—carts and trucks wrapped with professionally designed logos, often serving locally sourced gourmet fare—and help explain why other forms of vending continue to be viewed as marginal or even illicit but certainly not creative, such as the immigrant, working-class vendors in Chicago discussed by Martin (2014). In Vancouver, the newly formed Street Food Vendors Association excludes most hot dog vendors on the basis that the food that they serve is heavily loaded with preservatives and lacks homemade ingredients.

Such groups, like the jumble of Vancouver's hippie vendors in the 1970s, offer little perceived value to urban streets and sidewalks.

REFERENCES

Anderson, Kay. 1991. *Vancouver's Chinatown: Racial Discourse in Canada, 1875–1980*. Montreal: McGill-Queen's University Press.

Benson, Joshua. 2006. "Regulating Street Vendors in New York City: Case Studies." MS thesis, Department of Urban Planning, Columbia University.

Binkley, Sam. 2007. *Getting Loose: Lifestyle Consumption in the 1970s*. Durham, NC: Duke University Press.

Blomley, Nicholas. 2011. *Rights of Passage: Sidewalks and the Regulation of Public Flow*. London: Routledge.

Blomley, Nicholas. 2012. "Colored Rabbits, Dangerous Trees, and Public Sitting: Sidewalks, Police, and the City." *Urban Geography* 33 (7): 917–935.

Bluestone, Daniel. 1991. "The Pushcart Evil: Peddlers, Merchants, and New York City's Streets, 1880–1940." *Journal of Urban History* 18 (1): 68–92.

Boltanski, Luc, and Eve Chiapello. 2007. *The New Spirit of Capitalism*. New York: Verso.

Boyer, M. Christine. 1983. *Dreaming the Rational City: The Myth of American City Planning*. Cambridge, MA: MIT Press.

Bromley, Ray. 2000. "Street Vending and Public Policy: A Global Review." *International Journal of Sociology and Social Policy* 20 (1-2): 1–29.

Carroll, Rory. 2012. "Venice Beach Back to Bohemian Ideals after LAPD Cracks Down on Hawkers." *Guardian,* April 20. https://www.theguardian.com/world/2012/apr/20/venice-beach-bohemian-lapd-hawkers.

City of Vancouver. 2013. "Permit Applicant Resource Guide," http://vancouver.ca/files/cov/street-food-vending-permit-application-resource-guide.pdf.

Cross, John C. 1998. *Informal Politics: Street Vendors and the State in Mexico City*. Stanford, CA: Stanford University Press.

Devlin, Ryan. 2011. "'An Area That Governs ltself: lnformality, Uncertainty and the Management of Street Vending in New York City." *Planning Theory* 10 (1): 53–65.

Duneier, Mitchell. 1999. *Sidewalk*. New York: Farrar, Strauss and Giroux.

Estrada, Emir, and Pierrette Hondagneu-Sotelo. 2011. "lntersectional Dignities: Latino Immigrant Street Vendor Youth in Los Angeles." *Journal of Contemporary Ethnography* 40 (1): 102–131.

Florida, Richard. 2005. *Cities and the Creative Class*. New York: Routledge.

Foucault, Michel. 2009. *Security, Territory, Population: Lecture at the College de France 1977–1978*. New York: Palgrave Macmillan.

Frank, Thomas. 1997. *The Conquest of Cool: Business Culture, Counterculture, and the Rise of Hip Consumerism*. Chicago: University of Chicago Press.

Hanser, Amy, and Zachary Hyde. 2014. "Foodies Remaking Cities." *Contexts* 13 (3): 44–49.

Harms, Erik. 2009. "Vietnam's Civilizing Process and the Retreat from the Street." *City & Society* 21 (2): 182–206.

Hernandez-L6pez, Ernesto. 2011. "Las Taco Truck War: How Law Cooks Food Culture Contests." *University of Miami Inter-American Law Review* 43 (1): 233–268.

Hunt, Alan. 2006. "Police and the Regulation of Traffic: Policing as a Civilizing Process?" ln *The New Police Science: The Police Power* in *Domestic and International Governance,* edited by M. Dubber and M. Valverde, 168–184. Stanford, CA: Stanford University Press.

Hunt, Stacey. 2009. "Citizenship's Place: The State's Creation of Public Space and Street Vendors' Culture of Informality in Botoga, Colombia." *Environment and Planning: D, Society & Space* 27:331–351.

Johnston, Josèe, and Shyon Baumann. 2010. *Foodies: Democracy and Distinction in the Gourmet Foodscape*. New York: Routledge.

Kettles, Gregg W. 2007. "Legal Responses to Sidewalk Vending: The Case of Los Angeles, California." In *Street Entrepreneurs: People, Place and Politics in Local and Global Perspective,* edited by J. Cross and A. Morales, 58–78. London: Routledge.

Kim, Annette M. 2012. "The Mixed-Use Sidewalk." *Journal of the American Planning Association* 78 (3): 225–238.

Ley, David. 1987. "Styles of the Times: Liberal and Neo-conservative Landscapes in Inner Vancouver, 1968–1986." *Journal of Historical Geography* 13 (1): 40–56.

Ley, David. 1996. *The New Middle Class and the Remaking of the Central City*. Oxford: Oxford University Press.

Ley, David. 2003. "Artists, Aestheticisation and the Field of Gentrification." *Urban Studies* 40 (12): 2527–2544.

Loukaitou-Sideris, Anastasia, and Renia Lhrenfeucht. 2009. *Sidewalks: Conflict and Negotiation over Public Space*. Cambridge, MA: MIT Press.

Martin, Nina. 2014. "Food Fight! Immigrant Street Vendors, Gourmet Food Trucks and the Differential Valuation of Creative Producers in Chicago." *International Journal of Urban and Regional Research* 38 (5): 1867–1883.

Martinez, Ruben. 1991. "Sidewalk Wars: Why LA Street Vendors Won't Be Swept Away." *Los Angeles Weekly,* December 6–12, p. 20, 24.

Modan, Gabriella. 2008. "Mango Fufu Kimchi Yucca: The Depoliticization of 'Diversity' in Washington, D.C. Discourse." *City & Society* 20 (2): 188–221.

Parsons, Talcott. 1978. *Action Theory and the Human Condition*. New York: Free Press.

Peck, Jamie. 2012. "Recreative City: Amsterdam, Vehicular Ideas and the Adaptive Spaces of Creativity Policy." *International Journal of Urban and Regional Research* 36 (3): 462–485.

Punter, John. 2003. *The Vancouver Achievement: Urban Planning and Design*. Vancouver: UBC Press.

Southworth, Michael, and Eran Ben-Joseph. 1993. *Regulated Streets: The Evolution of Standards for Suburban Residential Streets*. Berkeley: University of California at Berkley, Institute of Urban and Regional Development.

Stillerman, Joel. 2006. "The Politics of Space and Culture in Santiago, Chile's Street Markets." *Qualitative Sociology* 29:507–530.

Stoller, Paul. 2002. *Money Has No Smell: The Africanization of New York City*. Chicago: University of Chicago Press.

Valverde, Mariana. 2012. *Everyday Law on the Street: City Governance in an Age of Diversity*. Chicago: University of Chicago Press.

Wang, Oliver. 2009. "To Live and Dine in Kogi L.A." *Contexts* 8 (4): 69–71.

Woo, Benjamin, Jamie Rennie, and Stuart R. Poyntz. 2015. "Scene Thinking." *Cultural Studies* 29 (3): 285–297.

Wouters, Cas. 2007. *Informalization: Manners and Emotions Since 1890*. Los Angeles: Sage.

Zukin, Sharon. 1991. *Landscapes of Power: From Detroit to Disney World*. Berkeley: University of California Press.

Zukin, Sharon. 1995. *The Cultures of Cities*. Malden, MA: Blackwell.

Zukin, Sharon. 2010. *Naked City: The Death and Life of Authentic Urban Places*. Oxford: Oxford University Press.

THINKING ABOUT THE READING

What was your understanding of street vending culture prior to reading this selection? Was it all based on the delicious food you have sampled from these vendors or had you given it deeper reflection? How might this new branding of the "informal" that once gave opportunity and access to marginalized groups, now be used to exclude them? Can formalization be done in a way that benefits and protects workers without excluding them? What is street vending's connection to historical and present day social justice issues? If we changed the context to include developing countries beyond Canada and the United States, would the issues mentioned in this selection stay the same or change?

CHAPTER 5

Building Identity

Socialization

Sociology teaches us that humans don't develop in a social vacuum. Other people, cultural practices, historical events, and social institutions shape what we do and say, what we value, and who we become. Our self-concept, identity, and sense of self-worth are derived from our interactions with other people. We are especially tuned in to the reactions, real or imagined, of others.

Socialization is the process by which individuals learn their culture and learn to live according to the norms of their society. Through socialization, we learn how to perceive our world, gain a sense of our own identity, and discover how to interact appropriately with others. This learning process occurs within the context of several social institutions—schools, religious institutions, the media, and the family—and it extends beyond childhood. Adults must be resocialized into a new galaxy of norms, values, and expectations each time they leave or abandon current positions and enter new ones.

The conditions into which we are born shape our initial socialization in profound ways. Circumstances such as race, ethnicity, gender, and social class are particularly significant factors in socialization processes. In "Life as the Maid's Daughter," sociologist Mary Romero describes a research interview with a young Chicana regarding her recollections of growing up as the daughter of a live-in maid for a white, upper-class family living in Los Angeles. Romero describes the many ways in which this girl learns to move between different social settings, adapt to different expectations, and occupy different social positions. This girl must constantly negotiate the boundaries of inclusion and exclusion, as she struggles between the socializing influence of her own ethnic group and that of the white, upper-class employers she and her mother live with. Through this juggling, she illustrates the ways in which we manage the different, often contradictory, identities that we take on in different situations.

Similar to race and ethnicity, gender and social class play an integral role in shaping our identities. In "Tiger Girls on the Soccer Field," Hilary Levy Friedman investigates the intersection of gender and social class in the socialization process of competitive afterschool activities. She finds that the type of gender socialization employed by parents is very much dependent on their socioeconomic status and has the potential to reproduce social inequality. Despite these different versions of femininity, Friedman notes that the type of gender socialization these kids receive in afterschool activities does not necessarily always determine their future attainment.

The third reading for this section is a contemporary study focusing on inner-city girls and their relationship to "the code." Nikki Jones suggests that these girls are no more immune to violence than boys. She provides narrative descriptions of some of the ways in which street life shapes the behavior and identity of the young women in her study.

Something to Consider as You Read

According to sociologists, we are shaped by our cultural environment and by the influences of significant people and groups in our lives. Consider some of the people or groups whose opinions matter to you. Can you imagine them as a kind of audience in your head, observing and reacting to your behavior? Think about the desire to feel included. To what extent has this desire shaped your participation in a group that has had an impact on your self-image? How important are "role models" in the socialization process? If someone is managing conflicting identities and has no role models or others in similar situations, how might this conflict affect her or his sense of self and relationships with others? What do these readings suggest about the importance of being the "right person in the right place" even if that's not all you feel yourself to be? How do power and authority affect people's sense of self and their right to be whoever they want to be in any situation? How do social conditions shape our choices and opportunities?

Life as the Maid's Daughter

MARY ROMERO

(1995)

Introduction

. . . My current research attempts to expand the socio-logical understanding of the dynamics of race, class, and gender in the everyday routines of family life and reproductive labor. . . . I am lured to the unique setting presented by domestic service . . . and I turn to the realities experienced by the children of private household workers. This focus is not entirely voluntary. While presenting my research on Chicana private household workers, I was approached repeatedly by Latina/os and African Americans who wanted to share their knowledge about domestic service—knowledge they obtained as the daughters and sons of household workers. Listening to their accounts about their mothers' employment presents another reality to understanding paid and unpaid reproductive labor and the way in which persons of color are socialized into a class-based, gendered, racist social structure. The following discussion explores issues of stratification in everyday life by analyzing the life story of a maid's daughter. This life story illustrates the potential of the standpoint of the maid's daughter for generating knowledge about race, class, and gender. . . .

Social Boundaries Presented in the Life Story

The first interview with Teresa,[1] the daughter of a live-in maid, eventually led to a life history project. I am intrigued by Teresa's experiences with her mother's white, upper-middle-class employers while maintaining close ties to her relatives in Juarez, Mexico, and Mexican friends in Los Angeles. While some may view Teresa's life as a freak accident, living a life of "rags to riches," and certainly not a common Chicana/o experience, her story represents a microcosm of power relationships in the larger society. Life as the maid's daughter in an upper-middle-class neighborhood exemplifies many aspects of the Chicano/Mexicano experience as "racial ethnics" in the United States, whereby the boundaries of inclusion and exclusion are constantly changing as we move from one social setting and one social role to another.

Teresa's narrative contains descriptive accounts of negotiating boundaries in the employers' homes and in their community. As the maid's daughter, the old adage "Just like one of the family" is a reality, and Teresa has to learn when she must act like the employer's child and when she must assume the appropriate behavior as the maid's daughter. She has to recognize all the social cues and interpret social settings correctly—when to expect the same rights and privileges as the employer's children and when to fulfill the expectations and obligations as the maid's daughter. Unlike the employers' families, Teresa and her mother rely on different ways of obtaining knowledge. The taken-for-granted reality of the employers' families do not contain conscious experiences of negotiating race and class status, particularly not in the intimate setting of the home. Teresa's status is constantly changing in response to the wide range of social settings she encounters—from employers' dinner parties with movie stars and corporate executives to Sunday dinners with Mexican garment workers in Los Angeles and factory workers in El Paso. Since Teresa remains bilingual and bicultural throughout her life, her story reflects the constant struggle and resistance to maintain her Mexican identity, claiming a reality that is neither rewarded nor acknowledged as valid.

Teresa's account of her life as the maid's daughter is symbolic of the way that racial ethnics participate in the United States; sometimes we are included and other times excluded or ignored. Teresa's story captures the reality of social stratification in the United States, that is, a racist, sexist, and class-structured society upheld by an ideology of equality. I will analyze the experiences of the maid's daughter in an upper-middle-class neighborhood in Los Angeles to investigate the ways that boundaries of race, class, and gender are maintained or diffused in everyday life. I have selected various excerpts from the transcripts that illustrate how knowledge about a class-based and gendered, racist social order is learned, the type of information that is conveyed, and how the boundaries between systems of domination impact everyday life. I begin with a brief history of Teresa and her mother, Carmen.

Learning Social Boundaries: Background

Teresa's mother was born in Piedras Negras, a small town in Aguas Calientes in Mexico. After her father was seriously injured in a railroad accident, the family moved to a small town outside Ciudad Juarez. . . . By the time she was fifteen she moved to Juarez and took a job as a domestic, making about eight dollars a week. She soon crossed the border and began working for Anglo families in the country club area in El Paso. Like other domestics in El Paso, Teresa's mother returned to Mexico on weekends and helped support her mother and sisters. In her late twenties she joined several of her friends in their search for better-paying jobs in Los Angeles. The women immediately found jobs in the garment industry. Yet, after six months in the sweatshops, Teresa's mother went to an agency in search of domestic work. She was placed in a very exclusive Los Angeles neighborhood. Several years later Teresa was born. Her friends took care of the baby while Carmen continued working; childcare became a burden, however, and she eventually returned to Mexico. At the age of thirty-six Teresa's mother returned to Mexico with her newborn baby. Leaving Teresa with her grandmother and aunts, her mother sought work in the country club area. Three years later Teresa and her mother returned to Los Angeles.

Over the next fifteen years Teresa lived with her mother in the employer's (Smith) home, usually the two sharing the maid's room located off the kitchen. From the age of three until Teresa started school, she accompanied her mother to work. She continued to live in the Smiths' home until she left for college. All of Teresa's live-in years were spent in one employer's household. The Smiths were unable to afford a full-time maid, however, so Teresa's mother began doing day work throughout the neighborhood. After school Teresa went to whatever house her mother was cleaning and waited until her mother finished working, around 4 or 6 P.M., and then returned to the Smiths' home with her mother. Many prominent families in the neighborhood knew Teresa as the maid's daughter and treated her accordingly. While Teresa wanted the relationship with the employers to cease when she went to college and left the neighborhood, her mother continued to work as a live-in maid with no residence other than the room in the employer's home; consequently, Teresa's social status as the maid's daughter continued. . . .

One of the Family

As Teresa got older, the boundaries between insider and outsider became more complicated, as employers referred to her and Carmen as "one of the family." Entering into an employer's world as the maid's daughter, Teresa was not only subjected to the rules of an outsider but also had to recognize when the rules changed, making her momentarily an insider. While the boundaries dictating Carmen's work became blurred between the obligations of an employee and that of a friend or family member, Teresa was forced into situations in which she was expected to be just like one of the employer's children, and yet she remained the maid's daughter. . . .

Living under conditions established by the employers made Teresa and her mother's efforts to maintain a distinction between their family life and an employer's family very difficult. Analyzing incidents in which the boundaries between the worker's family and employer's family were blurred highlights the issues that complicate the mother-daughter relationship. Teresa's account of her mother's hospitalization was the first of numerous conflicts between the two that stemmed from the live-in situation and their relationships with the employer's family. The following excerpt demonstrates the difficulty in interacting as a family unit and the degree of influence and power employers exerted over their daily lives:

> When I was about ten my mother got real sick. That summer, instead of sleeping downstairs in my mother's room when my mother wasn't there, one of the kids was gone away to college, so it was just Rosalyn, David and myself that were home. The other two were gone, so I was gonna sleep upstairs in one of the rooms. I was around eight or nine, ten I guess. I lived in the back room. It was a really

neat room because Rosalyn was allowed to paint it. She got her friend who was real good, painted a big tree and clouds and all this stuff on the walls. So I really loved it and I had my own room. I was with the Smiths all the time, as my parents, for about two months. My mother was in the hospital for about a month. Then when she came home, she really couldn't do anything. We would all have dinner, the Smiths were really, really supportive. I went to summer school and I took math and English and stuff like that. I was in this drama class and I did drama and I got to do the leading role. Everybody really liked me and Ms. Smith would come and see my play. So things started to change when I got a lot closer to them and I was with them alone. I would go see my mother everyday, and my cousin was there. I think that my cousin kind of resented all the time that the Smiths spent with me. I think my mother was really afraid that now that she wasn't there that they were going to steal me from her. I went to see her, but I could only stay a couple of hours and it was really weird. I didn't like seeing my mother in pain and she was in a lot of pain. I remember before she came home the Smiths said that they thought it would be a really good idea if I stayed upstairs and I had my own room now that my mother was going to be sick and I couldn't sleep in the same bed 'cause I might hurt her. It was important for my mother to be alone. And how did I feel about that? I was really excited about that [having her own room]—you know. They said, "Your mom she is probably not going to like it and she might get upset about it, but I think that we can convince her that it is ok." When my mom came home, she understood that she couldn't be touched and that she had to be really careful, but she wanted it [having her own room] to be temporary. Then my mother was really upset. She got into it with them and said, "No, I don't want it that way." She would tell me, "No, I want you to be down here. ¿Qué crees que eres hija de ellos? You're gonna be with me all the time, you can't do that." So I would tell Ms. Smith. She would ask me when we would go to the market together, "How does your mom seem, what does she feel, what does she say?" She would get me to relay that. I would say, "I think my mom is really upset about me moving upstairs. She doesn't like it and she just says no." I wouldn't tell her everything. They would talk to her and finally they convinced her, but my mom really, really resented it and was really angry about it. She was just generally afraid. All these times that my mother wasn't there, things happened and they would take me places with them, go out to dinner with them and their friends. So that was a real big change, in that I slept upstairs and had different rules. Everything changed. I was more independent. I did my own homework; they would open the back door and yell that dinner was ready—you know. Things were just real different.

The account illustrates how assuming the role of insider was an illusion because neither the worker's daughter nor the worker ever became a member of the white, middle-class family. Teresa was only allowed to move out of the maid's quarter, where she shared a bed with her mother, when two of the employer's children were leaving home, vacating two bedrooms. . . .

Teresa and Carmen did not experience the boundaries of insider and outsider in the same way. Teresa was in a position to assume a more active family role when employers made certain requests. Unlike her mother, she was not an employee and was not expected to clean and serve the employer. Carmen's responsibility for the housework never ceased, however, regardless of the emotional ties existing between employee and employers. She and her employers understood that, whatever family activity she might be participating in, if the situation called for someone to clean, pick up, or serve, that was Carmen's job. When the Smiths requested Teresa to sit at the dinner table with the family, they placed Teresa in a different class position than her mother, who was now expected to serve her daughter alongside her employer. Moving Teresa upstairs in a bedroom alongside the employer and their children was bound to drive a wedge between Teresa and Carmen. There is a long history of spatial deference in domestic service, including separate entrances, staircases, and eating and sleeping arrangements.

Carmen's room reflected her position in the household. As the maid's quarter, the room was separated from the rest of the bedrooms and was located near the maid's central work area, the kitchen. The room was obviously not large enough for two beds because Carmen and Teresa shared a bed. Once Teresa was moved upstairs, she no longer shared the same social space in the employer's home as her mother. Weakening the bonds between the maid and her daughter permitted the employers to broaden their range of relationships and interaction with Teresa.

Carmen's feelings of betrayal and loss underline how threatening the employers' actions were. She understood that the employers were in a position to buy her child's love. They had already attempted to socialize Teresa into Euro-American ideals by planning Teresa's education and deciding what courses she would take. Guided by the importance they place on European culture, the employers defined the Mexican Spanish spoken by Teresa and her mother as inadequate and classified Castillan Spanish as "proper" Spanish. As a Mexican immigrant woman working as a live-in maid, Carmen was able to experience certain middle-class privileges, but her only access to these privileges was through her relationship with employers. Therefore, without the employers' assistance, she did not have the necessary connections to enroll Teresa in private schools or provide her with upper-middle-class experiences to help her develop the skills needed to survive in elite schools. Carmen only gained these privileges for her daughter at a price; she relinquished many of her parental rights to her employers. To a large degree the Smiths determined Carmen's role as a parent, and the other employers restricted the time she had to attend school functions and the amount of energy left at the end of the day to mother her own child.

Carmen pointed to the myth of "being like one of the family" in her comment, "¿Qué crees que eres hija de ellos? You're gonna be with me all the time, you can't do that." The statement underlines the fact that the bond between mother and daughter is for life, whereas the pseudofamily relationship with employers is temporary and conditional. Carmen wanted her daughter to understand that taking on the role of being one of the employer's family did not relinquish her from the responsibility of fulfilling her "real" family obligations. The resentment Teresa felt from her cousin who was keeping vigil at his aunt's

hospital bed indicated that she had not been a dutiful daughter. The outside pressure from an employer did not remove her own family obligations and responsibilities. Teresa's relatives expected a daughter to be at her mother's side providing any assistance possible as a caretaker, even if it was limited to companionship. The employer determined Teresa's activity, however, and shaped her behavior into that of a middle-class child; consequently, she was kept away from the hospital and protected from the realities of her mother's illness. Furthermore, she was submerged into the employer's world, dining at the country club and interacting with their friends.

Her mother's accusation that Teresa wanted to be the Smiths' daughter signifies the feelings of betrayal or loss and the degree to which Carmen was threatened by the employer's power and authority. Yet Teresa also felt betrayal and loss and viewed herself in competition with the employers for her mother's time, attention, and love. In this excerpt Teresa accuses her mother of wanting to be part of employers' families and community:

> I couldn't understand it—you know—until I was about eighteen and then I said, "It is your fault. If I treat the Smiths differently, it is your fault. You chose to have me live in this situation. It was your decision to let me have two parents, and for me to balance things off, so you can't tell me that I said this. You are the one who wanted this." When I was about eighteen we got into a huge fight on Christmas. I hated the holidays because I hated spending them with the Smiths. My mother always worked. She worked on every holiday. She loved to work on the holidays! She would look forward to working. My mother just worked all the time! I think that part of it was that she wanted to have power and control over this community, and she wanted the network, and she wanted to go to different people's houses.

As employers, Mr. and Mrs. Smith were able to exert an enormous amount of power over the relationship between Teresa and her mother. Carmen was employed in an occupation in which the way to improve working conditions, pay, and benefits was through the manipulation of personal relationships with employers. Carmen obviously tried to take advantage of her relationship with the Smiths in order to provide the best for her daughter. The more intimate and interpersonal the relationship, the more likely employers were to give gifts, do favors, and provide financial assistance. Although speaking in anger and filled with hurt, Teresa accused her mother of choosing to be with employers and their families rather than with her own daughter. Underneath Teresa's accusation was the understanding that the only influence and status her mother had as a domestic was gained through her personal relationships with employers. Although her mother had limited power in rejecting the Smiths' demands, Teresa held her responsible for giving them too much control. Teresa argued that the positive relationship with the Smiths was done out of obedience to her mother and denied any familial feelings toward the employers. The web between employee and employers' families affected both mother and daughter, who were unable to separate the boundaries of work and family.

Maintaining Cultural Identity

A major theme in Teresa's narrative was her struggle to retain her Mexican culture and her political commitment to social justice. Rather than internalizing meaning attached to Euro-American practices and redefining Mexican culture and bilingualism as negative social traits, Teresa learned to be a competent social actor in both white, upper-middle-class environments and in working- and middle-class Chicano and Mexicano environments. To survive as a stranger in so many social settings, Teresa developed an acute skill for assessing the rules governing a particular social setting and acting accordingly. Her ability to be competent in diverse social settings was only possible, however, because of her life with the employers' children. Teresa and her mother maintained another life—one that was guarded and protected against any employer intrusion. Their other life was Mexican, not white, was Spanish speaking, not English speaking, was female dominated rather than male dominated, and was poor and working-class, not upper-middle-class. During the week Teresa and her mother visited the other Mexican maids in the neighborhoods, on weekends they occasionally took a bus into the Mexican barrio in Los Angeles to have dinner with friends, and

every summer they spent a month in Ciudad Juarez with their family. . . .

Teresa's description of evening activity with the Mexican maids in the neighborhood provides insight into her daily socialization and explains how she learned to live in the employer's home without internalizing all their negative attitudes toward Mexican and working-class culture. Within the white, upper-class neighborhood in which they worked, the Mexican maids got together on a regular basis and cooked Mexican food, listened to Mexican music, and gossiped in Spanish about their employers. Treated as invisible or as confidants, the maids were frequently exposed to the intimate details of their employers' marriages and family life. The Mexican maids voiced their disapproval of the lenient child-rearing practices and parental decisions, particularly surrounding drug usage and the importance of material possessions:

> Raquel was the only one [maid] in the neighborhood who had her own room and own TV set. So everybody would go over to Raquel's. . . . This was my mother's support system. After hours, they would go to different people's [maid's] rooms depending on what their rooms had. Some of them had kitchens and they would go and cook all together, or do things like play cards and talk all the time. I remember that in those situations they would sit, and my mother would talk about the Smiths, what they were like. When they were going to negotiate for raises, when they didn't like certain things, I would listen and hear all the different discussions about what was going on in different houses. And they would talk, also, about the family relationships. The way they interacted, the kids did this and that. At the time some of the kids were smoking pot and they would talk about who was smoking marijuana. How weird it was that the parents didn't care. They would talk about what they saw as being wrong. The marriage relationship, or how weird it was they would go off to the beauty shop and spend all this money, go shopping and do all these weird things and the effect that it had on the kids.

The interaction among the maids points to the existence of another culture operating invisibly within a Euro-American and male-dominated community. The workers' support system did not include employers and addressed their concerns as mothers, immigrants, workers, and women. They created a Mexican-dominated domain for themselves. Here they ate Mexican food, spoke Spanish, listened to the Spanish radio station, and watched novellas on TV. Here Teresa was not a cultural artifact but, instead, a member of the Mexican community.

In exchanging gossip and voicing their opinions about the employers' lifestyles, the maids rejected many of the employers' priorities in life. Sharing stories about the employers' families allowed the Mexican immigrant women to be critical of white, upper-middle-class families and to affirm and enhance their own cultural practices and beliefs. The regular evening sessions with other working-class Mexican immigrant women were essential in preserving Teresa and her mother's cultural values and were an important agency of socialization for Teresa. For instance, the maids had a much higher regard for their duties and responsibilities as mothers than as wives or lovers. In comparison to their mistresses, they were not financially dependent on men, nor did they engage in the expensive and time-consuming activity of being an ideal wife, such as dieting, exercising, and maintaining a certain standard of beauty in their dress, makeup, and hairdos. Unlike the employers' daughters, who attended cotillions and were socialized to acquire success through marriage, Teresa was constantly pushed to succeed academically in order to pursue a career. The gender identity cultivated among the maids did not include dependence on men or the learned helplessness that was enforced in the employers' homes but, rather, promoted self-sufficiency. However, both white women employers and Mexican women employees were expected to be nurturing and caring. These traits were further reinforced when employers asked Teresa to babysit for their children or to provide them with companionship during their husbands' absences.

So, while Teresa observed her mother adapting to the employers' standards in her interaction with their children, she learned that her mother did not approve of their lifestyle and understood that she had another set of expectations to adhere to. Teresa attended the same schools as employers' children, wore similar clothes, and conducted most of her social life within the same socioeconomic class, but she remained the maid's daughter—and learned the limitations of that position. Teresa watched her mother uphold higher standards for her and apply a different set of standards to the employers' children; most of the time, however, it appeared to Teresa as if they had no rules at all.

Sharing stories about the Smiths and other employers in a female, Mexican, and worker-dominated social setting provided Teresa with a clear image of the people she lived with as employers rather than as family members. Seeing the employers through the eyes of the employees forced Teresa to question their kindness and benevolence and to recognize their use of manipulation to obtain additional physical and emotional labor from the employees. She became aware of the workers' struggles and the long list of grievances, including no annual raises, no paid vacations, no social security or health benefits, little if any privacy, and sexual harassment. Teresa was also exposed to the price that working-class immigrant women employed as live-in maids paid in maintaining white, middle-class, patriarchal communities. Employers' careers and lifestyles, particularly the everyday rituals affirming male privilege, were made possible through the labor women provided for men's physical, social, and emotional needs. Female employers depended on the maid's labor to assist in the reproduction of their gendered class status. Household labor was expanded in order to accommodate the male members of the employers' families and to preserve their privilege. Additional work was created by rearranging meals around men's work and recreation schedules and by waiting on them and serving them. Teresa's mother was frequently called upon to provide emotional labor for the wife, husband, mother, and father within an employer's family, thus freeing members to work or increase their leisure time.

Discussion

Teresa's account offers insight into the ways racial ethnic women gain knowledge about the social order and use the knowledge to develop survival strategies. As the college-educated daughter of an immigrant Mexican woman employed as a live-in maid, Teresa's experiences in the employers' homes, neighborhood, and school and her experiences in the homes of working-class Mexicano families and barrios provided her with the skills to cross the class and cultural boundaries separating the two worlds. The process of negotiating social boundaries involved an evaluation of Euro-American culture and its belief system in light of an intimate knowledge of white, middle-class families. Being in the position to compare and contrast behavior within different communities, Teresa debunked notions of "American family values" and resisted efforts toward assimilation. Learning to function in the employers' world was accomplished without internalizing its belief system, which defined ethnic culture as inferior. Unlike the employers' families, Teresa's was not able to assume the taken-for-granted reality of her mother's employers because her experiences provided a different kind of knowledge about the social order.

While the employers' children were surrounded by positive images of their race and class status, Teresa faced negative sanctions against her culture and powerless images of her race. Among employers' families she quickly learned that her "mother tongue" was not valued and that her culture was denied. All the Mexican adults in the neighborhood were in subordinate positions to the white adults and were responsible for caring for and nurturing white children. Most of the female employers were full-time homemakers who enjoyed the financial security provided by their husbands, whereas the Mexican immigrant women in the neighborhood all worked as maids and were financially independent; in many cases they were supporting children, husbands, and other family members. By directly observing her mother serve, pick up after, and nurture employers and their families, Teresa learned about white, middle-class privileges. Her experiences with other working-class Mexicans were dominated by women's responsibility for their children and extended families. Here the major responsibility of mothering was financial; caring and nurturing were secondary and were provided by the extended family or children did without. Confronted with a working mother who was too tired to spend time with her, Teresa learned about the racial, class, and gender parameters of parenthood, including its privileges, rights, responsibilities, and obligations. She also learned that the role of a daughter included helping her mother with everyday household tasks and, eventually, with the financial needs of the extended family. Unlike her uncles and male cousins, Teresa was not exempt from cooking and housework, regardless of her financial contributions. Within the extended family Teresa was subjected to standards of beauty strongly weighted by male definitions of women as modest beings, many times restricted in her dress and physical movements. Her social worlds became clearly marked by race, ethnic, class, and gender differences.

Successfully negotiating movement from a white, male, and middle-class setting to one dominated by working-class, immigrant, Mexican women involved a socialization process that provided Teresa with the skills to be bicultural. Since neither setting was bicultural, Teresa had to become that in order to be a competent social actor in each. Being bicultural included having the ability to assess the rules governing each setting and to understand her ethnic, class, and gender position. Her early socialization in the employers' households was not guided by principles of creativity, independence, and leadership but, rather, was based on conformity and accommodation. Teresa's experiences in two different cultural groups allowed her to separate each and to fulfill the employers' expectations without necessarily internalizing the meaning attached to the act. Therefore, she was able to learn English without internalizing the idea that English is superior to Spanish or that monolingualism is normal. The existence of a Mexican community within the employers' neighborhood provided Teresa with a collective experience of class-based racism, and the maids' support system affirmed and enhanced their own belief system and culture. As Philomena Essed (1991, 294) points out, "The problem is not only how knowledge of racism is acquired but also what kind of knowledge is being transmitted."

Teresa's life story lends itself to a complex set of analyses because the pressures to assimilate were challenged by the positive interactions she experienced within her ethnic community. Like other bilingual persons in the United States, Teresa's linguistic abilities were shaped by the linguistic practices of the social settings she had access to. Teresa learned the appropriate behavior for each social setting, each marked by different class and cultural dynamics and in which women's economic roles and relationships to men were distinct. An overview of Teresa's socialization illustrates the process of biculturalism—a process that included different sets of standards and rules governing her actions as a woman, as a Chicana, and as the maid's daughter. . . .

NOTES

This essay was originally presented as a paper at the University of Michigan, "Feminist Scholarship: Thinking through the Disciplines," 30 January 1992.

I want to thank Abigail J. Stewart and Donna Stanton for their insightful comments and suggestions.

1. The names are pseudonyms.

REFERENCE

Essed, Philomena. 1991. *Understanding Everyday Racism.* Newbury Park, Calif.: Sage.

THINKING ABOUT THE READING

Teresa's childhood is unique in that she and her mother lived in the household of her mother's employer, requiring them to conform to the expectations of the employers even when her mother was "not at work." Her childhood was shaped by the need to read signals from others to determine her position in various social settings. What were some of the different influences in Teresa's early socialization? Did she accept people's attempts to mold her, or did she resist? How did she react to her mother's employers' referring to her as "one of the family"? Teresa came from a poor family, but she spent her childhood in affluent households. With respect to socialization, what advantages do you think these experiences provided her? What were the disadvantages? How do you think these experiences would have changed if she were a *son* of a live-in maid rather than a daughter? If she were a poor *white* girl rather than Latina?

Tiger Girls on the Soccer Field

HILARY LEVEY FRIEDMAN

(2013)

Charlotte, age 9, told me about her experiences playing competitive soccer: "At recess I'm like the only girl playing soccer. Everyone else is doing something else. So usually they call me a tomboy because I'm playing with the boys. But I'm NOT a tomboy. A tomboy is somebody who like wants to be a boy and is like always being with the boys and stuff. I have dolls and I like pink. I really like girl things, like I painted my nails."

To Charlotte, being a tomboy is a negative label. She is more eager to identify with her femininity, pointing out how she paints her nails and wears pink. She wants a strong femininity, the kind that lets her be an aggressive soccer player, too. "We play soccer against boys sometimes because it's better for the girls to learn to be more aggressive," she told me. While Charlotte thinks girls can be just as good as boys at soccer, she thinks they'll only improve if they become as tough as the boys.

Her mom Marie agrees. Looking ahead, she sees competitive sports as a way for her daughter to become aggressive—not just in the athletic arena, but also in life. Marie told me, "We have no illusions that our daughter is going to be a great athlete. But the team element [is important]. I worked for Morgan Stanley for 10 years, and I interviewed applicants, and that ability to work on a team was a crucial part of our hiring process. So it's a skill that comes into play much later. It's not just about ball skills or hand-eye coordination."

> "When I was interviewing job candidates at Morgan Stanley," Marie, a white woman with two Ivy League degrees told me, "if I got a female candidate—because it's banking and you need to be aggressive, you need to be tough—if she played, like, ice hockey, *done*. My daughter's playing, and I'm just a big believer in kids learning to be confidently aggressive, and I think that plays out in life assertiveness."

Many parents like Marie believe that being cutthroat and aggressive sets girls on a path to the corner office as a company executive. The higher up you go in the class hierarchy, the more likely you will encounter parents like Marie, who believe in teaching their daughters what I call "aggressive femininity." They are taught to be both physically and competitively forceful, actively subsuming aspects of their femininity; many of their parents define their daughters in opposition to "girly-girls."

As Sheryl Sandberg, CEO of Facebook and author of the bestseller, *Lean In,* declared, "Instead of calling our daughters bossy, let's say, 'My daughter has executive leadership skills!'" Girls today grow up in a world with an unprecedented set of educational and professional opportunities, and many look up to successful women like Sandberg. More girls will graduate from college and earn advanced degrees than ever before, and nearly all professions are open to them, even combat careers in the military.

Successful women want to raise daughters who share the qualities that have brought them success—qualities that some liken to bossiness.

Nice Girls Competing

When I studied 95 families with elementary school-age children who were involved in competitive after-school activities—chess, dance, and soccer—I met parents like Marie who saw their kids' participation in competitive afterschool activities as a way to develop certain values and skills: the importance of winning; the ability to bounce back from a loss to win in the future; to perform within time limits; to succeed in stressful situations; and to perform under the gaze of others—what I call "Competitive Kid Capital."

One of the most striking findings was that upper-middle-class parents of girls often perceive a link between aggression and success in athletics, and are more likely to enroll their daughters in soccer or chess, rather than dance—activities that are deemed more cooperative and less competitive. Like Sheryl Sandberg, they believe that executive leadership skills can be effectively developed and honed on soccer fields and basketball courts, even when the competitors are wearing pink shoes and jerseys.

Malcolm, an African-American lawyer with three Ivy League degrees, believes that sports don't just steer his seven-year-old daughter toward assertiveness, they actively drive her away from more traditionally feminine pursuits. "She's a cute little girl, but I don't like her to be a girly-girl," he explained. "You know, I don't want her to be a cheerleader—nothing against that—but I want her to prepare to have the option, if she wants to be an executive in a company, that she can play on that turf. And if she's kind of a girly-girl, maybe she'll be a secretary. There's nothing wrong with that, but let her have the option of doing something else if she wants."

Malcolm thinks being a "girly-girl" means less desirable, more traditionally feminine occupations. The images he evokes related to being an executive, such as "play on that turf," suggests the importance he places on athletics to help his daughter follow a historically male career path. And he identifies cheerleading—which was once a male-dominated area and still has an athletic and competitive component, even as the athletes are now expected to wear make-up, curl their hair, and often bare their midriffs—as being too much of a girly-girl activity.

Sports Make the Girl

Today, sports are important element of American upper-middle-class culture and child-rearing practices. But as recently as a century ago, organized team sports were limited to males. Women and girls were generally seen as physically inferior and mentally unable to handle competition. Even when they were allowed to participate, competition was off-limits, and seen as damaging.

When New York City's Public Schools Athletic Girls League was founded in 1905, for example, the director was opposed to keeping records, arguing that girls could easily injure themselves if they got too aggressive or tried to break a record. All-girls' elite schools were among the first to break with this view of women and competition, though they called competitive organizations "associations" instead of "leagues," lest people complain a league was too masculine.

Much of this changed, along with social attitudes, after the passage of Title IX 40 years ago. With time, young women who had once been focused on the arts came, in the twenty-first century, to see athletics as especially important tools for development. Two recent studies, one by the Women's Sports Foundation

and the other by the Oppenheimer Foundation, have found that 82 percent of executive businesswomen played organized sports in middle school and high school. Of female Fortune 500 executives, 80 percent said they were competitive tomboys during childhood. The Oppenheimer study also found that, while 16 percent of all American women describe themselves as athletic, among women who earn over $75,000 annually, the number rises to about 50 percent.

These conclusions are consistent with the studies like those of economist Betsy Stevenson, whose work on Title IX finds that participation in high school sports increases the likelihood that a girl will attend college, enter the labor market, and enter previously male-dominated occupations. She suggests that sports develops such skills as learning how to compete and how to become a team member, which are both key as women navigate the traditionally male-dominated labor market.

But competition, athletic or otherwise, is still seen as a masculine attribute. In 2010, the journal *Sex Roles* published a study on high school boys and girls that found that even today, "boys are 'trained' from an early age to be competitive . . . Research suggests that girls are less comfortable than boys in competitive circumstances and that girls are socialized to mask overt competitiveness and aggressiveness more generally." David Hibbard and Duane Buhrmester, both psychologists, argue that a mentality of "competing to win" is at odds with the "nice girl" ideal. Girls who engage in head-to-head competition may have more social difficulties, even as they become prepared for a fast-tracked, upper-middle-class life.

Pink Girls and Dancing Queens

Parents of chess-playing girls also encourage their daughters to be assertive and competitive. As one chess mom explained to me, "We're raising her . . . to be feminist. And so she says she wants to be a Grandmaster or the President [of the United States]. She doesn't have any ideas about gender limitations and I think that's a good thing."

Chess girls don't have to be as assertive as soccer girls like Charlotte. Partly because it is not a physical game, chess allows girls to be what one mother of two sons described to me as a "pink girl": "These girls have princess T-shirts on," she said. They have "rhinestones and bows in their hair—and they beat boys. And the boys come out completely deflated. That's the kind of thing I think is so funny. That girl Carolyn, I call her the killer chess player. She has bows in her hair, wears dresses, everything is pink, Barbie backpack, and she plays killer chess."

That a winning girl can look so feminine has an especially strong effect on boys, and sometimes their parents. Another chess mom told me how a father reacted negatively when his son lost to her daughter: "The father came out and was shocked. He said, 'You let a girl beat you!'"

In competitive dance, it's more common to see girls win, if only because the activity is dominated by girls. Dance is a physical activity that, like cheerleading, "no girly-girls" dad Malcolm would like his daughter to avoid. Competitive dancers are expected to wear make-up when they compete. While this has a practical purpose—to make sure the dancers' faces are not "washed out" by the stage lights—lipstick, blush, and mascara also accentuate feminine features—practices that are among those sociologist C. J. Pascoe would identify as part of "normative femininity."

As I sat in the audience at dance competitions, I often heard teachers and parents remark, "Wow, she looks beautiful up there," or, "They look very good." In addition to make-up, girl's dance costumes featured sequins, rhinestones, ribbons, and other decorative embellishments, and, at most competitions, costume and appearance are evaluated as part of the final score.

In contrast, in chess and soccer, appearance matters little to the outcome of the competition. Although soccer girls' appearances are regulated, it is done in a way that de-emphasizes femininity. Soccer girls must remove all jewelry (for safety reasons), and coaches direct girls to make sure all of their hair is out of their faces. To keep their view unimpeded, girls pull their hair back in ponytails, using headbands or elastic bands. This has become a fashion and identity statement itself—perhaps a way to assert femininity in a less-than-feminine environment, and to keep shorter hair and bangs off the face. And, of course, female soccer uniforms are not easily distinguishable from male uniforms. Many traditional markers of femininity are absent from the pitch.

It is not surprising, then, that although both soccer and dance parents mentioned lifelong fitness and health as a motivation for their young daughters' involvement with these activities, only dance moms linked their kids' participation to obesity and appearance. Dance mom Tiffany told me about her concerns about her daughter's future body: "My short-term goal for her is

to keep, believe it or not, physically fit. Because, she's an eater, across the board . . . [Dance] keeps her at a nice weight. You know what I mean? And she struggles with that [weight], that's going to be her struggle, I told her."

Gender Scripts and Classed Lessons

Another set of scripts—those about femininity—helps explain how parents (especially dance and soccer parents) choose among activities for their daughters. I call the dance script the "graceful girls," the soccer "aggressive girls," and the chess "pink warriors." When dance, soccer, and chess parents draw from different gender scripts, they are shaped by class, producing classed lessons in femininity for their girls.

Though nearly all of the families I met are part of the broadly defined middle class, parents higher up in the hierarchy of the middle class promote a more aggressive femininity, as seen in both soccer and chess families. Dance mothers, who generally have lower status than the chess and soccer parents, promote a femininity that is less competitively aggressive and prioritizes physical appearance. Lower-middle-class and working-class families place a greater emphasis on traditional femininity.

Among the 38 families I met who had competitive young girls, the vast majority of soccer families were upper-middle-class. None of the dance families were upper-middle-class, and over a third were lower-middle-class; dance was the only activity of the three that had any working-class participants. Chess families with daughters who compete tend to look the most like soccer families, as the majority of families are upper-middle-class.

These upper-middle-class families had at least one parent who has earned an advanced postgraduate degree and work in a professional or managerial occupation, and both parents had earned a four-year college degree. The lower-middle-class families have just one parent with a college degree; neither parent works in a professional or managerial occupation.

Recall Malcolm and Marie. The former is a lawyer, and the latter was an investment banker who recently stopped working to spend more time with her five children. Both attended elite universities, and were representative of the rest of the parents. Most of the soccer parents had similar occupations, or they were professors or doctors.

It is not surprising that these highly credentialed, competitive parents have similar occupational aspirations for their children, including their daughters. They are trying to impart particular skills and lessons to their daughters at a young age to help them succeed in the long term. As Malcolm made clear, upper-middle-class parents do not want their daughters to end up as secretaries, so participation in competitive activities, where aggression is inculcated, becomes a priority so the girls can maintain their family's status in the future.

Bossy Is Best?

Today, there are three times more female soccer players than Girl Scouts in the United States. This trend is due, in part, to the fact that upper-middle-class families are trying to strategically maintain their family's class position, preparing their daughters to enter what are traditionally male worlds. Parents are choosing afterschool activities that will give these girls an advantage in college admissions and beyond; they are more likely to have the resources to enable their daughters to travel and compete.

But aggressive femininity can come at a cost. A recent study of the long-term effects of sports participation on adolescent girls by psychologists Campbell Leaper and Elizabeth Daniels found that many girls "struggle to reconcile their athleticism with traditional standards of hegemonic femininity that emphasize maintaining a thin body ideal and adhering to a rigid definition of beauty." Aggressive and pink warrior girls, along with graceful girls, face what psychologist Stephen Hinshaw calls the "triple bind"

of being supportive, competitive, and successful—and effortlessly beautiful.

In her work on female litigators, sociologist Jennifer Pierce similarly found that successful women had to become either "very male" or "very caring." She describes this binary: "Whereas men are praised for using intimidation and strategic friendliness, women who are aggressive are censured for being too difficult to get along with, and women who are nice are considered 'not tough enough' to be good litigators." Women need to be aggressive to succeed, but not *so* aggressive that they get labeled bitchy. It's a delicate balancing act for women in the workforce, and for parents who want to raise girls who can be the boss.

These classed gender ideals also have long-term implications for inequality. Girls from upper-middle-class families seem better equipped with the skills they need to succeed in more lucrative careers, and in leadership roles as adults. Better understanding socialization practices at the upper end of the class structure may open up real opportunities for others as well.

Sheryl Sandberg wasn't a soccer player. She wasn't even athletic, in an aggressive sense, at all. She was once an aerobics instructor who succeeded by leading others in a silver leotard. Her story suggests that soccer and contact sports aren't a direct path to the corner office, and that dance and cheerleading don't shut the door on success.

The future is not cast in stone: Tiffany's dancing daughter may yet become an executive, and Malcolm's daughter may become her assistant. That doesn't stop many affluent parents from being convinced that leaning in while wearing pink cleats produces girls with executive leadership skills.

THINKING ABOUT THE READING

The socialization process is one of the most important aspects of sociology because it allows us to understand how society reproduces itself and why it is constantly changing. How does Friedman's article on children's participation in afterschool activities contribute to the nature (genetic inheritance) versus nurture (environmental influence) debate? What does socialization in these various afterschool activities—chess, dance, soccer—teach children about their self and place in the social world? In your answer, consider terms from the article like *aggressive femininity, normative femininity,* and *competitive kid capital*. According to the author, how does time and place in history influence the content of these socialization messages? How might a person's place in her or his life cycle shape these messages and the tools available to achieve them? Do other factors besides social class and gender influence your socialization process? What about race and ethnicity? Sexuality? Religion? Physical and mental abilities?

Working 'the Code'

On Girls, Gender, and Inner-City Violence

NIKKI JONES

(2008)

In mainstream American society, it is commonly assumed that women and girls shy away from conflict, are not physically aggressive, and do not fight like boys and men.

In this article, I draw on field research among African-American girls in the United States to argue that the circumstances of inner-city life have encouraged the development of uniquely situated femininities that simultaneously encourage and limit inner-city girls' use of physical aggression and violence. First, I begin by arguing that, in the urban environments that I studied, gender—being a girl—does not protect inner-city girls from much of the violence experienced by inner-city boys. In fact, teenaged boys and girls are both preoccupied with 'survival' as an ongoing project. I use my analysis of interviews with young people involved in violent incidents to demonstrate similarities in how young people work 'the code of the street' across perceived gender lines. This in-depth examination of young people's use of physical aggression and violence reveals that while young men and young women fight, survival is still a gendered project.

Race, Gender, and Inner-City Violence

Inner-city life has changed dramatically over the last century and especially over the last 30 years.

In his ethnographic account of life in inner-city Philadelphia, Elijah Anderson writes that the code of the street is 'a set of prescriptions and proscriptions, or informal rules, of behaviour organised around a desperate search for respect that governs public social relations, especially violence among so many residents, particularly young men and women' (Anderson, 1999, p. 10). Furthermore, the code is 'a system of accountability that promises "an eye for an eye," or a certain "payback" for transgressions' (Anderson, 1999, p. 10). Fundamental elements of the code include respect and 'a credible reputation for vengeance that works to deter aggression' (Anderson, 1999, p. 10). According to Anderson, it is this complex relationship between masculinity, respect and violence that, at times, encourages poor, urban young men to risk their lives in order to be recognised and respected by others *as a man.*

Black feminist scholar Patricia Hill Collins considers Anderson's discussion of masculinity and the 'code of the street' in her recent analysis of the relationship between hegemonic (and racialised) masculinities and femininities, violence and dominance (Collins, 2004, pp. 188–212). Collins argues that the hyper-criminalisation of urban spaces is exacerbated by the culture of the code. As young men from distressed urban areas cycle in and out of correctional facilities at historically remarkable rates, she argues, urban public schools, street concerns and homes have become a ' . . . nexus of street, prison and youth culture,' which exerts 'a tremendous amount of pressure on Black men, especially young, working class men, to avoid being classified as "weak"' (Collins, 2004, p. 211).

What about Girls?

Over the last few decades, feminist criminologists and gender and crime scholars have examined women's and girls' experiences with aggression and violence with increasing complexity. Emphasising how particular material circumstances influence women's and girls' relationship to violence shifts the focus from the consideration of dichotomous gender differences to the empirical examination of gender similarities and differences in experiences with violence among young women and men who live in poor, urban areas (Simpson, 1991). The analysis presented here follows in this tradition by recognising the influence of shared life circumstances on young people's use of violence.

The young people from Philadelphia's inner-city neighbourhoods that I encountered generally share similar life circumstances, yet how they respond to these structural and cultural circumstances—that is, how they work the code of the street—is also gendered in ways that reflect differences among inner-city girls' and boys' understanding of what you 'got to' do to 'survive.'

Methods

Each of the respondents featured in this study was enrolled in a city hospital-based violence intervention project that targeted youth aged 12 to 24 who presented in the emergency department as a result of an intentional violent incident and were considered to be at either moderate or high risk for involvement in future violent incidents. As a consequence of patterns of racial segregation within the city, almost the entire population of young women and men who voluntarily enrolled in the hospital's violence intervention project were African-American.

My fieldwork for this study took place in three phases over 3 years (2001–2003). During the first phase of the study, which lasted about a year and a half, I conducted 'ride alongs' with intervention counsellors who met with young people in their homes shortly after their initial visit to the emergency room. I also conducted a series of interviews with members of the intervention counselling staff. Most of the staff grew up in Philadelphia and were personally familiar with many of the neighbourhoods we visited. During this time and throughout the study, I also observed interactions in the spaces and places that were significant in the lives of the young people I met. These spaces included trolley cars and buses (transportation to and from school), a neighbourhood high school nicknamed 'the Prison on the Hill,' the city's family and criminal court, and various correctional facilities in the area. I also intentionally engaged in extended conversations with grandmothers and mothers, sisters, brothers, cousins and friends of the young people I visited and interviewed. I recorded this information in my fieldnotes and used it to complement, supplement, test and, at times, verify the information collected during interviews.

Shared Circumstances, Shared Code

While the problem of inner-city violence is believed to impact boys and men only, my interviews with teenaged inner-city girls revealed that young women are regularly exposed to many of the same forms of violence that men are exposed to in their everyday lives and are deeply influenced by its normative order. In the inner-city neighbourhoods I visited, which were often quite isolated from the rest of the city, I encountered young men and young women who could quickly recall a friend, relative or 'associate' who had been shot, robbed or stabbed. In the public high school I visited, I watched adolescent girls and boys begin their school day with the same ritual: they dropped their bags on security belts, stepped through a metal detector, and raised their arms and spread their legs for a police-style 'pat down' before entering the building. Repeatedly, I encountered teenaged girls who, like the young men they share space with in the inner city, had stories to tell about getting 'rolled on,' or getting 'jumped,' or about the 'fair one' gone bad. It is these shared circumstances of life that engender a shared understanding about how to survive in a setting where your safety is never guaranteed. In the following sections, I provide portraits of four young people involved in violent incidents in order to illustrate what was revealed to me during the course of field research and interviews: an appreciation of 'the code of the street' that cut across gender lines. The first two respondents, Billy and DeLisha, tell stories of recouping from a very public loss in a street fight. The second set of respondents, Danielle and Robert, highlight how even those who are averse to fighting must sometimes put forth a 'tough front' to deter potentially aggressive challenges in the future.

Billy and Delisha: 'I'm Not Looking over My Shoulder'

Billy was 'jumped' by a group of young men while in 'their' neighbourhood, which is within walking distance of his own. He tells me this story as we sit in the living room of his row home. Billy recently reached his 20s, although he looks older than his age. He is White but shares a class background that is similar to many of the young people I interviewed. His block, like most of the others I visited during this study, is a collection of row homes in various states of disrepair. Billy spends more time here than he would like. He is unemployed and when asked how best the intervention project he enrolled in could help him his request was simple: I need a job. As we talk, I think that Billy is polite—he offers me a drink (a beer, which I decline) before we begin our interview—and even quiet. He recalls two violent battles within the last year, both of which ended with him in the emergency room, without wavering too far from a measured, even tone. The first incident he recalls for me happened in South Philadelphia. He was walking down the block, when he came across a group of guys on the corner, guys who he had 'trouble' with in the past. As he stood talking to an acquaintance, Billy was approached from behind and punched in the back of the head. The force of the punch was multiplied exponentially by brass knuckles, 'splitting [his] head open.' Billy was knocked out instantly, fell face-first toward the ground and split his nose on a concrete step. The thin scar from this street-fight remains several months later.

In contrast to Billy's even tone, DeLisha is loud. She is thin with a medium-brown complexion. Her retelling of the story of her injury is more like a re-enactment as the adrenaline, anxiety and excitement of the day return. She comes across as fiercely independent, especially for a 17-year-old girl. DeLisha, a young mother with a 1-year-old daughter, has been unable to rely on her own drug-addicted mother for much of her life. After years of this independence, she is convinced that she does not need anyone's help to 'make it' in life. While she has been a 'fighter' for as long as she can remember, she was never hurt before. Not in school. Not in her neighbourhood, which is one of the most notorious in the city. And not like this. She had agreed to a fight with another neighbourhood girl. The younger girl, pressured by her family and peers to win the battle, shielded a box-cutter from DeLisha's sight until the very last minute. When it seemed that she would lose, the girl flashed the box-cutter and slashed DeLisha across the hand, tearing past skin and muscle into a tendon on her arm.

During my interviews with Billy and DeLisha, I asked each of them how these very public losses, which also resulted in serious physical injuries, would influence their mobility within the neighbourhood.

Would they avoid certain people and places? Would or could they shrug their loss off or would they seek vengeance for their lost battle? Billy's and DeLisha's responses were strikingly similar in tone, nearly identical at some points, and equally revealing of two of the most basic elements of the code of the street: the commitment to maintaining a 'tough front' and 'payback.'

> Billy: I mean, just like I say, I walk around this neighbourhood. I'm not looking over my shoulder . . . I'm not going to walk [and] look around my shoulder because I've got people looking for me. I mean you want me . . . you know where I live. They can call me at any time they want. That's how, that's how I think. . . . I'm not going to sit around my own neighbourhood and just say: 'Aww, I got to watch my back.' You want me? You got me.
>
> DeLisha: I'm not a scared type . . . I walk on the streets anytime I want to. I do anything I want to, anytime I want to do it. It's never been a problem walking on the street 3.00 in the morning. If I want to go home 3.00 in the morning, I'm going to go home. I'm not looking over my shoulder. My grandma never raised me to look over my shoulder. I'm not going to stop because of some little incident [being cut in the hand with a box cutter].

Billy and DeLisha's strikingly similar responses reveal their commitment to a shared 'system of accountability,' the code of the street, which, as Anderson argues, governs much of social life, especially violence, in distressed urban areas (Anderson, 1999). Billy and DeLisha hold themselves accountable to this system ('I'm not going to . . . ') and are also aware that others will hold them accountable for their behaviours and actions. Billy and DeLisha are acutely aware that someone who 'looks over their shoulder' while walking down the street is perceived as weak, a moving target, and both are determined to reject such a fate. Instead, Billy and DeLisha remain committed to managing their 'presentation of self' (Goffman, 1959) in a way that masks any signs of vulnerability.

In addition to their commitment to 'not looking over their shoulder,' Billy and DeLisha are also sensitive to the fact that the fights they were in were not 'fair.' These street-level injustices inform Billy and DeLisha's expectations for retaliation. Consistent with the code, both Billy and DeLisha—equally armed with long fight histories—realise the importance of 'payback' and consider future battles with their challengers to be inevitable. When I asked DeLisha if she anticipated another fight with the young woman who cut her, she replied with a strong yes, 'because I'm taking it there with her.' Billy was also equally committed to retaliation, telling me: '. . . one by one, I will get them.'

Danielle and Robert: 'Sometimes You Got to Fight'

In *Code of the Street* (1999), Anderson demonstrates how important it is for young people to prove publicly that they are not someone to be 'messed with.' One of the ways that young people prove this to others is by engaging in fights in public, when necessary. The following statements from Danielle and Robert, two young people who are adept at avoiding conflicts, illustrate teenaged girls' and boys' shared understanding of the importance of demonstrating that one is willing to fight as a way to deter ongoing challenges to one's well-being:

> Danielle: 'cause sometimes you got to fight, not fight, but get into that type of battle to let them know that I'm not scared of you and you can't keep harassing me thinking that it's okay.
>
> Robert: . . . you know, if someone keep picking on you like that, you gonna have to do something to prove a point to them: that you not going to be scared of them . . . So, sometimes you do got to, you do got to fight. Cause you just got to tell them that you not scared of them.

Like DeLisha and Billy, Danielle, a recent high-school graduate, and Robert, who is in the 11th grade, offer nearly identical explanations of the importance of physically protecting one's own boundaries by demonstrating to others that you will fight, if necessary. While neither Danielle nor Robert identify as 'fighters,' both are convinced that sometimes you 'got to fight.' Again, this shared language reveals an awareness and commitment to a shared system of accountability, 'the code of the street,' which encourages young people— teenaged girls and boys—to present a 'tough front' as a way to discourage on-going challenges to one's personal security. For the young people in this study, the value placed on maintaining a tough front or 'proving a point' cut across perceived gender lines.

In addition to possibly deterring future challenges, Anderson argues that presenting and ultimately proving oneself as someone who is not to be 'messed with' helps to build a young person's confidence and self-esteem: 'particularly for young men and perhaps increasingly among females . . . their identity, their self-respect, and their honor are often intricately tied up with the way they perform on the streets during and after such [violent] encounters' (Anderson, 1999, p. 76). Those young people who are able to perform well during these public encounters acquire a sense of confidence that will facilitate their movement throughout the neighbourhood. This boost to one's sense of self is not restricted to young men; young women who can fight and win may also demonstrate a strong sense of pride and confidence in their ability to 'handle' potentially aggressive or violent conflicts, as illustrated by the following interview with Nicole.

Nicole: 'I Feel Like I Can Defend Myself'

My conversation with Nicole typifies the confidence expressed by teenaged girls who can fight and win. Nicole is a smart, articulate young woman who attended some community college courses while still a senior in high school. She planned to attend a state university to study engineering after graduation. While in high school, she tells me, she felt confident in her ability to walk the hallways of her sometimes chaotic public school: 'I feel like I can defend myself.' Unlike some young women who walk the hallways constantly testing others, Nicole's was a quiet confidence: 'I don't, like, I mean, when I'm walking around school or something, I don't walk around talking about "yeah, I beat this girl up."' Nicole could, in fact, claim that she didn't beat up just one girl but several, at the same time. Nicole explained to me how her most recent fight began:

> We [she and another young woman] had got into two arguments in the hallway and then her friends were holding her back. So I just said, 'Forget it. I'm just going to my class.' So

I'm in class, I'm inside the classroom and I hear Nina say, 'Is this that bitch's class?' I came to the door and was like, 'Yes, this is my class.' And she puts her hands up [in fighting position] and she swings . . . And me and her was fighting, and then I got her on the wall, and then I felt somebody pulling my hair, and it turns out to be Jessica. Right? And then we fighting, and then I see Tasha, and it's me and all these three people and then they broke it all up.

Nicole's only injury in the fight came from the elbow of the school police officer who eventually ended the battle. As Nicole recalls this fight, and her performance in particular, I notice that she is smiling. This smile, together with the tone in which she tells the story of her earlier battle, makes it clear that she is proud of her ability to meet the challenge presented to her by these young women. Impressed at her ability to fight off three teenaged girls at the same time, I ask Nicole: 'How did you manage not to get jumped?' She quickly corrects my definition of the situation: 'No. I managed to beat them up.' After retelling her fight story, Nicole shakes her head from side to side and says: 'I had to end up beating them up. So sad.' I notice her sure smile return. 'You don't really look like you feel bad about that,' I say. 'I don't,' she replies.

The level of self-confidence that Nicole displays in this brief exchange contrasts with the passivity and submissiveness that is commonly expected of women and girls, especially white, middle-class women and girls (Collins, 2004). It is young men, not teenaged girls, who are expected to exude such confidence as they construct a 'tough front' to deter would-be challengers (Anderson, 1999). Nicole's confidence is also more than an expressive performance. Nicole knows that she is physically able to fight and win, when necessary, because she has done so in the past. For teenaged girls like Nicole and Sharmaine, whom I discuss below, this confidence is essential to their evaluation of how best to handle potential interpersonal conflicts in their everyday lives.

Sharmaine: '. . . I Have One Hand Left'

Sharmaine, an 8th grader, displayed a level of self-confidence similar to Nicole's after a fight with a boy in her classroom. Moments before the fight,

the boy approached Sharmaine while she was looking out her classroom window, and 'whispered something' in her ear. Sharmaine knew that this boy liked her, but she thought she had made it quite clear that she did not like him. Sharmaine quickly told him to back off and then looked to her teacher for reinforcement. Her teacher, Sharmaine recalls, just laughed at the boy's advances. After he whispered in Sharmaine's ear a second time, she turned around and punched him in the face. Sharmaine later ended up in the emergency room with a jammed finger from the punch. I asked Sharmaine if she was concerned about him getting back at her when she returned to school. She tells me that someone in the emergency room asked her the same question. 'What did you say?' I ask. 'I told them no . . . because I have one hand left.'

For young women like Nicole and Sharmaine, the proven ability to defend themselves translates into a level of self-confidence that is not typically expected in girls and young women. Those girls who are confident in their ability to 'take care of themselves' become more mobile as they come to believe, as DeLisha says, that they can 'do anything [they] want to, anytime [they] want to do it.' Girls who are able to gain and maintain this level of self-confidence are able to challenge the real and imagined gendered boundaries on space and place in the inner city.

'Boys Got to Go Get Guns'

The need to be 'distinguished as a man'—a benchmark of hegemonic masculinity—often fosters adolescent boys' preoccupation with distinguishing themselves *from* women (Anderson, 1999; Collins, 2004, p. 210; Connell & Messerschmidt, 2005). This is a gendered preoccupation that was not revealed in urban adolescent girls' accounts of physical aggression and violence. The following statement from Craig, a young man who has deliberately checked his readiness to fight after being shot in the hip, illustrates how the need to 'be a man' influences young men's consideration of violence:

Yeah, I don't fight no more. I can't fight [because of injury]. So, I really stop and think about stuff because it isn't even worth it . . . unless, I mean, you really want it [a fight] to happen . . . I'm going to turn the other cheek. But, I'm not going to be, like, wearing a skirt. That's the way you got to look at it.

While Craig is prepared to exit his life as a 'fighter,' he predicts that his newfound commitment to avoid fights will not stand up to the pressure of proving his manhood to a challenger. Craig is well aware of how another young man can communicate that he 'really want [a fight] to happen.' Once a challenger publicly escalates a battle in this way, young men like Craig have few choices. At this moment, a young man will have to demonstrate to his challenger, and his audience, that he isn't 'wearing a skirt.' Not only must he fight, he must also fight *like a man.*

Craig's admission is revealing of how a young man's concern with not being 'like' a woman influences his consideration of the appropriate use of physical aggression. While a similar type of preoccupation with intergender distinctions was not typically revealed in young women's accounts, I found that teenaged girls were generally aware of at least one significant difference in how young women and men were expected to work the code of the street. As is revealed in my conversation with Shante, a teenaged girl who was hit in the head with a brick by a neighbourhood girl, young men are generally expected to use more serious or lethal forms of violence than girls or women. I asked Shante what people in her neighbourhood thought about girls fighting.

'Today,' she asked, 'you mean like people on the street?'

'Yeah.'

'If [a girl] get beat up, you just get beat up. That's on you.'

'Do you think it's different for boys?' I asked.

'Umm, boys got to go get guns. They got to blow somebody's head off. They got to shoot. They don't fight these days. They use guns.'

Shante's perception of what boys 'got to' do is informed by years of observation and experience.

Shante has grown up in a neighbourhood marked by violence. Days before this interview, she saw a young man get shot in the head. She tells me he was dead by the time he hit the sidewalk. When I asked Shante whether or not girls used guns, she could recall just one young woman from the neighbourhood—the same young woman who hit Shante over the head with a brick—who had 'pistol whipped' another teenaged girl. While she certainly used the gun as a weapon, she didn't shoot her. These two incidents are actually quite typical of reported gender differences in the use of weapons in violent acts: boys and men are much more likely than girls and women to use guns to shoot and kill. Women and girls, like many of the young women I spoke with during this study, are far more likely to rely on knives and box-cutters, if they use a weapon at all (see also Miller, 1998 & 2001; Pastor et al., 1996, p. 28). Those young women who did use a weapon, such as a knife or box-cutter, explained that they did so for protection. For example, Shante told me that she carried a razor blade, 'because she doesn't trust people.'

Takeya: 'A Good Girl'

In contrast to the commitment to protecting one's manhood, which Craig alludes to and Elijah Anderson describes in great detail (Anderson, 1999), the young women I spoke to did not suggest that they fought because that's what *women* do. Furthermore, while young women deeply appreciated the utility of a 'tough front,' they were unlikely to use phrases like 'I don't want to be wearing a skirt.' In fact, while young men like Craig work to prove their manhood by distinguishing themselves from women, many of the young women I spoke with—including the 'toughest' among them—embraced popular notions of femininity, 'skirts' and all. For many of the girls I interviewed, an appreciation of some aspects of hegemonic femininity modulated their involvement in violent interactions.

My conversation with Takeya sheds light on how inner-city girls attempt to reconcile the contradictory concerns that emerge from intersecting survival and gender projects. When I asked Takeya, a slim 13-year-old girl with a light-brown complexion, about her fighting history, she replied, 'I'm not in no fights. I'm a good girl.' 'You are a good girl?' I asked. 'Yeah, I'm a good girl and I'm-a be a pretty girl at 18.'

Takeya's concern with being a 'pretty girl' reflects an appreciation of aspects of hegemonic femininity that place great value on beauty. Her understanding of what it means to be beautiful is also influenced by the locally placed value on skin colour, hair texture and body figure. While brown skin and textured hair may not fit hegemonic (White, middle-class) conceptions of beauty, in this setting, a light-brown skinned complexion, 'straight' or 'good' hair, and a slim figure help to make one 'pretty' and 'good' (Banks, 2000). Yet, Takeya also knows that one's ability to stay pretty—to be a pretty girl at age 18—is directly influenced by one's involvement in interpersonal aggression or violence.

In order to be considered a 'pretty girl' by her peers, Takeya knows that she must avoid those types of interpersonal conflicts that tend to result in cuts and scratches to young women's faces, especially the ones that others consider beautiful (in *Code of the Street* [1999] Anderson writes that such visible scars often result in heightened status for the young women who leave their mark on pretty girls). Yet, Takeya is also aware that the culture of the code requires her to become an able fighter and to maintain a reputation as such. After expressing her commitment to being a 'good' girl, Takeya is sure to inform me that not only does she know how to fight, others also recognise her as an able fighter: 'I don't want you to think I don't know how to fight. I mean everybody always come get me [for fights]. [I'm] the number one [person they come to get].'

Takeya's simultaneous embrace of the culture of code and some aspects of normative femininity, Craig's concern with distinguishing himself from women, and Shante's convincing disclosure regarding what boys 'got to' do highlight how masculinity and femininity projects overlap and intersect with the project of survival for young people in distressed inner-city neighbourhoods. Both Craig and Takeya appreciate fundamental elements of 'the code,' especially the importance of being known as an able fighter. Yet, Craig's use of physical aggression is likely to be encouraged by his commitment to a distinctive aspect of

hegemonic masculinity: being distinguished from a girl. Meanwhile, Takeya's use of physical aggression and violence is tempered—though not extinguished—by seemingly typical 'female' concerns: being a 'good' and 'pretty' girl. In contrast to the project of accomplishing masculinity, which overlaps and, at times, contradicts the project of survival for young men, the project of accomplishing femininity can, at times, facilitate young women's struggle to survive in this setting.

Gender, Survival, and 'The Code'

I have argued that gender does not protect young women from much of the violence young men experience in distressed inner-city neighbourhoods, and that given these shared circumstances, it becomes equally important for women and men to work 'the code of the street.' Like many adolescent boys, young women also recognise that reputation, respect and retaliation—the '3 Rs' of the code of the street—organise their social world (Anderson, 1999). Yet, as true as it is that, at times, young men and women work the code of the street in similar ways, it is also true that differences exist. These differences are rooted in the relationships between masculinity, femininity and the use of violence or aggression in distressed urban areas and emerge from overlapping and intersecting survival and gender projects.

In order to 'survive' in today's inner city, young women like DeLisha, Danielle, Shante and Takeya are encouraged to embrace some aspects of the 'code of the street' that organises much of inner-city life (Anderson, 1999). In doing so, these girls also embrace and accomplish some aspects of hegemonic masculinity that are embedded in the code. My analysis of interviews with teenaged girls and boys injured in intentional violent incidents reveals an appreciation of the importance of maintaining a tough front and demonstrating nerve across perceived gender lines. It is this appreciation of the cultural elements of the code that leads teenaged girls like Danielle to believe strongly that 'sometimes you got to fight.'

REFERENCES

Anderson, E. (1999). *Code of the street: Decency, violence and the moral life of the inner city*. New York: W. W. Norton.

Banks, I. (2000). *Hair matters: Beauty, power, and Black women's consciousness*. New York: New York University Press.

Collins, P. Hill. (2004). *Black sexual politics: African Americans, gender, and the new racism*. New York: Routledge.

Connell, R.W., & Messerschmidt, J.W. (2005). Hegemonic masculinity: Rethinking the concept. *Gender & Society, 19*(6), 829–859.

Goffman, E. (1959). *The presentation of self in everyday life*. New York: Anchor Books.

Miller, J. (1998). Up it up: Gender and the accomplishment of street robbery. *Criminology, 36*(1), 37–66.

Miller, J. (2001). *One of the guys: Girls, gangs, and gender*. Oxford: Oxford University Press.

Pastor, J., McCormick, J., & Fine, M. (1996). Makin' homes: An urban girl thing. In B. J. Ross Leadbeater & N. Way (Eds.), *Urban girls: Resisting stereotypes, creating identities*. New York: New York University Press.

Simpson, S. S. (1991). Caste, class, and violent crime: Explaining difference in female offending. *Criminology, 29*(1), 115–135.

THINKING ABOUT THE READING

This reading demonstrates that inner-city girls are also not as isolated from violence as is commonly thought. What are some of the reasons for their involvement with violence? What is the "code of the street"? How are violence and the "code" related to the ways in which these girls see themselves? How are they related to their survival? Does the way in which girls use and understand violence differ from the ways in which boys see it?

CHAPTER 6

Supporting Identity

The Presentation of Self

S ocial behavior is highly influenced by the images we form of others. We typically form impressions of people based on an initial assessment of their social group membership (ethnicity, age, gender, etc.), their personal attributes (e.g., physical attractiveness), and the verbal and nonverbal messages they provide. These assessments are usually accompanied by a set of expectations we've learned to associate with members of certain social groups or people with certain attributes. Such judgments allow us to place people in broad categories and provide a degree of predictability in interactions.

While we are forming impressions of others, we are fully aware that they are doing the same thing with us. Early in life, most of us learn that it is to our advantage to have people think highly of us. In "The Presentation of Self in Everyday Life," Erving Goffman describes a process called *impression management* in which we attempt to control and manipulate information about ourselves to influence the impressions others form of us. Impression management provides the link between the way we perceive ourselves and the way we want others to perceive us. We've all been in situations—a first date, a job interview, meeting a girlfriend's or boyfriend's family for the first time—in which we've felt compelled to "make a good impression." What we often fail to realize, however, is that personal impression management may be influenced by larger organizational and institutional forces.

How do trans and gender non-comforming young people learn social presentation? In the second reading in this chapter, sociologist Arlene Stein portrays trans youth who use social media to share tips and advice for self-presentation. Using venues such as YouTube, trans masculine youth post videos about chest binding and other techniques that enable them to feel more comfortable in their public gender presentation. As Stein points out, social media provides a new realm for these young people to learn from one another and creates new possibilities for expression.

Race is one of the central features (along with gender and age) of first impressions. In "Blue Chip Blacks: Managing Race in Public Spaces," Karyn R. Lacy presents research based on interviews with middle-class Blacks in Washington, who use their agency and cultural capital to produce "public identities" and control interactions with Whites that lead to positive outcomes in public arenas like shopping malls, real estate (house hunting), and the workplace. The use of public identities demonstrates how some middle-class Blacks can define their situation and avoid racial discrimination through the manipulation of their public interactions with Whites.

Something to Consider as You Read

As you read these selections on the presentation of self and identity, consider where people get their ideas about whom and what they can be in various settings. Consider a setting in which everyone present may be trying to create a certain impression because that's what they all think everyone else wants. What would have to happen for the "impression script" to change in this setting? In what ways do material resources and authority influence the impression we're able to make? Are there certain types of people who needn't be concerned about the impressions they give off? Compare and contrast the readings on public identities and the "trans masculinity." Are there similar cultural scripts operating in both these scenarios?

The Presentation of Self in Everyday Life

Selections

ERVING GOFFMAN

(1959)

Introduction

When an individual enters the presence of others, they commonly seek to acquire information about him or to bring into play information about him already possessed. They will be interested in his general socio-economic status, his conception of self, his attitude toward them, his competence, his trustworthiness, etc. Although some of this information seems to be sought almost as an end in itself, there are usually quite practical reasons for acquiring it. Information about the individual helps to define the situation, enabling others to know in advance what he will expect of them and what they may expect of him. Informed in these ways, the others will know how best to act in order to call forth a desired response from him.

For those present, many sources of information become accessible and many carriers (or "sign-vehicles") become available for conveying this information. If unacquainted with the individual, observers can glean clues from his conduct and appearance which allow them to apply their previous experience with individuals roughly similar to the one before them or, more important, to apply untested stereotypes to him. They can also assume from past experience that only individuals of a particular kind are likely to be found in a given social setting. They can rely on what the individual says about himself or on documentary evidence he provides as to who and what he is. If they know, or know of, the individual by virtue of experience prior to the interaction, they can rely on assumptions as to the persistence and generality of psychological traits as a means of predicting his present and future behavior.

The expressiveness of the individual (and therefore his capacity to give impressions) appears to involve two radically different kinds of sign activity: the expression that he *gives,* and the expression that he *gives off.* The first involves verbal symbols or their substitutes which he uses admittedly and solely to convey the information that he and the others are known to attach to these symbols. This is communication in the traditional and narrow sense. The second involves a wide range of action that others can treat as symptomatic of the actor, the expectation being that the action was performed for reasons other than the information conveyed in this way. As we shall have to see, this distinction has an only initial validity. The individual does of course intentionally convey misinformation by means of both of these types of communication, the first involving deceit, the second feigning.

Taking communication in both its narrow and broad sense, one finds that when the individual is in the immediate presence of others, his activity will have a promissory character. The others are likely to find that they must accept the individual on faith, offering him a just return while he is present before them in exchange for something whose true value will not be established until after he has left their presence. (Of course, the others also live by inference in their dealings with the physical world, but it is only in the world of social interaction that the objects about which they make inferences will purposely facilitate and hinder this inferential process.) The security that they justifiably feel in making inferences about the individual will vary, of course, depending on such factors as the amount of information they already possess about him, but no amount of such past evidence can entirely obviate the necessity of acting on the basis of inferences. As William I. Thomas suggested:

> It is also highly important for us to realize that we do not as a matter of fact lead our lives, make our decisions, and reach our goals in everyday life either statistically or scientifically. We live by inference. I am, let us say, your guest. You do not know, you cannot determine scientifically, that I will not steal your money or your spoons. But inferentially I will not and inferentially you have me as a guest.[1]

Let us now turn from the others to the point of view of the individual who presents himself before them. He may wish them to think highly of him, or to think that he thinks highly of them, or to perceive how in fact he feels toward them, or to obtain no clear-cut impression; he may wish to ensure sufficient harmony so that the interaction can be sustained, or to defraud, get rid of, confuse, mislead, antagonize, or insult them. Regardless of the particular objective which the individual has in mind and of his motive for having this objective, it will be in his interests to control the conduct of the others, especially their responsive treatment of him.[2] This control is achieved largely by influencing the definition of the situation which the others come to formulate, and he can influence this definition by expressing himself in such a way as to give them the kind of impression that will lead them to act voluntarily in accordance with his own plan. Thus, when an individual appears in the presence of others, there will usually be some reason for him to mobilize his activity so that it will convey an impression to others which it is in his interests to convey. . . .

I have said that when an individual appears before others his actions will influence the definition of the situation which they come to have. Sometimes the individual will act in a thoroughly calculating manner, expressing himself in a given way solely in order to give the kind of impression to others that is likely to evoke from them a specific response he is concerned to obtain. Sometimes the individual will be calculating in his activity but be relatively unaware that this is the case. Sometimes he will intentionally and consciously express himself in a particular way, but chiefly because the tradition of his group or social status require this kind of expression and not because of any particular response (other than vague acceptance or approval) that is likely to be evoked from those impressed by the expression. Sometimes the traditions of an individual's role will lead him to give a well-designed impression of a particular kind and yet he may be neither consciously nor unconsciously disposed to create such an impression. The others, in their turn, may be suitably impressed by the individual's efforts to convey something, or may misunderstand the situation and come to conclusions that are warranted neither by the individual's intent nor by the facts. In any case, in so far as the others act *as if* the individual had conveyed a particular impression, we may take a functional or pragmatic view and

say that the individual has "effectively" projected a given definition of the situation and "effectively" fostered the understanding that a given state of affairs obtains. . . .

When we allow that the individual projects a definition of the situation when he appears before others, we must also see that the others, however passive their role may seem to be, will themselves effectively project a definition of the situation by virtue of their response to the individual and by virtue of any lines of action they initiate to him. Ordinarily the definitions of the situation projected by the several different participants are sufficiently attuned to one another so that open contradiction will not occur. I do not mean that there will be the kind of consensus that arises when each individual present candidly expresses what he really feels and honestly agrees with the expressed feelings of the others present. This kind of harmony is an optimistic ideal and in any case not necessary for the smooth working of society. Rather, each participant is expected to suppress his immediate heartfelt feelings, conveying a view of the situation which he feels the others will be able to find at least temporarily acceptable. The maintenance of this surface of agreement, this veneer of consensus, is facilitated by each participant concealing his own wants behind statements which assert values to which everyone present feels obliged to give lip service. Further, there is usually a kind of division of definitional labor. Each participant is allowed to establish the tentative official ruling regarding matters which are vital to him but not immediately important to others, e.g., the rationalizations and justifications by which he accounts for his past activity. In exchange for this courtesy he remains silent or noncommittal on matters important to others but not immediately important to him. We have then a kind of interactional *modus vivendi*. Together the participants contribute to a single overall definition of the situation which involves not so much a real agreement as to what exists but rather a real agreement as to whose claims concerning what issues will be temporarily honored. Real agreement will also exist concerning the desirability of avoiding an open conflict of definitions of the situation.[3] I will refer to this level of agreement as a "working consensus." It is to be understood that the working consensus established in one interaction setting will be quite different in content from the working consensus established in a different type of setting. Thus, between two friends at lunch, a reciprocal show of affection, respect, and concern for the other is maintained. In service occupations, on the other hand, the specialist often maintains an image of disinterested involvement in the problem of the client, while the client responds with a show of respect for the competence and integrity of the specialist. Regardless of such differences in content, however, the general form of these working arrangements is the same. . . .

. . . Given the fact that the individual effectively projects a definition of the situation when he enters the presence of others, we can assume that events may occur within the interaction which contradict, discredit, or otherwise throw doubt upon this projection. When these disruptive events occur, the interaction itself may come to a confused and embarrassed halt. Some of the assumptions upon which the responses of the participants had been predicated become untenable, and the participants find themselves lodged in an interaction for which the situation has been wrongly defined and is now no longer defined. At such moments the individual whose presentation has been discredited may feel ashamed while the others present may feel hostile, and all the participants may come to feel ill at ease, nonplussed, out of countenance, embarrassed, experiencing the kind of anomy that is generated when the minute social system of face-to-face interaction breaks down. . . .

We find that preventive practices are constantly employed to avoid these embarrassments and that corrective practices are constantly employed to compensate for discrediting occurrences that have not been successfully avoided. When the individual employs these strategies and tactics to protect his own projections, we may refer to them as "defensive practices"; when a participant employs them to save the definition of the situation projected by another, we speak of "protective practices" or "tact." Together, defensive and protective practices comprise the techniques employed to safe-guard the impression fostered by an individual during his presence before others. It should be added that while we may be ready to see that no fostered impression would survive if defensive practices were not employed, we are less ready perhaps to see that few impressions could survive if those who received the impression did not exert tact in their reception of it.

In addition to the fact that precautions are taken to prevent disruption of projected definitions, we may also note that an intense interest in these disruptions comes to play a significant role in the social life of the group. Practical jokes and social games are played in which embarrassments which are to be taken unseriously are purposely engineered.[4] Fantasies are created in which devastating exposures occur. Anecdotes from the past—real, embroidered, or fictitious—are told and retold, detailing disruptions which occurred, almost occurred, or occurred and were admirably resolved. There seems to be no grouping which does not have a ready supply of these games, reveries, and cautionary tales, to be used as a source of humor, a catharsis for anxieties, and a sanction for inducing individuals to be modest in their claims and reasonable in their projected expectations. The individual may tell himself through dreams of getting into impossible positions. Families tell of the time a guest got his dates mixed and arrived when neither the house nor anyone in it was ready for him. Journalists tell of times when an all-too-meaningful misprint occurred, and the paper's assumption of objectivity or decorum was humorously discredited. Public servants tell of times a client ridiculously misunderstood form instructions, giving answers which implied an unanticipated and bizarre definition of the situation.[5] Seamen, whose home away from home is rigorously he-man, tell stories of coming back home and inadvertently asking mother to "pass the fucking butter."[6] Diplomats tell of the time a near-sighted queen asked a republican ambassador about the health of his king.[7]

To summarize, then, I assume that when an individual appears before others he will have many motives for trying to control the impression they receive of the situation. This report is concerned with some of the common techniques that persons employ to sustain such impressions and with some of the common contingencies associated with the employment of these techniques. It will be convenient to end this introduction with some definitions. . . . For the purpose of this report, interaction (that is, face-to-face interaction) may be roughly defined as the reciprocal influence of individuals upon one another's actions when in one another's immediate physical presence. An interaction may be defined as all the interaction which occurs throughout any one occasion when a given set of individuals are in one another's continuous presence; the term "an encounter" would do as well. A "performance" may be defined as all the activity of a given participant on a given occasion which serves to influence in any way any of the other participants. Taking a particular participant and his performance as a basic point of reference, we may refer to those who contribute the other performances as the audience, observers, or co-participants. The pre-established pattern of action which is unfolded during a performance and which may be presented or played through on other occasions may be called a "part" or "routine."[8] These situational terms can easily be related to conventional structural ones. When an individual or performer plays the same part to the same audience on different occasions, a social relationship is likely to arise. Defining social role as the enactment of rights and duties attached to a given status, we can say that a social role will involve one or more parts and that each of these different parts may be presented by the performer on a series of occasions to the same kinds of audience or to an audience of the same persons. . . .

Performances

Front

I [use] the term "performance" to refer to all the activity of an individual which occurs during a period marked by his continuous presence before a particular set of observers and which has some influence on the observers. It will be convenient to label as "front" that part of the individual's performance which regularly functions in a general and fixed fashion to define the situation for those who observe the performance. Front, then, is the expressive equipment of a standard kind intentionally or unwittingly employed by the individual during his performance. For preliminary purposes, it will be convenient to distinguish and label what seem to be the standard parts of front.

First, there is the "setting," involving furniture, décor, physical layout, and other background items which supply the scenery and stage props for the spate of human action played out before, within, or upon it. A setting tends to stay put, geographically speaking, so that those who would use a particular setting as part of their performance cannot begin their act until they have brought themselves to the appropriate place and must terminate their performance

when they leave it. It is only in exceptional circumstances that the setting follows along with the performers; we see this in the funeral cortège, the civic parade, and the dreamlike processions that kings and queens are made of. In the main, these exceptions seem to offer some kind of extra protection for performers who are, or who have momentarily become, highly sacred. . . .

It is sometimes convenient to divide the stimuli which make up personal front into "appearance" and "manner," according to the function performed by the information that these stimuli convey. "Appearance" may be taken to refer to those stimuli which function at the time to tell us of the performer's social statuses. These stimuli also tell us of the individual's temporary ritual state, that is, whether he is engaging in formal social activity, work, or informal recreation, whether or not he is celebrating a new phase in the season cycle or in his life-cycle. "Manner" may be taken to refer to those stimuli which function at the time to warn us of the interaction role the performer will expect to play in the oncoming situation. Thus a haughty, aggressive manner may give the impression that the performer expects to be the one who will initiate the verbal interaction and direct its course. A meek, apologetic manner may give the impression that the performer expects to follow the lead of others, or at least that he can be led to do so. . . .

Dramatic Realization

While in the presence of others, the individual typically infuses his activity with signs which dramatically highlight and portray confirmatory facts that might otherwise remain unapparent or obscure. For if the individual's activity is to become significant to others, he must mobilize his activity so that it will express *during the interaction* what he wishes to convey. In fact, the performer may be required not only to express his claimed capacities during the interaction but also to do so during a split second in the interaction. Thus, if a baseball umpire is to give the impression that he is sure of his judgment, he must forgo the moment of thought which might make him sure of his judgment; he must give an instantaneous decision so that the audience will be sure that he is sure of his judgment.[9] . . .

Similarly, the proprietor of a service establishment may find it difficult to dramatize what is actually being done for clients because the clients cannot "see" the overhead costs of the service rendered them. Undertakers must therefore charge a great deal for their highly visible product—a coffin that has been transformed into a casket—because many of the other costs of conducting a funeral are ones that cannot be readily dramatized.[10] Merchants, too, find that they must charge high prices for things that look intrinsically inexpensive in order to compensate the establishment for expensive things like insurance, slack periods, etc., that never appear before the customers' eyes. . . .

Idealization

. . . I want to consider here another important aspect of this socialization process—the tendency for performers to offer their observers an impression that is idealized in several different ways.

The notion that a performance presents an idealized view of the situation is, of course, quite common. Cooley's view may be taken as an illustration:

> If we never tried to seem a little better than we are, how could we improve or "train ourselves from the outside inward"? And the same impulse to show the world a better or idealized aspect of ourselves finds an organized expression in the various professions and classes, each of which has to some extent a cant or pose, which its members assume unconsciously, for the most part, but which has the effect of a conspiracy to work upon the credulity of the rest of the world. There is a cant not only of theology and of philanthropy, but also of law, medicine, teaching, even of science—perhaps especially of science, just now, since the more a particular kind of merit is recognized and admired, the more it is likely to be assumed by the unworthy.[11]

Thus, when the individual presents himself before others, his performance will tend to incorporate and exemplify the officially accredited values of the society, more so, in fact, than does his behavior as a whole.

To the degree that a performance highlights the common official values of the society in which it occurs, we may look upon it, in the manner of Durkheim and Radcliffe-Brown, as a ceremony—as an expressive rejuvenation and reaffirmation of the moral values of the community. Furthermore, insofar as the expressive bias of performances comes to be accepted as reality, then that which is accepted at the moment as reality will have some of the characteristics of a celebration. To stay in one's room away from the place where the party is given, or away from where the practitioner attends his client, is to stay away from where reality is being performed. The world, in truth, is a wedding.

One of the richest sources of data on the presentation of idealized performances is the literature on social mobility. In most societies there seems to be a major or general system of stratification, and in most stratified societies there is an idealization of the higher strata and some aspiration on the part of those in low places to move to higher ones. (One must be careful to appreciate that this involves not merely a desire for a prestigeful place but also a desire for a place close to the sacred center of the common values of the society.) Commonly we find that upward mobility involves the presentation of proper performances and that efforts to move upward and efforts to keep from moving downward are expressed in terms of sacrifices made for the maintenance of front. Once the proper sign-equipment has been obtained and familiarity gained in the management of it, then this equipment can be used to embellish and illumine one's daily performances with a favorable social style.

Perhaps the most important piece of sign-equipment associated with social class consists of the status symbols through which material wealth is expressed. American society is similar to others in this regard but seems to have been singled out as an extreme example of wealth-oriented class structure—perhaps because in America the license to employ symbols of wealth and financial capacity to do so are so widely distributed. . . .

Reality and Contrivance

. . . Some performances are carried off successfully with complete dishonesty, others with complete honesty; but for performances in general neither of these extremes is essential and neither, perhaps, is dramaturgically advisable.

The implication here is that an honest, sincere, serious performance is less firmly connected with the solid world than one might first assume. And this implication will be strengthened if we look again at the distance usually placed between quite honest performances and quite contrived ones. In this connection take, for example, the remarkable phenomenon of stage acting. It does take deep skill, long training, and psychological capacity to become a good stage actor. But this fact should not blind us to another one: that almost anyone can quickly learn a script well enough to give a charitable audience some sense of realness in what is being contrived before them. And it seems this is so because ordinary social intercourse is itself put together as a scene is put together, by the exchange of dramatically inflated actions, counteractions, and terminating replies. Scripts even in the hands of unpracticed players can come to life because life itself is a dramatically enacted thing. All the world is not, of course, a stage, but the crucial ways in which it isn't are not easy to specify. . . .

When the individual does move into a new position in society and obtains a new part to perform, he is not likely to be told in full detail how to conduct himself, nor will the facts of his new situation press sufficiently on him from the start to determine his conduct without his further giving thought to it. Ordinarily he will be given only a few cues, hints, and stage directions, and it will be assumed that he already has in his repertoire a large number of bits and pieces of performances that will be required in the new setting. The individual will already have a fair idea of what modesty, deference, or righteous indignation looks like, and can make a pass at playing these bits when necessary. He may even be able to play out the part of a hypnotic subject[12] or commit a "compulsive" crime[13] on the basis of models for these activities that he is already familiar with.

A theatrical performance or a staged confidence game requires a thorough scripting of the spoken content of the routine; but the vast part involving "expression given off" is often determined by meager stage directions. It is expected that the performer of illusions will already know a good deal about how to manage his voice, his face, and his body, although he—as well as any person who directs him—may find it difficult indeed to provide a detailed verbal statement of this kind of knowledge. And in this, of course, we approach the situation of the straightforward man in the street. Socialization may not so much involve a learning of the many specific details of a single concrete part—often there could not be enough time or energy for this. What does seem to be required of the individual is that he learn enough pieces of expression to be able to "fill in" and manage, more or less, any part that he is likely to be given. The legitimate performances of everyday life are not "acted" or "put on" in the sense that the performer knows in advance just what he is going to do, and does this solely because of the effect it is likely to have. The expressions it is felt he is giving off will be especially "inaccessible" to him.[14] But as in the case of less legitimate performers, the incapacity of the ordinary individual to formulate in advance the movements of his eyes and body does not mean that he will not express himself through these devices in a way that is dramatized and performed in his repertoire of actions. In short, we all act better than we know how.

When we watch a television wrestler gouge, foul, and snarl at his opponent we are quite ready to see that, in spite of the dust, he is, and knows he is, merely playing at being the "heavy," and that in another match he may be given the other role, that of clean-cut wrestler, and perform this with equal verve and proficiency. We seem less ready to see, however, that while such details as the number and character of the falls may be fixed beforehand, the details of the expressions and movements used do not come from a script but from command of an idiom, a command that is exercised from moment to moment with little calculation or forethought. . . .

Personality-Interaction-Society

In recent years there have been elaborate attempts to bring into one framework the concepts and findings derived from three different areas of inquiry: the individual personality, social interaction, and society. I would like to suggest here a simple addition to these inter-disciplinary attempts.

When an individual appears before others, he knowingly and unwittingly projects a definition of the situation, of which a conception of himself is an important part. When an event occurs which is expressively incompatible with this fostered impression, significant consequences are simultaneously felt in three levels of social reality, each of which involves a different point of reference and a different order of fact.

First, the social interaction, treated here as a dialogue between two teams, may come to an embarrassed and confused halt; the situation may cease to be defined. Previous positions may become no longer tenable, and participants may find themselves without a charted course of action. The participants typically sense a false note in the situation and come to feel awkward, flustered, and, literally, out of countenance. In other words, the minute social system created and sustained by orderly social interaction becomes disorganized. These are the consequences that the disruption has from the point of view of social interaction.

Secondly, in addition to these disorganizing consequences for action at the moment, performance disruptions may have consequences of a more far-reaching kind. Audiences tend to accept the self projected by the individual performer during any current performance as a responsible representative of his colleague-grouping, of his team, and of his social establishment. Audiences also accept the individual's particular performance as evidence of his capacity to perform the routine and even as evidence of his capacity to perform any routine. In a sense these larger social units—teams, establishments, etc.—become committed every time the individual performs his routine; with each performance the legitimacy of these units will tend to be tested anew and their permanent reputation put at stake. This kind of commitment is especially strong during some performances. Thus, when a surgeon and his nurse both turn from the operating table and the anesthetized patient accidentally rolls off the table to his death, not only is the operation disrupted in an embarrassing way, but the reputation of the doctor, as a doctor and as a man, and also the reputation of the hospital may be weakened. These are the consequences that disruptions may have from the point of view of social structure.

Finally, we often find that the individual may deeply involve his ego in his identification with a particular part, establishment, and group, and in his self-conception as someone who does not disrupt social interaction or let down the social units which depend upon that interaction. When a disruption occurs, then, we may find that the self-conceptions around which his personality has been built may become discredited. These are consequences that disruptions may have from the point of view of individual personality.

Performance disruptions, then, have consequences at three levels of abstraction: personality, interaction, and social structure. While the likelihood of disruption will vary widely from interaction to interaction, and while the social importance of likely disruptions will vary from interaction to interaction, still it seems that there is no interaction in which the participants do not take an appreciable chance of being slightly embarrassed or a slight chance of being deeply humiliated. Life may not be much of a gamble, but interaction is. Further, insofar as individuals make efforts to avoid disruptions or to correct for ones not avoided, these efforts, too, will have simultaneous consequences at the three levels. Here, then, we have one simple way of articulating three levels of abstraction and three perspectives from which social life has been studied.

Staging and the Self

The general notion that we make a presentation of ourselves to others is hardly novel; what ought to be stressed in conclusion is that the very structure of the self can be seen in terms of how we arrange for such performances in our Anglo-American society. . . .

The self, then, as a performed character, is not an organic thing that has a specific location, whose fundamental fate is to be born, to mature, and to die; it is a dramatic effect arising diffusely from a scene that is presented, and the characteristic issue, the crucial concern, is whether it will be credited or discredited.

In analyzing the self then we are drawn from its possessor, from the person who will profit or lose most by it, for he and his body merely provide the peg on which something of collaborative manufacture will be hung for a time. And the means for producing and maintaining selves do not reside inside the peg; in fact these means are often bolted down in social establishments. There will be a back region with its tools for shaping the body, and a front region with its fixed props. There will be a team of persons whose activity on stage in conjunction with available props will constitute the scene from which the performed character's self will emerge, and another team, the audience, whose interpretive activity will be necessary for this emergence. The self is a product of all of these arrangements, and in all of its parts bears the marks of this genesis.

The whole machinery of self-production is cumbersome, of course, and sometimes breaks down, exposing its separate components: back region control; team collusion; audience tact; and so forth. But, well oiled, impressions will flow from it fast enough to put us in the grips of one of our types of reality—the performance will come off and the firm self accorded each performed character will appear to emanate intrinsically from its performer.

Let us turn now from the individual as character performed to the individual as performer. He has a capacity to learn, this being exercised in the task of training for a part. He is given to having fantasies and dreams, some that pleasurably unfold a triumphant performance, others full of anxiety and dread that nervously deal with vital discreditings in a public front region. He often manifests a gregarious desire for teammates and audiences, a tactful considerateness for their concerns; and he has a capacity for deeply felt shame, leading him to minimize the chances he takes of exposure.

These attributes of the individual *qua* performer are not merely a depicted effect of particular performances; they are psychobiological in nature, and yet they seem to arise out of intimate interaction with the contingencies of staging performances.

And now a final comment. In developing the conceptual framework employed in this report, some language of the stage was used. I spoke of performers and audiences; of routines and parts; of performances coming off or falling flat; of cues, stage settings, and backstage; of dramaturgical needs, dramaturgical skills, and dramaturgical strategies. Now it should be admitted that this attempt to press a mere analogy so far was in part a rhetoric and a maneuver. . . .

And so here the language and mask of the stage will be dropped. Scaffolds, after all, are to build other things with, and should be erected with an eye to taking them down.

This report is not concerned with aspects of theater that creep into everyday life. It is concerned with the structure of social encounters—the structure of those entities in social life that come into being whenever persons enter one another's immediate physical presence. The key factor in this structure is the maintenance of a single definition of the situation, this definition having to be expressed, and this expression sustained in the face of a multitude of potential disruptions.

A character staged in a theater is not in some ways real, nor does it have the same kind of real consequences as does the thoroughly contrived character performed by a confidence man; but the *successful* staging of either of these types of false figures involves use of *real* techniques—the same techniques by which everyday persons sustain their real social situations. Those who conduct face to face interaction on a theater's stage must meet the key requirement of real situations; they must expressively sustain a definition of the situation: but this they do in circumstances that have facilitated their developing an apt terminology for the interactional tasks that all of us share.

NOTES

1. Quoted in E. H. Volkart, editor, *Social Behavior and Personality,* Contributions of W. I. Thomas to Theory and Social Research (New York: Social Science Research Council, 1951), p. 9.

2. Here I owe much to an unpublished paper by Tom Burns of the University of Edinburgh. He presents the argument that in all interactions a basic underlying theme is the desire of each participant to guide and control the responses made by the others present. A similar argument has been advanced by Jay Haley in a recent unpublished paper, but in regard to a special kind of control, that having to do with defining the nature of the relationship of those involved in the interaction.

3. An interaction can be purposely set up as a time and place for voicing differences in opinion. But in such cases participants *must* be careful to agree not to disagree on the proper tone of voice, vocabulary, and degree of seriousness in which all arguments are to be phrased, and upon the mutual respect which disagreeing participants must carefully continue to express toward one another. This debaters' or academic definition of the situation may also be invoked suddenly and judiciously as a way of translating a serious conflict of views into one that can be handled within a framework acceptable to all present.

4. Goffman, *op. cit.,* pp. 319–27.

5. Peter Blau, "Dynamics of Bureaucracy" (Ph.D. dissertation, Department of Sociology, Columbia University, forthcoming, University of Chicago Press), pp. 127–29.

6. Walter M. Beattie, Jr., "The Merchant Sea-man" (unpublished M.A. report, Department of Sociology, University of Chicago, 1950), p. 35.

7. Sir Frederick Ponsonby, *Recollections of Three Reigns* (New York: Dutton, 1952), p. 46.

8. For comments on the importance of distinguishing between a routine of interaction and any particular instance when this routine is played through, see John van Neumann and Oskar Morgenstern, *The Theory of Games and Economic Behaviour* (2nd ed.) (Princeton: Princeton University Press, 1947), p. 49.

9. See Babe Pinelli, as told to Joe King, *Mr. Ump* (Philadelphia: Westminster Press, 1953), p. 75.

10. Material on the burial business used throughout this report is taken from Robert W. Habenstein,

"The American Funeral Director" (unpublished Ph.D. dissertation, Department of Sociology, University of Chicago, 1954). I owe much to Mr. Habenstein's analysis of a funeral as a performance.

11. Charles H. Cooley, *Human Nature and the Social Order* (New York: Scribner's, 1922), pp. 352–53.

12. This view of hypnosis is neatly presented by T. R. Sarbin, "Contributions to Role-Taking Theory. I: Hypnotic Behavior," *Psychological Review,* 57, pp. 255–70.

13. See D. R. Cressey, "The Differential Association Theory and Compulsive Crimes," *Journal of Criminal Law, Criminology and Police Science,* 45, pp. 29–40.

14. This concept derives from T. R. Sarbin, "Role Theory," in Gardner Lindzey, *Handbook of Social Psychology* (Cambridge: Addison-Wesley, 1954), Vol. 1, pp. 235–36.

THINKING ABOUT THE READING

According to Goffman, why must everyone engage in impression management? What are some of the reasons we do this? What does he mean by the terms *definition of the situation, working consensus,* and *preventative strategies*? Consider a situation in which you were particularly aware of your own self-presentation. Do you think Goffman is interested primarily in the interactions between people or in their individual psychology? What is the source of the "scripts" that people use to determine what role they should play in a given situation or performance?

Performing Trans Masculinity Online

ARLENE STEIN

(2017)

Sixteen-year-old Kye dreams of having a masculine chest one day. "A big chest is extremely dysphoric for a lot of transguys," he says. Though he has small breasts, wearing a bra "enhanced them and made them look bigger," so he started binding them, flattening them to minimize their appearance. Like Kye, many trans men hope one day to have top surgery, but typically they must wait at least until they are 18, and gain access to sufficient funds, to do so. In the meantime, many bind, or flatten, their chests. In a four-minute You Tube video, Kye displays his flattened chest and instructs others on how to achieve a similar effect; over 75,000 viewers have seen it. "I'm a real boy!" he proclaims in the video, which was shot on his computer in his bedroom, poised in front of a dinosaur crossing poster, a series of hand-drawn animal cartoons, and the cover of a Broadway playbill.

"Wearing sports bras are better than nothing," says Kye in a video post, but "binders are what transmen need to start passing as men"—that is, to be seen by others as male. Kye, who lives in Illinois, can't afford commercially made binders, such as undershirts which have two or three layers of spandex, so he affixes Ace elastic compression bandages tightly across his chest with a safety pin, cautioning viewers of his vlog: "when wrapped too tightly, they can do damage." Compression wraps can tighten over time and restrict breathing, cause fluid build-up in the lungs, and even broken ribs. Many trans men bind their breasts for months, even years, often as a prelude to undergoing "top" surgery.

In his videos, Kye thinks out loud, figuring out ways of minimizing the social tension that occurs when gender presentation raises questions in public, and sharing what he's learned with others facing similar challenges. He's trying out a different body, helping others to do the same, and building an intimate community with other young trans men. These opportunities for public self-reflection are particularly important for those who live in the liminal space of their family homes. Being out in public can at times be difficult, if not dangerous. They can be bullied at school, or assaulted on the street if they disclose their transgender status to others. By narrating their life stories and sharing information they are creating a networked public comprised of young trans men, building emotional bonds with similar others.

Kye is among a growing number of young transgender males who are coming out of the shadows, at younger ages—and online. For increasing numbers of gender variant people, the Internet has become a community, a scattered web of gender-questioning peers, who are instantaneously connecting with one another, sharing knowledge, and foregoing the authority of experts at younger and younger ages. While looking for evidence of transgender men's lives online, I stumbled upon Kye's video, and an entire genre of YouTube video diaries that document the process of transition. I was struck by the ease with which individuals were willing to narrate the deepest recesses of their lives for an audience of unknown others.

In YouTube videos, trans men document their decision to publicly assume a male gender, disclose that decision to family and friends, and undergo surgical and nonsurgical body modifications. Over the course of three years, Kye has posted 20 videos on subjects ranging from "How Do You Know You're Trans?" to an interview with his girlfriend: "How to Date a Transman." People have viewed his YouTube channel, which has over 1,000 subscribers, over 145,000 times. His is one of thousands of video blogs, or vlogs, produced by young female-to-male individuals on the Internet. Today, those in their 20s and younger are likely to have first encountered the idea of transitioning online. Chest binding techniques are a particularly popular topic of discussion. Searching for the terms "transgender men" and "chest binding" on YouTube yielded over 4,000 videos.

In the first of over 40 videos documenting his transition, Connor introduces himself: "The name is Connor and like many other people in the world I am transgender. 1 know there are a million videos that you can watch about trans stuff but now you have another one. I am here to help and to entertain. DUUHH! A'ight so love you my friends. Enjoy the page." In a video entitled "Moment of Major Dysphoria," his room is dark, illuminated only by the glow of the computer, he discusses his estrangement from his natal body, others' inability to recognize him as the gender he truly feels himself to be, and his desire to transition. "I really need to get it done. It's hard to wait. I want to get on t (testosterone). It gets better, I think. It just takes time." He is crying.

When he went to work the other day, everyone called him by Connor, his chosen name, "that was really cool." A few people even "called me sir," he said, "but it doesn't fool me." He desperately wishes to be recognized by others for the gender he feels himself to be. "I want my parents to be ok with it, and I just want to get things done"—get access to chest surgery and hormones. "Looks like some of you are watching," Connor tells his unknown audience. "I hope everyone else who has this problem is hanging in there. Don't give up. Hopefully you guys are rooting for me, and I will root for you too. Peace and love, I'll talk to you guys soon."

He addresses his viewers, the "guys," with familiarity and affection, and describes "meeting buddies online," though they have never actually been in the physical presence of those they communicate with and probably never will be.

By producing and consuming YouTube vlogs, young trans men are creating a visual record of the transition process and creating what Internet researcher danah boyd calls "networked publics"— spaces that are structured by networked technologies for people to "gather, connect, and help construct society as we understand it."[1] They use vlogs and other social media to document the decisions to move away from their assigned gender, bind their breasts, change their pronouns, pass as male, and often, undergo chest surgery—and to work out the emotional challenges such choices pose.

Before the Internet age, it wasn't easy to find a community if you wanted to break out of your family, particularly if you were attracted to members of your own sex, or liked to cross-dress. As a teenager in the 1970s, I made my way to the local public library, where I found a medical textbook that told me all about the lurid world of homosexuality. Those scary pictures of naked people looking plaintively at the camera, arrayed like mugshots, probably set my own coming out process back at least a decade. Who would want to live such a sad, lonely life? College wasn't much better. In the late 1970s, none of my courses—I was a history major, and took lots of anthropology and sociology— mentioned queerness. And I was too scared to search for "abnormal psychology." Eventually, I ended up in

San Francisco, and joined a support group, basically a coming-out group, found my way to lesbian bars, and all was well.

During those pre-Internet days, even though I knew that I was attracted to other women, it took ages to admit it to myself, and even longer to act on it—until I found a subculture of my own. The fact that there was at least a five-year gap between that first realization to the time I eventually used the L-word to describe myself would be unthinkable today. The Internet has made it possible to articulate one's desires in the privacy of one's home, or childhood bedroom, and find others who share that interest practically instantly. Googling "1 am a girl but feel like a boy" turns up over eight million results.

***

To the outside observer, these young people seem extraordinarily willing to share the deepest aspects of their private lives—and even over-share, at times. When he first saw these videos on YouTube, sociologist Sal Johnston, a member of an earlier cohort of transgender men, admits that he thought their publicness would invite voyeurism, disdain, and mockery. "Why would you do that?" he recalls asking himself, he tells me. But today's young people lead lives online. Millennials who openly narrate their experiences online, even experiences that are at odds with the vast majority of those around them, are downright normal.

Young people's online and offline lives blur into one another. Many of them assume, too, that the sheer volume of information available online means that only like-minded others would be interested in viewing their videos, and that those who lack a direct investment in such concerns would have little interest in them.

While few barriers to public gawking actually exist, norms of mutual respect generally seem to operate on transgender vlog sites. "In networked publics, interactions are often public by default, private through effort," writes media theorist danah boyd. "What's at stake is not whether someone can listen in but whether one should."[2] Even though transgender vlogs tend to be open for all to see, the over 50 videos that I looked at revealed only a half dozen instances of negative feedback. In each of these cases, a member of the community, or an ally, came to the defense of those who were attacked. When someone named Ethan posted a vlog of his flattened chest, discussing the virtues of a particular type of chest binder, and was taunted: "If your [sic] a dude why can't you show your chest?" another viewer responded in Ethan's defense: "If you think it is wrong and/or nasty, then why would you search for it to begin with? Ethan is not a woman, he's a man. . . you deal with it."

Responding to one of Kye's videos, a viewer writes: "Ok so, I'm not FTM or MTF but my boyfriend is FTM and watching your videos has helped me. Thank you so much, and keep up the great Vlog." She adds: "PS. You're great for starting these to help people. Not just to bitch or try to get famous. You're an amazing guy, and I appreciate you!" Another viewer writes: "You inspire me beyond belief. Maybe one day I can come out, too."

A year after he began posting videos on YouTube, Kye underwent top surgery; his final video documents the effects of testosterone on his changing body. Today, Kye, an art student studying illustration, lives full-time as male, and no longer posts videos online. But only a few years ago, his vlog was a lifeline, enabling him to publicly document his transition and help others to do the same.

In theory, individual vloggers can control their privacy settings, deciding which videos to share and which to keep private. But creating boundaries around online spaces is difficult. The greater the number of viewers, the less isolated vloggers feel, and the more information they are able to share. For those who participate in these networked publics, coming out online can be personally powerful.

In their everyday lives, transgender people must be acutely aware of how they appear to others, particularly when they use bathrooms and travel through public places. Transgender women are particularly vulnerable to what sociologist Laurel Westbrook and Kristen Schilt call "penis panics"—perceptions of sexual threat in gender-segregated spaces such as bathrooms. Trans women are particularly threatening, they write, because they present the "terror of penises where they 'should not' be." In contrast, transgender men are seen as a sexual threat mainly insofar as they are a "source of homosexual contamination to heterosexual cis women." According to Westbrook and Schilt, trans men's "perceived lack of a natural penis renders them biologically female" and therefore "unable to be highly sexually threatening."[3]

Once they are perceived by others as men, transgender men report that they may be subject to homophobic violence from cisgender men who see them as insufficiently masculine. Black trans men also report feeling vulnerable when in the presence of men in positions of institutional power, such as police, according to interviews with 49 transgender men in the Midwestern and Western US conducted by sociologist Miriam Adelson.[4] Much of the violence directed against transgender men, in other words, is very similar in character to that which is directed against men in general. Men police other men, often in violent ways. "Moment to moment, day to day, you have to be careful," Sal Johnston tells me. "It's an exhausting way to live."

By openly narrating their lives on YouTube, young trans men are throwing off their internalized shame and making a claim for attention in a world where attention-getting is key to self-making. They have grown up with reality television and social media, in an age of publicity. Young people understand the search for attention as normal—and inseparable from our "brand culture," according to communications scholar Sarah Banet-Weiser. Brand relationships, she argues, have become cultural contexts for everyday living, individual identity, and personal relationships.[5]

FTM transition vlogs are a mash-up of coming out stories, *Consumer Reports* product reviews, and reality television self-revelations. Short, personal, and informational, they are embedded in the commercial culture in which they have sprouted, appearing next to videos instructing viewers on "How to get a flat stomach in a week," or ads for Epson printers, exemplifying the freedoms as well as constraints of self-making with new media. Those who master the art of attention-getting have some potential to earn money by directing traffic to ads and becoming "content management partners." Brandon has posted 43 videos, has 177 subscribers, and a YouTube channel of his own. "I have about four guys who are going to be doing videos," he says, "I'm still going to be doing videos here, and also on our channel. A 13-year-old is our youngest." He meets lots of his "buddies" online, he says, and plans "to get a couple more guys so that we can have a video every day."[6]

"The Internet changes everything," says Jamison Green, who organized FTM support groups in San Francisco in the 1980s the old-fashioned way—face to face. It breaks down barriers and allows people to communicate with others privately, but also enables them to be seen if they wish. An increasing number of younger people, so-called "digital natives," are completely at home in social media. They have never known a time before it was possible to access a deluge of information about what people are consuming, what they look like, what they're thinking. While peer groups have historically played an important role in exchanging information about the emotional, social and medical aspects of transitioning, it was not until those who were questioning their gender seized upon the Internet, and social media, in the 1990s, that the movement really took off. The Internet has enabled younger people to "break down barriers." Green (who is in his mid-60s) acknowledges. "It's had a huge impact," opening up possibilities for people to stand apart from their families and communities.

Green wonders whether social media also "creates a sense of isolation for people," and enables questionable information to enter circulation far too easily.

On the Internet, "you don't know if the advice you're getting is reasonable or not," he tells me. "It's very, very difficult to suss that out with the cold frame of the screen." He remembers how special, and at times electrifying, it has felt at times to sit across from someone you hardly know and utter a statement like "I think I am a man," and then spend the next hour with that person, and ten other people one barely knows, to process that information and use it to imagine alternative ways of being in the world.

Face to face gatherings have their problems, Green acknowledges, and some transgender support groups exert pressure on individuals who are gender questioning to "go all the way" and undergo a gender transition. Others send the message to certain individuals that "they are not masculine enough" or "trans enough." Still, he believes that there's no substitute for the physical presence of others.

NOTES

1. danah boyd, *It's Complicated: The Social Lives of Networked Teens.* New Haven: Yale University Press, 2014, 9.

2. danah boyd, *It's Complicated: The Social Lives of Networked Teens,* 58.

3. Laurel Westbrook and Kristen Schilt, "Penis Panics," in *Exploring Masculinities,* edited by C. J. Pascoe and Tristan Bridges. Oxford: Oxford University Press, 2016, 385, 387.

4. Miriam Abelson, "Negotiating Vulnerabilty and Fear," in Pascoe and Bridges, eds., *Exploring Masculinities,* 395.

5. Banet-Weiser, Sarah. *Authentic™: The Politics of Ambivalence in a Brand Culture.* New York: New York University Press, 2012.

6. Data were collected in May 2014.

THINKING ABOUT THE READING

According to Stein, what are "networked publics"? What role do they play in the impression management process for trans men? What role do they play in building community? What is unique about the online participation of Millennials? How does it compare to past generations and time periods?

Blue Chip Blacks

Managing Race in Public Spaces

KARYN R. LACY

(2007)

"They're trying to be like the whites instead of being who they are," Andrea Creighton, a forty-three-year-old information analyst with the federal government, told me when I asked whether she believed blacks had made it in the United States or still had a long way to go. Andrea is black, and she perceives irrepressible distinctions between middle-class blacks and whites, even though many aspects of her life appear to reflect membership in the suburban middle-class mainstream. She and her husband, Greg, have two teenage children: a girl, age seventeen, and a boy, age fifteen. They have lived on a quiet street in Sherwood Park, an upper-middle-class suburb of Washington, D.C., for seven years. Their four-bedroom home is an imposing red-brick-front colonial with shiny black shutters, nestled on an acre of neatly manicured lawn. The children are active members of the local soccer team, and Greg is one of the team's coaches. Andrea and her husband each drive midsize cars and have provided their daughter, who is old enough to drive unaccompanied by an adult, with her own car. At first blush, they seem nearly identical to their white middle-class counterparts. But unlike the nearly all-white neighborhood that the average middle-class white family calls home, the Creightons' upscale subdivision is predominantly black. Andrea and Greg are pleased that their children are growing up in a community filled with black professionals. The Creightons' residence in Sherwood Park is one indication of the kind of social differentiation Andrea employs to define her identity as a member of the black middle class. Though she shares many lifestyle characteristics with mainstream whites, she feels that middle-class blacks are not mirror images of middle-class whites, nor should they aspire to be.

In terms of occupational status, educational attainment, income, and housing, the top segment of the black middle class is equal to the white middle class. The key distinction between the white and black middle classes is thus a matter of degree. Middle-class whites fit the public image of the middle class and may therefore take their middle-class status for granted, but blacks who have "made it" must work harder, more deliberately, and more consistently to make their middle-class status known to others.

Instances of discrimination against blacks in stores, in the workplace, and in other public spaces occur every day, unobserved by potential sympathizers and unreported by black victims. As sociologist Joe Feagin's gripping study of the black middle-class experience shows, middle-class status does not automatically shield blacks from discrimination by whites in public spaces (Feagin 1991). His interviewees' reports of being denied seating in restaurants, accosted while shopping, and harassed by police officers lead Feagin to conclude that a middle-class status does not protect blacks from the threat of racial discrimination. Feagin's study documents the formal and informal mechanisms that contribute to persistent discrimination toward blacks in the public sphere. His perspective, which has been invaluable in shedding light on the dynamics of racial stratification in the United States, suggests that contemporary patterns of discrimination often prevent accomplished blacks from enjoying the taken-for-granted privileges associated with a middle-class status, such as a leisurely dinner out or a carefree shopping experience.

This study demonstrates that despite the ever-present possibility of stigmatization, not all middle-class blacks feel as overwhelmed by and as ill-equipped to grapple with perceived discrimination as racial stigma theory implies. Some perceive themselves as active agents capable of orchestrating public interactions with whites to their advantage in a variety of public settings. Study participants from Lakeview, Riverton, and Sherwood Park describe how the strategic deployment of cultural capital, including language, mannerisms, clothing, and credentials, allows them to create what I call *public identities* that effectively lessen or short-circuit potential discriminatory treatment.

White Americans typically equate race with class and then reflexively consign all blacks to the lowest class levels. The experiences of middle-class blacks in my study suggest that those who actively correct the misapprehensions of white strangers reduce the likelihood of discriminatory treatment. This invocation of a public identity is a deliberate, conscious act—one that entails psychological costs as well as rewards. As Charlotte, an elementary school teacher and Lakeview resident, explains, black people "have two faces," and learn to distinguish self-presentation strategies suitable in the white world from self-presentation strategies useful in the black world.

Most middle-class whites, on the other hand, pay little overt attention to their own race or class. For them, most activities such as shopping, working as a manager, or buying a house are routinized, psychologically neutral, and relatively conflict free. Public challenges to their class status are rare. Middle-class blacks face a different reality. When they leave the familiarity of their upscale suburban communities, many of the accoutrements associated with their middle-class lifestyle fade from view. Skin color persists. On occasions when race trumps class, blacks' everyday interactions with white store clerks, real estate agents, and office subordinates can become exercises in frustration or humiliation or both. Asserting public identities makes it possible for blacks to tip the balance of a public interaction so that class trumps race. Blacks who successfully bring their middle-class status firmly into focus pressure white strangers and workplace subordinates to adjust their own behaviors in light of this information. Public identities, then, are not so much prepared responses that permit individuals to skillfully avoid or ignore strangers or social deviants when in public as they are strategies for sustaining problem-free interactions involving strangers. The use of public identities allows some middle-class blacks to complete their shopping without being accosted by store clerks or security guards, to supervise workplace subordinates effectively, and to disarm hostile real estate agents.

Constructing Public Identities: Boundary-Work in the Public Sphere

A key component of the public identities asserted by middle-class blacks is based on class and involves differentiating themselves from lower-class blacks through what I call *exclusionary* boundary-work.

Washington-area middle-class blacks are firm in their belief that it is possible to minimize the probability of encountering racial discrimination if they can successfully convey their middle-class status to white strangers. To accomplish this feat, interviewees attempt to erect exclusionary boundaries against a bundle of stereotypes commonly associated with lower-class blacks. Exclusionary boundary-work is most readily apparent when middle-class blacks are shopping or managing employees in the workplace. Middle-class blacks also engage in *inclusionary* boundary-work in order to blur distinctions between themselves and white members of the middle class by emphasizing areas of consensus and shared experience. Efforts to highlight overlaps with the white middle class are common when middle-class blacks engage in house-hunting activities.

The construction and assertion of public identities varies according to social context and the basis of perceived discrimination. In the context of shopping, the middle-class blacks in this study perceive that race bias is operational, that is, that there is a failure by others to distinguish them from the black poor. Specifically, they know that whites wrongly assume that blacks are poor and that the poor are likely to be shoplifters. Consequently, when shopping, these middle-class blacks confront the stereotype of the street-savvy black shoplifter, which white store clerks often apply to blacks as a group. To disassociate themselves from this negative image and signal that they "belong" in the store (i.e., that they have money, can afford the merchandise, and have no need to steal), study participants report that they dress with care. "People make decisions about you based on how you're dressed and what you look like," Michelle says. "Because I know that," she elaborates, "I choose my dress depending on what the environment is." Interviewees contend that their decisions to eschew clothing associated with urban popular culture—for example, oversized gold earrings, baggy jeans, and designer tennis shoes—maximize their chances of enjoying a trouble-free shopping experience and signal their respectability to white strangers. This kind of exclusionary boundary-work helps middle-class blacks establish *social differentiation*—they make clear to store personnel that they are *not* like the poor.

Evidence of social differentiation emerges in the workplace as well. Just as the professions have used educational credentials to limit membership and to bring legitimacy to their discipline, professional blacks underscore their authority as managers by highlighting credentials such as job title and professional status. Holding positions of power, interviewees believe, makes them impervious to workplace discrimination.

In the context of house-hunting, middle-class blacks perceive that class, rather than race bias, operates. In order to maximize their range of residential options, public identities are constructed to be linked in an inclusionary manner with their white counterparts. With the dominant cultural code in mind, middle-class blacks rely on mainstream language and mannerisms to carry out interactions with real estate agents. In cases in which these interactions break down, respondents use their own resources and social networks to find an acceptable home on their own. Put simply, middle-class blacks engage in inclusionary boundary-work to establish *social unity*—to show that middle-class blacks are much like the white middle-class. These identity construction processes are mutually reinforcing in that they each help to affirm respondents' position as legitimate members of the American middle class.

Cultural Capital and Cultural Literacy

Cultural capital, a key signifier of middle-class status, constitutes the means by which public identities are staked out. Cultural capital theorists argue that an important mechanism in the reproduction of inequality is a lack of exposure to dominant cultural codes, behaviors, and practices (Bourdieu and Passeron 1977). Middle-class blacks have obviously secured a privileged position in the occupational structure. But cultural capital differs from such economic capital in that cultural capital indicates a "proficiency in and familiarity with dominant cultural codes and practices—for example, linguistic styles, aesthetic preferences, styles of interaction" (Aschaffenburg and Maas 1997). These signifiers of middle-class status are institutionalized and taken for granted as normative, hence the underlying assumption that groups that cannot activate cultural capital fall victim to systematic inequality.

The majority of the blacks in this study are first-generation middle-class or grew up in working-class families; therefore, they could not acquire cultural

capital through the process outlined by Bourdieu. They were not in a position to inherit from their parents the ability to signal their class position to whites via mainstream cultural resources because their parents either did not have access to middle-class cultural resources or they had views about black-white interaction that were informed by Jim Crow laws and other pillars of racial segregation. The few interviewees who did grow up in the middle class question how much their parents, who went about their everyday lives almost exclusively in black communities, could have effectively prepared them to negotiate routine interactions with whites as equals.

The blacks in my study were not endowed with the cultural capital useful in managing interactions with whites through their families of origin. As children, they were compelled to figure out these negotiations on their own through their immersion in white colleges, workplaces, and educational institutions, without involving their parents or other adults. They did so through two socialization processes that facilitate the construction of public identities: improvisation and script-switching.

Improvisations Socialization

During childhood, the blacks in this study were socialized into a set of informal strategies that allowed them to negotiate on their own the racial discrimination they faced at that time. In contrast to their parents' strategies of avoidance, deference, and unwillingness to confront authority, interviewees were more likely to fight back surreptitiously. For example, they often challenged indirectly the authority of white teachers and authority figures. When these middle-class blacks employed improvisational strategies, they left the impression that they were obeying the rules when they were, in fact, circumventing rules and established practices. This phenomenon is typified by Brad, who told me how a white guidance counselor had discouraged his applying to college: "My high school counselor told me that I should not go to Michigan because I probably wouldn't make it, and I should go to a trade school. [That way] I would have a job, [and] I could support my family." He pauses, visibly upset. Then, with sarcasm, he adds, "She was great."

I asked him, "This was a black woman telling you this?" He answered, "Uh-uh, she was a white woman.

Miss Blupper. I remember her name." Miss Blupper's lack of confidence in Brad's intellectual ability made him even more determined to go to college. Brad acquired on his own a knowledge of college rankings and the admissions process that his guidance counselor was unwilling to provide. He ended up graduating from high school early to attend the University of Michigan and went on to become a judge.

In addition to being discouraged from pursuing a college track by high school teachers, middle-class blacks frequently faced white teachers who were heavily invested in symbolically maintaining the racial boundaries that had been dismantled by desegregation policy. Looking back on his tenure as class president during his junior year at the predominantly white high school, Greg remembers that the tradition dictating who should escort the homecoming queen was abandoned by his white teacher when she realized that he was slotted to escort a white girl:

> My junior year in high school there was always the tradition that the juniors put on the prom for the seniors. . . . I was the class president, and I was 'spose to escort the queen. . . . Well, they made an exception that year. [He laughs.] Basically they said, well, they'd let me and my date lead the parade, and the queen and everybody else [were to] follow behind. Well, you know how I am, I'm saying, "What's up with this?" I'm 'spose to walk the queen, but the queen's white. They didn't want me walking a white queen. I guess they didn't want this black guy walking in with this white queen. So it's really funny that the girl that I happened to be dating at that time, she had naturally red hair, and [she was] just as white as almost snow. But she was black! Yeah, she was a black girl! [He laughs.] . . . So, anyway, I said, "I'll take her to the prom. I'll fake 'em all out." So I'm leading the prom, me [and the girl], we're going to the prom together. So nobody knew anything; so me and [the girl] showed up, and my, my, my, you talking about fine [attractive]!

Greg decided to "pay back" the teacher not by using official channels and reporting her to higher authorities or by insisting that in fact he would escort the white queen as tradition dictated, but by devising a scheme on his own that would both expose the absurdity of the black-white boundary and preserve his dignity. Brad also circumvented official channels in his quest for a college education.

By the time he entered high school, Greg possessed an insider's knowledge of mainstream culture; he knew whites would be baffled by the apparent racial identity of his fair-skinned date. He acquired this familiarity with dominant codes and practices through exposure to white cultural norms in integrated settings, settings that required him to manage interactions with whites. Greg improvised strategies for managing these interactions as the specific conflict arose, yet these incidents prepared him, as I will demonstrate, for later experiences with racial discrimination.

Script-Switching

Script-switching processes refer to the strategies middle-class blacks employ to demonstrate that they are knowledgeable about middle-class lifestyles and to communicate their social position to others.

Scholars now recognize that blacks and whites tend to "behave" different kinds of scripts. For example, Thomas Kochman observed that blacks tend to communicate in an "emotionally intense, dynamic, and demonstrative" style, whereas whites tend to communicate in a "more modest and emotionally constrained" style (Kochman 1981:106). Of course, Kochman's schema is a generalization of these racial groups. There are whites and blacks who do not fit neatly into the categories he lays out. But these exceptions do not erase the powerful impact of these stereotypes on everyday interactions across the color line. Because public interactions are governed by mainstream scripts, middle-class blacks are compelled to switch from black scripts to white scripts in public spaces. Thus, public interactions require a different presentation of self than those asserted in majority-black spaces. In short, the middle-class blacks sometimes downplay their racial identities in public interactions with whites. Jasmine is short, with a bouncy haircut in the shape of a trendy bob. She seems taller than she actually is because she is extroverted and somewhat bossy, whereas her husband Richard is quiet and shy. Jasmine, now forty-five, describes how she felt compelled to script-switch as a teenager when her parents enrolled her in a predominantly white high school:

> I remember wanting to do "the white thing" when I was there. I had iodine and baby oil, trying to get a tan, and why wasn't [my] hair blowing in the wind? They [the white girls] would be shaving their legs and that type of thing, and most African American girls aren't that particular. I felt I needed to be a part of them, I needed to do their thing. . . . To this day, I think I made the blend [between two cultures] pretty decent because I have plenty of friends who just hate going back to our high school reunion. They just see no purpose [in going], but I enjoyed it because I participated in everything. . . . I was homecoming queen, I was in their beauty pageant when no other black person would dare to be in their pageant. I was like, "If you can do it, I can do it!"

Charlotte, speaking with admiration of a worker in a predominantly white school system with very few other black teachers, outlined how a black male art teacher who declined to script-switch was harassed by the white principal. "[The] white principal can't *stand* him, and I think it's because he's this big, black guy, and he's loud. You know, 'Hey, how ya doing!' Kind of like that. He's real down to earth, and I think they're kind of envious of him, because he's been in books, he's been in the [*Washington*] *Post*, he's been on TV, and they're trying to get their little doctorates. And they're always demeaning him. . . . They are just awful to him."

According to Charlotte, this teacher is subjected to a different set of evaluation criteria than the other teachers working at the school. But because Charlotte and the few other black teachers have not been mistreated in the ways that she observes the black male teacher has been, Charlotte feels that the white principal is reacting not so much to the art teacher's race as to his refusal to display the appropriate command of cultural capital—in short, to switch scripts. By Charlotte's account, the white principal interprets the art teacher's behavior as gauche, even though there

may be no basis for this conclusion aside from the teacher's refusal to engage a white script. "He kinda doesn't make the—he's an artist, and he's eccentric, and he's just *him*, and he doesn't do the bullshit." Charlotte added parenthetically, "And see . . . they want that, they want him to do that."

As Charlotte's narrative makes clear, some middle-class blacks believe that social acceptance in the public sphere is contingent upon their ability to script-switch. They believe that they are less likely to be hassled in white settings if they are willing to script-switch. Blacks who refuse to do so or are uncomfortable doing so may be penalized, just as the teacher at Charlotte's school was targeted.

Asserting Public Identities

Undoubtedly, all persons attempting to cross class boundaries have to spend time thinking about clothing, language, tastes, and mannerisms; they risk being identified as a member of a lower class if they make a mistake. Concerns among the socially mobile about needing to properly appropriate the general skills and cultural styles of the middle class in a convincing way are well-documented in the sociological literature and in fictional accounts. However, middle-class blacks' ambiguous position in the racial hierarchy means that they have to spend more time thinking about what they will wear in public, work harder at pulling off a middle-class presentation of self, and be more demonstrative at it than white middle-class people who are also exhibiting their status and negotiating for deference. Moreover, while the fault line for upwardly mobile whites today is strictly class, middle-class blacks must negotiate class boundaries as well as the stereotypes associated with their racial group. In this section, I demonstrate how public identities are put to work in three public spaces, each with its own distinct pattern of black-white interaction. While shopping and in the workplace, these middle-class blacks employ public identities to establish their distinctiveness from the black poor and from subordinate workers. In the context of house-hunting, middle-class blacks perceive that class bias operates; therefore, public identities are constructed to establish their overlap with the white middle class.

Exclusionary Boundary-Work

Shopping

An obvious way for middle-class blacks to signal their class position is through physical appearance.

In real terms, this would mean selecting clothing that contrasts sharply with the attire associated with black popular culture. Philip, who wears a suit to his job as a corporate executive, observed: "Being black is a negative, particularly if you're not lookin' a certain way. You . . . go in an elevator dressed in what I have on now [he is wearing a blue polo shirt and white shorts], white women start holding their pocketbooks. But if I'm dressed like I normally go to work, then it's fine."

Philip implies that he can control the extent to which he will be evaluated on the basis of whites' stereotypes about poor blacks by the type of clothing he decides to wear to the store. If Philip decides to assert his public identity, he will shop in his suit. Once he begins to make purchases, additional signifiers of his social status such as credit cards and zip code assure the store clerk that he is a legitimate member of the middle class. Through his performance, Philip believes that he annuls a stigmatized racial identity. He believes that when he is dressed as a professional, whites see his class status first and respond to him as a member of that social group.

The assurance of these additional middle-class signifiers allows middle-class blacks to occasionally engage in subversive expressions of their class identity, much to their delight. Terry complained that store clerks react negatively to blacks who are "dressed down" under the assumption that they cannot afford to buy anything. "Going into a store, somebody follows you around the store. But [store clerks] don't help you [at all] if you go into a specialty store. They just refuse to walk up to you. Then you see a white person walk in and they immediately run to help them." However, as a member of the middle class, Terry is pleased that she has the leisure time and the requisite skills to voice a complaint:

Now lately I will write a complaint. I will find out who owns the store and write a complaint. Before I used to just tell the [salesperson, "I guess you didn't know who walked into your store. It's a shame that you treat people like this because you

don't know how much money I have." I love going to expensive stores in jeans and a T-shirt. Because they don't know how much money you have. And, you know, I may have a thousand dollars to give away that day. [She laughs.] They just don't know. And the way people treat you, I think it's a shame, based on your appearance.

Convinced that a store clerk ignored her because her clothing belied her actual class status, Terry went on to test her suspicion by varying the style of clothing that she sports while shopping. Terry enjoys "dressing down," but this subversive presentation of self appears to be enjoyable precisely because she can shed this role at a moment's notice, reassuming her actual middle-class identity. She then drew on her resources as a member of the middle class to file a formal complaint.

Because their performance as members of the middle class is perceived as legitimate when they are clothed in a way that signifies their social status, these blacks believe that using this strategy helps them to avoid the discrimination that blacks of a lower-class status experience. This perception is illustrated by Michael, a stylish corporate manager who suggested that his appearance, coupled with his Sherwood Park zip code and his assets, lead others to draw the conclusion that he is middle-class. He boasted, "When I apply for anything [that requires using] credit, I just give my name, address. . . . You have to fill out the credit application . . . you put your address down there, then you put down your collateral, IRA, all that stuff. So I don't know if I've been discriminated against that way. I mean, I can go to the store and buy what I want to buy."

In cases of racial discrimination, blacks are typically precluded from achieving a desired goal, such as obtaining a desired product or entering a particular establishment. Since middle-class blacks in this study enter stores and "buy what they want to buy, (when they are dressed in a manner that reflects their social status), they conclude that they have not experienced racial discrimination.

This suggests that when interviewees "buy what they want to buy" without interference from whites, they have successfully conveyed their class position to store clerks.

Others also suggested that when middle-class blacks are dressed down, that is, not engaging public identities, their shopping experience is often extremely unpleasant. Michelle attempted to shop while dressed down, and was dismissed by the store clerk: "I went somewhere and they tried to tell me how I couldn't afford something . . . I was in the mood to buy. They were saying, 'Well, it might cost this or that.' I mean I went there seriously looking to shop. But I wasn't dressed that way." In response to my question, "Was it clothing or race?" Michelle looked slightly puzzled, as if she hadn't consider this possibility, then waffled as to the explanation for the store clerk's behavior:

> Probably a mixture of both, I don't know. See, I don't know what it's like to be white and dressed poorly and [to] try and buy something. I've always had in my mind where someone told me that you could wear holey jeans as long as you have on two-hundred-dollar shoes. People know that you got money. That's when you're worried about what people think about you. But, you know, on a relaxed day, I don't care what they [white people] think. You either have the money or you don't.

Sorting out the store clerk's motivation is difficult for Michelle in part because whites' stereotypes of the face of poverty are conflated with race. When most whites think abstractly about the middle class, they see a white family, not a black one. This same image leads whites to associate poverty with blacks. In order for whites to believe that the blacks appearing before them are middle-class, they would have to erase the indelible image linking the concept "middle class" exclusively to whites. Middle-class blacks in the Washington, D.C., area convey this status by engaging their public identity, expressed through clothing that signals their middle-class status to others. In the workplace, middle-class blacks focus on a different form of cultural capital—professional title and credentials—to minimize racial tension in the workplace and to underscore their position as managers or supervisors.

The Workplace

Perhaps no public setting better reflects the cultural styles and preferences of the American mainstream than the corporate world. As Feagin and Sikes observe in *Living with Racism*, blacks "in corporate America are under constant pressure to adapt . . . to the values and ways of the white word" (Feagin and Sikes 1994: 135).

White colleagues and clients still register surprise when they encounter corporate blacks who speak intelligently about the topic at hand, black managers still confront "glass ceilings," and black managers still endure subjective critiques assessing their "fit" with the corporate culture. I focus here on two such problems faced by black managers today: managing white subordinates and negotiating racial disputes. Like shopping sites, workplace settings are characterized by a low regard for black cultural styles. According to Mary Jackman, many whites perceive black cultural styles as "inappropriate for occupational tasks involving responsibility or authority" (Jackman 1994: 130). This means that black managers' credibility resides in their ability to switch to the script associated with white cultural styles. Therefore, in the workplace, black managers assert public identities by demonstrating their command of the cultural capital appropriate for their title or position. Indeed, they must, since the workplace experiences of middle-class blacks are characterized by frequent episodes of discriminatory treatment.

Michael, a corporate manager, has a dry sense of humor and enjoys putting people in their place. He established his role as an authority figure at the outset by highlighting impermeable boundaries between himself and his receptionist. One such boundary is the telephone. Clearly annoyed, Michael explained, "The receptionist, always bitches about answering telephones, but that's her job. She's the receptionist. I ain't never gonna answer the telephone." Michael does not answer his own telephone because his conception of a manager means that subordinates handle mundane details such as phone messages. Answering the phone would reduce his social status to that of a subordinate.

In his position as corporate manager, Michael says he has never experienced any racial discrimination. He attributes this feat to the weight of his title and his ability to utilize it. "On *this* job . . . I always came in with some authority. Hey, you know, like, 'I'm corporate manager. You all can do whatever you want to do, but remember, I'm the one that signs [off]. I'm the one that signs.' And, when you're the one that signs, you got the power. So even if they don't like you, they got to smile, which is okay by me." Greg used a similar strategy with white employees who resented having to work under him after his company was awarded a lucrative contract. He begins to smile as he remembers how he handled the conflict:

> There are two folks that I know of that are stone redneck. I mean they're the biggest rednecks you ever did see. They now came over to work for me. They couldn't accept that. So we had several briefings and I said, "Okay, here's how we're gonna do this and here's how we're gonna work." Well, the people they work for . . . were also big rednecks, so they just sort of go along together. Well, they refused— not openly refused, but just subtly. They wouldn't come to meetings. . . . I ended up basically saying to them, "Look, y'all can do what you want to do. But when it comes time for bonuses, and it comes time for yearly wages and all that kind of stuff, now you can go to Jim [white supervisor who reports to Greg], and he can tell you what to do and y'all can go do it. But if he doesn't tell me that you did it, I won't know. So when it comes time for your annual evaluation, I'll just say, 'Didn't do nothing.' So, it's y'all's fault." Well, then they sort of opened up.

In contrast to previous studies of middle-class blacks in the workplace, those surveyed here feel empowered to negotiate workplace discrimination. Situated in positions of power, middle-class blacks rely on public identities—for example, their role as supervisor or manager—to solidify their identities as persons of considerable social status. Once their status is established, these middle-class blacks are in a position to extinguish racial conflicts in the workplace. In other instances, middle-class blacks decide that such effort is "not worth it," and juxtapose the pleasant aspects of their high-status occupations against such racial incidents as they arise. Though racial discrimination in the workplace has hardly disappeared, black professionals have become more adept at using class-based resources to resolve these kinds of conflicts.

Inclusionary Boundary-Work

House-Hunting

In *American Apartheid*, Douglas Massey and Nancy Denton argue that middle-class blacks have not had the opportunity to live wherever they want, to live "where people of their means and resources usually locate" (Massey and Denton 1993:138). They conclude that a major factor in blacks' exclusion is racial discrimination by real estate agents, who serve as the "gatekeepers" of predominantly white neighborhoods to which blacks, even those with the requisite resources, seldom gain entry.

Yet middle-class blacks interviewed for this study insist that one of the benefits of being middle-class is the option of living in any neighborhood one desires. Their housing decisions are no longer restricted by the behavior of real estate agents. John, who chose the majority-black but upper-middle-class Sherwood Park community, explained, "We could have lived anywhere we wanted to. We could have afforded to live a lot of different places, but we chose here." He and most of the middle-class blacks in this study minimize the likelihood that they have experienced racial discrimination while house-hunting because, in so many other aspects of their lives, they use class-based resources to secure a desired good. How do blacks use their public identity while house-hunting? To manage their interactions with white real estate agents, these middle-class blacks place a good deal of emphasis on displays of cultural capital—particularly appropriate clothing, apt language, and knowledge of the housing market. Yet house-hunting is a more complicated site for the construction and use of public identity because in house-hunting, unlike shopping and the workplace, respondents are unsure as to whether real estate agents are responding to their race or their class.

The preoccupation with presenting a middle-class appearance is evident in Lydia's description of her experience while viewing a model home in a predominantly white suburban subdivision located in the same greater metropolitan area where she and her husband eventually bought a home.

In response to the question "Have you ever experienced racial discrimination while house-hunting?" Lydia replied:

> I guess I never really thought about that in terms of racial, but economically, I think I have been. I tend not to be a person that dresses up. [She chuckles.] A couple times I've gone looking for houses and I'll just wear sweatpants. And you go out looking for a house that's in expensive neighborhoods, I

don't know what they expect me to drive up in. That has nothing to do with how much money I have in the bank. And I've had that happen . . . a couple times. . . . I went to a house. . . . I don't know what we were driving, probably an old beat-up car. So I pull into the driveway, and I had on sweatpants, my [baseball] hat, I go in and see the house. I'd asked [the real estate agent] about the house, asked her for the information, and I said I wanted to take a tour. She immediately said to me, "Is this your price range?" [Dramatic pause.] I asked her how much was the house. She told me, and it was my price range, no big deal. I asked, "Was this a black real estate agent?" Lydia answered, "White. She wanted to discuss my income before she would show me the house. Basically, I told her I'll take a look at the house, and I'll let her know when I'm finished."

Lydia felt that the real estate agent was attempting to discourage her from viewing the house. However, she believed that her choice of clothing, her baseball hat, and her old car all signaled the wrong social class status to the agent—not that the agent objected to black home-seekers. I attempted to clarify the kind of discrimination Lydia felt she had experienced by posing a follow-up question: "Is that standard procedure? Do real estate agents normally ask you how much you make before they show you the house?" Lydia responded, shaking her head slightly from side to side, "No, no. I had been looking at lots and lots of houses. And I *knew* what she was doing. It was her way of saying, 'Oh, *God*, who is this person coming in here?' Because when I was there, a white couple came in, and I stopped to listen to what [the agent] would say to them. None of that, none of that."

I asked, "Did they have on sweatpants too?"

"No, they were dressed up," she laughed.

I persisted, "But you think it was because you had on sweatpants, not because you were a black person?"

"I think she probably, maybe looked at me and felt maybe I didn't make enough money to afford the house. That was part of it. I'm not sure, looking at houses, that we ever experienced any kind of *racial* discrimination. Because the real estate agents

we had . . . they all took us to predominantly white neighborhoods. It wasn't that they were trying to steer us toward any type of neighborhood. They were willing to take our money anywhere." She burst into laughter.

I asked, "So do you think you could have actually bought one of those houses if you'd wanted to?"

"Oh yeah, oh yeah."

Lydia had an opportunity to test her suspicion that the real estate agent associated her with the poor when a white couple arrived to view the same home, even though the white couple had been well-dressed, not like her, and no comparison that controlled on clothing had been possible. Lydia concluded that the agent assessed the couple more favorably based on the quality of their clothing, and to support her position, Lydia identified occasions when white real estate agents had accepted her middle-class performance as a legitimate expression of who she is, showing her expensive homes in white neighborhoods.

Lydia's account illustrates the difficulty in pinpointing racial discrimination in the housing market. She did go on to view the model home. Though she was dressed in an overly casual way, Lydia used strong language to inform the real estate agent that she intended to tour the home. And the agent did not move to prevent her from walking through the model home. Consequently, in Lydia's view, the encounter did not qualify as a "racial" one. So long as they are permitted to view the homes of their choice, the middle-class blacks in this study do not perceive racial discrimination in the housing market as affecting their own housing choices.

For instance, Audrey, now sixty-four, remembers her disheartening experience with a real estate agent over twenty years ago, when she and her husband moved into the area from another city:

The agent took us down south [of the city] mostly, to . . . where more of the blacks lived . . . where they seemed to be feeding the black people that came into the area. . . . And when she started out showing us property [south of the city] . . . we told her we wanted to be closer. The things she showed us [that were closer] . . . it was gettin' worse. The properties . . . weren't as nice. So when she showed us the properties [in a black and Hispanic low-income section], we kind of like almost accepted the fact that this was what you're going to be getting.

Audrey and her family moved into the undesirable housing, but "from that day on," she said, "we never stopped looking at houses. We took it upon ourselves to continue just to look, to explore different areas." A year later, they moved to a more attractive neighborhood. Now distrustful of real estate agents, Audrey drew on cultural knowledge she'd acquired on her own—about desirable neighborhoods, schools, and the housing market in general— to locate a home in a neighborhood more suited to her family's tastes. Acquiring this kind of detailed information takes leisure time and research skills.

Greg and his wife found that their real estate agent also directed them to undesirable housing when they returned to the United States from a work assignment in Taiwan. Greg remembers:

> The agent kept showing us older homes. . . . They were ten-year-old homes, twelve-year-old homes, and they just weren't our style. . . . Some of the homes, they had beautician shops in the basement, and she thought that was a great deal, you know, you could wash, you could style your hair. And I'm thinking, "I don't need that." So Andrea [his wife] just said, "I'm not interested in those." So we came here [to Sherwood Park) just on a whim, I guess. And they had a girl [real estate agent] named [Liz], she said, "Let me show you these," and we looked at 'em. We went, "Oh," and, "Ah, yeah, okay." Then Andrea just said, "Hey, that's what I want."

In each of these examples, middle-class blacks confront discrimination from real estate agents. Audrey and her husband were steered to a section of the city where many blacks already lived. Greg and his wife were shown older, less attractive homes within their general area of choice. But the fact that these families were able to successfully find a home that did appeal to them leads them to the conclusion that widespread discrimination against blacks no longer effectively bars blacks of their social status from entering the neighborhood of their choice. Recall John's comment: "We could have lived anywhere we wanted to. . . . We chose here." When real

estate agents fail them, middle-class blacks simply find an attractive home by driving around on their own. As Audrey made clear, they "never stop looking," or they happen to find a desirable home "on a whim," as Greg and his wife did.

In cases where respondents do recognize discriminatory practices, they rely on two strategies to secure desirable housing, both of which require middle-class blacks to assert public identities. Some blacks confront real estate agents directly, the option Lydia chose when she advised the agent that she would "take a look at the house, and . . . let her know when [she had] finished." Though she was "dressed down," Lydia used unmistakable language to articulate her middle-class identity to the agent. In short, Lydia attempted to show that she belonged there, viewing the model home, just as much as the well-dressed white couple. In doing so, she relied on the class conviction that her access to cultural capital effectively challenged the real estate agent's potential roadblock.

Other middle-class blacks forgo the agent-client relationship completely, locating homes on their own as they drive through potential neighborhoods. Many already have friends living in the neighborhoods where they find their homes. Through these social networks, they are made aware of homes coming up for sale. This strategy can be likened to the self-reliant script that middle-class blacks make use of in the workplace. In the workplace, these middle-class blacks place little faith in the EEOC to resolve racial conflicts; instead, they resolve them on their own. While house-hunting, they dispense with real estate agents who are unwilling to help them find adequate housing. To locate a home on one's own requires skill and resources: a car, a working knowledge of the area's neighborhoods, leisure time to search, and so on. Thus, the middle-class blacks in this study realize that racial discrimination persists in the housing market, but they do not feel that their housing options are severely limited by it. After all, in the end, Lakeview and Riverton residents do locate a home that pleases them, and because they have no way to systematically assess whether their housing search compares unfavorably to that of their white counterparts, they tend to wave off the practices of prejudicial real estate agents as inconsequential in their housing decisions. Relying on middle-class resources and networks to negotiate these public interactions and to secure their dream home is a reasonably satisfying solution.

Conclusion

Although what makes the evening news is corporate discrimination scandals—multimillion-dollar lawsuits filed against companies accused of engaging in various forms of modern racism—the everyday instances of racial discrimination experienced by middle-class blacks warrant additional attention from scholars and the public. Feagin's racial stigma theory suggests that a middle-class standing does not protect blacks from racial discrimination. However, I have shown that this conclusion may not be invariantly true. Middle-class blacks in the Washington, D.C. area use public identities to reduce the probability that racial discrimination will determine important outcomes in their lives. By examining how public identities are employed in various public settings, we gain insight into the informal strategies blacks develop as a result of their experiences in a racialized society. These informal strategies are far more common than the occasional discrimination suits filed by blacks and profiled in the media.

Public identities constitute a form of cultural capital in which blacks with the knowledge and skills valorized by the American mainstream are in a position to manipulate public interactions to their advantage. Previous studies have not examined how high-status minority group members come to possess cultural capital. I introduced two conceptual devices to explain this process and to connect the acquisition of cultural capital to the construction and assertion of public identities in adulthood: improvisational processes and script-switching. To assert public identities, middle-class blacks first acquire cultural capital through their childhood introduction to integrated settings and through their ongoing interactions in the American mainstream, where white cultural styles rule the day. These improvisational and script-switching socialization processes allow middle-class blacks to demonstrate their familiarity with the cultural codes and practices associated with the white middle class. I also show that the cultural capital so critical to doing well in school is influential beyond the school setting as well: in shopping malls, the workplace, and to some extent, with real estate agents.

Among these middle-class blacks, projecting public identities is an opportunity to shore up their status as a group that is not merely black, but distinctly black and *middle-class*. Interviewees noted that "the world is not fair" and that "people will look at [them] in special ways because [they] are black." But these middle-class blacks also tend to associate persistent racial discrimination in public spaces with lower-class blacks, not their class grouping. As members of the middle class, they firmly believe in their ability to engage in strategies that minimize the amount and severity of discrimination directed toward their group. On the rare occasions when they believe that they do experience discrimination—from sales clerks, for example—middle-class blacks associate the incidents with an inability on their part to effectively signal their class position to store employees.

The findings presented in this chapter do not negate the racial stigma paradigm. Rather, these findings call attention to a neglected aspect of the model, namely, the mobilization of class-related strategies as a bulwark against racial discrimination. Indeed, the data suggest that social class may figure more centrally in middle-class blacks' subjective understanding of their public interactions than previous studies allow.

REFERENCES

Aschaffenburg, Karen, and Ineke Maas. 1997. "Cultural and Educational Careers: The Dynamics of Social Reproduction." *American Sociological Review* 62:573–87.

Bourdieu, Pierre, and Jean-Claude Passeron. 1977. *Reproduction in Education, Society, and Culture*. Beverly Hills, Calif.: Sage.

Feagin, Joe. 1991. "The Continuing Significance of Race: Antiblack Discrimination in Public Places." *American Sociological Review* 56: 101–16.

Feagin, Joe, and Melvin Sikes. 1994. *Living with Racism: The Black Middle-Class Experience*. Boston: Beacon Press.

Jackman, Mary. 1994. *The Velvet Glove*. Berkeley: University of California Press.

Kochman, Thomas. 1981. *Black and White Styles in Conflict*. Chicago: University of Chicago Press.

Massey, Douglas, and Nancy Denton. 1993. *American Apartheid*. Cambridge, Mass.: Harvard University Press.

THINKING ABOUT THE READING

According to Lacy, what was the key distinction between middle-class blacks and middle-class whites? What are public identities, and how did the study participants use these in their public interactions with whites? What is cultural capital, and how was it used in the creation of these public identities? What do the findings in the study mean for racial stigma theory? How might other minority groups use public identities in the architecture of their social environments?

CHAPTER 7

Building Social Relationships

Intimacy and Family

I n this culture, close, personal relationships are the standard by which we judge the quality and happiness of our everyday lives. Yet in a complex, individualistic society like ours, these relationships are becoming more difficult to establish and sustain. Although we like to think that the things we do in our relationships are completely private experiences, they are continually influenced by large-scale political interests and economic pressures. Like every other aspect of our lives, close relationships are best understood within the broader social context. Laws, customs, and social institutions often regulate the form relationships can take, our behavior in them, and even the ways in which we can exit them. At a more fundamental level, societies determine which relationships can be considered legitimate and therefore entitled to cultural and institutional recognition. Relationships that lack societal validation are often scorned and stigmatized.

If you were to ask couples applying for a marriage license why they were getting married, most, if not all, would no doubt mention the love they feel for one another. But, as Stephanie Coontz discusses in "The Radical Idea of Marrying for Love," love hasn't always been a prerequisite or even a justification for marriage. Until relatively recently, marriage was principally an economic arrangement, and love, if it existed at all, was a sometimes irrational emotion that was of secondary importance. In fact, in some past societies, falling in love before marriage was considered disruptive, even threatening, to the extended family. Today, however, it's hard to imagine a Western marriage that begins without love.

Speaking of love, gay fatherhood has presented a challenge to the socially constructed and legitimate images of paternity and masculinity in society. Even within the gay community, gay fatherhood has brought up questions around the sexual norms of gay culture. Stacey interviews gay fathers in Los Angeles to explore the growing social character of paternity and the deliberate as well as difficult terrain these men navigate as they become fathers. In the same way that Coontz shows how marriage has entered contested terrain, paths to planned parenthood for gay men are full of tensions as they negotiate both cultural and institutional recognition.

While certain groups like gay fathers have to navigate a complicated path to becoming a father, the same can be said for mixed-status couples in the United States. April M. Schueths explains that the myth of a citizenship binary is deeply harmful to couples and their families who live outside of it in contested terrain. While legal marriage is popularly thought of as a path to citizenship, scholars are finding that in many cases it creates a compromised citizenship for the citizen spouse, does not provide sufficient protections for the noncitizen spouse, and may actually create a higher risk for deportation and/or penalties for living in the U.S. as undocumented immigrants. Schueths argues that an increase in Latina/o populations has overlapped with an increase in punitive immigration laws, which has led to devastating inequalities for mixed-status couples and their families.

Something to Consider as You Read

Each of these selections emphasizes the significance of external or structural components in shaping family experiences. As you read, keep track of factors such as income level, job opportunities, citizenship status, and consider how these factors affect the choices families make. Consider some of the ways in which household income might be related to family choices. For example, consider what choices a family with a high income might have regarding how best to assist an ailing grandparent or how to deal with an unexpected teen pregnancy or in providing children with extracurricular activities. Or, how might a mixed-status couple decide whether to risk family separation to travel to family crises and celebrations. Consider how these choices are related to the appearance of traditional family values. How does legal marriage support families who have access to it? For instance, what kinds of benefits and social assistance do married couples receive that assists them in raising children? What kind of symbolic importance does legal marriage bestow? How might a redefinition of marriage impact different groups in society? How do different routes to parenthood affect the cultural and institutional recognition of families? How could public policy rectify the inequalities experienced by mixed status families?

The Radical Idea of Marrying for Love

STEPHANIE COONTZ

(2005)

The Real Traditional Marriage

To understand why the love-based marriage system was so unstable and how we ended up where we are today, we have to recognize that for most of history, marriage was not primarily about the individual needs and desires of a man and woman and the children they produced. Marriage had as much to do with getting good in-laws and increasing one's family labor force as it did with finding a lifetime companion and raising a beloved child.

Marriage, a History

Reviewing the role of marriage in different societies in the past and the theories of anthropologists and archaeologists about its origins, I came to reject two widespread, though diametrically opposed, theories about how marriage came into existence among our Stone Age ancestors: the idea that marriage was invented so men would protect women and the opposing idea that it was invented so men could exploit women. Instead, marriage spoke to the needs of the larger group. It converted strangers into relatives and extended cooperative relations beyond the immediate family or small band by creating far-flung networks of in-laws. . . .

Certainly, people fell in love during those thousands of years, sometimes even with their own spouses. But marriage was not fundamentally about love. It was too vital an economic and political institution to be entered into solely on the basis of something as irrational as love. For thousands of years the theme song for most weddings could have been "What's Love Got to Do with It?" . . .

For centuries, marriage did much of the work that markets and governments do today. It organized the production and distribution of goods and people. It set up political, economic, and military alliances. It coordinated the division of labor by gender and age. It orchestrated people's personal rights and obligations in everything from sexual relations to the inheritance of property. Most societies had very specific rules about how people should arrange their marriages to accomplish these tasks.

Of course there was always more to marriage than its institutional functions. At the end of the day—or at least in the middle of the night—marriage is also a face-to-face relationship between individuals. The actual experience of marriage for individuals or for particular couples seldom conforms exactly to the model of marriage codified in law, custom, and philosophy in any given period. But institutions do structure people's expectations, hopes, and constraints. For thousands of years, husbands had the right to beat their wives. Few men probably meted out anything more severe than a slap. But the law upheld the authority of husbands to punish their wives physically and to exercise forcibly their "marital right" to sex, and that structured the relations between men and women in *all* marriages, even loving ones.

The Radical Idea of Marrying for Love

George Bernard Shaw described marriage as an institution that brings together two people "under the influence of the most violent, most insane, most delusive, and most transient of passions. They are required to swear that they will remain in that excited, abnormal, and exhausting condition continuously until death do them part."[1]

Shaw's comment was amusing when he wrote it at the beginning of the twentieth century, and it still makes us smile today, because it pokes fun at the unrealistic expectations that spring from a dearly held cultural ideal—that marriage should be based on intense, profound love and a couple should maintain their ardor until death do them part. But for thousands of years the joke would have fallen flat.

For most of history it was inconceivable that people would choose their mates on the basis of something as fragile and irrational as love and then focus all their sexual, intimate, and altruistic desires on the resulting marriage. In fact, many historians, sociologists, and anthropologists used to think romantic love was a recent Western invention. This is not true. People have always fallen in love, and throughout the ages many couples have loved each other deeply.[2]

But only rarely in history has love been seen as the main reason for getting married. When someone did advocate such a strange belief, it was no laughing matter. Instead, it was considered a serious threat to social order.

In some cultures and times, true love was actually thought to be incompatible with marriage. Plato believed love was a wonderful emotion that led men to behave honorably. But the Greek philosopher was referring not to the love of women, "such as the meaner men feel," but to the love of one man for another.[3]

Other societies considered it good if love developed after marriage or thought love should be factored in along with the more serious considerations involved in choosing a mate. But even when past societies did welcome or encourage married love, they kept it on a short leash. Couples were not to put their feelings for each other above more important commitments, such as their ties to parents, siblings, cousins, neighbors, or God.

In ancient India, falling in love before marriage was seen as a disruptive, almost antisocial act. The Greeks thought lovesickness was a type of insanity, a view that was adopted by medieval commentators in Europe. In the Middle Ages the French defined love as a "derangement of the mind" that could be cured by sexual intercourse, either with the loved one or with a different partner.[4] This cure assumed, as Oscar Wilde once put it, that the quickest way to conquer yearning and temptation was to yield immediately and move on to more important matters.

In China, excessive love between husband and wife was seen as a threat to the solidarity of the extended family. Parents could force a son to divorce his wife if her behavior or work habits didn't please them, whether or not he loved her. They could also require him take a concubine if his wife did not produce a son. If a son's romantic attachment to his wife rivaled his parents' claims on the couple's time and labor, the parents might even send her back to her parents. In the Chinese language the term *love* did not traditionally apply to feelings between husband and wife. It was used to describe an illicit, socially disapproved relationship. In the 1920s a group of intellectuals invented a new word for love between spouses because they thought such a radical new idea required its own special label.[5]

In Europe, during the twelfth and thirteenth centuries, adultery became idealized as the highest form of love among the aristocracy. According to the Countess of Champagne, it was impossible for true love to "exert its powers between two people who are married to each other."[6]

In twelfth-century France, Andreas Capellanus, chaplain to Countess Marie of Troyes, wrote a treatise on the principles of courtly love. The first rule was that "marriage is no real excuse for not loving." But he meant loving someone outside the marriage. As late as the eighteenth century the French essayist Montaigne wrote that any man who was in love with his wife was a man so dull that no one else could love him.[7]

Courtly love probably loomed larger in literature than in real life. But for centuries, noblemen and kings fell in love with courtesans rather than the wives they married for political reasons. Queens and noblewomen had to be more discreet than their husbands, but they too looked beyond marriage for love and intimacy.

This sharp distinction between love and marriage was common among the lower and middle classes as well. Many of the songs and stories popular among peasants in medieval Europe mocked married love.

The most famous love affair of the Middle Ages was that of Peter Abelard, a well-known theologian in France, and Héloïse, the brilliant niece of a fellow churchman at Notre Dame. The two eloped without marrying, and she bore him a child. In an attempt to save his career but still placate Héloïse's furious uncle, Abelard proposed they marry in secret. This would mean that Héloïse would not be living in sin, while Abelard could still pursue his church ambitions. But Héloïse resisted the idea, arguing that marriage would not only harm his career but also undermine their love.[8] . . .

"Happily Ever After"

Through most of the past, individuals hoped to find love, or at least "tranquil affection," in marriage.[9] But nowhere did they have the same recipe for marital happiness that prevails in most contemporary Western countries. Today there is general agreement on what it takes for a couple to live "happily ever after." First, they must love each other deeply and choose each other unswayed by outside pressure. From then on, each must make the partner the top priority in life, putting that relationship above any and all competing ties. A husband and wife, we believe, owe their highest obligations and deepest loyalties to each other and the children they raise. Parents and in-laws should not be allowed to interfere in the marriage. Married couples should be best friends, sharing their most intimate feelings and secrets. They should express affection openly but also talk candidly about problems. And of course they should be sexually faithful to each other.

This package of expectations about love, marriage, and sex, however, is extremely rare. When we look at the historical record around the world, the customs of modern America and Western Europe appear exotic and exceptional. . . .

About two centuries ago Western Europe and North America developed a whole set of new values about the way to organize marriage and sexuality, and many of these values are now spreading across the globe. In this Western model, people expect marriage to satisfy more of their psychological and social needs than ever before. Marriage is supposed to be free of the coercion, violence, and gender inequalities that were tolerated in the past. Individuals want marriage to meet most of their needs for intimacy and affection and all their needs for sex.

Never before in history had societies thought that such a set of high expectations about marriage was either realistic or desirable. Although many Europeans and Americans found tremendous joy in building their relationships around these values, the adoption of these unprecedented goals for marriage had unanticipated and revolutionary consequences that have since come to threaten the stability of the entire institution.

The Era of Ozzie and Harriet: The Long Decade of "Traditional" Marriage

The long decade of the 1950s, stretching from 1947 to the early 1960s in the United States and from 1952 to the late 1960s in Western Europe, was a unique moment in the history of marriage. Never before had so many people shared the experience of courting their own mates, getting married at will, and setting up their own households. Never had married couples been so independent of extended family ties and community groups. And never before had so many people agreed that only one kind of family was "normal."

The cultural consensus that everyone should marry and form a male breadwinner family was like a steamroller that crushed every alternative view. By the end of the 1950s even people who had grown up in completely different family systems had come to believe that universal marriage at a young age into a male breadwinner family was the traditional and permanent form of marriage.

In Canada, says historian Doug Owram, "every magazine, every marriage manual, every advertisement . . . assumed the family was based on the . . . male wage-earner and the child-rearing, home-managing housewife." In the United States, marriage was seen as the only culturally acceptable route to adulthood and independence. Men who chose to remain bachelors were branded "narcissistic," "deviant," "infantile," or "pathological." Family advice expert Pat Landes argued that practically everyone, "except for the sick, the badly crippled, the deformed, the emotionally warped and the mentally defective," ought to marry. French anthropologist Martine Segalen writes that in Europe the postwar period was characterized by the overwhelming "weight of a single family model." Any departure from this model—whether it was late marriage, nonmarriage, divorce, single motherhood, or even delayed childbearing—was considered deviant. Everywhere psychiatrists agreed and the mass media affirmed that if a woman did not find her ultimate fulfillment in home-making, it was a sign of serious psychological problems.[10]

A 1957 survey in the United States reported that four out of five people believed that anyone who preferred to remain single was "sick," "neurotic," or "immoral." Even larger majorities agreed that once married, the husband should be the breadwinner and the wife should stay home. As late as 1962 one survey of young women found that almost all expected to be married by age twenty-two, most hoped to have four children, and all expected to quit work permanently when the first child was born.[11]

During the 1950s even women who had once been political activists, labor radicals, or feminists— people like my own mother, still proud of her work to free the Scottsboro Boys from legal lynching in the 1930s and her job in the shipyards during the 1940s—threw themselves into homemaking. It's hard for anyone under the age of sixty to realize how profoundly people's hunger for marriage and domesticity during the 1950s was shaped by their huge relief that two decades of depression and war were finally over and by their amazed delight at the benefits of the first real mass consumer economy in history. "It was like a miracle," my mother once told me, to see so many improvements, so quickly, in the quality of everyday life. . . .

This was the first chance many people had to try to live out the romanticized dream of a private family, happily ensconced in its own nest. They studied how the cheery husbands and wives on their favorite television programs organized their families (and where the crabby ones went wrong). They devoured articles and books on how to get the most out of marriage and their sex lives. They were even interested in advertisements that showed them how to use home appliances to make their family lives better. . . .

Today strong materialist aspirations often corrode family bonds. But in the 1950s, consumer aspirations were an integral part of constructing the postwar family. In its April 1954 issue, *McCall's* magazine heralded the era of "togetherness," in which men and women were constructing a "new and warmer way of life . . . as a family sharing a common experience." In women's magazines that togetherness was always pictured in a setting filled with modern appliances and other new consumer products. The essence of modern life, their women readers learned, was "abundance, emancipation, social progress, airy house, healthy children, the refrigerator, pasteurised milk, the washing-machine, comfort, quality and accessibility."[12] And of course marriage.

Television also equated consumer goods with family happiness. Ozzie and Harriet hugged each other in front of their Hotpoint appliances. A man who had been a young father in the 1950s told a student of mine that he had no clue how to cultivate the family "togetherness" that his wife kept talking about until he saw an episode of the sitcom *Leave It to Beaver,* which gave him the idea of washing the car with his son to get in some "father-son" time.

When people could not make their lives conform to those of the "normal" families they saw on TV, they blamed themselves—or their parents. . . . "Why didn't she clean the house in high heels and shirtwaist dresses like they did on television?"[13]

At this early stage of the consumer revolution, people saw marriage as the gateway to the good life. Americans married with the idea of quickly buying their first home, with the wife working for a few years to help accumulate the down payment or furnish it with the conveniences she would use once she became a full-time housewife. People's newfound spending money went to outfit their homes and families. In the five years after World War II, spending on food in the United States rose by a modest 33 percent and clothing expenditures by only 20 percent, but purchases of household furnishings and appliances jumped by 240 percent. In 1961, Phyllis Rosenteur, the author of an American advice book for single women, proclaimed: "Merchandise plus Marriage equals our economy."[14]

In retrospect, it's astonishing how confident most marriage and family experts of the 1950s were that they were witnessing a new stabilization of family life and marriage. The idea that marriage should provide both partners with sexual gratification, personal intimacy, and self-fulfillment was taken to new heights in that decade. Marriage was the place not only where people expected to find the deepest meaning in their lives but also where they would have the most fun. Sociologists noted that a new "fun morality," very different "from the older 'goodness morality,'" pervaded society. "Instead of feeling guilty for having too much fun, one is inclined to feel ashamed if one does not have enough." A leading motivational researcher of the day argued that the challenge for a consumer society was "to demonstrate that the hedonistic approach to life is a moral, not an immoral, one."[15]

But these trends did not cause social commentators the same worries about the neglect of societal duties that milder ideas about the pleasure principle had triggered in the 1920s. Most 1950s sociologists weren't even troubled by the fact that divorce rates were *higher* than they had been in the 1920s, when such rates had been said to threaten the very existence of marriage. The influential sociologists Ernest Burgess and Harvey Locke wrote matter-of-factly that "the companionship family relies upon divorce as a means of rectifying a mistake in mate selection."

They expressed none of the panic that earlier social scientists had felt when they first realized divorce was a permanent feature of the love-based marital landscape. Burgess and Locke saw a small amount of divorce as a safety valve for the "companionate" marriage and expected divorce rates to stabilize or decrease in the coming decades as "the services of family-life education and marriage counseling" became more widely available.[16]

The marriage counseling industry was happy to step up to the plate. By the 1950s Paul Popenoe's American Institute of Family Relations employed thirty-seven counselors and claimed to have helped twenty thousand people become "happily adjusted" in their marriages. "It doesn't require supermen or superwomen to succeed in marriage," wrote Popenoe in a 1960 book on saving marriages. "Success can be attained by almost anyone."[17]

There were a few dissenting voices. American sociologist Robert Nisbet warned in 1953 that people were loading too many "psychological and symbolic functions" on the nuclear family, an institution too fragile to bear such weight. In the same year, Mirra Komarovsky decried the overspecialization of gender roles in American marriage and its corrosive effects on women's self-confidence.[18]

But even when marriage and family experts acknowledged that the male breadwinner family created stresses for women, they seldom supported any change in its division of labor. The world-renowned American sociologist Talcott Parsons recognized that because most women were not able to forge careers, they might feel a need to attain status in other ways. He suggested that they had two alternatives. The first was to be a "glamour girl" and exert sexual sway over men. The second was to develop special expertise in "humanistic" fields, such as the arts or community volunteer work. The latter, Parsons thought, was socially preferable, posing less of a threat to society's moral standards and to a woman's own self-image as she aged. He never considered the third alternative: that women might actually win access to careers. Even Komarovsky advocated nothing more radical than expanding part-time occupations to give women work that didn't interfere with their primary role as wives and mothers.[19]

Marriage counselors took a different tack in dealing with housewives' unhappiness. Popenoe wrote dozens of marital advice books, pamphlets, and syndicated newspaper columns, and he pioneered the *Ladies' Home Journal* feature "Can This Marriage Be Saved?," which was based on case histories from his Institute of Family Relations. The answer was almost always yes, so long as the natural division of labor between husbands and wives was maintained or restored. . . .

In retrospect, the confidence these experts expressed in the stability of 1950s marriage and gender roles seems hopelessly myopic. Not only did divorce rates during the 1950s never drop below the highs reached in 1929, but as early as 1947 the number of women entering the labor force in the United States had begun to surpass the number of women leaving it.[20] Why were the experts so optimistic about the future of marriage and the demise of feminism?

Some were probably unconsciously soothed into complacency by the mass media, especially the new television shows that delivered nightly images of happy female homemakers in stable male breadwinner families. . . .

When divorce did occur, it was seen as a failure of individuals rather than of marriage. One reason people didn't find fault with the 1950s model of marriage and gender roles was that it was still so new that they weren't sure they were doing it right. Millions of people in Europe and America were looking for a crash course on how to attain the modern marriage. Confident that "science" could solve their problems, couples turned not just to popular culture and the mass media but also to marriage experts and advice columnists for help. If the advice didn't work, they blamed their own inadequacy.[21] . . .

At every turn, popular culture and intellectual elites alike discouraged women from seeing themselves as productive members of society. In 1956 a *Life* magazine article commented that women "have minds and should use them . . . so long as their primary interest is in the home." . . . Adlai Stevenson, the two-time Democratic Party candidate for president of the United States, told the all-female graduating class of Smith College that "most of you" are going to assume "the humble role of housewife," and "whether you like the idea or not just now," later on "you'll like it."[22]

Under these circumstances, women tried their best to "like it." By the mid-1950s American advertisers reported that wives were using housework as a way to express their individuality. It appeared that Talcott Parsons was right: Women were compensating for their lack of occupational status by expanding their role as consumer experts and arbiters of taste and style. First Lady Jackie Kennedy was the supreme exemplar of this role in the early 1960s.[23]

Youth in the 1950s saw nothing to rebel against in the dismissal of female aspirations for independence. The number of American high school students agreeing that it would be good "if girls could be as free as boys in asking for dates" fell from 37 percent in 1950 to 26 percent in 1961, while the percentage of those who thought it would be good for girls to share the expenses of dates declined from 25 percent to 18 percent. The popular image was that only hopeless losers would engage in such egalitarian behavior. A 1954 Philip Morris ad in the *Massachusetts Collegian* made fun of poor Finster, a boy who finally found a girl who shared his belief in "the equity of Dutch treat." As a result, the punch line ran, "today Finster goes everywhere and shares expenses fifty-fifty with Mary Alice Hematoma, a lovely three-legged girl with side-burns."[24]

No wonder so many social scientists and marriage counselors in the 1950s thought that the instabilities associated with the love-based "near-equality" revolution in gender roles and marriage had been successfully contained. Married women were working outside the home more often than in the past, but they still identified themselves primarily as housewives. Men seemed willing to support women financially even in the absence of their older patriarchal rights, as long as their meals were on the table and their wives kept themselves attractive. Moreover, although men and women aspired to personal fulfillment in marriage, most were willing to stay together even if they did not get it. Sociologist Mirra Komarovsky interviewed working-class couples at the end of the 1950s and found that "slightly less than one-third were happily or very happily married." In 1957, a study of a cross section of all social classes found that only 47 percent of U.S. married couples described themselves as "very happy." Although the proportion of "very happy" marriages was lower in 1957 than it was to be in 1976, the divorce rate was also lower.[25]

What the experts failed to notice was that this stability was the result of a unique moment of equilibrium in the expansion of economic, political, and personal options. Ironically, this one twenty-year period in the history of the love-based "near-equality"

marriage when people stopped predicting disaster turned out to be the final lull before the long-predicted storm.

The seeming stability of marriage in the 1950s was due in part to the thrill of exploring the new possibilities of married life and the size of the rewards that men and women received for playing by the rules of the postwar economic boom. But it was also due to the incomplete development of the "fun morality" and the consumer revolution. There were still many ways of penalizing nonconformity, tamping down aspirations, and containing discontent in the 1950s.

One source of containment was the economic and legal dependence of women. Postwar societies continued the century-long trend toward increasing women's legal and political rights outside the home and restraining husbands from exercising heavy-handed patriarchal power, but they stopped short of giving wives equal authority with their husbands. Legal scholar Mary Ann Glendon points out that right up until the 1960s, "nearly every legislative attempt to regulate the family decision-making process gave the husband and father the dominant role."[26]

Most American states retained their "head and master" laws, giving husbands the final say over questions like whether or not the family should move. Married women couldn't take out loans or credit cards in their own names. Everywhere in Europe and North America it was perfectly legal to pay women less than men for the same work. Nowhere was it illegal for a man to force his wife to have sex. One legal scholar argues that marriage law in the 1950s had more in common with the legal codes of the 1890s than the 1990s.[27]

Writers in the 1950s generally believed that the old-style husband and father was disappearing and that this was a good thing. The new-style husband, said one American commentator, was now "partner in the family firm, part-time man, part-time mother and part-time maid." Family experts and marital advice columnists advocated a "fifty-fifty design for living,"" emphasizing that a husband should "help out" with child rearing and make sure that sex with his wife was "mutually satisfying."[28]

But the 1950s definition of fifty-fifty would satisfy few modern couples. Dr. Benjamin Spock, the famous parenting advice expert, called for men to get more involved in parenting but added that he wasn't suggesting equal involvement. "Of course I don't mean that the father has to give just as many bottles, or change just as many diapers as the mother," he explained in a 1950s edition of his perennial best-seller *Baby and Child Care*. "But it's fine for him to do these things occasionally. He might make the formula on Sunday."[29]

The family therapist Paul Popenoe was equally cautious in his definition of what modern marriage required from the wife. A wife should be "sympathetic with her husband's work and a good listener," he wrote. But she must never consider herself "enough of an expert to criticize him."[30] . . .

Many 1950s men did not view male bread-winning as a source of power but as a burdensome responsibility made worthwhile by their love for their families. A man who worked three jobs to support his family told interviewers, "Although I am somewhat tired at the moment, I get pleasure out of thinking the family is dependent on me for their income." Another described how anxious he had been to finish college and "get to . . . acting as a husband and father should, namely, supporting my family." Men also remarked on how wonderful it felt to be able to give their children things their families had been unable to afford when they were young.[31]

A constant theme of men and women looking back on the 1950s was how much better their family lives were in that decade than during the Depression and World War II. But in assessing their situation against a backdrop of such turmoil and privation, they had modest expectations of comfort and happiness, so they were more inclined to count their blessings than to measure the distance between their dreams and their real lives.

Modest expectations are not necessarily a bad thing. Anyone who expects that marriage will always be joyous, that the division of labor will always be fair, and that the earth will move whenever you have sex is going to be often disappointed. Yet it is clear that in many 1950s marriages, low expectations could lead people to put up with truly terrible family lives.

Historian Elaine Tyler May comments that in the 1950s "the idea of 'working marriage' was one that often included constant day-to-day misery for one or both partners." Jessica Weiss recounts interviews conducted over many years in the Berkeley study with a woman whose husband beat her and their children. The wife often threw her body between her husband and the young ones, taking the brunt of the violence on herself because "I can take it much easier than the kids can." Her assessment of the marriage strikes the modern observer as a masterpiece of understatement: "We're really not as happy as we should be." She was not even indignant that her neighbors rebuffed her children when they fled the house to summon help. "I can't say I blame the neighbors," she commented. "They didn't want to get involved." Despite two decades of such violence, this woman did not divorce until the late 1960s.[32]

A 1950s family that looked well-functioning to the outside world could hide terrible secrets. Both movie star Sandra Dee and Miss America of 1958, Marilyn Van Derbur, kept silent about their fathers' incestuous abuse until many years had passed. If they had gone public in the 1950s or early 1960s, they might not even have been believed. Family "experts" of the day described incest as a "one-in-a-million occurrence," and many psychiatrists claimed that women who reported incest were simply expressing their own oedipal fantasies.[33]

In many states and countries a nonvirgin could not bring a charge of rape, and everywhere the idea that a man could rape his own wife was still considered absurd. Wife beating was hardly ever treated seriously. The trivialization of family violence was epitomized in a 1954 report of a Scotland Yard commander that "there are only about twenty murders a year in London and not all are serious—some are just husbands killing their wives."[34] . . .

Still, these signs of unhappiness did not ripple the placid waters of 1950s complacency. The male bread-winner marriage seemed so pervasive and popular that social scientists decided it was a necessary and inevitable result of modernization. Industrial societies, they argued, needed the division of labor embodied in the male breadwinner nuclear family to compensate for their personal demands of the modern workplace. The ideal family—or what Talcott Parsons called "the normal" family—consisted of a man who specialized in the practical, individualistic activities needed for subsistence and a woman who took care of the emotional needs of her husband and children.[35]

The close fit that most social scientists saw between the love-based male breadwinner family and the needs of industrial society led them to anticipate that this form of marriage would accompany the spread of industrialization across the globe and replace the wide array of other marriage and family systems in traditional societies. This view was articulated in a vastly influential 1963 book titled *World Revolution and Family Patterns,* by American sociologist William F. Goode. Goode's work became the basis for almost all high school and college classes on family life in the 1960s, and his ideas were popularized by journalists throughout the industrial world.[36]

Goode surveyed the most up-to-date family data in Europe and the United States, the Middle East, sub-Saharan Africa, India, China, and Japan and concluded that countries everywhere were evolving toward a conjugal family system characterized by the "love pattern" in mate selection. The new international marriage system, he said, focused people's material and psychic investments on the nuclear family and increased the "emotional demands which each spouse can legitimately make upon each other," elevating loyalty to spouse above obligations to parents. Goode argued that such ideals would inevitably eclipse other forms of marriage, such as polygamy. Monogamous marriage would become the norm all around the world.

The ideology of the love-based marriage, according to Goode, "is a radical one, destructive of the older traditions in almost every society." It "proclaims the right of the individual to choose his or her own spouse. . . . It asserts the worth of the *individual* as against the inherited elements of wealth or ethnic group." As such, it especially appealed "to intellectuals, young people, women, and the disadvantaged." . . .

Despite women's legal gains and the "radical" appeal of the love ideology to women and youth, Goode concluded that a destabilizing "full equality" was not in the cards. Women had not become more "career-minded" between 1900 and the early 1960s, he said. In his 380-page survey of world trends, Goode did not record even one piece of evidence to suggest that women might become more career-minded in the future.

Most social scientists agreed with Goode that the 1950s family represented the wave of the future. They thought that the history of marriage had in effect reached its culmination in Europe and North America and that the rest of the world would soon catch up. As late as 1963 nothing seemed more obvious to most family experts and to the general public than the preeminence of marriage in people's lives and the permanence of the male breadwinner family.

But clouds were already gathering on the horizon.

When sustained prosperity turned people's attention from gratitude for survival to a desire for greater personal satisfaction . . .

When the expanding economy of the 1960s needed women enough to offer them a living wage . . .

When the prepared foods and drip-dry shirts that had eased the work of homemakers also made it possible for men to live comfortable, if sloppy bachelor lives . . .

When the invention of the birth control pill allowed the sexualization of love to spill over the walls of marriage . . .

When the inflation of the 1970s made it harder for a man to be the sole breadwinner for a family . . .

When all these currents converged, the love-based male-provider marriage would find itself buffeted from all sides.

NOTES

1. Quoted in John Jacobs, *All You Need Is Love and Other Lies About Marriage* (New York: HarperCollins, 2004), p. 9.

2. William Jankowiak and Edward Fischer, "A Cross-Cultural Perspective on Romantic Love," *Ethnology* 31 (1992).

3. Ira Reiss and Gary Lee, *Family Systems in America* (New York: Holt, Rinehart and Winston, 1988), pp. 91–93.

4. Karen Dion and Kenneth Dion, "Cultural Perspectives on Romantic Love," *Personal Relationships* 3 (1996); Vern Bullough, "On Being a Male in the Middle Ages," in Clare Less, ed., *Medieval Masculinities* (Minneapolis: University of Minnesota Press, 1994); Hans-Werner Goetz, *Life in the Middle*

Ages, from the Seventh to the Thirteenth Century (Notre Dame, Ind.: University of Notre Dame Press, 1993).

5. Francis Hsu, "Kinship and Ways of Life," in Hsu, ed., *Psychological Anthropology* (Cambridge, U.K.: Schenkman, 1972), and *Americans and Chinese: Passage to Differences* (Honolulu: University Press of Hawaii, 1981); G. Robina Quale, *A History of Marriage Systems* (Westport, Conn.: Greenwood Press, 1988); Marilyn Yalom, "Biblical Models", in Yalom and Laura Carstensen, eds., *Inside the American Couple* (Berkeley: University of California Press, 2002).

6. Andreas Capellanus, *The Art of Courtly Love* (New York: W. W. Norton, 1969), pp. 106–07.

7. Ibid., pp. 106–07, 184. On the social context of courtly love, see Theodore Evergates, ed., *Aristocratic Women in Medieval France* (Philadelphia: University of Pennsylvania Press, 1999); Montaigne, quoted in Olwen Hufton, *The Prospect Before Her: A History of Women in Western Europe, 1500–1800* (New York: Alfred A. Knopf, 1996), p. 148.

8. Betty Radice, trans., *Letters of Abelard and Heloise* (Harmondsworth, U.K.: Penguin, 1974).

9. The phrase is from Chiara Saraceno, who argues that until the end of the nineteenth century, Italian families defined love as the development of such feelings over the course of a marriage. Saraceno, "The Italian Family," in Antoine Prost and Gerard Vincent, eds., *A History of Private Life: Riddles of Identity in Modern Times* (Cambridge, Mass.: Belknap Press, 1991), p. 487.

10. Owram, *Born at the Right Time*, p. 22 (see chap. 13, n. 20); Elaine Tyler May, *Homeward Bound: American Families in the Cold War Era* (New York: Basic Books, 1988); Barbara Ehrenreich, *The Hearts of Men: American Dreams and the Flight from Commitment* (Garden City, N.Y.: Anchor Press, 1983), pp. 14–28; Douglas Miller and Marson Nowak, *The Fifties: The Way We Really Were* (Garden City, N.Y.: Doubleday, 1977), p. 154; Duchen, *Women's Rights* (see chap. 13, n. 28); Marjorie Ferguson, *Forever Feminine: Women's Magazines and the Cult of Femininity* (London: Heinemann, 1983); Moeller, *Protecting Motherhood* (see chap. 13, n. 22); Martine Segalen, "The Family

in the Industrial Revolution," in Burguière et al., p. 401 (see chap. 8, n. 2).

11. Daniel Yankelovich, *New Rules: Searching for Self-Fulfillment in a World Turned Upside Down* (New York: Random House, 1981); Lois Gordon and Alan Gordon, *American Chronicle: Seven Decades in American Life, 1920–1989* (New York: Crown, 1990).

12. Alan Ehrenhalt, *The Lost City: Discovering the Forgotten Virtues of Community in the Chicago of the 1950s* (New York: Basic Books, 1995), p. 233; modernity quote from the French woman's magazine *Marie-Claire*, in Duchen, *Women's Rights and Women's Lives*, p. 73 (see chap. 13, n. 28).

13. Quoted in Ruth Rosen, *The World Split Open: How the Modern Women's Movement Changed America* (New York: Viking, 2000), p. 44.

14. Coontz, *The Way We Never Were*, p. 25; Rosenteur, quoted in Bailey, *From Front Porch to Back Seat*, p. 76 (see chap. 12, n. 11).

15. Martha Wolfenstein, "Fun Morality" [1955], in Warren Susman, ed., *Culture and Commitment, 1929–1945* (New York: George Braziller, 1973), pp. 84, 90; Coontz, *The Way We Never Were*, p. 171.

16. Ernest Burgess and Harvey Locke, *The Family: From Institution to Companionship* (New York: American Book Company, 1960), pp. 479, 985, 538.

17. Molly Ladd-Taylor, "Eugenics, Sterilisation and Modern Marriage in the USA," *Gender & History* 13 (2001), pp. 312, 318.

18. Nisbet, quoted in John Scanzoni, "From the Normal Family to Alternate Families to the Quest for Diversity with Interdependence," *Journal of Family Issues* 22 (2001); Mirra Komarovsky, *Women in the Modern World: Their Education and Their Dilemmas* (Boston: Little, Brown, 1953).

19. Talcott Parsons, "The Kinship System of the United States" in Parsons, *Essays in Sociological Theory* (Glencoe, Ill.: Free Press, 1954); Parsons and Robert Bales, *Family, Socialization, and Interaction Processes* (Glencoe, Ill.: Free Press, 1955).

20. *Historical Statistics of the United States: Colonial Times to the Present* (Washington, D.C.: U.S.

Department of Commerce, Bureau of the Census, 1975); Sheila Tobias and Lisa Anderson, "What Really Happened to Rosie the Riveter," *Mss Modular Publications* 9 (1973).

21. Beth Bailey, "Scientific Truth. . . and Love: The Marriage Education Movement in the United States," *Journal of Social History* 20 (1987).

22. Miller and Nowak, *The Fifties*, pp. 164–65; Weiss, *To Have and to Hold*, p. 19 (see chap. 13, n. 29); Rosen, *World Split Open*, p. 41.

23. Glenna Mathews, *"Just a Housewife": The Rise and Fall of Domesticity in America* (New York: Oxford University Press, 1987); Betty Friedan, *The Feminine Mystique* (New York: Dell, 1963).

24. Bailey, *From Front Porch to Back Seat*, p. 111.

25. Mirra Komarovsky, *Blue-Collar Marriage* (New Haven: Vintage, 1962), p. 331. Mintz and Kellogg, *Domestic Revolutions*, p. 194; Norval Glenn, "Marital Quality," in David Levinson, ed., *Encyclopedia of Marriage and the Family* (New York: Macmillan, 1995), vol. 2, p. 449.

26. Mary Ann Glendon, *The Transformation of Family Law* (Chicago: University of Chicago Press, 1989), p. 88. On Europe, Gisela Bock, *Women in European History* (Oxford, U.K.: Blackwell Publishers, 2002), p. 248; Bonnie Smith, *Changing Lives: Women in European History Since 1700* (Lexington, Mass.: D. C. Heath, 1989), p. 492.

27. Sara Evans, *Tidal Wave: How Women Changed America at Century's End* (New York: Free Press, 2003), pp. 1–20; John Ekelaar, "The End of an Era?," *Journal of Family History* 28 (2003), p. 109. See also Lenore Weitzman, *The Marriage Contract* (New York: Free Press, 1981).

28. Ehrenhalt, *Lost City*, p. 233.

29. Quoted in Michael Kimmell, *Manhood in America: A Cultural History* (New York: Free Press, 1996), p. 246.

30. Ladd-Taylor, "Eugenics," p. 319.

31. Ibid., p. 32; Robert Rutherdale, "Fatherhood, Masculinity, and the Good Life During Canada's Baby Boom," *Journal of Family History* 24 (1999), p. 367.

32. May, *Homeward Bound*, p. 202; Weiss, *To Have and to Hold*, pp. 136–38.

33. Marilyn Van Derbur Atler, "The Darkest Secret," *People* (June 10, 1991); Dodd Darin, *The Magnificent Shattered Life of Bobby Darin and Sandra Dee* (New York: Warner Books, 1995); Elizabeth Pleck, *Domestic Tyranny* (New York: Oxford University Press, 1987); Linda Gordon, *Heroes of Their Own Lives: The Politics and History of Family Violence, 1880–1960* (New York: Viking, 1988).

34. Coontz, *The Way We Never Were*, p. 35; Leonore Davidoff et al., *The Family Story* (London: Longmans, 1999), p. 215.

35. Parsons, "The Kinship System of the United States"; Parsons, "The Normal American Family," in Seymour Farber, Piero Mustacchi, and Roger Wilson, eds., *Man and Civilization: The Family's Search for Survival* (New York: McGraw-Hill, 1965); Parsons and Bales, *Family, Socialization, and Interaction Processes*. For similar theories in British sociology, see Michael Young and Peter Willmott's *The Symmetrical Family* (London: Pelican, 1973), pp. 28–30; *Family and Kinship in East London* (Glencoe, Ill.: The Free Press, 1957); and *Family and Class in a London Suburb*.

36. The quotations and figures in this and the following paragraphs are from Goode, *World Revolution*.

THINKING ABOUT THE READING

According to Coontz, if not for romance, what are some of the common reasons throughout history that people marry? What are the characteristics of the "male bread-winner, love-based marriage"? What social conditions are necessary for this kind of family arrangement to prevail? Does Coontz think this family form is viable in the long-term future? Do you?

Gay Parenthood and the End of Paternity as We Knew It

JUDITH STACEY

(2011)

Because let's face it, if men weren't always hungry for it, nothing would ever happen. There would be no sex, and our species would perish.

—Sean Elder, "Why My Wife Won't Sleep with Me," 2004

Because homosexuals are rarely monogamous, often having as many as three hundred or more partners in a lifetime—some studies say it is typically more than one thousand—children in those polyamorous situations are caught in a perpetual coming and going. It is devastating to kids, who by their nature are enormously conservative creatures.

—James Dobson, "Same-Sex Marriage Talking Points"

Unlucky in love and ready for a family, [Christie] Malcomson tried for 4½ years to get pregnant, eventually giving birth to the twins when she was 38. Four years later, again without a mate, she had Sarah. "I've always known that I was meant to be a mother," Malcomson, 44, said. "I tell people, I didn't choose to be a single parent. I choose to be a parent."

—Lornet Turnbull, "Family Is . . . Being Redefined All the Time," 2004

Gay fathers were once as unthinkable as they were invisible. Now they are an undeniable part of the contemporary family landscape. During the same time that the marriage promotion campaign in the United States was busy convincing politicians and the public to regard rising rates of fatherlessness as a national emergency (Stacey 1998), growing numbers of gay men were embracing fatherhood. Over the past two decades, they have built a cornucopia of family forms and supportive communities where they are raising children outside of the conventional family. Examining the experiences of gay men who have openly pursued parenthood against the odds can help us to understand forces that underlie the decline of paternity as we knew it. Contrary to the fears of many in the marriage-promotion movement, however, gay parenting is not a new symptom of the demise of fatherhood, but of its creative, if controversial, reinvention. When I paid close attention to gay men's parenting desires, efforts, challenges, and achievements, I unearthed crucial features of contemporary paternity and parenthood more generally. I also came upon some inspirational models of family that challenge widely held beliefs about parenthood and child welfare.

The Uncertainty of Paternity

Access to effective contraception, safe abortions, and assisted reproductive technologies (ART) unhitches traditional links between heterosexual love, marriage, and baby carriages. Parenthood, like intimacy more generally, is now contingent. Paths to parenthood no longer appear so natural, obligatory, or uniform as they used to but have become voluntary, plural, and politically embattled. Now that children impose immense economic and social responsibilities on their parents, rather than promising to become a reliable source of family labor or social security, the pursuit of parenthood depends on an emotional rather than an economic calculus. "The men and women who decide to have children today," German sociologists Ulrich Beck and Elisabeth Beck-Gernsheim correctly point out, "certainly do not do so because they expect any material advantages. Other motives closely linked with the emotional needs of the parents play a significant role; our children mainly have 'a psychological utility.'" (Beck and Beck-Gernsheim 1995:105). Amid the threatening upheavals, insecurities, and dislocations of life under global market and military forces, children can rekindle opportunities for hope, meaning, and connection. Adults who wish to become parents today typically seek the intimate bonds that children seem to promise. More reliably than a lover or spouse, parenthood beckons to many (like Christie Malcomson in the third epigraph to this chapter) who hunger for lasting love, intimacy, and kinship—for that elusive "haven in a heartless world" (Lasch 1995).

Gay men confront these features of post-modern parenthood in a magnified mode. They operate from cultural premises antithetical to what U.S. historian Nicholas Townsend termed "the package deal" of (now eroding) modern masculinity—marriage, work, and fatherhood (Townsend 2002). Gay men who choose to become primary parents challenge conventional definitions of masculinity and paternity and even dominant sexual norms of gay culture itself.

Gay fatherhood represents "planned parenthood" in extremis. Always deliberate and often difficult, it offers fertile ground for understanding why and how people do and do not choose to become parents today. Unlike most heterosexuals or even lesbians, gay men have to struggle for access to "the means of reproduction" without benefit of default scripts for achieving or practicing parenthood. They encounter a range of challenging, risky, uncertain options—foster care, public and private forms of domestic and 'international adoption, hired or volunteered forms of "traditional" or gestational surrogacy, contributing sperm to women friends, relatives, or strangers who agree to co-parent with them, or even resorting to an instrumental approach to old-fashioned heterosexual copulation.

Compared with maternity, the social character of paternity has always been more visible than its biological status. Indeed, that's why prior to DNA testing, most modern societies mandated a marital presumption of paternity. Whenever a married woman gave birth, her husband was the presumed and legal father. Gay male paternity intensifies this emphasis on social rather than biological definitions of parenthood. Because the available routes to genetic parenthood for gay men are formidably expensive, very difficult to negotiate, or both, most prospective gay male parents pursue the purely social paths of adoption or foster care (Brodzinsky, Patterson, and Vaziri 2002).

Stark racial, economic, and sexual asymmetries characterize the adoption marketplace. Prospective parents are primarily white, middle-class, and relatively affluent, but the available children are disproportionately from poorer and darker races and nations. Public and private adoption agencies, as well as birth mothers and fathers, generally consider married heterosexual couples to be the most desirable adoptive parents (Human Rights Campaign 2009). These favored straight married couples, for their part, typically seek healthy infants, preferably from their own race or ethnic background. Because there are not enough of these to meet the demand, most states and counties allow single adults, including gay men, to shop for parenthood in their overstocked warehouse of "hard to place" children. This is an index of expediency more than tolerance. The state's stockpiled children have been removed from parents who were judged to be negligent, abusive, or incompetent. Disproportionate numbers are children of color, and the very hardest of these to place are older boys with "special needs", such as physical, emotional, and cognitive disabilities.

The gross disjuncture between the market value of society's adoptable children and the supply of prospective adoptive parents allows gay men to parent a hefty share of them. Impressive numbers of gay men willingly rescue such children from failing or devastated families. Just as in their intimate adult relationships, gay men more readily accept children across boundaries of race, ethnicity, class, and even health.

The multi-racial membership of so many of gay men's families visually signals the social character of most gay fatherhood. In addition, as we will see, some gay men, like single-mother-by-choice Christie Malcomson, willingly unhitch their sexual and romantic desires from their domestic ones in order to become parents. For all of these reasons, gay men provide frontier terrain for exploring noteworthy changes in the meanings and motives for paternity and parenthood.

Finding Pop Luck in the City of Angels

Gay paternity is especially developed and prominent in L.A.—again, not the environment where most people would expect to find it, but which, for many reasons, became a multi-ethnic mecca for gay parenthood. According to data reported in Census 2000, both the greatest number of same-sex couple households in the United States and of such couples who were raising children were residing in Los Angeles County (Sears and Badgett 2004). It is likely, therefore, that the numbers there exceeded those of any metropolis in the world.

Local conditions in Los Angeles have been particularly favorable for gay and lesbian parenthood. L.A. County was among the first in the United States to openly allow gay men to foster or adopt children under its custody, and numerous local, private adoption agencies, lawyers, and services emerged that specialized in facilitating domestic and international adoptions for a gay clientele. In 2001 California enacted a domestic-partnership law that authorized second-parent adoptions, and several family-court judges in California pioneered the still-rare practice of granting pre-birth custody rights to same-sex couples who planned to co-parent. The City of Angels became the surrogacy capital of the gay globe, thanks especially to Growing Generations, the world's first gay- and lesbian-owned professional surrogacy agency founded to serve an international clientele of prospective gay parents (Strah and Margolis 2003).

The gay men I studied were among the first cohort of gay men young enough to even imagine parenthood outside heterosexuality and mature enough to be in a position to choose or reject it. I intentionally over-sampled for gay fathers. Nationally 22 percent of male same-sex-couple households recorded in Census 2000 included children under the age of eighteen (Simmons and O'Connell 2003:10). However, fathers composed half of my sample overall and more than 60 percent of the men who were then in same-sex couples. Depending on which definition of fatherhood one uses, between twenty-four and twenty-nine of my fifty primary interviewees were fathers of thirty-five children, and four men who were not yet parents declared their firm intention to become so.[1] Only sixteen men, in contrast, depicted themselves as childless more or less by choice. Also by design, I sampled to include the full gamut of contemporary paths to gay paternity. Although most children with gay fathers in the United States were born within heterosexual marriages before their fathers came out, this was true for only six of the thirty-four children that the men in my study were raising. All of the others were among the pioneer generation of children with gay dads who chose to parent after they had come out of the closet. Fifteen of the children had been adopted (or were in the process of becoming so) through county and private agencies or via independent, open adoption agreements with birth mothers; four were foster-care children; five children had been conceived through surrogacy contracts, both gestational and "traditional"; and four children had been born to lesbians who conceived with sperm

from gay men with whom they were co-parenting. In addition, five of the gay men in my study had served as foster parents to numerous teenagers, and several expected to continue to accept foster placements. Two men, however, were biological but not social parents, one by intention, the other unwittingly.[2]

The fathers and children in my study were racially and socially diverse, and their families, like gay-parent families generally, were much more likely to be multi-racial and multi-cultural than are other families in the United States, or perhaps anywhere in the world. Two-thirds of the gay-father families in my study were multi-racial. The majority (fifteen) of the twenty-four gay men who were parenting during the time of my study were white, but most (twenty-one) of their thirty-four children were not.[3] Even more striking, only two of the fifteen children they had adopted by 2003 were white, both of these through open adoption arrangements with birth mothers; seven adoptees were black or mixed race, and six were Latino. In contrast, nine of the twelve adoptive parents were white, and one each was black, Latino, and Asian American.

It is difficult to assess how racially representative this is of gay men, gay parents, and their families in the city, the state, or the nation. Although the dominant cultural stereotype of gay men and gay fathers is white and middle class, U.S. Census 2000 data surprisingly report that racial minorities represented a higher proportion of same-sex-couple-parent households in California than of heterosexual married couples (Sears and Badgett 2004). The vast majority of the children in these families, however, were born within their gay parents' former heterosexual relationship (Gates 2005). Contemporary gay paths to paternity are far more varied and complex.

Predestined Progenitors

Of the men I interviewed, eighteen who had become dads and four who planned to do so portrayed their passion for parenthood in terms so ardent that I classify them as predestined parents. The following two stories illustrate typical challenges and triumphs of different paths to predestined parenthood. The first depicts another blessedly compatible and privileged couple, and the second is about a courageous, much less affluent gay man who was "single by chance, parent by choice."

Predestined Pairing

Eddie Leary and Charles Tillery, a well-heeled, white, Catholic couple, had three children born through gestational surrogacy. Their firstborn was a genetic half-sibling to a younger set of twins. The same egg donor and the same gestational surrogate conceived and bore the three children, but Charles is the genetic father of the first child, and Eddie's sperm conceived the twins. At the time I first interviewed them in 2002, their first child was three years old, the twins were infants, and the couple had been together for eighteen years. Eddie told me that they had discussed their shared desire to parent on their very first date, In fact, by then Eddie had already entered a heterosexual marriage primarily for that purpose, but he came out to his wife and left the marriage before achieving it. Directly echoing Christie Malcomson, Eddie claimed that he always knew that he "was meant to be a parent." He recalled that during his childhood whenever adults had posed the clichéd question to him, "What do you want to be when you grow up?" his ready answer was 'a daddy.'"

Charles and Eddie met and spent their first ten years together on the East Coast, where they built successful careers in corporate law and were gliding through the glamorous DINC (double income, no children) fast lane of life. By their mid-thirties, however, they were bored and began to ask themselves the existential question, "Is this all there is?" They had already buried more friends than their parents had by their sixties, which, Eddie believed, "gives you a sense of gravitas." In addition, he reported, "My biological clock was definitely ticking." In the mid-1990s, the couple migrated to L.A., lured by the kind of gay family life style and the ample job opportunities it seemed to offer. They spent the next five years riding an emotional roller coaster attempting to become parents. At first Eddie and Charles considered adoption, but they became discouraged when they learned that then-governor Pete Wilson's administration was preventing joint adoptions by same-sex couples. Blessed with ample financial and social resources, they decided to shift their eggs, so to speak, into the surrogacy basket. One of Charles's many cousins put the couple in touch with her college roommate, Sally, a married mother of two in her mid-thirties who lived in Idaho. Sally was a woman who loved both bearing and rearing children, and Charles's cousin knew that she had been fantasizing about bestowing the gift of parenthood on a childless couple. Although Sally's imaginary couple

had not been gay, she agreed to meet them. Eddie and Sally both reported that they bonded instantly, and she agreed to serve as the men's gestational surrogate.

To secure an egg donor and manage the complex medical and legal processes that surrogacy requires at a moment just before Growing Generations had opened shop, Eddie and Charles became among the first gay clients of a surrogate parenthood agency that mainly served infertile heterosexual couples. Shopping for DNA in the agency's catalog of egg donors, they had selected Marya, a Dutch graduate student who had twice before served as an anonymous donor for married couples in order to subsidize her education. Marya had begun to long for maternity herself, however, and she was loathe to subject her body and soul yet again to the grueling and hormonally disruptive process that donating ova entails. Yet when she learned that the new candidates for her genes were gay men, she found herself taken with the prospect of openly aiding such a quest. Like Sally, she felt an immediate affinity with Eddie and agreed to enter a collaborative egg-donor relationship with him and Charles. When she had served as egg donor for infertile married couples, Marya explained, "the mother there can get a little jealous and a little threatened, because she's already feeling insecure about being infertile, and having another woman having that process and threatening the mother's role, I think is a big concern." With a gay couple, in contrast, "you get to be—there's no exclusion, and there's no threatened feelings."

Because Eddie is a few years older than Charles, he wanted to be the first to provide the sperm, and all four parties were thrilled when Sally became pregnant on the second in-vitro fertilization (IVF) attempt. Elation turned to despair, however, when the pregnancy miscarried in the thirteenth week. Eddie described himself as devastated, saying, "I grieved and mourned the loss of my child, just as if I'd been the one carrying it." In fact, Sally recovered from the trauma and was willing to try again before Eddie, who said, "I couldn't bear the risk of losing another of my children." Instead, Charles wound up supplying the sperm for what became the couple's firstborn child, Heather. Two years later, eager for a second child, the couple had persuaded both reluctant women to subject their bodies to one more IVF surrogacy, this time with Eddie's sperm. A pair of healthy twin boys arrived one year later, with all four procreative collaborators, as well as Sally's husband, present at the delivery to welcome the boys into what was to become a remarkable, surrogacy-extended family.

Occasionally Marya, the egg donor, continued to visit her genetic daughter, but Eddie and Sally quickly developed an extraordinary, deep, familial bond. They developed the habit of daily, long-distance phone calls that were often lengthy and intimate. "Mama Sally," as Heather started to call her, began to make regular use of the Leary-Tillery guest room, accompanied sometimes by her husband and their two children. Often she came to co-parent with Eddie as a substitute for Charles, who had to make frequent business trips. The two families began taking joint vacations skiing or camping together in the Rockies, and once Marya had come along. Sally's then ten-year-old daughter and eight-year-old son began to refer to Heather as their "surrogate sister."

Eddie and Charles jointly secured shared legal custody of all three children through some of the earliest pre-birth decrees granted in California. From the start, the couple had agreed that Eddie, a gourmet cook who had designed the family's state-of-the-culinary-art kitchen, would stay home as full-time parent, and Charles would be the family's sole breadwinner. After the twins arrived, they hired a daytime nanny to assist Eddie while Charles was out earning their sustenance, and she sometimes minded the twins when Eddie and Heather joined the weekly playgroup of the Pop Luck Club (PLC), composed of at-home dads and tots. Charles, for his part, blessed with Herculean energy and scant need for sleep, would plunge into his full-scale second shift of baby feedings, diapers, baths, and bedtime storytelling the moment he returned from the office. Although Eddie admitted to some nagging concerns that he "may have committed career suicide by joining the mom's club in the neighborhood," he also believed he'd met his calling: "I feel like this is who I was meant to be."

Parent Seeking Partner

Armando Hidalgo, a Mexican immigrant, was thirty-four years old when I interviewed him in 2001. At that point, he was in the final stages of adopting his four-year-old black foster son, Ramon. Armando had been a teenage sexual migrant to Los Angeles almost twenty years earlier. He had run away from home when he was only fifteen in order to conceal his unacceptable sexual desires from his large, commercially successful, urban Mexican family. The youthful Armando had paid a coyote to help him cross the border. He had survived a harrowing illegal immigration experience which culminated in a

Hollywood-style footrace across the California desert to escape an INS patrol in hot pursuit. By working at a Taco Bell in a coastal town, Armando put himself through high school. Drawing upon keen intelligence, linguistic facility, and a prodigious work ethic and drive, he had built a stable career managing a designer furniture showroom and he had managed to secure U.S. citizenship as well.

Four years after Armando's sudden disappearance from Mexico, he had returned there to come out to his family, cope with their painful reactions to his homosexuality and exile, and begin to restore his ruptured kinship bonds. He had made annual visits to his family ever since, and on one of these he fell in love with Juan, a Mexican language teacher. Armando said that he told Juan about his desire to parent right at the outset, and his new lover had seemed enthusiastic: "So, I thought we were the perfect match." Armando brought his boyfriend back to Los Angeles, and they lived together for five years.

However, when Armando began to pursue his lifelong goal of parenthood, things fell apart. To initiate the adoption process, Armando had enrolled the couple in the county's mandatory foster-care class. However, Juan kept skipping class and neglecting the homework, and so he failed to qualify for foster-parent status. This behavior jeopardized Armando's eligibility to adopt children as well as Juan's. The county then presented Armando with a "Sophie's choice." They would not place a child in his home unless Juan moved out. Despite Armando's primal passion for parenthood, "at the time," he self-critically explained to me, "I made the choice of staying with him, a choice that I regret. I chose him over continuing with my adoption." This decision ultimately exacted a fatal toll on the relationship. In Armando's eyes, Juan was preventing him from fulfilling his lifelong dream of having children. His resentment grew, but it took another couple of years before his passion for parenthood surpassed his diminishing passion for his partner. That is when Armando moved out and renewed the adoption application as a single parent.

Ramón was the first of three children that Armando told me he had "definitely decided" to adopt, whether or not he found another partner. His goal was to adopt two more children, preferably a daughter and another son, in that order. Removed at birth from crack-addicted parents, Ramón had lived in three foster homes in his first three years of life, before the county placed him with Armando through its fost-adopt program. Ramón had suffered from food allergies, anxiety, and hyperactivity when he arrived, and the social worker warned Armando to anticipate learning disabilities as well. Instead, after nine months under Armando's steady, patient, firm, and loving care, Ramón was learning rapidly and appeared to be thriving. And so was Armando. He felt so lucky to have Ramón, whom he no longer perceived as racially different from himself: "To me he's like my natural son. I love him a lot, and he loves me too much. Maybe I never felt so much unconditional love."

In fact, looking back, Armando attributed part of the pain of the years he spent struggling to accept his own homosexuality to his discomfort with gay male sexual culture and its emphasis on youth and beauty. "I think it made me fear that I was going to grow old alone," he reflected. "Now I don't have to worry that I'm gay and I'll be alone." For in addition to the intimacy that Armando savored with Ramón, his son proved to be a vehicle for building much closer bonds with most of his natal family. Several of Armando's eleven siblings had also migrated to Los Angeles. Among these were a married brother, his wife, and their children, who provided indispensable back-up support to the single working father. Ramón adored his cousins, and he and his father spent almost every weekend and holiday with them.

Ramón had acquired a devoted, long-distance *abuela* (grandmother) as well. Armando's mother had begun to travel regularly from Mexico to visit her dispersed brood, and, after years of disapproval and disappointment, she had grown to admire and appreciate her gay son above all her other children. Armando reported with sheepish pride that during a recent phone call his mother had stunned and thrilled him when she said, "You know what? I wish that all your brothers were like you. I mean that they liked guys." Astonished, Armando had asked her, "Why do you say that?" She replied, "I don't know. I just feel that you're really good to me, you're really kind. And you're such a good father." Then she apologized for how badly she had reacted when Armando told the family that he was gay, and she told him that now she was really proud of him. "'Now I don't have to accept it,'" Armando quoted her, "'because there's nothing to accept. You're natural, you're normal. You're my son, I don't have to accept you.' And she went on and on. It was so nice, it just came out of her. And now she talks about gay things, and she takes a cooking class from a gay guy and tells me how badly her gay

cooking teacher was treated by his family when they found out and how unfair it is and all."

Although Armando had begun to create the family he always wanted, he still dreamt of sharing parenthood with a mate who would be more compatible than Juan: "I would really love to meet someone, to fall in love." Of course, the man of his dreams was someone family-oriented: "Now that's really important, family-oriented, because I am very close to my family. I always do family things, like my nephews' birthday parties, going to the movies with them, family dinners, etcetera. But these are things that many gay men don't like to do. If they go to a straight family party, they get bored." Consequently, Armando was pessimistic about finding a love match. Being a parent, moreover, severely constrained his romantic pursuits. He didn't want to subject Ramón, who had suffered so much loss and instability in his life, to the risk of becoming attached to yet another new parental figure who might leave him. In addition, he didn't want Ramón "to think that gay men only have casual relationships, that there's no commitment." "But," he observed, with disappointment, "I haven't seen a lot of commitment among gay men." Armando took enormous comfort, however, in knowing that even if he never found another boyfriend, he will "never really be alone": "And I guess that's one of the joys that a family brings." Disappointingly, I may never learn whether Armando found a co-parent and adopted a sister and brother for Ramón, because I was unable to locate him again in 2008.

Adopting Diversity

While Eddie, Charles, and Armando all experienced irrepressible parental yearnings, they pursued very different routes to realizing this common "destiny." Gestational surrogacy, perhaps the newest, the most high-tech, and certainly the most expensive path to gay parenthood, is available primarily to affluent couples, the overwhelming majority of whom are white men who want to have genetic progeny. Adoption, on the other hand, is one of the oldest forms of "alternative" parenthood. It involves bureaucratic and social rather than medical technologies, and the county fost-adopt program which Armando and six other men in my study employed is generally the least expensive, most accessible route to gay paternity. Like Armando, most single, gay prospective parents pursue this avenue and adopt "hard-to-place" children who, like Ramón, are often boys of color with "special needs."

The demographics of contrasting routes to gay parenthood starkly expose the race and class disparities in the market value of children. Affluent, mainly white couples, like Charles and Eddie, can purchase the means to reproduce white infants in their own image, or even an enhanced, eugenic one, by selecting egg donors who have traits they desire with whom to mate their own DNA. In contrast, for gay men who are single, less privileged, or both, public agencies offer a grab bag of displaced children who are generally older, darker, and less healthy (U.S. Department of Health and Human Services 2003; Kapp, McDonald, and Diamond 2001). Somewhere in between these, two routes to gay paternity are forms of "gray market," open domestic or international adoptions, or privately negotiated sperm-donor agreements with women, especially lesbians, who want to co-parent with men. Independent adoption agencies and the Internet enable middle-class gay men, again typically white couples, to adopt newborns in a variety of hues.

Price does not always determine the route to parenthood that gay men choose, or the race, age, health, or pedigree of the children they agree to adopt. During the period of my initial research, only one white, middle-class couple in my study had chosen to adopt healthy white infants. Some affluent white men enthusiastically adopted children of color, even when they knew that the children had been exposed to drugs prenatally. Drew Greenwald, a very successful architect who could easily have afforded assisted reproductive technology (ART), was the most dramatic example of this. He claimed, "It never would have occurred to me to do surrogacy. I think it's outrageous because there are all these children who need good homes. And people have surrogacy, they say, in part it's because they want to avoid the complications of adoption, but in candor they are really in love with their own genes. . . . I just think there is a bit of narcissism about it."

Drew had opted for independent, open, transracial adoption instead. When I first interviewed him in 2002, he had just adopted his second of two multi-racial babies born to two different women who both had acknowledged using drugs during their pregnancies. Soon after adopting his first infant, Drew reunited with James, a former lover who had fallen "wildly in love" with Drew's new baby. James moved in while Drew was in the process of adopting a second child, and they have co-parented together ever since. Indeed, parenthood is the "glue" that cemented a relationship between the couple that Drew believed might otherwise have failed. Shared parenting provided them with a "joint project, a focus, and a source of commitment."

I was indulging in my guilty pleasure of reading the Style section of the Sunday *New York Times* one morning in the fall of 2008, when I stumbled across a wedding photo and announcement that Drew and James, "the parents of five adopted children," had just married. Several weeks later, on a conference trip to Los Angeles, I visited the bustling, expanded family household. I learned that the white birth mother of their second child had since had two more unwanted pregnancies, one with the same African American man as before and one with a black Latino. She had successfully appealed to Drew and James to add both of these mixed-race siblings to their family. After the first of these two new brothers had joined their brood, Drew and James began to worry that because only one of their children was a girl, she would find it difficult to grow up in a family with two dads and only brothers. And so they turned to the Internet, where they found a mixed-race sister for their first daughter. Three of the five children suffered from learning or attention-deficit difficulties, but Drew took this in stride. He was well aware, he said, that he and James had signed on "for all sorts of trauma, challenge, heartache" in the years ahead. He was both determined and financially able to secure the best help available for his children. Nonetheless, Drew acknowledged, "I fully expect that the kids will break my heart at some point in various ways, but it's so worth it." It was sufficiently worth it, apparently, that the year after my 2008 visit, I received an email from Drew announcing that their child head count had climbed to six, because their "jackpot birth mom" had given birth yet again. "We're up to four boys and two girls," Drew elaborated. "It's a lot, as you can imagine, but wonderful."

Situational Parents

Despite the fact that I over-sampled for gay parents, the majority of men in my study fell into the intermediate range on the passion-to-parent continuum. I would classify twenty-six of my fifty primary research subjects as having been situationally with or without children. Nine men whose personal desire to parent had ranged from reluctant, unenthusiastic, or indifferent to ambivalent, hesitant, or even mildly interested became situational parents after they succumbed to the persuasive entreaties of a fervently motivated mate, or if they fell in love with a man who was already a parent. Sixteen men who had remained childless expressed a similar range of sentiments, and in one case even a portion of regret. These men would have agreed to co-parent with a predestined partner or, in some cases, with even just a willing one. They had remained childless, however, either because they were single or because their partners were refuseniks or other situationists." None of them had a passion for parenthood that was potent enough to overcome the resistance of a reluctant mate or to confront alone the formidable challenges that prospective parents, and especially gay men, must meet.

Persuasive Partner

Glenn Miya, a Japanese American who was thirty-six years old when we first met, liked children enough to spend his workday life as a pediatrician. Nonetheless, he had not felt an independent desire to fill his home life with them as well. His long-term partner, Steven Llanusa, a Cuban-Italian elementary school teacher, however, was a predestined parent who, eight years into their relationship, had given Glenn an ultimatum to co-parent with him or part. Glenn's initial misgivings had been serious enough to rupture the couple's relationship for several months. Looking backward on this period, Glenn thought that he had been "suffering a bit of pre-parental panic," while Steven felt that he "was being forced to make a choice between his partner or being a parent," just the way Armando had felt. Although Steve had not wanted to face this choice, he had been determined that he "was not going to renege" on his commitment to parenthood. Fortunately for both men and, as it turns out, for the three Latino brothers whom they later adopted, couples counseling helped Glenn to work through his reservations and to reunite the couple.

Their co-parenting career began, Glenn said, by "parenting backwards." First they had signed up with a foster-care-parent program and taken in several teenagers, including one who was gay. Both the positive and negative aspects of their experiences as foster parents convinced them that they were ready to make a more permanent commitment to children. The couple's combined income was clearly sufficient to cover the expense of independent adoption, and

perhaps even surrogacy, had they wished to pursue these options. Instead, however, they had enrolled in the county's fost-adopt program, choosing "very consciously to adopt elementary-school-age kids," because they believed that they could not afford to stay home as full-time parents and did not want to hire a nanny to take care of infants or toddlers. They chose, in other words, to undertake what most authorities consider to be the most difficult form of adoptive parenthood. Nor had they chosen to start, or to stop, with one "difficult-to-place" child. Rather, they had accepted first a set of seven-year-old Mexican American twin boys and their five-year-old brother soon afterward. The county had removed the three boys from drug-addicted parents. Both twins had acquired learning disabilities from fetal alcohol syndrome, and one had a prosthetic leg. All three boys had suffered parental neglect and been physically abused by their father, who was serving a prison sentence for extensive and repeated domestic violence.

Despite the formidable challenges of transracially adopting three school-age abused and neglected children with cognitive, physical, and emotional disabilities, or perhaps partly because of these facts, the Miya-Llanusa family had become a literal California poster family for gay fatherhood. Both parents and their three sons played active leadership roles in the Pop Luck Club; they all participated in public education and outreach within the gay community and beyond; they spoke frequently to the popular media; they hosted massive community and holiday parties; and they served as general goodwill ambassadors for gay and multi-cultural family values in the boys' schools, sports teams, and dance classes and in their Catholic parish and their white, upper-middle-class suburban neighborhood.

Although Steve had been the predestined parent, and Glenn initially had been a reluctant, situational one, Glenn was the one who told me that he wouldn't mind emulating Eddie Leary's pattern of staying home to parent full-time, if his family had been able to afford forgoing the ample income that his pediatric practice earned.

The Miya-Llanusa clan was still going strong and still going public with their enduring love and family story when I caught up with them again in October 2008. Love certainly had come first for this family, but it had taken twenty-two years before the state of California briefly allowed marriage to follow. In August 2008, Steve and Glenn had seized the moment and held a glorious, almost-traditional, religious and legal wedding ceremony, with all three, now teenage sons as ushers, and more than one hundred of their beaming family and friends in attendance. By then, Proposition 8 was on the California ballot, and Glenn and Steve had contributed their time, resources, and a photo-album slide show portraying the history of their love, marriage, and family to that unsuccessful political campaign to keep marriage legal for other California families like theirs.

Poly-Parent Families

Independent adoption often generates complex family ties. Many pregnant women choose this option so that they can select adoptive parents whom they like for their babies and who will maintain contact with them after the adoption has been finalized. That is one of the reasons for the steady growth in the number of children Drew and James were raising. Although there are no reliable data on this, gay men seem to have an advantage over lesbian or single straight women who seek gray-market babies, because some birth mothers find it easier to relinquish their babies to men than to women, just as Marya had felt about donating her eggs. A pregnant woman who chooses gay men to adopt her offspring can hold on to her maternal status and avoid competitive, jealous feelings with infertile, adopting mothers.

It is true that most of the men in my study who adopted children through the gray market wanted their children to stay in touch with their birth mothers, and sometimes with their birth fathers as well. Drew and James even chose to operate "on a first-name basis" with their six (so far!) adopted children in order to reserve the terms *Mommy and Daddy* for their children's various genetic parents. Poly-parenting families do not always spring from such contingencies, however. Pursuing parenthood outside the box inspires some people to create intentional multi-parent families.

Front House/Back House

After thirteen years of close friendship, Paul (a white gay man) and Nancy (a white lesbian) decided to try to start a family together through alternative insemination. The two self-employed professionals spent the next two years carefully discussing their familial visions, values, expectations, anxieties, and limits. In October 1999, when Nancy began attempting to conceive their first child, they composed and signed a co-parenting agreement. They understood that the document would lack legal force but believed that going through the process of devising it would lay a crucial foundation for co-parenting. This agreement could serve as a model of ethical, sensitive planning for egalitarian, responsible co-parenting. In fact, it has already done so for several lesbian and gay friends of Paul's and Nancy's, and for two of mine. I do not know of any heterosexual couples who have approached the decision to parent together so thoughtfully. Perhaps this agreement can inspire some of them to do so too. Nancy and Paul were delighted, devoted biological and legal co-parents of a preschool-age son and an infant daughter when I interviewed them in 2001. They were not, however, the children's only parents. Before Nancy became pregnant with their first child, Cupid tested Paul's ability to live up to the sixth of the pair's prenatal pledges. Nancy had met and entered a romantic relationship with Liza, a woman who long had wanted to have children. Paul had risen to the challenge of supporting and incorporating Liza into his parenting alliance with Nancy, and so their son and daughter were born into a three-parent family. Nancy and Paul more than honored all of the pertinent terms in their shared parenting plan. Jointly they had purchased a duplex residential property. During the period of my study, Nancy and Liza lived together in the front house, Paul inhabited the back house, their toddler was sleeping alternate nights in each, and the breastfed infant still was sharing her two mothers' bedroom every night. Paul and Nancy, the two primary parents, were fully sharing the major responsibilities and expenses along with the joys of parenthood. Both had reduced their weekly work schedules to three days so that each could devote two days weekly to full-time parenting. A hired nanny cared for the children on the fifth day. Liza, who was employed full-time, did early evening child care on the days that Nancy and Paul worked late, and she fully co-parented with them on weekends and holidays.

This three-parent family enjoyed the support of a thick community of kith and kin. One of Paul's former lovers was godfather to the children, and he visited frequently. The three-parent family celebrated holidays with extended formal and chosen kin, including another gay-parent family.

The family was still intact when I contacted Paul and Nancy again in October 2008. Nancy and Liza had just celebrated their tenth anniversary as a couple, and Paul was still single.

Careful Fourplay

A second successfully planned poly-parent family included two moms, two dads, and two homes. Lisa and Kat, a monogamous, white lesbian couple, had initiated this family when after fifteen years together, they had asked their dear friend and former housemate, Michael Harwood, to serve as the sperm donor and an acknowledged father to the children they wished to rear. It had taken Michael, a white gay man who was single at that time, five years of serious reflection and discussions before he finally agreed to do so. "There is really no way to express the complexity of my journey," Michael related in an account he wrote for a gay magazine, "or to impart the richness of the experience. Given the rare opportunity to truly think about whether or not I wanted to be a parent (as opposed to having it sprung upon me), I left no rock unturned—no hiking trail was untread."[4]

Gradually Michael had realized that he did not wish to become a parent unless he too had a committed mate: "I told them that I could not do it alone (without a partner). I thought about what it would be like going through parenthood without a significant partner with whom to discuss and share things. It seemed too isolating."[5] Fortuitously, just when his lesbian friends were reaching the end of their patience, Michael met and fell in love with Joaquin, a Chicano, gay predestined parent who had always wanted children. The new lovers asked Lisa and Kat to give them a year to solidify their union before embarking on co-parenthood. Both couples reported that they spent that year in a four-way parental courtship:

> Joaquin and I had many talks and all four of us were, quite frankly, falling in love with each other in a way that can only be described as romantic love. There were flowers, there were candlelight dinners, and there were many beach walks and much laughter. There were many brave conversations about our needs and our fears and our excitement. There was nothing that could prepare us for the first night when Joaquin and I went to Lisa and Kat's home to make love and leave a specimen. . . . By the way, it is not a turkey baster but a syringe that is used. Love was the main ingredient, though, and Joaquin and I experienced a transcendent epiphany as we walked along the beach after the exchange. We knew that our lives and our relationship to Lisa and Kat would never be the same even if the conception did not happen. We shared, perhaps, the most intimate of experiences with Lisa and Kat.[6]

Since that magical night, the two couples also had shared many of the intimate joys and burdens of parenting two children. Unlike Nancy and Paul, however, they did not try to equalize parental rights and responsibilities. Lisa and Michael are the children's biological and legal parents, with both of their names on both of the birth certificates. The children resided, however, with Lisa and Kat, who are their primary, daily caretakers and their chief providers. Lisa, who gave birth to and breast-fed both children, also spent the most time with them, primarily because Kat's employment demanded more time outside the home. Although Michael and Joaquin lived and worked more than seventy-five miles away, they had visited their children every single weekend of the children's lives as well as on occasional weeknights. They also conferred with the co-moms and spoke, sang, read, or sent emails to their preschooler almost daily. In addition, the adults consciously sustained, monitored, and nurtured their co-parenting alliance and friendship by scheduling periodic "parent time" for the four adults to spend together while the children slept.

This four-parent family, like the three-parent front-house/back-house family and like the surrogacy-extended family that Eddie and Mama Sally nurtured, regularly shared holidays and social occasions with a wide array of legal and chosen kin. They too were immersed in a large local community of lesbian- and gay-parent families, a community which Lisa had taken the initiative to organize. Three proud sets of doting grandparents were constantly vying for visits, photos, and contact with their grandchildren. In painful contrast, Kat's parents had rejected her when she came out, and they refused to incorporate, or even to recognize, their grandchildren or any of their lesbian daughter's family members within their more rigid, ideological understanding of family.

The Contingency of Contemporary Parenthood

This colorful quilt of lucky, and less lucky, gay pop stories from my research opens a window onto the vagaries of contemporary paths to parenthood generally and to paternity specifically. Because I intentionally over-sampled for fathers when I was recruiting participants for my study, I wound up including a disproportion-ate number of predestined parents. Their stories help us to understand some complex connections between romantic partnership and parenthood today. Most, if not all, of the fervently motivated dads strongly wished to combine the two forms of intimacy. Some even had made parenthood a pivotal courtship criterion, and the luckiest of these, like Eddie and Charles, found com-patible predestined partners. However, if push comes to shove for a predestined parent, children will trump coupledom and can even thwart it, as we have seen. Although Armando deeply desired and attempted to combine partnership with parenthood, he was ulti-mately unwilling to sacrifice the latter on the pyre of adult intimacy. On the other hand, parenthood can prove a pathway to coupling for a fortunate few who, like Drew and Bernardo, find that their parental status enhances their appeal to other predestined parents.

There are numerous reasons to believe that fewer straight men than gay men feel a predestined urge to parent. For one thing, by definition, if not by dispo-sition, gay men are already gender dissidents. Living without wives or girlfriends, they have to participate in caretaking and domestic chores more than straight men do and are less likely to find these activities threatening to their masculine identities. Second, gay men are more likely to be single than are straight men or than are women of whatever sexual orienta-tion (Bell and Weinberg 1978). That translates into a higher percentage of men like Armando, who are apt to feel drawn to seek compensatory intimacy through parenthood. On the carrot side of the ledger, gay dads enjoy easier access than most straight dads do to primary parenting status and its rewards and to support networks for their families.

Gay men also face less pressure to conform to gender scripts for parenting or to defer to women's biological and cultural advantages for nurturing young children. Gay fatherhood, that is to say, occu-pies terrain more akin to conventional motherhood than to dominant forms of paternity.

The unmooring of masculinity from pater-nity exposes the situational character of contem-porary fatherhood and fatherlessness. No longer a mandatory route to masculine adult social status, paternity today is increasingly contingent on the fate of men's romantic attachments. In fact, to attain any form of parenthood today requires either the unequivocal yearning of at least one adult or a more or less accidental pregnancy, like egg donor Marya's. In other words, contemporary maternity has also become increasingly situational, a fact that is reflected in declining fertility rates.

Nonetheless, the majority of women still skew toward the predestined pole of the desire-to-parent continuum. Men, in contrast, regardless of their sexual inclinations, generally cluster along the situa-tional bandwidth. Heterosexual "situations" lead most straight men into paternity (and straight women to maternity). Homosexual situations, on the other hand, lead most gay men to forgo parenthood (Lesbian situa-tions likely are somewhere in between) (Simmons and O'Connell 2003). If this contrast seems obvious, even tautological, it was not always the case. Instead, most contemporary gay fathers became parents while they were enmeshed in closeted homosexual "situations." The past few decades of hard-won gains in gay strug-gles for social acceptance have diminished the need for men with homoerotic desires to resort to this ruse.

Paradoxically, the same shift from closeted to open homosexuality which has made gay fatherhood so vis-ible might also reduce its incidence. Beyond the closet, far fewer gay men than before will become situational parents because they entered heterosexual marriages to pass as straight. Openly gay paternity, by definition, is never accidental. It requires the determined efforts of at least one gay man, like Armando. Eddie, whose passion for parenthood feels predestined—a man, that is, whose parental desires more conventionally might be labeled maternal rather than paternal.

The gay dads I studied did not feel that parent-ing made them less, or more, of a man. Instead, most felt free to express a full palette of gender options. As Drew put it, "I feel that I have a wider emotional range available to me than maybe most of the straight men I know. And I feel comfortable being mother, father, silly gay man, silly queen, tough negotiator in business. I feel like I'm not bound by rules." Rather than a bid for legitimate masculine status, or a rejection of it, inten-tional gay parenthood represents a search for enduring love and intimacy in a world of contingency and flux.

Of course, there is nothing distinctively gay or masculine about this quest. Heterosexual masculin-ity also no longer depends upon marriage or parent-hood. Indirectly, therefore, gay male paths to planned parenthood highlight the waning of traditional incentives for pursuing the status of fatherhood as we knew it. Parenthood, like marriage and mating practices, has entered contingent terrain.

The fact that gay men now pursue parenthood outside social conventions of gender, marriage, and procreation catapults them into the vanguard of contemporary parenting. Just as gay men are at once freer and more obliged than most of the rest of us to craft the basic terms of their romantic and domestic unions, so too they have to make more self-conscious decisions about whether to parent, with whom, and how. I hope that the thoughtful, magnanimous, child-centered co-parenting agreement that Paul and Nancy devised will inspire throngs of prospective parents to undertake similar discussions before deciding whether baby should make three, or four or more, for that matter.

NOTES

1. Twenty-four men were actively parenting children. In addition, two men were step-fathers to a partner's non-residential children; one man with his mother formerly co-foster-parented teenagers; four of the adoptive fathers had also formerly fostered teenagers, and two of these intended to resume this practice in the future; one man served as a known sperm donor for lesbian-couple friends; and one man was a genetic father who does not parent his offspring.

2. One man, a sperm dad who nicknamed himself a "spad," had facilitated a lesbian friend's desire to conceive a child with a donor willing to be an avuncular presence in her child's life. The other unwittingly impregnated a former girlfriend who chose to keep the child and agreed not to reveal its paternity.

3. Of the gay parents, five are Latino, three are black or Caribbean, and one is Asian American. Thirteen of the thirty-four children are white; nine are Latino; eight are black, Caribbean, or mixed race; and four are multi-racial Asian.

4. "Love Makes a Family," unpublished speech to a gay community group, on file with author. Additional information about this speech is withheld to protect the anonymity of my informant.

5. Ibid.

6. Ibid.

REFERENCES

Beck, Ulrich, and Elizabeth Beck-Gernsheim. 1995. *The Normal Chaos of Love*. Cambridge, UK: Polity.

Bell, Alan P., and Martin S. Weinberg. 1978. *Homosexualities: A Study of Diversity among Men and Women*. New York: Simon & Schuster.

Brodzinsky, David, Charlotte J. Patterson, and Mahnoush Vaziri. 2002. "Adoption Agency Perspectives on Lesbian and Gay Prospective Parents: A National Study." *Adoption Quarterly* 5(3): 5–23.

Gates, Gary. Distinguished Scholar at the Williams Institute, UCLA Law School, personal communication, May 17, 2005.

Human Rights Campaign. 2009. "Equality from State to State 2009." http://www.hrc.org/documents/HRC_States_Report_09.pdf.

Kapp, Stephen, Thomas P. McDonald, and Kandi L. Diamond. 2001. "The Path to Adoption for Children of Color." *Child Abuse and Neglect* 25(2): 215–229.

Lasch, Christopher. 1995. *Haven in a Heartless World: The Family Besieged*. New York: Norton.

Sears, R. Bradley, and M.V. Lee Badgett. 2004. "Same-Sex Couples and Same-Sex Couples Raising Children in California: Data from Census 2000." Williams Project on Sexual Orientation and the Law, UCLA Law School.

Simmons, Tavia, and Martin O'Connell. 2003. "Married-Couple and Unmarried-Partner Households: 2000." U.S. Census Bureau, February.

Stacey, Judith. 1998. "Dada-ism in the Nineties: Getting Past Baby Talk about Fatherlessness."

In *Lost Fathers: The Politics of Fatherlessness*, ed. Cynthia Daniels. New York: St. Martin's.

Strah, David, and Susanna Margolis. 2003. *Gay Dads*. New York: J.T. Tacher/Putnam.

Townsend, Nicholas. 2002. *The Package Deal: Marriage, Work, and Fatherhood in Men's Lives*. Philadelphia: Temple University Press.

U.S. Department of Health and Human Services, Administration for Children and Families, Administration on Children, Youth, and Families, Children's Bureau. 2003. *The AFCARS Report*. http://www.acf.hhs.gov/programs/cb/publications/afcars/report8.pdf.

THINKING ABOUT THE READING

According to Stacey, how do gay men who choose to parent challenge conventional definitions of masculinity and paternity? How have these men made the "social character of paternity" more visible? How do the stories of Stacey's interviewees compare with images of gay male families you have observed in the media? Stacey's interviewees all lived in Los Angeles, a city that she notes is one of the most favorable cities for the architectures of gay and lesbian parenthood. Due to different legal and social restrictions on gay parenthood and families in other areas of the United States, how might the experiences of gay men who wish to parent and form families be different in these places?

Life and Love outside the Citizenship Binary

APRIL M. SCHUETHS

(2015)

A popular myth is harming families in the United States. The notion that families are split into mutually exclusive groups of citizens and noncitizens is false. The belief in such a citizenship binary hides the interconnections between Americans, both documented and undocumented, in the same family. While scholars are beginning to discuss the important challenges surrounding mixed-status families, few have documented the experiences of mixed-status couples (i.e., undocumented immigrants partnered with US citizens). The public mistakenly assumes that mixed-status marriage confers legalization to the undocumented partner (Schueths 2012). However, marriage alone does not provide the protections of citizenship for undocumented spouses and in many cases creates a compromised citizenship for the citizen spouse (Mercer 2008; Schueths 2012). Misunderstood and hidden in the shadows, mixed-status couples quietly suffer injustice.

The increase in immigrant Latino/a populations, particularly Mexican immigrants (Ennis, Rios-Vargas, and Albert 2011), has coincided with the growth of punitive immigration laws that promote family inequality. Navigating confusing immigration policies that vilify undocumented immigrants and their families is essentially like walking through a minefield, as one misstep can cost a family their life as they know it. Accordingly, the stories of mixed-status couples have become complex and important to understand. Thus my work is focused on the following research question: How do thirty-nine participants, representing twenty mixed-status couples, construct and understand their subjective experiences within the United States as they attempt to negotiate their position?

Self-Reflections of My Work with Mixed-Status Couples

The impetus for this research took place on my friend Jacqueline's front porch one chilly fall evening. We were talking about her partner, Aaron, and how hard it was for him living as an undocumented immigrant and the profound impact it had on their relationship. As we sat on her porch, it occurred to me that this educated, successful woman was not the only person I knew who was in a relationship with or married to an undocumented Latino/a. There were others including another close friend, a circle of acquaintances, and also former students. These educated women, many who identified as white, did not seem to fit the "media profile" of an individual married or partnered with an undocumented person. I wondered why no one was talking about these issues, in the same way these women were, especially in the light of intense immigration debates.

On December 12, 2006, about two months after I started my research, large-scale immigration raids of Swift meatpacking plants took place in six states, including Nebraska, the state I was residing in at the time. Both large-scale and less publicized raids continued, creating an environment of fear and uncertainty for undocumented individuals and their families. Participants were well aware of the anti-immigrant sentiment and during interviews often commented on specific incidences in their communities and within the United States. Thus my recruitment flyers were in English and Spanish and stated, "No human being is illegal!,"[1] and included an excerpt that stated, "Undocumented and formerly undocumented individuals and their families contribute to our society and deserve to tell their story in a safe environment."

I was naturally concerned that families would be reluctant to tell their stories. I am a middle-class, heterosexual, white woman who receives numerous privileges because of my status set; I have never been undocumented, nor am I currently a member of a mixed-status couple. My Spanish-language skills are basic, at best. Before my personal experiences with mixed-status couples, I too believed the stereotype that marriage was an easy antidote for legalization. I know now that I was mistaken.

My privileged position affects my perceptions and interpretations; therefore it has been my goal to remain self-reflective throughout the entire research process. I used reflective journals to record my impressions, thoughts, and, ideas. I relied heavily on the guidance of my immigration scholar colleagues, especially my interpreter, who grew up in a mixed-status family. Most importantly, I returned to my participants for their feedback on my findings.

Even with my blind spots I strive, albeit imperfectly, to be an advocate of social justice. I must acknowledge that I may have unknowingly had greater rapport with English-speaking participants, regardless of legal status. Yet, regardless of language, individuals welcomed the opportunity to tell their story, and some even expressed gratitude that "someone was actually looking at this." As more than one participant stated, "It's relieving to tell your story, because who really cares? Nobody."

Stories of Mixed-Status Couples

My research on mixed-status couples was collected over a two-year period (2007–9) and examines the lived experiences of undocumented and formerly undocumented Latino/a immigrants partnered or married to US native-born citizens of any race and ethnicity (Schueths 2009). Latino/a participants reported that they left their country of origin because of scarce job opportunities in Mexico, or the desire to be closer to their family members who were already in the United States, or both. Several male participants stated that they were seeking a sense of adventure, while one female participant stated that she was fleeing political persecution.

I conducted interviews with thirty-nine participants (twenty couples). One couple included only the female partner because the male partner was living in Mexico and did not choose to participate. I interviewed participants in person (twenty-seven) or, because of distance, on the telephone (twelve) and either one-on-one (seven couples) or with their partner present (thirteen couples). Twenty-two participants reported that Spanish was their first language. Of these, four participants requested a Spanish interpreter. I used the same interpreter, a bilingual male colleague, who self-identifies as Mexican and, at the time, was studying Latino/a immigration. In-person interviews generally took place in the couples' homes (twenty) or at private community settings (seven).

Due to the sensitivity of this research, participants were not required to provide their names; only verbal consent was required. The interviews typically averaged sixty to ninety minutes, and I used aliases to protect the privacy and safety of the families.

Participants lived in seven states (Illinois, Iowa, Minnesota, Missouri, Nebraska, Texas, and Wisconsin), and three participants were residing in Mexico at the time of the interview. In general, participants tended to be undocumented Mexican men married to Anglo women. One Latina participant reported being from Central America. An overwhelming majority of couples were married and reported being married for about three years on average and together for a total of five. Couples that were not married or engaged were together from one to three years. Ninety percent of the couples in my sample self-identified as interracial, while 10 percent self-identified as Mexican/Mexican-American/Hispanic. The average participant was thirty-one years old, and the women were slightly older than the men. Couples tended to either have no children or be part of a blended family. On average, the women in this sample tended to have more education than the men, regardless of their legal status. The median family income reported was $59,000 per year, and about half of the couples owned their own home.

We'll Be Together Somehow

Nearly two-thirds of the couples in this study included a partner who was undocumented at the time of this study. The remaining one-third consisted of seven couples with a formerly undocumented spouse who now has permanent residence. In order to gain permanent residence, five of the seven couples spent time physically divided (typically for at least one year) in two different countries.[2] Not surprisingly, the foreboding threat of deportation and family separation weighs heavily on many participants' minds. The majority of US citizen partners, in particular women, suggested that regardless of what happens they will find a way to remain with their partner, even if it means relocating beyond the United States. Some of the participants were very matter-of-fact about stating their position, while others expressed more impassioned views.

Lola and Eduardo, an engaged interracial couple, have not yet started the immigration paperwork process but have spoken with an attorney, who gave them devastating news. Eduardo is facing a ten-year ban, and possibly a lifetime ban, for previous arrests when attempting to cross the Mexico-US border "illegally." He was barely an adult at the time. Although they plan to consult a different attorney, they know that it will likely be an uphill battle. Regardless of pending legal difficulties, their wedding was around the corner when I interviewed them and they were fully prepared to do what it takes to be together, even if that means being forced to move to Mexico.

Antonio and Rebecca, a newly married interracial couple, are in a similar predicament. Although moving to Mexico is not the goal, Rebecca, an Anglo citizen, expresses faith that things will be okay: "I know that it will be fine because, worst case scenario, he has to go back to Mexico. Well, I could live in Mexico. We'll be together somehow."

Donna and Alfonso, also a married interracial couple and self-described "best friends," are in the midst of immigration proceedings and have been living in two different countries for months. Alfonso is in Mexico waiting to learn whether his immigration case will be approved. Donna echoes the majority of citizen women in this study: "Like if [for] some reason we get a ban and he isn't able to come back to the US, then he knows I'll move down there [Mexico] in a heartbeat to just be together, and he knows that if he moves back here that we'll figure things out, whatever happens."

Kate, a biracial citizen, however, is not willing to be separated from her husband, Jorge, an undocumented Mexican immigrant. She passionately explains that she will not lose her spouse without a fight:

My thing is, and I've always been blunt about this, I won't lose my husband. Somebody else will lose their life before I lose my husband. Because that's like me going into their house and taking their wife away or their husband away They're not gonna like it either. I won't lose my husband, because if I lose him, I lose one of my best friends, I lose myself, basically because what am I gonna have when I come home? I won't have him to talk to. I won't have him to do things with, I won't lose my husband.

Filing immigration paperwork with the US Citizenship and Immigration Services does not guarantee that a spouse will be granted legal residence, and it is extremely risky because individuals who have lived in the United States without status for an extended period of time are subject to harsh penalties, including being banned from the United States for ten years or even life (Mercer 2008). Few options exist for couples who want to remain in the United States together. Acceptance of an extreme hardship waiver is one of the only ways for a US citizen to adjust his or her spouses undocumented status, which is very difficult (and costly) to obtain. Family separation in itself is not grounds for approval of the waiver; the hardship must be extraordinary. In some cases, families are not even eligible to apply for the waiver.

Manuel and Abby's immigration case seemed straightforward (i.e., no major law violations), and their attorney thought that Manuel had a good chance of being allowed to remain in the United States. Because of his extended unlawful presence, he was subject to a ten-year bar from the United States and was required to document that his deportation would cause extreme hardship to his citizen wife and child. Manuel and Abby were devastated when they learned that their case had been denied. Abby recounts an emotional good-bye with her husband as he boarded a plane for Mexico, his country of origin:

I can't even describe it. I'm going to start crying if I talk about it. I hate to even think about it. It was the hardest thing I had ever been through in my life. That day in the airport, when we had to say good-bye to each other, I totally broke down and freaked out. . . . I could hardly get my emotions under control to get him on the plane. Because I had no idea how long I'd be away from him. I literally think, since the day we started dating, we were never apart for more than forty-eight hours. It was like love at first sight.

After being forced to be a transnational family for several excruciating months, they had no choice but to relocate the entire family to Mexico, including their five-year-old daughter. This move was not part of their plan. Manuel explains, "You never know where you might be ending up."

Challenges with separation were not limited to the couples and their immediate family but also included stories of extended family members divided by international borders, primarily Mexico and the

United States. The circumstances for transnational families are complicated by strict border enforcement and harsh US immigration laws, making it extremely risky for undocumented individuals to travel back and forth between Mexico and the United States. Physical borders and legalities clearly play a role in participants' lives and travel decisions; however, emotional connections with extended family members can sometimes trump legal risks. These dilemmas are never easy. Antonio described his divided loyalties between family members in two countries. He is pretty sure that he will eventually have to return to Mexico with his US citizen wife, Rebecca, in hopes of adjusting his undocumented legal status. Even though he would prefer to stay in the United States, he is conflicted: "Like I told her [Rebecca], if I go back [to Mexico], I'm gonna go to my mom. But my sister is getting old, and my sister lives here [in the United States] by herself, with [a child]. Now it's like, I don't even know what to do. It's like a balance." The decision to stay in the United States or return to Mexico becomes particularly difficult to negotiate when family crises and celebrations arise. Participants in the process of applying for their residency or considering application for residency risk being barred from the United States, should they get caught crossing the Mexico-US border. These risks must be carefully weighed.

When Raul received word that his father was ill and would not likely make it, he and Trim, his Mexican-American US citizen wife, decided that it was best for him to return to Mexico to be with his extended family. This return was particularly risky because Raul was undocumented at the time. Raul described traveling alone to Mexico: "Because my father passed away, I had to go see my family one last time. It was very painful, first of all because she [Trini] wasn't with me to support me."

Trini explained that, despite legal risks, they determined that it was best for Raul to be with his family: "He had never gone back and forth, he had always been here in the states, and when they called him and told him his dad was sick we decided that he should go and see his dad even though we knew the, you know, what was gonna happen. We didn't really know what was all entailed in bringing him [Raul] back until we got immersed in it."

Raul recently returned to the United States after being separated from Trini for eighteen months. Fortunately his immigration case was eventually approved. He reported, "I wanted to come back; my life is here [in the United States) now." He went on to explain, "It's the same situation—you can never be with both at the same time."

Chelsea, an Anglo citizen spouse, traveled to Mexico without her undocumented husband, Juan, to attend his family members wedding. She echoes the challenges of extended family separation: "It's not just about our family here—there's a whole 'nother family missing their family member."

Finally, the inherent inhumanity of the immigration system is highlighted. Tiffany, an Anglo citizen spouse, who has traveled back and forth to Mexico for three years to be with her undocumented husband, illustrates that it is easier to legally bring a dog across the Mexico-US border than it is to bring a person. "So I could go down there [to Mexico] and pay $300 and bring two dogs across [to] the United States. And I can't even pay $30,000 and bring my husband across [to] the United States. That's sad."

Stuck behind Invisible Bars

Participants described dealing with the byzantine immigration system as confusing, difficult, arbitrary, expensive, timely, and ultimately a "nightmare." Constant changes to policies, laws, and paperwork create the need for diligent understanding if one ever hopes to successfully maneuver the system. The ambiguous immigration process prevented many families from even trying to adjust a spouse's legal status; they simply had too much to lose since there are no guarantees that permanent residency will be approved.

Due to an extended unlawful presence in the United States, Eduardo, a college student who is engaged to Lola, will face a ten-year or even a lifetime bar from the United States. Lola, an Anglo citizen, shares what they heard about the possible shadiness of the system: "We've kind of heard that it's like however much money you're willing to pay, the less amount of time you have to spend in Mexico or the faster you get them [papers]. It's kind of like the system may be corrupt. I'm not for sure." Eduardo describes a sense of hopelessness that his current circumstance can ever improve. "My situation, how I feel, it's like in a two-by-two closet with one door and it's up in the ceiling, you know, because how I see the system, from what I've read, there is no way out." Similarly, Anna, an Anglo citizen, explains that she wishes she could help her undocumented partner, Carlos, and his family, who have not yet attempted to adjust their legal status. She says, "They're stuck behind invisible bars because they're just held back, they can't excel."

A great deal of misinformation also contributes to keeping families "stuck." Consequently, mixed-status couples are vulnerable to being taken advantage of even by those who claim to be advocates. Some couples stumbled their way through the process, while others became overnight immigration experts. Alfonso and Donna, an interracial married couple, were forced to decipher the immigration system on their own. They were told by a paralegal that Alfonso, an undocumented immigrant, would not have to leave the country to adjust his legal status; however, this information was not correct. At the time of my interview, Alfonso was in Mexico waiting to learn whether his case would be approved. Donna says: "I wish we had done a lot more research when we started. I definitely could have gotten all this on my own without even hiring the lawyer, and we probably paid them $1000 for them doing basically nothing." Mariano and Faith, also an interracial married couple, paid $3,000 despite having worked without an attorney up to their first immigration appointment. Because Mariano could face a ten-year bar from the United States, they have been advised to stall their immigration paperwork. Although their attorney is a well-known immigrant advocate in their community, Faith says, "She exploited me a little."

Even when couples have access to correct information, the process of attempting to adjust a spouse's legal status can create a sense of anxiety. Jackie, an Anglo citizen spouse, described the overall absurdity of the immigration process: "I remember receiving a letter one day that said the case would be resolved in 999 days. And I just about fell out of my chair. And I laughed because—it wasn't really a funny laugh, it was just . . . just the whole procedure was insane."

Families with an undocumented partner, who travel abroad, attempting to adjust their legal status, confront further emotional and financial strain because their family's income is often cut in half. While Cruz, who now has permanent residency, was in Mexico attempting to adjust his legal status, Jackie, his spouse, says, "I was at my breaking point because I was desperate, I was broke." She had solid credit before her husband left for Mexico. In less than a year, their credit card debt climbed from $3,000 to $20,000. Because

remittances are often sent from the United States to Mexico, many people might be surprised to learn that during their time apart, Cruz ended up sending money back to the United States to help support Jackie:

He [Cruz] couldn't help me. There was no work; I think he maybe worked twice. He picked tomatoes or something. There's no work where he was [In Mexico]. I was making all these payments on my own, and I ended up relying on credit cards and reserve lines of credit to get me through things. He sold our car, the car that he took down . . . he kept a car that—it was paid off—it was the car that I had for a long time, and [he] ended up selling it and sending me money It was kind of ironic—usually money goes into Mexico. He ended up sending me some money to help me get through.

In general, families' quality of life improves if a spouse is able to gain permanent residence, yet it is important to understand that their struggles do not immediately disappear. For example, Vanessa described the drawn-out immigration process: "So that took, ah, that took years. That immigration process, like I find it to be very difficult, you know, lengthy, ah, just, just like a nightmare." She is also extremely private about her previous legal status. Her teenage children do not even know that she was once undocumented. She reported, "I will not, do not, say it to anyone." Although her husband, David, an Anglo citizen, would like her to pursue US citizenship, Vanessa explains that she is fearful that working under a false Social Security number years ago could come back to haunt her: "And now I'm even more scared because with all the things, things that they do on immigration, all the times. I even have nightmares. I have nightmares, and they send me back to my country."

Sue, an Anglo citizen spouse, clarified that, technically, permanent residents can still face legal risks for deportation:

What a lot of people don't understand is that even with residency, he [Alejandro, her husband] has his resident status, but still, if he were picked up on a certain crime that may be a misdemeanor on the local level, if they decided to pursue it and immigration had a question about it, they could charge him at a federal level, and it may not be a misdemeanor anymore, it might be an aggravated misdemeanor, or it might even be classified as a felony. Or if he would drink and get two DUIs in less than a five-year period, that also could be a deportable crime, and they would deport him. Or if they just don't like the way he looks, you know, depending on what the immigration officer wanted to bring up.

Despite dealing with an immigration system that operates within unclear boundaries, few people would trade their permanent residency for their former undocumented status. The risks are much greater for families with an undocumented partner.

The majority of mixed-status couples with an undocumented partner dream of the day their status issues disappear. They desperately want "to do the right thing." For example, Antonio, an undocumented spouse, says: "Even in the news, you know, why illegal people, they should do the right thing, you know. And we try to do the right things, and it's not working." Rebecca, his citizen spouse, expressed her frustration with seemingly arbitrary immigration rules: "You can't just look up the rules and follow the rules. I'm a rule follower. And, you know, it doesn't work like that. I mean, there's so many roadblocks, it's like they make you work the system."

In addition, participants frequently perceived immigration workers as having a great deal of discretion, often making arbitrary decisions. They argued that workers have entirely too much power. According to mixed-status families, catching someone on a bad day can literally have detrimental consequences. As Abby, a citizen spouse whose husband's case was denied, points out: "Those people have way too much power in their hands." She continues:

You can go to one person and you will get your papers, but if you go to someone that's in a bad mood, you're not going to get your papers. There should be rules and regulations, like a How chart: if you've done this, then this is what's going to happen; if you've done this, this is what's going to happen. It shouldn't just be every case for itself, I don't think. Literally, he (Manuel) got somebody that was in a bad mood and he got denied.

Other mixed-status couples felt that immigration workers were impolite and purposely looked for reasons to deny their case. Trini and Raul discussed their experience with immigration workers at the consulate in Ciudad Juarez, Mexico. Trini, a Mexican-American citizen, explained: "I think, actually at the consulate, people are not helpful at all. It's really like they'll try to find, from some experiences that we heard, they'll find any reason . . . to say no." Raul, now a legal permanent resident, described waiting for hours in the reception area at the consulate. He could hear other people meeting with immigration workers, crying, pleading their cases. He, too, expressed that immigration workers tend to be unhelpful. "They're all very rude; they don't treat you with respect." He continued: "It's psychological, accusing and scaring people. They ask about everything you've done. I was always scared that they would find something wrong, accuse you of something you didn't do."

Lilly, an undocumented spouse, knows firsthand what it is like to be accused of something she did not do. She described growing up on the border and frequently traveling back and forth between Mexico and the United States because she had family on both sides. Her family had actually lived in the United States at one point and had initiated residency for the family; therefore she had a travel visa and a Social Security card but was not authorized to work in the United States."[3]

She described her attempt to do the right thing:

1 went to get another permit because I was going to be here [in the United States] two days longer than my permit was going to be good for and I didn't want to get in trouble- This is how stupid this is: I didn't want to get into trouble, so I go into the office, at the border—by the way I usually left my car on the US side, I left it on the US side and left to get a permit, which was half a block [away]. So, anyway, I went in there and I asked for a permit, and she was like, "Oh, can I have your ID?" I open my wallet and the first thing she saw was [a business card from a US college]. She took my wallet, she took my bag, they put me in a room, they shook everything out, and they told me: "You're not getting out of here until God knows when." At that point I was trying to figure out what I wanted to

study aside from the career that I didn't like . . . I visited [the college], and I was interested in [discipline], and I went and I got a card, a business card, from the international department of admissions. *International,* as in from another country; so I had that and I had my Social [Security card] in my wallet, and then I had my [temporary] driver's license, so she assumed that I was living, working, and studying here. First of all, if you look at my Social it says, "Not valid for work."

Lilly continues, "So, basically, they throw me in this room, and you don't get the right to call anybody, its freezing cold, and they're telling you you're going to stay a week." After being interrogated for nearly four hours, she gave in and signed their papers. Although she was innocent and barely an adult at the time, her immigration record is forever marked. In addition, her travel visa was taken from her, and therefore she no longer had the ability to travel back and forth between Mexico and the United States. "Anyway, I signed whatever paper so they could let me go—this was after four hours—and they fingerprinted me, they handcuffed me." She continues: "I honestly believed in justice. I believed I wasn't doing anything wrong, so they had to see it, but of course they didn't care to see it, and why would they? They don't care."

Juan, an undocumented spouse, echoes the sentiment I heard from nearly all the participants; he calls for a workable solution to legalization: "I know there's a lot of illegal people here. . . . I don't want anything free. I would be happy to pay $5,000 for a visa." Sue, a citizen spouse, points out, "If they could go back to just taking the money and letting families be together . . . we'd have families that would be unified and the government would be making more money." Simply paying a fine is likely an impractical immigration solution since mixed-status families are more likely to be low-income when compared with other families (Fix and Zimmermann 2001). Although the majority of couples in this study were not low-income, like many middle-class families they often faced financial hardships, which were exacerbated by their mixed status. Even if some families could pay the fine, this sum would likely be prohibitive to most.

Where Do We Go from Here?

This work illuminates the omitted or misunderstood narratives of couples living outside the citizenship binary. Mixed-status couples discuss the threat of impending separation as well as the struggles of surviving living apart from their loved ones. For example, Kate, a citizen, points out, "I've always been blunt about this, I won't lose my husband." Couples also reveal stories of extended family members divided by international borders. In the participants' views, the dense immigration system is overflowing with injustice and is ultimately a "nightmare." Participants explain their desire to "do the right thing"; however, they point out that there is often no rhyme or reason for many of the immigration decisions made. As Eduardo, an undocumented immigrant, powerfully explains, "There is no way out." Furthermore, without citizenship, families who secure permanent residency for a spouse often continue to live within unclear boundaries.

Current public policy disregards the consequences of family separation and the lack of options available to "legally" adjust an undocumented spouse's legal status. Increasing racial and ethnic diversity from nonwhite groups and the growth of undocumented immigration appear to have infused a sense of anger on the part of some members of the dominant group, leading to increasingly restrictive policies (Hero 2010). Paradoxically, these unjust policy shifts also negatively affect the citizen partners of undocumented immigrants, many of whom are from the dominant racial group (Schueths 2012, 2014).

Consistent with Julie Mercer's (2008) research, this study found that enforcement-based immigration policies promote separation of mixed-status spouses and are inherently contradictory to US pro-marriage initiatives. This situation is an example of how the US legal system subtly reinforces the dominant cultural values while marginalizing the experiences of nondominant individuals and their families. The hardships of family separation and an opaque immigration system validate recommendations to remove the bars for unlawful presence and to permit a greater number of family visas (Cruz 2010, 181). Findings from this research also acknowledge the potential economic benefits of returning to the payment of a penalty fee for unlawful entry into the United States (Mercer 2008, 325). Undocumented immigrants and their citizen partners consistently expressed their willingness to pay a penalty fee as opposed to being forced to leave the country. However, many (perhaps most) mixed-status families would not have the financial means to pay a penalty fee. Returning to the $5,000-fine policy may create a divided opportunity structure where the most affluent couples reap the benefit of legalization, while their lower-income counterparts remain trapped in their current state of legal limbo.

Mixed-status couples must be conceptualized in new and more accurate ways that acknowledge their humanity. Outdated narratives must be replaced with the current realities of mixed-status couples in the context of destructive immigration policies. I conclude with the words of a participant, Chelsea, who evocatively compares her husband, Juan, and herself to Romeo and Juliet: "Instead of our parents keeping us apart, it's our countries."

REFERENCES

Cruz, Evelyn H. 2010. "Because You're Mine, I Walk the Line; The Trials and Tribulations of the Family Visa Program." *Fordham Urban Law Journal* 38 (1); 155–85.

Ennis, Sharon R., Merarys Rios-Vargas, and Nora G. Albert. 2011. *The Hispanic Population; 2010.* Census Brief, C2010BR-04, Washington, DC US Census Bureau. http://www.census.gov/prod/cen2010/brief/2010br-04.pdf

Fix, Michael E., and Wendy Zimmermann, 2001. "All under One Root: Mixed-Status Families in an Era of Reform." *International Migration Review* 35(2): 397–419.

Hero. Rodney E. *2010.* "Immigration and Social Policy in the United States." *Annual Review of Political Science* 13: 445–68.

Mercer, Julie. 2008, "The Marriage Myth: Why Mixed-Status Marriages Need an Immigration Remedy" *Golden Gate University Law Review 38(2):* 293–325.

Schueths, April M. 2009. "Public Policies, Social Myths and Private Vulnerabilities: The Lives of Mixed Citizenship Status Families in the United States." PhD diss., University of Nebraska-Lincoln Paper AAI3350756.

_____2012. "'Where Are My Rights?': Compromised Citizenship in Mixed-Status Marriage: A Research Note." *Journal of Sociology and Social Welfare.*39 (4): 97–109.

_____2014. "'It's Almost like While Supremacy': Interracial Mixed-Status Couples Facing Racist Nativism." *Ethnic and Racial Studies* 37(13); 2438–56.

US Customs and Border Protection, n.d. "'Definition of an I-94." https//help-cbp.gov/app/answers/detail/a_id/88o/~/definition-of-an-i-94.

US Department of Homeland Security n.d. Homeland Security. http://www.dhs.gov/dhsgov-z-index.

NOTES

1. This chapter draws from my dissertation, titled "Public Policies, Social Myths, and Private Vulnerabilities: 'The Lives of Mixed Citizenship Status Families in the United States" (Schueths 2009). My research was supported by the University of Nebraska-Lincoln's Department of Sociology, the Center for Great Plains Studies, and the Office of Graduate Studies.

2. Typically, immigrants with extended undocumented presence in the United States must return to their country of origin to adjust their legal status.

3. Lilly was a temporary visitor to the United States and used an arrival-departure record (Form 1–94). For more information, see US Customs and Border Protection, n.d.

THINKING ABOUT THE READING

What is the citizenship binary? How does it cause family inequalities and what role does public policy play in this process? How does it compromise commonly held values and norms around what married couples and their families should embody? Do institutions in the United States need to be reframed in order to support families?

Constructing Difference
Social Deviance

According to most sociologists, deviance is not an inherent feature or personality trait. Instead, it is a consequence of a definitional process. Like beauty, it is in the eye of the beholder. Deviant labels can impede everyday social life by forming expectations in the minds of others. Some sociologists argue that the definition of *deviance* is a form of social control exerted by more powerful people and groups over less powerful ones.

At the structural level, the treatment of people defined as deviant is often more a function of *who* they are than of *what* they did. In particular, racial, ethnic, gender, and poverty stereotypes often combine to influence social reactions to individuals who have broken the law. In "Imprisoned Black Women in Popular Media," Cheryle D. Snead-Greene and Michael D. Royster provide explanations for the disproportionate number of women of color in the prison system. They examine the war on drugs, aggressive policing, the emphasis of punishment over treatment, and the impact that prison has on women of color. Using the television series, *Orange Is the New Black* (*OITNB*) as their case study, the authors demonstrate how media representations of prisons, like the ones in *OITNB*, shape people's view of women's incarceration, while also sending messages about social injustice, gender inequalities, and racial disparities in prison.

The definitional process that results in the labelling of some acts as deviant can occur at the institutional as well as the individual level. Powerful institutions are capable of creating a definition of deviance that the public comes to accept as truth. One such institution is religion, and one topic rampant with tensions and conflict in evangelical Christian communities is that of sexual activity. Once considered to only be acceptable within the confines of a monogamous heterosexual marriage and for the sole purpose of procreation, Kelsy Burke shows how Christian sexuality websites are using technology to advocate for "godly sex." This concept combines the traditional notions of gender and sexuality with more current views on sexual identities, practices, and desires. Thus, on one hand, these website creators are challenging tradition but on the other, they are also finding innovative ways to positively shape religious expression, practices, and beliefs that affect the daily lives of their Christian users.

Since deviant labels are defined, they can also be redefined. Nonetheless, these labels still have a powerful impact on the people they are assigned to, especially when they have gained widespread acceptance across the social world. People whose bodies do not reflect socially accepted norms on size are often labelled as deviant because their bodies represent culturally assigned images of laziness, unattractiveness, and therefore are labelled as nonsexual. In this selection, "Fat Shame to Fat Pride: Fat Women's Sexual and Dating Experiences," Jeannine A. Gailey interviews fat-identified women to learn more about their perceptions of body image, the size acceptance movement, and their dating and sexual histories. While body shame and fat hatred did have meaningful effects on the lives of these women, she also finds that is not the whole story.

Something to Consider as You Read

In reading and comparing these selections, consider who has the power to define others as deviant. Think about the role of social institutions in establishing definitions of deviance. For example, how does medicine or religion or law participate in describing certain behaviors as abnormal and/or immoral and/or illegal? Does it make a difference which social institution defines certain behaviors as deviant? Why do you think certain deviant behaviors fall under the domain of medicine and others fall under the domain of the law? And do these classifications change with time? For instance, during Prohibition, alcohol consumption was illegal; subsequent to its reinstatement as a legal substance, overconsumption among certain social classes symbolized depravity, and now alcohol abuse is often treated as a medical condition. Who makes the decisions to define certain behaviors not only as deviant, but as deviant within a particular social domain?

Imprisoned Black Women in Popular Media

CHERYLE D. SNEAD-GREENE AND MICHAEL D. ROYSTER

(2018)

The term *War on Drugs* was first used by President Richard Nixon on June 17, 1971, at which time he described illegal drugs as "public enemy number one in the United States." Nixon's drug initiative dramatically increased the size and presence of federal drug control agencies and pushed through measures such as mandatory sentencing and no-knock warrants. According to Human Rights Watch, the *War on Drugs* caused soaring arrest rates that disproportionately targeted African Americans; studies indicate that Nixon may have used the *war on drugs* to criminalize and disrupt Black and hippie communities and their leaders (NPR, 2007). In her book, *The New Jim Crow: Mass Incarceration in the Age of Colorblindness* (2010), Michelle Alexander proclaims that the drug war has never been focused on rooting out drug kingpins or violent offenders. She contends federal funding flows to those agencies that increase dramatically the volume of drug arrests, not the agencies most successful in bringing down the bosses.

The War on Drugs impacts people differently based on gender and race. With more than one million women behind bars or under the control of the criminal justice system, women are the fastest growing segment of the incarcerated population, increasing at nearly double the rate of men since 1985. Nationally, there are more than eight times as many women incarcerated in state and federal prisons and local jails as there were in 1980, increasing in number from 12,300 in 1980 to 182,271 by 2002. The racial disparities that exist in incarceration are just as startling but not surprising. The NAACP (2016) reports that women of color are significantly overrepresented in the criminal justice system. African Americans (men and women) now constitute nearly 1 million of the total 2.3 million incarcerated population. According to the Bureau of Justice Statistics (BJS) the total female prison population in 2011 was 1,598,780 (equating to approximately 1 in 100 African American women in prison). More specifically, the ACLU finds that Black women represent 30 percent of all incarcerated women in the U.S, although they represent 13 percent of the female population generally; and, Hispanic women represent 16 percent of incarcerated women, although they make up only 11 percent of all women in the U.S.

Black women within the prison system deal with various sociological issues and influences that precede their tenure within the walls of confinement. In the Netflix comedy drama series *Orange Is the New Black* (*OITNB*) there are several characters who share with its audience experiences with racial disparities prior to prison. In this chapter we will look into the lives of several Black female characters in the series that were incarcerated for drug abuse. We will briefly discuss the War on Drugs as a war on women. We will discuss how female, Black prisoners, who were victims of the prison system and the internal dynamics of imprisonment, endured prison culture while serving their terms. Finally, we will address the physical, psychological, and internal impact that prison had on these women.

Impact of the War on Drugs Mandate

One of the effects of President Nixon's War on Drugs entailed a broad depletion of significant proportions of African American men from the homes and their respective communities through means of differential justice. The series *OITNB* functions as a testament to how African American women have endured the effects of the removal of targeted men, through their own loss of social capital. The absence of African American men has contributed towards families headed solely by women under economically deprived conditions. Michelle Alexander contends, "The criminalization and demonization of black men has turned the black community against itself, unraveling community and family relationships, decimating networks of mutual support, and intensifying the shame and self-hate experienced by the current pariah caste" (2010: 120–121). Furthermore, such conditions have created a shortage in viable male companions within a predominantly endogamous culture. Such combined factors have created conditions in which women become accustomed to life without significant bonds to men as a source of meaningful emotional and economic support. This dynamic is exacerbated by the scarcity of sustainable employment and eroding of public assistance.

In the 1980s, Ronald Reagan reignited the War on Drugs at a time when drug related crimes were in decline. During that time, says law professor Michelle Alexander (2010), "the media was saturated with images that seemed to confirm the worst negative racial stereotypes." The legacy of Nixon's War on Drugs had a direct impact on many of the drug reform policies made by the Reagan, Bush, Clinton, and Obama administrations. For example, Ronald Reagan escalated the war with "tough on crime" mandatory minimum sentences. George H.W. Bush advised the country that drugs were the greatest domestic threat facing the nation while holding up a bag of seized cocaine. Bill Clinton signed laws that pushed for tougher prison sentences and stripped prison inmates of much of their legal defense rights. The Obama administration alone worked to reshape how America fights its war on drugs—to treat drugs more as a public health issue than a punitive criminal justice undertaking (Lopez, 2017).

The War on Drugs Is a War on Women

The *War on Drugs* policy has had a critical impact on the lives of women in the criminal justice system. Not only has the policy punished women disproportionately to the harm they cause society, the policy has also branded these women as pariahs or social outcasts. The drug war severely punishes women, particularly mothers. Even women who do not use drugs may be punished, for example, by welfare regulations that require recipients to submit to invasive and embarrassing monitored drug testing in order to obtain public assistance. Drug use and drug selling occur at similar rates across racial and ethnic groups, yet Black and Latina women are far more likely to be criminalized for drug law violations than White women. The Drug Policy Alliance (2016) finds that Black women are more than twice as likely—and Latinas are 25 percent more likely—to be incarcerated than White women.

Researchers have found that about half of women offenders confined in state prisons had been using alcohol, drugs, or both at the time of the offense for which they had been incarcerated. These women usually share a similar sociodemographic profile: Most of the women are poor, undereducated, unskilled, single mothers and disproportionately women of color, and their paths to crime are usually marked by abuse, poverty, and addiction.

The emphasis on punishment rather than treatment has brought many low-income women and women of color into the criminal justice system. Women offenders who in the past decades would have been given community sanctions are now being sentenced to prison. Mandatory minimum sentencing for drug offenses has increased the numbers of women in state and federal prisons. Between 1995 and 1996, female drug arrests increased by 95%, while male drug arrests increased by 55%. In 1979, the Bureau of Justice Studies reports that approximately one in ten women in U.S. prisons were serving a sentence for a drug conviction; in 1999, this figure was approximately one in three.

Orange Is the New Black and the Imprisoned Black Woman Drug Offender

In the late eighteenth century, most punishment moved behind prison walls; what took place there was a mystery to most. In the modern era, people often turn to the media and popular culture to feed their curiosity about what sociologist Erving Goffman calls the total institution. In real life, prison life is ugly, grisly, and unpredictable. Not wanting to get their hands truly dirty, people have opted to view the macabre of prison life on the big screen or on the small screen in the comfort of their own homes. They would rather get their "fix" by turning on the television to watch marathons of the prison documentary series *Lockup* on the cable news station MSNBC or by binge-watching *Orange Is the New Black* (*OITNB*) on Netflix. No matter how they choose to ingest it, criminologist Dawn Cecil (2015) contends there are ample opportunities on television to satisfy people's curiosity about life behind bars.

The series *OITNB* depicts the story of Piper Chapman, a White woman in her thirties who is sentenced to fifteen months in prison after being convicted of a decade-old crime of drug trafficking. The show takes place in Litchfield Penitentiary, a minimum-security women's federal prison, and pays close attention to how instances of corruption, drug smuggling, funding cuts, overcrowding, and correctional officer brutality adversely impact not only the prisoners' health and well-being, but also the prison's basic ability to fulfill its fundamental responsibilities and ethical obligations as a federal corrections institution.

In this essay we focus on several dynamic, yet unique women of color, featured in the series that were imprisoned for drug abuse. Tasha "Taystee" Jefferson, Dayanara "Daya" Diaz, and Poussey Washington are convicted drug offenders in the fictional Litchfield Prison system; they are women of color who are victims of both the external and internal dynamics of the War in Drugs policy and imprisonment.

Criminal justice researcher Barbara Bloom and her colleagues Barbara Owen and Stephanie Covington (2004) note that as the United States increased the criminal penalties through mandatory sentencing and longer sentence lengths, huge increases in the imprisonment of women have resulted. Drug use by any woman, whether she lives in suburban or urban areas, often violates gender expectations for women in our society. Poor women who use street-level drugs experience additional societal stigma because they do not have the protective societal buffer enjoyed by women who are insulated by their families, friends, and economic status. Those who use street-level drugs are also less protected from becoming prisoners of the War on Drugs because of their high visibility. Although Whites use drugs at the same rate as African Americans according to public health data, African Americans make up almost half of those arrested for drug offenses and more than half of those convicted of drug offenses, causing critics such as Michelle Alexander (2010) to call the War on Drugs the "New Jim Crow." Between 1982 and 1996, drug law violation sentences got longer and the African American prison population doubled.

Viewers first meet Tasha Taystee Jefferson in prison in Season 1; she works in the hair salon. Almost immediately, the show encourages viewers to see past the orange jumpsuit and recognize that the Taystee character is witty, intelligent, and creative. Jefferson is also, unfortunately, a young Black woman who is incarcerated due to her reluctant participation in a drug ring culminating in a drug trafficking conviction. In Season 1, Episode 9, Jefferson is released from Litchfield but finds that her support network is missing. By Episode 12 in the same season, unable to adjust to life outside, Jefferson commits a crime and returns to Litchfield. Jefferson's story serves to illustrate the often untelevised reality of the never-ending "merry-go-round" from the time prisoners are sentenced to the time they are released and then resentenced again. Likewise, the rate of recidivism among women prisoners is on the rise. In July 2002, the Bureau of Justice Statistics (BJS) released a Special Report, *Recidivism of Prisoners Released in 1994*, describing the recidivism patterns of 272,111 female and male former prisoners (Langan & Levin, 2002). Within three years, almost 68% of all released prisoners were rearrested; 47% were reconvicted; and 25% were resentenced to prison. There are many external factors that contribute to recidivism for women offenders, with the most common factors being substance abuse and mental illness, especially posttraumatic stress disorder.

Dayanara "Daya" Diaz is also in prison for drug related offenses. She was unwittingly involved in a drug operation literally taking place on her kitchen table. Daya was sentenced to 36 months in prison. Mandatory minimum sentencing strips judicial discretion and imposes unduly long prison sentences on minor offenders, violating common sense and fundamental notions of justice and morality. It is important to note that according to Drug Policy Alliance, the most egregious example of mandatory minimum sentencing is the sentencing disparity between crack cocaine and powder cocaine drug law violations.

In Season 4, we learn that Daya's mother, Aleida, who is also incarcerated in Litchfield, was a silent partner in the drug ring operation taking place in Daya's home. While inside Litchfield, Daya and her mother continue to clash. Although rare, there are a few relatives sharing prison dorms and even prison cells. Of the estimated 600,000 parents of minor children in the nation's state prisons in 2004, half had a relative who was currently or used to be incarcerated, according to a Bureau of Justice Statistics report.

Poussey Washington, well-educated and from a middle-class family with a military officer father, is in prison after being busted over a small amount of marijuana. Studies have shown that African Americans and Hispanics are significantly more likely than Whites to be arrested for possession and sale of marijuana, targeted for arrest by the police, and to receive a conviction and criminal record, despite the fact that the majority of regular marijuana users are non-Hispanic Whites. Cannabis is the most widely used illicit substance, with 29 million Americans using it at least once a year. Though 74% of regular marijuana users are non-Hispanic Whites and 14% are Black, Drug Policy Alliance reports that African Americans make up 30% of all marijuana arrests.

While in prison, Poussey becomes depressed and turns to alcohol, even making her own "hooch" to satisfy this addiction. In Season 2, another inmate approaches Poussey about selling her homemade "toilet hooch", but Poussey rejects the offer and, as a result, is psychologically and emotionally punished by the inmate. The toll that this abuse takes on Poussey is revealed in many of the uncharacteristic behaviors that she exhibits in later seasons. Like Poussey, many prisoners are forced to undergo increasingly harsh policies and conditions of confinement in order to survive in the prison. These prolonged adaptations to the deprivations and frustrations of life inside prison lead to certain psychological changes. The person who suffers the acute pains of psychological or emotional abuse from other inmates may develop posttraumatic stress disorder or other forms of disability, which may be in the form of what criminology scholar Gresham Sykes has referred to as diminished sense of self-worth and personal values.

Whether their crimes were petty or significant, all three of these women will likely be forever labeled as drug offenders and face stigmatization long after leaving prison. The War on Drugs mandate continues to haunt drug offenders far beyond the prison walls or the parole officer's office. According to Michelle Alexander, author of *The New Jim Crow: Mass Incarceration in the Age of Colorblindness* (2010) this scenario is not unique. Alexander argues that this war has been waged almost exclusively in poor communities of color and that today we see millions of poor people and folks of color who are trapped, yet again, in a criminal justice system that is treating them like commodities, like people who are easily disposable.

Education may be one way to reduce the incarceration rates of Black women. According to educational statistics from *The Sentencing Project* of women in the criminal justice system:

- 44% of women in state prisons have neither graduated from high school nor received a GED.

- 14% of women in state prisons have had some college-level education.

- Half of women in prison participate in educational or vocational programming – only one of every five women takes high school or GED classes.

- Only half of women's correctional facilities offer post-secondary education (2007).

Some prisons offer limited educational programs to model inmates. Vocational training or career technical education programs in prison are designed to teach inmates about general employment skills or skills needed for specific jobs and industries. The overall goal of vocational training is to reduce risk of inmates' recidivating by teaching them marketable skills they can use to find and retain employment following release from prison. In their research on educational programs, researchers David Wilson, Catherine Gallagher, and Doris MacKenzie found vocational and technical training programs can also reduce institutional problem behaviors by replacing inmates' idle time with constructive work (2000).

On *OITNB*, the warden attempts to offer educational courses to the Litchfield inmates in order to give them something useful to do during their incarceration; as a result of budget cuts, the formal education program is replaced with a more cost-effective vocational training program. Only a few of the women in Litchfield choose to take advantage of the training program; however, in a Season 4 flashback, we see Taystee and other inmates using the vocational training program to prepare for Litchfield's Mock Job Fair, an annual event sponsored by a nonprofit called Dress for Success. The mock job fair gives Taystee a chance to show off her business smarts with a Philip Morris representative in a mock interview (interestingly, she manages to spin her drug-running experience as a net positive). She is named the Job Fair's winner to a thunderous ovation only to learn that the coveted job is a fake . . . simply a prison myth.

Conclusions

The United States has the highest incarcerations rates per capita in the world, with 2.2 million people currently in the nation's prisons and jails—a 500% increase over the last forty years according to *The Sentencing Project*. The first feature of mass incarceration is simply the sheer number of African Americans behind bars. From 1995 to 2002 the average annual rate of growth of the female inmate population was 5.2%, higher than the average 3.5% increase in the male inmate population. Since 1995 the total number of male prisoners has grown 27%; the number of female prisoners 42%. By year end in 2002, women accounted for 6.8% of all prisoners, up from 6.1% in 1995. More than 60% of the people in prison today are people of color. Black men are nearly six times as likely to be incarcerated as White men and Hispanic men are 2.3 times as likely. For Black men in their thirties, 1 in every 10 is in prison or jail on any given day. The rate of imprisonment for Black women far outpaces that of both White and Latina women; for example, in 2014, *The Sentencing Project* reports the imprisonment rate for African American women (109 per 100,000) was more than twice the rate of imprisonment for White women (53 per 100,000), as compared to Hispanic women who were incarcerated at 1.2 times the rate of White women (64 vs. 53 per 100,000). The explosion of both the prison population and its racial disparity are largely attributable to aggressive street-level enforcement of the drug laws and harsh sentencing of drug offenders.

Punishment changed in the United States in the last third of the twentieth century. The indicators of this change are well-documented and widely agreed upon. Prison populations soared, correctional and rehabilitative goals were largely supplanted in official and popular discourse by concerns with public safety and victims' rights, penal policy became highly politicized, and public sentiment toward criminals hardened. As a consequence, criminal punishment touched the lives of more Americans than ever before in the 1990s, a decade characterized by "mass imprisonment." For women, life in prison is a harsh reality. U.S. studies on women in prison reveal that female inmates incarcerated in U.S. prisons and jails share a "superfecta" of characteristics: undereducated, low-income, unskilled with sporadic employment histories, and histories of alcohol and substance dependency.

Although incarceration is wide spread across the world and increasingly common in the U.S., for many people what they know about life in prison is through media and cinema representations. Prison representations such as those on *OITNB* play an important role in shaping people's views of women's incarceration. *OITNB* takes place in a fictional prison setting, thus, serving as entertainment for the viewers. People have long been enamoured with crime and punishment, and *OITNB* glamorizes life in prison. Viewers can laugh and cry with TV prisoners and either shun and support them, but at the end of the hour they can shut off the television set and forget about these characters until the next episode.

Prison life experienced by, and seen through the eyes of, inmates like Taystee, Daya, and Poussey may be shaped for television, but the view is also revealing. African American women have many challenges to overcome if they find themselves confined by prison walls. *OITNB* attempts to give these women a voice; it attempts to share with its audience the social injustice, the gender inequalities, and the racial disparities that exist in prison. All of the imprisoned women of Litchfield are different, yet they share similar stores, and these stories give viewers a glimpse into the U.S. prison system with an emphasis on the gender and racial effects of the War on Drugs policy.

REFERENCES

Alexander, M. (2010). *The new Jim Crow: Mass incarceration in the age of colorblindness*. New York: New Press.

Bloom, B., Owen, B., & Covington, S. (2004). Women offenders and the gendered effects of public policy. *Review of Policy Research, 21*(1), 31–48.

Cecil, D.K. (2015). *Prison life in popular culture: From the big house to* Orange Is the New Black. Boulder, CO: Lynne Rienner Publishers.

Drug Policy Alliance. (2016). Fact sheet: Women, prison and the drug war. Retrieved at http://www.drugpolicy.org/sites/default/files/DPA_Fact%20

Sheet_Women%20Prison%20and%20Drug%20War%20%28Feb.%202016%29.pdf

Harrison, P. M., & Beck, A.J. (2003). *Prisoners in 2002.* Bureau of Justice Statistics Special Report, NCJ-193427, U.S. Department of Justice, Washington, DC.

Irwin, J. (2005). *The warehouse prison: Disposal of the new dangerous class.* Los Angeles, CA: Roxbury Publishing Company.

Kerman, P. (2013). *Orange is the new black: My year in a women's prison.* New York: Spiegel & Grau Trade Paperbacks.

Langan, P. A., & Levin, D.J. (2002). *Recidivism of prisoners released in 1994.* Bureau of Justice Statistics Bulletin, NCJ-200248, U.S. Department of Justice, Washington, DC.

Lochner, L., & Moretti, E. (2003). The effect of education on crime: Evidence from prison inmates, arrests, and self-reports. Retrieved at https://eml.berkeley.edu//~moretti/lm46.pdf

Lopez, G. (2017). How Obama quietly reshaped America's war on drugs. Retrieved at https://www.vox.com/identities/2016/12/19/13903532/obama-war-on-drugs-legacy

NAACP. (2016). Criminal justice fact sheet. Retrieved at http://www.naacp.org/criminal-justice-fact-sheet/

NPR. (2007). Timeline: America's war on drugs. Retrieved at http://www.npr.org/templates/story/story.php?storyId=9252490

The Sentencing Project. (2007). Women in the criminal justice system: Briefing sheets. Retrieved from https://www.sentencingproject.org/wp-content/uploads/2016/01/Women-in-the-Criminal-Justice-System-Briefing-Sheets.pdf

Wilson, D. B., Gallagher, C. A., & MacKenzie, D. L. (2000, November 1). A meta-analysis of corrections-based education, vocation, and work programs for adult offenders. *Journal of Research in Crime and Delinquency, 37*(4), 347–368.

THINKING ABOUT THE READING

According to the authors, how has the War on Drugs impacted poor women of color? In what way have institutions played a role in defining these women as deviant? Are the behaviors used to classify them as deviant also used in the same way for other groups? How have definitions of deviance changed over time in the criminal justice system?

Overcoming the Obscene in Evangelical Sex Websites

KELSY BURKE

(2016)

Cyberspace has the power to both reflect the larger world's norms and values and shape and reimagine these norms and values, creating new realities for its participants. Through in-depth analysis of websites and their content, observations of online activity in real time, and online interviews with website creators and users, Christians under Covers shows how religious conservatives use the Internet, as both a producer and a product of their faith.

BetweenTheSheets.com, LustyChristianLadies.com, LovingGroom.com, AffectionateMarriage.com, StoreOfSolomon.com, and MaribelsMarriage.com are all examples of Christian sexuality websites—sites that are easily recognizable as Christian with content focused specifically and explicitly on positive expressions of sex/sexuality within marriage.

When it comes to sex, the result is a new evangelical sexual logic, what I call the logic of godly sex, reflecting traditional beliefs about gender and sexuality but accommodating a contemporary understanding of sexual identities, practices, and desires. At the heart of this twenty-first century sexual logic is the ability, and indeed the prerogative, of married Christians to have "good" sex. This "goodness" incorporates dual meanings—"good" meaning normal, allowed, and sanctioned by God and "good" in the sense of feelings of pleasure and satisfaction. Both dimensions are important in constructing the logic of godly sex; the former instructs who is allowed to have sex, and the latter tells couples how they can enjoy sex. Conservative Christians, especially when using the Internet, merge these philosophies, allowing them to align their specific sexual interests—so long as they are married, monogamous, and heterosexual—with their moral framework.

Spreading the message of godly sex is not an easy task. Even though the majority of Americans use the Internet—more than half of all American adults are members of Facebook, for example—it comes with perceived dangers, many of which have to do with sexuality. Media stories about pornography, perverts, cyberstalking, and cyberbullying give the impression that virtual reality is one where innocence is lost. "Family values" have declined and risk is paramount. It is no wonder that 50 percent of parents of American teens with Internet access use parental controls to block or monitor online activity. On her blog, WeddingNights.com, Lisa writes candidly about the risky relationship between cyberspace and sex: "Typing 'sex' online quickly lures some of the most appalling junk you can imagine." She describes blogging about Christian sexuality as a struggle: "There is so much out there crying to impair marriage. We who blog about this face outrageous obstacles online." Lisa, like many others, considers the Internet to be a space of perversion. Those who want to use it to blend messages about sexuality with Christian values have much work to do.

A common way Christian sexuality website creators justified running their sites was to explain that they believe they were the right kind of Christians to do it—because they were women, because of their happy and secure marriages, or because of their devotion to God. This hints at the logic of godly sex, wherein some conservative Christians make sense of sexuality distinctly for themselves—combining religious and secular ideas to privilege their status as married, monogamous, heterosexual Christians and making their sexual lives appear to be without limits because they obediently live within God's rules about sexuality. Website creators draw from the logic of godly sex that is presented in popular evangelical literature to establish a place for themselves in the secular and sinful Internet. They use their beliefs in God to determine who is allowed to be sexual and expand the kinds of sexual dialogue that are possible online. In doing so, they extend their religious beliefs in order to legitimize the spaces they create online as authentically Christian.

Displaying personal piety, marital exceptionalism, God's omniscience reflects what Bourdieu calls dispositions—versus positions. The creators of Christian sexuality websites gain traction with a Christian audience by constructing religious authority outside of formal institutions. This is in contrast to evangelicals, who write sex advice books and rely largely on their positions—as, for example, doctors, psychologists, or pastors (credentials that are often displayed prominently on the jackets of evangelical sex advice books)—to write about sex from a Christian perspective. Online, however, website creators are uniquely situated to construct forms of religious authority in different ways than evangelical authors. They rely not on traditional forms of religious authority but rather on an online presentation of religious knowledge that validates their Christian status. Personal piety, marital exceptionalism, and God's omniscience resemble familiar and generally accepted Protestant Christian belief, but website creators extend them in a way that juxtaposes openings and closures within the logic of godly sex. These beliefs keep out certain others from participating in godly sex and legitimize the actions of those who fit within its framework. "Wayside in my marriage. And I vowed to encourage other women and make the church a safe place to talk and be heard."

Lisa describes herself as a wife, mom, Midwesterner, and writer, but first and foremost a "follower of Christ." She does not call herself a leader, teacher, or counselor but instead points to a passion she has for "speaking hope" to others by sharing her own experiences and beliefs. After her Bible study ended, she felt called by God to continue to share her message, and so she decided to start a blog. In describing this decision, she gives credit to a higher power rather than to her own abilities or credentials: "I know that I have a heart to encourage, so I think God wanted to use me in this particular way."

Personal Piety

Lisa started her blog, Wedding Nights.com, to share her story with other Christian women. Her first marriage ended because of problems related to sexuality. While she was struggling in that relationship, she turned to women in her church for advice. These women were like family to her; they saw each other several times a week at church and in small group Bible studies. They were sympathetic, having suffered themselves from many of the problems Lisa described—such as miscommunication about sex and difficulty prioritizing it in their daily lives—but they offered few helpful remedies. After she divorced, Lisa spent time in prayer and read Christian books about marriage and relationships. This prompted the revelation that her marriage had ended in part because she hadn't been sexually available to her husband. When she remarried a few years later, she made a commitment to herself, to her marriage, and to other women: "I vowed that I wouldn't let sex just

fall by the wayside in my marriage. And I vowed to encourage other women and make the church a safe place to talk and be heard."

Christian sexuality websites also differ from popular evangelical literature by giving a distinct voice to women. Men almost always author evangelical sex advice books, if not as single authors then as husband and wife teams in which they usually take the lead. Shannon Ethridge, Linda Dillow, and Lorraine Pintus, although frequently mentioned in this book and on Christian sexuality websites, are outnumbered by their male counterparts. Yet the gender distribution of people who create Christian sexuality websites is quite different. Women appear to have much control of the web; they make up a disproportionate number of bloggers and online sex toy store owners. Of the blogs in my study, eight are run by women, four are run by men, and four are run by husband-and-wife teams. Of the sex toy stores, twelve are operated by husband-and-wife teams and five are operated by women. None of the online scores in my study were solely operated by men, probably due to what Holly described at the beginning of the chapter about men's perceived weaknesses when it comes to pornography.

The significant number of women running these sites supports the gender-equal language that is a hallmark of the logic of godly sex, but it does not offer substantial authority to women over men. Women who start up their own blogs or sex toy stores do so as a service to God, not because they feel they have specific expertise on the subject of sex. Blogger Maribel explained to me that she started her website to "share" what she's learned from her own marriage. A couple of years after she began blogging, she started to feel overwhelmed by the amount of emails she received asking her for advice. She decided to set up an online payment system so that she could be compensated for the time she spent writing to her readers. In describing this decision, however, Maribel repeatedly emphasized that she does not consider herself a professional authority on sex:

> I was spending several days in a row working on one person's issue and emailing back and forth with them, and I'm not a licensed marriage counselor or anything like this or a therapist, but I just needed to be compensated for my time a little bit to move people up the line who specifically needed more help. Generally, I refer people to a counselor. I say, "You

should go talk to a therapist, but I'm happy to give you my input." So it [the compensation] was kind of a little supplement to help me get the people who really wanted desperately somebody to talk to. I think a lot of times women need to hash it out with somebody.

Maribel, like other bloggers, emphasized the value of sharing and listening and stressed the fact that this required no expertise. And like Holly and Samantha, other store owners I interviewed, Maribel framed what she sells (her time and attention) as a "supplement" to help in Christians' marriages, something extra that could help couples along. If professional advice is the cake, Maribel's support is the icing.

Website creators reinforce a piety that is personal rather than prescriptive, ordinary rather than expert. All of the creators I interviewed emphasized the importance of sharing pieces of their individual stories with website users. Maribel, for example, says very little about herself on her "About Me" page—only that she is a married Christian woman who loves God and her husband. Yet her posts reveal tidbits about her life: she is a mom; she leads a women's group at her church; she and her husband are relatively newly married. We also learn mundane details about her life: she is a horrible dancer, likes to cook, and doesn't like her downstairs neighbors. This information gives readers a sense that they are reading the stories and advice of a real person—someone who is who she says she is and with whom they can relate.

Many website creators choose not to disclose any identifying information (such as their names or photographs of themselves) on their sites. Of the eight website creators I interviewed, only half gave their names on their websites, and only about 30 percent of all sites in my study (eleven out of thirty-six) included their creators' first and last names. Some creators I spoke with said that protecting their real-life relationships was their motivation for keeping their online activity private. Holly, the owner of StoreOfSolomon.com, is open with many of her friends and family members about how she makes a living, but she doesn't disclose her identity on the site. She explained to me that even though she is not ashamed of her business, she realizes that some people might make assumptions about her character based on what she does. "I need time to explain what I do. If I don't have time to explain what I do, I don't broadcast it. It isn't the same at a PTA meeting as saying you sell Mary Kay [cosmetics]." Holly feels

that others in her community (like fellow members of a Parent Teacher Association) might pass judgment on her based on how she makes a living, which is very different from a seemingly innocuous and uncontroversial career of selling cosmetics. Kitty, the pen name of a blogger on LustyChristianLadies.com, told me that she and her fellow bloggers intentionally keep their identities private: "We feel that it is enough for the readers to know our love for God and our message through our writing without needing to show them pictures of ourselves or tell everyone our names." Some website creators do not identify themselves on their sites because, in their minds, it is their Christian message that is important, not their identities.

By de-emphasizing the importance of their identities, website creators frame the work they do on their sites as undeserving of high praise or personal glory. Instead, they justify their sites by stating that they were simply driven to answer God's call. They believe that God uses the Internet to reach Christians who need to receive important information about sexuality. The owners of one online store, Corinthians.com, share on their homepage that they created their business to "help the body of Christ through education and provision of written, audio, or video material and also more literal means of help through marital aids." They go on to say that married couples who "become more intimate with each other" will also become more intimate with Christ. These kinds of declarations insist that Christian sexuality websites serve the ultimate evangelical project—helping others become closer to Jesus—vis-à-vis helping couples have good sex in their marriage. Bloggers and owners of online stores refer to the work they do in creating and managing their sites as forms of ministry and service, not unlike missionary work in a foreign country or a soup kitchen run by a church. WeddingNights.com's creator, Lisa, explained why she decided to start her blog by stating, simply, "God wanted to use me in this particular way."

The piety that Christian sexuality website creators construct on their sites is utterly personal—whether they create it through sharing anecdotes from their lives and relationships; emphasizing their "ordinariness"; or describing their intimate conversations with God about His call to create the sites. Protestant Christian beliefs demand a personal relationship with Jesus that is up to the individual, and the logic of godly sex applies similar spiritual reasoning to matters of sexual ministries. Website creators see themselves as called and inspired by God, and this way of thinking enables them to rationalize and validate their websites and businesses. The logic of godly sex appears when these website creators justify explicit discussions about sex by citing their piety and faith in God. This excludes online discussions led by those without this piety.

Marital Exceptionalism

Though a money-making business, MarriageLove Toys.com boldly and unapologetically turns away some potential customers. Visitors to the site find this message clearly displayed on the homepage: "This site should NOT be viewed if you are unmarried! Only married couples should view these products as they are intended to be used for sex as God intentionally designed it: for husband and wife." The owners of the site feel that limiting their customer base to align their business model with their religious beliefs is more important than potential profit. Similarly, creators of other sites usually offer guidelines for how they envision their sites to be used, and these often state explicitly that their sites are intended exclusively for married couples (both husbands and wives). Before becoming a member of BetweenTheSheets.com, users must agree to the site's terms of use, which include confirming that they are married or soon-to-be married. John and Barbara informally encourage both husbands and wives to join the site, and they advise users who look at the message boards alone to disclose their online activity to their spouses. Couples who are engaged (with a "ring and a date") but not yet married are restricted to posting in the "Engaged" section of the site.

Website creators use marriage, which they consider to be a spiritually exceptional relationship, to justify the sexual content on their sites. Their logic goes like this: since God allows married couples, and married couples only, to have sex, God also allows married couples, and married couples only, to think and talk about sex. Doing, thinking, and talking are inevitably linked within a marriage relationship, as website creators emphasize that couples must communicate and contemplate in order to have good sex. But thinking and talking about sex also extends beyond a marriage relationship to include others within the Christian community. Website creators treat the marriage relationship as a holy and exceptional form of religious devotion, constructing a form of spiritual capital I call marital exceptionalism. This means that website users can participate on Christian sexuality sites while remaining faithful to their spouses because their marriages are the reference points they use to frame all thoughts, discussions, and actions related to sexuality.

Website creators who write about sex believe that imagination helps within the context of marital exceptionalism but hurts in any other situation. Reinforcing the conviction that godly sex applies only to the right kind of relationships, imagination is appropriate and encouraged only when it is focused on sexually enticing and pleasing one's spouse. It is fundamentally inappropriate in all other sexual situations. This is why Chariot, a blogger for LustyChristianLadies.com, encourages women readers to take boudoir-style photographs of themselves to share with husbands. Boudoir photography, referencing the French term for a woman's private dressing room, allows women to pose in sexually suggestive ways, wearing little to no clothing. On LCL, Chariot invokes the imagination when describing her favorite setup for a photograph: "My favorite pose is seriously sensual. Lay on your back wearing bra and panties. Have the photographer straddle you and point the lens down so that the photograph looks as if your husband is on top of you. HOT! HOT! HOT!" Chariot says that the image is effective because of its positioning, which allows the recipient of the photo, her husband, to imagine that he is on top of her, his wife. This makes the image "seriously sensual" while remaining appropriate within the guidelines of Chariot's faith. Erotic images within a marriage relationship become one possibility available to the sexual repertoires of Christian couples in the quest for godly sex.

The imaginative possibilities when it comes to marital sexuality are what fuel one online business, GodOfLove.com, which sells customized erotic stories for married couples. The owners noted the popularity of erotica and explained why people find it appealing: "Some non-Christian therapists suggest that erotica can help get couples eager for intimacy. They may suggest sexually explicit fiction or even films." These Christians understand the appeal of erotica, which can add excitement to the tedium of everyday life and help individuals get turned on. They even suggest that trained authorities, such as therapists, would recommend the practice. Yet GodOfLove.com cautions Christians against using secularly produced erotica: "Nearly every Christian pastor would firmly disagree with this approach.

There are too many risks and disadvantages of [secular] sexual books or videos." These risks stem from the fact that consuming erotica typically means that one imagines the people in the story, people other than one's spouse. GodOfLove.com notes, "while the emotions can be there, the intimacy with your spouse is not. These can pull people onto a possibly destructive path of unrealistic illusion." Here, GodOfLove.com has constructed a dilemma for conservative Christians: erotica can help add excitement and arousal but is ultimately off-limits in its commonly found, secular form. This is where GodOfLove.com provides a Christian solution, offering personalized erotic stories for married couples.

Like Christian proponents of boudoir photography, GodOfLove.com distinguishes between godly and sinful fantasies. Those that involve just husband and wife as leading characters are okay, while those that involve anyone other than a husband and wife are not. "At GodOfLove, we believe that fantasies are not sin if they involve just the married couple reading the story. Sexual imagination in this context can improve desire and prompt the great sex that God wants for Christian marriages." Far from committing sin, they contend, fantasizing about one's spouse actually improves a marriage relationship in a way that receives God's approval. The products the site offers provide a way for married Christians to fantasize about their spouses without relying solely on their own creativity. The owners of GodOfLove.com frame their site as a service for fellow Christians that pleases God because it directs and enhances the Christian imagination within marriage, which enhances a couple's intimacy.

The creators of Christian sexuality websites believe that married Christians are given special permission by God to be sexual and experience pleasure, which gives them access to thoughts and deeds that they believe to be off limits to anyone else. Bunny, an LCL blogger, writes that "sex is a gift from God and something to be shared in fidelity between a husband and wife." Therefore, she believes that GodOfLove.com provides erotic stories "with a twist that we fully support." She explains that "in all of these stories, the man and woman are Christian and married." Much like the "innovators" sociologist Robert Merton describes in his theory of social deviance, creators of Christian sexuality websites have created an exceptional case in which they can achieve what they want—sex that is good and godly—through a

range of means that remain deviant and unacceptable for all others. So long as they remain within the confines of their own monogamous, heterosexual marriages, these Christians insist that they are free to consume and produce erotica, purchase sex toys, and even read about the sex lives of others on message boards. This marital exceptionalism establishes Christian sexuality websites as spaces that uphold religious values rather than undermine them. Website creators use this belief as a form of spiritual capital to make a place for themselves in the secular and sexualized spaces of the Internet, optimizing both the sexual pleasure and the sense of religious devotion of their users.

God's Omniscience

Despite their best efforts to regulate who views Christian sexuality websites and to what ends, the creators of these sites cannot prevent their online content from being used for sinful purposes. This is true, of course, for evangelical sex advice books, as well, but online spaces exacerbate the problem of an unknowable audience. Anyone may stumble upon these sites—perhaps a friend shared a link to one of them on Facebook, or a Google search for "married sexuality" returned one of the sites as a top result. This is part of what makes the Internet seem risky. Advice given on Christian sexuality sites or sex toys purchased from online Christian stores may be used for sexual relationships not supported by the creators of these sites. Even Christian users of these sites may fall to temptation while reading posts and fantasize about someone other than their spouses. Language and images that seem utterly unsexual (like a photograph of a car with its trunk open to accompany instructions for the sexual position "Doggy Style") can still connote sexual scenarios. Christian sexuality website creators cannot deny that their sites may—however unintentionally—provoke sinful thoughts.

Website creators must reconcile themselves with the unknowable uses of sexual content associated with their sites. How they do this has to do with the basic Christian belief that God is omniscient. This belief becomes a unique source of spiritual capital for believers who create Christian sexuality websites. Followers of God lack knowledge that God naturally possesses about other people's thoughts and intentions. Focusing on God's judgment, they assert their fundamental inability to control how others use their sites. They draw from biblical scripture—for example, I Samuel 2:3 (KJV), "For the Lord is a God of knowledge, and by Him actions are weighed." Having established a sense of religious positioning through personal piety and marital exceptionalism, the creators of the sites reason that it is God's job, not their own, to do the regulatory work of monitoring and possibly punishing those who use Christian sexuality websites in ways other than they are intended.

Holly, owner of StoreOfSolomon.com, explained her relationship with her mostly unknown customer base: "What they choose to do with what they order is ultimately between them and God." When I commented that she didn't seem too concerned about not being able to monitor them, she responded, "I have a link [on my site] called 'Better Than Sex' that explains what it means to be a Christian and follow Christ. If someone comes to my site who isn't a Christian, my hope is that they would be exposed to a little bit of God's love."

Website creators use the familiar evangelical Protestant belief that individuals are accountable only to an all-knowing God to excuse themselves from the responsibility of monitoring how their sites are used. This means their sites may be complicit in sins committed by users without reducing the creators' confidence that their sites are authentically Christian. As an effective form of spiritual capital, God's omniscience creates a division among those who use Christian sexuality websites. It legitimizes the actions of website creators as good and holy and delegitimizes the actions of those who use the sites

for sin, considering their actions beyond the control of creators of the sites.

Overcoming the Obscene

The combination of personal piety, marital exceptionalism, and God's omniscience supports the foundations of godly sex and God's approval of Christian sexuality websites.

Religious persons who create virtual communities have unique opportunities to shape the meaning of religious expression. In this way, their online communities display similar beliefs to those of evangelical churchgoers, which cultural anthropologist Omri Elisha describes as reflecting "varying degrees of plasticity as well as constancy." Individuals who prescribe to Christianity are at least somewhat limited in the kinds of spiritual capital (religious knowledge and dispositions) they express, since the religion has well-established beliefs and customs that have been developed over two thousand years. Yet lived religion, online or otherwise, confronts, as Elisha writes, "a host of quotidian dilemmas, aspirations, innovations, and frustrations that are not always easily explained (or dismissed) by a single, cohesive, uniformly authorized system of doctrine." Online religion in particular allows website creators to construct new forms of participatory religious expression; they are able to shape what religion looks like, how it is practiced, and how their beliefs affect daily life. It is this balance between tradition and innovation that makes the logic of godly sex so compelling: it reinforces believers' religious beliefs while extending the possibilities of their sexual lives.

THINKING ABOUT THE READING

According to Burke, how has the institution of religion through evangelical Christianity helped create and enforce "normal" sexual activity and relationships? What is "godly sex"? Is it blurring definitions of deviance? Is it empowering or oppressive? How is digital media being used by evangelical Christians as both a producer and a product of their faith?

Fat Shame to Fat Pride

Fat Women's Sexual and Dating Experiences

JEANNINE A. GAILEY

(2012)

The television sitcom *Mike and Molly* about a "clinically obese" couple spurred quite a fury when the lead characters kissed on television. Viewers responded unabashedly by indicating that they did not want to see fat people kissing. In fact, a *Marie Claire* writer wrote, 'I would be grossed out if I had to watch two characters with rolls and rolls of fat kissing each other" (Kelly, 2010). Kelly later apologized for her statements, but her reaction exemplifies the cultural attitude that fat bodies are not typically viewed as attractive or sexual. "Culturally, we're taught to believe that sexual activity happens as a result of sexual desire. Sexual desire, in turn, happens as a result of beauty, sexiness, sex appeal, love" (Blank, 2000, 2). The message is that fat people are not sexy and should not be portrayed as such on television.

Women who are fat are generally viewed as deviant, lazy, unattractive, and nonsexual (Regan, 1996). Not surprisingly, there is a dearth of literature about fat women and their dating and sexual histories. Using a feminist perspective, North American fat-identified women were interviewed about their body image, involvement in the size acceptance movement, and their dating and sexual experiences. This study offers an important contribution because women's perspectives are the focus here—not men's or outsiders as in previous literature.

Literature Review

Body Image and Sex

Body image concerns play an important role in sexual pleasure and functioning (Wiederman and Hurst, 2008): If women are distracted by concerns about their physical appearance, they may be unable to relax and focus on their own sexual pleasure. A societal emphasis on bodily flaws works to keep women, especially marginalized women, in their place, that is passive, submissive, and other-oriented. Greater body self-consciousness leads to lower levels of sexual pleasure and arousal, sexual assertiveness, sexual functioning, sexual self-esteem, and higher levels of sexual avoidance, ambivalence in sexual decision making and sexual risk taking (Wiederman and Hurst, 1998; Sanchez and Kiefer, 2007). Body shame results from a perceived failure to meet the ideals of the cultural system and has been found to result in the avoidance of sex (Trapnell, Meston, and Gorzalta, 1997). The way a woman perceives her own level of attractiveness influences her comfort in and enjoyment of sexual relationships (Hoyt and Kogan, 2002). In sum, when women accept their bodies they tend to become more agentic in their sexuality.

Sex and Fat Women

Recently, there has been an increase in the literature regarding size discrimination and in the emerging area of fat studies. However, the research is scant regarding fat women's sexuality. Several studies have focused on people's perceptions of fat women's sexuality. Regan (1996) found that participants viewed a fat woman differently compared to an average-weight woman and a fat and average-weight man. The fat woman was perceived to experience less sexual desire, intercourse, and oral sex and to be less sexually attractive, desirable, warm, responsive, and skilled compared with the other three groups. Similarly, Harris (1990) found that fatter women were judged to be less attractive, less likely to date, and less erotic, as well as to have lower self-esteem and deserve a fatter, uglier romantic partner. The research, although limited, indicates that participants perceived fat women as nonsexual.

Gimlin (2002) interviewed women involved with the National Association to Advance Fat Acceptance (NAAFA) about negotiating the stigma associated with being fat. Participants reported not feeling sexually attractive until they started attending NAAFA events and met fat admirers (FAs). She found that some members reported distrust and mistreatment by men they dated, but Gimlin was not investigating dating behaviors so the insight she was able to provide is limited.

Sex with Fat Women

Fat represents a challenge to the identification as sexual (Murray, 2004) because weight is connected to the heteronormative system of meaning and value that constitutes what it means to be feminine or masculine. The Western configuration of the gender order has been referred to as *hegemonic masculinity*. Hegemonic masculinity provides the blueprint for the way men should behave and the goals to which they should aspire (Connell, 1987). In the context of hegemonic masculinity, the tendency is for males to dominate other males and subordinate females. According to Connell, emphasized femininity, the normative pressure for women to accommodate the interests and needs of men, is an important component for sustaining hegemonic masculinity. The fat female body is frequently not considered to align with the feminine ideal because it symbolizes domination or resistance to idealized femininity and over-consumption. Moreover, fat women are perceived as out of control, which represents resistance and a threat to hegemonic masculinity and the patriarchal order of society. Likewise, men who date fat women are seen as having lesser status and are thus stigmatized (Goode and Preissler, 1983).

Given that heteronormativity emphasizes men's pleasure in sex, it is not surprising that scholarship has largely focused on men's experiences as FAs or the sexual mistreatment of fat women. Swami and Tovée's (2009) FAs rated the bodies labeled "overweight" or ""obese"" as more attractive than the control group. The FAs also rated a wider range of body sizes attractive compared with the control group, which suggests that FAs may reject the cultural norms associated with beauty (cf. Goode and Preissler, 1983). However, the largest proportion of the men Goode and Preissler interviewed were "closet" and not "overt" FAs (180). Very few of the men identified as exclusively dating fat women, and most reported it was a preference.

Gailey and Prohaska (2006) studied "hogging"—a practice in which men sometimes place bets in groups about who can take home the largest woman, or they state that they settle for a fat woman at the end of the night because they are horny or reportedly "hard-up." The men sometimes engage in behaviors in which they humiliate women they deem fat (cf. Flood, 2008). Participants indicated that they thought fat women were "easy" because they are desperate for attention or insecure. In sum, the literature indicates that fat women are viewed as nonsexual or as less sexual than "normal" weight persons but has largely ignored fat women's experiences and firsthand accounts of their sexuality.

Method

The sample consisted of 36 fat-identified North American women who were involved in one or more of the various size acceptance organizations. Twenty-three indicated that they "aren't that involved" but do subscribe to blogs, social networking sites, or listservs. Five women identified as activists, and eight indicated that their involvement includes attending social events, research, art, and performance art. Participants' ages ranged from 23 to 60 years, 33 women identified as Caucasian and three as African American. All participants had engaged in heterosexual relationships, even though one identified as lesbian and three identified as bisexual. Nineteen women indicated that they were single, eight were married, five were cohabitating, and four were divorced. Their weights ranged from 215 to 500 pounds and, according to body mass index (BMI), all were "obese," most "morbidly obese."

Study information was widely disseminated to a number of size acceptance listservs. Women self-selected by contacting me via e-mail, and I provided information about the study and consent forms. The interviews were semi-structured, and all but one took place over the phone. The interviews focused on women's body image, involvement in size acceptance, and dating and sexual histories. All of the interviews were digitally recorded and transcribed verbatim. Interviews ranged from 45 minutes to two-and-a-half hours.

I recorded my thoughts and feelings during and after each interview session because, as Kleinman and Copp (1993) noted, emotions are an inevitable part of fieldwork. Some of the stories made me cry, others were energizing and invigorating, and a few had very little impact on my mood. A number of interviewees thanked me, noting that the experience was cathartic and that they appreciated having someone listen and the chance to recall events and people they had not thought about in years. Intensive interviews with marginalized groups raises interesting ethical issues, but can be somewhat overcome if the interview setting is one of mutual respect (Oakley, 1981). Therefore, when numerous participants asked me if I am a fat woman and what sparked my interest in the topic, I responded that I am 5 feet 3 inches and about 120 pounds. I also noted that I became interested in the topic because of my previous research on men who mistreat fat women, and because of the lack of scholarship about fat women's sex lives from fat women's perspectives.

Following the principles of grounded theory (Glaser and Strauss, 1967), I studied these data searching for patterns in the women's experiences with size acceptance, their body image, and their sexual histories. As patterns emerged, I restructured my focus to draw out conceptual distinctions. Some of the data supported my working analysis, whereas others contradicted it. The transcripts were reread and coded by the emerging categories that were informed by the themes that stemmed from other interviews and the issues raised in the scholarly literature. The completed interviews were then rechecked for the presence or absence of the themes and for variation among the participants. I used all of the information to improve my analytic model accordingly, continuing the process until the data yielded no new conceptual patterns. I concluded interviewing new participants when I reached a point of theoretical saturation. All names are pseudonyms to ensure confidentiality.

Results

Thirty-four women (94% of the sample) indicated that they experienced a life of ridicule, body shame, and numerous attempts to lose weight. Moreover, they reported that their relationships and sex lives suffered as a result. Twenty-six reported a change when they embodied the size acceptance ideology. In other words, they went through a transition from feeling awful about their body and having less than satisfactory sex to feeling better about their bodies and sex lives. Seven women indicated that they are not comfortable with their bodies and are actively trying to lose weight; in addition, they reported either a nonexistent sex life or negative sexual experiences. There were three women whose accounts do not fit into the theory that emerged: one because

she reported an overwhelmingly negative view of her body, but an extremely satisfying sex life, and two others reported always having a positive body image with no history of dieting or fat hatred and positive sex lives. The following themes represent feelings of body shame, fat as a threat to femininity and masculinity, embodiment of fat, and difficulties embodying fat.

Body Shame and Sexual Relationships

The majority of the participants were told from a young age that they should be ashamed of their fat body and that they needed to change it at any cost. Body shame and fat hatred developed and influenced other aspects of their social lives. Body shame is conceptualized as negative evaluations of one's body with an emotional component, including a desire to hide oneself and one's body (Schooler et al., 2005). In nearly all of the accounts of negative sexual experiences, there was also an emphasis on their body:

> I would find these random, like, mostly disgusting men and I would let them take me out to dinner and then I would have sex with them, because then I would be able to eat, you know? And I started getting a really awful image again, because, for most of those men, fat was a fetish. It wasn't, like, an acceptable thing. It was a fetish thing. Like, "Obviously, lady, I would never date you, but I will screw you because I have this weird fetish thing." (Karen, 24, single)

Karen was turned into a fetishistic object by men who were using her as a means to an end. Her experience demonstrates that when a person is objectified by others they feel dehumanized— that is, their feelings, thoughts, or desires are not considered by others. Understanding how others, especially men, view them, numerous women were wary of the intentions of the men they met online or at BBW (Big Beautiful Women) events because they knew that the attraction may be a fetish. With a fetish, the fat woman becomes an object, not a person, and is no longer an autonomous body or equal to the man. The devastating emotional impact of objectification is demonstrated by the following respondent who stated that she was afraid to date when she was younger.

When I say I didn't date, I didn't. I went to bars, and I met guys, and I slept with them and woke up with an emotional hangover. I can remember sitting in a doctor's office, and I was flipping through a *Reader's Digest,* and you know how they have all those funny little things in there? And one of them was a story, and it said, "If it wasn't for alcohol, fat girls would never get laid." And I remember sitting in that office, and the tears coming to my eyes, and feeling so exposed, even though nobody knew what I had just read. I just felt like yeah, that's how I saw myself. I didn't see myself as desirable. I didn't see myself as—I just didn't see myself as someone who men dated. I saw myself as someone who got drunk and men slept with. (Ronnie, 51, divorced)

Patti, a 28-year-old who is married, answered my question about whether men she "slept around with" when she was younger mistreated her or if they were simply looking for sex. She said, "I think it was both, it was kind of like they're looking for a lay, and they felt a big girl is an easy target." Similarly, Marissa, a 34-year-old who is married, said, "I think I've had negative responses from men. I've also had men think I'm shitty because I'm fat, and poke me and pinch me and do those types of things, and I really, really hated that." Both women indicated that some of the men mistreated them or used them for sex; they attributed it to their weight because of the perception that fat women are sexually desperate and because they do not meet cultural standards of beauty.

Fat as a Threat to Femininity and Masculinity

The self is displayed to the social world through our outward appearance. Therefore, it is not just the messages that women receive, it is also the messages that men receive about what their partner "should" look like. Men who fail to or resist embodiment of masculinity achieve a subordinate male status because masculinity is enacted through a set of negotiations in the context of relationships between men and women. Men who are attracted to fat women are ridiculed because fat women are considered ugly, overindulgent, and out of control. FAs must decide whether they can cope with the stigma or not, and if not they often claim to "hog" or covertly date fat women (Gailey and Prohaska, 2006).

Mary, a 40-year-old, said "some [of the men she dated] seemed embarrassed because being seen with a fat person sort of lowers your street credit somehow, or like your perceived masculinity, or it's a desire that [men] are ashamed to have." Beth, a 60-year-old married woman, talked about Western culture and the stigma men receive for their attraction to fat women, "In our society, it's a shameful thing to be attracted to a fat woman—there's got to be something the matter with you." The theme of shamed partners was also echoed in a 23-year-old pregnant woman, who is in a positive relationship. Abigail reflected on her past and said, "I mean, I always thought when I was younger, that men don't want to sleep with fat girls. But it's the opposite. It's just that they don't tell anybody about it." Participants tended to internalize fat hatred, and many grew up believing that men are not attracted to fat women. As a result, they struggled with trying to form relationships while negotiating the fear that men might reject them, make fun of them, or use them. A few of the women became desperate for attention and sexual satisfaction and reported that they engaged in experiences that they normally would not have to meet their sexual needs.

Transformation through Embodiment of Fat Pride

Although it is true that participants still struggle with their bodies and have bad days, 26 (72%) indicated that they have less body shame since they embodied fat pride. Embodiment reflects how we understand ourselves, including our interactions with others, and is deeply enmeshed in social and political forces (Turner, 1996). In other words, embodiment of fat pride involves self-transformation through political and community participation.

> I met a lot of really interesting people in fat acceptance that opened my mind into the body is a beautiful thing and not something that we should be torturing ourselves over. I had that kind of epiphany moment where I said, "my God, I've spent my entire life worrying about whether I'm fat or not. I think I'm going to stop." (Marissa, 34, married)

Not only did fat acceptance help her and 25 other participants with body image, it also helped many attain the confidence they needed to get out of relationships that were disrespectful and abusive. Again, self-transformation is an underlying theme:

> I think during that time I was starting to make more connections in the fat acceptance movement, and so I started getting a little bit more confidence, and I just sort of started drifting away and putting him off, and like whenever he'd call me, I'd be like oh I'm busy, or whatever. He just didn't respect me that much, like he refused to use condoms and things like that. It first started like, okay I can deal with that, and then as I started getting a little more confident, I was like well, no, why should I deal with that? (Rachel, 26, single)

The movement helped Rachel develop the confidence she needed to end the relationship and realize that she can and should stand up for herself. Numerous women had similar experiences in which they realized that they maintained relationships with men who treated them disrespectfully because they were afraid that they would not meet anyone who would find them attractive. One interviewee summed it up nicely by stating:

> Yeah, because that's what we're told. It's so—it's so the fear thing that we're told. No one will ever, ever, ever desire you, and anybody who does desire you is out of their mind or crazy or has no friends or is utterly desperate or wants to hurt you, and I have no doubt that stuff is out there. It's just not the whole story. (Michelle, 27, divorced)

Clearly, Michelle not only realizes that there are men who engage in behaviors such as hogging (Gailey and Prohaska, 2006), but she is also aware that stories about those behaviors are used as techniques of social control. Family members frequently warned participants, especially as adolescents, that if they did not lose weight that they would never get married. According to 26 participants, the embodiment of fat pride has helped them feel better about their social position by improving their view of self,

gain confidence to end abusive relationships, and improve current relationships.

Tina, 35, discussed "retraining" her husband to better suit her sexual needs and desires, something that she reportedly could not do before she found the size acceptance movement because she lacked the confidence.

"As I get more comfortable with my body, I figure out more what I want, and what satisfies me better, and then it's retraining him. Because when he married me eight years ago, I was a very different person than I am now." Corina, a woman in her early forties, explained that even though she discovered size acceptance in the late 1980s, she was unable to accept that she is sexually attractive to men. Therefore, she refrained from engaging in sexual activity until her late thirties. She stated,

> About three years ago, I met somebody online and became sexually active with him. He was not somebody that I would want to have a continued relationship with, because he's little loopy, but it was a very, very positive experience to become sexually active as an older person, I think I was much more confident in myself by the time it happened. I think having been exposed to size acceptance by that point really helped the whole process be very positive. (Corina, 41, single)

Another woman who reported that she spent the majority of her early twenties lonely and ashamed of her weight eventually met her current husband. After they met, but before their marriage, she discovered the size acceptance movement.

> I found that all of my experience in fat acceptance was really helpful during wedding planning as well—I was able to completely ignore all of the standard messages of losing weight before the wedding. I bought a dress that fit perfectly off the rack, and had no body anxiety, even wearing a strapless dress, and looking at the pictures brings me a lot of happiness. I was really grateful to the fat acceptance movement for allowing me to build the self-confidence to buck those kinds of expectations. (Jessica, 35, married)

The fat acceptance movement affected 26 participants' self-confidence and bodily acceptance. It would be naive to assume that the movement has countered all of the negative messages women are inundated with daily, but there is a predominant theme of feeling better than they did before they discovered the movement: To embody a fat identity is subversive and a form of political resistance. Acts of subversion and resistance to dominant social forces can become empowering. The women who embody, or are working to embody, fat pride, can move beyond trying to change their bodies and focus on developing satisfying relationships with lovers and themselves.

Relationships and Sex after Embodiment of Fat Pride

Twenty-six women reported positive sexual experiences and relationships after discovering the fat acceptance movement and beginning to embody fat pride. In fact, several indicated that there is never a shortage of willing and appreciative partners. Most met men online, or at NAAFA or BBW events, whereas others said they met men at the grocery store, exercise facilities, and work. The following is from a woman who shared a broad range of positive and fulfilling sexual experiences.

> I had a lot of really good sex with a lot of different kinds of people, and people that surprised me, and people that had less shame than I thought they would, and some people who had shame, but you know, especially if you're not in a serious relationship, you can have a certain kind of room for it. (Mary, 40, single)

These data revealed that the way women view their bodies and their satisfaction with their body often translates into happier sexual relationships. One woman discussed her own internal struggle between how she feels about her body and how a recent partner treated her compared with previous sexual partners.

> We hooked up and had sex, and like he was very into oral sex, and I just remember being a little bit kind of "weirded out" that the first night that we hooked up. I wasn't expecting

for us to do that, and it was I think like the last day of my period, and he insisted on going down on me, and I was like, "No! I have my period!" And he was like, "I don't care," And I was amazed that he did that, and then he did it again the next morning, before I'd showered, and I was like what is with this guy? But he was a different sexual partner in that he spent a lot of time paying attention to my body in ways that I felt like my previous sexual partners had not. (Jodi, 30, cohabitating)

Rachel expressed a similar situation when she talked about her present sexual relationship. "I think a lot of it has to do with the fact I'm in a really good relationship now that's very respectful and loving, and it's just hard to think about what I settled for, before" (Rachel, 26, single). Both are now enjoying mutually satisfying sexual relationships, something neither reportedly had before they embodied fat pride. With increased confidence, they are seeking partners who treat them well and satisfy them sexually.

Carrie, in her fifties, discussed a lover she met after her divorce from a man who she felt took advantage of her low self-esteem. "Aside from that, the way he touches me, the way he looks at me, the way he kisses me, the way he'll let his hand just rest on my abdomen, and when we're having sex there's just such an appreciation." She reported that this was the first really good sexual experience she has ever had. She has since had several relationships with men and women and reportedly is finally satisfied sexually. She is enjoying sex, enjoying her body, and discovering her sexuality.

Jenna discussed how her involvement in size acceptance not only changed her views of her body, but also opened up sexual relationships and a brief business venture; she ran a dating service for BBW and their admirers before Internet dating was readily available.

> But yeah, as far as impacting my body, and also being in a particular dating and social business, I had a chance to meet several guys who impacted the way I looked at my body, because they were very—not just accepting, but enamored. That really has an impact when somebody sees you that positively and takes a lot of time with

you physically—it changes the way you see yourself. (Jenna, 58, single)

Women who accept their bodies, or are beginning to, not only experience freedom from the pressure to diet or change their bodies, but also the freedom to be sexual. As the women experience less body shame and increased confidence, they also seek out or attract partners who treat them better and truly appreciate them. Participants who have begun to see their bodies as beautiful and desired seem to enjoy their sexual relationships and have better experiences than those who do not.

Not Quite There

Seven women (19% of the sample) have not embodied fat pride, but do subscribe to size acceptance listservs or blogs. They reported not feeling comfortable removing their clothing in the presence of another and also did not feel sexually desirable. Many women have reservations about nudity, but they are able to overcome it to engage in sexual intimacy (Weinberg and Williams, 2010). It should be noted that all seven women are single, which could have an impact on their comfort level. One woman stated:

I've gained 37 pounds and it's all in my stomach, and I don't want anybody to see it. I mean, honest to goodness, if Mel Gibson came here and he said I worship your stomach, and I'd say, well, you'll have to do it from afar, because you're not going to see it. That's how bad it is. (Sophie, 55)

Sophie will not engage in sexual relationships, even with an actor she finds extremely attractive, because of her poor body image. A woman who has tried to change her body said:

I've only had sex once since I had gastric bypass surgery. and I felt very self-conscious about it because I have a lot of excess skin from the weight loss. I like to keep the lights out, and I was again disappointed with the experience. It was very boring. I didn't enjoy it. (Janet, 36)

Janet is still not conventionally thin; in fact, she is still "obese" according to the BMI. She thought that

having surgery would make her thinner and contribute to body acceptance; unfortunately, she reports it has not worked. Pam, a 29-year-old, had a sexual partner make fun of her because of her weight. As she described the story, she ended with, "It was part that, but partly being insecure about my body, and not feeling desirable. I just avoided it [sex]." Given the stigma and marginalized identity that fat persons experience, it is not surprising that those who arc unsatisfied with their appearance are unable or unwilling to engage in sexual relationships.

Discussion and Conclusion

The present article is grounded in fat women's experiences with dating and sex. The interviews revolved around their discovery and involvement in the size acceptance movement, their view of their bodies, and their dating and sexual histories. Previous research indicates that fat women are mistreated in sexual relationships (Gailey and Prohaska, 2006), which is certainly the case for some fat women, but as one participant stated, "it's not the whole story."

Twenty-six women, about three-quarters of the sample, reported that when they embodied fat pride that they tended to experience an increase in self-confidence and better sexual relationships, whereas women who were still struggling with their body size tended to report less sexual fulfillment and were more likely to report that they felt men used them sexually. Wiederman and Hurst (1998) found that women's sexual self-schemas were related to women's sense of feeling attractive; these data appear to reflect that as well. Based on participants' accounts and several previous studies, one can speculate that the differences exist not because of actual weight, but because of the woman's satisfaction with their body.

I do not attempt to generalize these findings to all fat women, and these data do not represent all fat women's dating and sexual experiences, especially given that the sample was relatively homogenous (racially and sexually) and respondents self-selected. Also, I was unable to record the body language of participants because interviews were conducted over the phone. However, it may have been easier for participants to discuss embarrassing moments or to share personal information because I could not see them. Future researchers could investigate the sexual and dating histories of fat women who have not been exposed to fat pride or those who reject it. Additionally, future researchers would benefit by focusing on the sexual and dating histories of women who identify as lesbian and for whom the majority of their sexual experiences have been with other women.

Despite the limitations, the results offer important contributions to the fat studies and feminist literature. First, the conventional wisdom that women of size are either nonsexual or sexually desperate was not confirmed for this sample. The present sample was quire diverse in their dating histories and sexual experiences. There were reports of alternative sexual lifestyles, near celibacy, sexual abuse, and the number of sexual partners ranged from one to over 100. Participants seem to align with the overall trends for women's sexual experiences in the United States, fat or not (Lindberg and Singh, 2008).

Second, involvement with size acceptance groups appears to improve the way some women view their bodies and their sexual satisfaction. Women, fat or not, are critical of their bodies and the number of women who engage in dangerous dieting practices or disordered eating is increasing. Perhaps involvement in body positive messages has the potential for combating some of the insidious messages women are inundated with daily. Twenty-six participants who experienced severe body shame and outright fat hatred were able to embrace and embody fat pride, which has transformed their view of self and led to increased sexual agency and satisfaction.

Based on previous research and popular culture, one might assume that sex is nonexistent in the lives of fat women, or if it does exist, that the relationships are colored by abuse, disrespect, or shame. Participants revealed that despite the tremendous social stigma associated with fat, 28 have had and continue to experience satisfying sexual relationships. The size acceptance movement has played a key role in helping these women resist patriarchal control by subverting the hegemonic view of women's bodies and their sexuality.

REFERENCES

Blank, Hanne. 2000. *Big Big Love: A Sourcebook on Sex for People of Size and Those Who Love Them*. Eugene, OR: Greenery Press.

Connell, R.W. 1987. *Gender and Power*. Stanford, CA: Stanford University Press.

Flood, Michael. 2008. "Men, Sex and Homosociality; How Bonds Between Men Shape Their Sexual Relations with Women." *Men and Masculinities* 10: 339–359.

Gailey, Jeannine A., and Ariane Prohaska. 2006, "'Knocking Off a Fat Girl': An Exploration of Hogging, Male Sexuality, and Neutralizations," *Deviant Behavior* 27: 31–49.

Gimlin, Debra. 2002. *Body Work. Beauty and Self-Image in American Culture*. Berkeley: University of California Press.

Glaser, Barney G., and Anselm C. Strauss. 1967. *The Discovery of Grounded Theory: Strategies for Qualitative Research*. New York: Aldine.

Goode, Erich, and Joanne Preissler. 1983. "The Fat Admirer." *Deviant Behavior* 4: 175–202.

Harris, Mary B. 1990, "Is Love Seen as Different for the Obese?" *Journal of Applied Social Psychology* 20: 1209–1224.

Hoyt, Wendy D., and Lori R. Kogan. 2002. "Satisfaction with Body Image and Peer Relationships for Males and Females in a College Environment." *Sex Roles* 45: 199–215.

Kelly, Maura. 2010. "Should Fatties Get a Room? (Even on TV)?" *Marie Claire*, October 25.

Kleinman, Sherryl, and Martha Copp. 1993. *Emotions and Fieldwork*. Thousand Oaks, CA: Sage.

Lindberg, Laura Duberstein, and Susheela Singh. 2008. "Sexual Behavior of Single Adult American Women." *Perspectives on Sexual and Reproductive Health* 40: 27–33.

Murray. Samantha. 2004. "Locating Aesthetics: Sexing the Fat Woman." *Social Semiotics* 14: 237–247.

Oakley, Ann. 1981. "Interviewing Women: A Contradiction in Terms." In *Doing Feminist Research*, ed. Helen Roberts, 147–161. London: Heinemann.

Regan, Pamela C. 1996. "Sexual Outcasts: The Perceived Impact of Body Weight and Gender on Sexuality." *Journal of Applied Social Psychology* 26: 1803–1815.

Sanchez, Diana T., and Amy K, Kiefer. 2007. "Body Concerns In and Out of the Bedroom: Implications for Sexual Pleasure and Problems." *Archives of Sexual Behavior* 36: 808–820.

Schooler, Deborah. L., Monique Ward, Ann Merriwethcr, and Allison S. Caruthers. 2005. "Cycles of Shame: Menstrual Shame, Body Shame, and Sexual Decision-Making." *Journal of Sex Research* 42: 324–334.

Swami, Viren, and Martin, Tovée. 2009. "Big Beautiful Women: The Body Size Preferences of Male Fat Admirers." *Journal of Sex Research* 46: 89–96.

Trapnell, Paul D., Cindy M. Meston, and Boris B. Gorzalta. 1997. "Spectatoring and the Relation Between Body Image and Sexual Experience: Self-Focus or Self-Valence?" *Journal of Sex Research* 34: 267–278.

Turner, Bryan S. 1996. *The Body and Society*. 2nd ed. Thousand Oaks, CA: Sage.

Weinberg, Martin S., and Colin J. Williams. 2010. "Bare Bodies: Nudity, Gender, and the Looking Glass Body." *Sociological Forum* 25: 47–67.

Wiederman, Michael W,, and Shannon R. Hurst. 1998. "Body Size, Physical Attractiveness, and Body Image Among Young Adult Women: Relationships to Sexual Experience and Sexual Esteem." *Journal of Sex Research* 35: 272–281.

THINKING ABOUT THE READING

What is body (fat) shame? Why are fat people labelled as deviant? What culturally prescribed norms do they transgress and challenge? What other body markers are constructed as deviant in the social world? Do any of these examples vary by time and place? What is fat pride and how did the women in this study display it? What role do institutions and organizations play in shaping definitions of normal bodies? What other aspects of identity intersect with body size that either increase the assignment of deviance and discrimination, or offset some of it?

PART

III

Social Structure, Institutions, and Everyday Life

The Structure of Society
Organizations and Social Institutions

One of the great sociological paradoxes is that we live in a society that so fiercely extols the virtues of rugged individualism and personal accomplishment, yet we spend most of our lives responding to the influence of larger organizations and social institutions. These include both nurturing organizations, such as churches and schools, and larger, more impersonal bureaucratic institutions.

No matter how powerful and influential they are, organizations are more than structures, rules, policies, goals, job descriptions, and standard operating procedures. Each organization, and each division within an organization, develops its own norms, values, and language. This is usually referred to as organizational culture. Organizational cultures are pervasive and entrenched, yet, even so, individuals often find ways to exert some control over their lives within the confines of these organizations. Accordingly, organizations are dynamic entities in which individuals struggle for personal freedom and expression while also existing under the rules and procedures that make up the organization. Given this dynamic activity, an organization is rarely what it appears to be on the surface.

In her article "Cool Stores, Bad Jobs," Yasemin Besen-Cassino looks at the ways in which corporations like Starbucks and Banana Republic attract young people into low-wage, no-benefit jobs through the allure of working in trendy environments. These chains target affluent young people and market the jobs as fashionable and desirable.

Despite claims of impartiality, fairness, and color-blind justice, the organizational culture of the criminal court system in Chicago is one ripe with racialized injustice. In her article, "Separate and Unequal," Nicole Gonzalez Van Cleve details how the court system is marked by a separate and unequal divide between black and white in the groups, processes, and outcomes. She describes the "White Castle" type of justice the system embodies inside a court and jail complex jokingly referred to as the "Hotel California" for the way it represents the gateway of mass incarceration. Indeed, she shows us a system riddled with racial discrimination that was connected to other structural issues like the war on drugs, poverty, educational disparities, family disruption, and the emphasis on punishment over rehabilitation.

The military institution provides a compelling example of what sociologist Erving Goffman called a total institution. A total institution is a closed entity that is organized around stringent values, norms, and rules that are the foundation for resocializing the individuals who enter this institutional culture. These institutions and organizations believe that in order for them to function smoothly and achieve their goals, that all members must fall in line with the values and rules. In Gwynne Dyer's article, "Anybody's Son Will Do," she describes the long-standing tradition of how the military resocializes men from their civilian role to the killer/soldier role. Similar to how some religious faiths resocialize new entrants, the assimilation process for new citizens, or the processing of prisoners in prisons, this resocialization process is paramount to maintaining the institutional culture.

Something to Consider as You Read

As you read these selections, think about a job you've had and the new procedures you had to learn when you started. Was the job just about the procedures, or did you also have to learn new (and perhaps informal) cultural norms? Think about some of the ways in which the organizational environment induces you to behave in ways that are very specific to that situation. As you read, compare some of these organizational environments to the ones discussed in this chapter. How might other social institutions such as sports and religion shape behavior and beliefs?

Cool Stores, Bad Jobs

YASEMIN BESEN-CASSINO

(2013)

"I just came in to get coffee one day, but got a job with it." Josh, a 19-year-old college student, had settled into his dorm room and headed into town, figuring he might like to work where he usually hangs out. He wanted to make some money and hopefully some friends. After chatting with the shift manager about music and movies, he was offered a job—just like that.

Josh's new job at the Coffee Bean, a pseudonym for a national coffee chain, is typical of a part-time student job: it offers low pay, limited hours, no benefits, and non-standard shifts involving nights and weekends, but it's a job. You'd expect his coworkers would be other struggling students or "adults" who can't do any better. Instead, Josh is pretty much the norm. Affluent students like Josh, with his fashionable clothes, stylish haircut, and brand-new cell phone, are becoming typical workers in places like Coffee Bean.

According to the 2000 Department of Labor's Report on the Youth Labor Force, youth from higher socio-economic status backgrounds are *more* likely to work than their less affluent counterparts (40 percent of higher income 15-year-olds, compared to 32 percent from the lowest income quartile). According to the Current Population Survey, among older teenagers, those from the lowest income groups are the ones least likely to work. In fact, the lowest SES citizens are less likely to work at every age group.

We wouldn't be surprised to see that poor students must work to put themselves through school or to help with basic expenses. But why do affluent students like Josh choose to give up their free time to work in part-time jobs they don't really need?

To answer that question, I hung out at the Coffee Bean, interviewing current and former student workers—40 in all. I also interviewed dozens of college students about their work experiences, perception of brands and consumption habits, and experiences in the aftermath of the recent economic recession.

What I found is that young people see low-paid chain stores as places to socialize with friends away from watchful parental eyes. They can try on adult roles and be associated with their favorite brands. Corporations like Starbucks and Old Navy, in turn, target such kids, marketing their jobs as cool, fashionable, and desirable. Soon, their workers match their desired consumers.

"Every Shift Was Like a Party"

Jamie, a 19-year-old full-time student and the employee at the Coffee Bean, told me his work "is not something you do for money or experience, you know. It's where I hang out. And my parents are okay with it." Since he lives at home, work provides a central space to socialize and see friends without adult supervision, and his parents encourage his employment (though Jamie admits to using work as an excuse to get out of family obligations and house chores).

Not all parents are oblivious to such motives, however. Sarah started working at the Coffee Bean when she turned 18. Her mother knows she works at the coffee shop so that she can see her friends. Wiping dirty tables, washing dishes, carrying trash bags, and dealing with needy and annoying customers was not how she thought her daughter would develop her skills and utilize her knowledge. She characterized her daughter's time at the shop as a "waste of time," even as she admitted that the job kept Sarah "busy" and "out of trouble."

Suburbs are social wastelands for many young people, offering little public transportation and limited chances to hang out with friends or meet new people. Many young people turn to malls and shopping centers, socializing in front of stores and congregating in mall parking lots.

In response, many malls, shopping centers, and movie theaters recently began to ban unattended teenagers, implementing a "parental escort policy." While the owners seek out young customers, they see young people hanging out together as a "counter-productive activity" which can encourage illegal behavior, drug use, or alcohol consumption. It's closed off the few public spaces young people had for socializing outside of school.

Given limited public space for socializing in the suburbs, more and more young people are turning to work as a safe, central place to socialize, free of parental supervision and adult scrutiny.

Sarah loved the people she worked with and thought her job was fun. She scheduled her shifts so that she could work with her friends, and many acquaintances trickled in over the course of the day. She spent so much time at the coffee shop that she felt as though she lived there. Where else could she go that would both welcome her and her friends?

Jules, who is now in college, remembers that the high-end clothing store where she worked part-time during high school didn't even seem like a job. Instead, every shift was like a "party." She would schedule her shifts to see her friends, who were also employees. Her workplace was the place to be.

Representing the Brand That Represents You

Monica, the daughter of two doctors, grew up in an affluent suburb of a large city. When it came to getting a job, she said she wouldn't work just anywhere. Individually owned, family businesses, or "mom and pop" places were out of the question. They might offer more money and better working conditions, but in Monica's words: "It's not the same." Her friends don't work at such places, and those shops don't have the right brand, the cool, desirable image she hoped she would gain by working at someplace hipper (like the one where she eventually did take a job).

Just as consuming certain brands distinguishes young people from others, so, too, does choosing a workplace. In addition to social benefits, well-known chains can offer social distinction and function as identity markers. When asked why she prefers one store's job over the other, Brianna, a 19-year-old college student, said, "I shop there." Like Josh, her motto is "If I shop there, I'll work there." During the past few decades, as a result of unfettered markets, more and more aspects of life have become commodified, including social spaces in the suburbs. In late capitalism, young people search for identities through the brands of the products they buy—and sell. Many young affluent people also self-identify through the brands of the stores they work for: "I am a typical Coffee Bean guy." When working conditions are comparable, many young people gravitate toward those jobs they associate with better branding, or with their own "personal brand."

Employers use this hunt for social space and prestige to their advantage, advertising job openings so that they can target affluent young people. Companies can seek out workers to perform both basic tasks *and* aesthetic labor to represent their brand—workers who "look good and sound right," according to British scholars Dennis Nickson and Chris Warhurst. Many retail and service jobs now require their workers to embody the look of their brands.

For high-end clothing shops, sociologist Mary Gatta wrote in a 2011 article, the best workers are affluent, female workers who look and sound like potential consumers of the brand. Sociologist David Wright has described how bookstore employees are expected to seem like avid readers. The perfectly tailored workforce helps build authenticity and brand loyalty.

Making Bad Jobs Look Good

"What is it like to work at Starbucks?" asks a 2012 advertisement. "It is a lot like working with friends. For one thing, the people, who work here are not employees, we're partners. . . ." Instead of working conditions, pay, benefits, or advancement opportunities, the ad touts opportunity to work with friends. Spencer's, a store that specializes in retail and entertainment, ad emphasizes fun: "Join the Party!"

The thing is, it can be hard to recruit affluent, good looking, and social young people to work at relatively low-paying jobs that offer few advancement opportunities. So job ads must frequently emphasize the coolness and desirability of the brand. A 2011 Old Navy recruitment ad proclaims: "Cool Jobs are in our jeans." A job at Old Navy must be as cool as their denim. Another Old Navy ad reads: "If you love fashion and fun, you're in the right place." A 2012 H&M job ad tells prospective employees: "A great job is always in fashion." We're fashionable, the ad says, and if you work here, you can be, too.

Job advertisements market employment just as the stores market products. When Old Navy says "Try us on," they are suggesting young people can try on the job just as they try on the clothes in the store. Cotton On's 2012 ad compares the person and the product—"I am Cotton On, Are You? Be a Part of the Crew! Join us Today!"—explicitly reinforcing a link between the products and the workers: if you like to consume these goods, you'll like selling them.

By working there, young people are entitled to discounts, which further bolsters consumption of the brand. A 2012 employment ad for Express reads,

"We're looking for people with style, people who love fashion and people who want an Express discount. We're looking for people like you." By mentioning a store discount, stores show that they want to attract workers who already like and use their products. "Must Love Make-up," a 2012 Bare Escentuals ad reads, while H&M asks: "You Obviously like Shopping Here, Why not Work Here?"

Working for a retail shop often creates a high level of brand loyalty and insider status. If customers are trying to associate themselves with a desired brand (Ecko even offers additional discounts to customers if they can show off a tattoo—a real tattoo—of the company's logo), workers are associated with it even more strongly. As a 2012 Cache recruitment puts it: "Cache Careers: The only thing that is more amazing that shopping at Cache is working at Cache." By working at these stores, young people can become associated with a cool brand. Employee discounts create even greater brand loyalty.

Interviewing affluent young people, employers rarely ask about qualifications or talents, nor do they speak of the power or control these youth will enjoy on the job. Rather, they're asked about their favorite music and movies. It's all about the fun environment and the cool brand.

Branding the Self

Will, a 19-year-old white male, talks about Coffee Bean. "A typical employee," he says, "is usually a teenager or an adult in their early 20s, who feels they are more sophisticated for serving overpriced coffee." They did not see it as an opportunity to make money. They saw how popular Coffee Bean was and wanted to be a part of the popular chain of coffee shops.

A marker of identity, the job can help define the person—something many young people struggle to do. Ashley, a 19-year-old white female, notices that people working at the coffee shop have a certain look and personality. "They are artsy, somewhat nerdy. The guys that work there usually play the guitar. Smart people usually work at Coffee Bean." For Ashley and other workers, this "vibe" is a social marker that says a lot about their own personalities as employees. Eric says the other Coffee Bean baristas "are classy hippies, who listen to the Grateful Dead and memorize the script to *Rent* and *Rocky Horror Picture Show*." And for Mike, Coffee Bean

workers are, "liberal, artsy, upper-to-middle class, earring, tattoos, drives a green car, hates the war and loves trees." Employees' interests, social and political preferences, and other consumption habits are all deduced from where they work.

"Fast Food Employees Are Dumb"

Of course not all working students are affluent. Mason is a 21-year-old social science major who resides in a predominantly African-American, low-income city. When he applied for jobs, he had difficulty finding a job in the stores affluent kids could work—he didn't have the "right" look. More economically disadvantaged youth like Mason often end up in fast food jobs. Keeping up with aesthetic demands alongside bills can require a hefty investment.

In fact, many students who work at the Coffee Bean and similar business do so to put themselves through school or help their families—they're not all like the young people I've described above, even though that is a growing segment of workers. But many employers prefer to hire the affluent students because they "look good and sound right."

Sociologists Christine Williams and Catherine Connell, in a 2010 article, reported that employers intentionally locate affluent workers by shutting less affluent workers out: they offer part-time jobs that pay too little to live on. They construct long interview processes (remember Josh's "interview-over-coffee," a wandering conversation that determined he would get a job at the Coffee Bean?) designed to weed out those who don't have time to wait.

So, even as more affluent young people use certain jobs to accumulate social prestige and see their friends, less affluent young people who really *need* these jobs are less likely to get them. More often, the lower-SES students will have to settle for the less desirable fast food jobs.

In the words of Sean, an affluent, white, 20-year-old male, "a typical [fast food] employee is a teenage student or an adult with problems and no education. Most [fast food] employees are dumb." When working at a particular store, however badly paid, is seen as a status marker, those who work in food service are believed to be inferior, lacking in requisite skills and intelligence. But even affluent workers report having trouble keeping up with the aesthetic requirements of their jobs, and sometimes chasing that cool factor plunges them into high levels of debt.

Jules, a white, 20-year-old female, remembers that the upscale clothing store where she worked during her high school years was *the* place to be seen. Working there meant that she was a part of an exclusive club. However, trying to keep up with the aesthetic requirements—she needed to look fashionable and put-together, and wearing the store's latest looks made them easier to sell (Oh, you like this shirt? We have it in green . . .) meant she would buy new clothes from the shop every week. Despite the employee discount, by the time she left the job, she had accumulated credit card debt that rivaled her student loans.

Affluent young workers, who think of their jobs as an extension of their social lives, are less likely to speak up when their jobs are problematic, when they experience sexual harassment, or when they see gender or racial discrimination. Viewing them as just "part-time jobs," as ways of associating themselves with a cool brand rather than support themselves or families, this growing group of affluent young workers is also less likely to complain about how little they're paid. These days, it's hip workers and their disdain for fast-food employees that are tilting the labor market in unexpected ways.

THINKING ABOUT THE READING

Besen-Cassino focuses on contemporary corporations that target affluent youth as employees. What are some of the strategies these companies use to convince young people to work for low wages and few benefits, that is, what do these companies do to make bad jobs look cool? How does the company benefit from this arrangement? What about employees, do they benefit? How does a brand's popularity influence the choice to work for that company? When young people see their jobs as "cool" or as a party, how likely are they to speak up about poor working conditions? What might some of the social theorists say about these tactics and working conditions under capitalism?

Separate and Unequal Justice

NICOLE GONZALEZ VAN CLEVE

(2016)

TO DRIVE TO THE NATION'S BIGGEST and busiest courthouse, take I-55 South from the "Loop"—the center of the city—as though you are making your way to Midway Airport. Drive toward poverty; until the neighborhoods get more racially homogeneous, more black and brown; until the regal Chicago skyline is small but visible in your rearview mirror. Exit at California Avenue, just a few exits shy of Cicero, and start navigating by artifacts of concentrated poverty: look for trash, broken glass, discarded hubcaps on the side of the road, worn gym shoes thrown over electrical wires, and bars on the windows of homes. Look for storefront churches advertising salvation and redemption for a modest fee adjacent to liquor stores offering another type of escapism. Look for graffiti on brick walls of buildings; spray-painted murals memorializing the honorable deaths of young men, women, and children who died in local violence—sacred shrines depicted upon the profane markers of deterioration and disadvantage.

The criminal courthouse is situated in a predominantly Mexican neighborhood with concentrations of violence, gangs, and drugs. Storefront lawyers' offices are among the few businesses in sight. With bars on the windows of their offices, even the few local lawyers who set up shop here seem imprisoned. Mothers push babies in worn umbrella strollers, and the elderly cart groceries home against a backdrop of cement walls, spiked barbed wire, and chain-link fences that surround the adjacent jail. Daily life goes by these fixtures of incarceration.

On my first day driving to the courthouse on 26th and California Avenue (Leighton Criminal Court Building), the Chicago weather served a brutal bite.

Beyond the white structure of the Greco-Roman courthouse was what looked like a Depression-era breadline. Umbrellas were tilted and angled, making the breadline appear like a shantytown fortress in defense of the weather. Those without umbrellas buddied under newspapers and jackets, extended in contorted directions like a modern sculpture, to protect themselves from the wind and ice. It was the 8:30 A.M. courthouse "rush hour" and the breadline was the security queue for the general public—a line that included defendants, families, witnesses, and children. This group, which stretched far outside the building, was almost entirely comprised of people of color.

Adjacent to this line was a separate entrance for attorneys and personnel who had identification badges. While the general public was left to withstand the elements, the flow of professional traffic moved swiftly through, flashing credentials with sheriff's officers nodding and helping to expedite and to avoid inconvenience. The personnel and professionals in this group tended to be white.

Such adjacencies of a black and brown breadline braving the elements and a VIP lane for white professionals instantly demarcated a Jim Crow-style social arrangement on the outside perimeter of the courthouse. This visual of a black and brown entrance and a separate entrance for whites was my first clue of a double system of justice—one for people of color and the poor, and one for wealthy whites.

Introducing the All-White Cast

A small population of mostly white attorneys must commute to this space and manage a system foreign to their personal lives and communities. Cases in Cook County are handled by an "all-white cast." Eighty-four percent of state's attorneys (SAs), 69 percent of public defenders (PDs), and 74 percent of trial court judges are white. This is in stark contrast to the cases and people they process. In 2004, 86.2 percent of felony defendants were male, 69 percent were African American, 17 percent were white, and 11.2 percent were Latino. The Public Defender's Office represents about 23,000 indigent defendants each year. These individuals are determined by a judge to be too poor to secure private counsel.

Such an imbalance quickly presents in visual terms as racial segregation in and around the courthouse. Even outside the building, I observed that segregation was not just spatially arranged but extended to separate and unequal rules and practices between white professionals and the people of color who defined the consumers of criminal justice. On the east side of California Avenue (facing the courthouse) is a five-story parking garage known for the aroma of urine and for being the only free parking in the area. This lot is restricted for jurors, lawyers, cops, and courthouse employees. An older sheriff sits at the gate. On some days, the security gate is propped up and you can find the sheriff napping. Like the courthouse entrance, white drivers with flashy cars are assumed to be lawyers and rarely get stopped—except if the driver chooses to stop. Usually, those who stop are "outsiders" or jurors who *believe* the posted sign that states that a courthouse badge is necessary for entry.

Courthouse insiders will tell you a separate set of rules. If you drive with authority and give a wave to the sheriff, you should have no trouble passing through to the garage—regardless of what the sign says. Such advice travels through social networks of mostly white attorneys, interns, and students. This tip speaks nothing of race, but the unspoken privilege is delineated along a racial divide. The professionals who give out the tip tend to be educated and white. The jurors and outsiders who stop, then pass through the gate with little scrutiny, are also white.

The outsiders who may or may not be aware of these unspoken rules tend to be black, Latino, and poor. Where does that leave them in this urban landscape in and around the courthouse? Unlike the white professionals, blacks and Latinos arrive at the criminal courthouse on foot, travel by city bus (which may take several transfers), or get dropped off in front of the courthouse by a friend or relative.

For the lucky few who have cars, metered lots play a cruel joke on the unsuspecting. High-priced meters have a maximum time limit that barely allows for the time it takes to stand in the security line and find your courtroom. Because leaving the courtroom to feed the meter may cause a defendant or victim to miss his or her case (thereby, forfeiting bond and causing a defendant, in particular, to go to jail), a parking subculture emerged to cope with this cruel catch-22. Some relatives, neighbors, and friends wait in well-worn cars for friends and strangers alike. The cars have rusted paint and loud mufflers that rattle and bark when the car is turned on to idle for warmth. The occupants periodically feed the meters on behalf of friends and strangers—creating a make-shift parking arrangement for the poor. In contrast to the mild indignity of the parking garage smelling of urine, this parking charade has a circus-like feel, with children playing outside the cars while adults chat and compare notes. What is obvious to outsiders and first-time visitors to 26th and Cal is that this charade is racially defined. These separate and unequal structural divides between white and black are firm boundaries that are rigid, unbending, and policed by white courtroom insiders—especially Cook County sheriff's officers. Such rigid boundaries extend inside and around the building—delineating black, brown, and poor from educated, privileged, and white. It is an isolated ecosystem that thrives on segregation.

Criminal Courts as a Complex of Punishment

Once you've driven to 26th and Cal, an impressive white Greco-Roman courthouse casts an imposing presence upon the surrounding desolation. Vacant lots, railroad tracks, and abandoned industry define what appears to be a post-apocalyptic landscape. It's difficult to comprehend that you're only six miles from the center of the city, but far from the view and access of most Chicagoans, tourists, and downtown lawyers. This is not the mayor's Chicago: the pristine version of a metropolis with glorious fountains, museums, and the Magnificent Mile. And it's not Obama's Chicago, which extends beyond Hyde Park's mini-mansions all the way to Grant Park, the site of Obama's Election Day speech—a place synonymous with an emotionally searing visual of the hope of a post-racial America. No. This part of Chicago is built like Alcatraz Island, a prison of justice encircled not by a moat of water but by impenetrable poverty and violence.

Crook County and the White Castle

One of the puns associated with Chicago's criminal justice system is to call it "Crook County"— a term that dismantles the lines of punishment between the court and the jail. Outsiders may think that the "crooks" refer to the pretrial detainees who are charged (and not convicted of their crimes) but too poor to post their bond. However, in this narrative, the "crooks" in the county are actually the professionals—the guards, prosecutors, judges, and even the defense attorneys who are sometimes laughed at as public "pretenders"—the true hustlers who rigged the system.

In the 1970s, Jonathan Casper conducted a series of studies that captured the "consumer" perspective of justice, which appraised the criminal justice system from the vantage point of the system's consumers. This was an important intervention at a time when the "Due Process Revolution" was extending myriad new rights and protections to the criminally accused. He noted that defendants viewed the system as having the same lack of integrity as trying to survive on the streets—a system where the law and the lawless converged in a courthouse where attorneys played the same immoral "games" as a common street hustler. These perceptions of illegitimacy live on in these cultural quips about the "crooks of Cook County," where the boundaries of punishment and due process are not the only things broken down; the boundaries of criminality and civility, the law and the lawless, the moral and the immoral are all blurred as part of the social features of the "Crook County" criminal justice system.

Some of the locals call the court the "White Castle." This term critiques the speed of delivering justice and the mechanisms for achieving it. White Castle is a fast-food chain that is often a fixture of many impoverished neighborhoods. They serve up slider hamburgers, named not just for their size but also for the urban legend that they make you sick, sliding out the next day. This nickname designated the court as a place of drive-thru justice that is not about truth, wisdom, peace, and other symbolic pillars associated with the statues outside the building but instead connotes an assembly line of plea bargains. Beyond the sheer speed of justice, the quality is more like a Hobbesian vision, "poor, nasty, brutish, and short."

Welcome to the Hotel California

Locals also call the jail the "Hotel California." On the surface, it is a play on the Eagles' 1976 hit and a euphemism for a jail located on California Avenue. The lyrics provide a powerful social commentary on the jail and the larger criminal justice system that was reappropriated by the accused and their families. Inmates mock the conditions of "living it up" in one of the most notorious jails in the nation and the legal need to bring your "alibis." Those few who can post bond can metaphorically "check out any time" they want, but they "can never leave."

Ordinary Dysfunction

While criminal courts vary from jurisdiction to jurisdiction, there are some similarities in all criminal court processes. All courtroom workgroups are tasked with "doing justice" while disposing of cases—two goals that are often conflicting and difficult to balance. All workgroups also have a common composition: judge, prosecutors, and defense attorneys who are familiar with one another's specialized roles but who retain their own unique tasks and vantage points in the system.

In the case of jails, most jails in large urban localities are subject to overcrowding. Bond court judges face the task of assessing risk of the accused with little information on defendants, little time to consider it, and little concern regardless of the level of resources. As such, Cook County may be ordinary in its dysfunction—facing the same struggles and burdens that mass incarceration has created for frontline practitioners throughout the nation. There are generalizable features that make Cook County-Chicago an excellent case to understand the experience of justice and the ideological vantage points of those who make justice run in our criminal courts, especially in an era of mass incarceration and the scarcity of resources it has produced in local state courts and jails.

However, the nickname "Hotel California" raises questions about segregation and isolation of this court complex and what it has done to make Chicago an elegant case for examining the racialized effects of criminal justice in urban spaces—where those who are held accountable to the courts tend to be impoverished people of color and those who manage the courts are white, educated, and from places outside of the communities they hold accountable. When a criminal courthouse and a jail are placed in a segregated space, and the space is surrounded by impoverishment and violence, when, if ever, does imprisonment end and freedom begin? When is the supposed deliberative nature of due process distinct from the punitive nature of punishment? And, if surveillance in these neighborhoods is omnipresent, then the sheer proximity of the court and jail to the community disciplines everyone—even the children who have to walk by the court and jail on route to school, church, and other daily fixtures of life.

Us versus Them

An elderly black woman sat silent and still in a courtroom. She hypnotically gazed at the courtroom proceedings through bulletproof glass as white professionals shuffled papers, walked between attorney tables, and casually navigated the daily exchanges that defined the court call: plea bargains, probation violation cases, bond forfeitures, and status updates that defined the mundane features of the business of the courtroom workgroup. The microphone *was* off, so you couldn't hear, but you could see the professionals laugh and smile as if they were in a casual workplace. The interaction was like watching a silent movie, and the audience of mostly black and brown people who sat watching the bulletproof glass—and the professionals beyond it—were like obedient churchgoers at a solemn funeral.

A white court watcher, dressed in jeans and a hoodie, sat among the public, discreetly writing notes with a pen on a form that was a bit crinkled from being in his pocket. The ominous and awkward silence in the court gallery was thick—the type of silence where you are conscious of your own breath. As the court watcher jotted notes, the elderly woman glanced over, taking quick peeks at what he was writing. At court recess, she asked boldly, "What are *you* doing here?" He was one of the few white observers of the court, and despite his hoodie and jeans, his race made it difficult for him to blend in. What was unclear was whether she was asking him why he was writing notes, or a more direct question: What is a white boy like *you* doing in the public gallery with everyone like *me?*

He revealed that he was "court watching" for a study. She revealed that she was related to a victim and a defendant. She asked him specifically to "remember" what he saw "here." As he was trained to do, the court watcher asked a follow-up question: "What do you want me to remember and I will write it down." She turned to the bulletproof glass and responded, "What do *you* see is wrong with this picture?" There was a long pause. "They're [attorneys] *all* white."

Like the outside perimeter of the court with its breadlines and parking shantytowns, the inside of the courthouse and the courtrooms themselves are demarcated and divided along racial lines. People of color stood in separate and longer lines; they were treated as criminals, searched, scrutinized, and mocked. In this space, race is a basic division— delineating the professionals from the public, the "insiders" from the "outsiders," and the power to act informally versus formally.

Distinctions need to be made about social boundaries—what they are, how they are maintained, and how they operate—to understand the segregated social arrangements that define the courthouse. Boundaries maybe "symbolic" where social actors make conceptual distinctions between people or practices. These symbolic boundaries help separate people into groups, generate feelings and ideologies about those groups, and may impact status and, therefore, access to resources and privileges. Once symbolic boundaries become entrenched, rigid and socially agreed upon, they congeal in an institutional form of "social boundaries," where social differences lead to unequal access and opportunity.

While officers yelled orders to all outsiders, security enforcement unapologetically highlighted racial disparity. White researchers were often asked why they were in the building, as though they were out of place. In many instances, these white observers were asked whether they were students or lawyers even when they were not wearing business attire. If they could provide a student ID, they received a host of quality-of-life privileges; they could bring in drinks and snacks and could violate other small security measures. As one court watcher observed:

> Passing through security was very easy— there was barely a line at all and the security personnel let us through with no problems. However, I did notice that the personnel were not as "carefree" with certain other people (primarily African Americans) who they made empty out their entire purses/bags.

Beyond this assumption of criminality, people of color were overtly treated in separate and unequal ways. After setting off the metal detector, a white researcher noted that she was checked, matter-of-factly, with a detecting wand and promptly allowed to proceed. Behind her, a Latino man set off the same alarm and was instead asked, "Do you have a knife?" by a sheriff. A separate incident involved a black man. He emptied his pockets for security but subsequently forgot to collect his money. Upon remembering, he asked the deputy to retrieve it. As he left, another deputy asked his co-worker, "Were you trying to steal that guy's change?" "No," replied the first deputy. He then continued, "But he'd earn it back on the street corner tonight anyway." These abusive remarks were made within earshot of the target.

The hallmarks of modern racism are its subtlety, especially in contrast to the overt abuses of the Jim

Crow era. Yet at the threshold of this courthouse, racialized comments or singling out people of color was an unabashed part of the social arrangements of the space and immediately positioned the armed sheriff's officers as "the police" of this boundary work. The racialized mocking and differential treatment occurred within earshot of other people of color and researchers—demonstrating a distinct culture so brazenly hostile that the niceties of modern racism break down.

Space and Race Divisions in the Courtrooms

The racial demarcation in the courthouse extends into the courtrooms where professionals practice law. On two floors, the courtrooms are nicknamed "fishbowls," because the public galleries are partitioned off from the courtroom professionals by bulletproof glass. The glass divides the courtroom into two parts, separating the minority consumers of justice from the white purveyors of justice. Even in courtrooms without a physical barrier, sheriffs exert a constant threat of violence that polices the professional space from the public gallery with symbolic boundaries as impenetrable as the bulletproof glass itself.

Sheriffs act as henchmen as they aggressively police this racial line by limiting the public access to the court proceedings. Visitors view the court proceedings from behind this soundproof barrier and rely on a microphone at the judge's bench to pipe sound to the gallery. Researchers noted that the sound was periodically turned off either by oversight of court personnel or for professionals to have sidebar discussions. There was no explanation to the public.

Given the limited access to the proceedings, defendants, victims, and their families had many questions for attorneys, clerks, and sheriffs. *Am I in the correct courtroom? Who is my public defender? Is my son on today's court call?* In these cases, a family member would try to ask questions during recess periods, by slowly approaching the partition door, or signaling for a defense attorney, clerk, or sheriff. In the best of circumstances, these signals were ignored. In other circumstances, the move to cross the barrier was matched with the hostility of a physical threat.

Such hostility was so intimidating that I observed an elderly Latina walk toward the professionals with her arms up in a surrender position like she might get shot. Viewing me as a court professional and clerk, she asked me, in Spanish, whether she was in the correct courtroom to see her son, who was a defendant *"Mi hijo es Alejandro Villarreal. ¿Dónde queda su cita de corte? ¿Me puedes ayudar?"* As I began to answer her question, the sheriff barked for her to "sit down and step back" while aggressively walking toward her as though she had a weapon. I averted my eyes from the woman so that our further interaction would not escalate what was already a frightening response.

My actions weighed on my conscience. It was difficult to erase the memory of an elderly woman raising her hands like she was the criminal. There was also the trauma of the sheriff's violent reaction to the possibility of me helping her. The violence conditioned me to the culture of the courts while it made an example out of the woman to the entire public gallery—a public lesson that disciplined us all into maintaining the segregation of the court. I knew that averting my eyes not only saved the woman, but also saved me from losing the very street cred that allowed me to witness such abuse for my field notes. Complicity through silence maintained my research access, hut it weighed heavily. I wrote my confessions in field notes: *What is the cost of this research? When is my silence abuse? Have I become one of the insiders?*

In another case, an elderly black woman came into a courtroom that did not have bulletproof glass. The judge was not on the bench, and only a few prosecutors had started to thumb through files to begin the day. The gallery was nearly empty. The elderly woman slowly, yet defiantly, walked across the boundary into the professional space and went to the prosecutor to inquire if her son's case would be heard in that courtroom. The prosecutor referred her to the clerk. Before she could redirect her question, the sheriff yelled for her to step back. He pointed to the symbolic division between the public and the professional space as though there was a line drawn on the floor as powerful as bulletproof glass.

With so few people in the court, it was confusing where he was pointing. The woman walked backward to the gallery and stood obediently behind the imaginary line. The sheriff scanned the names of the inmates in the courtroom's adjacent lockup and snapped at the woman, "He's not here." He set the papers down and turned his head, which emphasized that his veiled effort was over. In defeat, the woman left the court, but persistently asked one more prosecutor walking into the courtroom where to go next. Seeing this, the sheriff tore the woman up with insults.

That lady felt compelled to ask everyone along the way . . . [he spoke to the prosecutor] Tell her: "Your son is executed."

In earshot of other members of the public, such cruel threats disciplined others from making the same mistake of crossing boundaries or asking questions.

Unable to speak with professionals, the public often tried to whisper questions to one another for support and clarification. If the public tried to whisper and talk in the gallery, this too was met with a threat of violence. In court, the gallery should be neither seen nor heard. For instance, a court watcher noted the following:

> One sheriff was particularly brusque. In response to some muffled chatter, she pointed rather menacingly at the "offenders" and mouthed "Stop talking!" while making a throat-slashing gesture with her hand. On another occasion, the same officer rudely directed a mother to step back from the partition, without providing an explanation as to why her moving was needed. Instead, the officer merely repeated, "Backup!"

Laughing Like No One's Watching

Beyond affecting access to justice, the courtroom boundaries corresponded to boundaries of behavior. They reinforced the "us" versus "them" divisions that defined the culture and the Jim Crow–like separation between white professionals and the public gallery of predominantly people of color. Professionals who were seasoned insiders could joke and act in casual ways that minimized the gravity of processing cases and people through the system, while racial minorities in the public gallery were policed into formal, obedient behavior. They were either criminalized for participating and asking questions or ignored to the point of invisibility.

Laughter, jokes, and mocking of defendants during court proceedings defined the professionals'

informality and occurred with the microphones on. At other times, laughter was visible but the jokes were inaudible. One court watcher noted that the judge stopped the court record "to tell personal jokes to the sheriff, clerk, and prosecutor." In another courtroom, a court watcher described the sheriff as akin to the judge's "sidekick" (like Ed McMahon to Johnny Carson), rather than an officer of the law. In another courtroom, when the proceedings ended for the day, the courtroom deputy started playing a Michael Jackson song over computer speakers while other court personnel and the general public remained in the courtroom. And another court watcher recorded that "attorneys and court staff retreated to an adjacent room during a break. Through the open door, they appeared to be watching TV (based on their conversations, it may have been the U.S Open)."

Even judges contributed to this outlandish behavior, some by their joking and some by their indifference. One court watcher noted the following:

> The minute I was walking in [the court] the judge was disparaging a defendant, and the judge, sheriff, and gallery were all laughing at defendant's expense. I noticed this a lot. It was like the judge did not take anyone seriously—defendants or attorneys. . . the judge took out Girl Scout cookies. He passed them out to the attorneys and even to one defendant . . . Often, he turned the microphone off when it was time to make a decision. This made it so that anyone in the gallery had no idea what was going on. Many people in the gallery made comments when the judge did this like, "Then he goes again" or "He always does this."

This theme of indifference, neglect, and disregard for the seriousness of cases was a pervasive pattern and occurred with little regard for people in the public gallery who were watching it unfold.

THINKING ABOUT THE READING

According to the author, what is separate and unequal in the Cook County criminal justice system? In what ways is racism deeply entrenched in this system? What roles do different groups—prosecutors, judges, defense attorneys—play in this process? How does understanding the racial injustice in the criminal justice system allow us to understand various social inequalities that extend beyond it? What are your ideas for solutions on how to address the problems in this racist and unequal system?

Anybody's Son Will Do

GWYNNE DYER

(1985)

Yet he did kill the Japanese soldier, just as he had been trained to—the revulsion only came afterward. And even after Manchester knew what it was like to kill another human being, a young man like himself, he went on trying to kill his "enemies" until the war was over. Like all the other tens of millions of soldiers who had been taught from infancy that killing was wrong, and had then been sent off to kill for their countries, he was almost helpless to disobey, for he had fallen into the hands of an institution so powerful and so subtle that it could quickly reverse the moral training of a lifetime.

The whole vast edifice of the military institution rests on its ability to obtain obedience from its members even into death—and the killing of others. It has enormous powers of compulsion at its command, of course, but all authority must be based ultimately on consent. The task of extracting that consent from its members has probably grown harder in recent times, for the gulf between the military and the civilian worlds has undoubtedly widened: Civilians no longer perceive the threat of violent death as an everyday hazard of existence, and the categories of people whom it is not morally permissible to kill have broadened to include (in peacetime) the entire human race. Yet the armed forces of every country can still take almost any young male civilian and turn him into a soldier with all the right reflexes and attitudes in only a few weeks. Their recruits usually have no more than twenty years' experience of the world, most of it as children, while the armies have had all or history to practice and perfect their techniques.

> *Just think of how the soldier is treated. While still a child he is shut up in the barracks. During his training, he is always being knocked about. If he makes the least mistake he is beaten, a burning blow on his body, another on his eye, perhaps his head is laid open with a wound. He is battered and bruised with flogging. On the march. . . they hang heavy loads round his neck like that of an ass.*
>
> —EGYPTIAN, CIRCA 1500 B.C.

> *The moment I talk to the new conscripts about the homeland I strike a land mine. So I kept quiet. Instead, I try to make soldiers of them. I give them hell from morning to sunset. They begin to curse me, curse the army, curse the state. Then they begin to curse together, and become a truly cohesive group, a unit, a fighting unit.*
>
> —ISRAELI, CIRCA A.D. 1970

Human beings are fairly malleable, especially when they are young, and in every young man there are attitudes for any army to work with: the inherited values and postures, more or less dimly recalled, of the tribal warriors who were once the model for every young boy to emulate. Civilization did not involve a sudden clean break in the way people behave, but merely the progressive distortion and redirection of all the ways in which people in the old tribal societies used to behave, and modern definitions of maleness still contain a great deal of the old warrior ethic. The anarchic machismo of the primitive warrior is not what modern armies really need in their soldiers, but it does provide them with promising raw material for the transformation they must work in their recruits.

Just how this transformation is wrought varies from time to time and from country to country. In totally militarized societies—ancient Sparta, the samurai class of medieval Japan, the areas controlled by organizations like the Eritrean People's Liberation Front today—it begins at puberty or before, when the young boy is immersed in a disciplined society in which only the military values are allowed to penetrate. In more sophisticated modern societies, the process is briefer and more concentrated, and the way it works is much more visible. It is, essentially, a conversion process in an almost religious sense—and as in all conversion phenomena, the emotions are far more important than the specific ideas. . . .

Armies know this. It is their business to get men to fight, and they have had a long time to work out the best way of doing it. All of them pay lip service to the symbols and slogans of their political masters, though the amount of time they must devote to this activity varies from country to country. . . . Nor should it be thought that the armies are hypocritical—most of their members really do believe in their particular national symbols and slogans. But their secret is that they know these are not the things that sustain men in combat.

What really enables men to fight is their own self-respect, and a special kind of love that has nothing to do with sex or idealism. Very few men have died in battle, when the moment actually arrived, for the United States of America or for the sacred cause of Communism, or even for their homes and families; if they had any choice in the matter at all, they chose to die for each other and for their own vision of themselves. . . .

The way armies produce this sense of brotherhood in a peacetime environment is basic training: a feat of psychological manipulation on the grand scale which has been so consistently successful and so universal that we fail to notice it as remarkable. In countries where the army must extract its recruits in their late teens, whether voluntarily or by conscription, from a civilian environment that does not share the military values, basic training involves a brief but intense period of indoctrination whose purpose is not really to teach the recruits basic military skills, but rather to change their values and their loyalties. "I guess you could say we brainwash them a little bit," admitted a U.S. Marine drill instructor, "but you know they're good people."

The duration and intensity of basic training, and even its major emphases, depend on what kind of society the recruits are coming from, and on what sort of military organization they are going to. It is obviously quicker to train men from a martial culture than from one in which the dominant values are civilian and commercial, and easier to deal with volunteers than with reluctant conscripts. Conscripts are not always unwilling, however; there are many instances in which the army is popular for economic reasons. . . .

It's easier if you catch them young. You can train older men lo be soldiers; it's done in every major war. But you can never get them to believe that they like it, which is the major reason armies try to get their recruits before they are 20. There are other reasons too, of course, like the physical fitness, lack of dependents, and economic dispensability of teenagers, that make armies prefer them, but the most important qualities teenagers bring to basic training are enthusiasm and naiveté. Many of them actively want the discipline and the closely structured environment that the armed forces will provide, so there is no need for the recruiters to deceive the kids about what will happen to them after they join.

There is discipline. There is drill. . . . When you are relying on your mates and they are relying on you, there's no room for slackness or sloppiness. If you're not prepared to accept the rules, you're better off where you are.
—British Army Recruiting Advertisement, 1976

People are not born soldiers, they become soldiers. . . . And it should not begin at the moment a new recruit is enlisted into the ranks, but rather much earlier, at the time of the first signs of maturity, during the lime of adolescent dreams.
—Red Star (Soviet Army Newspaper), 1973

Young civilians who have volunteered and have been accepted by the Marine Corps arrive at Parris Island, the Corps's East Coast facility for basic training, in a state of considerable excitement and apprehension: Most are aware that they are about to undergo an extraordinary and very difficult experience. But they do not make their own way to the base; rather, they trickle in to Charleston airport on various flights throughout the day on which their training platoon is due to form, and are held there, in a state of suppressed but mounting nervous tension, until late in the evening. When the buses finally come to carry them the 76 miles to Parris Island, it is often after midnight—and this is not an administrative oversight. The shock treatment they are about to receive will work most efficiently if they are worn out and somewhat disoriented when they arrive.

The basic training organization is a machine, processing several thousand young men every month, and every facet and gear of it has been designed with the sole purpose of turning civilians into Marines as efficiently as possible. Provided it can have total control over their bodies and their environment for approximately three months, it can practically guarantee converts. Parris Island provides that controlled environment, and the recruits do not set foot outside it again until they graduate as Marine privates 11 weeks later.

They're allowed to call home, so long as it doesn't get out of hand—every three weeks or so they can call home and make sure everything's all right, if they haven't gotten a letter or there's a particular set of circumstances. If it's a case of an emergency call coming in, then they're allowed to accept that call; if not, one of my staff will take the message. . . .

In some cases I'll get calls from parents who haven't quite gotten adjusted to the idea that their son had cut the strings—and in a lot of cases that's what they're doing. The military provides them with an opportunity to leave home but they're still in a rather secure environment.

—Captain Brassington, USMC

Basic training is not really about teaching people skills; it's about changing them so that they can do things they wouldn't have dreamt of otherwise. It works by applying enormous physical and mental pressure to men who have been isolated from their normal civilian environment and placed in one where the only right way to think and behave is the way the Marine Corps wants them to. The key word the men who run the machine use to describe this process is *motivation.*

I can motivate a recruit and in the third phase, if I tell him to jump off the third deck, he'll jump off the third deck. Like I said before, it's a captive audience and I can train that guy; I can get him to do anything I want him to do. . . . They're good kids and they're out to do the right thing. We get some bad kids, but you know, we weed those out. But as far as motivation—here, we can motivate them to do anything you want in recruit training.

—USMC Drill Instructor, Parris Island

The first three days the raw recruits spend at Parris Island are actually relatively easy, though they are hustled and shouted at continuously. It is during this time that they are documented and inoculated, receive uniforms, and learn the basic orders of drill that will enable young Americans (who are not very accustomed to this aspect of life) to do everything simultaneously in large groups. But the most important thing that happens in "forming" is the surrender of the recruits' own clothes, their hair—all the physical evidence of their individual civilian identities.

During a period of only 72 hours, in which they are allowed little sleep, recruits lay aside their former lives in a series of hasty rituals (like being shaven to the scalp) whose symbolic significance is quite clear to them even though they are quite deliberately given absolutely no time for reflection, or any hint that they might have the option of turning back from their commitment. The men in charge of them know how delicate a tightrope they are walking, though, because at this stage the recruits are still newly caught civilians who have not yet made their ultimate inward submission to the discipline of the Corps.

Forming Day One makes me nervous. You've got a whole new mob of recruits, you know, 60 or 70 depending, and they don't know anything. You don't know what kind of a reaction you're going to get from the stress you're going to lay on them, and it just worries me the first day. . . .

Things could happen, I'm not going to lie to you. Something might happen. A recruit might decide he doesn't want any part of this stuff and maybe take a poke at you or something like that. In a situation like that it's going to be a spur-of-the moment thing and that worries me.

—USMC Drill Instructor

But it rarely happens. The frantic bustle of forming is designed to give the recruit no time to think about resisting what is happening to him. And so the recruits emerge from their initiation into the system, stripped of their civilian clothes, shorn of their hair, and deprived of whatever confidence in their own identity they may previously have had as 18-year-olds, like so many blanks ready to have the Marine identity impressed upon them.

The first stage in any conversion process is the destruction of an individual's former beliefs and confidence, and his reduction to a position of helplessness and need. It isn't really as drastic as all that, of course, for three days cannot cancel out 18 years; the inner thoughts and the basic character are not erased. But the recruits have already learned that the only acceptable behavior is to repress any unorthodox thoughts and to mimic the character the Marine Corps wants. Nor are they, on the whole, reluctant to do so, for they *want* to be Marines. From the moment they arrive at Parris Island, the vague notion that has been passed down for a thousand generations that masculinity means being a warrior becomes an explicit article of faith, relentlessly preached: To be a man means to be a Marine.

There are very few 18-year-old boys who do not have highly romanticized ideas of what it means to be a man, so the Marine Corps has plenty of buttons to push. And it starts pushing them on the first day of real training: The officer in charge of the formation appears before them for the first time, in full dress uniform with medals, and tells them how to become men.

The United States Marine Corps has 205 years of illustrious history to speak for itself. You have made the most important decision in your life . . . by signing your name, your life, your pledge to the Government of the United States, and even more importantly, to the United States Marine Corps—a brotherhood, an elite unit. In 10.3 weeks you are going to become a member of that history, those traditions, this organization—if you have what it takes . . .

All of you want to do that by virtue of your signing your name as a man. 'The Marine Corps says that we build men. Well, I'll go a little bit further. We develop the tools that you have—and everybody has those tools to a certain extent right now. We're going to give you the blueprints, and we are going to show you how to build a Marine. You've got to build a Marine—you understand?

—Captain Pingree, USMC

The recruits, gazing at him in awe and adoration, shout in unison, "Yes, sir!" just as they have been taught. They do it willingly, because they are volunteers—but even conscripts tend to have the romantic fervor of volunteers if they are only 18 years old. Basic training, whatever its hardships, is a quick way to become a man among men, with an undeniable status, and beyond the initial consent to undergo it, it doesn't even require any decisions.

I had just dropped out of high school and I wasn't doing much on the street except hanging out, as most teenagers would be doing. So they gave me an opportunity: a recruiter picked me up, gave me a good line, and said that I could make it in the Marines, that I have a future ahead of me. And since I was living with my parents, I figured that I could start my own life here and grow up a little.

—USMC recruit, 1982

I like the hand-to-hand combat and . . . things like that. It's a little rough going on me, and since I have a small frame I would like to become deadly, as I would put it. I like to have them words, especially the way they've been teaching me here.

—USMC Recruit (From Brooklyn), Parris Island, 1982

The training, when it starts, seems impossibly demanding physically for most of the recruits—and then it gets harder week by week. There is a constant barrage of abuse and insults aimed at the recruits, with the deliberate purpose of breaking down their pride and so destroying their ability to resist the transformation of values and attitudes that the Corps intends them to

undergo. At the same time, the demands for constant alertness and for instant obedience are continuously stepped up, and the standards by which the dress and behavior of the recruits are judged become steadily more unforgiving. But it is all carefully calculated by the men who run the machine, who think and talk in terms of the stress they are placing on the recruits: *We take so many c.c.'s of stress and we administer it to each man—they should be a little bit scared and they should be unsure, but they're adjusting.* The aim is to keep the training arduous but just within most of the recruits' capability to withstand. One of the most striking achievements of the drill instructors is to create and maintain the illusion that basic training is an extraordinary challenge, one that will set those who graduate apart from others, when in fact almost everyone can succeed.

There has been some preliminary weeding out of potential recruits even before they begin basic training, to eliminate the obviously unsuitable minority, and some people do "fail" basic training and get sent home, at least in peacetime. The standards of acceptable performance in the U.S. armed forces, for example, tend to rise and fall in inverse proportion to the number and quality of recruits available to fill the forces to the authorized manpower levels. (In 1980, about 15% of Marine recruits did not graduate from basic training.) But there are very few young men who cannot be turned into passable soldiers if the forces are willing to invest enough effort in it.

Not even physical violence is necessary to effect the transformation, though it has been used by most armies at most times.

It's not what it was 15 years ago down here. The Marine corps still occupies the position of a tool which the society uses when it feels like that is a resort that they have to fall to. Our society changes, as all societies do, and our society felt that through enlightened training methods we could still produce the same product—and when you examine it, they're right. . . . Our 100 c.c.'s of stress is really all we need, not two gallons of it, which is what used to be. . . . In some cases with some of the younger drill instructors it was more an initiation than it was an acute test, and so we introduced extra officers and we select our drill instructors to "fine-tune" it.

—Captain Brassington, USMC

There is, indeed, a good deal of fine-tuning in the roles that the men in charge of training any specific group of recruits assume. At the simplest level, there is a sort of "good cop–bad cop" manipulation of recruits' attitudes toward those applying the stress. The three younger drill instructors with a particular serial are quite close to them in age and unremittingly harsh in their demands for ever higher performance, but the senior drill instructor, a man almost old enough to be their father, plays a more benevolent and understanding part and is available for individual counseling. And generally offstage, but always looming in the background, is the company commander, an impossibly austere and almost godlike personage.

At least these are the images conveyed to the recruits, although of course all these men cooperate closely with an identical goal in view. It works: In the end they become not just role models and authority figures, but the focus of the recruits' developing loyalty to the organization.

> *I imagine there's some fear; especially in the beginning, because they don't know what to expect. . . . I think they hate you at first, at least for a week or two, but it turns to respect . . . They're seeking discipline, they're seeking someone to take charge, 'cause at home they never got it. . . . They're looking to be told what to do and then someone is standing there enforcing what they tell them to do, and it's kind of like the father-and-son game, all the way through. They form a fatherly image of the DI {drill instructor] whether they want to or not.*
>
> —Sergeant Carrington, USMC

Just the sheer physical exercise, administered in massive doses, soon has recruits feeling stronger and more competent than ever before. Inspections, often several times daily, quickly build up their ability to wear the uniform and carry themselves like real Marines, which is a considerable source of pride. The inspections also help to set up the pattern in the recruits of unquestioning submission to military authority: Standing stock-still, staring straight ahead, while somebody else examines you closely for faults is about as extreme a ritual act of submission as you can make with your clothes on.

But they are not submitting themselves merely to the abusive sergeant making unpleasant remarks about the hair in their nostrils. All around them are deliberate reminders—the flags and insignia displayed on parade, the military music, the marching formations and drill instructors' cadenced calls—of the idealized organization, the "brotherhood" to

which they will be admitted as full members if they submit and conform. Nowhere in the armed forces are the military courtesies so elaborately observed, the staffs' uniforms so immaculate (some DIs change several times a day), and the ritual aspects of military life so highly visible as on a basic training establishment.

Even the seeming inanity of close-order drill has a practical role in the conversion process. It has been over a century since mass formations of men were of any use on the battlefield, but every army in the world still drills it, troops, especially during basic training, because marching in formation, with every man moving his body in the same way at the same moment, is a direct physical way of learning two things a soldier must believe: that orders have to be obeyed automatically and instantly, and that you are no longer an individual, but part of a group.

The recruits' total identification with the other members of their unit is the most important lesson of all, and everything possible is done to foster it. They spend almost every waking moment together—a recruit alone is an anomaly to be looked into at once—and during most of that time they are enduring shared hardships. They also undergo collective punishments, often for the misdeed or omission of a single individual (talking in the ranks, a bed not swept under during barracks inspection), which is a highly effective way of suppressing any tendencies toward individualism. And, of course, the DIs place relentless emphasis on competition with other "serials" in training: There may be something infinitely pathetic to outsiders about a marching group of anonymous recruits chanting, "Lift your heads and hold them high, 3313 is a-passin' by," but it doesn't seem like that to the men in the ranks.

Nothing is quite so effective in building up a group's morale and solidarity, though, as a steady diet of small triumphs. Quite early in basic training, the recruits begin to do things that seem, at first sight, quite dangerous: descend by ropes from 50-foot towers, cross yawning gaps hand-over-hand on high wires (known as the Slide for Life, of course), and the like. The common denominator is that these activities are daunting but not really dangerous: The ropes will prevent anyone from falling to his death off the rappelling tower, and there is a pond of just the right depth—deep enough to cushion a falling man, but not deep enough that he is likely to drown—under the Slide for Life. The goal is not to kill recruits, but to build up their confidence as individuals and as a group by allowing them to overcome apparently frightening obstacles.

You have an enemy here at Parris Island. The enemy that you're going to have at Parris Island is in every one of us. It's in the form of cowardice. The most rewarding experience you're going to have in recruit training is standing on line every evening, and you'll be able to look into each other's eyes, and you'll be able to say to each other with your eyes: "By God, we've made it one more day! We've defeated the coward."

—Captain Pingree, USMC

Number on deck, sir, 45 . . . highly motivated, truly dedicated, rompin; stompin; bloodthirsty, kill-crazy United States Marine Corps recruits, SIR!

—Marine Chant, Parris Island, 1982

If somebody does fail a particular test, he tends to be alone, for the hurdles *are* deliberately set low enough that most recruits can clear them if they try. In any large group of people there is usually a goat: someone whose intelligence or manner or lack of physical stamina marks him for failure and contempt. The competent drill instructor, without deliberately setting up this unfortunate individual for disgrace, will use his failure to strengthen the solidarity and confidence of the rest. When one hapless young man fell off the Slide for Life into the pond, for example, his drill instructor shouted the usual invective—Well, *get out the water. Don't contaminate* it *all day*—and then delivered the payoff line: *Go back and change your clothes. You're useless to your unit now.*

"Useless to your unit" is the key phrase, and all the recruits know that what it means is "useless *in battle.*" The Marine drill instructors at Parris Island know exactly what they are doing to the recruits, and why. They are not rear-echelon people filling comfortable jobs, but the most dedicated and intelligent NCOs [non-commissioned officers] the Marine Corps can find; even now, many of them have combat experience. The Corps has a clear-eyed understanding of precisely what it is training its recruits for—combat—and it ensures that those who do the training keep that objective constantly in sight

The DIs stress the recruits, feed them their daily ration of synthetic triumphs over apparent obstacles, and bear in mind all the time that the goal is to instill the foundations for the instinctive, selfless reactions and the fierce group loyalty that is what the recruits will need if they ever see combat. They are

arch-manipulators, fully conscious of it, and utterly unashamed. These kids have signed up as Marines, and they could well see combat; this is the way they have to think if they want to live.

I've seen guys come to Vietnam from all over. They were all sorts of people that had been scared—some of them had been scared all their life and still scared. Some of them had been a country boy, city boys—you know, all different kinds of people but when they got in combat they all reacted the same—99 percent of them reacted the same. . . A. lot of it is training here at Parris Island, but the other part of it is survival. They know if they don't conform—conform I call it, but if they don't react in the same way other people are reacting, they won't survive. That's just it. You know, if you don't react together, then nobody survives.

—USMC Drill Instructor, Parris Island, 1982

"When I went to boot camp and did individual combat training, they said if you walk into an ambush what you want to do is just do a right face—you just turn right or left, whichever way the fire is coming from, and assault. I said, "Man, that's crazy. I'd never do anything like that. It's stupid". . .

The first time we came under fire, on Hill 1044 in Operation Beauty Canyon in Laos, we did it automatically. Just like you look at your watch to see what time it is. We done a right face, assaulted the hill—a fortified position with concrete bunkers emplaced, machine guns, automatic weapons and we took it. And we killed—I'd estimate probably 35 North Vietnamese soldiers in the assault, and we only lost three killed. I think it was about two or three, and about eight or ten wounded. . . .

But you know, what they teach you, it doesn't faze you until it comes down to the time to use it, but it's in the back of your head, like, What do you do when you come to a stop sign? It's in the back of your head, and you react automatically.

—USMC sergeant, 1982

Combat is the ultimate reality that Marines—or any other soldiers, under any flag—have to deal with. Physical fitness, weapons training, and battle drills are all indispensable elements of basic training, and it is absolutely essential that the recruits learn the attitudes of group loyalty and interdependency which will be their sole hope of survival and success in combat. The training inculcates or fosters all of those things, and even by the halfway point in the 11-week course, the recruits are generally responding with enthusiasm to their tasks. . . .

In basic training establishments, . . . the malleability is all one way: in the direction of submission to military authority and the internalization of military values. What a place like Parris Island produces when it is successful, as it usually is, is a soldier who will kill because that is his job.

THINKING ABOUT THE READING

Describe the norms, values, and language of the organizational culture in the military. What are the methods used in the military to resocialize men into soldiers? What happens if recruits resist that resocialization process? Is it possible for the recruits to exercise any control over their lives in this total institution? How might the contemporary military institution reflect this organizational culture but also display some changes from the time period of Dyer's article? Consider some of the pressing social problems associated with the military in recent years (PTSD, suicide, substance abuse, homelessness, sexual harassment, and assault) and think about what influence the organizational social culture may have had on these issues.

CHAPTER 10

The Architecture of Stratification

Social Class and Inequality

I nequality is woven into the fabric of all societies through a structured system of *social stratification*. Social stratification is a ranking of entire groups of people that perpetuates unequal rewards and life chances in society. The structural-functionalist explanation of stratification is that the stability of society depends on all social positions being filled—that is, there are people around to do all the jobs that need to be done. Higher rewards, such as prestige and large salaries, are afforded to the most important positions, thereby ensuring that the most qualified individuals will occupy the highest positions. In contrast, conflict theory argues that stratification reflects an unequal distribution of power in society and is a primary source of conflict and tension.

Social class is the primary means of stratification in American society. Contemporary sociologists are likely to define a person's class standing as a combination of income, wealth, occupational prestige, and educational attainment. It is tempting to see class differences as simply the result of an economic stratification system that exists at a level above the individual. Although inequality is created and maintained by larger social institutions, it is often felt most forcefully and is reinforced most effectively in the chain of interactions that take place in our day-to-day lives.

The face of American poverty has changed somewhat over the past several decades. The economic status of single mothers and their children has deteriorated while that of people older than age 65 has improved somewhat. What hasn't changed is the ever-widening gap between the rich and the poor. Poverty persists because in a free market and competitive society, it serves economic and social functions. In addition, poverty receives institutional "support" in the form of segmented labor markets and inadequate educational systems. The ideology of competitive individualism—that to succeed in life, all one has to do is work hard and win in competition with others—creates a belief that poor people are to blame for their own suffering. So, although the problem of poverty remains serious, public attitudes toward poverty and poor people are frequently indifferent or even hostile. Sociologists such as Fred Block and his colleagues call this attitude "the compassion gap." According to their research, this cultural attitude of indifference or disdain is rooted in individualism and a lack of understanding of economic conditions over time (e.g., the relative difficulty of owning a home today as compared with the period just after World War II when much government assistance was available). The authors see the "compassion gap" as an attitude that gets in the way of establishing more workable social policies for the poor.

This attitude extends to the ways in which we perceive people's status based on characteristics such as clothing, personal hygiene, and physical traits, such as scars or blemishes. In "Branded With Infamy" Vivyan Adair describes the various ways in which poor women's bodies are marked as "unclean" or "unacceptable." These markings are the result of a life of poverty: a lack of access to proper health care, nutrition, and shelter; and demanding physical and emotional labor. But instead of seeing the impact of economic circumstances on the lives of these women, more affluent people tend to view them (and their children) as members of an undesirable social class that should be disciplined, controlled, and punished.

Due to the possibility of social mobility, many believe that when people move from one social class to another, that their new location means their past one is left behind and forgotten. In "Marrying Across Class Lines," Jessi Streib shows how social class is never a relic of the past and that it permeates the relationships of middle-class married couples who came from different social class origins. Streib describes contrasting approaches—"laissez-faire" and "managerial"—to various facets of daily life including money, paid work, housework, time, leisure, parenting, and emotions. In some cases, these opposing approaches led to an appreciation and admiration of their spouse and other times to tension and conflict.

Social reproduction theory suggests that the social class you are born into will most likely be the one you die in. When social class privileges and the associated family resources are intertwined with racial privilege and residential segregation, it becomes evident how this cycle is reproduced over generations. Lauren Alfrey and France Winddance Twine show the cultural and social advantages that upper middle-class White and Asian tech workers in Silicon Valley have over their Black and working-class White colleagues. This investigation highlights the "experience gap" that occurs "outside the pipeline" between these groups that came from early and crucial exposure to computers and technological training while growing up in economically affluent communities. This combination of racial and class segregation was plainly visible in both their formal educational and occupational trajectories as tech workers.

Something to Consider as You Read

In reading these selections, pay careful attention to the small ways in which economic resources affect everyday choices and behavior. For instance, how might poverty, including the lack of access to nice clothing, affect one's ability to portray the best possible image at a job interview? How might poverty impact a person's intimate relationships? How might early exposure to forms of cultural capital (e.g., computer knowledge) affect a person's chance at certain jobs? Consider further the connection between media portrayals and self-image. Where do people get their ideas about their own self-worth, their sense of entitlement, and how they fit into society generally? How do these ideals differ across social class and how are they similar? Some observers have suggested that people in the United States don't know how to talk about class, except in stereotypical terms. How might this lack of "class discourse" perpetuate stereotypes and the myth that the poor deserve their fate? Consider examples of the "compassion gap" in your own life and as reflected in recent news and policy decisions. Does the compassion gap relate to the failure to fully understand social issues such as teenage pregnancy?

Branded With Infamy

Inscriptions of Poverty and Class in America

VIVYAN ADAIR

(2002)

"My kids and I been chopped up and spit out just like when I was a kid. My rotten teeth, my kids' twisted feet. My son's dull skin and blank stare. My oldest girl's stooped posture and the way she can't look no one in the eye no more. This all says we got nothing and we deserve what we got. On the street good families look at us and see right away what they'd be if they don't follow the rules. They're scared too, real scared."
—Welfare recipient and activist, Olympia, Washington, 1998

I begin with the words of a poor, White, single mother of three. Although officially she has only a tenth-grade education, she expertly reads and articulates a complex theory of power, bodily inscription, and socialization that arose directly from material conditions of her own life. She sees what many far more "educated" scholars and citizens fail to recognize: that the bodies of poor women and children are produced and positioned as texts that facilitate the mandates of a . . . profoundly brutal and mean-spirited political regime. . . .

Over the past decade or so, a host of inspired feminist welfare scholars and activists have addressed and examined the relationship between state power and the lives of poor women and children. As important and insightful as these exposés are, with few exceptions, they do not get at the closed circuit that fuses together systems of power, the material conditions of poverty, and the bodily experiences that allow for the perpetuation—and indeed the justification—of these systems. They fail to consider what the speaker of my opening passage recognized so astutely: that systems of power produce and patrol poverty through the reproduction of both social and bodily markers. . . .

. . . [In this article I employ the theory of Michel Foucault to describe how the body is] the product of historically specific power relations. Feminists have used this notion of social inscription to explain a range of bodily operations from cosmetic surgery (Morgan 1991), prostitution (Bell 1994), and Anorexia Nervosa (Hopwood 1995, Bordo 1993) to motherhood (Chandler 1999, Smart 1992), race (Stoler 1995, Ford-Smith 1995), and cultural imperialism (Desmond 1991). As these analyses illustrate, Foucault allows us to consider and critique the body as it is invested with meaning and inserted into regimes of truth via the operations of power and knowledge. . . .

Foucault clarifies and expands on this process of bodily/social inscription in his early work. In "Nietzsche, Genealogy, History," he positions the physical body as virtual text, accounting for the fact that "the body is the inscribed surface of events that are traced by language and dissolved by ideas" (1984, 83). . . . For Foucault, the body and [power] are inseparable. In his logic, power constructs and holds bodies. . . .

In *Discipline and Punish* Foucault sets out to depict the genealogy of torture and discipline as it reflects a public display of power on the body of subjects in the 17th and 18th centuries. In graphic detail Foucault begins his book with the description of a criminal being tortured and then drawn and quartered in a public square. The crowds of good parents and their growing children watch and learn. The public spectacle works as a patrolling image, socializing and controlling bodies within the body politic. Eighteenth century torture "must mark the victim: it is intended, either by the scar it leaves on the body or by the spectacle that accompanies it, to brand the victim with infamy . . . it traces around or rather on the very body of the condemned man signs that can not be effaced" (1984, 179). For Foucault, public exhibitions of punishment served as a socializing process, writing culture's codes and values on the minds and bodies of its subjects. In the process punishment . . . rearranged bodies.

. . . Foucault's point in *Discipline and Punish* is . . . that public exhibition and inscription have been replaced in contemporary society by a much more effective process of socialization and self-inscription. According to Foucault, today discipline has replaced torture as the privileged punishment, but the body continues to be written on. Discipline produces "subjected and practiced bodies, docile bodies" (1984,

182). We become subjects . . . of ideology, disciplining and inscribing our own bodies/minds in the process of becoming stable and singular subjects. . . . The body continues to be the site and operation of ideology. . . .

Indeed, while we are all marked discursively by ideology in Foucault's paradigm, in the United States today poor women and children of all races are marked with multiple signs of both discipline and punishment that cannot be erased or effaced. They are systematically produced through both 20th century forces of socialization and discipline and 18th century exhibitions of public mutilation. In addition to coming into being as disciplined and docile bodies, poor single welfare mothers and their children are physically inscribed, punished, and displayed as dangerous and pathological "other." It is important to note when considering the contemporary inscription of poverty as moral pathology etched onto the bodies of profoundly poor women and children, that these are more than metaphoric and self-patrolling marks of discipline. Rather on myriad levels—sexual, social, material, and physical—poor women and their children, like the "deviants" publicly punished in Foucault's scenes of torture, are marked, mutilated, and made to bear and transmit signs in a public spectacle that brands the victim with infamy. . . .

The (Not So) Hidden Injuries of Class

Recycled images of poor, welfare women permeate and shape our national consciousness.[1] Yet—as is so often the case—these images and narratives tell us more about the culture that spawned and embraced them than they do about the object of the culture's obsession . . . .

These productions orchestrate the story of poverty as one of moral and intellectual lack and of chaos, pathology, promiscuity, illogic, and sloth, juxtaposed always against the order, progress, and decency of "deserving" citizens. . . .

I am, and will probably always be, marked as a poor woman. I was raised by a poor, single, White mother who had to struggle to keep her four children fed, sheltered, and clothed by working at what seemed like an endless stream of minimum wage, exhausting, and demeaning jobs. As a child poverty was written onto and into my being at the level of private and public thought and body. At an early age my body bore witness to and emitted signs of the painful devaluation carved

into my flesh; that same devaluation became integral to my being in the world. I came into being as disciplined body/mind while at the same time I was taught to read my abject body as the site of my own punishment and erasure. In this excess of meaning the space between private body and public sign was collapsed.

For many poor children this double exposure results in debilitating . . . shame and lack. As Carolyn Kay Steedman reminds us in *Landscape for a Good Woman,* the mental life of poor children flows from material deprivation. Steedman speaks of the "relentless laying down of guilt" she experienced as a poor child living in a world where identity was shaped through envy and unfulfilled desire and where her own body "told me stories of the terrible unfairness of things, of the subterranean culture of longing for that which one can never have" (1987, 8). For Steedman, public devaluation and punishment "demonstrated to us all the hierarchies of our illegality, the impropriety of our existence, our marginality within the social system" (1987, 9). Even as an adult she recalls that:

> . . . the baggage will never lighten for me or my sister. We were born, and had no choice in the matter; but we were social burdens, expensive, unworthy, never grateful enough. There was nothing we could do to pay back the debt of our existence. (1987, 19)

Indeed, poor children are often marked with bodily signs that cannot be forgotten or erased. Their bodies are physically inscribed as "other" and then read as pathological, dangerous, and undeserving. What I recall most vividly about being a child in a profoundly poor family was that we were constantly hurt and ill, and because we could not afford medical care, small illnesses and accidents spiraled into more dangerous illnesses and complications that became both a part of who we were and written proof that we were of no value in the world.

In spite of my mother's heroic efforts, at an early age my brothers and sister and I were stooped, bore scars that never healed properly, and limped with feet mangled by ill-fitting, used Salvation Army shoes. When my sister's forehead was split open by a door slammed in frustration, my mother "pasted" the angry wound together on her own, leaving a mark of our inability to afford medical attention, of our lack, on her very forehead. When I suffered from a concussion, my mother simply put borrowed ice on my head and tried to keep me awake for a night. And when throughout elementary school we were sent to the office for mandatory and very public yearly checks, the school nurse sucked air through her teeth as she donned surgical gloves to check only the hair of poor children for lice.

We were read as unworthy, laughable, and often dangerous. Our school mates laughed at our "ugly shoes," our crooked and ill-serviced teeth, and the way we "stank," as teachers excoriated us for inability to concentrate in school, our "refusal" to come to class prepared with proper school supplies, and our unethical behavior when we tried to take more than our allocated share of "free lunch."[2] Whenever backpacks or library books came up missing, we were publicly interrogated and sent home to "think about" our offences, often accompanied by notes that reminded my mother that as a poor single parent she should be working twice as hard to make up for the discipline that allegedly walked out the door with my father. When we sat glued to our seats, afraid to stand in front of the class in ragged and ill-fitting hand-me-downs, we were held up as examples of unprepared and uncooperative children. And when our grades reflected our otherness, they were used to justify even more elaborate punishment. . . .

Friends who were poor as children, and respondents to a survey I conducted in 1998,[3] tell similar stories of the branding they received at the hands of teachers, administrators, and peers. An African-American woman raised in Yesler Terrace, a public housing complex in Seattle, Washington, writes:

> Poor was all over our faces. My glasses were taped and too weak. My big brother had missing teeth. My mom was dull and ashy. It was like a story of how poor we were that anyone could see. My sister Evie's lip was bit by a dog and we just had dime store stuff to put on it. Her lip was a big scar. Then she never smiled and no one smiled at her cause she never smiled. Kids called her "Scarface." Teachers never smiled at her. The princip[al] put her in detention all the time because she was mean and bad (they said).

And, a White woman in the Utica, New York, area remembers:

> We lived in dilapidated and unsafe housing that had fleas no matter how clean my mom tried to be. We had bites all over us. Living in our car between evictions was even worse—then we didn't have a bathroom so I got kidney problems that I never had doctor's help for. When my teachers wouldn't let me got to the bathroom every hour or so I would wet my pants in class. You can imagine what the kids did to me about that. And the teachers would refuse to let me go to the bathroom because they said I was willful.

Material deprivation is publicly written on the bodies of poor children in the world. In the United States poor families experience violent crime, hunger, lack of medical and dental care, utility shut-offs, the effects of living in unsafe housing and/or of being homeless, chronic illness, and insufficient winter clothing (Edin and Lein 1997, 224–231). According to Jody Raphael of the Taylor Institute, poor women and their children are also at five times the risk of experiencing domestic violence (Raphael, 2000).

As children, our disheveled and broken bodies were produced and read as signs of our inferiority and undeservedness. As adults, our mutilated bodies are read as signs of inner chaos, immaturity, and indecency as we are punished and then read as proof of need for further discipline and punishment. When my already bad teeth started to rot and I was out of my head with pain, my choices as an adult welfare recipient were to either let my teeth fall out or have them pulled out. In either case the culture would then read me as a "toothless illiterate," as a fearful joke. In order to pay my rent and to put shoes on my daughter's feet, I sold blood at two or three different clinics on a monthly basis until I became so anemic that they refused to buy it from me. A neighbor of mine went back to the man who continued to beat her and her children after being denied welfare benefits, when she realized that she could not adequately feed, clothe, and house her family on her own minimum wage income. My good friend sold her ovum to a fertility clinic in a painful and potentially damaging process. Other friends exposed themselves to all manner of danger and disease by selling their bodies for sex in order to feed and clothe their babies.

Exhaustion also marks the bodies of poor women in indelible script. Rest becomes a privilege we simply cannot afford. After working full shifts each day, poor mothers trying to support themselves at minimum wage jobs continue to work to a point of exhaustion that is inscribed on their faces, their bodies, their posture, and their diminishing sense of self and value in the world. My former neighbor recently recalled:

> I had to take connecting buses to bring and pick up my daughters at childcare after working on my feet all day. As soon as we arrived at home, we would head out again by bus to do laundry. Pick up groceries. Try to get to the food bank. Beg the electric company to not turn off our lights and heat again. Find free winter clothing. Sell my blood. I would be home at nine or ten o'clock at night. I was loaded down with one baby asleep and one crying. Carrying lots of heavy bags and ready to drop on my feet. I had bags under my eyes and no shampoo to wash my hair so I used soap. Anyway I had to stay up to wash diapers in the sink. Otherwise they wouldn't be dry when I left the house in the dark with my girls. In the morning I start all over again.

This bruised and lifeless body, hauling sniffling babies and bags of dirty laundry on the bus, was then read as a sign that she was a bad mother and a threat that needed to be disciplined and made to work even harder for her own good. Those who need the respite less go away for weekends, take drives in the woods, take their kids to the beach. Poor women without education are pushed into minimum wage jobs and have no money, no car, no time, no energy, and little support, as their bodies are made to display marks of their material deprivation as a socializing and patrolling force.

Ultimately, we come to recognize that our bodies are not our own; that they are rather public property. State-mandated blood tests, interrogation of the most private aspects of our lives, the public humiliation of having to beg officials for food and medicine, and the loss of all right to privacy, teach us that our bodies are only useful as lessons, warnings, and signs of degradation that everyone loves to hate. In "From Welfare to Academe: Welfare Reform as College-Educated Welfare Mothers Know It," Sandy Smith-Madsen describes the erosion of her privacy as a poor welfare mother:

> I was investigated. I was spied upon. A welfare investigator came into my home and after thoughtful deliberation, granted me permission to keep my belongings. . . . Like the witch hunts of old, if a neighbor reports you as a welfare queen, the guardians of the state's compelling interest come into your home and interrogate you. While they do not have the right to set your body ablaze on the public square, they can forever devastate heart and soul by snatching away children. Just like a police officer, they may use whatever they happen to see against you, including sexual orientation. Full-fledged citizens have the right to deny an officer entry into their home unless they possess a search warrant; welfare mothers fork over citizenship rights for the price of a welfare check. In Tennessee, constitutional rights go for a cash value of $185 per month for a family of three. (2000, 185)

Welfare reform policy is designed to publicly expose, humiliate, punish, and display "deviant" welfare mothers. "Workfare" and "Learnfare"—two alleged successes of welfare reform—require that landlords, teachers, and employers be made explicitly aware of the second-class status of these very public bodies. In Ohio, the Department of Human Services uses tax dollars to pay for advertisements on the side of Cleveland's RTA busses that show a "Welfare Queen" behind bars with a logo that proclaims "Crime does not pay. Welfare fraud is a crime" (Robinson 1999). In Michigan a pilot program mandating drug tests for all welfare recipients began on October 1, 1999. Recipients who refuse the test will lose their benefits immediately (Simon 1999). In Buffalo, New York, a County Executive proudly announced that his county will begin intensive investigation of all parents who refuse minimum wage jobs that are offered to them by the state. He warned: "We have many ways of investigating and exposing these errant parents who choose to exploit their children in this way" (Anderson 1999). And, welfare reform legislation enacted in 1996 as the Personal Responsibility and Work Opportunities Reconciliation Act (PRWORA), requires that poor mothers work full-time, earning minimum wage salaries with which they cannot support their children. Often denied medical, dental, and childcare benefits, and unable to provide their families with adequate food, heat, or clothing, through this legislation the state mandates child neglect and abuse. The crowds of good parents and their growing children watch and learn. . . .

Reading and Rewriting the Body . . .

The bodies of poor women and children, scarred and mutilated by state-mandated material deprivation and public exhibition, work as spectacles, as patrolling images socializing and controlling bodies within the body politic. . . .

Spectacular cover stories of the "Welfare Queen" play and re-play in the national mind's eye, becoming a prescriptive lens through which the American public as a whole reads the individual dramas of the bodies of poor women and their place and value in the world. These dramas produce "normative" citizens as singular, stable, rational, ordered, and free. In this dichotomous, hierarchical frame the poor welfare mother is juxtaposed against a logic of "normative" subjectivity as the embodiment of disorder, disarray, and other-ness. Her broken and scarred body becomes proof of her inner pathology and chaos, suggesting the need for further punishment and discipline.

In contemporary narrative welfare women are imagined to be dangerous because they refuse to sacrifice their desires and fail to participate in legally sanctioned heterosexual relationships; theirs is read, as a result, as a selfish, "unnatural," and immature sexuality. In this script, the bodies of poor women are viewed as being dangerously beyond the control of men and are as a result construed as the bearers of perverse desire. In this androcentric equation fathers become the sole bearers of order and of law, defending poor women and children against their own unchecked sexuality and lawlessness.

For Republican Senator and former US Attorney General John Ashcroft writing in *The St. Louis Dispatch,* the inner city is the site of "rampant illegitimacy" and a "space devoid of discipline" where all values are askew. For Ashcroft, what is insidious is not material poverty, but an entitlement system that has allowed "out-of-control" poor women to rupture traditional patriarchal authority, valuation, and boundaries (1995, A:23). Impoverished communities then become a site of chaos because without fathers they allegedly lack any organizing or patrolling principle. George Gilder agrees with Ashcroft when he writes in the conservative *American Spectator* that:

> The key problem of the welfare culture is not unemployed women and poor children.

It is the women's skewed and traumatic relationships with men. In a reversal of the pattern of civilized societies, the women have the income and the ties to government authority and support. . . . This balance of power virtually prohibits marriage, which is everywhere based on the provider role of men, counterbalancing the sexual and domestic superiority of women. (1995, B:6)

For Gilder, the imprimatur of welfare women's sordid bodies unacceptably shifts the focus of the narrative from a male presence to a feminized absence.

In positioning welfare mothers as sexually chaotic, irrational, and unstable, their figures are temporarily immobilized and made to yield meaning as a space that must be brought under control and transformed through public displays of punishment. Poor single mothers and children who have been abandoned, have fled physical, sexual, and/or psychological abuse, or have in general refused to capitulate to male control within the home are mythologized as dangerous, pathological, out of control, and selfishly unable—or unwilling—to sacrifice their "naturally" unnatural desires. They are understood and punished as a danger to a culture resting on a foundation of inviolate male authority and absolute privilege in both public and private spheres.

William Raspberry disposes of poor women as selfish and immature, when in "Ms. Smith Goes After Washington," he warrants that:

> . . . unfortunately AFDC [Aid to Families with Dependent Children] is paid to an unaccountable, accidental and unprepared parent who has chosen her head of household status as a personal form of satisfaction, while lacking the simple life skills and maturity to achieve love and job fulfillment from any other source. I submit that all of our other social ills—crime, drugs, violence, failing schools . . . are a direct result of the degradation of parenthood by emotionally immature recipients. (1995, A:19)

Raspberry goes on to assert that like poor children, poor mothers must be made visible reminders to the rest of the culture of the "poor choices" they have made. He claims that rather than "coddling" her, we have a responsibility to "shame her" and to use her failure to teach other young women that it is "morally wrong for unmarried women to bear children," as we "cast single motherhood as a selfish and immature act" (1995, A:19).

Continuous, multiple, and often seamless public inscription, punishing policy, and lives of unbearable material lack leave poor women and their children scarred, exhausted, and confused. As a result, their bodies are imagined as an embodiment of decay and cultural disease that threatens the health and progress of our nation. . . . In a 1995 *USA Today* article entitled "America at Risk: Can We Survive Without Moral Values?" for example, the inner city is portrayed as a "*dark*" realm of "*decay* rooted in the *loss* of values, the *death* of work ethics, and the *deterioration* of families and communities." Allegedly here, "all morality has *rotted* due to a *breakdown* in gender discipline." This space of disorder and disease is marked with tropes of race and gender. It is also associated with the imagery of "communities of women *without* male leadership, cultural values and initiative [emphasis added]" (1995, C:3). In George Will's *Newsweek* editorial he proclaims that "*illogical* feminist and racial *anger* coupled with *misplaced* American emotion may be part or a cause of the *irresponsible* behavior *rampant* in poor neighborhoods." Will continues, proclaiming that here "mothers *lack* control over their children and have *selfishly* taught them to embrace a *pathological* ethos that values *self-need* and *self-expression* over self-control [emphasis added]" (1995, 23).

Poor women and children's bodies, publicly scarred and mutilated by material deprivation, are read as expressions of an essential lack of discipline and order. In response to this perception, journalist Ronald Brownstein of the *L.A. Times* proposed that the *Republican Contract with America* will "*restore* America to its path, *enforcing* social *order* and common *standards* of behavior, and replacing *stagnation* and *decay* with *movement* and *forward* thinking *energy* [emphasis added]" (1994, A:20). In these rhetorical fields poverty is . . . linked to lack of progress that would allegedly otherwise order, stabilize, and restore the culture. What emerges from these diatribes is the positioning of patriarchal, racist, capitalist, hierarchical, and heterosexist "order" and movement against the alleged stagnation and decay of the body of the "Welfare Queen."

Race is clearly written on the body of the poor single mother. The welfare mother, imagined as young, never married, and Black (contrary to statistical evidence[4]), is framed as dangerous and in need of punishment because she "naturally" emasculates her own men,

refuses to service White men, and passes on—rather than appropriate codes of subservience and submission—a disruptive culture of resistance, survival, and "misplaced" pride to her children (Collins 1990). In stark contrast, widowed women with social security and divorced women with child support and alimony are imaged as White, legal, and propertied mothers whose value rests on their abilities to stay in their homes, care for their own children, and impart traditional cultural morals to their offspring, all for the betterment of the culture. In this narrative welfare mothers have only an "outlaw" culture to impart. Here the welfare mother is read as both the product and the producer of a culture of disease and disorder. These narratives imagine poor women as powerful contagion capable of, perhaps even lying in wait to infect their own children as raced, gendered, and classed agents of their "diseased" nature. In contemporary discourses of poverty, racial tropes position poor women's bodies as dangerous sites of "naturalized chaos" and as potentially valuable economic commodities who refuse their proper role.

Gary McDougal in "The Missing Half of the Welfare Debate" furthers this image by referring to the "crab effect of poverty" through which mothers and friends of individuals striving to break free of economic dependency allegedly "pull them back down." McDougal affirms—again despite statistical evidence to the contrary—that the mothers of welfare recipients are most often themselves "generational welfare freeloaders lacking traditional values and family ties who cannot, and will not, teach their children right from wrong." "These women" he asserts "would be better off doing any kind of labor regardless of how little it pays, just to get them out of the house, to break their cycles of degeneracy" (1996, A:16).

In this plenitude of images of evil mothers, the poor welfare mother threatens not just her own children, but all children. The Welfare Queen is made to signify moral aberration and economic drain; her figure becomes even more impacted once responsibility for the destruction of the "American Way of Life" is attributed to her. Ronald Brownstein reads her "spider web of dependency" as a "crisis of character development that leads to a morally bankrupt American ideology" (1994, A:6).

These representations position welfare mothers' bodies as sites of destruction and as catalysts for a culture of depravity and disobedience; in the process they produce a reading of the writing on the body of the poor woman that calls for further punishment and discipline. In New York City, "Workfare" programs force *lazy* poor women to take a job—"any job"—including working for the city wearing orange surplus prison uniforms picking up garbage on the highway and in parks for about $1.10 per hour (Dreier 1999). "Bridefare" programs in Wisconsin give added benefits to *licentious* welfare women who marry a man—"any man"—and publish a celebration of their "reform" in local newspapers (Dresang 1996). "Tidyfare" programs across the nation allow state workers to enter and inspect the homes of poor *slovenly* women so that they can monetarily sanction families whose homes are deemed to be appropriately tidied.[5] "Learnfare" programs in many states publicly expose and fine *undisciplined* mothers who for any reason have children who don't (or can't) attend school on a regular basis (Muir 1993). All of these welfare reform programs are designed to expose and publicly punish the *misfits* whose bodies are read as proof of their refusal or inability to capitulate to androcentric, capitalist, racist, and heterosexism values and mores.

The Power of Poor Women's Communal Resistance

Despite the rhetoric and policy that mark and mutilate our bodies, poor women survive. Hundreds of thousands of us are somehow good parents despite the systems that are designed to prohibit us from being so. We live on the unlivable and teach our children love, strength, and grace. We network, solve irresolvable dilemmas, and support each other and our families. If we somehow manage to find a decent pair of shoes, or save our food stamps to buy our children a birthday cake, we are accused of being cheats or living too high. If our children suffer, it is read as proof of our inferiority and bad mothering; if they succeed we are suspect for being too pushy, for taking more than our share of free services, or for having too much free time to devote to them. Yet, as former welfare recipient Janet Diamond says in the introduction to *For Crying Out Loud:*

> In spite of public censure, welfare mothers graduate from school, get decent jobs, watch their children achieve, make good lives for themselves . . . welfare mothers continue to be my inspiration, not because they survive, but because they dare to dream. Because when you are a welfare recipient, laughter is an act of rebellion. (1986, 1)

. . . Because power is diffuse, heterogeneous, and contradictory, poor women struggle against the marks of their degradation. . . .

Poor women rebel by organizing for physical and emotional respite, and eventually for political power. My own resistance was born in the space between self-loathing and my love of and respect for poor women who were fighting together against oppression. In the throes of political activism (at first I was dragged blindly into such actions, ironically, in a protest that required, according to the organizer, just so many poor women's bodies) I became caught up in the contradiction between my body's meaning as despised public sign, and our shared sense of communal power, knowledge, authority, and beauty. Learning about labor movements, fighting for rent control, demanding fair treatment at the welfare office, sharing the costs, burdens, and joys of raising children, forming good cooperatives, working with other poor women to go to college, and organizing for political change, became addictive and life affirming acts of resistance.

Communal affiliation among poor women is discouraged, indeed in many cases prohibited, by those with power over our lives. Welfare offices, for example, are designed to prevent poor women from talking together; uncomfortable plastic chairs are secured to the ground in arrangements that make it difficult to communicate, silence is maintained in waiting rooms, case workers are rotated so that they do not become too "attached" to their clients, and, reinforced by "Welfare Fraud" signs covering industrially painted walls, we are daily reminded not to trust anyone with the details of our lives for fear of further exposure and punishment. And so, like most poor women, I had remained isolated, ashamed, and convinced that I was alone in, and responsible for, my suffering.

Through shared activism we became increasingly aware of our individual bodies as sites of contestation and of our collective body as a site of resistance and as a source power.

Noemy Vides (Vides and Steinitz, 1996) in "Together We Are Getting Freedom," reminds us that "by talking and writing about learned shame together, [poor women] pursue their own liberation" (305). Vides adds that it is through this process that she learned to challenge the dominant explanations that decreed her value in the world,

> provoking an awareness that the labels— ignorant peasant, abandoned woman, bro-

ken-English speaker, welfare cheat—have nothing to do with who one really is, but serve to keep women subjugated and divided. [This communal process] gives women tools to understand the uses of power; it emboldens us to move beyond the imposed shame that silences, to speak out and join together in a common liberatory struggle. (305)

In struggling together, we contest the marks of our bodily inscription, disrupt the use of our bodies as public sign, change the conditions of our lives, and survive. In the process, we come to understand that the shaping of our bodies is not coterminous with our beings or abilities as a whole. Contestation and the deployment of new truths cannot erase the marks of our poverty, but the process does transform the ways in which we are able to interrogate and critique our bodies and the systems that have branded them with infamy. As a result, these signs are rendered fragile, unstable, and ultimately malleable.

NOTES

1. Throughout this paper I use the terms "welfare recipients" and "poor working women" interchangeably because as the recent *Urban Institute* study made clear, today these populations are, in fact, one and the same. (Loprest 1999)

2. As recently as 1995, in my daughter's public elementary school cafeteria, "free lunchers" (poor children who could not otherwise afford to eat lunch, including my daughter) were reminded with a large and colorful sign to "line up last."

3. The goal of my survey was to measure the impact of the 1996 welfare reform legislation on the lives of profoundly poor women and children in the United States. Early in 1998 I sent fifty questionnaires and narrative surveys to four groups of poor women on the West and the East coasts; thirty-nine were returned to me. I followed these surveys with forty-five minute interviews with twenty of the surveyed women.

4. In the two years directly preceding the passage of the PRWORA, as a part of sweeping welfare reform, in the United States the largest percentage of people on welfare were white (39%) and fewer than 10% were teen mothers. (1994. U.S. Department of Health and Human Services, "An Overview of Entitlement Programs")

5. *Tidyfare* programs additionally required that caseworkers inventory the belongings of AFDC recipients so that they could require them to "sell-down" their assets. In my own case, in 1994 a HUD inspector came into my home, counted my daughter's books, checked them against his list to see that as a nine-year-old she was only entitled to have twelve books, calculated what he perceived to be the value of the excess books, and then had my AFDC check reduced by that amount in the following month.

REFERENCES

Abramovitz, Mimi. 1989. *Regulating the lives of women: Social welfare policy from colonial times to the present.* Boston: South End Press.

_____. 2000. *Under attack, fighting back.* New York: Monthly Review Press.

Albelda, Randy. 1997. *Glass ceilings and bottomless pits: Women's work, women's poverty.* Boston: South End Press.

"America at risk: Can we survive without moral values?" 1995. *USA Today.* October, Sec. C: 3.

Amott, Teresa. 1993. *Caught in the crises: Women and the U.S. economy today.* New York: Monthly Review Press.

Anderson, Dale. 1999. "County to investigate some welfare recipients." *The Buffalo News.* August 18, Sec. B: 5.

Ashcroft, John. 1995. "Illegitimacy rampant." *The St. Louis Dispatch.* July 2, Sec. A: 23.

Bell, Shannon. 1994. *Reading, writing and rewriting the prostitute body.* Bloomington and Indianapolis: Indiana University Press.

Bordo, Susan, 1993. *Unbearable weight: Feminism, Western culture and the body.* Berkeley: University of California Press.

Brownstein, Ronald. 1994. "GOP welfare proposals more conservative." *Los Angeles Times,* May 20, Sec. A: 20.

_____. 1994. "Latest welfare reform plan reflects liberals' priorities." *Los Angeles Times.* May 20, Sec. A: 6.

Chandler, Mielle. 1999. "Queering maternity." *Journal of the Association for Research on Mothering.* Vol. 1, no. 2, (21–32).

Collins, Patricia Hill. 1990. *Black feminist thought: Knowledge, consciousness, and the politics of empowerment.* New York: Routledge.

Crompton, Rosemary. 1986. *Gender and stratification.* New York: Polity Press.

Desmond, Jane. 1991. "Dancing out the difference; cultural imperialism and Ruth St. Denis's Radna of 1906." *Signs.* Vol. 17, no. 1, Autumn, (28–49).

Diamond, Janet. 1986. *For crying out loud: Women and poverty in the United States.* Boston: Pilgrim Press.

Dreier, Peter. 1999. "Treat welfare recipients like workers." *Los Angeles Times.* August 29, Sec. M: 6.

Dresang, Joel. 1996. "Bridefare designer, reform beneficiary have role in governor's address." *Milwaukee Journal Sentinel.* August 14, Sec. 9.

Dujon, Diane and Ann Withorn. 1996. *For crying out loud: Women's poverty in the United States.* Boston: South End Press.

Edin, Kathryn and Laura Lein. 1997. *Making ends meet: How single mothers survive welfare and low wage work.* New York: Russell Sage Foundation.

Ford-Smith, Honor. 1995. "Making white ladies: Race, gender and the production of identity in late colonial Jamaica." *Resources for Feminist Research,* Vol. 23, no. 4, Winter (55–67).

Foucault, Michel. 1984. "Discipline and punish." In P. Rabinow (ed.) *The Foucault reader.* New York: Pantheon Books.

_____. 1978. *The history of sexuality: An introduction.* Trans. R. Hurley. Harmondsworth: Penguin.

_____. 1977. "Nietzsche, genealogy, history." In P. Rabinow (ed.) *The Foucault reader.* New York: Pantheon Books.

_____. 1980. *Power/knowledge: Selected interviews and other writings 1972–1977.* C. Gordon (ed.). Brighton: Harvester.

Funiciello, Theresa. 1998. "The brutality of bureaucracy." *Race, class and gender: An anthology,* 3rd ed. Eds. Margaret L. Andersen and Patricia Hill Collins. Belmont: Wadsworth Publishing Company, (377–381).

Gilder, George. 1995. "Welfare fraud today." *American Spectator.* September 5, Sec. B: 6.

Gordon, Linda. 1995. *Pitied, but not entitled: Single mothers and the history of welfare.* New York: Belknap Press, 1995.

hooks, bell. "Thinking about race, class, gender and ethics" 1999. Presentation at Hamilton College, Clinton, New York.

Hopwood, Catherine. 1995. "My discourse/myself: Therapy as possibility (for women who eat compulsively)." *Feminist Review.* No. 49, Spring, (66–82).

Langston, Donna. 1998. "Tired of playing monopoly?" In *Race, class and gender: An anthology, 3rd ed.* Eds. Margaret L. Andersen and Patricia Hill Collins. Belmont: Wadsworth Publishing Company, (126–136).

Lerman, Robert. 1995. "And for fathers?" *The Washington Post.* August 7, Sec. A: 19.

Loprest, Pamela. 1999. "Families who left welfare: Who are they and how are they doing?" *The Urban Institute,* Washington, DC. August, No. B-1.

McDougal, Gary. 1996. "The missing half of the welfare debate." *The Wall Street Journal.* September 6, Sec. A: 16 (W).

McNay, Lois. 1992. *Foucault and feminism: Power, gender and the self.* Boston: Northeastern University Press.

Mink, Gwendoly. 1998. *Welfare's end.* Ithaca, NY: Cornell University Press.

_____. 1996. *The wages of motherhood: Inequality in the welfare state 1917–1942.* Ithaca, NY: Cornell University Press.

Morgan, Kathryn. 1991. "Women and the knife: Cosmetic surgery and the colonization of women's bodies." *Hepatia*. V6, no 3. Fall, (25–53).

Muir, Kate. 1993. "Runaway fathers at welfare's final frontier. *The Times*. Times Newspapers Limited. July 19, Sec. A: 2.

"An overview of entitlement programs." 1994. U.S. Department of Health and Human Services. Washington, DC: U.S. Government Printing Office.

Piven, Frances Fox and Richard Cloward. 1993. *Regulating the poor: The functions of public welfare*. New York: Vintage Books.

Raphael, Jody. (2000). *Saving Bernice: Battered women, welfare, and poverty*. Lebanon, NH: Northeastern University Press.

Raspberry, William. 1995. "Ms. Smith goes after Washington." *The Washington Post*. February 1, Sec. A: 19.

_____. 1996. "Uplifting the human spirit." *The Washington Post*. August 8, Sec. A: 31.

Robinson, Valerie. 1999. "State's ad attacks the poor." *The Plain Dealer,* November 2, Sec. B: 8.

Sennett, Richard and Jonathan Cobb. 1972. *The hidden injuries of class*. New York: Vintage Books.

Sidel, Ruth. 1998. *Keeping women and children last: America's war on the poor*. New York: Penguin Books.

Simon, Stephanie. 1999. "Drug tests for welfare applicants." *The Los Angeles Times*. December 18, Sec. A: 1. National Desk.

Smart, Carol. 1997. *Regulating womanhood: Essays on marriage, motherhood and sexuality*. New York: Routledge.

_____. 1992. *Disruptive bodies and unruly sex: the regulation of reproduction and sexuality in the nineteenth century*. New York: Routledge, (7–32).

Smith-Madsen, Sandy. 2000. "From welfare to academe: Welfare reform as college-educated welfare mothers know it." *Reclaiming class: Women, poverty and the promise of education in America*. Vivyan Adair and Sandra Dahlberg (eds.). Philadelphia: Temple University Press, (160–186).

Steedman, Carolyn Kay. 1987. *Landscape for a good woman*. New Brunswick, NJ: Rutgers University Press.

Stoler, Ann Laura. 1995. *Race and the education of desire: Foucault's history of sexuality and the colonial order of things*. Durham, NC: Duke University Press.

Sylvester, Kathleen. 1995. "Welfare debate." *The Washington Post*. September 3, Sec. E: 15.

Tanner, Michael. 1995. "Why welfare pays." *The Wall Street Journal*. September 28, Sec. A: 18 (W).

Vides, Noemy and Victoria Steinitz. 1996. "Together we are getting freedom." *For crying out loud*. Diane Dujon and Ann Withorn (eds.). Boston: South End Press, (295–306).

Will, George. 1995. "Welfare gate." *Newsweek*. February 5, Sec. 23.

THINKING ABOUT THE READING

When we think of people's bodies being labeled as deviant, we usually assume the bodies in question either deviate from cultural standards of shape and size or are marked by some noticeable physical handicap. However, Adair shows us that poor women's and children's bodies are tagged as undesirable in ways that are just as profound and just as hard to erase. What does she mean when she says that the illnesses and accidents of youth became part of a visible reminder of who poor people are in the eyes of others? How do the public degradations suffered by poor people (for instance, having a school nurse wear surgical gloves to check only the hair of poor children for lice) reinforce their subordinate status in society? Why do you think Adair continually evokes the images of "danger," "discipline," and "punishment" in describing the ways non-poor people perceive and respond to the physical appearance of poor people? Explain how focusing on the "deviance" of poor people deflects public attention away from the harmful acts committed by more affluent citizens.

Marrying across Class Lines

JESSI STREIB

(2015)

Christie, a cheerful social worker in her mid-40s, told me about the first time she met her husband, Mike. It was over thirty years ago, when they were in junior high school. She used to watch Mike as he wiped off the tables before the next round of students entered the school cafeteria. She thought he was cute and smart. And she was not fooled by his job—she knew that it was people like her who usually cleaned tables, not people like Mike. In fact, her father worked on the maintenance crew at their school.

Mike's father, by contrast, was a productive professor who authored famous books and traveled the world attending conferences and giving lectures. As Christie knew, Mike washed tables in exchange for being allowed to go to the front of the line to collect his food, not because he needed the money.

> Although respondents tended to think their class differences were behind them, they left a deep imprint that their marriage, shared resources, and thousands of days together did not erase.

When the couple began dating, their class differences became obvious. Her parents rarely bought new items; their cars were used and the ping pong table they gave her for Christmas was put together with items they found. Pop Tarts were her favorite food, but one that they could rarely afford. Mike's family bought expensive new cars, went on annual vacations, had cable TV, and had enough money left over to tuck a good amount away in Mike's trust fund. But while they had grown up with different amounts of resources, by the time we talked, Christie did not feel that their differences mattered. Over 25 years of marriage, they shared a house, a bank account, a level of educational attainment, and, later, three children. Their lives had merged, and so had their resources. To Christie, their class differences were part of their pasts, and, in any case, never mattered much: "I don't think that it was the actual economic part that made the tension for Mike and I. It was personality style more than class or money."

Christie was one of the 64 adults in 32 couples I interviewed about their marriages, their current families, and their pasts. In order to focus on how class background matters in a small sample, all respondents were white college-educated adults in heterosexual marriages. Half were like Christie—they had grown up in the working-class. The other half were like Mike—they had grown up in the middle-class. All were married to a partner whose class origin was different than their own. My goal was to discern how what most respondents, like Christie, did not think mattered—their class background—was related to their ways of attending to their own lives and to their marriages. Although respondents tended to think their class differences were behind them, irrelevant to their current lives, instead they left a deep imprint that their marriage, their shared resources, and their thousands of days together did not erase.

Social Class and Family Life

It is common knowledge that families located in different social classes develop different ways of going about daily life. Such differences were made famous in the 1970s by sociologist and psychologist Lillian Rubin in her classic book, *Worlds of Pain*. Rubin interviewed couples and demonstrated that the texture of family life, as well as ideas of what it means to be a good parent, child, and spouse, are all shaped by the resources and jobs available to families. Later, sociologist Annette Lareau offered another in-depth look, observing that the daily interactions between parents and children, and, to some degree, between adult members of the family, differed by social class. Middle-class parents, she found, tended to manage their children's lives, while working-class parents more often let their children grow. French sociologist Pierre Bourdieu also observed wide class differences. He theorized that class not only shapes family life, but also individuals' ideas and instincts about how to use resources, spend time, and interact with others. Sociologists do not see each family as wholly unique, but shaped by the resources available to them in their class position.

Such work suggests that people like Christie and Mike, who grew up in different social classes, were likely to have different experiences of family and develop different ideas about a "good life." However, when scholars of social class and family life conduct research, they usually focus on the divide between college-educated couples and everyone else. This divide is critical for understanding inequality, but it is problematic to simply call couples like Christie and Mike a college-educated, middle-class couple. The label erases that Christie and Mike spent two decades in a class apart, and that upwardly mobile people like Christie may carry their ideas of family and a good life with them into their marriage and the middle class.

Indeed, simply referring to Christie and Mike as a college-educated, middle-class couple ignores that Christie knew what it was like to grow up with limited savings, watch a parent go to a job that was consistently framed as a means to an end, and grow up in a family that expressed their emotions immediately and intensely. It ignores that Mike knew of none of these things. He knew, instead, of family safety nets, jobs that were enjoyed beyond their financial ends, and emotions that were rationalized and guarded.

When social scientists ignore these background differences, they present only differences between college-educated and high-school educated couples, overlooking differences within college-educated couples. And when married couples ignore these differences, they ignore that the class of each partner's past organizes and shapes the contours of their marriage.

The Organization of Difference

Christie believed that her differences from Mike were driven by their personalities. She wasn't wrong. What she did not realize, however, was that what she called their personalities were, in turn, related to their class trajectory. People like Christie—born into the working-class but now college-educated—tended to prefer taking what I call a laissez-faire approach to their daily lives. They preferred to go with the flow, enjoy the moment, and live free from self-imposed constraints. They assumed things would work out without their intervention. People like Mike—those born into the middle class—instead tended to prefer to take what I call a managerial approach to their daily lives. They preferred to plan, monitor, organize, and oversee. They assumed that things would not work out without their active intervention.

The people I interviewed did not just apply laissez-faire and managerial tendencies to one aspect of their lives, but seven. When it came to how to attend to their money, paid work, housework, time, leisure, parenting, and emotions, middle-class-origin respondents tended to want to plan, organize, and oversee. Working-class-origin respondents more often preferred to let things take their own course without as much intervention.

Take, for example, how Christie and Mike thought about money. When I met them, they had shared a bank account for over two decades, but they did not share ideas of how to use the money in it. Referring to money, Christie repeatedly told Mike: "Live for the day!" Growing up, saving for long-range plans was not possible. Christie's family had to spend what they had to pay their bills today. A small amount in savings was also normal to her as a child, and continued to be normal to her as a college-educated adult. Christie said that she learned from her parents' experience that worrying about money was unnecessary: even without much money, things would work out. Now that she and Mike were both college-educated professionals who earned much more than her parents, this seemed especially true. Free from concerns over necessities, she now made a point to be free from worrying about money.

Mike, however, grew up in a family with more money and more options. His family could pay for their daily needs, then choose how to save for college tuition, retirement, rainy days, and leisure. For him, thinking about how to manage money was normal and he learned that management could make a difference. As an adult, Mike budgeted, monitored their current expenditures, forecasted their future expenses, and worried about whether he was earning enough. When Christie told him to "live for the day" and worry less, he reported responding: "I see that. But at the same time, we had three kids in college, and we're in our mid-forties. We have a lot of expenses." He felt that Christie's laissez-faire philosophy was reasonable, but he felt more comfortable with a managerial one.

> Just as taking the person out of the class did not take the class out of the person, a marriage was not a new beginning that removed the imprints of each partner's class past.

Their differences also extended to work. Christie grew up observing her father work in a job as a maintenance worker at her public school while her mother did unpaid labor at home. There was no career ladder for her father to climb. Hours were circumscribed by a time clock, and putting in more hours would not lead to more status or opportunities. Mike also saw his mother doing unpaid home labor, but observed his father, a professor, on a career ladder—from graduate student, to assistant, associate, and then full professor. More hours could lead to more books published, more prestige, and more opportunities to share his ideas.

Such differences likely shaped Christie and Mike's ideas of work. Mike felt he had to prod Christie, a social worker, to not be "status quo"—to work longer hours and think about how moving to a new place might give them opportunities to get ahead. Christie, for her part, admired Mike's dedication to work, but did not understand it. Mike owned his own business. He worked long hours (despite not being paid by the hour) and he constantly felt pressure to achieve more. Christie asked him to work fewer hours and have more faith that his business would do fine without his planning, strategizing, and long hours. So, just as Mike asked Christie to take a more managerial approach to work—one where she organized and planned her *career* trajectory—Christie asked Mike to take a more laissez-faire approach—one where he put in less time, did less planning, and assumed his career would be okay. Though each understood the other's perspective, neither adopted it. Christie maintained her hands-off approach to work. Mike maintained his hands-on one.

This hands-on/hands-off, or managerial/ laissez-faire divide organized many other aspects of their lives. Mike wanted to manage the division of housework by putting "more structure in the whole idea of who is going to do what" around the house. Christie wanted each to do the household tasks as they got around to them. Mike preferred to manage his feelings—to slowly process and weigh how to express them. Christie felt it was more genuine to express emotions as they were felt and in the way they were felt. Christie summarized their differences when she described Mike as Type A, driven, and organized—all things that she felt she was not.

Some of the differences that Christie and Mike expressed might sound like gender differences. Gender certainly shapes how much time each spouse spends on each task and how much power they have over decisions in different spheres. But with the exception of the highly gendered spheres of housework and parenting in which it was mainly women who followed the managerial/laissez-faire divide, class origin alone shaped how each partner wanted to tackle each task and use each resource. Take, for example, Leslie and Tom. They proudly proclaim that they are nerds: they met at a science-fiction convention, continued their courtship though singing together in a science-fiction themed choir, and, as a married couple, engage in role-playing games together. Their shared interests and college degrees, however, could not mask the lingering ways their class backgrounds shaped their lives and their marriage.

> Class origin shaped how each partner wanted to tackle each task and use each resource.

Leslie, a fit forty-year-old with short brown hair and glasses, was raised by a graduate-school-educated middle-manager and a college-educated homemaker. She attended private school with the sons and daughters of celebrities, judges, and politicians—where, she said, "famous and rich were people were the norm." Her husband, Tom, a shy, dark-haired forty-eight-year-old grew up as the son of a high-school-educated security guard and a nurse. He attended public school. While their childhood class differences certainly could have been wider, they still mapped onto ways of organizing their lives. Leslie, like Mike, preferred a managerial approach to her life—scheduling, planning, organizing, and monitoring, Tom, like Christie, felt that a hands-off approach was a better way to live.

The differences that Leslie and Tom described about money mirrored those that Mike and Christie expressed. Leslie stated simply: "I'm the saver and he's the spender." But it was not just how much Tom spent that bothered Leslie, it was also that Tom did not actively think about managing their money. Leslie complained: "I do the lion's share of work. Beyond the lion's share of the work . . . Balancing stuff, actually paying the bills, keeping track of things, saying we need to have some goals. Both big picture and small picture stuff." She said that Tom did not manage money; he spent without thinking.

Tom knew of Leslie's concern: "She worries a lot more about money than I do. About how we're doing . . . I think she would like it if I paid more attention to what our expenses are and how the money is going out." They had been having these debates for the past 20 years, but their differences had not gone away. Leslie said she still couldn't get Tom to set financial goals or think about how each expense fit in with their overall plan. Their compromise was that Tom checked with Leslie before making big purchases. But this was not an optimal solution for Leslie, who called herself the "superego"—the one who still had to make the decisions about how to manage their money, about what they really needed and what they could forego. Tom still assumed it would all work out, that a hands-off approach would do just fine.

Leslie also noted that she took a managerial approach to work, whereas Tom took a laissez-faire one. At the time of the interview, Leslie was a college-educated, part-time secretary at her children's school. Tom was a college-educated computer programmer. Though Leslie's job was less prestigious, she found much more satisfaction in it, talking about the sense of accomplishment she had at work, the meaning of doing good work, and her goals for the future. She was not sure what her next career move would be, but she knew one thing; "I want to get somewhere." Tom didn't want to get anywhere with work. Leslie cried as she explained; "He's been at the same job for quite a while and only moves when forced to."

Leslie clarified that her concern was not about how much Tom earned, but about his approach to his career: "I can totally understand being content. It's more that sometimes I just don't know what he wants and I'm not sure he knows. And this may sound dumb, but the actual goals, what they are, worry me less than not having any." To Leslie, careers were to be managed. Goals were to be created and worked toward. Tom did not have the same sense.

Their differences also extended past what is directly related to class—money and work—to other parts of their lives. Like Mike, Leslie wanted to structure housework more than Tom did, so she delegated tasks and monitored his work. Tom, like Christie, figured the housework could be done when he got to it, without as much of a schedule. Leslie and Mike liked to plan and organize in general. However, while Mike appreciated that Christie got him to pause his planning and "stop to smell the roses," Leslie was upset that Tom did not plan. She expressed it as a deficiency: "If you plan, if you're a planner, you do that mental projecting all the time. You're thinking ahead, saying, 'What's going to happen if I do this?' I really don't think he does that. I don't know if it's because he doesn't want to, it's too hard, he doesn't have the capacity, I don't know. But he just doesn't do that." Tom defended his approach: "She definitely wants more structure in things we do. More planning. I'm more of a 'Let's just do it' [person] and it will get done the best way we can get it done."

Leslie also insisted that their children's time be structured by adults, guided by routines, and directed at learning-related outcomes. But Tom, again, questioned this approach: "Leslie thinks they need more structure than they really do." As such, when he was in charge of parenting, he did not ask their daughters to have a regular reading time or strict bedtime. He did not view each of the kids' behaviors as in need of monitoring, assessing, or guiding. As sociologist Annette Lareau observed of people currently in the working-class, Tom, who was born into the working-class but no longer a member, felt that the kids would be fine without parents' constant management.

Navigating Difference

The laissez-faire/managerial differences that couples like Christie and Mike and Leslie and Tom navigated were common to the couples I interviewed—college-educated couples in which each partner grew up in a different class. The systematic differences that these couples faced meant that class infused their marriages, usually without their knowledge. These differences, however, were not experienced in a uniform way.

Most of the people I interviewed appreciated their spouse's differences, or at least found them understandable and valid. A minority of couples, however, found their differences to be more divisive. In these couples, middle-class-origin respondents disdained their spouse's attitudes and asked their spouse to change.

Christie and Mike were one of the couples who dealt with their differences with respect and even admiration. Mike did not always agree with Christie's laissez-faire approach, but he appreciated her sense that he sometimes needed to manage less and live in the moment more. Christie sometimes found Mike's managerial style frustrating, but she also admired how organized he was. She appreciated how well Mike had done in his career and respected that he needed more planning, organization, and monitoring lo feel secure. They preferred different approaches, but they saw the benefits of the other's way and tried to accommodate their partner's differences.

Leslie and Tom did not navigate their differences with such ease. Leslie defined Tom's hands-off approach as deeply flawed. As such, her strategy was to get him to change—to get him to do things in a more managerial way. But her strategy left them both unhappy. Tom resented being asked to change; Leslie fumed that Tom would say he would change, but did not. She explained: "Mostly what happens is he says, 'You're right. That would be better.' But the implementation is just not always there." Leslie remained frustrated with what she saw as the inadequacy of Tom's style, and Tom remained frustrated that Leslie did not see the benefits of living a life that was less structured, scheduled, and planned. Asking for assimilation was a failed strategy, both in that it did not work and in that respondents said that it left them disappointed and dissatisfied.

Regardless of how they navigated their differences—with respect or demands for change—couples like Mike and Christie and Leslie and Tom had to navigate the subtle ways that the class of their pasts still shaped their lives and their marriages. The decades that each couple was together, their shared college degrees, and their shared resources did not erase the fact that the middle-class-origin partners preferred to take a managerial approach to their lives while working-class-origin partners favored a laissez-faire one. Just as taking the person out of the class did not take the class out of the person, a marriage was not a new beginning that removed the imprints of each partner's class past.

THINKING ABOUT THE READING

How do the different social class backgrounds of these couples shape their relationships and contribute to the architecture of the lives they have built together? Describe the "laissez-faire" and "managerial" approaches to everyday life that these individuals embodied. Is there anything ironic about these approaches and what social class positions they were aligned with? While Streib's focus is on social class, reflect on how an intersectionality analysis could uncover other interesting aspects of the influence of class origin. How, if at all, could you see the effects of the "compassion gap" operating in these relationships? What implications do these findings have for larger ideologies like the "American Dream"?

Becoming a Geek Girl

Race, Inequality and the Social Geography of Childhood

LAUREN ALFREY AND FRANCE WINDDANCE TWINE

(2018)

The notion of social geography suggest that the physical landscape is peopled and that it is constituted and perceived by . . . . social rather than natural processes.[1]

—*Ruth Frankenberg*

In Los Altos, a suburb of San Francisco, just about everyone was an engineer or worked in electronics. A childhood spent here—in the future Silicon Valley—was the first key lucky break in Steve Jobs' young life.[2]

—*Demetri Goritsas,* One Last Thing

[We] can have a meritocratic market in a deeply unfair society, if "merit" is developed highly unequally and largely as a result of the lottery of birth.[3]

—*Richard Reeves*

Steve Jobs grew up in Los Altos, an affluent and predominantly White suburb in Silicon Valley, where he and his childhood friends could stroll to neighbor's homes to be tutored in electronics.[4] As a teen, this upper middle class and racially exclusive residential community was where Jobs formed friendships with the sons of electrical engineers. He spent his weekends building electronic equipment with fathers whose occupations had brought them to the same Silicon Valley neighborhood. Was growing up in Los Altos really a "lucky break"? Or an unearned benefit of racial and class privilege?[5] Communities like Los Altos are the product of structural racism and class inequality. Federal and local housing policies, de facto segregation, and real estate practices sustain hyper-segregated communities.

The computing experiences and technological skills that Steve Jobs acquired in his childhood was facilitated by a *social and economic universe* that gave him privileged proximity to upper middle-class White engineers. In other words, his *social proximity to the engineers* was a form of cultural capital, a type of currency that could be converted into a life-long advantage. This proximity was produced by federal policies, local real estate practices, and structural racism. Living in a neighborhood in Silicon Valley, where engineers with relevant occupational expertise also lived, provided an early resource that Jobs drew upon and that was denied to his peers of diverse racial backgrounds residing in poorer communities.

Segregation by race, class and space shapes opportunities to develop one's talents. The forms of capital that Steve Jobs and Bill Gates enjoyed include the financial, educational, and social resources necessary to "play" with electronics equipment as teenagers, and thus to develop life-long skills. While these men were clearly talented and are considered revolutionaries in the field of computing, their *pathways* to success are far from unique. In our study, nearly all the White and Asian engineers we interviewed reported childhood experiences similar to Jobs and Gates. Their career trajectories into technology stood in stark contrast to the Black participants in our study. We found that masculinity, class privilege, residential segregation and access to informal tutoring as well as formal education, played a crucial role in who becomes a technology entrepreneur and innovator.

Childhood exposure to computers flows into young adulthood, as their parents engage in what sociologists call "opportunity hoarding." In his book, *Dream Hoarders: How the American Upper Middle Class Is Leaving Everyone Else in the Dust* (2017), Richard Reeves details the cultural mechanisms that reproduce class inequality and restrict upward mobility for the lower middle-classes in the contemporary United States. As a member of the upper middle class himself, Reeves identifies three major opportunity hoarding mechanisms used by this group:

Not all upper-middle class advantage results from an open contest. We also engage in some opportunity hoarding, accessing valuable, finite opportunities by unfair means. [. . .] Three opportunity hoarding mechanisms stand out in particular: exclusionary zoning in residential areas; unfair mechanisms influencing college admissions, including legacy preferences, and the informal allocation of internships.[6]

Reeves is challenging the idea that the US is a simple meritocratic and classless society. Instead, he details how unearned class advantages give the children of upper middle class families unique opportunities. He argues that:

> Many of the things we do for our kids – reading stories, helping with homework . . . supporting their sports and extracurricular activities – will equip them to be more successful in the world and increase their chances of remaining in the upper middle class. . . . The problem comes when we use our power to distort competition.[7]

A nuanced analysis of inequality in the tech industry must consider the significant role that residential and social segregation continue to play in the ability of the upper middle class to hoard the opportunities that facilitate the social accomplishments of children. Drawing upon the childhood experiences narrated by tech workers, we examine the ways that class privilege, racial privilege, and social geography intersect and provide life-long advantages for tech workers in our study. We argue that the skills and experiences necessary to become an engineer in Silicon Valley are over determined by an individual's class privileges, family resources, and social networks.

We begin by asking: Who can become a geek girl? Drawing upon interviews with Asian, Black and White tech workers, we analyze their childhood experiences. Building upon the theoretical work in critical race studies, we examine how racial privilege, class inequality, and residential segregation by race, structures the informal and formal learning experiences and future career opportunities of girls.

We begin our analysis with Ruth Frankenberg's concept of the "social geography of race" and the literature on residential segregation to examine the childhood experiences of children who became technology workers. Our goal is to provide an intersectional analysis that illuminates the significant role that leisure activities, formal education, and informal mentoring play in the lives of children who later become technology workers. Here we offer the childhood portraits of six American tech workers: 2 Asians, 2 Blacks, and 2 unhyphenated Whites.[8]

The Social Geography of Race

In *White Women, Race Matters: The Social Construction of Whiteness* (1993), Frankenberg employed the concept of "social geography of race" in her analysis of the racial consciousness of White women. Drawing upon interviews with 30 white women, Frankenberg analyzed the life narratives of white women. Frankenberg identifies her goals as "attempt as theoretically as possible to situate them in relation both to the material relations of racism at specific times and places in the United States, and to the circulation and shifting salience of a range of discourses on race."[9] Frankenberg argues that "it is clear that, indeed, race privilege translated directly into forms of social organization that shaped daily life . . . the de jure, and later de facto, residential, social and educational segregation that characterized most of these women's childhoods, and that these in turn shaped the women's perceptions of race."[10] Introducing the analytical concept of "social geography," Frankenberg writes:

> Geography here refers to the physical landscape – the home, the street, the neighborhood, the school, parts of town visited or driven through rarely or regularly, places visited on vacation. My interest was in how physical space was divided and who inhabited it, and . . . To what extent, for example, did they have relationships of closeness or distance, equality or inequality, with people of color? What were they encouraged or taught by example to make of the variously "raced" people in their environments. *Racial social geography,* in short, refers to the racial and ethnic mapping of environments in physical and social terms and enables

also the beginning of an understanding of the conceptual mappings of self and other operating in white women's lives.[11]

Following Frankenberg, we give careful attention to the ways that tech workers described their childhood environments. The non-Black tech workers interviewed tended to employ what Frankenberg refers to as "color- and race-evasive" discourses that suggested that they perceived residential segregation by race and class as "normal" and as taken-for-granted. White and Asian technology workers had to be prompted and asked to specifically describe the demographics of their childhood networks in order for them to name and recognize that their residential, educational and social universe excluded Blacks and Latinos. They had learned not to see their hypersegregated neighborhoods as socially produced and perhaps as a problem. Their mono-cultural upper middle-class social worlds facilitated their acquisition of experiences, skills and other accomplishments, as children who were able to spend their youth building computers and learning coding with the resources provided by their parents and communities.

Residential Segregation in Silicon Valley

Throughout the 20th century, private developers, real estate agents and the federal government worked together to systematically deny blacks, regardless of their income and occupational status, access to single family housing in newly built communities. In *The Color of Law: A Forgotten History of How Our Government Segregated America,* Richard Rothstein (2017) details the ways that the local communities, that were not yet racially segregated, were denied loans by the federal government. Rothstein begins his analysis by detailing the central role the federal government played in the implementation and enforcement of racially segregated housing in suburban areas where new housing was being constructed. We learn that in Palo Alto, only seven miles from the childhood home of Steve Jobs, middle-class Black professionals were systematically shut out of the housing market and forced into either the East Bay (Richmond) and later East Palo Alto.

The story of racial segregation in Palo Alto begins in the late 1940s, during the post–WWII era of suburbanization. A multiracial group of residents created the Peninsula Housing Association of Palo Alto, a co-op whose goal was to build a racially integrated middle-class residential community. They purchased a 260-acre ranch adjacent to the Stanford campus with a plan to build 400 homes, including community recreational facilities, a shopping area, a gas station, and a restaurant on commonly owned land. When they applied for a loan, local banks refused to finance construction costs or to issue mortgages to co-op members without government approval. The Federal Housing Authority (FHA) would not insure loans to a cooperative that included Blacks.

In response to pressures to reconstitute themselves as an all-White cooperative by the federal government, the membership voted in favor of a compromise: a quota system that would limit the number of Blacks that could join the Peninsula Housing Association to the proportion of African Americans in California's overall population. This decision was so controversial that it led board members to resign. Following this decision, the cooperative was forced to disband because it could not obtain financing without government approval. In 1950, the association sold its land to a private developer whose FHA agreement specified that no properties be sold to African Americans. The builder then constructed individual homes for sale to Whites in "Ladera," a subdivision that still adjoins the Stanford campus.[12]

California has a long history of racial and ethnic segregation including the removal and segregation of Native Americans onto reservations, Asian immigrants, and other groups in its early history.[13] Blacks were segregated in urban San Francisco, Los Angeles and other communities. In the years following 1950, the number of Blacks seeking jobs and homes in and near Palo Alto increased, but developers using federal government loan insurance refused to sell to them, and no California state-licensed real estate agent would show them houses.[14]

In 1954, one resident of a Whites-only area in East Palo, across a highway from the Stanford campus, sold his house to a Black family. The sale of a single home to a Black family by a White family provoked a racial panic that generated White flight. This panic was fueled by White real estate agents who bought their homes at a steep discount and sold them for a much higher amount to Blacks who had been locked out of other communities. What followed was a familiar story—the creation of a racially segregated school system for Blacks by a White school board. A formerly racially integrated school became segregated when a district map was drawn that forced Black students to attend a newly constructed school. In 1958, the school board decided to end integration by creating another school district and locating the new school in the heart of East Palo Alto. As Rothstein writes:

> The district decided to construct the new school in the heart of what had become the East Palo Alto ghetto, so black students in Palo Alto's existing integrated building would have to withdraw, creating a segregated African American school in the eastern section, a white one to the west. The board ignored the pleas of African American and liberal white activists that it draw an east-west school boundary to establish two integrated secondary schools.[15]

Sociologists have documented similar patterns of pervasive hyper-segregation, throughout U.S. cities and suburbs, that keeps Blacks, poorer Latinos, and some immigrant grounds socially and residentially segregated from Whites who reside and attend schools in upper middle-class communities.[16]

Life-long advantages accrue to the Asian and White children of middle and upper middle-class people who are able to send their children to well-resourced public schools in racially and class exclusive zip codes. These advantages include: access to the highest paid teachers, advanced placement courses, private tutors, and childhood friendship networks that include engineers. Children like Steve Jobs and his White childhood friends would have had virtually no contact with Blacks living in surrounding neighborhoods. The result is for Whites living in these kinds of socially segregated environments is what Bonilla-Silva and Embrick conceptualize as "White habitus."

White Habitus

Residential segregation by race and class has produced what Bonilla-Silva and Embrick refer to as "White habitus."[17] They argue that this social and residential segregation produces a form of consciousness in which, "members of the dominant racial group, will be oblivious to the racial components of their own socialization and how that may affect their perceptions of Blacks."[18]

Steve Jobs was adopted by a White middle-class family as an infant. He spent most of his youth up in Los Altos, California, an upper middle-class and predominantly White suburban community in the heart of Silicon Valley. Los Altos is located 20 miles south of San Francisco on the peninsula. As Demetri Goritsas explains in the film, *One Last Thing,* the neighborhood of Job's childhood in the early 1970s was such that, "just about everybody was an engineer, or worked in electronics."

Jobs' childhood best friend, Bill Fernandez, lived on the same block and his family shared a love of electronics. Fernandez, who later became a user interface architect, knew his neighbor's son, Steve Wozniak, whom he described as an "electronics geek." Fernandez introduced Jobs and Wozniak for the first time and they later began working on electronics projects together. Explaining the significance of this meeting between two White male geeks, Fernandez said, simply: "If Woz and Jobs had never met, there wouldn't have been an Apple computer."

The meeting of Woz and Jobs, who later founded Apple and became the legendary titans of a burgeoning computer industry, is less coincidental when we consider the racial and class geography of their childhood residential community. As Fernandez recalled, this meant that he could "go up and down the street to the various Dads on the street, and get mentored in electronics. And Steve Wozniak's father was one of the people who mentored me."

The childhoods of Steve Jobs and his male friends, spent in predominantly or exclusively White residential neighborhoods, provided them with life-long advantages that included interactions with the children of computer engineers. This meant they could easily acquire mentorship and the training to further develop coding skills, and could translate these lessons into a future career—all outside the boundaries of an actual classroom. As Jobs himself told biographer Walter Isaacson, "Most of the dads in the neighborhood did really neat stuff, like photovoltaics and batteries and radar. I grew up in awe of that stuff and I asked people about it."[19] Noting this, is it any surprise that these three boys became computer engineers?

Such upbringings sit in striking contrast to Black, Latino and those Asian Americans who share a passion for electronics, but live in an under-resourced neighborhood. Our research found that invisibility and exclusion of Blacks and Latinos from their childhood friendship groups, classrooms, and neighborhoods was as an unremarkable feature of life for the non-Blacks interviewed. The consequences were that the later exclusion of Blacks and Latinos from the workplace also functioned as an unremarkable feature of their professional experience.

Neighborhood and family resources also mattered in Mark Zuckerberg's story, the CEO and co-founder of Facebook, and one of the most powerful figures of the 21st software industry. Mark Zuckerberg ended his college career at Harvard to develop Facebook. In contrast to Black and Latino college drop-outs, Zuckerberg, as an upper middle-class White college dropout from Harvard, possessed the racial, social, economic and cultural capital to secure the financial resources to found a company. Most importantly, his friendships with his former wealthy Harvard classmates, Eduardo Saverin, enabled him to implement his vision.

Like Steve Jobs, Zuckerberg also spent his childhood in a predominantly White, upper middle-class universe of privilege. He had access to a computer during a time when few American families had a home computer. Using his father's office computer Zuckerberg taught himself basic programming at the age of twelve. When his interest in programming caught the attention of his parents, they hired a computer tutor and paid them to visit the family home every week. Eventually, the Zuckerbergs enrolled their son in Exeter Academy, one of the most exclusive and prestigious private college preparatory schools on the East Coast. In today's dollars, enrollment costs approximately $46,000 annually.

Women in Computing

Radia Perlman, known as the "mother of the internet," was born in 1951 and grew up in New Jersey.[20] Both of her parents worked in the burgeoning tech industry. The daughter of a mother who was a programmer and held the title of "mathematician," Perlman was not encouraged to study science and math in school. In striking contrast to the experiences of Jobs and Zuckerberg, she described her childhood in the following way:

I always liked logic puzzles and I found math and science classes in school effortless and fascinating. However, I did not fit the stereotype of the "engineer." I never took things apart or built a computer out of spare parts. Although my mother was a programmer, I didn't really talk to her about programming. Mostly I remember talking to her about literature and music, although she did help me with my math homework in high school. A teacher commented that when the class was going over the homework problems, the other kids would say, "my father said it should be done this way." I'd say "My mother said it should be done this way."[21]

Perlman was introduced to computer programming by a high school teacher who succeeded in getting her and several of her classmates enrolled in a programming class at the Stevens Institute of Technology. According to Perlman, the teacher drove her to the classes. As a White undergraduate at MIT, Perlman benefitted from another opportunity offered to her by a male teaching assistant:

The way I actually learned how to program was that as a sophomore at MIT. I was taking a physics class and the TA said to me "I need a programmer for a project. Would you like to be my programmer?" I said "I don't know how to program." He said "Yes, I know. That's why I'm asking you. You're obviously bright, so I'm sure you can learn (I was doing very well in the class), and I have no money to pay you. If you knew how to program I'd have to pay you." At that time, I had a boyfriend who knew how to program. So even though learning programming seemed scary to me, it would be a safe way to learn.[22]

Perlman's biography illustrates the several advantages she possessed during her childhood, including: class privilege, racial privilege and two parents who were industry insiders and thus had the financial resources to send her to well-resourced private schools. Her teachers and later graduate student teaching assistants gave her unique access to educational experiences and knowledge not available to her peers who lived in poorer or under-resourced communities.

Yet in contrast to the dominant narratives circulating in Silicon Valley, that positions White male founders as geniuses, Perlman did not describe herself as being smarter than her peers. Instead, she explained how she lacked basic confidence when she entered her first university computer programming class:

> I walked into the class, and all the other students were talking about how they had built ham radios when they were seven. I didn't even know what a ham radio was. They were also asking questions using scary words like "input" I had no idea what that meant, and it felt like I was so far behind that I'd never catch up. I wound up not getting anything out of that class.[23]

The childhood experiences of Steve Jobs, Mark Zuckerberg, and Radia Perlman illuminate the racial, class, and educational advantages that these titans of computing received early in their life. The forms of social and capital that their parents possessed is what sociologist Pierre Bourdieu calls an *intergenerational transfer of life chances*.[24] This equipped them with early exposure and experiences to develop their interests and cultivate their skills. In the following section, we turn to six technology workers of diverse backgrounds to show how their childhood access to educational, social and other resources generated experiences that similarly prepared them for jobs in the technology industry.

Joelle: Dads and Robots

Joelle is a 26-year old White software engineer who has worked at a top technology firm in San Francisco for five months. As the daughter of a mechanical engineer and a geologist, Joelle secured her current position after completing an internship at the company that now employs her. Her sister interned at this same company and now works as an engineer for Google. Internships like these, in which students are trained for full-time employment, are essential for securing an entry-level position after college graduation. The role of Joelle's sister in helping her secure an internship is an example of an opportunity hoarding mechanism that what Reeves calls "informal allocation of internships."[25]

Like the other engineers we interviewed, Joelle's parents provided her with experiences that introduced her to the field of electrical engineering. As a very young child, Joelle began working on electrical engineering projects with her father. When she was six years old, she and her father began working on soldering projects where they made computer circuit boards. Later as a high school student, Joelle joined a robotics club. She described how her robotics club solidified her interest in pursuing engineering as a career:

> And I was also one of the original members on our robotics teams that formed during our junior year. These robots would be 5 feet tall and like 120 pounds. They're big robots. There was a big component of mechanical engineering. Just kind of figure out where the electricity needs to go and lay everything out. From what I saw there, I thought that electrical engineering would be the most interesting.

Joelle reported that when her father learned that his daughter had joined the robotics club, he volunteered to serve as a mentor. Like other White women interviewed, fathers and men played a key role in supporting their childhood informal education through play and coursework.

> My dad – when he found out I was on the robotics team, he started mentoring. It was good. Everybody learned how to . . . do whatever they needed to do to make the robot happen. . . . Mentors helped the team by breaking down the new problem. Each year you got a new problem. Shooting basketballs into targets might be one of them. Or balancing on some sort of balance board. . . .They have a couple of different ways that you do offense and defense. So they would help break down what was just announced to us. Everybody would say all

the ideas they had for making theirs the best strategy. They would kind of guide us through it.

Like other tech workers, Joelle described a social and educational universe in which the absence of Blacks and Latinos was taken for granted. While she was able to identify an occasional Asian American, and one Hispanic classmate, the absence of Blacks and brown-skinned Latinos was continuous throughout her childhood and later as an adult employed in the industry.

Monique: How Robotics Saved a Ward of the State

Monique is a 28-year old software engineer who grew up in Virginia and earned a degree at Rochester Institute of Technology. At the age of 12, she became a ward of the State of Virginia. Her older sister was designated as her guardian when Monique was in the foster care system. It was not until graduate school that Monique taught herself to code. Her career path illustrates one of the patterns we uncovered among the Black and Black Latinas in our sample. Like these interviewees, Monique attended public schools without the same advantages of her parents or peers who went to private school. Although she had a strong interest in mechanical engineering, she did not have the grades in mathematics, nor the help of private tutors, to help her develop her math skills. When it came time to attend college, she was denied entry into her preferred major at university.

Like Joelle, Monique became inspired by robotics. Although she grew up without parents in foster homes, Monique received the educational and emotional support of a White female teacher who served as a mentor. She attended a public high school that had a Career Tech Program, an engineering program that provided engineering coursework throughout high school. Describing the gender demographics in her classes, Monique said:

At the time it was just mechanical and automotive stuff, where all the boys went; dentistry and cosmetology where all the girls went. And then there was business

which was split between boys and girls . . . and then an engineering class where there were all boys, but it was taught by a White woman . . . she kind of grabbed me in there, because she saw my eyes light up over the robotics piece. We had robotics at our school due to that program. I sacrificed my social status, or what little I had and joined engineering. It was honestly the best part of my high school years. That engineering program sustained me above all else to get through it.

Having a White female mentor provided a source of emotional support and inspired Monique to embrace engineering. In striking contrast to the White and Asian women interviewed, Monique did not have parents embedded in the industry, thus, she was more dependent upon adult mentors at school.

Saraswati: A Daughter of South Asian Engineers

Saraswati, a 40-something Indian American entrepreneur and computer scientist, earned a joint degree in software and electrical engineering from Duke University. The daughter of engineers, Saraswati grew up in Silicon Valley and was exposed to computing culture. As a child, she built her first computer with her father. She later co-founded a financial services software company with a university friend after college. It grew into a multi-million-dollar business that has allowed Saraswati to retire from the business in her 30s and pursue start-up endeavors.

During her interview, Saraswati described how gender-segregated forms of play characterized her childhood leisure activities. In contrast her brother, Saraswati, did not play video games. Instead, white Barbie dolls were the preferred toys among Saraswati and her upper middle-class female peers. While her brother learned to program, Saraswati joined the Speech and Debate team in high school—cultivating a love of writing and public speaking. She did not learn computer programming until college. After her first year, she changed her major from economics to a joint major in software and electrical engineering based on her father's advice. Saraswati characterized this as a "wayward" path to computer engineering, saying:

> My Dad was a hardware engineer so I learned a lot about tech early on [. . .] He was getting his masters at San Jose State, and I would sit in on lectures . . . I knew what a circuit board was, and we built our first computer together. I was always working on little things. But I always saw it as a hobby. I never thought I wanted to be an engineer because it seemed dull. Like my Dad would goes to work 9–5 and sit a cubicle. That didn't seem like a fit for me. . . . when I got to college I was majoring in economics, and I wasn't excited about it. . . . my Dad was like, "Maybe you should think about taking computer science classes because you like all these techie gadgets, you have a Kindle, and you have all this stuff."

Describing her childhood, Saraswati noted that she was "always programming little things." However, her father did not actively encourage her to pursue computer engineering as he did with her younger brother. Now an electrical engineer, her brother was the one to "break stuff, build stuff." While he was building his skills in computing, she was guided towards more gender appropriate endeavors, such as creative writing.

Britney: Following in Her Father's Footsteps

Britney is a 26-year-old Chinese-American, who grew up in the 1990s in an upper middle-class and racially exclusive residential neighborhood in Silicon Valley. During her interview Britney wore the standard tech uniform—a dark t-shirt, with no makeup, and no visible jewelry. Both of Britney's parents worked in tech. Her mother was a chip layout designer, who later retired to become a full-time home-maker. Her father, who had studied physics in college, switched to electrical engineering in graduate school, with the hopes of finding a

higher-paying job, outside of academia. Her father has worked in the tech industry for most of this life. Like other female engineers interviewed, Britney described her father as a central figure in her pathway to a technology career:

> He's always been on top of the tech industry. And so he's probably the one who said to my mom that she could probably learn this, and make a lot more money and do less hours. He was also the one who pushed me to do the Computer Science AP test – the class and then the AP test, because he thought that would be a good fit for me. I was originally not interested in that at all.

As a child, she attended distinguished and high-ranking public schools. Britney described having *no interest in computer science or technology as a child*. Despite her uninterest in STEM, her father demanded that she enroll in computer science classes in high school. He pushed her into the technology field. He bought the family a home computer, and later, a personal laptop for Britney to do her school work. On her 14th birthday, Britney's father bought her two video game systems—an X-Box and a Halo 2. She admitted to rarely playing, and noted that they were more often used by her friends. Although gaming is often thought of as a leisure activity, Britney's father considered gaming a strategic resource to build his daughter's technical competence. As she described:

> [The video games] was his trying to get me interested in tech. And I think, knowing that I was not taking this kind of bait, he was pretty confident I was not going to be interested in electrical engineering, which is at such a low-level in terms of like circuits and things like that. It's just very math-y. In a sense, it's almost non-creative. There's definitely a right answer to put the circuits together, otherwise, nothing works.

Britney attended an elite high school that offered an elective course in computer programming, which was designed and led by one of the school's English teachers. It was a course that

Britney described as his passion project—one that was unusual for high schools of this era. She felt the class would not have been offered without the interest of this particular teacher, who, like his students, lived in the heart of Silicon Valley. Initially, Britney was a reluctant student of computer science. She recalls:

> I didn't want to take this computer science class. My dad made me [. . .] [I learned that] computer science is much more creative. You're developing something. You're using this language to write out what you're trying to do. There are multiple right ways to do the same thing. One is more elegant. One is more straight-forward. . . . And so [my father] felt that it was artistic enough to interest me. And that yes, later on it would turn into a good career if I continued with that. So he convinced me to take [an] AP class [in computer science].

Later, as an undergraduate, Britney majored in computer science at the University of California. Her undergraduate program offered a general overview of computer science as a field, but provided very limited technical training. After graduation, Britney entered Stanford University where she pursued a Master's degree in the same field. This move from a public university to Stanford illuminated the exceptional resources available at private university.

Britney reported that her sister, Lisa, later followed the same route through high school. Britney's parents went even further by enrolling her younger sister in a tech-coding camp, which in today's dollars can cost as much as $3,000, and encouraged her to build her own website. Britney reported that, her sister "was never interested in" STEM. Yet her parents still demanded Britney's sister take the same Advanced Placement courses to equip her with skills that could translate into a well-paying career.[26] Today, Lisa is an undergraduate at Pomona College, where she is studying to be a computer science major.

The childhood experiences of Joelle, Saraswati and Britney demonstrate that their parents' investment in engineering and their occupations constituted a crucial form of capital. As children, their parents embedded them in a social landscape of engineers.

Despite any gendered barriers, all three women were exposed to computing as children, which provided them with experiences that laid the foundation for a future career in the technology industry. Residential segregation by race, ethnicity and class, also structures the distribution of these forms of childhood knowledge. These class-based childhood experiences, as the family members of engineers, combined with on-going access to the best education in public and private schools, produces life-long cultural advantages for "computer geeks."

In the next section, we introduce three geek girls who either did not express an early interest in computing or did not have the cultural capital and social resources to secure a job in technology without a lot of struggle. We begin with a well-educated Black woman who had an early interest in computing, but who lacked the resources and parental networks that her Asian and White peers reported. She did not grow up in a household of engineers that could provide social and educational capital. We compare her experiences to those of a White woman who entered the technology industry as a lifestyle choice and did not report having any early interest or passion for computing.

Jasmine: A Black Unicorn

Nearly six feet tall, Jasmine is the 29-year-old middle daughter in a family of 5 children. Jasmine grew up in Kentucky in a working-class community. Her mother, a Head Start teacher, was a teen mom and raised Jasmine as a single mother. Jasmine earned her degree in informative assurance and security engineering. She has since held a number of positions in the technology industry. Prior to working for her current employer, she worked for Google as a systems administrator and security engineer. She provides infrastructure that apps (applications) run on, and she makes sure that they are stable enough to keep running.

Jasmine is a millennial who became passionate about computing as an early teen. When she was 12 years old and in middle school, Jasmine began to actively develop her skills and knowledge in computing by seeking out coursework beyond the boundaries of her school. In her words:

I was very, very curious and liked to work with my hands.[. . .] I saw computers and I wanted to know how they worked. [. . .] In middle school, there was a program called the Student Technology Leadership Program. It's an organization in Kentucky. So I got involved in that . . . And it taught me kind of the basics – as computers were becoming a kind of big thing . . . The Internet was becoming a big thing.[. . .] And I started teaching older teachers how to use a computer and how to use a mouse. And how to interface with the desktop. And this was when I was 12, 13 years old.

In contrast to the White and Asian tech workers interviewed, Jasmine lived in a neighborhood with a poorly resourced public school. Since her neighborhood school did not offer a Student Technology Leadership Program (STLP), Jasmine had to strategize to find alternative education. Eventually, through her own tenacity, she was admitted to another middle school.

I lived a mile down from [name of school] but it wasn't considered a good school . . . At the same time, I really wanted to go to [high school] because of the STLP program that they had. And from there, I learned a lot. . . . I had a very, very rigorous networking program because they literally went through the curriculum I had, was basically going through different types of certifications. [. . .] so I was going through industry-level certification in high school.

In contrast to the White and Asian geek girls in our sample, Jasmine had neither females nor co-ethnics in any of her CS classes. She was a gender and racial/ethnic minority. Describing the demographics of her classmates, she noted that "I was actually the only woman in my classes until I graduated."

Tiffany: Sister of a Tech Firm VP

Tiffany is a 27-year-old White woman, who is thin with long, straight brown hair and bangs. At the time of her interview she was employed as a recruiting coordinator for a major tech firm in San Francisco. She earned her degree in Geology and Physics at a private university on the East Coast. Upon graduation, she was recruited to work as a teacher in an under-resourced public school. She is the daughter of an editor and a university professor, and the sister of a Vice President of a technology firm in San Francisco. Her career trajectory and childhood experiences illuminate one of the recurring patterns that we found among White women who reported no specific interest in computing or technology as children. Instead, they had fathers, boyfriends or siblings who entered the industry and achieved increases in their wages, job benefits, and lifestyles. Their social connections, combined with their race and class position, enabled these women to secure jobs in tech without enduring the same rigorous interview process described by Black participants and others who were not embedded in these networks.

When asked, "What was appealing to you about working for a tech company?", Tiffany replied, "I mostly did it because of the people I would be working with and their descriptions of what working in tech was like." She reported being bored and unhappy in her former job in Texas and wanted to return to California to be near her family. In our research, we found that the Asian and White women typically reported having had familial and social relationships that provided unearned access to six figure internships and permanent full-time jobs in the industry. In Tiffany's case, she was referred for a position at her brother's company. According to her own analysis, she was hired even after she failed to adequately answer tough questions during her interview. Familial and social connections provided individuals like Tiffany with unearned advantages that distinguished their experiences from the rigorous screening and interview process, often lasting several months, that Black tech workers endured.

As a child, she attended an exclusive private school. Like Britney, Tiffany grew up in an upper middle-class and exclusive California community. Describing her childhood community, Tiffany said: . . . "We also lived in this really awesome neighborhood – it was like a UCLA faculty neighborhood . . . up in the hills." Like many of the White and Asian technology workers in our sample, she grew up in a racially segregated community that provided her with life-long advantages in terms of her access to economic, cultural, and social capital.

Like Britney, Tiffany did not engage in computer related activities or hobbies as a child. The difference between Tiffany and Britney is that Tiffany's father did not push her to study computer science. However, at the private school that she attended, she was offered AP classes in physics. And she did not have a "minority" experience as a girl. Instead, she belonged to a cohort of other girls in her high school class who also studied AP Physics. Describing her interests at this time:

> I wasn't really at the computer. And I wasn't really doing video games either. [. . .] I did a lot of just hanging out with my family. *A really big piece of my childhood was doing homework or doing study groups with friends or whatever. It really felt like my childhood circled around academics. . . . It was more focused on getting A's in my classes. It wasn't like I had a deep passion for a certain topic. I liked them all.*

When asked about her experiences during high school, Tiffany never mentioned race or ethnicity as significant. Like the other White women interviewed, she typically employed race-evasive and color-evasive language when describing her classmates. Instead, she emphasized that girls were adequately represented in Advanced Placement Physics courses. In this sense, her experiences diverged from some of the other White millennials interviewed. As she said:

> I did end up going to a pretty small private high school . . . I think everyone had to take physics, but not everyone took AP Physics . . . I think those classes . . . actually had a pretty good gender ratio. Maybe it was 1/3 women to 2/3 men. But I think it was between 1/3 and 1/2. So I didn't even really feel like the minority in my class in terms of gender.

In her description of her pathway to technology, Tiffany identified her brother as the central player in securing her a job in the industry. She described a particular visit with her brother in which she expressed feeling disenchanted and bored with her career in teaching. Her brother encouraged Tiffany to move to San Francisco and build a new life. He set up an interview for her at his company which included a conversation with his boss, the CEO. With an older sibling who had worked at three top technology firms and holds a leadership position at his current company, Tiffany was hired for a competitive position in recruiting, despite having no prior experience and performing poorly in her interview. Tiffany is notably not an engineer. She does not code or program. As we will see later, her pathway into tech sits in stark contrast to the Black tech workers interviewed and Whites from lower-middle or working-class backgrounds.

When she was asked during her interview, "What was appealing to you about working for a tech company?" she replied:

> . . . I knew someone there, right? My brother worked there so that's a more comfortable environment to get started in. [. . .] I had been to visit [my brother] once before and had . . . seen the office and seen that it had a very fun vibe. And you know they give you meals . . . a lot of the stupid stuff that had been hard about living alone in Texas would be made a lot easier by joining a tech company . . . I was like "Oh, I need new friends and so this would be a great way to have a job that pays reasonably well and have friends."

Tiffany moved across the country and secured a six-figure job with no coding experience, no previous internship experience and no real passion for the field. Her description of her motivations demonstrates the significance of social connections, regardless of one's degree. Her trajectory suggests that a social referral from a male employed in a leadership position can be more powerful than having either a degree in CS, or experience as an intern.

Who Gets to Be a Geek: The Costs of Race and Poverty

Maya is a 29-year old Black tech worker. She grew up in Baltimore and now works as an engineer at one of the top technology firms in the United States. Her childhood experiences and trajectory to a tech job differ from the White, Asian and Latinx Americans in our sample. In contrast to the non-Blacks in our sample, she had no family members, siblings, husbands, or boyfriends working in the industry. As a child, her parents did not have the resources to engage in "opportunity hoarding." Neither of her parents worked in the technology industry. Maya did not have the economic and social resources that a middle-class family could provide. Nevertheless, her mother succeeded in getting her enrolled in a slightly better public school. Describing her childhood, Maya said:

> I grew up in Baltimore in a poor neighborhood. My mother was a single mom and worked two jobs. I'm the oldest of six kids . . . I left Baltimore when I was 12 years. I didn't have any computer classes or anything like that until the 6th grade. I left Baltimore in the sixth grade. . . . But the crazy part is that I didn't have computer classes either . . . I didn't get into my Excel class until I moved in my senior class in high school when we moved to Delaware. And I only spent one year there. And in that one year, I had Microsoft Excel classes. Everything else I learned on my own. I didn't have any computer software experience until then.

Due to her family's economic status and lack of resources, Maya did not have the same resources and educational experiences as her middle and upper middle-class White or Asian peers. Recalling her feelings during this time, she noted:

> My childhood memory is that I didn't have the internet at all when I lived in Baltimore . . . . And I just desperately wanted to do things on the internet and play games. . . . I desperately wanted to be a part of that world and I couldn't. I didn't have the internet. . . . And so when I moved and my mom married my stepdad, he had the internet. And there was this longing for several years. And finally I got a chance to be on the internet and I never let it go.

After her mother remarried, she moved the family to Delaware. Describing her friendship and social universe, Maya recounted a multiracial friendship network. This represents another pattern that distinguished Black tech workers from their non-Black peers. They were more likely to be immersed in and to cultivate a multiracial friendship network. Unlike the White and Asian tech workers we interviewed, they had to negotiate a tech ecosystem in which rarely, if ever, had co-ethnics or individuals from their same cultural background.

The Experience Gap

In their research on computer science students attending Carnegie Mellon, Jane Margolis, Allan Fisher, and Faye Miller found that there was an "experience gap" among male and female students. They argued:

> Despite the fact that most of the women students educated in the U.S. had computers in their homes growing up and enjoyed using them, their interest in computing was usually one among several and developed more gradually than it does for the male students. As the women describe their enjoyment of programming, most compare themselves to a male member of their family, and note that he was the one who was "really into computers." More female students in our sample report watching while a male family member (father or brother) played games, tinkered, or took the computer apart.[27]

Computing skills among engineers were often cultivated well before college. In a profession in which ten years of programming skills is described as normative for an entry-level position, early childhood exposure for Asians and Whites emerged as a key dimension of cultural capital. The childhood experiences of the middle and upper middle-class Asian and White women in our sample, support the findings of Margolis, Fisher, and Miller. They argued that their gender-segregated play in childhood produces a "gap" in experience, which inhibits women from pursuing technical careers. However, by interviewing women from diverse racial and class backgrounds, we provide a more nuanced analysis of divergent pathways into technology careers and challenge the myth that the "pipeline" is the primary obstacle to Blacks, Latinos and women entering the industry. In addition to gender-segregated forms of play, we show how residential segregation by race and class, and disparate financial resources during childhood, influence a young person's exposure to computers as "toys" for skill-building. In the next section, we discuss the role of parents in our interviewees' trajectories into tech.

Parental Resources: A Form of Educational and Economic Capital

Parents were central figures in the childhood narratives of White and Asian engineers raised in middle or upper middle-class communities. In this section, we discuss how childhood exposure to technology was a source of advantage for the economically privileged White and Asian participants we interviewed. The role of their parents and the resources available to them during childhood stood in stark contrast to the working-class White and Black tech workers in our sample.

The childhood resources of individuals who became engineers challenge a dominant discourse of meritocracy that circulates in the media and the tech industry. This discourse shifts the analytical lens away from structural inequality, racism, and a male supremacist corporate culture by suggesting that only the "best and the brightest" are hired for jobs in the technology industry. This is a myth. Our research illuminates the significant resources that parents invested in their children's technical skills. These parents were often engineers, technicians, or computer programmers in the early computing industry. In addition to parents, many of our participants detailed how their skills with and interest in technology were further enhanced by siblings, neighbors, and peers of similar race and class backgrounds. Having access to these resources prepared the way for a future career. This was taken for granted by the non-Blacks interviewed, as they interpreted their childhood experiences as typical for engineers.

Conclusion

Being primed for the technology pipeline is, in part, a product of ongoing racial inequality, class inequality, and residential segregation in the United States. Early experiences with computer coding is valuable,

in part, because it was exclusive. This may change as learning to code becomes a more central part of the curriculum for students. In the case of the Generation X and Millennials interviewed (particularly the engineers), their early exposure to computer programming, "gaming" culture, or electrical engineering via assembling or dissembling computers was a significant experience that prepared them for a career in the technology industry.

Women employed in the jobs in the tech industry that did not require coding reported having fathers, brothers, boyfriends or former classmates who were employed in the industry. In these cases, racial and class privilege appeared to operate in concert with social connections to compensate for their lack of coding experience and lack of internships.

Those children who became engineers were more likely to have had high levels of exposure to informal tech training at home. These childhood experiences produced lifelong advantages. We have identified several important variables in the experiences that prepared children for a career in tech. These include the following: 1) access to personal computers, 2) formal classes in computing, 3) informal knowledge learned through play, and 4) parental interventions and childhood friendship networks.

In striking contrast to the Black tech workers, Asians and Whites reported having access to well-resourced public and private schools, early exposure to computers and gaming systems, and parental encouragement of computing related classes and hobbies. These experiences were central in the life histories of Asian and White engineers and non-engineers as well. The forms of access detailed in this chapter were available only to individuals who grow up in racially and class segregated upper middle-class communities. These resources operate "outside the pipeline," meaning that Whites and Asians, particularly engineers, were more likely to: 1) have parents, siblings, or friends, who enabled them to secure internships and full-time jobs in the technological industry, 2) have grown up in residential neighborhoods where they established friendships with the children of tech workers, and 3) had access to informal and formal mentoring and training in computing and engineering at an early age.

These childhood experiences provided cultural and social advantages, as well as technical knowledge. They produced what Jane Margolis and Fisher call an "experience gap" because these experiences were not available to the Black[28] tech workers interviewed, who had worked very hard to acquire programming or electrical engineering skills in creative ways. These taken-for-granted advantages flow from class privilege, racial privilege and residential segregation, which sorts upper middle-class Whites and Asians into wealthier and more resourced school districts. This prepared Asians and Whites for the pipeline into the tech industry, in ways that distinguish them from working-class White and Blacks in our sample.

NOTES

1. See pages 43–44 in Ruth Frankenberg (1993), *White Women, Race Matters: The Social Construction of Whiteness.* Minneapolis, MN: University of Minnesota.

2. See *One Last Thing* (2011), a documentary directed by Sarah Hunt and Mimi O'Connor. Demetri Goritsas narrates. 55 minutes, United States. Produced by Pioneer Productions. Distributed by PBS and Channel 4 (BBC) as well as others.

3. See Richard Reeves. 2017. *Dream Hoarders: How the American Upper Middle Class Is Leaving Everyone Else in the Dust, Why That Is a Problem and What to Do About It.* Washington, DC: The Brookings Institute.

4. This was reported by Bill Hernandez, a childhood friend of Steve Jobs. Bill Hernandez, interviewed in the film *One Last Thing.*

5. See Peggy McIntosh, "Unpacking the Invisible Knapsack of White Privilege," in *Peace and Freedom Magazine* (July/August 1989, 10–12).

6. See Richard Reeves. *Dream Hoarders* (p. 12).

7. See Reeves. *Dream Hoarders* (p. 13).

8. All of the workers interviewed were US citizens or naturalized citizens. None were working on Hl–Visas.

9. See Ruth Frankenberg. 1993. *White Women, Race Matters: The Social Construction of Whiteness.* Minneapolis: University of Minnesota Press (p. 11).

10. See Frankenberg, *White Women* (p. 11).

11. See Frankenberg, *White Women* (p. 43–44).

12. See Richard Rothstein. 2017. *The Color of Law: A Forgotten History of How Our Government Segregated America.* New York, NY: Liveright Publishing (p. 11–12).

13. See *Racial Faultlines: The Historical Origins of White Supremacy in California* by Tomas Almaguer. (1994, first edition) Berkeley/Los Angeles: University of California Press.

14. See Rothstein, *The Color of Law* (p. 11–12).

15. See Rothstein, *The Color of Law* (p. 13).

16. See Doug Massey and Nancy Denton, 1998. *American Apartheid: Segregation and the Making of the Underclass.* Cambridge, MA: Harvard University Press.

17. In "Every Place Has a Ghetto": The Significance of Whites' Social and Residential Segregation, Eduardo Bonilla-Silva and David Embrick, argue that. See Vol. 30, No. 3: 323–345 in *Symbolic Interaction.*

18. See Bonilla-Silva and David Embrick, "Every Place has a Ghetto" (p. 325).

19. See Walter Isaacson. 2015. *Steve Jobs.* New York, NY: Simon & Schuster.

20. See "Radia Perlman: Don't Call Me the Mother of the Internet," by Rebecca J. Rosen, published in *The Atlantic Monthly,* March 3, 2013. https://www.theatlantic.com/technology/archive/2014/03/radia-perlman-dont-call-me-the-mother-of-the-internet/284146/

21. See Rosen, "Radia Perlman."

22. See Rosen, "Radia Perlman."

23. See Rosen, "Radia Perlman."

24. See *Distinction: A Social Critique of the judgement of Taste,* 1984, by Pierre Bourdieu

25. See Reeves, *Dream Hoarders* (p. 12).

26. In the United States and Canada, Advanced Placement (AP) courses, created by the College Board, offer college-level curricula and examinations to high school students. Enrollment in these courses is elective, and high school students must earn a high enough score on placement exams to be accepted into AP classes.

27. See "The Anatomy of Interest: Women in Undergraduate Computer Science," by Jane Margolis, Allan Fisher, and Faye Miller.

28. The Latinos in our sample included upper middle-class White Latinos who were born and grew up in Mexico and Black Latinas who grew up in the United States and had experiences more similar to US Black Natives. The White Latinos in our sample, despite having accents that would mark them as non-native, reported having similar class and racial advantages to the upper middle-class White Americans in our sample.

THINKING ABOUT THE READING

How does this selection challenge the myth that there just are not enough people of color and individuals from lower socioeconomic origins in the pipeline for certain types of occupations? What does it say about the notion of "competitive individualism"? What early experiences were significant factors in a tech worker's occupational success? How did race intersect with class and space in the stories of these tech workers? Do you think similar dynamics operate in access to other types of occupations? How might different paths to these prestigious occupations affect the culture for the workers in them?

CHAPTER 11

The Architecture of Inequality

Race and Ethnicity

The history of race in the United States is an ambivalent one. Cultural beliefs about equality conflict with the experiences of most racial and ethnic minorities: oppression, violence, and exploitation. Opportunities for life, liberty, and the pursuit of happiness have always been distributed along racial and ethnic lines. U.S. society is built on the assumption that different immigrant groups will ultimately assimilate, changing their way of life to conform to that of the dominant culture. But the increasing diversity of the population has shaped people's ideas about what it means to be an American and has influenced our relationships with one another and with our social institutions.

It has been said that White people in the United States have the luxury of "having no color." When someone is described with no mention of race, the default assumption is that he or she is White. In other words, *white* is used far less often as a modifying adjective than *black, Asian,* or *Latino.* As a result, "whiteness" is rarely questioned or examined as a racial or ethnic category. In her article "Optional Ethnicities," Mary C. Waters argues that unlike members of other groups, U.S. Whites can choose whether or not to include their specific ancestry in descriptions of their own identities. For Whites of European descent, claiming an ethnic identity is a voluntary "leisure-time activity" with few social implications. Indeed, the option of being able *not* to claim any ethnicity is available only to the majority group in a society.

Bart Landry explores the intersections of race and gender in "Black Women and a New Definition of Womanhood." This article provides a fascinating picture of women's struggle for equality from the perspective of Black women, a group that is often ignored and marginalized in discussions of the women's movement. Although much of the article focuses on Black women's activism in the 19th century, it provides important insight into the intersection of race and gender today. Landry raises an important contrast between the way in which 19th-century middle-class White women and middle-class Black women framed the relationship between family and public life.

The diversity of our population has rapidly occurred along racial and ethnic lines and had a profound impact on relationships in all spheres of social life. When other forms of diversity like sexuality, that are becoming more visible in these spheres are included, we see an even more complicated picture of relationships and shared spaces. Shaeleya Miller explores the conflict and tensions over Queer People of Color (QPOC) spaces and anti-racist politics in a group of queer university student leaders. She finds how ironically, identity management processes can reinforce structural inequalities, even in communities like this one, focused on social justice.

Something to Consider as You Read

As you read these selections, consider the differences between individual prejudice and institutional racism. Is it possible for someone not to be racist and still participate in practices that perpetuate racism? Compare these readings with those in other chapters. Consider the connections between access to economic resources, social class, and race. How might socioeconomic status influence attitudes and behaviors toward others who may share your ethnicity but not your class position? Think also about how you identify your own race or ethnicity. When you fill out a questionnaire that asks you to select a racial/ethnic category, do you think the category adequately reflects you? When you go somewhere, do you assume you will easily find others of your own race or ethnicity? When you watch television or a movie, how likely is it that the central characters will be people who share your racial background? Practice asking yourself similar questions as a way of enhancing your racial awareness.

Optional Ethnicities

MARY C. WATERS

(1996)

What does it mean to talk about ethnicity as an option for an individual? To argue that an individual has some degree of choice in their ethnic identity flies in the face of the commonsense notion of ethnicity many of us believe in—that one's ethnic identity is a fixed characteristic, reflective of blood ties and given at birth. However, social scientists who study ethnicity have long concluded that while ethnicity is based on a *belief* in a common ancestry, ethnicity is primarily a *social* phenomenon, not a biological one (Alba 1985, 1990; Barth 1969; Weber [1921] 1968, p. 389). The belief that members of an ethnic group have that they share a common ancestry may not be a fact. There is a great deal of change in ethnic identities across generations through intermarriage, changing allegiances, and changing social categories. There is also a much larger amount of change in the identities of individuals over their lives than is commonly believed. While most people are aware of the phenomenon known as "passing"—people raised as one race who change at some point and claim a different race as their identity—there are similar life course changes in ethnicity that happen all the time and are not given the same degree of attention as "racial passing."

White Americans of European ancestry can be described as having a great deal of choice in terms of their ethnic identities. The two major types of options White Americans can exercise are (1) the option of whether to claim any specific ancestry, or to just be "White" or American, (Lieberson [1985] called these people "unhyphenated Whites") and (2) the choice of which of their European ancestries to choose to include in their description of their own identities. In both cases, the option of choosing how to present yourself on surveys and in everyday social interactions exists for Whites because of social changes and societal conditions that have created a great deal of social mobility, immigrant assimilation, and political and economic power for Whites in the United States. Specifically, the option of being able to not claim any ethnic identity exists for Whites of European background in the United States because they are the majority group—in terms of holding political and social power, as well as being a numerical majority. The option of choosing among different ethnicities in their family backgrounds exists because the degree of discrimination and social distance attached to specific European backgrounds has diminished over time . . . .

Symbolic Ethnicities for White Americans

What do these ethnic identities mean to people and why do they cling to them rather than just abandoning the tie and calling themselves American? My own field research with suburban Whites in California and Pennsylvania found that later-generation descendants of European origin maintain what are called "symbolic ethnicities." Symbolic ethnicity is a term coined by Herbert Gans (1979) to refer to ethnicity that is individualistic in nature and without real social cost for the individual. These symbolic identifications are essentially leisure-time activities, rooted in nuclear family traditions and reinforced by the voluntary enjoyable aspects of being ethnic (Waters 1990). Richard Alba (1990) also found later-generation Whites in Albany, New York, who chose to keep a tie with an ethnic identity because of the enjoyable and voluntary aspects to those identities, along with the feelings of specialness they entailed. An example of symbolic ethnicity is individuals who identify as Irish, for example, on occasions such as Saint Patrick's Day, on family holidays, or for vacations. They do not usually belong to Irish American organizations, live in Irish neighborhoods, work in Irish jobs, or marry other Irish people. The symbolic meaning of being Irish American can be constructed by individuals from mass media images, family traditions, or other intermittent social activities. In other words, for later-generation White ethnics, ethnicity is not something that influences their lives unless they want it to. In the world of work and school and neighborhood, individuals do not have to admit to being ethnic unless they choose to. And for an increasing number of European-origin individuals whose parents and grandparents have intermarried, the ethnicity they claim is largely a matter of personal choice as they sort through all of the possible combinations of groups in their genealogies. . . .

Race Relations and Symbolic Ethnicity

However much symbolic ethnicity is without cost for the individual, there is a cost associated with symbolic ethnicity for the society. That is because symbolic ethnicities of the type described here are confined to White Americans of European origin. Black Americans, Hispanic Americans, Asian Americans, and American Indians do not have the option of a symbolic ethnicity at present in the United States. For all of the ways in which ethnicity does not matter for White Americans, it does matter for non-Whites. Who your ancestors are does affect your choice of spouse, where you live, what job you have, who your friends are, and what your chances are for success in American society, if those ancestors happen not to be from Europe. The reality is that White ethnics have a lot more choice and room to maneuver than they themselves think they do. The situation is very different for members of racial minorities, whose lives are strongly influenced by their race or national origin regardless of how much they may choose not to identify themselves in terms of their ancestries.

When White Americans learn the stories of how their grandparents and great-grandparents triumphed in the United States over adversity, they are usually told in terms of their individual efforts and triumphs. The important role of labor unions and other organized political and economic actors in their social and economic successes are left out of the story in favor of a generational story of individual Americans rising up against communitarian, Old World intolerance, and New World resistance. As a result, the "individualized" voluntary, cultural view of ethnicity for Whites is what is remembered.

One important implication of these identities is that they tend to be very individualistic. There is a tendency to view valuing diversity in a pluralist environment as equating all groups. The symbolic ethnic tends to think that all groups are equal; everyone has a background that is their right to celebrate and pass on to their children. This leads to the conclusion that all identities are equal and all identities in some sense are interchangeable—"I'm Italian American, you're Polish American. I'm Irish American, you're African American." The important thing is to treat people as individuals and all equally. However, this assumption ignores the very big difference between an individualistic symbolic ethnic identity and a socially enforced and imposed racial identity.

My favorite example of how this type of thinking can lead to some severe misunderstandings between people of different backgrounds is from the *Dear Abby* advice column. A few years back a person wrote in who had asked an acquaintance of Asian background where his family was from. His acquaintance answered that this was a rude question and he would not reply. The bewildered White asked Abby why it was rude, since he thought it was a sign of respect to wonder where people were from, and he certainly would not mind anyone asking HIM about where his family was from. Abby asked her readers to write in to say whether it was rude to ask about a person's ethnic background. She reported that she got a large response, that most non-Whites thought it was a sign of disrespect, and Whites thought it was flattering:

Dear Abby,

I am 100 percent American and because I am of Asian ancestry I am often asked "What are you?" It's not the personal nature of this question that bothers me, it's the question itself. This query seems to question my very humanity. "What am I? Why I am a person like everyone else!"

Signed, A REAL AMERICAN

Dear Abby,

Why do people resent being asked what they are? The Irish are so proud of being

Irish, they tell you before you even ask.
Tip O'Neill has never tried to hide his Irish
ancestry.

Signed, JIMMY
(Reprinted by permission of
Universal Press Syndicate)

In this exchange Jimmy cannot understand why Asians are not as happy to be asked about their ethnicity as he is, because he understands his ethnicity and theirs to be separate but equal. Everyone has to come from somewhere—his family from Ireland, another's family from Asia—each has a history and each should be proud of it. But the reason he cannot understand the perspective of the Asian American is that all ethnicities are not equal; all are not symbolic, costless, and voluntary. When White Americans equate their own symbolic ethnicities with the socially enforced identities of non-White Americans, they obscure the fact that the experiences of Whites and non-Whites have been qualitatively different in the United States and that the current identities of individuals partly reflect that unequal history.

In the next section I describe how relations between Black and White students on college campuses reflect some of these asymmetries in the understanding of what a racial or ethnic identity means. While I focus on Black and White students in the following discussion, you should be aware that the myriad other groups in the United States—Mexican Americans, American Indians, Japanese Americans—all have some degree of social and individual influences on their identities, which reflect the group's social and economic history and present circumstance.

Relations on College Campuses

Both Black and White students face the task of developing their race and ethnic identities. Sociologists and psychologists note that at the time people leave home and begin to live independently from their parents, often ages eighteen to twenty-two, they report a heightened sense of racial and ethnic identity as they sort through how much of their beliefs and behaviors are idiosyncratic to their families and how much are shared with other people.

It is not until one comes in close contact with many people who are different from oneself that individuals realize the ways in which their backgrounds may influence their individual personality. This involves coming into contact with people who are different in terms of their ethnicity, class, religion, region, and race. For White students, the ethnicity they claim is more often than not a symbolic one—with all of the voluntary, enjoyable, and intermittent characteristics I have described above.

Black students at the university are also developing identities through interactions with others who are different from them. Their identity development is more complicated than that of Whites because of the added element of racial discrimination and racism, along with the "ethnic" developments of finding others who share their background. Thus Black students have the positive attraction of being around other Black students who share some cultural elements, as well as the need to band together with other students in a reactive and oppositional way in the face of racist incidents on campus.

Colleges and universities across the country have been increasing diversity among their student bodies in the last few decades. This has led in many cases to strained relations among students from different racial and ethnic backgrounds. The 1980s and 1990s produced a great number of racial incidents and high racial tensions on campuses. While there were a number of racial incidents that were due to bigotry, unlawful behavior, and violent or vicious attacks, much of what happens among students on campuses involves a low level of tension and awkwardness in social interaction.

Many Black students experience racism personally for the first time on campus. The upper-middle-class students from White suburbs were often isolated enough that their presence was not threatening to racists in their high schools. Also, their class background was known by their residence and this may have prevented attacks being directed at them. Often Black students at the university who begin talking with other students and recognizing racial slights will remember incidents that happened to them earlier that they might not have thought were related to race.

Black college students across the country experience a sizeable number of incidents that are clearly the result of racism. Many of the most blatant ones that occur between students are the result of drinking. Sometimes late at night, drunken groups of White students coming home from parties will yell slurs at single Black students on the street. The other types of incidents that happen include being singled out for special treatment by employees, such as being followed when shopping at the campus bookstore, or going to the art museum with your class and the guard stops you and asks for your I.D. Others involve impersonal encounters on the street—being called a nigger by a truck driver while crossing the street, or seeing old ladies clutch their pocketbooks and shake in terror as you pass them on the street. For the most part these incidents are not specific to the university environment, they are the types of incidents middle-class Blacks face every day throughout American society, and they have been documented by sociologists (Feagin 1991).

In such a climate, however, with students experiencing these types of incidents and talking with each other about them, Black students do experience a tension and a feeling of being singled out. It is unfair that this is part of their college experience and not that of White students. Dealing with incidents like this, or the ever-present threat of such incidents, is an ongoing developmental task for Black students that takes energy, attention, and strength of character. It should be clearly understood that this is an asymmetry in the "college experience" for Black and White students. It is one of the unfair aspects of life that results from living in a society with ongoing racial prejudice and discrimination. It is also very understandable that it makes some students angry at the unfairness of it all, even if there is no one to blame specifically. It is also very troubling because, while most Whites do not create these incidents, some do, and it is never clear until you know someone well whether they are the type of person who could do something like this. So one of the reactions of Black students to these incidents is to band together.

In some sense then, as Blauner (1992) has argued, you can see Black students coming together on campus as both an "ethnic" pull of wanting to be together to share common experiences and community, and a "racial" push of banding together defensively because of perceived rejection and tension from Whites. In this way the ethnic identities of Black students are in some sense similar to, say, Korean students wanting to be together to share experiences. And it is an ethnicity that is generally much stronger than, say, Italian Americans. But for Koreans who come together there is generally a definition of themselves as "different from" Whites. For Blacks reacting to exclusion there

is a tendency for the coming together to involve both being "different from" but also "opposed to" Whites.

The anthropologist John Ogbu (1990) has documented the tendency of minorities in a variety of societies around the world, who have experienced severe blocked mobility for long periods of time, to develop such oppositional identities. An important component of having such an identity is to describe others of your group who do not join in the group solidarity as devaluing and denying their very core identity. This is why it is not common for successful Asians to be accused by others of "acting White" in the United States, but it is quite common for such a term to be used by Blacks and Latinos. The oppositional component of a Black identity also explains how Black people can question whether others are acting "Black enough." On campus, it explains some of the intense pressures felt by Black students who do not make their racial identity central and who choose to hang out primarily with non-Blacks. This pressure from the group, which is partly defining itself by not being White, is exacerbated by the fact that race is a physical marker in American society. No one immediately notices the Jewish students sitting together in the dining hall, or the one Jewish student sitting surrounded by non-Jews, or the Texan sitting with the Californians, but everyone notices the Black student who is or is not at the "Black table" in the cafeteria.

An example of the kinds of misunderstandings that can arise because of different understandings of the meanings and implications of symbolic versus oppositional identities concerns questions students ask one another in the dorms about personal appearances and customs. A very common type of interaction in the dorm concerns questions Whites ask Blacks about their hair. Because Whites tend to know little about Blacks, and Blacks know a lot about Whites, there is a general asymmetry in the level of curiosity people have about one another. Whites, as the numerical majority, have had little contact with Black culture; Blacks, especially those who are in college, have had to develop bicultural skills—knowledge about the social worlds of both Whites and Blacks. Miscommunication and hurt feelings about White students' questions about Black students' hair illustrate this point. One of the things that happens freshman year is that White students are around Black students as they fix their hair. White students are generally quite curious about Black students' hair—they have basic questions such as how often Blacks wash their hair, how they get it straightened or curled, what products they use on their hair, how they comb it, etc. Whites often wonder to themselves whether they should ask these questions. One thought experiment Whites perform is to ask themselves whether a particular question would upset them. Adopting the "do unto others" rule, they ask themselves, "If a Black person was curious about my hair would I get upset?" The answer usually is "No, I would be happy to tell them." Another example is an Italian American student wondering to herself, "Would I be upset if someone asked me about calamari?" The answer is no, so she asks her Black roommate about collard greens, and the roommate explodes with an angry response such as, "Do you think all Black people eat watermelon too?" Note that if this Italian American knew her friend was Trinidadian American and asked about peas and rice the situation would be more similar and would not necessarily ignite underlying tensions.

Like the debate in *Dear Abby,* these innocent questions are likely to lead to resentment. The issue of stereotypes about Black Americans and the assumption that all Blacks are alike and have the same stereotypical cultural traits has more power to hurt or offend a Black person than vice versa. The innocent questions about Black hair also bring up a number of asymmetries between the Black and White experience. Because Blacks tend to have more knowledge about Whites than vice versa, there is not an even exchange going on; the Black freshman is likely to have fewer basic questions about his White roommate than his White roommate has about him. Because of the differences historically in the group experiences of Blacks and Whites there are some connotations to Black hair that don't exist about White hair. (For instance, is straightening your hair a form of assimilation, do some people distinguish between women having "good hair" and "bad hair" in terms of beauty and how is that related to looking "White"?) Finally, even a Black freshman who cheerfully disregards or is unaware that there are these asymmetries will soon slam into another asymmetry if she willingly answers every innocent question asked of her. In a situation where Blacks make up only 10 percent of the student body, if every non-Black needs to be educated about hair, she will have to explain it to nine other students. As one Black student explained to me, after you've been asked a couple of times about something so personal, you begin to feel like you are an attraction in a zoo, that you are at the university for the education of the White students.

Institutional Responses

Our society asks a lot of young people. We ask young people to do something that no one else does as successfully on such a wide scale—that is to live together with people from very different backgrounds, to respect one another, to appreciate one another, and to enjoy and learn from one another. The successes that occur every day in this endeavor are many, and they are too often overlooked. However, the problems and tensions are also real, and they will not vanish on their own. We tend to see pluralism working in the United States in much the same way some people expect capitalism to work. If you put together people with various interests and abilities and resources, the "invisible hand" of capitalism is supposed to make all the parts work together in an economy for the common good.

There is much to be said for such a model—the invisible hand of the market can solve complicated problems of production and distribution better than any "visible hand" of a state plan. However, we have learned that unequal power relations among the actors in the capitalist marketplace, as well as "externalities" that the market cannot account for, such as long-term pollution, or collusion between corporations, or the exploitation of child labor, means that state regulation is often needed. Pluralism and the relations between groups are very similar. There is a lot to be said for the idea that bringing people who belong to different ethnic or racial groups together in institutions with no interference will have good consequences. Students from different backgrounds will make friends if they share a dorm room or corridor, and there is no need for the institution to do any more than provide the locale. But like capitalism, the invisible hand of pluralism does not do well when power relations and externalities are ignored. When you bring together individuals from groups that are differentially valued in the wider society and provide no guidance, there will be problems. In these cases the "invisible hand" of pluralist relations does not work, and tensions and disagreements can arise without any particular individual or group of individuals being "to blame." On college campuses in the 1990s some of the tensions between students are of this sort. They arise from honest misunderstandings, lack of a common background, and very different experiences of what race and ethnicity mean to the individual.

The implications of symbolic ethnicities for thinking about race relations are subtle but consequential. If your understanding of your own ethnicity and its relationship to society and politics is one of individual choice, it becomes harder to understand the need for programs like affirmative action, which recognize the ongoing need for group struggle and group recognition, in order to bring about social change. It also is hard for a White college student to understand the need that minority students feel to band together against discrimination. It also is easy, on the individual level, to expect everyone else to be able to turn their ethnicity on and off at will, the way you are able to, without understanding that ongoing discrimination and societal attention to minority status makes that impossible for individuals from minority groups to do. The paradox of symbolic ethnicity is that it depends upon the ultimate goal of a pluralist society, and at the same time makes it more difficult to achieve that ultimate goal. It is dependent upon the concept that all ethnicities mean the same thing, that enjoying the traditions of one's heritage is an option available to a group or an individual, but that such a heritage should not have any social costs associated with it.

As the Asian Americans who wrote to *Dear Abby* make clear, there are many societal issues and involuntary ascriptions associated with non-White identities. The developments necessary for this to change are not individual but societal in nature. Social mobility and declining racial and ethnic sensitivity are closely associated. The legacy and the present reality of discrimination on the basis of race or ethnicity must be overcome before the ideal of a pluralist society, where all heritages are treated equally and are equally available for individuals to choose or discard at will, is realized.

REFERENCES

Alba, Richard D. 1985. *Italian Americans: Into the Twilight of Ethnicity.* Englewood Cliffs, NJ: Prentice Hall.

_____. 1990. *Ethnic Identity: The Transformation of White America.* New Haven, CT: Yale University Press.

Barth, Frederick. 1969. *Ethnic Groups and Boundaries.* Boston: Little, Brown.

Blauner, Robert. 1992. "Talking Past Each Other: Black and White Languages of Race." *American Prospect* (Summer): 55–64.

Feagin, Joe R. 1991. "The Continuing Significance of Race: Anti-Black Discrimination in Public Places." *American Sociological Review* 56: 101–17.

Gans, Herbert. 1979. "Symbolic Ethnicity: The Future of Ethnic Groups and Cultures in America." *Ethnic and Racial Studies* 2: 1–20.

Lieberson, Stanley. 1985. *Making It Count: The Improvement of Social Research and Theory.* Berkeley: University of California Press.

Ogbu, John. 1990. "Minority Status and Literacy in Comparative Perspective." *Daedalus* 119: 141–69.

Waters, Mary C. 1990. *Ethnic Options: Choosing Identities in America.* Berkeley: University of California Press.

Weber, Max. [1921]/1968. *Economy and Society: An Outline of Interpretive Sociology.* Eds. Guenther Roth and Claus Wittich, trans. Ephraim Fischoff. New York: Bedminister Press.

THINKING ABOUT THE READING

What is "symbolic ethnicity" according to Waters? Why is this form of ethnic expression optional for some and not others? Based on Waters's thesis, would a campus club for Norwegian Americans be the same as one for African Americans? Consider the slogan "different but equal." Do you think this idea can be applied to racial and ethnic relations in contemporary society? Why are some ethnic and racial groups the subject of discrimination and oppression while others are a source of group membership and belonging? When might an ethnic identity be both? How would you describe the ethnic and racial climate of your college campus?

Black Women and a New Definition of Womanhood

BART LANDRY

(2000)

A popular novel of 1852 chirped that the white heroine, Eoline, "with her fair hair, and celestial blue eyes bending over the harp . . . really seemed 'little lower than the angels,' and an aureola of purity and piety appeared to beam around her brow."[1] By contrast, in another popular antebellum novel, *Maum Guinea and Her Plantation Children* (1861), black women are excluded from the category of true womanhood without debate: "The idea of modesty and virtue in a Louisiana colored-girl might well be ridiculed; as a general thing, she has neither."[2] Decades later, in 1902, a commentator for the popular magazine *The Independent* noted, "I sometimes hear of a virtuous Negro woman, but the idea is absolutely inconceivable to me. . . . I cannot imagine such a creature as a virtuous Negro woman."[3] Another writer, reflecting early-twentieth-century white male stereotypes of black and white women, remarked that, like white women, "Black women had the brains of a child, [and] the passions of a woman" but, unlike white women, were "steeped in centuries of ignorance and savagery, and wrapped about with immoral vices."[4]

Faced with the prevailing views of white society that placed them outside the boundaries of true womanhood, black women had no choice but to defend their virtue. Middle-class black women led this defense, communicating their response in words and in the actions of their daily lives. In doing so they went well beyond defending their own virtue to espouse a broader conception of womanhood that anticipated modern views by more than half a century. Their vision of womanhood combined the public and the private spheres and eventually took for granted a role for women as paid workers outside the home. More than merely an abstract vision, it was a philosophy of womanhood embodied in the lives of countless middle-class black women in both the late nineteenth and the early twentieth centuries.

Virtue Defended

Although black women were seen as devoid of all four of the cardinal virtues of true womanhood—piety, purity, submissiveness, and domesticity—white attention centered on purity. As Hazel Carby suggests, this stemmed in part from the role assigned to black women in the plantation economy. She argues that "two very different but interdependent codes of sexuality operated in the antebellum South, producing opposite definitions of motherhood and womanhood for white and black women which coalesce in the figures of the slave and the mistress."[5] In this scheme, white mistresses gave birth to heirs, slave women to property. A slave woman who attempted to preserve her virtue or sexual autonomy was a threat to the plantation economy. In the words of Harriet Jacobs's slave narrative, *Incidents in the Life of a Slave Girl* (1861), it was "deemed a crime in her [the slave woman] to wish to be virtuous."[6]

Linda Brent, the pseudonym Jacobs used to portray her own life, was an ex-slave struggling to survive economically and protect herself and her daughter from sexual exploitation. In telling her story, she recounts the difficulty all black women faced in practicing the virtues of true womanhood. The contrasting contexts of black and white women's lives called for different, even opposite, responses. While submissiveness and passivity brought protection to the white mistress, these characteristics merely exposed black women to sexual and economic exploitation. Black women, therefore, had to develop strength rather than glory in fragility, and had to be active and assertive rather than passive and submissive. . . .

Three decades later, in the 1890s, black women found reasons to defend their moral integrity with new urgency against attacks from all sides. Views such as those in *The Independent* noted earlier were given respectability by a report of the Slater Fund, a foundation that supported welfare projects for blacks in this period. The foundation asserted without argument, "The negro women of the South are subject to temptations

... which come to them from the days of their race enslavement.... To meet such temptations the negro woman can only offer the resistance of a low moral standard, an inheritance from the system of slavery, made still lower from a lifelong residence in a one-room cabin."[7]

At the 1893 World Columbian Exposition in Chicago, where black women were effectively barred from the exhibits on the achievements of American women, the few black women allowed to address a women's convention there felt compelled to publicly challenge these views. One speaker, Fannie Barrier Williams, shocked her audience by her forthrightness. "I regret the necessity of speaking of the moral question of our women," but "the morality of our home life has been commented on so disparagingly and meanly that we are placed in the unfortunate position of being defenders of our name."[8] She went on to emphasize that black women continued to be the victims of sexual harassment by white men and chided her white female audience for failing to protect their black sisters. In the same vein, black activist and educator Anna Julia Cooper told the audience that it was not a question of "temptations" as much as it was "the painful, patient, and silent toil of mothers to gain title to the bodies of their daughters."[9] Williams was later to write on the same theme. "It is a significant and shameful fact that I am constantly in receipt of letters from the still unprotected women in the South, begging me to find employment for their daughters . . . to save them from going into the homes of the South as servants as there is nothing to save them from dishonor and degradation."[10] Another black male writer was moved to reveal in *The Independent:* "I know of more than one colored woman who was openly importuned by White women to become the mistress of their husbands, on the ground that they, the white wives, were afraid that, if their husbands did not associate with colored women they would certainly do so with outside white women.... And the white wives, for reasons which ought to be perfectly obvious, preferred to have all their husbands do wrong with colored women in order to keep their husbands *straight!*"[11] The attacks on black women's virtue came to a head with a letter written by James Jacks, president of the Missouri Press Association, in which he alleged, "The Negroes in this country were wholly devoid of morality, the women were prostitutes and all were natural thieves and liars."[12] These remarks, coming from such a prominent individual, drew an immediate reaction

from black women throughout the country. The most visible was Josephine St. Pierre Ruffin's invitation to black club women to a national convention in Boston in 1895; one hundred women from ten states came to Boston in response. In a memorable address to representatives of some twenty clubs, Ruffin directly attacked the scurrilous accusations:

> Now for the sake of the thousands of self-sacrificing young women teaching and preaching in lonely southern backwoods, for the noble army of mothers who gave birth to these girls, mothers whose intelligence is only limited by their opportunity to get at books, for the cultured women who have carried off the honors at school here and often abroad, for the sake of our own dignity, the dignity of our race and the future good name of our children, it is "meet, right and our bounden duty" to stand forth and declare ourselves and our principles, to teach an ignorant and suspicious world that our aims and interests are identical with those of all good, aspiring women. Too long have we been silent under unjust and unholy charges.... It is to break this silence, not by noisy protestations of what we are not, but by a dignified showing of what we are and hope to become, that we are impelled to take this step, to make of this gathering an object lesson to the world.[13]

At the end of three days of meetings, the National Federation of Afro-American Women was founded, uniting thirty-six black women's clubs in twelve states.[14] The following year, the National Federation merged with the National League of Colored Women to form the National Association of Colored Women (NACW).

Racial Uplift: In Defense of the Black Community

While the catalyst for these national organizations was in part the felt need of black women to defend themselves against moral attacks by whites, they soon went beyond this narrow goal. Twenty years after its founding, the NACW had grown to fifty thousand members in twenty-eight federations and more than one thousand clubs.[15] The founding of these organizations represented a steady movement by middle-class black women to assume more active roles in the community. Historian Deborah Gray White argues that black club women "insisted that only black women could save the black race," a position that inspired them to pursue an almost feverish pace of activities.[16]

These clubs, however, were not the first attempts by black women to participate actively in their communities. Since the late 1700s black women had been active in mutual-aid societies in the North, and in the 1830s northern black women organized anti-slavery societies. In 1880 Mary Ann Shadd Cary and six other women founded the Colored Women's Progressive Franchise Association in Washington, D.C. Among its stated goals were equal rights for women, including the vote, and the even broader feminist objective of taking "an aggressive stand against the assumption that men only begin and conduct industrial and other things."[17] Giving expression to this goal were a growing number of black women professionals, including the first female physicians to practice in the South.[18] By the turn of the twentieth century, the National Business League, founded by Booker T. Washington, could report that there were "160 Black female physicians, seven dentists, ten lawyers, 164 ministers, assorted journalists, writers, artists, 1,185 musicians and teachers of music, and 13,525 school instructors."[19]

Black women's activism was spurred by the urgency of the struggle for equality, which had led to a greater acceptance of black female involvement in the abolitionist movement. At a time when patriarchal notions of women's domestic role dominated, historian Paula Giddings asserts, "There is no question that there was greater acceptance among Black men of women in activist roles than there was in the broader society."[20] This is not to say that all black men accepted women as equals or the activist roles that many were taking. But when faced with resistance, black women often *demanded* acceptance of their involvement. In 1849, for example, at a black convention in Ohio, "Black women, led by Jane P. Merritt, threatened to boycott the meetings if they were not given a more substantial voice in the proceedings."[21]

In the postbellum period black women continued their struggle for an equal voice in activities for racial uplift in both secular and religious organizations. . . . These women's organizations then played a significant role not only in missionary activities, but also in general racial uplift activities in both rural and urban areas.[22] . . .

Black Women and the Suffrage Movement

In their struggle for their own rights, black women moved into the political fray and eagerly joined the movement for passage of a constitutional amendment giving women the right to vote. Unlike white women suffragists, who focused exclusively on the benefits of the vote for their sex, black women saw the franchise as a means of improving the condition of the black community generally. For them, race and gender issues were inseparable. As historian Rosalyn Terborg-Penn emphasizes, black feminists believed that by "increasing the black electorate" they "would not only uplift the women of the race, but help the children and the men as well."[23]

Prominent black women leaders as well as national and regional organizations threw their support behind the suffrage movement. At least twenty black suffrage organizations were founded, and black women participated in rallies and demonstrations and gave public speeches.[24] Ironically, they often found themselves battling white women suffragists as well as men. Southern white women opposed including black women under a federal suffrage as a matter of principle. Northern white women suffragists, eager to retain the support of southern white women, leaned toward accepting a wording of the amendment that would have allowed the southern states to determine their own position on giving black women the vote, a move that would have certainly led to their exclusion.[25]

After the Nineteenth Amendment was ratified in 1920 in its original form, black women braved formidable obstacles in registering to vote. All across the South white registrars used "subterfuge and trickery" to hinder them from registering, including a "grandmother clause" in North Carolina, literacy tests in Virginia, and a $300 poll tax in Columbia, South Carolina. In Columbia, black women "waited up to twelve hours to register" while white women were registered first.[26] In their struggle to register, black women appealed to the NAACP, signed affidavits against registrars who disqualified them, and finally asked for assistance from national white women suffrage leaders. They were especially disappointed in this last attempt. After fighting side by side with white women suffragists for passage of the Nineteenth Amendment, they were rebuffed by the National Woman's Party leadership with the argument that theirs was a race rather than a women's rights issue.[27] Thus, white women continued to separate issues of race and sex that black women saw as inseparable.

Challenging the Primacy of Domesticity

A conflicting conception of the relationship between gender and race issues was not the only major difference in the approaches of black and white women to their roles in the family and society. For most white women, their domestic roles as wives and mothers remained primary. In the late nineteenth century, as they began increasingly to argue for acceptance of their involvement on behalf of child-labor reform and growing urban problems, white women often defended these activities as extensions of their housekeeping role. Historian Barbara Harris comments, "The [white women] pioneers in women's education, who probably did more than anyone else in this period to effect change in the female sphere, advocated education for women and their entrance into the teaching profession on the basis of the values proclaimed by the cult of true womanhood. In a similar way, females defended their careers as authors and their involvement in charitable, religious, temperance, and moral reform societies."[28] Paula Giddings notes that in this way white women were able "to become more active outside the home while still preserving the probity of 'true womanhood.'"[29] From the birth of white feminism at the Seneca Falls Convention in 1848, white feminists had a difficult time advancing their goals. Their numbers were few and their members often divided over the propriety of challenging the cult of domesticity. . . .

In the late nineteenth century the cult of domesticity remained primary even for white women graduates of progressive women's colleges such as Vassar, Smith, and Wellesley. For them, no less than for those with only a high-school education, "A Woman's Kingdom" was "a well-ordered home."[30] In a student essay, one Vassar student answered her rhetorical question, "Has the educated woman a duty towards the kitchen?" by emphasizing that the kitchen was "exactly where the college woman belonged" for "the orderly, disciplined, independent graduate is the woman best prepared to manage the home, in which lies the salvation of the world."[31] This essay reflects the dilemma faced by these young white women graduates. They found little support in white society to combine marriage and career. . . . Society sanctioned only three courses for the middle-class white woman in the Progressive period: "marriage, charity work or teaching."[32] Marriage and motherhood stood as the highest calling. If there were no economic need for them to work, single women were encouraged to do volunteer charity work. For those who needed an independent income, teaching was the only acceptable occupation.

Historian John Rousmaniere suggests that the white college-educated women involved in the early settlement house movement saw themselves as fulfilling the "service norm" so prominent among middle-class women of the day. At the same time, he argues, it was their sense of uniqueness as college-educated women and their felt isolation upon returning home that led them to this form of service. The settlement houses, located as they were in white immigrant, working-class slums, catered to these women's sense of noblesse oblige; they derived a sense of accomplishment from providing an example of genteel middle-class virtues to the poor. Yet the settlement houses also played into a sense of adventure, leading one resident to write, "We feel that we know life for the first time."[33] For all their felt uniqueness, however, with some notable exceptions these women's lives usually offered no fundamental challenge to the basic assumptions of true womanhood. Residency in settlement houses was for the most part of short duration, and most volunteers eventually embraced their true roles of wife and mother without significant outside involvement. The exceptions were women like Jane Addams, Florence Kelley, Julia Lathrop, and Grace Abbott, who became major figures in the public sphere. Although their lives disputed the doctrine of white women's confinement to the private sphere, the challenge was limited in that most of them did not themselves combine the two spheres of marriage and a public life. Although Florence Kelley was a divorced mother, she nevertheless upheld "the American tradition that men support their families, their wives throughout life," and bemoaned the "retrograde movement" against man as the breadwinner.[34]

Most college-educated black middle-class women also felt a unique sense of mission. They accepted Lucy Laney's 1899 challenge to lift up their race and saw themselves walking in the footsteps of black women activists and feminists of previous generations. But their efforts were not simply "charity work"; their focus was on "racial uplift" on behalf of themselves as well as of the economically less fortunate members of their race.[35] The black women's club movement, in contrast to the white women's, tended to concern themselves from the beginning with the "social and legal problems that confronted both black women and men."[36] While there was certainly some elitism in the NACW's motto, "Lifting as We Climb," these activists were always conscious that they shared a common experience of exploitation and discrimination with the masses and could not completely retreat to the safe haven of their middle-class homes.[37] On the way to meetings they shared the black experience of riding in segregated cars or of being ejected if they tried to do otherwise, as Ida B. Wells did in 1884.[38] Unlike white women for whom, as black feminist Frances Ellen Watkins Harper had emphasized in 1869, "the priorities in the struggle for human rights were sex, not race,"[39] black women could not separate these twin sources of their oppression. They understood that, together with their working-class sisters, they were assumed by whites to have "low animalistic urges." Their exclusion from the category of true womanhood was no less complete than for their less educated black sisters.

It is not surprising, therefore, that the most independent and radical of black female activists led the way in challenging the icons of true womanhood, including on occasion motherhood and marriage. Not only did they chafe under their exclusion from true womanhood, they viewed its tenets as strictures to their efforts on behalf of racial uplift and their own freedom and integrity as women. In 1894 *The Woman's Era* (a black women's magazine) set forth the heretical opinion that "not all women are intended for mothers. Some of us have not the temperament for family life. . . . Clubs will make women think seriously of their future lives, and not make girls think their only alternative is to marry."[40] Anna Julia Cooper, one of the most dynamic women of the period, who had been married and widowed, added

that a woman was not "compelled to look to sexual love as the one sensation capable of giving tone and relish, movement and vim to the life she leads. Her horizon is extended."[41] Elsewhere Cooper advised black women that if they married they should seek egalitarian relationships. "The question is not now with the woman 'How shall I so cramp, stunt, and simplify and nullify myself as to make me eligible to the honor of being swallowed up into some little man?' but the problem . . . rests with the man as to how he can so develop . . . to reach the ideal of a generation of women who demand the noblest, grandest and best achievements of which he is capable."[42]

. . . Black activists were far more likely to combine marriage and activism than white activists. . . . Historian Linda Gordon found this to be the case in her study of sixty-nine black and seventy-six white activists in national welfare reform between 1890 and 1945. Only 34 percent of the white activists had ever been married, compared to 85 percent of the black activists. Most of these women (83 percent of blacks and 86 percent of whites) were college educated.[43] She also found that "The white women [reformers], with few exceptions, tended to view married women's economic dependence on men as desirable, and their employment as a misfortune. . . ."[44] On the other hand, although there were exceptions, Gordon writes, ". . . most black women activists projected a favorable view of working women and women's professional aspirations."[45] Nor could it be claimed that these black activists worked out of necessity, since the majority were married to prominent men "who could support them."[46]

Witness Ida B. Wells-Barnett (married to the publisher of Chicago's leading black newspaper) in 1896, her six-month-old son in tow, stumping from city to city making political speeches on behalf of the Illinois Women's State Central Committee. And Mary Church Terrell dismissing the opinion of those who suggested that studying higher mathematics would make her unappealing as a marriage partner with a curt, "I'd take a chance and run the risk."[47] She did eventually marry and raised a daughter and an adopted child. Her husband, Robert Terrell, a Harvard graduate, was a school principal, a lawyer, and eventually a municipal court judge in Washington, D.C. A biographer later wrote of Mary Terrell's life, "But absorbing as motherhood was, it never became a full-time occupation."[48] While this could also be said of Stanton, perhaps what most distinguished black from white feminists and activists was the larger number of the former who unequivocally challenged domesticity and the greater receptivity they found for their views in the black community. As a result, while the cult of domesticity remained dominant in the white community at the turn of the twentieth century, it did not hold sway within the black community.

Rejection of the Public/Private Dichotomy

Black women of the nineteenth and early twentieth centuries saw their efforts on behalf of the black community as necessary for their own survival, rather than as noblesse oblige. "Self preservation," wrote Mary Church Terrell in 1902, "demands that [black women] go among the lowly, illiterate and even the vicious, to whom they are bound by ties of race and sex . . . to reclaim them."[49] These women rejected the confinement to the private sphere mandated by the cult of domesticity. They felt women could enter the public sphere without detriment to the home. As historian Elsa Barkley Brown has emphasized, black women believed that "Only a strong and unified community made up of both women and men could wield the power necessary to allow black people to shape their own lives. Therefore, only when women were able to exercise their full strength would the community be at its full strength. . . ."[50]

In her study of black communities in Illinois during the late Victorian era (1880–1910), historian Shirley Carlson contrasts the black and white communities' expectations of the "ideal woman" at that time:

> The black community's appreciation for and development of the feminine intellect contrasted sharply with the views of the larger society. In the latter, intelligence was regarded as a masculine quality that would "defeminize" women. The ideal white woman, being married, confined herself almost exclusively to the private domain of the household. She was demure, perhaps even self-effacing. She often deferred to her husband's presumably superior judgment, rather than formulating her own views and vocally expressing them,

as black women often did. A woman in the larger society might skillfully manipulate her husband for her own purposes, but she was not supposed to confront or challenge him directly. Black women were often direct, and frequently won community approval for this quality, especially when such a characteristic was directed toward achieving racial uplift. Further, even after her marriage, a black woman might remain in the public domain, possibly in paid employment. The ideal black woman's domain, then, was both the private and public spheres. She was wife and mother, but she could also assume other roles such as schoolteacher, social activist, or businesswoman, among others. And she was intelligent.[51]

. . . Although many black males, like most white males, opposed the expansion of black women's roles, many other black males supported women's activism and even criticized their brethren for their opposition. Echoing Maggie Walker's sentiments, T. Thomas Fortune wrote, "The race could not succeed nor build strong citizens, until we have a race of women competent to do more than hear a brood of negative men."[52] Support for women's suffrage was especially strong among black males. . . . Black men saw women's suffrage as advancing the political empowerment of the race. For black women, suffrage promised to be a potent weapon in their fight for their rights, for education and jobs.[53]

A Threefold Commitment

An expanded role for black women did not end at the ballot box or in activities promoting racial uplift. Black middle-class women demanded a place for themselves in the paid labor force. Theirs was a threefold commitment to family, career, and social movements. According to historian Rosalyn Terborg-Penn, "most black feminists and leaders had been wives and mothers who worked yet found time not only to struggle for the good of their sex, but for their race." Such a threefold commitment "was not common among white women."[54]

In her study of eighty African American women throughout the country who worked in "the feminized professions" (such as teaching) between the

1880s and the 1950s, historian Stephanie Shaw comments on the way they were socialized to lives dedicated to home, work, and community. When these women were children, she indicates, "the model of womanhood held before [them] was one of achievement in *both* public and private spheres. Parents cast domesticity as a complement rather than a contradiction to success in public arenas."[55] . . .

An analysis of the lives of 108 of the first generation of black clubwomen bears this out. "The career-oriented clubwomen," comments Paula Giddings, "seemed to have no ambivalence concerning their right to work, whether necessity dictated it or not."[56] According to Giddings, three-quarters of these 108 early clubwomen were married, and almost three-quarters worked outside the home, while one-quarter had children.

A number of these clubwomen and other black women activists not only had careers but also spoke forcefully about the importance of work, demonstrating surprisingly progressive attitudes with a very modern ring. "The old doctrine that a man marries a woman to support her," quipped Walker, "is pretty nearly thread-bare to-day."[57] "Every dollar a woman makes," she declared in a 1912 speech to the Federation of Colored Women's Clubs, "some man gets the direct benefit of same. Every woman was by Divine Providence created for some man; not for some man to marry, take home and support, but for the purpose of using her powers, ability, health and strength, to forward the financial . . . success of the partnership into which she may go, if she will. . . ."[58] Being married with three sons and an adopted daughter did not in any way dampen her commitment to gender equality and an expanded role for wives.

Such views were not new. In a pamphlet entitled *The Awakening of the Afro-American Woman*, written in 1897 to celebrate the earlier founding of the National Association of Colored Women, Victoria Earle Matthews referred to black women as "co-breadwinners in their families."[59] Almost twenty years earlier, in 1878, feminist writer and activist Frances Ellen Harper sounded a similar theme of equality when she insisted, "The women as a class are quite equal to the men in energy and executive ability." She went on to recount instances of black women managing small and large farms in the postbellum period.[60]

It is clear that in the process of racial uplift work, black middle-class women also included membership in the labor force as part of their identity. They were well ahead of their time in realizing that their membership in the paid labor force was critical to achieving true equality with men. For this reason, the National Association of Wage Earners insisted that all black women should be able to support themselves.[61] . . .

As W. E. B. DuBois commented as early as 1924, "Negro women more than the women of any other group in America are the protagonists in the fight for an economically independent womanhood in modern countries. . . . The matter of economic independence is, of course, the central fact in the struggle of women for equality."[62]

Defining Black Womanhood

In the late 1930s when Mary McLeod Bethune, the acknowledged leader of black women at the time and an adviser to President Franklin Roosevelt on matters affecting the black community, referred to herself as the representative of "Negro womanhood" and asserted that black women had "room in their lives to be wives and mothers as well as to have careers," she was not announcing a new idea.[63] As Terborg-Penn emphasizes:

> . . . most black feminists and leaders had been wives and mothers who worked yet found time not only to struggle for the good of their sex, but for their race. Until the 1970s, however, this threefold commitment—to family and to career and to one or more social movements—was not common among white women. The key to the uniqueness among black feminists of this period appears to be their link with the past. The generation of the woman suffrage era had learned from their late nineteenth-century foremothers in the black women's club movement, just as the generation of the post-World War I era had learned and accepted the experiences of the preceding generation. Theirs was a sense of continuity, a sense of group consciousness that transcended class.[64]

This "sense of continuity" with past generations of black women was clearly articulated in 1917 by Mary Talbert, president of the NACW. Launching an NACW campaign to save the home of the late Frederick Douglass, she said, "We realize today is the psychological moment for us women to show our true worth and prove the Negro women of today measure up to those sainted women of our race, who passed through the fire of slavery and its galling remembrances."[65] Talbert certainly lived up to her words, going on to direct the NAACP's anti-lynching campaign and becoming the first woman to receive the NAACP's Spingarn Medal for her achievements.

What then is the expanded definition of true womanhood found in these black middle-class women's words and embodied in their lives? First, they tended to define womanhood in an inclusive rather than exclusive sense. Within white society, true womanhood was defined so narrowly that it excluded all but a small minority of white upper- and upper-middle-class women with husbands who were able to support them economically. Immigrant women and poor women—of any color—did not fit this definition. Nor did black women as a whole, regardless of class, because they were all seen as lacking an essential characteristic of true womanhood—virtue. For black women, however, true womanhood transcended class and race boundaries. Anna Julia Cooper called for "reverence for woman as woman regardless of rank, wealth, or culture."[66] Unlike white women, black women refused to isolate gender issues from other forms of oppression such as race and nationality, including the struggles of colonized nations of Africa and other parts of the world. Women's issues, they suggested, were tied to issues of oppression, whatever form that oppression might assume. . . .

The traditional white ideology of true womanhood separated the active world of men from the passive world of women. As we have seen, women's activities were confined to the home, where their greatest achievement was maintaining their own virtue and decorum and rearing future generations of male leaders. Although elite black women did not reject their domestic roles as such, many expanded permissible public activities beyond charity work to encompass employment and participation in social progress. They founded such organizations as the Atlanta Congress of Colored Women, which historian Erlene Stetson claims was the first grassroots women's movement organized "for social and political good."[67]

The tendency of black women to define womanhood inclusively and to see their roles extending beyond the boundaries of the home led them naturally to include other characteristics in their vision. One of these was intellectual equality. While the "true" woman was portrayed as submissive ("conscious of inferiority, and therefore grateful for support"),[68] according to literary scholar Hazel Carby, black women such as Anna Julia Cooper argued for a "partnership with husbands on a plane of intellectual equality."[69] Such equality could not exist without the pursuit of education, particularly higher education, and participation in the labor force. Cooper, like many other black women, saw men's opposition to higher education for women as an attempt to make them conform to a narrow view of women as "sexual objects for exchange in the marriage market."[70] Education for women at all levels became a preoccupation for many black feminists and activists. Not a few—like Anna Cooper, Mary L. Europe, and Estelle Pinckney Webster—devoted their entire lives to promoting it, especially among young girls. Womanhood, as conceived by black women, was compatible with—indeed, required—intellectual equality. In this they were supported by the black community. While expansion of educational opportunities for women was a preoccupation of white feminists in the nineteenth century, as I noted above, a college education tended to create a dilemma in the lives of white women who found little community support for combining marriage and career. In contrast, as Shirley Carlson emphasizes, "The black community did not regard intelligence and femininity as conflicting values, as the larger society did. That society often expressed the fear that intelligent women would develop masculine characteristics—a thickening waist, a diminution of breasts and hips, and finally, even the growth of facial hair. Blacks seemed to have had no such trepidations, or at least they were willing to have their women take these risks."[71]

In addition to women's rights to an education, Cooper, Walker, Alexander, Terrell, the leaders of the National Association of Wage Earners, and countless other black feminists and activists insisted on their right to work outside the home. They dared to continue very active lives after marriage. Middle-class black women's insistence on the right to pursue careers paralleled their view that a true woman could move in both the private and the public spheres and that marriage did not require submissiveness or subordination. In fact, as Shirley Carlson has observed in her study of black women in Illinois in the late

Victorian period, many activist black women "continued to be identified by their maiden names—usually as their middle names or as part of their hyphenated surnames—indicating that their own identities were not subsumed in their husbands."[72]

While the views of black women on womanhood were all unusual for their time, their insistence on the right of all women—including wives and mothers—to work outside the home was the most revolutionary. In their view the need for paid work was not merely a response to economic circumstances, but the fulfillment of women's right to self-actualization. Middle-class black women like Ida B. Wells-Barnett, Margaret Washington, and Mary Church Terrell, married to men who were well able to support them, continued to pursue careers throughout their lives, and some did so even as they reared children. These women were far ahead of their time, foreshadowing societal changes that would not occur within the white community for several generations. . . .

Rather than accepting white society's views of paid work outside the home as deviant, therefore, black women fashioned a competing ideology of womanhood—one that supported the needs of an oppressed black community and their own desire for gender equality. Middle-class black women, especially, often supported by the black community, developed a consciousness of themselves as persons who were competent and capable of being influential. They believed in higher education as a means of sharpening their talents, and in a sexist world that looked on men as superior, they dared to see themselves as equals both in and out of marriage.

This new ideology of womanhood came to have a profound impact on the conception of black families and gender roles. Black women's insistence on their role as co-breadwinners clearly foreshadows today's dual-career and dual-worker families. Since our conception of the family is inseparably tied to our views of women's and men's roles, the broader definition of womanhood advocated by black women was also an argument against the traditional family. The cult of domesticity was anchored in a patriarchal notion of women as subordinate to men in both the family and the larger society. The broader definition of womanhood championed by black middle-class women struck a blow for an expansion of women's rights in society and a more egalitarian position in the home, making for a far more progressive system among blacks at this time than among whites.

NOTES

1. Quoted in Hazel V. Carby, *Reconstructing Womanhood: The Emergence of the Afro-American Woman Novelist* (New York: Oxford University Press, 1987), p. 26.

2. Ibid.

3. Quoted in Paula Giddings, *When and Where I Enter: The Impact of Black Women and Race and Sex in America* (New York: Bantam Books, 1985), p. 82.

4. Ibid., p. 82.

5. Carby, *Reconstructing Womanhood*, p. 20.

6. Harriet Jacobs, *Incidents in the Life of a Slave Girl*, L. Baria Child, ed. (1861; paperback reprint, New York: Harcourt Brace Jovanovich, 1973), p. 29.

7. Quoted in Giddings, *When and Where I Enter*, p. 82.

8. Ibid., p. 86.

9. Ibid., p. 87.

10. Ibid., pp. 86–87.

11. Ibid., p. 87.

12. Quoted in Sharon Harley, "Black Women in a Southern City: Washington, D.C., 1890–1920," pp. 59–78 in Joanne V. Hawks and Sheila L. Skemp, eds., *Sex, Race, and the Role of Women in the South* (Jackson, Miss.: University Press of Mississippi, 1983), p. 72.

13. Eleanor Flexner, *Century of Struggle: The Woman's Rights Movement in the United States* (Cambridge: Harvard University Press, 1959), p. 194.

14. Giddings, *When and Where I Enter*, p. 93.

15. Ibid., p. 95. For a discussion of elitism in the "uplift" movement and organizations, see Kevin K. Gains, *Uplifting the Race: Black Leadership, Politics, and Culture in the Twentieth Century* (Chapel Hill, N.C.: University of North Carolina Press, 1996). Black reformers, enlightened as they were, could

not entirely escape being influenced by Social Darwinist currents of the times.

16. Deborah Gray White, *Too Heavy a Load: Black Women in Defense of Themselves, 1894–1994* (New York: W. W. Norton & Company, 1999), p. 36.

17. Quoted in Giddings, *When and Where I Enter,* p. 75.

18. Ibid.

19. Ibid.

20. Ibid., p. 59.

21. Ibid.

22. Evelyn Brooks Higginbotham, *Righteous Discontent: The Women's Movement in the Black Baptist Church, 1880–1920* (Cambridge: Harvard University Press, 1993).

23. Rosalyn Terborg-Penn, "Discontented Black Feminists: Prelude and Postscript to the Passage of the Nineteenth Amendment," pp. 261–278 in Lois Scharf and Joan M. Jensen, eds., *Decades of Discontent: The Woman's Movement, 1920–1940* (Westport, Conn.: Greenwood Press, 1983), p. 264.

24. Ibid., p. 261.

25. Ibid., p. 264.

26. Ibid., p. 266.

27. Ibid., pp. 266–267.

28. Barbara J. Harris, *Beyond Her Sphere: Women and the Professions in American History* (Westport, Conn.: Greenwood Press, 1978), pp. 85–86.

29. Giddings, *When and Where I Enter,* p. 81.

30. John P. Rousmaniere, "Cultural Hybrid in the Slums: The College Woman and the Settlement House, 1889–1984," *American Quarterly* 22 (Spring 1970): p. 56.

31. Ibid., p. 55.

32. Rousmaniere, "Cultural Hybrid in the Slums," p. 56.

33. Ibid., p. 61.

34. Quoted in Linda Gordon, "Black and White Visions of Welfare: Women's Welfare Activism, 1890–1945," *Journal of American History* 78 (September 1991): 583.

35. Giddings, *When and Where I Enter,* p. 97.

36. Estelle Freedman, "Separatism as Strategy: Female Institution Building and American Feminism, 1870–1930," pp. 445–462 in Nancy F. Cott, ed., *Women Together: Organizational Life* (New Providence, RI: K. G. Saur, 1994), p. 450; Nancy Forderhase, "'Limited Only by Earth and Sky': The Louisville Woman's Club and Progressive Reform, 1900–1910," pp. 365–381 in Cott, ed. *Women Together: Organizational Life* (New Providence, RI: K. G. Saur, 1994); . . . Mary Dell Brady, "Kansas Federation of Colored Women's Clubs, 1900–1930," pp. 382–408 in Nancy F. Cott, *Women Together.*

37. Higginbotham, *Righteous Discontent,* pp. 206–207.

38. Giddings, *When and Where I Enter,* p. 22.

39. Terborg-Penn, "Discontented Black Feminists," p. 267.

40. Giddings, *When and Where I Enter,* p. 108.

41. Ibid., pp. 108–109.

42. Ibid., p. 113.

43. Linda Gordon, "Black and Whites Visions of Welfare," p. 583.

44. Ibid., p. 582.

45. Ibid., p. 585.

46. Ibid., pp. 568–69.

47. Ibid., p. 109.

48. Quoted in Giddings, ibid., p. 110.

49. Ibid., p. 97.

50. Elsa Barkley Brown, "Womanist Consciousness: Maggie Lena Walker and the Independent Order of Saint Luke," *Signs: Journal of Women in Culture and Society* 14, no. 3 (1989): 188.

51. Shirley J. Carlson, "Black Ideals of Womanhood in the Late Victorian Era," *Journal of Negro History* 77, no. 2 (Spring 1992): 62. Carlson notes that these black women of the late Victorian era also observed the proprieties of Victorian womanhood in their deportment and appearance but combined them with the expectations of the black community for intelligence, education, and active involvement in racial uplift.

52. Quoted in Giddings, *When and Where I Enter*, p. 117.

53. See Rosalyn Terborg-Penn, *African American Women in the Struggle for the Vote, 1850–1920* (Bloomington, Ind.: Indiana University Press, 1998).

54. Rosalyn Terborg-Penn, "Discontented Black Feminists," p. 274.

55. Stephanie J. Shaw, *What a Woman Ought to Be and to Do: Black Professional Women Workers During the Jim Crow Era* (Chicago: University of Chicago Press, 1996), p. 29. Shaw details the efforts of family and community to socialize these women for both personal achievement and community service. The sacrifices some families made included sending them to private schools and sometimes relocating the entire family near a desired school.

56. Giddings, *When and Where I Enter*, p. 108.

57. Brown, "Womanist Consciousness," p. 622.

58. Ibid., p. 623.

59. Carby, *Reconstructing Womanhood*, p. 117.

60. Quoted in Giddings, *When and Where I Enter*, p. 72.

61. Brown, "Womanist Consciousness," p. 182.

62. Quoted in Giddings, *Where and When I Enter*, p. 197.

63. Quoted in Terborg-Penn, "Discontented Black Feminists," p. 274.

64. Ibid., p. 274.

65. Quoted in Giddings, *Where and When I Enter*, p. 138.

66. Quoted in Carby, *Reconstructing Womanhood*, p. 98.

67. Erlene Stetson, "Black Feminism in Indiana, 1893–1933," *Phylon* 44 (December 1983): 294.

68. Quoted in Barbara Welter, "The Cult of True Womanhood: 1820–1860," p. 318.

69. Carby, *Reconstructing Womanhood*, p. 100.

70. Ibid., p. 99.

71. Carlson, "Black Ideals of Womanhood in the Late Victorian Era," p. 69. This view is supported by historian Evelyn Brooks Higginbotham's analysis of schools for blacks established by northern Baptists in the postbellum period, schools that encouraged the attendance of both girls and boys. Although, as Higginbotham observes, northern Baptists founded these schools in part to spread white middle-class values among blacks, blacks nevertheless came to see higher education as an instrument of their own liberation (*Righteous Discontent*, p. 20).

72. Ibid., p. 67.

THINKING ABOUT THE READING

How were the needs and goals of black women during the 19th-century movement for gender equality different from those of white women? How did their lives differ with regard to the importance of marriage, motherhood, and employment? What does Landry mean when he says that for these women, "race and gender are inseparable"? What was the significance of the "clubs" for these black women? How does this article change what you previously thought about the contemporary women's movement?

Racial Exclusion in Queer Student Organizations

SHAELEYA MILLER

(2018)

In 2012, leaders from three queer people of color (QPOC) organizations hosted an open dialogue on race in the queer community at a large university in California. These leaders hoped to prioritize QPOC voices while including white allies in a discussion about the need for QPOC-only spaces. Sitting in a circle of approximately three-dozen people, queer students of color shared their experiences of racism within the queer community, and expressed a desire for "closed spaces" where they could simultaneously discuss their racial and sexual identities without fear of backlash from their white peers. Many of them expressed concerns that discussions about racial discrimination were discouraged in LGBTQ spaces, in favor of focusing solely on the sexual and gender discrimination that all members were presumed to have in common. Underlying these concerns was distress among queer students of color, over prevailing sentiments that community members should not detract from the solidarity of shared gender and sexual marginalization by bringing up "other" identities, such as race.

Brooke (Korean-American queer woman, 22, 4th year) lamented that she often heard people groaning as soon as she started to speak about communities of color, and would think to herself "No! This is a queer space! Don't ruin it by talking about race!" Grace (Taiwanese American, bisexual woman, 22, 4th year) agreed, sharing a story about a white student telling two queer students of color in the campus LGBTQ center to "'shush' . . . 'keep it chill' and 'not bring up racism and get angry about it in the space'" but to "unify instead." As each student of color spoke, others nodded in agreement, while a small number of white students sat quietly in the crowd and Dane, a white gay man who was co-chair of the queer Chicanx/Latinx organization, La Familia De Colores, wrote notes on the board and all but directed the conversation.

Months later, similar conversations continued to take place, but QPOC-only spaces remained few and far between. People also remarked on Dane's controversial behaviors as the white co-chair of a Latinx/Chicanx organization, and the leadership role he had taken in what was meant to be a QPOC space. Over the course of the next year, the resistance to QPOC-only spaces and discussions focused on race seemed to grow more contentious. The more QPOC leaders pushed for recognition, the more they faced opposition from their peers.

So what do we make of resistance to anti-racist politics and closed spaces in what was otherwise considered a progressive social justice community? With special attention to students' articulations of diversity, inclusion, and solidarity, this research provides an empirical study of how identity management processes can reinforce structural inequalities—even within communities focused on promoting social justice.

Theoretical Overview

Identity theorists suggest that identity-verification plays a significant role in each individual's sense of self and belonging in relation to others. Starting from the assumption that individuals take into account others' perceptions of them, symbolic interactionists suggest that people tend to behave in ways designed to elicit interpretations from others that match the ways they would like to be perceived (Cooley 1902; Mead 1934). The set of shared group meanings attached to a particular identity constitute an identity standard that people can use as a reference point when attempting to present themselves to others.

When managing one identity at a time, cues for what constitutes successful enactment of an identity can be categorized with relative ease. However, when multiple identities intersect, they produce new meanings and expectations (Collins 1989; Crenshaw 1982) so that identity-verification requires a more complex set of guides for behavior. Some identities carry salience across multiple contexts and operate as master statuses for individuals attempting to participate in various meaningful communities (Sandoval 2000). While sexual identities may be the primary concern of white gay and lesbian activists, sexual identities may be complexly interwoven with or secondary to racial identities for queer people of color (QPOC) whose race is always visible (Alimahomed 2010; Lorde 1984; Anzaldúa 1983).

Whereas *person* identities represent an individual's internal sense of self as a unique person, *social* identities have to do with the ways that individuals see themselves as members of social categories such as race, gender, class, or sexuality. People can view themselves as belonging to a social category without identifying with the perceived ideas and values of other members. But when members of a group develop a common culture, shared values, and behavioral expectations through interactions with one another, they form a *group* identity. This group identity can derive from being part of an organization, a family, a religious group, or any other collective. When members formulate this shared identity around a common cause, such as shared grievances, and the connection of members' everyday experiences to larger social injustices, social movement scholars refer to this as a *collective* identity (Taylor and Whittier 1992; Rupp and Taylor 1999: 365). Sometimes collective identities derive from categories that are projected onto the group from the outside and are reclaimed by members as a source of empowerment and pride.

In this research, I examine the impact of identity-verification processes among queer students in a large California state university as they worked to facilitate an inclusive and diverse movement community. Since queerness critiques the establishment of specific identity definitions and meanings, I look to commonly cherished ideologies instead of discrete identities in order to distinguish the source of solidarity among queer students in this site. Building on Ghaziani's (2011) assertion that movement cultures can be identified through conflicts over values and investments, I focus my analysis on disharmony over QPOC spaces and anti-racist politics that took place among queer student leaders during the 2012–2013 school year. Taking seriously the social psychological assertion that people's perceptions of reality guide their actions and behaviors, I closely analyze students' interpretations of one another's actions, and their responses to the appraisals they believed they were receiving from their peers (Cooley 1902). To this end, I explicitly attended to the ideological commitments that students on this campus associated with queerness, and analyzed students' claims about racial inclusion in relation to these commitments. I identify the ways that students evaluated their peers and attempted to restore identity congruence for themselves in the face of contentious racial politics. I suggest that the racial ideologies embedded within the queer community at UCSB privileged whiteness and white experiences as "common sense" while rendering QPOC logics as counterintuitive to "what ought to be" (Bonilla-Silva 2010: 10).

Consolidated around students' shared sexual and gender marginalization, queer collective identity was often articulated to the exclusion of intersecting racial identities and, subsequently, through implicitly white ways of conceptualizing queerness. Though whiteness in the queer community was largely invisible, students who talked about race and established QPOC-only spaces marked whiteness as a meaningful category. This shift forced white students to grapple with new ideas that complicated their own self-views, often in undesirable ways. Recognizing white racial privilege made many white queer students hyperaware of their own racial identities in a community where they had sought reprieve from stigmas associated with queerness. In a community where shared marginalization was a source of solidarity, being identified as a potential oppressor was in direct conflict with group values. The moral identity conflict that white students experienced when confronted with their privileges thus led many of them to resist discussions about racism within the queer community. Based on my findings, I argue that because queer solidarity in this community was formed around shared marginalization, white students experienced dissonance when challenged to interrogate aspects of their identity that afforded them privilege. In attempts to restore their self views, these same students often repositioned themselves as the victims of racial discrimination and subsequently reinforced white-normative approaches to queer politics.

The Study

Between 2011 and 2013, I conducted over 100 hours of participant observation and 53 interviews with queer undergraduate students attending a university in California. I began announcing my research agenda at queer student meetings and events in 2011, and

I soon became well known through word of mouth as "the researcher" among them. For two years, I attended as many social and campus related events as possible, fielding invitations both in person and on Facebook to attend students' parties, workshops, and campus groups. I also made myself available to students who wanted to talk about their work within queer student spaces, experiences with family and friends, and coming out processes. My recruitment strategies yielded participants who were likely to be involved in queer community spaces, allowing me to focus on students' perceptions of the ways their peers handled racial inclusion and diversity within specifically queer group contexts. Students whom I interviewed were diverse across gender, sexuality, and race. Campus-wide statistics on students' transgender and sexual identities at the time were unavailable, but the racial diversity of my sample was roughly representative of the racial diversity of the campus as a whole.

Inclusive Queer Identities: Solidarity and Group Expectations

Students who identified as queer tended to do so as a result of their participation in queer student spaces and organizations. While only fourteen percent of the students I interviewed identified themselves solely as queer, most used queer as a social identity to convey that, "the LGBTQQIA community is one that I'm a part of" (Christina—White lesbian, 19, 1st year). Queer was used as "a blanket term . . . to insinuate that everyone is welcome" (Julia—biracial White/Hawaiian lesbian woman, 18, 1st year), and to acknowledge "all of these different identities that should be celebrated or included" (Om—White, queer genderqueer, 20 years old, 3rd year).

Elias (Chicana queer genderqueer, 21, 4th year) suggested that "[Queer] doesn't break down by individual identity . . . it, fortifies, if anything, the community . . . It's just like: 'We're queer.'" Thus, for most of the students I interviewed, queer reinforced solidarity among members of the campus community and allowed people with multiple identities and experiences to feel that they were a part of the group.

Students who did not initially identify as queer eventually learned to do so through feedback from their peers. Elena (Biracial Puerto Rican/Salvadorian

bisexual woman, 21, 4th year) described having been openly criticized for identifying as bisexual because "lesbian," "gay," or "bisexual" identities were perceived as reinforcing gender and sexual binaries. Subsequently, she now identified as queer and reported feeling "more solidarity" with others who "seem to be more positive when I say 'queer.'" Since queer was appraised more positively than other identities, every student that I interviewed said they identified as queer in community spaces, even if they privately identified as gay, lesbian, or bisexual. For example, David (Filipino gay man, 21, 4th year) told me he identified as gay among close friends but publicly used "queer as an umbrella term just for someone who's not heterosexual" because "some people are offended by smaller, more narrow labels."

As these accounts suggest, the very act of labeling oneself queer instead of using distinct sexual identities allowed students a degree of control over others' perceptions and appraisals of them. Students suggested that identifying as queer confirmed they were part of a cohesive community and increased their sense of solidarity with others. But, there was an implicit whiteness in the ways queer students celebrated queer solidarity. The construction of a cohesive queer group identity relied on assumptions about what queer students shared in common. Offense is taken when students used "more narrow labels," even in reference to themselves, extended beyond sexual identities to encompass sanctions against emphasizing any form of difference between group members. As a result, queer students of color, for whom racial experiences were often salient, were often dissuaded from talking about those experiences in queer spaces. In the following section, I discuss the ways that these expectations reflected distinctly white queer investments and how QPOC identities were managed in this context.

"Queer is just Something on Top": QPOC Identities in a (White) Queer Community

Most queer students of color told me that being "person of color" (POC) was not a salient identity before coming to college. But on a predominantly white campus, many of them adopted POC as an identity. "Back home in Hacienda Heights, I was the white kid because all my friends were Asian," Tee (biracial Taiwanese/White queer genderqueer, 22, 5th year) explained. "Now here in [university town], I'm the Asian kid because there are so many white people around. And I feel like I need to represent the Asians." In connection with their newfound racial consciousness, queer students of color who felt the queer community was permeated with white ideals also began to identify as "queer people of color" or "QPOC" in order to acknowledge their racial and sexual identities, while claiming solidarity with other queer students of color.

Identity politics are characterized by the transformation of stigmatized identities into sources of empowerment. It is therefore unsurprising that students involved in the queer community tended to emphasize the subordinated, or "marked," aspects of their identity. Marked identities are those that differ from unmarked (or unacknowledged) societal norms such as whiteness, masculinity, heterosexuality, or cisgender identity. While the identities and experiences of queer people of color were racially marked in this space, the identities and experiences of white queer students were simply coded as queer—unracialized in their whiteness. "For me it's been harder to recognize . . . because whiteness is unmarked" Max (White queer gender queer, 21, 4th year) explained, "whereas if you were a person of color, I think it would be more obvious because you're not the unmarked norm of society." Amaya (Chicana queer woman, 19, 2nd year) noted that the general absence of racial awareness in the queer community was likely because, "A lot of times, for white folks, being queer is the first time that they're different." On the other hand, she explained, "for us—being QPOC—being a person of color is the first thing that we're different about. And like, being queer is just something on top."

Because being queer was a source of "difference" for otherwise unmarked white students, queer identity was an extremely important and salient identity for most of the white queer students I interviewed. For many of them, it was the only significant identity that they spoke of at all. When they did invoke whiteness, white students often did so in order to compare their own experiences with the stereotypically negative experiences they imagined people of color were subjected to in communities of color. Many white students assumed that in communities of color "being queer was a huge 'no'" (Patrick—White

gay/homosexual man, 19, 2nd year), a belief that served to situate the queer campus community as a safe haven while simultaneously framing non-white racial categories as inherently antagonistic to queer identities.

The prevailing stereotype that communities of color are inherently homophobic also framed white queer students as potential "saviors" for queers of color who were perceived as outcasts from their presumably homophobic communities of origin. In reality, both queer students of color and white queer students described difficulties coming out to their families because of cultural, religious, or political ideologies. Moreover, queer students of color tended to say they experienced empowerment in spaces where both their racial and sexual identities were acknowledged. Dalton (Black queer man, 21, 4th year), who came out among queer Black and Latino friends in the Los Angeles ball culture, said that "they actually made me feel good about my sexuality and . . . what it meant to be Black and queer . . . It's kinda just like, oh my God I have a history! . . . There are people out there like me, who are accepting of sexuality."

Unfortunately, many white students failed to recognize how rendering queer and of color identities as irreconcilably in conflict with one another reproduced discourses that further marginalized queer students of color as other. When QPOC organizers set out to establish closed QPOC spaces, however, white queer students were forced to recognize, or mark, their own whiteness. As a result, many white queer students found themselves in the uncomfortable position of having to either reconsider or defend their self-views as solely marginalized individuals.

Marking White Queerness: Marginalized Identities in Crisis

Self-esteem is highly contextual: negative self-evaluations are heightened in settings where individuals perceive that others might evaluate them as being inferior. When individuals' expectations concerning culturally agreed upon identities are perceived as being unmet, negative emotions can result (Goodwin and Jasper 2006: 625). Social movement participants with discordant identity expectations often engage in a great deal of work around their collective identities in order to facilitate ongoing solidarity (Taylor 2000).

While queer students of color were often keenly aware of their racial identities in multiple spaces, race only became salient to white queer students when discussed in queer spaces. For some white queer students, acknowledging racism in the queer community made them think about their own whiteness for the first time. "I never thought really about being white," said Patrick (White homosexual/gay man, 19, 2nd year) "so it's very interesting coming here and people alerting myself [sic] of my whiteness." For white students, being informed of their whiteness often meant being told they had white privilege, which implicated them as beneficiaries of racism. As a result, whiteness was experienced by many white students as a "spoiled" racial identity in that it was no longer invisible and neutral, but visible and linked to the oppression of others.

Since shared marginalization was a source of solidarity among community members, being told they had white privilege posed a crisis of identity for some white students. This was especially true for students who wanted to ally with queer students of color but who were discouraged by the expectations associated with being a "good" ally. As Myers suggests,

> Ally activism is a natural means of verifying that one is indeed a 'good' person. Sometimes, though, the challenges of being an ally prevent self-verification. If activists do not get the confirmation or appreciation from beneficiaries that they expect, they may exit the activist environment and find another site for self-verification. The same can result simply because allies grow weary of the ongoing self-presentation and identity maintenance tasks. (2008: 177)

Attending QPOC events was the most visible method through which white queer students could demonstrate their moral identities to others, making it the preferred method for engaging in allyship. But white students' attempts to recuperate spoiled identities through participation in QPOC spaces often made matters worse. Several QPOC leaders were critical of "passive" forms of allyship that entailed showing up but did not include critical self-awareness. "A lot of times it's like people don't think that they're racist when they really are," Amaya (Chicana queer woman, 19, 2nd year) told me, adding that she took issue with people who identified as "radical queers" while maintaining distinct silence on matters of race. "I'm just like, 'well, you're a radical *white* queer.'"

Some white students described feeling overwhelmed by the expectations associated with active allyship. "I always have to remind myself that I am white, so I have to be careful what I say in certain aspects," Patrick (White homosexual/gay man, 19, 2nd year) said:

> I am white, so I have to come off as a certain kind of person. Or I am white, so I have to really make sure I don't talk too much, you know? . . . A lot of it is trial and error and just observation. . . . A lot of checking your privilege is if your privilege is not being checked then people will snap at you or kinda put you in line.

As Patrick suggested, eliciting feedback for being a good ally required continual awareness of one's own behaviors in relation to others, commonly referred to as "checking your privilege." This reflected a degree of informal social control, in that students were socialized through involvement in the group and learned what constituted appropriate and inappropriate behaviors. As a result, those who perceived the risk that someone would "put you in line" behaved in ways that they believed would minimize the threat of negative appraisals. But some students reported that having their privilege under constant surveillance was frustrating. While a number of white queer students expressed a strong desire to be anti-racist allies, they were often silent about racial inequalities so as not to take up too much space. As Om (White queer genderqueer, 20, 3rd year) explained, "I feel educated to talk about topics that deal with race, but on the other hand, I don't wanna overstep my bounds . . . dominate conversations about race . . . if there are people there that can talk about their actual experiences as a non-white person." While being cognizant of how they occupied space was a common form of allyship in this site, it also justified whites' evasiveness when it came to directly confronting racism and implicitly sanctioned expectations that students of color should be the ones to educate others.

The salience of students' individual racial identities played a significant role in how they perceived racial justice. For some white students, close friendships with anti-racist QPOC leaders increased the salience of their own racial identities while helping them to depersonalize critiques of white privilege. The feedback that one is a close friend and ally to queers of color likely played a role in this phenomenon. Luke (White queer/pansexual trans man, 20, 3rd year) had grown up in a primarily black neighborhood and was accustomed to being the only white person in his group of friends. "I have friends that very much hate white people. And, like, are very open about it. . . . They're like: 'I hate white people,'" he laughed. "And I'm standing right here, kind of like: 'Eh! Okay' (laughing). But I mean, I guess for me I just separate that more like, institutional whiteness as opposed to me as a white individual." Luke recognized that criticisms of "institutional whiteness" were not the same as being negatively appraised "as a white individual." He credited this to his social network, which made up mostly of QPOC leaders. "They talk to me about their views on it" he explained, "and so that impacts how I see it . . . and why I feel upset with white folks—because they're not acknowledging these feelings that are coming from queer people of color." By interpreting his friends' comments as critiques of "whiteness as an institution," rather than as critiques of whiteness as a social identity, Luke was thus able to acknowledge white privilege without experiencing them as threatening to his own view of himself.

One of the most significant impacts of racial discussions on white students was that it contradicted their self-views as wholly marginalized individuals. As McCall (2003) suggests, in addition to positive self-views, people identify themselves in opposition to "not me" identities, those identities that are counter to their own self-views. In this case, students not only identified as "marginalized" subjects but also as "not oppressors," and "not privileged" in contrast to positions they perceived that others accused them of occupying. Brown (1993) argues that one of the pitfalls of identity politics is the propensity for marginalized subjects to become so wedded to their pain and oppression that they can only understand themselves and their identities in the context of their own subjugation. This limits marginalized subjects' capacities for acknowledging where they themselves are complicit in perpetuating the marginalization

and subordination of others. To counter this effect, many white students emphasized their own marginalization, deploying various rhetorical strategies to accuse QPOC leaders of discriminating against them because they were white. This helped to mitigate the identity discordance they experienced, reinforcing both the positive "marginalized" identity and negative "not oppressor" identity in relation to other queer students.

While all members of the queer community emphasized the value of inclusion as a shared group standard, their interpretations of what inclusion looked like varied drastically. When queer people of color resisted closed spaces, it was symbolically significant because their identities added veracity to their claims. "I can't believe we're being exclusive, like, we're not letting other people into our meetings" Dan (Biracial Black/Puerto Rican queer man, 19, 1st year) exclaimed in reference to QPOC-only meetings. Reid (Filipino gay man, 19, 2nd year), who described privilege as a "hot topic" in the queer community told me: "I don't know if I like the whole idea of quantifying someone's privilege over another . . . I have friends who definitely are involved in the community . . . and have been pushed away because of their race or because they're male." Likewise, Sarah (Mexican-American gay woman, 21, 4th year) said that increased QPOC leadership had resulted in an inclination within organizations to exclude white people. While she said that privilege was a "legitimate issue," she added that she was "above it" and tried to "keep away" from those politics in attempts to "be as inclusive as I can be."

Students' continuous use of the term "inclusive" to couch their critiques of closed spaces and to restore their positive self-views suggests that inclusion was a highly valued quality in this community. Based on the assumption that queers should come together around shared oppression, students often interpreted QPOC-only spaces as a form of exclusion against their white peers. Critiques of closed spaces thus bolstered white queers' moral identities by framing them as the victims of QPOC hostility, while lowering the moral statuses of QPOC leaders for being "exclusionary." The prevailing sentiments that QPOC-only spaces were exclusive, and therefore antithetical to queer solidarity, provided strong incentives for queer students of color to distance themselves from QPOC leadership. "Coming to college we gain a lot of realization and insight into those experiences that we've had, and it can be angering," Peter (biracial Filipino/White gay man, 21, 4th year) told me. "I feel like this anger in the [QPOC] leadership is affecting the image of the community, and that negative image of the community is something that people kinda wanna dissociate from . . . I personally don't want to be a part of it anymore."

When nonwhite people's accounts are provided as evidence of their own exclusion from various communities, they are generally perceived as being overly subjective, anecdotal, or angry (Ahmed 2012; Bonilla-Silva 2010). This pattern of dismissal is indicative of how white normative frames permeate both academic and everyday discourses and influence how some (white) discourses are read as objective while others (nonwhite) are read as subjective (Bonilla-Silva 2010). While he supported and even desired QPOC-only spaces, Ross (Latino queer man, 19, 2nd year) qualified his interest with the caveat that he wasn't "against anyone being allowed to go," and that it was more about being able to "chill with my peeps" than about excluding others. While this statement may seem like a minor point, his assertion that he was not trying to be exclusive illustrated the power of group norms to influence individuals' behavior. Even while they knew that closed spaces were important, QPOC leaders were nonetheless beholden to group norms that demanded inclusion take priority over differences.

Queer Organizations as Self-Verification Opportunities

Individuals join social movement communities to act in concert with others as well as to convey particular information about themselves: that they are invested in social justice, have a moral commitment to equality, or that they are dedicated to certain ideologies common to the group. Acceptance within these communities signals to members that they are being perceived in ways that match their own self views. However, negative feedback can lead to identity discordance at which point individuals either work to recover their status (Goffman 1955), or leave in pursuit of more affirming associations.

Since inclusion was valued over the delineation of group boundaries in this community (Ghaziani

2011), adopting a queer identity entailed a willingness to include everyone. As Christina (White lesbian woman, 19, 1st year) explained: "The bigger the community gets, the more influential we are for queer issues on campus." But as movements become more broadly defined, conflicts are likely to arise over which investments to prioritize.

UCSB boasted a wide range of queer student organizations catering to a number of different identities and interests. There was a queer Asian Pacific Islander group (QAPI), a queer Chicanx/Latinx group (La Familia De Colores), a queer Black and African diaspora group (Black Quare), a queer Jewish group (Keshet), the Kinky Undergraduate Fetish Fellowship (KUFF), and a trans and genderqueer group called the Society for Accessible and Safe Spaces (SASS). While the umbrella organizations (Queer Student Union (QSU), Queer Commission (QComm), and Friendly Undergraduate Queers in it Together (FUQIT) were all reputed to have white agendas at the time of my research, students explained that in previous years these organizations had prioritized intersectional politics.

"I don't know if QSU addressed QPOC issues specifically," Elias (Chicana genderqueer, 21, 4th year) said of her first year on campus in 2008, "I think it was just an organization that was like, try'na welcome people. And the folks were queer people of color, so the folks who were getting involved were queer people of color." Amaya (Chicana queer woman, 19, 2nd year) suggested that the prevalence of students of color in queer leadership positions had likely resulted from their abilities to affirm racial identities in other contexts. "A lot of us, I think, tend to gravitate more towards queer spaces than we do to people of color spaces," she explained. "I can talk about being a person of color at home, but I can't talk about being queer at home. So I think, like, a lot of times in college we find those spaces—those queer spaces—a lot more."

By mid-2008, however, new discourses had begun to emerge in queer organization meetings. "I remember very clearly one officer meeting, and someone brought up that QSU meetings weren't the safest space for gay white men—like, they didn't feel comfortable" Elias recalled of a conversation she'd had with a fellow officer at that time. He described this as "a turning point" for him in terms of his racial awareness:

I wasn't as aware of things back then . . . But it's true, [white gay men] really just didn't come to events . . . [QPOC leaders] were addressing QPOC issues and being critical of white queer movements . . . I think the people who weren't feeling too comfortable were people who weren't willing to acknowledge their privilege. I think within those spaces people were forced to acknowledge their privilege. Or asked to. Or required.

Under the guidance of QPOC leaders, the agendas of queer umbrella organizations had taken for granted the significance of intersecting oppressions in the queer community. But when white gay men seeking validation of their marginalized sexual identities expressed discomfort at being "forced to acknowledge their privilege," new efforts at inclusion shifted to facilitate the safety of white queers. These efforts involved educating white queer students about racial inequality and explaining to them why racism was an important issue for queer students.

As a result, queer students of color began to feel tokenized and excluded within the mainstream queer community. They were often asked not to speak about race unless it was to educate white queer students, and even then they were asked to prioritize white people's feelings and to be "kind" in their framing of racial politics. Though queer umbrella organizations were described as having a white agenda, many students struggled to explain what this meant in concrete terms. "I understand that a black female queer is not going to have the same experience as a white male queer . . . but when they say that [organizations] have a 'white agenda,' I don't know what that means," Peter (biracial Filipino/White, gay man, 21, 4th year) told me. "I don't know if by like, 'white agenda' they mean that it just doesn't accommodate the experiences of people who don't identify as white? . . . I don't know."

Students' difficulties describing a "white agenda" pointed to a white hegemony in queer community spaces, such as the taken-for-granted and invisible ways in which whiteness permeated queer students' everyday interactions and methods for sustaining community on campus. Unlike the white gay men who were reportedly uncomfortable about racial discussions, several queer of color students said that

not talking about race got in the way of their feeling included in queer spaces. "Especially within QSU," Amaya (Chicana queer woman, 19, 2nd year) said, "it's supposed to be more of an umbrella organization. Sometimes when the issues of race are brought up people will be like, 'Well what does race have anything to do with it?'" Luke (White, queer/pansexual trans man, 20, 3rd year) expressed similar sentiments. "You go into a QSU meeting, and it's all white gay guys," he said, "That's just like, the way it is . . . you can just see that." It was in this context that queer students of color had begun to form alternative organizations where they could address their concurrent experiences of racial and sexual marginalization.

White Queer Politics and QPOC Organizations

In a community where race was treated as an outgroup concern, identifying as QPOC empowered queer students of color to articulate the specificities of their queer experiences while simultaneously marking their systematic exclusion from white queer spaces. But despite couching their strategies within socially valued social justice frameworks, QPOC leaders were held primarily accountable to ideologies of tolerance and inclusion. The consistent pattern was as follows: 1) Queer students of color in leadership positions would emphasize the need for racial awareness in the queer community; 2) White queer students and their friends would suggest that racial discussions detracted from queer solidarity; 3) In attempts to recover from accusations that were failing to align with queer group expectations, QPOC leaders would redirect their energies away from their own work and towards educating white queer students.

By 2009 queer students of color had established Black Quare (2008), De Colores (2008), and QAPI (Queer Asian Pacific Islanders) (2009). Many of them maintained leadership positions within QSU and QComm as well as in QPOC organizations, serving as "bridge leaders" (Robnett 1997) who connected other students of color with queer events and resources. QPOC students reported that these new affiliations allowed them to simultaneously validate their sexual and racial identities without fear of repercussions in the midst of an otherwise white-centric community. Ross (Latino queer man, 19, 2nd year) said he was most likely to attend De

Colores events than QSU or QComm events because his racial and sexual identities were both integral to his sense of self. Since being a queer woman of color (QWOC) came "with a different territory . . . and different experience," Elena (Latina bisexual/queer woman, 21, 4th year) shared that "having solidarity [with] other QWOC, and being able to talk about our experiences and stuff has been very empowering and . . . amazing." Dalton (Black queer man, 21, 4th year) said that since "a lot of people don't understand like what it means to be black, what it means to be queer, what it means to be low-income" organizations like Black Quare were "seriously imperative" to the continued growth of the community. Amaya (Chicana queer woman, 19, 2nd year) recalled her first experience in queer Chicanx spaces, which provided respite from the white queer norms:

> I think for a really long time I was used to seeing white queerness and what queerness meant in a white sphere. Um, and to see [queerness] kind of manifested in these QPOC, especially in Chicano spaces, and like, just to be able to speak Spanish, and talk queer stuff in Spanish was really cool . . . . Cause I do feel like sometimes I have to compromise certain identities in certain spaces.

Amaya's sentiment that she had to "compromise certain identities in certain spaces" suggested that in non-QPOC spaces, queer students of color believed they would be negatively appraised or scrutinized if they did not adhere to white norms. QPOC spaces thus offered queer students of color more resonant possibilities for celebrating what it meant to be *both* queer *and* of color.

But even in QPOC spaces, white norms still materialized. Through the lens of inclusion, white students like Patrick suggested they were taking the high road by attempting to participate in QPOC spaces. "I had this whole preconceived notion that if I go to QAPI they're going to be looking at me like, 'Why the hell is this white kid here?' he laughed. "But now I know better. Now I know you have to go in there with your own voice and educate them and be like, 'No, you know, it's a possibility we can all be friends, I promise.'" Because he perceived queer student of color leaders as being hostile towards white people, Peter expressed feeling justified in attending

QPOC spaces not in order to learn more but in order to "educate them" about how "we can all be friends." By framing queer students of color in need of educating, he thus recuperated his moral status as a white person who was helping to promote group sanctioned methods of inclusion in the community.

Because they experienced defensive responses to racial discussions, queer students of color were often reticent about discussing their racial identities and experiences around white students. These sentiments became increasingly salient when Dane, a white gay man, assumed a co-chair position in La Familia De Colores. The other co-chair, Emilia (Latina queer/lesbian woman, 19, 2nd year) reported that attendance had been low since Dane had taken an officer position. "It's been expressed to me recently that there are people that are interested but don't feel safe with him being in that space," she told me. In a separate interview Renee (biracial Mexican/Italian queer woman, 19, 2nd year) told me that she was not opposed to having allies in QPOC spaces but had stopped attending De Colores because "the person in charge of it was this white male . . . and it was just really weird to me . . . Like, the idea of a white male being a co-chair position of a Latino/Latina queer org kinda turned me off."

Although some students suggested that Dane was "just trying to be helpful" and was being unfairly discriminated against because he was white, stories abounded regarding Dane's unchecked racial privilege and blatant racism in QPOC spaces. One student was offended that Dane had co-opted the term "transracial"—used to describe cross-culturally adopted infants—to denote his belief that he was Latino at heart. Alternately he was rumored to have said that he was "Latino by association" because his boyfriend was Latino. On yet another occasion I observed for myself that he had posted a photo of himself on Facebook in which he was smiling as he donned a sombrero, a fake mustache, a poncho, and held a large gardening rake over the caption "Mi carrara future: un Mexicano" (My future career: a Mexican)—as though sombreros and manual labor are what make a person Mexican.

Dane was not the only white person who posed a concern for QPOC leaders, but his racial insensitivity, combined with his position as leader in a QPOC organization, had caused "A stir within QPOC leadership" so that the dialogue among QPOC leaders had shifted from how to facilitate open collaborations to the importance of QPOC-only spaces (Grace—Taiwanese-American bisexual woman, 21, 4th year) "How are you gonna say that, you know, the space is safe for [queer people of color] when people like you—like this white person—are oppressing them and they can't freely talk about how they *feel* because they feel awkward that the person in leadership is a white person?" she asked. "So I guess that's where the discussion about like open vs. closed spaces happened. And I mean—how's he gonna help hold a space he's not allowed to be in?"

To complicate matters, Keshet entered its inaugural year the first year that QPOC leaders were establishing QPOC-only spaces. Seizing the opportunity to collaborate with other marginalized students Derek, the co-chair for Keshet, requested that his organization be included in closed spaces on the basis of cultural oppression, despite the fact that most of their members were not QPOC identified (when asked about his own identity, Derek confirmed that he identified as QPOC on the basis of his Jewish heritage). To complicate issues further, Keshet was invested in familiarizing queer Jewish students with their Israeli homeland, a political stake that some QPOC leaders feared would alienate queer Palestinian students. Already under a great deal of pressure to justify their desire for closed spaces, QPOC leaders were exasperated by this latest development. "It's interesting that they're like, arguing for being a part of QPOC because they have oppression as well," Grace (Taiwanese-American bisexual woman, 21, 4th year) said, "which I dunno if that really makes sense. Um, cause they're *not* people of color. . . . So I mean they could say that they strongly ally *with* QPOC . . . but not that they *are,* or that they belong in it and that they need to be included."

QPOC-Only Spaces and the Specter of Exclusion

Stigmatized groups sometimes respond to disenfranchisement by creating "free spaces" where they can organize in spaces free from the judgment or suppression of outside groups. Queer students of color who felt pressured to educate white queer students about racial inequality often described QPOC-only spaces as the only way they could prioritize their own needs. "There comes a point where it's like I need to stop . . . where I'm not explaining myself, I'm just being" Renee (biracial Mexican/Italian queer woman, 19, 2nd year) explained, "and that only exists in closed spaces."

When they were asked to refrain from attending QPOC-only spaces, many white students interpreted those requests as negative, signaling that they were not good enough allies. "People don't always know which spaces are open," Om (White queer genderqueer, 20, 3rd year) told me. "Allies don't know when to show up . . . and then of course you have the closed spaces and then people feel excluded and left out and that 'I wasn't a good enough ally [so] you couldn't let me be there.'" Elena (Latina bisexual woman, 21, 4th year) suggested that feelings of rejection might limit white students' abilities to respect QPOC-only spaces:

> I guess people misinterpret what closed means and . . . maybe they have good intentions and really wanna learn about a community. . . . or be a[n] active ally. But I guess they feel almost like, rejected or—I dunno how they feel—but I guess they feel really angry that they can't go or . . . can't assert themselves in that space.

But QPOC leaders said white students who wanted to be included rarely attended open meetings, even when explicitly invited. "When we do have events that are open, the person—specifically the person that has made certain comments—doesn't go to Black Quare events," Kacy (Black Costa Rican gay/genderqueer 21, 4th year) explained. "It's like, 'You *did* get the invite," he laughed. "I made sure we invited *you!*"

Through inclusive ideologies and practices, white hegemony continued to function and was even strengthened through the methods used to implement inclusion in this site. By the end of the 2012–2013 academic year, QPOC leaders had begun to resign in the face of overwhelmingly negative feedback. Brooke (Taiwanese-American queer woman, 22, 4th year) told me that a fellow QPOC leader had recently described the state of the QPOC community as "dead air—like nothing's happening . . . [H]e was telling me 'It's almost like they won . . . Like, you feel it . . . we stopped. We stopped completely.'" That student leaders were eventually shut down despite their best efforts to revitalize the QPOC community suggests that the criticisms they were subjected to carried substantial weight with regards to their self-views in relation to queer group membership.

The findings from this study contribute to scholarly understanding of identity processes and conflicts within diverse social movement communities, providing an empirical case for how identity management processes can reinforce structural inequalities—even within communities focused on promoting social justice. While scholarship has attended to how white anti-racists manage their own identities among themselves, there has been little attention to the interactional effects of managing the privileges associated with whiteness in a racially and culturally diverse social movement community. Under an ever-expanding queer group identity that emphasizes inclusion, queers of color are often made invisible rather than explicitly excluded from queer spaces. Because their racial experiences tend to become submerged within broad, white-centric frameworks for what it means to be queer, queers of color often remain invisible until they challenge the norms that render their sexual and racial identities as irreconcilable. But when queers of color contest ideologies that reinforce queer solidarity at the expense of their full participation in queer spaces, they were often perceived as threatening the cohesion of the queer community.

Early in this research, it became clear that the ideology of "solidarity through inclusion" embedded in the queer group identity was implicit in shutting down discussions of race within queer spaces. Since identifying as queer suggested that one was dedicated to inclusive practices, the assertion that closed spaces were exclusionary towards whites fit nicely within the queer ideological standards for critiquing the queer identities of QPOC leaders.

The findings from this research suggest that inclusive ideologies, when deployed in diverse social movement communities, can actually reproduce inequalities from within. These inequalities are made visible through the processes by which members attempt to verify group membership in the face of multiple identities and investments. Significantly, identity-verification processes in this site reproduced white hegemonic norms that discounted the experiences of queer students of color. The same inclusive politics that protected white students from scrutiny fostered a climate that limited queer of color students' abilities to develop their own self-verifying opportunity structures through QPOC-only spaces. Inclusion ultimately functioned as a mechanism for maintaining the invisibility and hegemony of white queer norms.

REFERENCES

Ahmed, Sarah. 2012. "On Being Included: Racism and Diversity in Institutional Life." Durham: Duke University Press.

Alimahomed, Sabrina. 2010. "Thinking Outside the Rainbow: Women of Color Redefining Queer Politics and Identity." *Social Identities* 16: 151–168.

Anzaldúa, Gloria. 2007. *Borderlands/La Frontera: The New Mestiza, Third Edition*. San Francisco: Aunt Lute Books.

Bonilla-Silva, Eduardo. 2010. *Racism Without Racists,3rd Edition*. New York: Rowan & Littlefield.

Brown, Wendy. 1993. "Wounded Attachments." *Political Theory*, 21(3), 390–410.

Collins, Patricia Hill. 1993. "Toward a New Vision: Race, Class, and Gender as Categories of Analysis and Connection." *Race, Sex & Class* 1(1): 25–45

Cooley, Charles Horton. 1902. *Human Nature and the Social Order*. New York: Scribner's.

Crenshaw, Kimberlé Williams. 1991. "Mapping the Margins: Intersectionality, Identity Politics, and Violence Against Women of Color." *Stanford Law Review* 43(6): 1241–1299.

Gamson, William. 1992. "The Social Psychology of Collective Action." Pp. 53–76 in *Frontiers of Social Movement Theory*, edited by A. D. Morris and C. McClurg Mueller. New Haven: Yale University Press.

Ghaziani, Ami. 2011. "Post-Gay Collective Identity Construction." *Social Problems*, 58:99–125.

Goffman, Erving. 1955. "On face-work: an analysis of ritual elements in social interaction." *Psychiatry:*

Journal for the Study of Interpersonal Processes, 18, 213–231.

Goodwin, Jeff and James M. Jasper. 2006. "Emotions and Social Movements." Pp. 611–635 in *Handbook of the Sociology of Emotions*, edited by J. C. Stets and J. H. Turner. New York: Springer.

Lorde, A. 1984/2007. *Sister Outsider: Essays and Speeches*. Trumansburg, NY: The Crossing Press.

McCall, George J. 2003. "The Me and the Not-Me: Positive and Negative Poles of Identity." Pp. 11–25 in *Advances in Identity Theory and Research*, edited by P.J. Burke, T.J. Owens, R.T. Serpe and P.A. Thoits. New York: Plenum Publishers.

Mead, George Herbert. 1934. *Mind, Self and Society.* Chicago: Chicago University Press.

Misa, Cristina M. 2001. "Where Have All the Queer Students of Color Gone?: Negotiated Identity of Queer Chican/o Students" pp. 67–80 in *Troubling Intersections of Race and Sexuality: Queer Students of Color and Anti-Oppressive Education*, edited by K.K. Kumashiro. Lanham: Rowman and Littlefield Press.

Robnett, Belinda. 1997. *How Long? How Long? African-American Women in the Struggle for Civil Rights.* New York: Oxford University Press.

Rupp, Leila and Verta Taylor. 1999. "Forging Feminist Identity in an International Movement: A Collective Identity Approach to Twentieth-Century Feminism." *Signs* 24(2): 363–386.

Sandoval, Chela. 2000. *Methodology of the Oppressed.* Minneapolis: University of Minnesota Press.

Stets, Jan E. and Richard T. Serpe. 2013. "Identity Theory." Pp. 31–60 in *Handbook of Social Psychology, Second Edition*, edited by J. DeLamater and A. Ward. New York: Springer.

Stryker, Sheldon. 2000. "Identity Competition: Key to Differential Social Movement Participation?" Pp. 21–40 in *Self, Identity, and Social Movements.* edited by S. Stryker, T.J. Owens and R. White. Minneapolis: University of Minnesota Press.

Tajfel, Henri. 1981. *Human Groups and Social Categories: Studies in Social Psychology.* New York: Cambridge University Press.

Taylor, Verta. 2000. "Emotions and Identity in Women's Self-Help Movements." Pp. 271–299 in *Self, Identity and Social Movements.* Edited by S. Stryker, T. J. Owens, and R. W. White. Minneapolis: University of Minnesota Press.

Taylor, Verta and Nancy Whittier. 1992. "Collective Identity in Social Movement Communities: Lesbian Feminist Mobilization." Pp. 104–129 in *Frontiers in Social Movement Theory*, edited by A.D. Morris and C. McClurg Mueller. New Haven: Yale University Press.

THINKING ABOUT THE READING

How did inclusion ultimately become an instrument for reproducing white queer power, inequalities, and rendering QPOC invisible in this article? What kind of tensions did Miller observe among these queer student leaders? Should we automatically see closed spaces as exclusive? Is it acceptable for some groups to have closed spaces but not others? How do these dynamics impact alliances among groups who are committed to social justice work? What are some of the issues that identity based groups on your campus are working on? Have you observed similar tensions and conflict between these groups? If so, in what ways are they visible? How have these groups contributed to the architecture and climate of your campus space? Are there separate domains for them or do they share a space together?

CHAPTER 12

The Architecture of Inequality

Sex and Gender

I n addition to racial and class inequality, gender inequality—and the struggle against it—has been a fundamental part of the historical development of our national identity. Gender ideology has influenced the lives
and dreams of individual people, shaped popular culture, and created or maintained social institutions. Gender is a major criterion for the distribution of important economic, political, and educational resources in most
societies. Gender inequality is perpetuated by a dominant cultural ideology that devalues women on the basis
of presumed biological differences between men and women. This ideology overlooks the equally important
role of social forces in determining male and female behavior.

Gender inequality exists at the institutional level as well, in the law, in the family (in terms of such things
as the domestic division of labor), and in economics. Not only are social institutions sexist, in that women
are systematically segregated, exploited, and excluded, but they are also gendered. Institutions themselves are
structured along gender lines so that traits associated with success are usually stereotypically male characteristics: tough-mindedness, rationality, assertiveness, competitiveness, and so forth.

Women have made significant advances politically, economically, educationally, and socially over the past
decades. The traditional obstacles to advancement continue to fall. Women have entered the labor force in
unprecedented numbers. Yet despite their growing presence in the labor force and their entry into historically
male occupations, rarely do women work alongside men or perform the same tasks and functions.

Jobs within an occupation still tend to be divided into "men's work" and "women's work." Such gender
segregation has serious consequences for women in the form of blocked advancement and lower salaries. But
looking at gender segregation on the job as something that happens only to women gives us an incomplete
picture of the situation. It is just as important to examine what keeps men out of "female" jobs as it is to
examine what keeps women out of "male" jobs. The proportion of women in male jobs has increased over the
past several decades, but the proportion of men in female jobs has remained virtually unchanged. In "Still a
Man's World," Christine L. Williams looks at the experiences of male nurses, social workers, elementary school
teachers, and librarians. She finds that although these men do feel somewhat stigmatized by their nontraditional career choices, they still enjoy significant gender advantages.

However, gender advantages are not always easy to attain and opportunities are largely impacted by context and other components of identity. Young boys and men learn the socially approved masculine traits to
embody in their socialization process. And while the dominant image of masculinity is often the same for most
boys and men, many of them realize they do not have access to the resources necessary to attain this ideal.
In "Synthesized Masculinities: The Mechanics of Manhood Among Delinquent Boys," Victor Rios and Rachel
Sarabia explored the world of "synthesized masculinities" for young, urban boys and men of color. They find
that larger social forces and institutions often block these boys from attaining success and a respected place in
their communities. As a result, they used synthesized masculinities to gain power and respect but this process
creates a negative impact on those around them and ultimately, themselves.

Teenage sexuality holds a very ambivalent and tension-filled place in U.S. society. Various institutions—legal,
political, religious—have contributed to the construction of a topic that has a long history of debate. In "Parents'
Constructions of Teen Sexuality," Sinikka Elliott explores parents' subjective understanding of teenage sexuality for
their own teen children as well as other teens. She finds a distinctive sense of binary thinking among these parents
who see their own teens as sexually innocent and other teens as hypersexual predators. Social constructions of deviance with gender, racial, and class signifiers drive parental fears and lead to the reproduction of social inequalities.

Something to Consider as You Read

While reading these selections, think about the significance of gender as a social category. A child's gender is the single most important thing people want to know when it is born. "What is it?" is a commonly understood shorthand for "Is it a boy or a girl?" From the time children are born, they learn that certain behaviors, feelings, and expectations are associated with the gender category to which they have been assigned. Think about some of the behaviors associated with specific gender categories. Make a list of stereotypical gender expectations. Upon reflection, do these seem reasonable to you? What are some recollections you have about doing something that was considered inappropriate for your gender? Think about ways in which these stereotypical expectations affect people's perceptions, especially in settings such as school or jobs.

Still a Man's World

Men Who Do "Women's Work"

CHRISTINE L. WILLIAMS

(1995)

Gendered Jobs and Gendered Workers

A 1959 article in *Library Journal* entitled "The Male Librarian—An Anomaly?" begins this way:

> My friends keep trying to get me out of the library. . . .Library work is fine, they agree, but they smile and shake their heads benevolently and charitably, as if it were unnecessary to add that it is one of the dullest, most poorly paid, unrewarding, off-beat activities any man could be consigned to. If you have a heart condition, if you're physically handicapped in other ways, well, such a job is a blessing. And for women there's no question library work is fine; there are some wonderful women in libraries and we all ought to be thankful to them. But let's face it, no healthy man of normal intelligence should go into it.[1]

Male librarians still face this treatment today, as do other men who work in predominantly female occupations. In 1990, my local newspaper featured a story entitled "Men Still Avoiding Women's Work" that described my research on men in nursing, librarianship, teaching, and social work. Soon afterwards, a humor columnist for the same paper wrote a spoof on the story that he titled, "Most Men Avoid Women's Work Because It Is Usually So Boring."[2] The columnist poked fun at hairdressing, librarianship, nursing, and babysitting—in his view, all "lousy" jobs requiring low intelligence and a high tolerance for boredom. Evidently people still wonder why any "healthy man of normal intelligence" would willingly work in a "woman's occupation."

In fact, not very many men do work in these fields, although their numbers are growing. In 1990, over 500,000 men were employed in these four occupations, constituting approximately 6 percent of all registered nurses, 15 percent of all elementary school teachers, 17 percent of all librarians, and 32 percent of all social workers. These percentages have fluctuated in recent years: As Table 12.1 indicates, librarianship and social work have undergone slight declines in the proportions of men since 1975; teaching has remained somewhat stable; while nursing has experienced noticeable gains. The number of men in nursing actually doubled between 1980 and 1990; however, their overall proportional representation remains very low.

Very little is known about these men who "cross over" into these nontraditional occupations. While numerous books have been written about women entering male-dominated occupations, few have asked why men are underrepresented in traditionally female jobs.[3] The underlying assumption in most research on gender and work is that, given a free choice, both men and women would work in predominantly male occupations, as they are generally better paying and more prestigious than predominantly female occupations. The few men who willingly "cross over" must be, as the 1959 article suggests, "anomalies."

Popular culture reinforces the belief that these men are "anomalies." Men are rarely portrayed working in these occupations, and when they are, they are represented in extremely stereotypical ways. For example, in the 1990 movie *Kindergarten Cop,* muscle-man Arnold Schwarzenegger played a detective forced to work undercover as a kindergarten teacher; the otherwise competent Schwarzenegger was completely overwhelmed by the five-year-old children in his class. . . .

I challenge these stereotypes about men who do "women's work" through case studies of men in four predominantly female occupations: nursing, elementary school teaching, librarianship, and social work. I show that men maintain their masculinity in these occupations, despite the popular stereotypes. Moreover, male power and privilege is preserved and reproduced in these occupations through a complex interplay between gendered expectations embedded in organizations, and the gendered interests workers bring with them to their jobs. Each of these occupations is "still a man's world" even though mostly women work in them.

I selected these four professions as case studies of men who do "women's work" for a variety of reasons. First, because they are so strongly associated with women and femininity in our popular culture, these professions highlight and perhaps even exaggerate the barriers and advantages men face when entering predominantly female environments. Second, they each require extended periods of educational training and apprenticeship, requiring individuals in these occupations to be at

least somewhat committed to their work (unlike those employed in, say, clerical or domestic work). Therefore I thought they would be reflective about their decisions to join these "nontraditional" occupations, making them "acute observers" and, hence, ideal informants about the sort of social and psychological processes I am interested in describing.[4] Third, these occupations vary a great deal in the proportion of men working in them. Although my aim was not to engage in between-group comparisons, I believed that the proportions of men in a work setting would strongly influence the degree to which they felt accepted and satisfied with their jobs.[5]

I traveled across the United States conducting in-depth interviews with seventy-six men and twenty-three women who work in nursing, teaching, librarianship, and social work. Like the people employed in these professions generally, those in my sample were predominantly white (90 percent). Their ages ranged from twenty to sixty-six, and the average age was thirty-eight. I interviewed women as well as men to gauge their feelings and reactions to men's entry into "their" professions. Respondents were intentionally selected to represent a wide range of specialties and levels of education and experience. I interviewed students in professional schools, "front line" practitioners, administrators, and retirees, asking them about their motivations to enter these professions, their on-the-job experiences, and their opinions about men's status and prospects in these fields. . . .

Riding the Glass Escalator

Men earn more money than women in every occupation—even in predominantly female jobs (with the possible exceptions of fashion modeling and prostitution).[6] Table 12.2 shows that men outearn women in teaching, librarianship, and social work; their salaries in nursing are virtually identical. The ratios between women's and men's earnings in these occupations are higher than those found in the "male" professions, where women earn 74 to 90 percent of men's salaries. That there is a wage gap at all in predominantly female professions, however, attests to asymmetries in the workplace experiences of male and female tokens. These salary figures

Table 12.2   Median Weekly Earnings of Full-Time Professional Workers, by Sex, and Ratio of Female: Male Earnings, 1990

Occupation	Both	Men	Women	Ratio
Registered Nurses	608	616	608	.99
Elementary Teachers	519	575	513	.89
Librarians	489	—*	479	—
Social Workers	445	483	427	.88
Engineers	814	822	736	.90
Physicians	892	978	802	.82
College Teachers	747	808	620	.77
Lawyers	1,045	1,178	875	.74

Sources: U.S. Department of Labor, Bureau of Labor Statistics, Employment and Earnings 38, no. 1 (January 1991), table 56, p. 223.

*The Labor Department does not report income averages for base sample sizes consisting of fewer than 50,000 individuals.

indicate that the men who do "women's work" fare as well as, and often better than, the women who work in these fields. . . .

Hiring Decisions

Contrary to the experience of many women in the male-dominated professions, many of the men and women I spoke to indicated that there is a *preference* for hiring men in these four occupations. A Texas librarian at a junior high school said that his school district "would hire a male over a female":

[CW: Why do you think that is?]

Because there are so few, and the . . . ones that they do have, the library directors seem to really. . . think they're doing great jobs. I don't know, maybe they just feel they're being progressive or something, [but] I have had a real sense that they really appreciate having a male, particularly at the junior high. . . . As I said, when seven of us lost our jobs from the high schools and were redistributed, there were only four positions at junior high, and I got one of them. Three of the librarians,

some who had been here longer than I had with the school district, were put down in elementary school as librarians. And I definitely think that being male made a difference in my being moved to the junior high rather than an elementary school.

Many of the men perceived their token status as males in predominantly female occupations as an *advantage* in hiring and promotions. When I asked an Arizona teacher whether his specialty (elementary special education) was an unusual area for men compared to other areas within education, he said,

Much more so. I am extremely marketable in special education. That's not why I got into the field. But I am extremely marketable because I am a man.

. . . Sometimes the preference for men in these occupations is institutionalized. One man landed his first job in teaching before he earned the appropriate credential "because I was a wrestler and they wanted a wrestling coach." A female math teacher similarly told of her inability to find a full-time teaching position because the schools she applied to reserved the math jobs for people (presumably men) who could double as coaches. . . .

. . . Some men described being "tracked" into practice areas within their professions which were considered more legitimate for men. For example, one Texas man described how he was pushed into administration and planning in social work, even though "I'm not interested in writing policy; I'm much more interested in research and clinical stuff." A nurse who is interested in pursuing graduate study in family and child health in Boston said he was dissuaded from entering the program specialty in favor of a concentration in "adult nursing." And a kindergarten teacher described his difficulty finding a job in his specialty after graduation: "I was recruited immediately to start getting into a track to become an administrator. And it was men who recruited me. It was men that ran the system at that time, especially in Los Angeles."

This tracking may bar men from the most female-identified specialties within these professions. But men are effectively being "kicked upstairs" in the process. Those specialties considered more legitimate practice areas for men also tend to be the most prestigious, and better-paying specialties as well. For example, men in nursing are overrepresented in critical care and psychiatric specialties, which tend to be higher paying than the others.[7] The highest paying and most prestigious library types are the academic libraries (where men are 35 percent of librarians) and the special libraries which are typically associated with businesses or other private organizations (where men constitute 20 percent of librarians).[8]

A distinguished kindergarten teacher, who had been voted citywide "Teacher of the Year," described the informal pressures he faced to advance in his field. He told me that even though people were pleased to see him in the classroom, "there's been some encouragement to think about administration, and there's been some encouragement to think about teaching at the university level or something like that, or supervisory-type position."

The effect of this "tracking" is the opposite of that experienced by women in male-dominated occupations. Researchers have reported that many women encounter "glass ceilings" in their efforts to scale organizational and professional hierarchies. That is, they reach invisible barriers to promotion in their careers, caused mainly by the sexist attitudes

of men in the highest positions.[9] In contrast to this "glass ceiling," many of the men I interviewed seem to encounter a "glass escalator." Often, despite their intentions, they face invisible pressures to move up in their professions. Like being on a moving escalator, they have to work to stay in place. . . .

Supervisors and Colleagues: The Working Environment

. . . Respondents in this study were asked about their relationships with supervisors and female colleagues to ascertain whether men also experienced "poisoned" work environments when entering nontraditional occupations.

A major difference in the experience of men and women in nontraditional occupations is that men are far more likely to be supervised by a member of their own sex. In each of the four professions I studied, men are overrepresented in administrative and managerial capacities, or, as in the case of nursing, the organizational hierarchy is governed by men. For example, 15 percent of all elementary school teachers are men, but men make up over 80 percent of all elementary school principals and 96 percent of all public school superintendents and assistant superintendents.[10] Likewise, over 40 percent of all male social workers hold administrative or managerial positions, compared to 30 percent of all female social workers.[11] And 50 percent of male librarians hold administrative positions, compared to 30 percent of female librarians, and the majority of deans and directors of major university and public libraries are men.[12] Thus, unlike women who enter "male fields," the men in these professions often work under the direct supervision of other men.

Many of the men interviewed reported that they had good rapport with their male supervisors. It was not uncommon in education, for example, for the male principal to informally socialize with the male staff, as a Texas special education teacher describes:

> Occasionally I've had a principal who would regard me as "the other man on the campus" and "it's us against them," you know? I mean, nothing really that extreme, except that some male principals feel like there's nobody there to talk to except the other man. So I've been in that position.

These personal ties can have important consequences for men's careers. For example, one California nurse, whose performance was judged marginal by his nursing superiors, was transferred to the emergency room staff (a prestigious promotion) due to his personal friendship with the physician in charge. And a Massachusetts teacher acknowledged that his principal's personal interest in him landed him his current job:

[CW: You had mentioned that your principal had sort of spotted you at your previous job and had wanted to bring you here [to this school]. Do you think that has anything to do with the fact that you're a man, aside from your skills as a teacher?]

Yes, I would say in that particular case, that was part of it. . . . We have certain things in common, certain interests that really lined up.

[CW: Vis-à-vis teaching?]

Well, more extraneous things—running specifically, and music. And we just seemed to get along real well right off the bat. It is just kind of a guy thing; we just liked each other. . . .

Interviewees did not report many instances of male supervisors discriminating against them, or refusing to accept them because they were male. Indeed, these men were much more likely to report that their male bosses discriminated against the *females* in their professions. . . .

Of course, not all the men who work in these occupations are supervised by men. Many of the men interviewed who had female bosses also reported high levels of acceptance—although the level of intimacy they achieved with women did not seem as great as with other men. But in some cases, men reported feeling shut out from decision-making when the higher administration was constituted entirely by women. I asked this Arizona librarian whether men in the library profession were discriminated against in hiring because of their sex:

Professionally speaking, people go to considerable lengths to keep that kind of thing out of their [hiring] deliberations.

Personally, it is another matter. It's pretty common around here to talk about the "old girl network." This is one of the few libraries that I've had any intimate knowledge of which is actually controlled by women. . . . Most of the department heads and upper level administrators are women. And there's an "old girl network" that works just like the "old boy network," except that the important conferences take place in the women's room rather than on the golf course. But the political mechanism is the same, the exclusion of the other sex from decision-making is the same. The reasons are the same. It's somewhat discouraging. . . .

Although I did not interview many supervisors, I did include twenty-three women in my sample to ascertain their perspectives about the presence of men in their professions. All of the women I interviewed claimed to be supportive of their male colleagues, but some conveyed ambivalence. For example, a social work professor said she would like to see more men enter the social work profession, particularly in the clinical specialty (where they are underrepresented). She said she would favor affirmative action hiring guidelines for men in the profession, and yet, she resented the fact that her department hired "another white male" during a recent search. I confronted her about this apparent ambivalence:

[CW: I find it very interesting that, on the one hand, you sort of perceive this preference and perhaps even sexism with regard to how men are evaluated and how they achieve higher positions within the profession, yet, on the other hand, you would be encouraging of more men to enter the field. Is that contradictory to you, or. . . ?]

Yeah, it's contradictory. . . .

Men's reception by their female colleagues is thus somewhat mixed. It appears that women are generally eager to see men enter "their" occupations, and the women I interviewed claimed they were supportive of their male peers. Indeed, several men agreed with this social worker that their female colleagues had facilitated their careers in various ways (including college mentorship). At the same time, however, women often resent the apparent ease with which men seem to advance within these professions, sensing that men at the higher levels receive preferential treatment, and thus close off advancement opportunities for women.

But this ambivalence does not seem to translate into the "poisoned" work environment described by many women who work in male-dominated occupations. Among the male interviewees, there were no accounts of sexual harassment (indeed, one man claimed this was a disappointment to him!) However, women do treat their male colleagues differently on occasion. It is not uncommon in nursing, for example, for men to be called upon to help catheterize male patients, or to lift especially heavy patients. Some librarians also said that women asked them to lift and move heavy boxes of books because they were men. . . .

Another stereotype confronting men, in nursing and social work in particular, is the expectation that they are better able than women to handle aggressive individuals and diffuse violent situations. An Arizona social worker who was the first male caseworker in a rural district, described this preference for men:

They welcomed a man, particularly in child welfare. Sometimes you have to go into some tough parts of towns and cities, and they felt it was nice to have a man around to accompany them or be present when they were dealing with a difficult client. Or just doing things that males can do. I always felt very welcomed.

But this special treatment bothered some respondents: Getting assigned all the violent patients or discipline problems can make for difficult and unpleasant working conditions. Nurses, for example, described how they were called upon to subdue violent patients. A traveling psychiatric nurse I interviewed in Texas told how his female colleagues gave him "plenty of opportunities" to use his wrestling skills. . . .

But many men claimed that this differential treatment did not distress them. In fact, several said they liked being appreciated for the special traits and abilities (such as strength) they could contribute to their professions.

Furthermore, women's special treatment of men sometimes enhanced—rather than detracted from—the men's work environments. One Texas librarian said he felt "more comfortable working with women than men" because "I think it has something to do with control. Maybe it's that women will let me take control more than men will." Several men reported that their female colleagues often cast them into leadership roles. . . .

The interviews suggest that the working environment encountered by "nontraditional" male workers is quite unlike that faced by women who work in traditionally male fields. Because it is not uncommon for men in predominantly female professions to be supervised by other men, they tend to have closer rapport and more intimate social relationships with people in management. These ties can facilitate men's careers by smoothing the way for future promotions. Relationships with female supervisors were also described for the most part in positive terms, although in some cases, men perceived an "old girls" network in place that excluded them from decision-making. But in sharp contrast to the reports of women in nontraditional occupations, men in these fields did not complain of feeling discriminated against because they were men. If anything, they felt that being male was an asset that enhanced their career prospects.

Those men interviewed for this study also described congenial workplaces, and a very high level of acceptance from their female colleagues. The sentiment was echoed by women I spoke to who said that they were pleased to see more men enter "their" professions. Some women, however, did express resentment over the "fast-tracking" that their male colleagues seem to experience. But this ambivalence did not translate into a hostile work environment for men: Women generally included men in their informal social events and, in some ways, even facilitated men's careers. By casting men into leadership roles, presuming they were more knowledgeable and qualified, or relying on them to perform certain critical tasks, women unwittingly contributed to the "glass escalator effect" facing men who do "women's work."

Relationships with Clients

Workers in these service-oriented occupations come into frequent contact with the public during the course of their work day. Nurses treat patients; social workers usually have client caseloads; librarians serve patrons; and teachers are in constant contact with children, and often with parents as well.

Many of those interviewed claimed that the clients they served had different expectations of men and women in these occupations, and often treated them differently.

People react with surprise and often disbelief when they encounter a man in nursing, elementary school teaching, and, to a lesser extent, librarianship. (Usually people have no clear expectations about the sex of social workers.) The stereotypes men face are often negative. For example, according to this Massachusetts nurse, it is frequently assumed that male nurses are gay:

> Fortunately, I carry one thing with me that protects me from [the stereotype that male nurses are gay], and the one thing I carry with me is a wedding ring, and it makes a big difference. The perfect example was conversations before I was married. . . . [People would ask], "Oh, do you have a girl-friend?" Or you'd hear patients asking questions along that idea, and they were simply implying, "Why is this guy in nursing? Is it because he's gay and he's a pervert?" And I'm not associating the two by any means, but this is the thought process.

. . . It is not uncommon for both gay and straight men in these occupations to encounter people who believe that they are "gay 'til proven otherwise," as one nurse put it. In fact, there are many gay men employed in these occupations. But gender stereotypes are at least as responsible for this general belief as any "empirical" assessment of men's sexual lifestyles. To the degree that men in these professions are perceived as not "measuring up" to the supposedly more challenging occupational roles and standards demanded of "real" men, they are immediately suspected of being effeminate—"like women"—and thus, homosexual.

An equally prevalent sexual stereotype about men in these occupations is that they are potentially dangerous and abusive. Several men described special rules they followed to guard against the widespread presumption of sexual abuse. For example, nurses were sometimes required to have a female "chaperone" present when performing certain procedures or working with specific populations. This psychiatric nurse described a former workplace:

> I worked on a floor for the criminally insane. Pretty threatening work. So you have to have a certain number of females on the floor just to balance out. Because there were female patients on the floor too. And you didn't want to be accused of rape or any sex crimes.

Teachers and librarians described the steps they took to protect themselves from suspicions of sexual impropriety. A kindergarten teacher said:

> I know that I'm careful about how I respond to students. I'm careful in a number of ways—in my physical interaction with students. It's mainly to reassure parents. . . .For example, a little girl was very affectionate, very anxious to give me a hug. She'll just throw herself at me. I need to tell her very carefully: "Sonia, you need to tell me when you want to hug me." That way I can come down, crouch down. Because you don't want a child giving you a hug on your hip. You just don't want to do that. So I'm very careful about body position.

. . . Although negative stereotypes about men who do "women's work" can push men out of specific jobs, their effects can actually benefit men. Instead of being a source of negative discrimination, these prejudices can add to the "glass escalator effect" by pressuring men to move *out* of the most feminine-identified areas and *up* to those regarded as more legitimate for men.

The public's reactions to men working in these occupations, however, are by no means always negative. Several men and women reported that people often assume that men in these occupations are more competent than women, or that they bring special skills and expertise to their professional practice. For example, a female academic librarian told me that patrons usually address their questions to the male reference librarian when there is a choice between asking a male or a female. A male clinical social worker in private practice claimed that both men and women generally preferred male psychotherapists. And several male nurses told me that people often assume that they are physicians and direct their medical inquiries to them instead of to the female nurses.[13]

The presumption that men are more competent than women is another difference in the experience of token men and women. Women who work in nontraditional occupations are often suspected of being incompetent, unable to survive the pressures of "men's work." As a consequence, these women often report feeling compelled to prove themselves and, as the saying goes, "work twice as hard as men to be considered half as good." To the degree that men are assumed to be competent and in control, they may have to be twice as incompetent to be considered half as bad. One man claimed that "if you're a mediocre male teacher, you're considered a better teacher than if you're a female and a mediocre teacher. I think there's that prejudice there.". . .

There are different standards and assumptions about men's competence that follow them into nontraditional occupations. In contrast, women in both traditional and nontraditional occupations must contend with the presumption that they are neither competent nor qualified. . . .

The reasons that clients give for preferring or rejecting men reflect the complexity of our society's stereotypes about masculinity and femininity. Masculinity is often associated with competence and mastery, in contrast to femininity, which is often associated with instrumental incompetence. Because of these stereotypes, men are perceived as being stricter disciplinarians and stronger than women, and thus better able to handle violent or potentially violent situations. . . .

Conclusion

Both men and women who work in nontraditional occupations encounter discrimination, but the forms and the consequences of this discrimination are very different for the two groups. Unlike "nontraditional" women workers, most of the discrimination and prejudice facing men in the "female" professions comes from clients. For the most part, the men and women I interviewed believed that men are given fair—if not preferential—treatment in hiring and promotion decisions, are accepted by their supervisors and colleagues, and are well-integrated into the workplace subculture. Indeed, there seem to be subtle mechanisms in place that enhance men's positions in these professions—a phenomenon I refer to as a "glass escalator effect."

Men encounter their most "mixed" reception in their dealings with clients, who often react negatively to male nurses, teachers, and to a lesser extent, librarians. Many people assume that the men are sexually suspect if they are employed in these "feminine" occupations either because they do or they do not conform to stereotypical masculine characteristics.

Dealing with the stress of these negative stereotypes can be overwhelming, and it probably pushes some men out of these occupations.[14] The challenge facing the men who stay in these fields is to accentuate their positive contribution to what our society defines as essentially "women's work.". . .

NOTES

1. Allan Angoff, "The Male Librarian—An Anomaly?" *Library Journal*, February 15, 1959, p. 553.

2. *Austin-American Statesman*, January 16, 1990; response by John Kelso, January 18, 1990.

3. Some of the most important studies of women in male-dominated occupations are: Rosabeth Moss Kanter, *Men and Women of the Corporation* (New York: Basic Books, 1977); Susan Martin, *Breaking and Entering: Policewomen on Patrol* (Berkeley: University of California Press, 1980); Cynthia Fuchs Epstein, *Women in Law* (New York: Basic Books, 1981); Kay Deaux and Joseph Ullman, *Women of Steel* (New York: Praeger, 1983); Judith Hicks Stiehm, *Arms and the Enlisted Woman* (Philadelphia: Temple University Press, 1989);

Jerry Jacobs, *Revolving Doors: Sex Segregation and Women's Careers* (Stanford: Stanford University Press, 1989); Barbara Reskin and Patricia Roos, *Job Queues, Gender Queues: Explaining Women's Inroads into Male Occupations* (Philadelphia: Temple University Press, 1990).

Among the few books that do examine men's status in predominantly female occupations are Carol Tropp Schreiber, *Changing Places: Men and Women in Transitional Occupations* (Cambridge: MIT Press, 1979); Christine L. Williams, *Gender Differences at Work: Women and Men in Nontraditional Occupations* (Berkeley: University of California Press, 1989); and Christine L. Williams, ed., *Doing "Women's Work": Men in Nontraditional Occupations* (Newbury Park, CA: Sage, 1993).

4. In an influential essay on methodological principles, Herbert Blumer counseled sociologists to "sedulously seek participants in the sphere of life who are acute observers and who are well informed. One such person is worth a hundred others who are merely unobservant participants." See "The Methodological Position of Symbolic Interactionism," in *Symbolic Interactionism: Perspective and Method* (Berkeley: University of California Press, 1969), p. 41.

5. The overall proportions in the population do not necessarily represent the experiences of individuals in my sample. Some nurses, for example, worked in groups that were composed almost entirely of men, while some social workers had the experience of being the only man in their group. The overall statistics provide a general guide, but relying on them exclusively can distort the actual experiences of individuals in the workplace. The statistics available for research on occupational sex segregation are not specific enough to measure internal divisions among workers. Research that uses firm-level data finds a far greater degree of segregation than research that uses national data. See William T. Bielby and James N. Baron, "A Woman's Place Is with Other Women: Sex Segregation within Organizations," in *Sex Segregation in the Workplace: Trends, Explanations, Remedies,* ed. Barbara Reskin (Washington, D.C.: National Academy Press, 1984), pp. 27–55.

6. Catharine MacKinnon, *Feminism Unmodified* (Cambridge: Harvard University Press, 1987), pp. 24–25.

7. Howard S. Rowland, *The Nurse's Almanac,* 2d ed. (Rockville, MD: Aspen Systems Corp., 1984), p. 153; John W. Wright, *The American Almanac of Jobs and Salaries,* 2d ed. (New York: Avon, 1984), p. 639.

8. King Research, Inc., *Library Human Resources: A Study of Supply and Demand* (Chicago: American Library Association, 1983), p. 41.

9. See, for example, Sue J. M. Freeman, *Managing Lives: Corporate Women and Social Change* (Amherst: University of Massachusetts Press, 1990).

10. Patricia A. Schmuck, "Women School Employees in the United States," in *Women Educators: Employees of Schools in Western Countries* (Albany: State University of New York Press, 1987), p. 85; James W. Grimm and Robert N. Stern, "Sex Roles and Internal Labor Market Structures: The Female Semi-Professions," *Social Problems* 21(1974): 690–705.

11. David A. Hardcastle and Arthur J. Katz, *Employment and Unemployment in Social Work: A Study of NASW Members* (Washington, D.C.: NASW, 1979), p. 41; Reginald O. York, H. Carl Henley and Dorothy N. Gamble, "Sexual Discrimination in Social Work: Is It Salary or Advancement?" *Social Work* 32 (1987): 336–340; Grimm and Stern, "Sex Roles and Internal Labor Market Structures."

12. Leigh Estabrook, "Women's Work in the Library/Information Sector," in *My Troubles Are Going to Have Trouble with Me,* ed. Karen Brodkin Sacks and Dorothy Remy (New Brunswick, NJ: Rutgers University Press, 1984), p. 165.

13. Liliane Floge and D. M. Merrill found a similar phenomenon in their study of male nurses. See "Tokenism Reconsidered: Male Nurses and Female Physicians in a Hospital Setting," *Social Forces* 64 (1986): 931–932.

14. Jim Allan makes this argument in "Male Elementary Teachers: Experiences and Perspectives," in *Doing "Women's Work": Men in Nontraditional Occupations,* ed. Christine L. Williams (Newbury Park, CA: Sage Publications, 1993), pp. 113–127.

THINKING ABOUT THE READING

Compare the discrimination men experience in traditionally female occupations to that experienced by women in traditionally male occupations. What is the "glass escalator effect"? In what ways can the glass escalator actually be harmful to men? What do you suppose might happen to the structure of the American labor force if men did in fact begin to enter predominantly female occupations in the same proportion as women entering predominantly male occupations?

The Mechanics of Manhood among Delinquent Boys

VICTOR RIOS AND RACHEL SARABIA

(2016)

"I gotta be a man on the street, a man with the cops, a man at work, and a man with my son and my lady."
—20-year-old Jason

Masculinity is a central vehicle by which marginalized young men attempt to compensate for race and class subordination. Differing forms of masculinity (i.e. subordinate, street, working-class, dominant, and hyper-masculinity) are used by young men to access resources for maintaining dignity and respect, a process we refer to as "synthesized masculinities." The young men we studied synthesized masculinities to acquire social status and to contest various forms of subordination.[1] Like other forms of gender and sexuality practice, the masculinities they practiced were fluid, situated, and shifting. By uncovering the processes through which differing types of masculinity are utilised and identifying when these practices become perilous or productive in the lives of street life-oriented young men and the women in their lives, we can begin to explore ways to develop policy and programs that encourage productive forms of masculinity.

In addition to the morals and values of manhood the young men we studied learned from being on the streets, they found masculinity-making resources through the process of criminalization—specifically negative encounters with school discipline, police, juvenile hall, and probation officers. One consequence of criminalization and punitive social control for these boys was the development of a specific set of gendered practices that worked in ways that obstructed desistance, social relations, and social mobility. By analyzing the perceptions and actions of these young men, we uncover how masculinity produces and was produced by race, class, and gender subordination.

Jason's discussion of "being a man" represents how many of the boys in our studies developed *synthesized masculinities,* a strategic and situational display of various *masculinities.* As of 2011, Jason was a 20-year-ofd young man with a criminal record.[2] He considered himself an "active gang member." We compared self-reports with a law enforcement gang database, and police, probation officers, or media accounts often confirmed these young men's assessments of themselves as gang members.

Jason garnered respect among his "homies because he spent much of his teenage years on the streets, "putting in work" (fighting, dealing drugs, stealing, and "earning respect" within the gang). Jason explains,

> Well you have to earn respect, nobody gives it to you. If you give respect to the right people you get respect from the right people . . . you hold your ground you know, just throw down [fighting] . . . like some fool tries make you look like a bitch then you throw down [fight] and that's how they look at respect you know?

In our observations we saw Jason "calling shots" in the neighborhood, giving orders to other young men, and avoiding victimization and incarceration by having other young men look out for him when conflict arose. But we also noticed that Jason was one of the few active gang members *not* searched and harassed by police. One day, we were standing in front of Golden State Liquors (one of the local hangout spots) with a group of six boys. Four of the boys were drinking tall cans of Arizona Iced Tea. A Gang Task Force officer pulled up to the curb, stepped out of his vehicle, and asked the boys, "What are you drinking?" Most of the boys ignored him; two shrugged their shoulders. The officer signaled to one of the boys, Julio, to come closer to him. Julio ignored him. The officer warned him, "If you don't come here, I'm gonna' make you look really bad in front of your homies." Julio walked up and the officer grabbed him by the shirt, pressuring him to sit on the curb. He lifted him up by the shirt and emptied Julio's pockets. He used his radio to gather information about Julio (whether he had a record or outstanding warrants). The officer proceeded to check the others' records, except for Jason. Before driving off, the officer looked at Jason and said, "I'll see you at the bagel shop . . . tell these boys they need to get a job like you."

Jason believed that the police gave him more respect after he acquired a job: he worked at a local bagel shop where police officers who patrolled the neighborhood stopped. "Police know I am a hard worker. That's what they expect of me. I'm a family man and I don't commit crime anymore." Jason was one of six homies who held a steady job of a gang of more than 80 young men.

Jason's four-year-old son, Junior, was often on the streets with him, hanging out at the park and in front of the liquor store. Junior often wore a blue bandana in' his rear pocket, a sign representing the largest Mexican American prison and street organization in the country, the Mexican Mafia. Jason sometimes had Junior play fight with older kids in the neighborhood; he wanted Junior to learn to "be a man." This entailed introducing Junior to street life, teaching him how to protect himself and showing him how to demand respect from others.

Although Jason believed that gang parents and older gang members sometimes played a negative role in the life of their younger kin, he did not realize that his own actions of socializing his son to be a tough man might also play a role in this process: "It's like the families and older guys force them to join [the gang], it's like a circle that can offer protection . . . well not just force them, but also they don't have the money to buy this and that so people join gangs for protection and go rob and shit." Jason wanted his son to have a bright future and was an active father. We observed him pushing his son in a stroller throughout the neighborhood, feeding, and changing him. Yet, he did not as often consider how the actions and lessons of manhood performed around his boy might encourage Junior to join a gang in the future. To Jason, Junior was partaking in "child's play." He did not understand this as part of a larger process that might eventually help his son participate in the very behavior from which he seemed intent on protecting him.

Jason was also incredibly loyal and respectful to his girlfriend, even on the street, where other young women were called "bitches" and "hoes" by their partners or other boys and were physically or symbolically attacked. Jason developed the ability to balance various forms of masculinity, providing him diverse benefits: respect on the streets, acknowledgment from police, a "manly son," and a healthy romantic relationship. Jason's experience, however, was unique. Whereas all of the young men in this study adopted different forms of masculinity, Jason was one of the few young men who experienced positive outcomes associated with his masculine performances. A much more common outcome was being arrested for challenging and assaulting others and police officers. By understanding Jason's experience and comparing him with the other young men, we find concrete examples of the various practices of masculinity that exist in this contest.[3]

Like Jason, many of the other boys relied on masculinity to obtain respect and cope with race and class marginality. However, their approaches often also led to victimization, stigmatization, and incarceration. With limited access to traditional pathways to accomplish conventional masculinity, the boys *in* this study sought alternative forms of achieving manhood. And what we refer to as "synthesized masculinities" allowed these young men to creatively accomplish masculinity throughout their lives. *Synthesized* masculinities address marginalized men's adoption of various forms of masculinities to access resources they perceive themselves to be lacking and to compensate for other forms of domination.

Background

Masculinities studies inquire into the ways that "different ideologies about manhood develop, change, are combined, amended and contested" (Bederman 1995). Masculinity is dynamic, constructed and realized through interactions with others (Carrigan et al. 1985; Kimmel 2003). Kimmel (2003) argues that manhood is accomplished through cultural symbols and the subordination of women. Among American men, achieving masculinity is a "relentless test." Failure to embody, affirm, or accomplish masculinity is a "source of men's confusion and pain" (Kimmel 2003: 58). But masculinities are also "subject positions taken up by different men in different cultural contexts" (Cooper 2009, 685). Because masculinity is always intersecting with sexuality, race, and class, there exists a plurality of masculine identities, not one form of masculine identity (Carrigan et al. 1985; Connell 1987, 1995).

Connell theorized "hegemonic masculinity" is the dominant form of masculinity, articulating a hierarchy of masculinities and a constant struggle for dominance (Connell and Messerschmidt 2005). Hegemonic masculinity refers to the historical process by which privileged males have dominated women and other marginalized men. The ability to produce wealth, to become recognized by mainstream institutions, and to demonstrate oneself as a respectable patriarchal person are key features of hegemonic masculinity. Accomplishing hegemonic masculinity is almost impossible for less affluent men of color (e.g., Carter 2005; Lopez 2003; Rios 2009). Thus, working-class men, non-white men, or gay men may seek other avenues to achieve manhood. As Adams and Savran (2002) argue, all men attempt to accomplish masculinity. But not all men desire the same type of masculinity, nor do they accomplish it at the same rate or with the same level of ease. When marginalized men feel unable to accomplish it at the same forms of masculinity that privileged men acquire, they enact "compensatory masculinities" (e.g., Pyke 1996). Compensatory masculinities are attempts to compensate by participating in other—often deviant—behavior (drugs, alcohol, sexual carousing, etc.) to illustrate resistance toward, and independence from, institutions and existing power structures (Pyke 1996). Toughness, dominance, and the willingness to resort to violence to resolve interpersonal conflicts are central resources for men less able to acquire mainstream masculinity-making resources (e.g., Anderson 1999; Harris 2000; Messerschmidt 1993; Rios 2009).

Whereas some marginalized men enact compensatory forms of masculinity, however, others also embrace more conventional forms. These various types of masculinity are not fixed; rather they are "synthesized," depending heavily on context and type of interaction (i.e., peer-peer, male-female, youth-authority figure). Working-class masculinity, hyper-masculinity, and street masculinity are not only compensatory behaviors; they are also components of fluid processes that street life-oriented young men draw on as they navigate across social contexts.

We examine how gang members' interactions with authorities shape a localized masculinity. But beyond the dominant-subordinate dichotomy often discussed, we provide a new framework for understanding the accomplishment of masculinity among a group of marginalized young men by complicating notions of dominant and subordinate masculinities. We theorize this framework by arguing that a dominant-synthesized Interaction occurs between police and youth. These synthesized performances critically highlight the negotiation of street, working-class, dominant, and subordinate masculinity. Like Young, we argue that these men are more than just "violent-prone individuals who mindlessly lash out at the world with hostility and aggression" (2004: 5). They are complex individuals negotiating barriers and creatively exploring opportunities in the world around them. In this chapter, we examine how poor Latino youth weigh various possibilities for their futures and how they make conscious choices during this process.

Law Enforcement, Masculinity Enforcement

Ninety-two of the 96 young men we studied and 22 of 35 young women we interviewed held negative worldviews about police. They all reported at least one negative interaction where they felt victimized, either through physical or through verbal abuse. In our observations on the street—and later in four months of ride-alongs with police—most of the interactions between youth and police were neutral. Often police simply questioned or cited the boys and let them go. We also observed a handful of positive interactions and many negative interactions with police as well. We witnessed police verbally degrade hoys and use excessive force and illegal search tactics. The police, for many of the young men in this study, signified one of many obstacles in their development and ability to integrate into the community. In the minds of these young men, the police represented a set of social forces that grouped them into a criminal status, facilitating their criminalization by community members, potential employers, and in school.

They described the police as a force that consistently tested, challenged, and degraded their masculinity, often through instilling fear of violence and incarceration. Dreamy—a 17-year-old Latino male once arrested for being in possession of a marijuana pipe—represented the perceptions of the rest of the boys in the study:

Cops are a bunch of bullies . . . They are always trying to act like they are bigger men than you . . . They think we are organized crime or something, and, like, damn, we are just a bunch of homies that are kicking it . . . 1 mean I think when you see a cop you should feel safe and, you know, kind of make you feel good, but hell no, when 1 see a cop I gel fuckin' scared as hell, even if I'm not doing anything wrong I'm still fuckin' scared as hell!

Angel, an 18-year-old Latino male, arrested twice—once for being involved in a gang fight and a second time for violating probation—voiced similar interactions with police:

They always say some fucked up shit to me. Once they told me, "Why don't you come work with us puta bitch?" And sometimes they're like, "I promise I won't take you in if you do something for me [like giving them information on criminal activity]." Pinche pendejos [fucking idiots]. It's all a trick. They are always on top of us . . . They're like "look, 1 know you're on probation," and they just keep talking shit, talking shit. Cops don't respect us. They laugh at us. En serio [seriously], they're just like, oh look at these fools.

Joker, a 16-year-old young man who hung out with the gang, but did well in school and avoided fighting, drinking, and being out late at night, discussed an incident where an officer used physical force on him:

The cops do nothing but harass. I go to school. 1 try to stay out of trouble. Narc [undercover police] cars are always around. I see them driving back and forth on my way to school. Sometimes I think I'm just trippin. It's like, fuck, why are they stopping here? You always gotta look over your shoulder, dog, you know what I mean? They roll up and they just stare at us. One time, they tried to stop me. I ran. I bounced because it was curfew. I tried to hide. They found me. I tried to tell them 1 got a fucked up back, that I had been in a car accident. I told them

not to slam me. That fool grabbed me from the neck, mother fucker, started cussing me out, fool. He fuckin slams the shit out of me dog, fuckin scraped my face, my chin and shit. And I'in just like, fuck, 1 got all dizzy. He was just talking shit. He was mad. He was like, "Yeah I fucked, you up, mother fucker, keep running from me, you fuckin little bitch, I'm gonna fuckin bust you this time." They always mistreating us.

Even one of the young women, Jessica, reported feeling treated like one of the guys by police as a punishment for hanging out with them:

They told me that if 1 was gonna' hang out with them [the guys] they were gonna' search me and disrespect me like how they do them. So they started to frisk me and feel up on me [she; motions her right hand under her left armpit, above her ribcage, and around her breast] . . . then one day the cops tackled me down because they thought I was going to run after a fight that I had with some girl . . . I messed up my arm and had to go to the hospital because of the tackle.

Although we do not have consistent data to confirm that this is a process that unfolds for all the young women that hang out with gang-associated boys, we believe that police utilized masculinity not only to socialize and discipline young boys but also to symbolically relegate women to the domestic sphere. When on the street with the boys, women in our study reported being treated like the boys. This might explain some of the expansion in incarceration rates for girls and young women during the era of mass incarceration.[4]

During our fieldwork, 4 of the boys in this study were arrested one afternoon in front of a community clinic. Three police officers were called to disperse a crowd of 20 suspected gang members loitering outside. Five additional officers were called into provide backup. The local newspaper reported the incident in this way:

One individual started taking pictures of the officers with his cell phone; a police officer noticed, and started taking pictures of the suspected gang members. One of the individuals, Oscar, 19, tried to take the officer's cell phone away and was arrested for attempted robbery, resisting an officer, battery on a police officer, and participation in a criminal street gang. Four other boys were arrested for petty infractions. (Fernandez 2009)

We interviewed Oscar after he spent four months in jail for this incident. He told us he was tired of being photographed by police. He responded by taking a picture of the officers. "Why can't we take pictures of them, but they can take them of us? It's a bunch of bullshit. They just slap a bunch of shit on us. They always try to put us in the wrong and make it look they are the innocent ones, the good guys." The officers responded by telling him to put his phone away. Oscar claimed that he was attempting to cover his face so that the officer could not take a picture of him. The officer, according to Oscar, pretended to have been assaulted and this led to his arrest.

Police consistently challenged and mocked the boys for their way of talking, their dress, with whom they chose to hang out, and for not displaying conventional forms of masculinity. This process made many of the young men feel as though they were engaged in a battle for manhood with police. The camera incident demonstrates the sorts of masculinity battles waged between officers and the boys. Police demanded respect, and when it was not given, they reacted quickly and harshly. According to the boys, police "create bogus charges": attempted robbery, resisting an officer, battery of a police officer, or participation in a criminal street gang.

On another occasion, we witnessed a negative police encounter with three of the boys in this study:

A Sheriff's car approached with two officers. Jessie was just about to light a cigarette. He put it in his mouth and then out again because his lighter did not work. The driver from the Sheriff's car yells from the car to Jessie asking him how old he is. Jessie tells him his age, "Nineteen." The cop yells at him to wait on the corner. We all stopped . . . The officer asked, "Why are you out and about?" He approached Jessie from behind, pulled his hands behind his back and patted him down, emptying his pockets. They then started telling him to show them any tattoos he had, making him lift his shirt in front of several folks eating on the patio of a nearby restaurant . . . 'The officers started asking the boys if they were on probation and put Jessie's name into the car's computer. They found a pocketknife in Jessie's pocket and asked him about it while the Sheriff was checking the name . . . The sheriff came back after running Jessie's name, walked him over to the curb and told him to sit down . . . *By this* time two other police cars pulled up. Juan [a friend of Jessie's] told the officer, "We're trying to do good things, we come to school."]The officer pulled his hands behind him and patted him down like he did Jessie, lifted his shirt, checked for tattoos, asked if he's on probation, sat him down on the curb, then got in his face, and yelled, "I'm not going to take any shit from a 16-year-old punk."

(from author's field notes)

The group was allegedly stopped because one of the boys "looked suspicious" and underage to be smoking. But the situation quickly escalated to all of them being questioned, searched, and put on display as criminals. Scenes like this are one way officers "policed" this area—by reaffirming their authority and masculinity over these boys. The officers asserted dominance by raising their voices and displaying immediate distrust, suspicion, and disrespect toward the youth. The officers also tried to aggravate the boys so they would respond with anger, giving the cops a reason to take them in. They did this by making threats to send Jessie to county jail if the rest of the group did not obey: "Tell those little punks we're gonna' take you to county if they don't man up and listen to our commands."

Policing is a male-dominated and masculine field (Cooper 2009; Dodsworth 2007; Harris 2000). Machismo has also been found to be a central element of police culture (Herbert 2006). Many of the police-youth encounters we witnessed involved masculinity challenges. Police officers were "doing" gender through their performances of dominance (e.g., Martin 1999). Many police-youth interactions involved officers symbolically claiming to be the "real" men by strategically emasculating boys and young men.

Consistent with Angela Harris's (2000) findings, police in our study responded to perceived attacks on their masculine self-identity with the use of violence or threats of violence. When they felt their honor or dignity was being disrespected, they restored it by using or threatening violence. Police officers got "macho" with youth, staging masculinity contests with male youth—contests ripe with meaning in these young men's lives. Youth often interpreted such actions by police as attempts to get them mad, get them to talk back, or do something that could later be used to justify arrest (Gau and Brunson 2010; Harris 2000; Sollund 2006).

The boys recognized police officers as enforcers of masculinity. They viewed police as acting more out of a desire to preserve their authority over youth, prove their manhood, and maintain dominant status on the streets than to enforce the law (Cooper 2009; Hahn 1971). They described officers as power-hungry individuals who had something to prove to the boys: that they were "manlier" than the gang. Criticizing police for overcompensating was an integral part of the boys' performances masculinity. They believed that they were the real men and that the police were weak individuals hiding behind badges and guns. Simultaneously, police attempted to reinforce a particular form of working-class masculinity—a form less available in this context and to these young men than police often seemed to understand. They pushed the idea that "a real man gets a job and provides for his family." Yet these boys' age and education put them in the company of a 40 percent unemployment rate. Jobs might exist; but these boys are not among those getting hired.

Most of the officers in their community are white. The boys saw them as "rich" men with "good jobs" even as they despised some of the officers. When officers gave advice to the boys, they often relied on their profession. "Right now you're just on probation for small stuff. You can still clean your record and become a cop one day," one police officer told a group of four of the boys, as they loitered in front of the liquor store. Officers consistently made references to being "a real man when giving boys advice. "Be a real man, get a job, leave the homies, go to school, and provide for your family," an officer told one boy as he stopped and searched him.

All of the boys understood what it took to "become a man," even if they had yet to acquire the resources to do so themselves. The following

descriptions of normative ideals are representative of all of the interviewees' perceptions:

A man is someone that can support their family.,. even with the struggle . . . having a job . . . putting support . . . having food on the table, a roof over their head, and clothes on their backs . . . that's a man. (Raul, 14)

Knowing how to work makes you a man. Being responsible. A man is somebody that, you know, doesn't back down. To be a man, you gotta be down for whatever. You stick around, or stick to what you say you're gonna do. You don't learn this stuff overnight though; becoming a man is a process. (Tito, 17)

I would want to be successful you know, and come back and help people that need it the most, like people that were or kids that went through the same shit that I went through or something you know, just trying to give back to the community . . . I mean hopefully college can help me figure that out you know cause . . . a lot of people don't even know what they want to do you know, and when they go to college that's where they figure shit out. So that's what Im'a try to do. (Jose, 16)

The boys believed that gang life was just *a* stage in their lives, that one day they might be able to transition. They had to wait to acquire the resources to become men capable of providing for their families by going to college or working. Although this kind of masculinity—working hard, finishing school, and providing for families—can place boys on a better trajectory and help them resist crime, the boys in this study encountered various obstacles on this path. These included a lack of entry-level jobs in Riverland, a dearth of community programs to help them transition back into school, and zero-tolerance school policies that led many to expulsion for gang activity. Many of the boys viewed school as a place where they were criminalized, not cared for. Twelve of the boys told us that they decided to drop out because they fell they did not belong, that schools did not care for them. Thirty-two [of the 57] had dropped out of school or been kicked out. On the streets, police gang units stopped, "tagged" (entered into a gang database), harassed, and arrested the boys, sometimes for something as simple as walking to the store to buy groceries.

Although the boys attempted to get jobs or complete school, their avenues for opportunities often turned out to be dead ends. They were not able to accomplish the manhood that mainstream society expected from them, and this realization was associated with stress, anger, and pain. As a result, they adopted and forged alternative forms of manhood—forms that often stressed being tough, gaining status and respect, and—like the police—demonstrating dominance over others.

Synthesized-Masculinity

Cooper (2009) argues that men gain masculine esteem and status from other men's acknowledgment of their masculinity. With limited access to traditional avenues used to accomplish masculinity, the Latino boys in this study negotiated alternative masculinities. In police-youth interactions in particular, these young men forged what we refer to as *synthesized masculinities*. Youths' interactions with police encouraged the performance of a masculinity that involved aspects of dominant, street, working-class, and subordinate masculinity, and the boys and young men in our study were adept at navigating this complicated enactment. They practiced deviant behavior (chest bumping police officers, attempting to block police from taking pictures, protesting their potential arrests, etc.) in a response to police officers' mistreatment, symbolically claiming to not be dominated, controlled, and harassed without a fight. They defied authority to gain masculine status and esteem.

Officers used toughness, dominance, disrespect, humiliation, and aggressive force to try to control boys upon arrest—a tactic that often proved counterproductive. Youth lost respect for cops with every negative interaction and perceived wrongful conviction. Those who encountered negative police interactions reported feeling wrongfully treated through the court process; those who experienced positive or neutral interactions with police reported feeling that the courts and the rest of the justice system treated them fairly throughout the process, despite similar "juvi" or jail sentences. Although the boys aspired to acquire culturally dominant forms of masculinity,

they embraced forms of synthesized masculinity. Fifteen-year-old Elias exemplifies this process. He defined being a man as follows:

> A real man is a leader, not a follower. He has backbone. He stands up for himself. He is able to protect himself. He doesn't go out and look for trouble just because. He lives for his own satisfaction and no one else's. He works when he can and when he can't find work he finds a way to make it work.

This redefinition of masculinity allowed the boys to see masculinity as within reach, as achievable. They could be leaders, they could stand up for themselves, and they could be themselves—guys who appreciated a street orientation. This synthesized masculinity allowed them to fill in the gaps—to access resources and mitigate race and class privileges/markers they perceived themselves to be lacking. The performances of synthesized masculinities differed by boy, unique to each of their situations and perceived strengths and weaknesses.

James Messerschmidt argues that men are constantly faced with "masculinity challenges," a process that can lead to crime when other "masculine resources" are in short supply:

> Masculinity challenges arise from interactional threats and insults from peers, teachers, parents, and from situationally defined masculine expectations that are not achievable . . . Masculinity challenges may motivate social action towards masculine resources (e.g., bullying, fighting) that correct the subordinating social situation, and various forms of crime can be the result. (2000: 13)

Crime is one available resource men rely on to communicate their manhood. Indeed, criminal activity constitutes a gendered practice. As such, crime is more likely when men need to prove themselves and when they are held accountable to a strict set of expectations. Furthermore, West and Zimmerman (1987) contend that accountability—the gendered actions that people develop in response to what they perceive others will expect of them—is encountered in interactions between individuals and institutions. Conceptualizing gender as structured by interactions with specific types of institutions enables an exploration of how the criminal justice system shapes the development of specific forms of masculinity.

The young men in both studies faced constant interrogation of and challenges to their manhood on the streets. Questions such as "Is he really a homey?" and "Is he really a man?" if answered in the negative, resulted in stigmatization or victimization. At the core of growing up in their community, the boys felt a constant necessity to prove their manhood. Institutions, also, often challenged their masculinity in the process of attempting to "reform" young men. Examples included being told that they were not "man enough" for having committed crime or that being in the system meant that they risked being emasculated. The boys responded to gendered institutional practices by synthesizing new gendered practices, identities, and models of masculinity.

There are a variety of underacknowledged collateral consequences of the criminalization and punitive social control of inner-city boys: constant surveillance and stigma imposed by schools, community centers, and families; permanent criminal credentials that exclude black and Latino males from the labor market; and the boys' mistrust and resentment toward police and the rest of the criminal justice system (see Rios 2011). In this study, we found that an additional consequence of enhanced policing, surveillance, and punitive treatment of marginalized boys is the development of a specific set of gendered practices, heavily influenced by interactions with police, detention facilities, and probation officers.

Encounters with white female teachers often created an "angry male of color" attacking a "white damsel in distress" phenomenon. Encounters with police were often a contest between who was a "bigger man," and probation officers interacted in either a motherly or a heavy-handed way. These patterns of punishment provided a constant backdrop against which these young men's understandings and performances of masculinity were formed.

Although race determines how a young person is treated in the criminal justice system, masculinity plays a role in how they desist or recidivate as they pass through that system. One of the outcomes of pervasive criminal justice contact for young black and Latino men is the production of a hypermasculinity. Harris (2000) defines hypermasculinity as an "exaggerated exhibition of physical strength and personal aggression," which is often responding to a gender threat "expressed through physical and sexual domination of others." Although not knowingly, we found that the criminal justice system encourages expressions of hypermasculinity by threatening and misunderstanding these young men's masculinity. This leads many boys and young men to rely on violence, crime, and a school and criminal justice counterculture. Detrimental forms of masculinity are partly developed through youths' interaction with police, juvenile hall, and probation officers. Thus, although we traditionally think of officers as *policing* these forms of behavior, we came to find that police often played a crucial role in producing these forms of behavior and their attendant meaning and significance.

Masculinity, Criminalization, and Punitive Social Control

Each of us shapes our behavior according to gendered expectations, and each of us is subject to a system of accountability that is gendered, raced, and classed (West and Fenstermaker 1995). The boys in this study were inculcated into a set of hypermasculine expectations that often encouraged behavior that conflicted with dominant institutions. On the street they would take on a tough persona. They described these acts as a tool for survival "You can't act weak, or you'll get taken out," Jose explained. "I can't act like a bitch . . . 'cause if I do, suckas will try to swoop up on me and take me out. So I gotta handle my business. Even if I am trying to change, I can't look weak," Tyrell explained.

In front of probation officers and police, they perceived two choices: engage in a masculinity battle or submit to their authority. The boys in our study understood this as a lose-lose predicament. If they acted tough, officers might hesitate to harass them. But, they might get arrested. If they acted passively, they risked humiliation and often took out this frustration on themselves or others through drug use or violence. Many of the boys had a "default" manhood they knew best, most involving masculine resources that had purchase on the streets.

To be assigned "real man" stains by relevant others and institutions, men must pass multiple litmus tests among peers, family, and these institutions. Contemporary urban ethnographers emphasize this point. For example, Elijah Anderson (1999) describes the "young male syndrome" as the perceived, expected, and often necessary pressure to perform a tough, violent, and deviant manhood to receive and maintain respect. Sandra Pyke (1996) argues that whereas wealthy men can prove masculinity through an ability to make money and consume products, poor young men rely on toughness, violence, and survival as a means of proving masculinity. Nikki Jones (2010) has even found that lower-income young women use masculinity as a resource for protecting themselves and gaining respect. Jones finds young women in a double bind: they have to act tough on the streets while simultaneously meeting feminine gendered expectations (Jones 2009). Although they are not fighting for masculinity per se, they perceive masculinity as a primary vehicle to maintain respect. Kenya—a 19-year-old Latina previously in a gang but now trying to help some of the boys in this study—explains the toughness exhibited by the few young women visible on the streets:

V.R.: You work with these boys; they are disrespectful of women at times. How do you deal with it?

Kenya: I . . . had an understanding of feminism before I had a term for it . . . You see young women in urban areas fighting for it in different ways, without the terms to define it, but it's still the same thing, fighting I had to fight dudes. . . . I've fought fella dudes . . .That's what made hella people scared of me. And, even though he won physically, the story got around that he was a punk for fighting a girl. One time, my friend got raped by this dude. So we beat the shit out of him and took a baseball bat with nails in it to his ass, taking justice into our own hands. I mean, not justice, 'cause beating his ass is not enough. . . . it sent a message out there that . . . that shit, it's just not acceptable.

Observing Kenya and other street-oriented young women interact with the boys made us realize that masculinity does not always correspond to biological sex; instead, it is a resource used by young people in specific settings to accomplish specific goals. Kenya took on the most masculine of boys to gain respect. Although we did not formally observe young women, we did find that masculinity was used by young women in similar ways: to survive and to resist forms of criminalization they encountered.

Toughness, dominance, and the willingness to resort to violence to resolve interpersonal conflicts are central characteristics of masculine identity. Kimmel and Mahler argue that most violent youths are not psychopaths but, rather, "overconformists to a particular normative construction of masculinity" (2003: 1440). We discovered that mainstream institutions and the criminal justice system expect a masculinity emphasizing hard work, law abidance, and an acceptance of subordinate social positions. Indeed, many of the boys were familiar with this form of masculinity from growing up with fathers or father figures who worked hard, respected authority, etc. Some of them attempted to embrace this masculinity as a means to reform. More commonly, however, when they tried to live up to this form of masculinity, to transform their lives, they found a dearth of viable jobs to "prove" they were hard workers. As Kimmel (1996) argues, an underacknowledged consequence of deindustrialization is that "proving" masculinity through success at work has become less possible for larger numbers of men.

The boys realized that embracing this "positive" working-class masculinity did not provide resources to survive on the streets, a place to which they constantly returned. In attempts to manage young men's criminality, institutions develop practices heavily influenced by masculinity. In response, the boys in this study became socialized to specific meanings of manhood at odds with those of dominant institutions of control. Gendered interactions with the criminal justice system placed the boys in a double bind. Most bought into the system's ideals of reform by attempting to become "hard-working men." However, frustration with the lack of viable employment and guidance opportunities led them right back to the seductive arms of hypermasculinity. The stories and actions of the young men in this study provide insight into how this double bind is partially generated by the criminal justice system.

Police officers are themselves embedded in a logic that embraces masculinity. For example, criminologists Prokos and Padavic (2002) found that academies train officers to practice a rogue and hostile masculinity. This training reverberates in the inner city. As Angela Harris explains, "Police officers in poor minority neighborhoods may come to see themselves as law enforcers in a community of savages, as outposts of the law in a jungle" (2002: 442). In this context, punitive police treatment of men of color is not only racial violence; it is gender violence. Young people in Oakland encountered these forms of violence regularly from police on the street, at school, at community centers, and in front of their apartment complexes. The boys often became victims of police officers attempting to uphold the law. Many officers sought to "teach" the young men by feminizing and emasculating them: they manhandled them, called them "little bitches," humiliated them in front of female peers, challenged them to fights, and more.

> Castro: Dude [the officer] was pointing his gun. "i give up, give up." He hit him [Castro's friend] with a stick and broke his arm, and this other fool had his knee on my neck. All 'cause we were smoking some weed . . . They beat us down and call us "little bitches."
>
> Rapa: They kick your ass, pistol whip you, even try to kill you. . . . Them bustas [cowards] just trying to prove themselves, you feel me? They trying to prove they are more manly than us, but if they didn't have guns or jails, they would end up being the bitches.

Gendered police interactions begin at an early age. The boys consistently reported early interactions with disciplinary authorities at school and by police. They learned that "being a man" meant not relying on the police, learning to take a beating from police, and—sometimes—desisting from committing crime and resisting the seductions of street life.

At the epicenter of the police-youth interactions we observed was a form of hypermasculinity—taught and learned, challenged and embraced. In attempting to teach the young men to be law-abiding citizens, officers helped support toughness, violence, and hypermasculinity in the boys. These forms of masculinity play a role in influencing young men toward violence and crime.

Conclusion

As adolescent boys practiced masculinity on the street, the institutions of control that "managed" the boys also generated meanings of manhood, informing and reinforcing the identities these youth formed on the street. In this case, the criminalization of black and Latino men and the criminal justice system's expectations of masculinity provided the young men with gender resources that limited their mobility, affected their families and relationships, and made them much more likely to end up in the criminal Justice system. The gendered behavior and ideals promoted by police, probation officers, and others was often less possible for these boys than authorities seemed to imagine. In this context, hypermasculinity served both as resistance and as a resource for self-affirmation. This survival strategy impeded social mobility and created a ready-made rationalization entitling the system to further criminalize and punish them.

The boys in this study, however, did not passively submit to police officers in all of their interactions. They actively resisted police officers' challenges to their masculinity. This resistance demonstrated the boys' "synthesized masculinities"—a process that made the accomplishment of masculinity more attainable. Neither dominant masculinity nor subordinate masculinity alone helps to explain the actions and meanings that gang-involved Latino boys navigate and create. In this study, we found that Latino boys constantly negotiated between subordinate, street, working-class, and dominant masculinity. With few resources and diverse constraints placed on them by families, police, and schools, the young men in this study often perceived failure as their only option. In this context, demonstrations of masculinity were a last-resort effort to acquire social status and alleviate other forms of subordination. For these boys, masculinity (more so than race and class) was a coping mechanism they relied on to survive in a world that they believed attacked them for being poor and brown. Masculinity was utilized as a vehicle for attempting to alleviate forms of social marginalization and subordination based on their race and class.

As Latino boys developed this synthesized masculinity, however, others (women, in particular) often fell victim to their subordination. For instance, we found that when men found themselves battling institutions of control, they often responded to this emasculation by symbolically remasculinizing themselves by subjecting young women to physical and symbolic violence (Rios 2009). Synthesized masculinity became a vehicle by which lower-status Latino youth living in Riverland were able to feel accomplished and develop self-affirmation. Similar to Cooper's (2009) work, this study highlights the need to change the gender dynamics of policing and deconstruct the toxic definitions of what it means to be a man. We must move away from punitive models of policing. Some steps that can be taken to begin to eliminate the patterns of policing observe include establishing extensive police training programs designed to challenge a macho police culture and address racial and gendered, raced, and classed stereotypes. Officers can also benefit from training that teaches them how to effectively communicate even when their authority is being challenged and to think about the consequences of prematurely presuming violence and acting upon that assumption.

REFERENCES

Adams, Rachel, and David Savran. 2002. *The Masculinity Studies Reader*. Oxford: Blackwell.

Anderson, Elijah, 1999. *Code of the Street: Decency, Violence, and Moral Life in the Inner City*. New York: Norton.

Bederman, Gail. 1995. *Manliness and Civilization: A Cultural History of Gender and Race in the United States, 1880–1917*. Chicago: University of Chicago Press.

Carrigan, Tim, R, W. Connell, and John Lee. 1985. "Toward a New Sociology of Masculinity." *Theory and Society* 14: 551–604.

Carter, Prudence L. 2005. *Keepin' it Real: School Success beyond Black and White*. New York: Oxford University Press.

Connell, R. W. 1987. *Gender and Power*. Stanford, CA: Stanford University Press.

Connell, R. W. 1995, *Masculinities*. Los Angeles: University of California Press.

Connell, R. W., and J. W. Messerschmidt. 2005. "Hegemonic Masculinity: Rethinking the Concept." *Gender & Society* 19: 629–59.

Cooper, Prank R. 2009. "'Who's the Man?': Masculinities Studies, Terry Stops, and Police Training." *Columbia Journal of Gender and Law* 18 (3): 671.

Dodsworth, Francis. 2007. "Police and the Prevention of Crime: Commerce, Temptation and the Corruption of the Body Politic, from Fielding to Colquhoun." *The British Journal of Criminology* 47 (3): 439–454.

Fernandez,Sonia. 2009. "4 Arrested in Franklin Clinic Gang Incident, Police Disperse Crowd of Suspected Gang Members Awaiting Rival Gang Members." April 6, 2009, https://www.noozhawk.com/article/040609_four_arrested_in_franklin_clinic_gang_incident

Being Treated Inside. "*Noozhawk,* 7 April, www.noozhawk.com/noozhawk/article/040609„ four_arrested_ in_franklin_clinic_gang_incident/

Gau, Jacinta, and Rod K. Brunson. 2010. "Procedural Justice and Order Maintenance Policing; A Study of Inner-City Young Men's Perceptions of Police Legitimacy." *Justice Quarterly* 27 (2): 255–79.

Hahn, Harlao. 1971. "Ghetto Assessments of Police Protection and Authority." *Law & Society Review* 183 (6): 1971–72.

Harris, Angela P. 2000. "Gender, Violence, Race, and Criminal Justice." *Stanford Law Review* 52 (4): 777–807.

Herbert, Steve. 2006. "Tangled up in Blue: Conflicting Paths to Police Legitimacy" *Theoretical Criminology* 10 (4): 481–504.

Jones, Nikki. 2009. "'I Was Aggressive for the Streets, Pretty for the Pictures': Gender, Difference and the Inner-City Girl." *Gender Society* 23 (1): 89–93.

Jones, Nikki. 2010. *Between Good and Ghetto: African American Girls and Inner-City Violence*. New Brunswick, NJ: Rutgers University Press.

Kimmel, Michael S. 1996. *Manhood in America: A Cultural History*. New York: Oxford University Press.

Kimmel, Michael S. 2003. "Masculinity as Homophobia: Fear, Shame, and Silence in the Construction of Gender Identity." In *Race, Class, and Gender in the United States: An Integrated Study*, edited by Paula S. Rothenberg, 6th ed., 81–93. New York: Worth.

Kimmel, Michael S., and Matthew Mahler. 2003. "Adolescent Masculinity, Homophobia, and Violence: Random School Shootings, 1982–2001." *American Behavioral Scientist* 46 (10): 1439–58.

Lopez, N. 2003. *Hopeful Girls, Troubled Boys: Race and Gender Disparity in Urban Education*. New York: Routledge.

Martin, Susan E. 1999. Police Force or Police Service? Gender and Emotional Labor. *The Annals of the American Academy of Political and Social Sciences* 561 (1): 111–2G.

Messerschmidt, James W. 1993. *Masculinities and Crime: Critique and Reconceptualizatian of Theory*. Lanham, MD: Rowman & Littlefield.

Messerschmidt, James W. 2000. "Becoming 'Real Men': Adolescent Masculinity Challenges and Sexual Violence," *Men and Masculinities* 2 (3): 286–307.

Prokos, Anastasia and Irene Padavic. 2002. "'There Oughtta Be a Law Against Bitches': Masculinity Lessons in Police Academy Training." *Gender, Work & Organization* 9 (4): 439–59.

Pyke, Karen D. 1996, "Class-Based Masculinities: The Interdependence of Gender, Class, and Interpersonal Power." *Gender & Society* 10: 527–49.

Rios, Victor M. 2009. "The Consequences of the Criminal Justice Pipeline on Black and Latino Masculinity." *The Annals of the American Academy of Political and Social Sciences* 623 (1): 150–62.

Rios, Victor M. 2011. *Punished: Policing the Lives of Black and Latino Boys*. New York: New York University Press.

Sollund, Ragnhild. 2006. "Racialisation in Police Stop and Search Practice—The Norwegian Case." *Critical Criminology* 14 (3): 265–92.

West, Candace and Sarah Fenstermaker. 1995. "Doing Difference." *Gender & Society* 9 (1): 8–37.

West, Candace and Don Zimmerman. 1987. "Doing Gender." *Gender & Society* 1: 125–51.

Yin, Robert K. 2002. *Case Study Research*. Thousand Oaks, CA: SAGE.

Young, Alford A., Jr. 2009. *The Minds of Marginalized Black Men: Making Sense of Mobility, Opportunity, and Future Life Changes*. Princeton, NJ: Princeton University Press.

NOTES

1. Insight for the ideas I present comes from nearly a decade of field work: a three-year ethnographic project in Northern California, 2002-2005, and a four-year ethnographic project in Southern California, 2007-2012. Both studies were designed to shadow young men who were caught up in the criminal justice system across institutional settings: at schools, parks, the streets, court, home, and community centers.

2. Youths' names and the names of places have been changed to protect subjects' safely and their confidentiality.

3. Yin argues that unique cases are a crucial area of study: "in case studies, rare situations are often precisely what the researcher wants" (Yin 2002).

4. The era of mass incarceration is the time period [circa 1970s to present] in which the United States has drastically expanded its incarceration and where a crackdown on crime, specifically among racialized and poor populations, has led to more criminal sanctions and criminalization than ever before.

THINKING ABOUT THE READING

What are synthesized masculinities? How do urban boys of color use this process to shape the architecture of their lives and attain power and respect in their lives? Are the outcomes good or bad? Gordon Murray described a concept called "the sting" that referred to when young boys are hurt by older boys or men (sting) and then take that sting and pass it on to another boy in order to heal themselves. What aspects of "the sting" do you see in the process of synthesized masculinities? What was unique about Jason's experiences with masculinity? Using your sociological imagination, what larger forces do the authors point to that are connected to the individual experiences of these young boys and men?

Parents' Constructions of Teen Sexuality

SINIKKA ELLIOTT

(2010)

Teen sexuality in the United States is routinely depicted as a dangerous enterprise, full of perils and pitfalls, yet sexuality is a pervasive aspect of the American cultural landscape and is considered key to individual identity and personal fulfillment. Social policy, sex educators, teachers, and other adults construct teenagers as both too young to know about sex and too sexually driven to be trusted with sexual information. How do parents negotiate these sex panics and contradictory discourses in making sense of teen sexuality? Drawing on in-depth interviews with forty-seven parents of teenagers, this article examines parents' subjective understandings of the sexuality of their own teenagers as well as teenagers in general.

Parents and Teen Sexuality: Sexual Scripts and Social Inequality

I follow an interactionist perspective that views sexuality not as biological or immutable but as intimately tied to sociocultural and psychological processes. In particular, I use Simon and Gagnon's (1986) sexual scripting theory. Simon and Gagnon posit three levels on which sexual scripting occurs: the cultural, interpersonal, and intrapsychic. On the cultural level, discourses are a culture's "instructional guides." They are the taken-for-granted ways to understand the social world and social practices that "shape our imaginings of the world and of ourselves" (McCormack 2005:663). For example, the discourse of teen sexuality as risky and hormonally fueled shapes how adults respond to teen sexual activity. Discourses are not accidental or neutral; rather, they reflect dominant interests. "Experts" and moral entrepreneurs in the scientific, medical, political, and religious communities, among others, play a prominent role in crafting and promulgating discourses of sexuality. Yet discourses are not monolithic or omnipotent: competing discourses may vie for prominence and may contest and contradict one another.

Discourses are often too broad or abstract to fit the nuances and complexities of everyday life. Thus individuals craft their own interpersonal scripts to fit the context of their particular situation and interactions. These interpersonal scripts play out on the interactional arena. On the level of the psyche, individuals engage in intrapsychic scripting. This concept captures internal motivations, desires, and anxieties in the construction of sexual subjectivities, what Simon and Gagnon (1986:99) refer to as an individual's "many-layered and sometimes multivoiced wishes."

Sexual scripting theory has primarily been used to explain how individuals develop a sense of themselves as sexual beings (e.g., Martin 1996). In the research presented here, I use this framework to attend to the multilayered process by which parents make sense of teenagers as sexual subjects.

Sex Education and Sex Panics

The first calls for sex education in the United States emerged in the early 1900s in conjunction with the notion that sex is dangerous for the young and the unmarried and a newfound developmental stage in the life course—adolescence. The discovery of adolescence was accompanied by a flurry of scientific research to bolster the notion that adolescents are neither physically nor developmentally suited for many adult responsibilities, including working, marrying, and bearing children (Luker 1996), and eventually to institute mandatory high school attendance (Palladino 1996). School-based sex education, however, was not widely implemented until the late 1970s when it almost immediately emerged as central to the culture wars between conservative and liberal interests (Irvine 2002; Luker, 2006).

Local and national debates over sex education have unfolded in this "broader context of high anxiety about potential dangers to children" (Irvine 2002:135). Indeed, although national polls show that most Americans support sex education (National Public Radio 2004; Rose and Gallup 1998), and despite greater openness about sexuality in popular culture since the 1960s, battles over sex education have increased in intensity over the past four decades (Irvine 2002)—a period marked by "sex panics," explosive political and local clashes over sexuality, including gay rights, censorship, and sex education (Vance 1984:434). These debates, are about far more than the sex education curriculum—they are fueled by and reproduce deep anxieties about childhood, sexuality, gender, marriage, and the institution of the family (Fields 2008; Irvine 2002; Luker 2006; Rubin 1984).

How do parents navigate the discourses of danger and sexual and personal responsibility in making sense of teen sexuality?

Binary Thinking and the Reproduction of Inequality

The debates over sex education have profoundly shaped not only sex education curricula but also the discourses of child and teen sexuality (Irvine 2002). In their rhetorical battles over sex education, conservative and liberal groups have engaged in "making up children" (Irvine 2002:108). Through this discursive work, children became socially defined as "innocent, vulnerable, and in need of protection from adult sexual knowledge and practice" (Thorne and Luria 1986:177; see also Rubin 1984). The seemingly generic notions of childhood innocence and asexuality promulgated in these debates, however, belie the racist, sexist, classist, and heterosexist foundations of sex education and the construction of the innocent child (Fields 2005, 2008; Irvine 2002). In particular, the lens of child innocence is used mostly to construct white, middle-class children (Fields 2008). Children without this race and class privilege are construed as hypersexual, "unsalvageable," and a corrupting influence (Fields 2008). Debates about teen sexuality "reflect the twin assumptions that American teens are too innocent to know about sexuality and too sexual to be trusted with information" (Pascoe 2007:29). Teenagers are both discursively "made up" as innocent and endangered by sexual information and "made up" as hormonally fueled and sexually driven (Schalet 2000) with race, class, and gender meanings etched through these constructions.

In the research presented here, I explore how parents' understandings of teen sexuality reflect binary thinking. Recognizing that parents' constructions do not take place in a discursive void, I contextualize their narratives within broader societal discourses of normal, acceptable sexual expression (e.g., Personal Responsibility 1996). My focus is on how these norms build on and contribute to gender and sexual, as well as race and class, inequalities. As I discuss in the conclusion, through their binary thinking, parents do not simply imply that their teens are sexually innocent but also that, as such, they are worthy of social resources and recognition, suggesting linkages between sexuality and citizenship (Fields and Hirschman 2007; Plummer 2003).

Constructing the Asexual Teen: Naïveté, Danger, and Dependence

In this section, I examine how and why parents think of their own children as asexual while constructing their children's peers as hypersexual. By asexual, I mean that parents did not describe their teenage children as sexually agentic, desiring subjects. In the first part, I suggest that parents depend on their understanding of their children as young, naive, and economically dependent in making this judgment. This part also reveals the extent to which parents think of teen sexual activity in largely negative ways. The second part shows that parents think of other people's children as highly sexual and sexualized, and underscores the extent to which they rely on gendered, but also raced and classed, sexual meanings to construct this asexual-sexual binary.

The parents in this study consistently characterized their children as young, immature, and naive. In doing so, they often compared their children with other teenagers. Beatrice (fifty-two, white, lower middle class) typifies this viewpoint in her comment about her sixteen-year-old daughter: "One thing I've noticed is that she's probably a little bit more immature than some of her friends, and that's okay, I think it will come." Echoing Beatrice, Ellena (forty-one, Latina, working class) said her sixteen-year-old daughter "seems very young or immature at times." Although I interviewed far more mothers than fathers, the few fathers also view their children as less mature than their peers. Ron (fifty, white, working class) sees both his fifteen-year-old son and his seventeen-year-old daughter as immature:

> They're a little immature for their ages. Well, my daughter especially. She still acts a little younger than most seventeen-year-olds. She looks younger than [seventeen] to me too. Which, we really don't mind though. We don't mind that. Because, we can sort of regulate it a little bit easier when she gets little questions and things like that.

Ron constructs his daughter, in particular, as younger than her peers, both in terms of how she acts and how she looks. Importantly, he observed that this has made parenting easier because his daughter has not asked difficult questions about sex and has seemingly acquiesced to her parents' answers in that department. He expressed relief that, in his assessment, her immaturity relative to her peers has delayed her interest in sex.

Indeed, many parents rely on their understanding of their children as young and immature in constructing their children as asexual and not yet capable of handling the responsibilities that accompany sexual activity. For example, Beth (thirty-nine, white, upper middle class) believes that her sixteen-year-old son is a virgin because he has told her as much and because he has not dated, but she also added:

> When you look at your child, they're just so little and young. You just don't think of them ever even thinking about [sex]. It's hard to even think about what you should be saying to kids. You don't think they are old enough when you think about those things.

Beth's view is shared with most of the parents in this study. Despite the fact that her son "surprises her a lot" (in the past few years, he has been caught smoking marijuana, drinking alcohol, and watching pornography), she cannot imagine him as a sexual being. She said she should probably talk to her son about sex, but has no idea of what to say or how to go about it; in her words, "It's hard to even think about what you should be saying."

Similarly, Kate (forty-three, white, lower middle class) said that her fourteen-year-old son is too young to have sex: "I don't think it's safe for his age. Maybe it's just him, I don't know. But he's a little naive." As she spoke of her fears for her son, it became clear that peer pressure is an important component of Kate's concerns for her son's sexual innocence and wellbeing:

SE: What is it about his age or his naïveté that you don't feel he'd be safe?

Kate: I don't know. I . . . [sighs].

SE: Is it that he wouldn't use protection?

Kate: Yeah? Or maybe, I guess, [that] he'd do something he didn't want to do. Get pushed into something or let himself be pushed into something. I think he would definitely do that. "I'm not going to be cool if I don't do this."

Here we see that Kate has a difficult time imagining her son might experience sexual desire of his own accord, at least not at his age. Like Ron, she views her teenager as asexual. However, she is concerned that he might succumb to sexual activity to appear cool in the eyes of his peers. Her fears center less on whether he will use contraception and more on her son finding himself in a sexual situation that he may not be ready to handle. In the same vein, Rosalia (forty-three, Latina, poor), who has five daughters ages nine to twenty-two, does not allow them to date or go out on their own until they are eighteen because, before that, "They're gullible. They'll just believe anything. They're naive, I guess."

Hence age and maturity are crucial to parents' understandings of their children's (a)sexuality: they posit their own teen children, at least until the age of eighteen, as young, immature, and naive, and, by association, sexually innocent. Their narratives also underscore the extent to which a danger discourse of teen sexuality underlies this understanding. Based on this hegemonic paradigm, teen sex equals (hetero) sexual intercourse and also equals danger, risk, and negative consequences. Kim (forty-five, black, lower middle class) said she emphasizes consequences when she talks to her seventeen-year-old son, twelve-year-old niece, and ten-year-old daughter: "[I tell them] 'Procreation is real. I don't care what anybody says, when you have sex, there's only the potential for a baby to pop up, no matter what precautions you take." As Melissa (forty-three, white, upper middle class) put it, "You're dealing with life and death issues" (emphasis as stated). Consistent with the danger discourse, which is constitutive of the larger panic over teen sexuality, parents regularly described teen sexual activity in terms of catastrophic consequences that no amount of information or safety measures can prevent.

Some of the narratives also reveal that parents equate teen sexual activity with deviance. For example, when Portia's (forty-six, Latina, upper middle class) then fifteen-year-old son came to her with the news that his girlfriend might be pregnant, Portia was in shock: "Because he was such a young teenager and I really didn't think. And again, this is a really good solid kid." The way Portia described her son suggests that he does not fit her stereotype of a sexually active teen. Indeed, Portia has not yet talked to her now sixteen-year-old son about contraception and does not plan to until he leaves for college, because "he's just a good kid who got in over his head." Portia's reluctance to view her son as a sexual subject because he is a "good kid" implies that she connotes teen sexual activity with badness.

Finally, in line with the legislative discourse that poses financial self-sufficiency as a precedent for sexual activity (Personal Responsibility 1996), parents link their understandings of their teens' sexuality to economic wherewithal. Beth, who earlier described her sixteen-year-old son as "little and young," for example, has told her son that he can watch pornography when he is eighteen and economically independent: "[I said] 'When you're eighteen and on your own computer, you pay for your own computer and your own TV and your own service, you can do whatever you want. But whenever you're in our house you live by our rules.'" Like Beth, many parents said their children can be sexually desiring subjects when they no longer live at home and are paying their own bills (most prefer that this also coincides with a time when they are married). Thus, while age clearly plays an important role in how parents think about their children's sexuality—parents often indicated precise ages when their children may date; some, like Beth, pinpointed when they may watch pornography; and many identified an age range during which they think of their children as particularly naive and immature, for example—age is not simply about developmental trajectories; it is

intertwined with economic dependence and a deep sense of parental responsibility to usher their children safely to adulthood. As I discuss in more detail in the following, parents' understandings of teen sexuality are also shaped by complex notions of difference and destruction.

Constructing the Hypersexual Teen: Promiscuity, Hormones, and Predation

Although parents have a difficult time envisioning their own teens as sexual subjects, they described their children's peers as highly sexual. Sylvia (forty-four, Latina, lower middle class), for example, characterized her fifteen- and fourteen-year-old daughters' peers in the following manner: "The way the teens are now, I know they're out they're doing it [having sex]. But I wouldn't want it for my girls." Other parents described their children's peers as "real sexual" (Gina, fifty-one, white, upper middle class) and "promiscuous" (Rosalia). Corina (thirty-nine, black, working class) put it this way: "[Teenagers] got their cute little bodies and their raging hormones. They're like raring to go." This understanding reflects a dominant discourse of sex as an uncontrollable drive to which teenagers, in particular, because of their raging hormones and lack of impulse control, are susceptible (Schalet 2000). This discourse often runs alongside a risk-based discourse of teen sexuality.

Some parents construct their own children's goodness and asexuality in part by contrasting it with other hedonistic teens. Kelly (thirty-seven, white, working class) described her sixteen-year-old niece, who lived with Kelly and her sixteen-and fourteen-year-old sons for six months, as follows: "I realized that my boys are pretty good, and I have no major complaints about how they act. Because this girl, she was very openly sexual and all she could think about was the next time she got to go see this guy." In general, Kelly said, "Kids are moving too fast these days." By contrast, her sons are not "even interested in acting like that. They have higher goals for themselves." In this way, Kelly separates her goal-oriented sons, who she believes are not sexual, from other "openly sexual" teenagers like her niece, who are, presumably, easily sidetracked by sexual activity.

Thus parents differentiate between their asexual teen children and their teens' sexual peers. However, this binary thinking does more than simply establish their teens as asexual and, therefore, good; it also creates a scenario in which their teenagers are imperiled by their peers. Indeed, parents described their children's peers as not simply sexual but as sexually predatory, with gender, race, and class meanings often woven through their descriptions. In what follows, I first analyze the fears parents expressed in relation to their sons' sexual well-being and then examine their fears for their daughters. In contrast to previous research suggesting that parents stress sexual vulnerability to their daughters while giving their sons more leeway to explore their sexuality underscoring the panic around teen sexuality, the parents in this study consider sex to be dangerous for both their sons and their daughters.

"You Need to Watch Out for Girls": Girls as Sexual Aggressors

Parents of sons consistently described their sons' female peers as hypersexual, sexually aggressive, and more sexually advanced than their sons. Rose (forty-three, white, upper middle class), who has three sons ages eight to fourteen, regularly talks to her oldest son about puberty, dating, and sex. "[I tell him], 'You need to watch out for girls.' And, of course he's not allowed to date yet, at his age. And he won't be able to date till he's sixteen, but I want to start telling him now 'cause I think a lot of times girls are more [sexually] aggressive than boys are." Despite being a woman herself, Rose warns her son away from girls. Like other parents I interviewed who have sons in their early teens, she said girls mature faster than boys and often pressure boys to have sex to solidify a relationship. As Kate cautions her fourteen-year-old son, "'Girls can manipulate you or be controlling.' Because he is one that would let a woman walk right over him." One father, Scott (thirty-four, white, lower middle class), also expressed concern about sexually assertive girls. Scott said that his fourteen-year-old adopted son is "not the type to initiate sex, [but] there are girls out there that would. And he's not a oh no, I can't do that [type of person]."

Research shows that young women face a limited range of acceptable behaviors when it comes to sexuality (Tolman 1994). If they violate the cultural construction of girls as naturally less interested in sex than boys, they risk being labeled sluts. Young women constantly skirt the Madonna-whore

dichotomy: either they are sexually innocent Madonnas or they are sexually lascivious whores. As more young women have sought sexual pleasure and agency, many adults have responded with alarm, underscoring the tremendous anxiety about female sexuality that persists in the United States (Wilkins 2004). Parents, hence, may rely on the Madonna-whore dichotomy in maintaining their own children's sexual innocence. By casting "other" girls as sexual temptresses, they maintain their understanding of their sons, and also their daughters, as asexual and innocent.

Parents' depictions of girls as sexual temptresses of ten had class overtones, though rarely directly articulated in terms of class (Bettie 2003). For example, Rose said she initiated a conversation with her son about the dangers of oral sex around the time he transitioned from a private to a public school: "I wanted to tell him, so he'll know, when a girl puts her mouth on a boy's pee-pee—somehow, by saying pee-pee that kind of makes it more gentle to me, but he gets the idea . . . [I said], 'Boys really lose respect for girls who act like that.'" When asked why she felt it was important to have this conversation, Rose explained that when her son attended private school, "There was talk among the moms that some of the kids at the public school, not our school, of course, were meeting at the movies and having oral sex in the back row." Now that Rose's son is at a public school, she worries that he may confront this situation, suggesting that the girls whom Rose deems sexual (and sexually threatening to her son) are those who attend public, not private, school.

Like Rose, Renae (forty-three, black, working class) said she instructs her nineteen- and thirteen-year-old sons to watch out for girls. Her warning evokes the cultural archetype of the female gold digger: "[I say], 'You better stay away, stay away. Sometimes girls trap you.'" Indeed, last year Renae's older son, Cameron, who was a senior in high school at the time, claimed that his girlfriend, who, like Cameron, was black, feigned a pregnancy. Had this been true, Renae feared it might have prevented Cameron from going to college. Renae insisted that Cameron accompany his girlfriend to Planned Parenthood where she took a pregnancy test that came back negative. Upon learning this, with his mother's insistence, Cameron broke up with the young woman. Cameron is now in his first year of college and has told Renae that his ex-girlfriend's pregnancy scare "really kind of woke me up to women. I'm scared of women." Although pleased that her son is focusing on his education, Renae hopes that he will remain open to women in the future:

> [I tell him], "Get your education. You going to meet a whole lot [of women] out there in different careers and different, well, attitudes and all that. Educated and everything. And on your level. Because I didn't feel [his ex-girlfriend] was on his level to be honest. She was more streetwise."

Renae's narrative reveals that it is not all women Cameron should stay away from, just a certain kind of woman. Like other parents, Renae did not overtly talk about class, but instead used code words like "streetwise" that have strong class overtones, imbued with gender and race meanings. The gold digger narrative, prevalent in mainstream hip-hop, meshes with contemporary and long-standing stereotypes of working-class and poor African American women, making them targets for parental (and social) anxieties (Collins 2004; Luker 1996). In encouraging her son to find girlfriends who share his career aspirations and intellectual abilities, Renae implicitly urges him to seek out women, and suggests there are many, who will share his future social class location.

"I Was a Teen Boy and I Want to Protect My Girls from That": Boys as Sexual Aggressors

Whereas the parents cast girls as the aggressors in talking to their sons about sexuality, in discussing sexuality with their daughters, parents consistently position their daughters as victimized and vulnerable rather than as desiring subjects— essentially as Madonnas. In this discourse, boys are the sexual aggressors. Many parents spoke extensively about their fears for their daughters' safety in relation to their male peers and dating relationships. Greg's (forty-three, white, lower middle class) advice to his eighteen-year-old stepdaughter exemplifies this concern. He frequently tells his stepdaughter that she is better off in a group than paired up with a boy:

> If the news has something about date rape on it or these girls turn up missing or dead and, not that it only happens on dates, we're not telling her that, but it's like, there's safety in numbers. [I tell her], "If you're with a group of friends and you stay with a group of friends, there's less chance something's going to happen to you. . . . If you're in a group you are better protected.

In addition to relying on the news and other sources of information, Greg, who has a biological teenage daughter as well as to two teenage step-daughters, bases his belief about predatory boys on his own experience as a male: "I feel like I have to protect my girls. I was a guy and I want to protect my girls from that." Greg carefully monitors his daughters' friendships with boys, has a rule that they cannot date until they are eighteen, and has made it clear that boys are not to be trusted.

The parents' discussions with their daughters about dating and relationships paint a fairly grim picture. Many parents view relationships, in general, as a hindrance to their daughter's well-being. Gabriela (forty-four, Latina, upper middle class) said she tells her three daughters (ages seven to sixteen): "Take care of yourself first, then seek out a relationship with someone else. Make sure that you're taking care of yourself first. Be self-sufficient, have your own job, your own career, travel, have your own interests." Some fear that even a responsible, trustworthy daughter might be lured in over her head by a boyfriend (most parents assume that their children are heterosexual) who is less focused, less responsible, and more sexually driven. Corina, who has a fourteen-year-old daughter as well as two daughters in their early twenties, said she regularly warns her daughters not to trust boys: "[I tell them], 'He just wants you for your body. And then after he get it, he's going to be done with you.'" She also asked her single brother to talk to her daughters about the "male point of view": "And he told them the truth: [He said], 'I just want them for their body. I'm using them and if any other man tells you that's not what they're doing, then they're lying to you. Basically they're users.'" Corina instructs her daughters instead to have "something left to save for your husband on your wedding night."

Parents' depictions of their daughters' potential dating relationships were often not only gendered but also raced and classed. Race was especially salient for some of these parents—white parents in particular—suggesting the continued linkages between race, gender, and sexuality. Historically, depictions of hypersexual black men corrupting white women's purity and innocence ignited and galvanized racist fears. Some of the white parents' narratives suggest the persistence of this trope. Pamela (forty-seven, white, lower middle class) was blunt about the prospect of her fifteen-year-old daughter dating interracially: "[My husband and I] do not want her to go out with a black person. I would be okay with the Hispanics. I just, the issue with a white person and a black person, I just think there's a lot of issues with that and so we won't let that happen." Pamela explained why she feels this way: "Where I grew up, people were shunned and bad names were called to the girls that were going out with the black guys. And it was mostly white girls with black guys, not the other way around." Pamela's explanation reflects a legacy of racial and sexual politics in which white women who dated men of color were deemed race traitors and fallen women, essentially whores (Collins 2004; Nagel 2001).

Most parents, however, were not as direct as Pamela in voicing concerns about interracial dating. Sheila (forty-eight, white, lower middle class) expressed ambivalence about the black boys her sixteen-year-old daughter dates. She said she does not mind that her daughter currently dates only black boys, but indicated that she thinks it is just a phase and frequently emphasized that her daughter "does not embrace their cultural values as a whole," implying that blacks have different (possibly inferior) cultural values compared with whites. Sheila also shared a story with me about one black boy who apparently exposed himself to her daughter two years ago, suggesting she wanted me to see that her worries about black boys were not unfounded. The story exposes the particular dilemmas parents face and how their interpretations are shaped by race, gender, and current understandings of teen sexuality. The boy and her daughter were standing in the yard talking when Sheila's husband, who was watching them from a window, saw the boy "acting suspicious." Her husband bolted out of the house and ran the "kid off our property." Their daughter admitted that he had exposed himself to her and that it was "gross." In response, Sheila's husband "sat out in our driveway in the back of our van for two nights with a rifle in his hand (laughs)." In addition to being vigilant at home, Sheila and her husband also tried to get their daughter transferred to another school.

Although it is difficult to say whether Sheila and her husband would have responded in a similar manner if the gender of the teenagers in this story had been reversed—that is, if a girl had exposed herself to their son—or if the boy in the story had been white, it seems as though racial and gendered sexual politics and discourse shaped their reaction. Female sexuality, especially white girls' sexuality, is often associated with (and may be experienced as) vulnerability and victimization while the sexuality of African American boys and men has historically been framed as excessive, dangerous, and out of control. Sheila and her husband's attempt to transfer their daughter to another school underscores their sense that she could not be safe near this boy. Their daughter, however, was unwilling to divulge the boy's name, suggesting some resistance on her part to her parents' efforts to characterize her as a victim.

Discussion and Conclusion

My analysis of interviews with forty-seven parents of teenagers reveals that parents do not think of their own teenagers as sexual subjects. A number of cultural, structural, and psychological forces shape this understanding, with the danger discourse of teen sexuality being perhaps paramount. This discourse is shaped by the debates over sex education, which are themselves part of a broad moral panic around child and teen sexuality characteristic of the last several decades. In line with this discourse, parents cannot envision any good coming from teen sexual activity; rather, they articulated innumerable negative consequences, including death. As one parent (Sandra, forty-five, white, upper middle class) put it, "There are diseases that will kill you. They will kill you." This produces a tremendous social and psychological incentive for parents to asexualize their teens (Simon and Gagnon 1986). Parents also indicated that economic independence is an important criterion for sexual activity; their ability to think of their teenagers as sexual subjects is hindered by their teens' economic dependence. Finally, parents' descriptions of teen sexual activity reveal that they equate it with deviance, something they do not associate with their "good" teenagers.

Yet, even as parents construct their own teens as asexual, they posit other teens as highly sexual and sexualized. That is, parents do not think of their children as sexually desiring subjects, but they construct their children's peers as sexually agentic and even predatory. Parents exhibited this binary thinking across gender, race, and class, and regardless of their children's actual behavior. Even the three parents in this study who have children who became teen parents subscribe to this understanding. This discourse appears to be so hegemonic that it transcends racial or class differences and is an everyday commonsense understanding. In this article, I have argued that parents' binary thinking is shaped by the contradictory discourses of teen sexuality that discursively construct teens as not only sexually innocent and vulnerable but also sexually driven and rapacious.

The data also show that the parents in this study often use gender, racial, and class signifiers in casting their children's peers as hypersexual. A long history of binary thinking around sexuality has shaped understandings of sexuality in U.S. society. As social historians have documented, the poor, new immigrants, blacks, Latinos, Asians, gays and lesbians, and those deemed mentally "unfit" to reproduce have long borne the mantle of "bad" (i.e., promiscuous) sexuality. Today, many of these sexual stereotypes endure and have become so entrenched that they are taken for granted. Collins (2004), for instance, argues that the persistent hypersexualization of black men and women can be seen in policymakers' and academics' intense concern over and scrutiny of black teenage motherhood. I argue these stereotypes enable parents to project their anxieties about teen sexuality onto gendered, and also raced and classed, Others. This othering of their children's peers preserves their notions of their own children as asexual and innocent. But this also means that parents see their children as potential victims in their intimate relationships. Based on this equation, their children's peers are not fellow innocents on a path of mutual self-discovery and pleasure. Instead, peers are potential predators, abusers, and entrappers, with gender, race, and class meanings woven through these depictions. Following well-worn gendered tropes, parents of sons expressed concerns about sexually voracious girls seducing and trapping their gullible sons. Parents of daughters worry about sexually predatory boys using, and sullying the reputations of, their heretofore innocent daughters.

Through their binary thinking, parents also contribute to the notion that teen sexuality is bad; hence, teenagers who have sex are bad, and any negative consequences that befall them are their own fault. For example, one mother, in talking to her sixteen-year-old daughter about a pregnant girl at her daughter's school, said, "She made a choice and her life's going to be harder because of that" (Beatrice). Thus, in line with the discourse of personal responsibility, parents assign agency to other teens' sexual behavior, but they conceive of their own teens as sexually vulnerable and potential victims. This suggests that one unintended consequences of legislation designed to promote personal responsibility in a society riven through with inequalities may be the scapegoating of others. By constructing their teenagers as asexual but other teenagers as hypersexual, parents may effectively create an "out" for their children if they behave "irresponsibly": their peers are to blame. In this model of responsibility, everyone but one's own child(ren) is held accountable.

REFERENCES

Bettie, Julie. 2003. *Women without Class: Girls, Race, and Identity*. Berkeley: University of California Press.

Collins, Patricia Hill 2004. *Black Sexual Politics: African Americans, Gender, and the New Racism*. New York: Routledge.

Fields, Jessica. 2005. 'Children Having Children': Race, Innocence, and Sexuality Education." *Social Problems* 52(4):549–1.

_____.2008. *Risky Lessons: Sex Education and Social Inequality*. New Brunswick, NJ: Rutgers University Press.

Fields, Jessica and Celeste Hirschman. 2007. "Citizenship Lessons in Abstinence-Only Sexuality Education." *American Journal of Sexuality Education* 2(2):3–25.

Irvine, Janice, ed. l994. *Sexual Cultures and the Construction of Adolescent Identities*. Philadelphia: Temple University Press.

_____.2002. *Talk about Sex: The Battles over Sex Education in the United States*. Berkeley: University of California Press.

Luker, Kristin. 1996. *Dubious Conceptions: The Politics of Teenage Pregnancy*. Cambridge, MA: Harvard University Press.

_____.2006. *When Sex Goes to School: Warring Views on Sex—and Sex Edcuation—since the Sixties*. New York: Norton.

Martin, Karin. 1996. *Puberty, Sexuality, and the Self: Boys and Girls at Adolescence*. New York: Routledge.

McCormack, Karen. 2005. "Stratified Reproduction and Poor Women's Resistance." *Gender & Society* 19(5):660–79.

Nagel, Joane. 2001. "Racial, Ethnic, and National Boundaries: Sexual Intersections and Symbolic Interactions." *Symbolic Interaction* 24(2):123–39.

Nathanson, Constance A. 1991. *Dangerous Passage: The Social Control of Sexuality in Women's Adolescence*. Philadelphia: Temple University Press.

National Public Radio, Kaiser Family Foundation, Harvard Kennedy School of Government Poll. 2004. *Sex Education in America*. Publication no. 7015, January. Retrieved from http://www.kff.org/newsmedia/7015.cfm.

Palladino, Grace. 1996. *Teenagers: An American History*. New York: Basic Books.

Pascoe, C. J. 2007. *Dude, You're a Fag: Masculinity and Sexuality in High School*. Berkeley: University of California Press.

Personal Responsibility and Work Opportunity Reconciliation Act. 1996. Pub. L. No. 104–193, sec. 912, 110 Stat. 2105–2355.

Plummer, Ken. 2003. *Intimate Citizenship: Private Decisions and Public Dialogues*. Seattle: University of Washington Press.

Rubin, Gayle. 1984. "Thinking Sex: Notes for a Radical Theory of the Politics of Sexuality." Pp. 267–319 in *Pleasure and Danger: Exploring Female Sexuality*, edited by C. S. Vance. Boston: Routledge and Kegan Paul.

Schalet, Amy T. 2000. "Raging Hormones, Regulated Love: Adolescent Sexuality and the Constitution of the Modern Individual in the United States and the Netherlands." *Body and Society* 6(1):75–105.

Simon, William and John Gagnon. 1986. "Sexual Scripts: Permanence and Change." *Archives of Sexual Behavior* 15(2):97–120.

Thorne, Barrie and Zella Luria. 1986. "Sexuality and Gender in Children's Daily Worlds." *Social Problems* 33(3):176–90.

Tolman, Deborah. 1994. "Doing Desire: Adolescent Girls' Struggle for with Sexuality." *Gender & Society* 8(3):324–42.

Vance, Carole S., ed. 1984. *Pleasure and Danger: Exploring Female Sexuality*. Boston: Routledge and Kegan Paul.

Wilkins, Amy. 2004. "'So Full of Myself as a Chick': Goth Women, Sexual Independence, and Gender Egalitarianism." *Gender & Society* 18(3):328–49.

THINKING ABOUT THE READING

What is the binary thought process that Elliott describes in the parents she studied? How do these parents' views of teenage sexuality and the notion of "personal responsibility" contribute to the reproduction of social inequalities? What kinds of long-term anxieties do these parents connect to teenage sexuality? How have social institutions participated in the meaning and norms assigned to teenage sexuality? How might the findings from this study contribute to the development of sex education in schools?

CHAPTER 13

Global Dynamics and Population Demographic Trends

I n the past several chapters, we have examined the various interrelated sources of social stratification. Race, class, and gender continue to determine access to cultural, economic, and political opportunities and as technology has rapidly advanced, we have a new lens through which to view these concepts. Indeed, technology has proven to be a paradox in terms of providing a new vehicle for constructing identity and building community but also a tool that can be used to reproduce social inequalities.

As we have noted in several selections throughout the book, sources of inequality are often interrelated. One area of inequality that is overlooked is ageism, and with the demographics shifts in recent years, the older segment of our population is getting increasingly larger and more racially and ethnically diverse. Yet, our knowledge of how the aging process plays out for certain minority groups like the LGBT community or people with disabilities is scarce.

Some other large-scale demographic phenomena affect people regardless of their age. Take, for instance, immigration. As social and demographic conditions in poor, developing countries grow worse, pressures to migrate increase. Countries on the receiving end of this migration often experience high levels of cultural, political, and economic fear. Immigration—both legal and illegal—has become one of the most contentious political issues in the United States today. While politicians debate proposed immigration restrictions, people from all corners of the globe continue to come to this country looking for a better life. An informed understanding of this phenomenon requires an awareness of the reasons for migration and the connection between the choices individuals make to immigrate and larger economic conditions that reflect global markets.

As Arlie Russell Hochschild points out in "Love and Gold," immigration can create serious problems in the families people leave behind. Many destitute mothers in places such as the Philippines, Mexico, and Sri Lanka leave their children for long periods of time to work abroad because they cannot make ends meet at home. Ironically, the jobs these women typically take when they leave their families—nannies, maids, service workers—involve caring for and nurturing other people's families. So while migrant women provide much-needed income for their own families and valuable "care work" for their employers, they leave an emotional vacuum in their home countries. Hochschild asks us to consider the toll this phenomenon is taking on the children of these absent mothers. Not surprisingly, most of the women feel a profound sense of guilt and remorse that is largely invisible to the families they work for.

With the advances in the medical field, individuals in the U.S. are living longer lives, especially when their socioeconomic position gives them access to important resources like quality healthcare, the time and safe space for physical activity, and proper nutrition. As life expectancy increases, so do cultural issues connected to age. In "The Embodied Experiences of Old Lesbians," Kathleen F. Slevin explores ageism and the everyday body experiences of a group of white, economically privileged lesbians. These women display a mixture of optimism and ambivalence about the "cultural imperialism of youth" and their aging bodies, which indicate that like other components of identity, age is a complex and fluid one. Their bodies are used as a site for assigning meaning to aging along with gender and sexuality.

In "The Algorithmic Rise of the 'Alt-Right,'" Jessie Daniels argues that the spread of white supremacy and the Alt-Right is happening through algorithms and social media platforms. Digital technologies are increasingly being used to build and expand membership in groups. He suggests that events like the "Unite the Right" rally in Charlottesville and the Emanuel AME Church massacre were facilitated by the algorithms of search engines and social media platforms. A combination of a belief in the "racelessness" of the Internet and the restriction of the flow of information along with profit motives has helped fuel the growth of groups like the Alt-Right.

Something to Consider as You Read

Global or demographic perspectives are big-picture perspectives. As you read these selections, practice thinking about the ways that demographic and global processes may shape individual experiences and choices. For example, consider your personal networks. Do they show signs of age segregation? How has immigration affected your everyday life? Do you know the story of how your family arrived in this country? How many generations have they been here? Is there a substantial immigrant population in your hometown? How has their presence been received by others? How do your personal experiences with immigrants compare to the largely negative images that are often presented in the media? Beyond immigration, think about the ways in which big economic and political changes affect the choices individuals make. Now, add wealth and technology to the equation and consider which countries are going to be in the best position to adjust to these global changes. Who is going to be most affected, possibly even exploited, in this global adjustment?

Love and Gold

ARLIE RUSSELL HOCHSCHILD

(2002)

Whether they know it or not, Clinton and Princela Bautista, two children growing up in a small town in the Philippines apart from their two migrant parents, are the recipients of an international pledge. It says that a child "should grow up in a family environment, in an atmosphere of happiness, love, and understanding," and "not be separated from his or her parents against their will . . . " Part of Article 9 of the United Nations Declaration on the Rights of the Child (1959), these words stand now as a fairy-tale ideal, the promise of a shield between children and the costs of globalization.

At the moment this shield is not protecting the Bautista family from those human costs. In the basement bedroom of her employer's home in Washington, D.C., Rowena Bautista keeps four pictures on her dresser: two of her own children, back in Camiling, a Philippine farming village, and two of her children she has cared for as a nanny in the United States. The pictures of her own children, Clinton and Princela, are from five years ago. As she recently told *Wall Street Journal* reporter Robert Frank, the recent photos "remind me how much I've missed." She has missed the last two Christmases, and on her last visit home, her son Clinton, now eight, refused to touch his mother. "Why," he asked, "did you come back?"

The daughter of a teacher and an engineer, Rowena Bautista worked three years toward an engineering degree before she quit and went abroad for work and adventure. A few years later, during her travels, she fell in love with a Ghanaian construction worker, had two children with him, and returned to the Philippines with them. Unable to find a job in the Philippines, the father of her children went to Korea in search of work and, over time, he faded from his children's lives.

Rowena again traveled north, joining the growing ranks of Third World mothers who work abroad for long periods of time because they cannot make ends meet at home. She left her children with her mother, hired a nanny to help out at home, and flew to Washington, D.C., where she took a job as a nanny for the same pay that a small-town doctor would make in the Philippines. Of the 792,000 legal household workers in the United States, 40 percent were born abroad, like Rowena. Of Filipino migrants, 70 percent, like Rowena, are women.

Rowena calls Noa, the American child she tends, "my baby." One of Noa's first words was "Ena," short for Rowena. And Noa has started babbling in Tagalog, the language Rowena spoke in the Philippines. Rowena lifts Noa from her crib mornings at 7:00 A.M., takes her to the library, pushes her on the swing at the playground, and curls up with her for naps. As Rowena explained to Frank, "I give Noa what I can't give to my children." In turn, the American child gives Rowena what she doesn't get at home. As Rowena puts it, "She makes me feel like a mother."

Rowena's own children live in a four-bedroom house with her parents and twelve other family members—eight of them children, some of whom also have mothers who work abroad. The central figure in the children's lives—the person they call "Mama"—is Grandma, Rowena's mother. But Grandma works surprisingly long hours as a teacher—from 7:00 A.M. to 9:00 P.M. As Rowena tells her story to Frank, she says little about her father, the children's grandfather (men are discouraged from participating actively in child rearing in the Philippines). And Rowena's father is not much involved with his grandchildren. So, she has hired Anna de la Cruz, who arrives daily at 8:00 A.M. to cook, clean, and care for the children. Meanwhile, Anna de la Cruz leaves her teenage son in the care of her eighty-year-old mother-in-law.

Rowena's life reflects an important and growing global trend: the importation of care and love from poor countries to rich ones. For some time now, promising and highly trained professionals have been moving from ill-equipped hospitals, impoverished schools, antiquated banks, and other beleaguered workplaces of the Third World to better opportunities and higher pay in the First World. As rich nations become richer and poor nations become poorer, this one-way flow of talent and training continuously widens the gap between the two. But in addition to this brain drain, there is now a parallel but more hidden and wrenching trend, as women who normally care for the young, the old, and the sick in their own poor countries move to care for the young, the old, and the sick in rich countries, whether as maids and nannies or as day-care and nursing-home aides. It's a care drain.

The movement of care workers from south to north is not altogether new. What is unprecedented, however, is the scope and speed of women's migration to these jobs. Many factors contribute to the growing feminization of migration. One is the growing split between the global rich and poor. . . .

[For example] domestic workers [who] migrated from the Philippines to the United States and Italy [in the 1990s] had averaged $176 a month, often as teachers, nurses, and administrative and clerical workers. But by doing less skilled—though no less difficult—work as nannies, maids, and care-service workers, they can earn $200 a month in Singapore, $410 a month in Hong Kong, $700 a month in Italy, or $1,400 a month in Los Angeles. To take one example, as a fifth-grade dropout in Colombo, Sri Lanka, a woman could earn $30 a month plus room and board as a housemaid, or she could earn $30 a month as a salesgirl in a shop, without food or lodging. But as a nanny in Athens she could earn $500 a month, plus room and board.

The remittances these women send home provide food and shelter for their families and often a nest egg with which to start a small business. Of the $750 Rowena Bautista earns each month in the United States, she mails $400 home for her children's food, clothes, and schooling, and $50 to Anna de la Cruz, who shares some of that with her mother-in-law and her children. As Rowena's story demonstrates, one way to respond to the gap between rich and poor countries is to close it privately—by moving to a better paying job. . . .

The International Organization for Migration estimates that 120 million people moved from one country to another, legally or illegally, in 1994. Of this group, about 2 percent of the world's population, 15 to 23 million are refugees and asylum seekers. Of the rest, some move to join family members who have previously migrated. But most move to find work.

As a number of studies show, most migration takes place through personal contact with networks of migrants composed of relatives and friends and relatives and friends of relatives and friends. One migrant inducts another. Whole networks and neighborhoods leave to work abroad, bringing back stories, money, know-how, and contacts. Just as men form networks along which information about jobs are passed, so one domestic worker in New York, Dubai, or Paris passes on information to female relatives or friends about how to arrange papers, travel, find a job, and settle. Today, half of all the world's migrants are women. . . .

The trends outlined above—global polarization, increasing contact, and the establishment of transcontinental female networks—have caused more women to migrate. They have also changed women's motives for migrating. Fewer women move for "family reunification" and more move in search of work. And when they find work, it is often within the growing "care sector," which, according to the economist Nancy Folbre, currently encompasses 20 percent of all American jobs.

A good number of the women who migrate to fill these positions seem to be single mothers. After all, about a fifth of the world's households are headed by women: 24 percent in the industrial world, 19 percent in Africa, 18 percent in Latin America and the Caribbean, and 13 percent in Asia and the Pacific. . . .

Many if not most women migrants have children. The average age of women migrants into the United States is twenty-nine, and most come from countries, such as the Philippines and Sri Lanka, where female identity centers on motherhood, and where the birth rate is high. Often migrants, especially the undocumented ones, cannot bring their children with them. Most mothers try to leave their children in the care of grandmothers, aunts, and fathers, in roughly that order. An orphanage is a last resort. A number of nannies working in rich countries hire nannies to care for their own children back home either as solo caretakers or as aides to the female relatives left in charge back home. Carmen Ronquillo, for example, migrated from the Philippines to Rome to work as a maid for an architect and single mother of two. She left behind her husband, two teenagers—and a maid.

Whatever arrangements these mothers make for their children, however, most feel the separation acutely, expressing guilt and remorse to the researchers who interview them. Says one migrant mother who left her two-month-old baby in the care of a relative. "The first two years I felt like I was going crazy. You have to believe me when I say that it was like I was having intense psychological problems. I would catch myself gazing at nothing, thinking about my child." Recounted another migrant nanny through tears, "When I saw my children again, I thought, 'Oh children do grow up even without their mother.' I left my youngest when she was only five years old. She was already nine when I saw her again, but she still wanted me to carry her."

Many more migrant female workers than migrant male workers stay in their adopted countries—in fact, most do. In staying, these mothers remain separated from their children, a choice freighted, for many, with a terrible sadness. Some migrant nannies, isolated in their employers' homes and faced with what is often depressing work, find solace in lavishing their affluent charges with the love and care they wish they could provide their own children. In an interview with Rhacel Parreñas, Vicky Diaz, a college-educated school teacher who left behind five children in the Philippines, said, "the only thing you can do is to give all your love to the child [in your care]. In my absence from my children, the most I could do with my situation was to give all my love to that child." Without intending it, she has taken part in a global heart transplant.

As much as these mothers suffer, their children suffer more. And there are a lot of them. An estimated 30 percent of Filipino children—some eight million—live in households where at least one parent has gone overseas. These children have counterparts in Africa, India, Sri Lanka, Latin America, and the former Soviet Union. How are these children doing? Not very well, according to a survey Manila's Scalabrini Migration Center conducted with more than seven hundred children in 1996. Compared to their classmates, the children of migrant workers more frequently fell ill; they were more likely to express anger, confusion, and apathy; and they performed particularly poorly in school. Other studies of this population show a rise in delinquency and child suicide. When such children were asked whether they would also migrate when they grew up, leaving their own children in the care of others, they all said no.

Faced with these facts, one senses some sort of injustice at work, linking the emotional deprivation of these children with the surfeit of affection their First World counterparts enjoy. In her study of native-born women of color who do domestic work, Sau-Ling Wong argues that the time and energy these workers devote to the children of their employers

is diverted from their own children. But time and energy are not all that's involved; so, too, is love. In this sense, we can speak about love as an unfairly distributed resource—extracted from one place and enjoyed somewhere else.

Is love really a "resource" to which a child has a right? Certainly the United Nations Declaration on the Rights of the Child asserts all children's right to an "atmosphere of happiness, love, and understanding." Yet in some ways, this claim is hard to make. The more we love and are loved, the more deeply we can love. Love is not fixed in the same way that most material resources are fixed. Put another way, if love is a resource, it's a *renewable* resource; it creates more of itself. And yet Rowena Bautista can't be in two places at once. Her day has only so many hours. It may also be true that the more love she gives to Noa, the less she gives to her own three children back in the Philippines. Noa in the First World gets more love, and Clinton and Princela in the Third World get less. In this sense, love does appear scarce and limited, like a mineral extracted from the earth.

Perhaps, then, feelings *are* distributable resources, but they behave somewhat differently from either scarce or renewable material resources. According to Freud, we don't "withdraw" and "invest" feeling but rather *displace* or redirect it. The process is an unconscious one, whereby we don't actually give up a feeling of, say, love or hate, so much as we find a new object for it—in the case of sexual feeling, a more appropriate object than the original one, whom Freud presumed to be our opposite-sex parent. While Freud applied the idea of displacement mainly to relationships within the nuclear family, it seems only a small stretch to apply it to relationships like Rowena's to Noa. As Rowena told Frank, the *Wall Street Journal* reporter, "I give Noa what I can't give my children."

Understandably, First World parents welcome and even invite nannies to redirect their love in this manner. The way some employers describe it, a nanny's love of her employer's child is a natural product of her more loving Third World culture, with its warm family ties, strong community life, and long tradition of patient maternal love of children. In hiring a nanny, many such employers implicitly hope to import a poor country's "native culture," thereby replenishing their own rich country's depleted culture of care. They import the benefits of Third World "family values." Says the director of a coop nursery in the San Francisco Bay Area, "This may be odd to say, but the teacher's aides we hire from Mexico and Guatemala know how to love a child better than the middle-class white parents. They are more relaxed, patient, and joyful. They enjoy the kids more. These professional parents are pressured for time and anxious to develop their kids' talents. I tell the parents that they can really learn how to love from the Latinas and the Filipinas."

When asked why Anglo mothers should relate to children so differently than do Filipina teacher's aides, the nursery director speculated, "The Filipinas are brought up in a more relaxed, loving environment. They aren't as rich as we are, but they aren't so pressured for time, so materialistic, so anxious. They have a more loving, family-oriented culture." One mother, an American lawyer, expressed a similar view:

Carmen just enjoys my son. She doesn't worry whether. . . he's learning his letters, or whether he'll get into a good preschool. She just enjoys him. And actually, with anxious busy parents like us, that's really what Thomas needs. I love my son more than anyone in this world. But at this stage Carmen is better for him.

Filipina nannies I have interviewed in California paint a very different picture of the love they share with their First World charges. Theirs is not an import of happy peasant mothering but a love that partly develops on American shores, informed by an American ideology of mother-child bonding and fostered by intense loneliness and longing for their own children. If love is a precious resource, it is not one simply extracted from the Third World and implanted in the First; rather, it owes its very existence to a peculiar cultural alchemy that occurs in the land to which it is imported.

For María Gutierrez, who cares for the eight-month-old baby of two hardworking professionals (a lawyer and a doctor, born in the Philippines but now living in San Jose, California), loneliness and long work hours feed a love for her employers' child. "I love Ana more than my own two children.

Yes, more! It's strange, I know. But I have time to be with her. I'm paid. I am lonely here. I work ten hours a day, with one day off. I don't know any neighbors on the block. And so this child gives me what I need."

Not only that, but she is able to provide her employer's child with a different sort of attention and nurturance than she could deliver to her own children. "I'm more patient," she explains, "more relaxed. I put the child first. My kids, I treated them the way my mother treated me."

I asked her how her mother had treated her and she replied:

My mother grew up in a farming family. It was a hard life. My mother wasn't warm to me. She didn't touch me or say "I love you." She didn't think she should do that. Before I was born she had lost four babies—two in miscarriage and two died as babies. I think she was afraid to love me as a baby because she thought I might die too. Then she put me to work as a "little mother" caring for my four younger brothers and sisters. I didn't have time to play.

Fortunately, an older woman who lived next door took an affectionate interest in María, often feeding her and even taking her in overnight when she was sick. María felt closer to this woman's relatives than she did to her biological aunts and cousins. She had been, in some measure, informally adopted—a practice she describes as common in the Philippine countryside and even in some towns during the 1960s and 1970s.

In a sense, María experienced a premodern childhood, marked by high infant mortality, child labor, and an absence of sentimentality, set within a culture of strong family commitment and community support. Reminiscent of fifteenth-century France, as Philippe Ariès describes it in *Centuries of Childhood*, this was a childhood before the romanticization of the child and before the modern middle-class ideology of intensive mothering. Sentiment wasn't the point; commitment was.

María's commitment to her own children, aged twelve and thirteen when she left to work abroad, bears the mark of that upbringing. Through all of their anger and tears, María sends remittances and calls, come hell or high water. The commitment is there. The sentiment, she has to work at. When she calls home now, María says, "I tell my daughter 'I love you.' At first it sounded fake. But after a while it became natural. And now she says it back. It's strange, but I think I learned that it was okay to say that from being in the United States."

María's story points to a paradox. On the one hand, the First World extracts love from the Third World. But what is being extracted is partly produced or "assembled" here: the leisure, the money, the ideology of the child, the intense loneliness and yearning for one's own children. In María's case, a premodern childhood in the Philippines, a postmodern ideology of mothering and childhood in the United States, and the loneliness of migration blend to produce the love she gives to her employers' child. That love is also a product of the nanny's freedom from the time pressure and school anxiety parents feel in a culture that lacks a social safety net—one where both parent and child have to "make it" at work because no state policy, community, or marital tie is reliable enough to sustain them. In that sense, the love María gives as a nanny does not suffer from the disabling effects of the American version of late capitalism.

If all this is true—if, in fact, the nanny's love is something at least partially produced by the conditions under which it is given—is María's love of a First World child really being extracted from her own Third World children? Yes, because her daily presence has been removed, and with it the daily expression of her love. It is, of course, the nanny herself who is doing the extracting. Still, if her children suffer the loss of her affection, she suffers with them. This, indeed, is globalization's pound of flesh.

Curiously, the suffering of migrant women and their children is rarely visible to the First World beneficiaries of nanny love. Noa's mother focuses on her daughter's relationship with Rowena. Ana's mother focuses on her daughter's relationship with María. Rowena loves Noa, María loves Ana. That's all there is to it. The nanny's love is a thing in itself. It is unique, private—fetishized. Marx talked about the fetishization of things, not feelings. When we make a fetish of an object—an SUV, for example—we see that object as independent of its context. We

disregard, he would argue, the men who harvested the rubber latex, the assembly-line workers who bolted on the tires, and so on. Just as we mentally isolate our idea of an object from the human scene within which it was made, so, too, we unwittingly separate the love between nanny and child from the global capitalist order of love to which it very much belongs.

The notion of extracting resources from the Third World in order to enrich the First World is hardly new. It harks back to imperialism in its most literal form: the nineteenth-century extraction of gold, ivory, and rubber from the Third World. . . .Today, as love and care become the "new gold," the female part of the story has grown in prominence. In both cases, through the death or displacement of their parents, Third World children pay the price.

Imperialism in its classic form involved the north's plunder of physical resources from the south. Its main protagonists were virtually all men: explorers, kings, missionaries, soldiers, and the local men who were forced at gunpoint to harvest wild rubber latex and the like. . . .

Today's north does not extract love from the south by force: there are no colonial officers in tan helmets, no invading armies, no ships bearing arms sailing off to the colonies. Instead, we see a benign scene of Third World women pushing baby carriages, elder care workers patiently walking, arms linked, with elderly clients on streets or sitting beside them in First World parks.

Today, coercion operates differently. While the sex trade and some domestic service is brutally enforced, in the main the new emotional imperialism does not issue from the barrel of a gun. Women choose to migrate for domestic work. But they choose it because economic pressures all but coerce them to. That yawning gap between rich and poor countries is itself a form of coercion, pushing Third World mothers to seek work in the First for lack of options closer to home. But given the prevailing free market ideology, migration is viewed as a "personal choice." Its consequences are seen as "personal problems.". . .

Some children of migrant mothers in the Philippines, Sri Lanka, Mexico, and elsewhere may be well cared for by loving kin in their communities. We need more data if we are to find out how such children are really doing. But if we discover that they aren't doing very well, how are we to respond? I can think of three possible approaches. First, we might say that all women everywhere should stay home and take care of their own families. The problem with Rowena is not migration but neglect of her traditional role. A second approach might be to deny that a problem exists: the care drain is an inevitable outcome of globalization, which is itself good for the world. A supply of labor has met a demand—what's the problem? If the first approach condemns global migration, the second celebrates it. Neither acknowledges its human costs.

According to a third approach—the one I take—loving, paid child care with reasonable hours is a very good thing. And globalization brings with it new opportunities, such as a nanny's access to good pay. But it also introduces painful new emotional realities for Third World children. We need to embrace the needs of Third World societies, including their children. We need to develop a global sense of ethics to match emerging global economic realities. If we go out to buy a pair of Nike shoes, we want to know how low the wage and how long the hours were for the Third World worker who made them. Likewise, if Rowena is taking care of a two-year-old six thousand miles from her home, we should want to know what is happening to her own children.

If we take this third approach, what should we or others in the Third World do? One obvious course would be to develop the Philippine and other Third World economies to such a degree that their citizens can earn as much money inside their countries as outside them. Then the Rowenas of the world could support their children in jobs they'd find at home. While such an obvious solution would seem ideal—if not easily achieved—Douglas Massey, a specialist in migration, points to some unexpected problems, at least in the short run. In Massey's view, it is not underdevelopment that sends migrants like Rowena off to the First World but development itself. The higher the percentage of women working in local manufacturing, he finds, the greater the chance that any one woman will leave on a first, undocumented trip abroad. Perhaps these women's horizons broaden. Perhaps they meet others who have gone abroad. Perhaps

they come to want better jobs and more goods. Whatever the original motive, the more people in one's community migrate, the more likely one is to migrate too.

If development creates migration, and if we favor some form of development, we need to find more humane responses to the migration such development is likely to cause. For those women who migrate in order to flee abusive husbands, one part of the answer would be to create solutions to that problem closer to home—domestic-violence shelters in these women's home countries, for instance. Another might be to find ways to make it easier for migrating nannies to bring their children with them. Or as a last resort, employers could be required to finance a nanny's regular visits home.

A more basic solution, of course, is to raise the value of caring work itself, so that whoever does it gets more rewards for it. Care, in this case, would no longer be such a "pass-on" job. And now here's the rub: the value of the labor of raising a child—always low relative to the value of other kinds of labor—has, under the impact of globalization, sunk lower still. Children matter to their parents immeasurably, of course, but the labor of raising them does not earn much credit in the eyes of the world. When middle-class housewives raised children as an unpaid, full-time role, the work was dignified by its aura of middle-classness. That was the one upside to the otherwise confining cult of middle-class, nineteenth- and early-twentieth-century American womanhood. But when the unpaid work of raising a child became the paid work of child-care workers, its low market value revealed the abidingly low value of caring work generally—and further lowered it.

The low value placed on caring work results neither from an absence of a need for it nor from the simplicity or ease of doing it. Rather, the declining value of child care results from a cultural politics of inequality. It can be compared with the declining value of basic food crops relative to manufactured goods on the international market. Though clearly more necessary to life, crops such as wheat and rice fetch low and declining prices, while manufactured goods are more highly valued. Just as the market price of primary produce keeps the Third World low in the community of nations, so the low market value of care keeps the status of the women who do it—and, ultimately, all women—low.

One excellent way to raise the value of care is to involve fathers in it. If men shared the care of family members worldwide, care would spread laterally instead of being passed down a social class ladder. In Norway, for example, all employed men are eligible for a year's paternity leave at 90 percent pay. Some 80 percent of Norwegian men now take over a month of parental leave. In this way, Norway is a model to the world. For indeed it is men who have for the most part stepped aside from caring work, and it is with them that the "care drain" truly begins.

In all developed societies, women work at paid jobs. According to the International Labor Organization, half of the world's women between ages fifteen and sixty-four do paid work. Between 1960 and 1980, sixty-nine out of eighty-eight countries surveyed showed a growing proportion of women in paid work. Since 1950, the rate of increase has skyrocketed in the United States, while remaining high in Scandinavia and the United Kingdom and moderate in France and Germany. If we want developed societies with women doctors, political leaders, teachers, bus drivers, and computer programmers, we will need qualified people to give loving care to their children. And there is no reason why every society should not enjoy such loving paid child care. It may even be true that Rowena Bautista or María Guttierez are the people to provide it, so long as their own children either come with them or otherwise receive all the care they need. In the end, Article 9 of the United Nations Declaration on the Rights of the Child—which the United States has not yet signed—states an important goal. . . . It says we need to value care as our most precious resource, and to notice where it comes from and ends up. For, these days, the personal is global.

THINKING ABOUT THE READING

Why do women leave their own families to work in other countries? Why is there such great demand for nannies and other care workers in some countries? Discuss the concept of care work as a commodity available for sale on a global market. What other services are available on a global market that used to be considered something one got "for free" from family members? Before such services were hired out, who, traditionally, was expected to provide them? What has changed? Discuss some reasons why women make up so much of the global labor force today. If these trends in global labor continue, what do you think families will look like in the near future?

Embodied Experiences of Older Lesbians

KATHLEEN SLEVIN

(2006)

Introduction

In this chapter I explore the bodily experiences of aging through the narratives of a group of old, white lesbians who are economically privileged. I particularly focus on exploring how ageism is both manifested and contested or resisted in the daily lives of these old women. Both feminist and life-course perspectives guide me in this analysis. The former framework focuses on ways that lives are shaped, by the intersections of power relations, including race, class, gender, sexual orientation, and age. The life-course perspective emphasizes sensitivity to how historical periods and personal biography shape lives (Stolier and Gibson 1994). My overall goal is to illustrate how feminist understandings of the body are deepened when we focus on old women and their bodily experiences. The narratives of the old lesbians in this study bring attention to a group that is "triply invisible" because they are old, female, and lesbian (Barker 2004). This focus also allows us to examine heteronormative and ageist notions about aging and being old and to explore how these notions shape the aging experiences of these old lesbians.

A key assumption is that the story of aging begins with the meanings we ascribe to our aging bodies. Thus, through intensive interviews with these old women, we come to see how they understand, articulate, and negotiate the *corporeal* aspects of growing old, and we come to appreciate how embodiment is critical to making sense of age and aging (Laz 2003). Because they are old and lesbian, we also see how age intersects with sexual orientation and gender to shape their ongoing corporeal understandings and negotiations. As well, we grasp more fully that our current state of knowledge promotes, even if implicitly, an essentialized and one-dimensional understanding of old people in general and of old women and lesbians in particular. Consequently, as we explore these women's experiences with aging and old age, we take care to not assume a universal or single aging experience shared by all old lesbians or by all of the old lesbians who compose this study.

Aging, Ageism, and the Body

Aging is increasingly constructed as a problem in our culture, and old age is stigmatized as a personal failure—especially for those who lack the requisite economic resources or physical abilities to participate in consumerism (Katz 2005). In a youth-oriented consumer society, the body is central in the framing of age-resisting cultural practices; the body is privileged as both a focus of consumption and the key to defining individuality (Gilleard and Higgs 2000). Certainly consumer ads with their metaphors of defying aging invite us to believe that growing old and, in particular, *looking old* are to be avoided at all costs. In addition to antiaging cosmetics and technologies, there is a growing emphasis on "staying young" through physical fitness. *Appearing* fit is a modern virtue that has, in the space of a few decades, become highly valued currency and a way to be judged productive in old age (Oberg and Tornstam 2001; Faircloth 2003). "Busy bodies" are now an integral part of active, "successful" aging—overshadowing how different social locations create difficulties and challenges for many old individuals (see Katz 2005; 136–38). Furthermore, we are led to believe that choice, the hallmark of a consumer society, is ours to make about how we grow old—indeed whether we do it at all, biology has been trumped by technology, including cosmetics that promise to help us resist old age and aging. Growing old has become the new century's solvable problem (Cruikshank 2003).

In recent decades we have witnessed an enormous upsurge in interdisciplinary attention to the body, and feminist scholars have been on the forefront. Though attentive to exploring intersections between gender, race, class, and sexual orientation, this scholarship ignores aging bodies (Katz 2005; Faircloth 2003; Calasanti and Slevin 2001). Despite the fact that the body is a critical marker of age, even social gerontologists have given it scant attention in understanding how we experience its aging, except in cases of disease and illness (Cruikshank 2003). Attention to the old people's bodily experiences has been scarce in general, and old women's bodies have been ignored especially (Katz 2005). When researchers do focus on old bodies, they have primarily emphasized loss of function and engage in a "narrative of decline" (Gullette 1997). Consequently, mundane physical experiences with aging bodies go unstudied, and old people experience their bodies in the context of a "profound cultural silence" (Twigg 2000: 115).

The body is central to ageist notions and practices; as Laws (1995) reminds us, ageism is an embodied form of oppression. Yet responses to aging bodies are gendered in various ways. For example, men are judged as a physical whole (face and body) while women are identified with their faces (Cruikshank 2003). In addition, ageism disempowers all women by not only dividing young from old but also "instilling the dread of age earlier and earlier in women's lives" (Weil 2001: x). While gendered in its manifestations and consequences, ageism varies greatly—it is shaped by multiple and changing forces and by various other social locations such as race, class, and sexual orientation. As a form of oppression it is both complex and unique because, unlike racism or sexism, we will all live to experience ageism, if we live long enough; as well, unlike racism and sexism, ageism fits only part of the life span and its victims may also be its perpetrators (Laws 1995).

For the most part, these women perceive that being lesbian and largely in the company of other lesbians shapes their aging experiences positively; Donna's assertion that to grow old as a lesbian is much easier than for heterosexual women captures the general sentiment. Beth's comment that "physical appearance is not as big an issue in the lesbian world as it is in the heterosexual world" gives an indication of how sexual orientation might matter. Barbara (age sixty-eight) provides an additional argument (that reinforces this notion: "I don't think lesbians require of each other as much as men require of their women." Finally, Eliza (age seventy-one) reminds us of the role of age relations. Her comment suggests that she is quite conscious about how being lesbian frees her from unrealistic expectations about maintaining a youthful appearance: "Lesbians worry less about aging, about how they look." Perhaps it is this perceived freedom to worry less than heterosexual women about looking old that allows Eliza to declare enthusiastically, "I love my gray hair."

Their comments also reveal that most of these women are conscious of how coping with the stigma of being lesbian has helped them to accept being old women. The authors of a recent study of old lesbians conclude that facing adversity has helped their interviewees "face the reality of their aging with a certain frankness and optimism" (Clunis et al. 2005: 170). Two respondents express similar notions:

I guess whatever got me through knowing . . . that it was not good to be lesbian, has gotten me past [the idea that] it's not good to be old. In other words, I've had practice with this from [day one]. (Beth, age sixty-seven)

Lesbians had to learn to cope with being different so [being old] is not such a shock . . . You've developed coping mechanisms . . . one is to accept your situation. Another is to choose not to be invisible at times and to say, "Hey, I have something to say." (Eliza, age seventy-one)

Like several interviewees, Sara (age sixty-five) is generally very comfortable with her aging, and her discussions throughout the interview reflect that she has given much thought to how age and gender shape women's identities: "I think there is something very sad about a woman who obviously can't accept the aging process and can't be comfortable with it." In coming out as lesbians, most of these women talked about how they learned to recognize the dominant society's stigmatization of their lesbianism for what it is—oppression. Just as most learned to contest the negative stereotype of being lesbian, they may also have learned to transfer such resistance to certain ageist notions of aging women. This may help explain Sara's feisty resistance: "I told myself for many years that the one thing I looked forward to in getting older was that I'd have a 'Fuck you' attitude!"

Still, this comment hints at the fact that Sara sees negative aspects associated with getting old. She is not alone in the struggle to reconcile contradictory attitudes about aging. Indeed, these narratives reveal multiple contradictions and underscore how much our experiences of ourselves is shaped by hegemonic ideas that valorize youth and denigrate old people, especially old women. The paradoxes about bodily aging that unfold in the narratives of these old lesbians lend credence to Barker's (2004) argument that lesbian claims to be more accepting (than gay males) of the bodily changes that accompany aging (wrinkles, sagging body parts, etc.) is a foundational myth rather than an empirically verified reality. The section that follows provides us an opportunity to examine these ideas in more depth, to explore what Copper calls the "endless unexamined contradictions in the prejudice which women feel toward the old women they themselves are or are becoming" (Copper 1988: 14).

"I'm Not Old." Like Hurd's (1999) interviewees, all the women in this study took great pleasure in their belief that they look and feel younger than their chronological ages. Such attitudes reproduce ageism by reinforcing the idea that to be old is bad and that to be seen as more youthful than one's chronological age is good. In other words, they "define themselves in light of that which they are not" (Hurd 1999: 425); they "pass" as younger than they are. Indeed, the further the distance between their chronological ages and their appearances as judged by others, the greater the delight expressed. Becca (age sixty-eight) talks about how young it makes her feel when people comment, "You don't look your age, I thought you were fifty-eight." Rita (age seventy-eight) tells a similar story about how great she felt to be told that she looks ten years younger than she is. Rita's explanation for being seen as younger than her chronological age has to do with "my energy and the vitality with which I . . . live my life." Rita's notion of being energetic and active is critical to the distancing tactics to which other women also allude; such conceptions illuminate the extent to which these women have internalized negative notions about old age and about looking one's chronological age. The comments also underscore how attractiveness is based on youthful standards that emphasize being active and involved while also implying negative stereotypes of old people as inactive and dull. Thus, age relations dictate that we uphold and value youth and recognize nothing positive in being old. Others also described their own aging by negotiating a self-image that accommodates ageist stereotypes by separating themselves from their same-age peers. For instance, here is how Eliza (age seventy-one) explains why she has aged "very well"; "a lot has to do with [the fact] that I'm still interested in things and still active and I enjoy life." The women I interviewed, as in previous research (Hurd 1999, 2000;

Minichiello et al. 2000), also define the markers of being "not old" as keeping busy and being intellectually engaged, active, fit, and productive. All rely too on being healthy enough to sustain the level of activity needed to be judged positively—something that Hurd (1999) reminds us is tenuous and is something that will inevitably diminish If these women live long enough.

Old Age as a Contagion. Another strategy to avoid being old is to create social distance between oneself and other old people. Becca (age sixty-eight) demonstrates this idea when she says, "Well, I don't really relate to anybody in my own age group. I mean it really is kind of interesting that . . . in a way I'm happy that I don't because I don't want to get pulled down by that and I think I could." Becca's strategy of spending time only with younger people and her rejection of her own age cohort is manifested in this description of what she experienced when she arrived at a lesbian dance one evening:

> We got there and said, "God, this is kind of depressing" because there were some older lesbians there and they were all overweight and it's like, "God, why am I here?" We left shortly thereafter . . . because the group was depressing. They were overweight . . . and they were not active, they were not involved in any kind of physical activity that would give them, I think . . . a younger attitude. It was scary. (Becca, age sixty-eight)

Becca's description, in which she reproduces ageist and sexist stereotypes, suggests several things worth noting. First, she employs the gaze of youth when she assesses the party scene and concludes that the old lesbians she saw embody old age in all its repulsiveness. Like Hurd's (2000) interviewees, Becca has internalized ageist cultural conceptions of attractiveness and, like them, she sees old women's bodies as ugly. Part of her revulsion is also tied to how she sees these old women as being overweight and inactive—both negative stereotypes of old people. But the stereotypes are also gendered and sexist (and likely class related, too) because we sense that some of her revulsion is connected to the fact that the old people in question are women from whom she distances herself and also stigmatizes for their lack of youthful vitality.

Becca is not alone in her desire to separate herself from her peers. Rita (seventy-eight) also claims to avoid her own age group because they are "conservative, afraid of living." Stating, "I always surround myself with younger people," Rita demonstrates a strategy of rejection and an active, explicit form of ageism. Yet in other contexts Rita is openly critical of prejudice against old people. Her contradictory positions remind us of the importance of considering context as we explore manifestations of ageism. Similarly, Gail (age seventy-three), who expressed the least ageist attitudes of all the women interviewed, still distances herself from other old women with this comment: "I don't dress like an old lady!"

Weight

The women I interviewed expressed complicated and sometimes contradictory responses to aging and their aging bodies. We hear their ambivalence toward being old in their narratives and how they waiver between positive and negative bodily assessments. Perhaps Miriam most powerfully illustrates the ambivalence that others struggled to explain. In one moment of the interview she declares, "I think I have aged really well. This is really the best time of my life, you know." Yet when she responds to the question "How do you feel overall about your body?" her words illustrate that she sees her aging body as problematic:

> I would say it's kind of 50-50 in that I still have a lot of energy; I still feel more good than I feel bad. But I certainly do not feel good about gaining weight. I've been struggling so with my weight. I have not had a waistline in ten years. (Miriam, age sixty-one)

Even among those who give every indication of being quite comfortable with aging, the negative theme raised by Miriam—weight—is a dominant issue when it comes to body image concerns for these women. They resemble Hurd's (1999) interviewees, who were uniformly dissatisfied with their weight and who expressed a sense of failure or defeat in their attempts to discipline their aging bodies. Taken as a whole, Miriam's words show how complex assessments of aging can be. When she talks positively about her aging, she is talking *not* about her body but about other aspects of aging, such as retirement. As well, when she talks about her body, she separates her bodily assessment into the distinct categories of body performance and body appearance concerns; she is happy with the former but not the latter.

By attending to body appearance issues, we see that these women's weight obsession and their body images are shaped by youthful and gendered standards of attractiveness. Per all of the nine women interviewed, weight emerged as a nagging, problematic concern that surfaced repeatedly in our conversations. That these women are lesbian provides them little, if any, relief from the never-ending obsession with weight issues. Only one, Gail (age seventy-three), talked little about weight concerns during the interview because, as she proudly made the point early in our conversation, she had lost thirty-five pounds in the past year and felt no need to lose more weight. The remaining women reported an average difference of twenty-three pounds between their ideal and real weights. They each talk in different ways about the obligation they feel to discipline their bodies: to exercise regularly and to restrict their eating. Talking about good health, fitness, and activity allows these women to perform "active" aging. Being well educated, healthy, and health conscious provides them a language that justifies their disciplinary activities, and like Hurd's (2000) respondents, they frequently emphasize health and not physical attractiveness as the motivator for staying active. But engaging in these activities also highlights how relentlessly coercive are the norms of thinness and youthfulness among some privileged old women in our culture. Being financially very comfortable provides them the means to work on their bodies on a regular basis, and their healthy habits and choices are intimately shaped by their class privilege—a privilege that allows some women to resist being old longer than those who do not have such means. Being female ensures a lifelong obligation to be ever vigilant and invested in their appearance, and it illuminates the ways that aging is "shrouded in denial or shame" (Cruikshank 2003: 7). Being old and lesbian provides little relief from the gendered and ageist demands to be trim and nonmatronly—if not thin.

Disciplining the Body

Disciplining the body to strive to meet youthful standards of attractive bodies thus emerges as a strategy of accommodation to ageist potions of what acceptable female bodies look like. As well, social class privilege reinforces this need to engage in body discipline because the means are available, and to not avail of them signals "moral failure or laxity" (Hurd 2000:91).

The following quotes by the women in my study illustrate the complexities of body image, weight, and body discipline. First, we hear the voice of two women who do not actively discipline their bodies, but not because they think they do not need to do so. On the contrary, they express unhappiness and disappointment as they have internalized these ageist standards but have, by their own judgment, shirked what they see as their obligation to discipline their bodies:

I am not very happy right now. I guess I weigh too much. I don't like the fact that I have gained weight . . . and I may get busy and do something about it. (Eliza, age seventy-one)

Deborah (age sixty) is no less happy with her lack of action:

[Sighs.] Well, unless I start to do something about my weight, it's going to get heavier. . . . I really would like my body to be thinner. I'm gonna actually get into an exercise program.

Finally, women who work to discipline their bodies also express unhappiness. Rita's discontent and her sense of loss for a younger body that was thinner are expressed in her regret that weight has robbed her of her more youthful appearance:

Since I gained weight my body lost some of its charm. I don't like it. I'm trying to lose weight and I'm looking at not a diet but a [new] way of life, a way of eating. So, I've changed my way of eating. (Rita, age seventy-eight, swims a few times a week)

Two other women who work hard on their bodies are still dissatisfied, and they anticipate failure, despite their efforts:

I want to continue to get stronger, to develop some muscles. I want to get about ten pounds off. I kind of got stuck. I'd like to get some off this abdomen. I don't know that it will ever happen [laughs]. (Beth, age sixty-seven, started exercising two years ago; she goes to the gym three times a week and has a personal trainer who helps her do strength training one of those days)

At this point I'm a little concerned about myself because . . . four years ago I was eight pounds lighter and a lot stronger and that stresses me some. I am working on that. I want to get to four days a week [in the gym] and then five maybe. (Becca, age sixty-eight)

Among all the noteworthy aspects of these quotes, perhaps what stands out most is the agelessness of many women's weight obsession (particularly white, affluent women of all ages). As well, we come to appreciate the fact that some affluent, healthy women feel obligated to exercise into their seventies and beyond to approximate the youthful body standards that our culture requires of women. Even when the language they call on to justify their body discipline is one that centers on health concerns rather than physical attractiveness, the narratives of these women convey self-disapproval.

However, the pressures they feel to strive for elusive, thinner bodies coexist with attempts to reduce the stigma of aging. Hurd (2000) sees this phenomenon as representing a developing pragmatism among older women who realize that the loss of youthful physical attractiveness is inevitable. The words of two women demonstrate how age relations shape approaches to aging, how some old women negotiate the inevitable decline in their bodies by accommodation. Miriam (age sixty-one), a former homecoming queen who is the most invested in her appearance and the most unhappy with how she looks at this stage of her life, speaks with "stoic resignation" (Cruikshank 2003:7).

I guess I don't feel quite as much pressure about it now. I'm more accepting of it in a way than I was even when I was young. I was more critical of it back then; now I am more accepting. I'm not happy about it but I am more accepting. It's OK as long as I have elastic in the waist. As long as I'm comfortable, I'm OK.

By contrast, Sara (age sixty-five), who accepts growing old and looking old, also suggests that women need to resist the notion that their physical appearance is a proxy for self-worth:

At the end of the day when you come home from the gym [your body] still may not look like what you want it to look like and that's the point at which we have to start learning how to love ourselves as we are.

Sara's advice to old women about learning to love who they are (as opposed to striving for an unobtainable youthful ideal) raises the interesting issue of how these women respond to cosmetic surgery as another antiaging strategy that allows aging women (and men) to alter their bodies so that they can pass as younger or more youthful than their chronological age.

Conclusions

This study advances feminist scholarship by revealing the age relations that render the body a site of struggle and ambivalence, even among old lesbians who are generally committed to challenging hegemonic gender norms. My findings illustrate the complexity of the embodied aging experience, and the narratives of these women remind us that their aging is not homogenous but varied; not only are there different views on aging but there are different approaches to growing and being old. Thus, not all of the women interviewed use the same strategies as they negotiate aging, and they do not all share the same experiences with or attitudes toward being old women. Being lesbian and living a lesbian lifestyle allows many of these women to resist and to be more positive about some aspects of being old women.

At the same time, this study reveals important commonalities among these women that demonstrate the oppressive nature of age relations. Their bodies are vehicles for creating meaning about aging and about old age, and their accounts reveal strategies they employ to manage the ageism that shapes their responses to their own bodies and to the bodies of others. We learn that ageism is not monolithic but dynamic, as their narratives contain various manifestations and intensities of ageism. Like the old women that Hurd (1999, 2000) studied, the old lesbians in my study teach us that ageism is a complex phenomenon (Minichiello et al. 2000) that requires constant negotiation of contradictory messages. Like Hurd's old heterosexual women, they engage in various distancing strategies, such as seeing themselves as "not old" and actively passing for younger than their chronological ages; they are also uniformly concerned with weight and with losing it, although most justify their concerns for health reasons rather than physical appearance. The majority also approve of cosmetic surgery as a way to fight looking old.

My data lend support to Copper's (1988) claim that old lesbians are socialized to adhere to many of the same gender norms as heterosexual women—an argument that reinforces the notion that gender trumps sexual orientation at least some of the time. As well, these narratives illuminate how deeply age matters; they allow us to see how ageist norms prevail and how feminism is limited in its influence in these regards. "Successful" aging requires that women—especially if they are privileged—age as slender, healthy and fit, energetic, and independent people (Ruddick 1999). This dictate underscores the power of heterosexual notions of youthful and thin bodies and reminds us also that social class privilege provides some in our society the means to resist being old or being seen as old for longer than the less advantaged can. Especially for those who have the means to seek the valued currency of being or appearing fit, the power of the youth gaze is insidious—whether one seeks a body that attempts to satisfy it because one wants to garner a male gaze or a female gaze. The words of these lesbians thus illuminate the facts that like all old women, they live in a society where the "cultural imperialism of youthfulness" is pervasive and that ageism plays a central role in identity (Laws 1995). Consequently, attachment to other women may provide some benefits in growing old, but such attachments provide little protection from the-"twin prejudices" (Daniluk 1998: 317) of ageism and sexism. Thus, the voices of the old lesbians in this study point to the centrality of age relations in understanding bodily experiences.

REFERENCES

Abell. S.C., and Richards, M.H. (1996) "The Relationship between Body Shape and Satisfaction and Self-Esteem: An Investigation of Gender and Class Differences," *Journal of Youth and Adolescence* 25 (5): 691–703.

Altabe, M., and Thompson, J.K. (1992) "Size Estimation versus Figural Reactions of Body Image Disturbance: Relation to Body Dissatisfaction and Eating Dysfunction," *International Journal of Eating Disorders* 11:397–402.

Arber, S., and Ginn, J. (1991) "The Invisibility of Age: Gender and Class in Later Life," *Sociological Review* 39 (2): 260–91.

Barker, J.C. (2004) "Lesbian Aging: An Agenda for Social Research," in *Gay and Lesbian Aging; Research and Future Directions*, ed. G. Herdt and B. de Vries, 29–72. New York: Springer.

Bordo, S. (1993) *Unbearable Weight: Feminism, Western Culture, and the Body*. Berkeley: University of California Press.

Brand, P., Rothblum, E., and Soloman, L. (1992) "A Comparison of Lesbians, Gay Men, and Heterosexuals on Weight and Restricted Eating," *International Journal of Eating Disorders* 11:253–59.

Calasanti, T.M., and Slevin, K.R. (2001) *Gender, Social Inequalities, and Aging*. Walnut Creek, CA; AltaMira Press.

Cash, T.B. (2000) "Women's Body Images: For Better or for Worse." Unpublished manuscript.

Clunis, M.D., Fredriksen-Goldsen, K.I., Freeman, P. A., and Nystrom, N. (2005) *Lives of Lesbian Elders: Looking Back, Looking Forward*. New York: Haworth Press.

Conncil, R.W. (1995) *Masculinities*. Berkeley; University of California Press.

Copper, B. (1988) *Over the Hill: Reflections on Ageism between Women*. Freedom, CA: Crossing Press.

Cruikshank, M. (2003) *Learning to Be Old: Gender, Culture, and Aging*. Lanham, MD: Rowman and Littlefield.

Daniluk, J.C. (1988) *Women's Sexuality across the Life Span*. New York: Guilford Press.

Faircloth, C.A., ed. (2003) *Aging Bodies: Images and Everyday Experience*. Walnut Creek, CA: AltaMira Press.

Furman, F.K (1997) *Facing the Mirror: Older Women and Beauty Shop Culture*. New York: Routledge.

Gagne, P., and McGaughey, D. (2002) "Designing Women: Cultural Hegemony and the Exercise of Power among Women Who Have Undergone Elective Mammoplasty," *Gender & Society* 16 (6): 814–38.

Gilleard, C, and Higgs, P. (2000) *Cultures of Ageing: Self, Citizen and the Body*. Harlow, England: Prentice Hall.

Glaser, B., and Strauss, A.L. (1967) *The Discovery of Grounded Theory. Strategies for Qualitative Research*. Chicago: Aldine.

Gullette, M.M. (1997) *Declining to Decline: Cultural Combat and the Politics of the Midlife*. Charlottesville: University Press of Virginia.

Herdt, G., and dc Vries, B. (2004) *Gay and Lesbian Aging: Research and Future Directions*. New York: Springer.

Hurd, L.C. (1999) "'We're Not Old!': Older Women's Negotiation of Aging and Oldness." *Journal of Aging Studies* 13 (4): 419–39.

Hurd, L.C. (2000) "Older Women's Body Image and Embodied Experience An Exploration," *Journal of Women and Aging* 12 (3/4): 77–97.

Katz, S. (2005) *Cultural Aging: Life Course, Lifestyle, and Senior Worlds*. Ontario, Canada; Broadview Press.

Laws, G. (1995) "Understanding Ageism: Lessons from Feminism and Postmodernism." *The Gerontologist* 35 (1): 112–18.

Laz, C. (2003) "Age Embodied," *Journal of Aging Studies* 17:503–19.

Minichiello, V., Browne, J., and Kendig, H. (2000) "Perceptions and Consequences of Ageism: Views of Older People," *Ageing & Society* 20 (3); 253–78.

Nettleion, S., and Wittson, J. (1998) *The Body in Everyday Life*. London and New York: Routledge.

Oberg, P, (2003) "Images versus Experience of the Aging Body," in *Aging Bodies: Images and Everyday Experience,* ed. C.A. Faircloth, 103–39. Walnut Creek, CA; AltaMira Press.

Oberg, P., and Tornstam, L. (2001) "Youthfulness and Fitness—Identity Ideals for All Ages!" *Journal of Aging and Identity* 6 (1): 15–29.

Rosenfeld, D (2003) "The Homosexual Body in Lesbian and Gay Elders' Narratives," in *Aging Bodies: Images and Everyday Experience,* ed. C.A. Faircloth, 171–203. Walnut Creek, CA: AltaMitra Press.

Ruddick, S. (1999) "Virtues and Age," in *Mother Time: Women, Aging, and Ethics,* ed. M.U. Walker, 45–60. Lanham, MD: Rowman & Littlefield.

Slevin, K.F., and Wingrove, C.W. (1998) *From Stumbling Blocks to Stepping Stones: The Life Experience of Fifty Professional African American Women*. New York: New York University Press.

Stein, A. (1997) *Sex and Sensibility: Stories of a Lesbian Generation*. Berkeley: University of California Press.

Stolier, E.P., and Gibson, R.C. (1994) *Worlds of Difference: Inequality in Aging Experience*. Thousand Oaks, CA: Pine Forge Press.

Twigg, J. (2000) *Bathing the Body and Community Care,* London and New York: Routledge.

Weil, L. (2001) "In the Service of Truth: Remembering Barbara Macdonald," foreword to *Look Me in the Eye: Old Women Aging and Ageism,* by B. Macdonald and C. Rich. Denver, CO: Spinsters, Ink.

Weinstock, J.S. (2004) "Lesbian Friendships at and beyond Midlife Patterns and Possibilities for the 21st Century," in *Gay and Lesbian Aging: Research and Future Directions,* ed. G. Herdt and B. de Vries, 177–210. New York: Springer.

West, C., and Zimmerman, D.H. (1987) "Doing Gender," *Gender & Society* (1): 125–51.

Williams, S.J., and Bendelcv, G. (1998) *The Lived Body. Sociological Themes, Embodied Issue*. London and New York: Routledge.

THINKING ABOUT THE READING

What do the narratives of these older, white, economically privileged lesbians tell us about cultural norms for gender, sexuality, and aging? What are some of the contradictions and feelings of ambivalence experienced by these women? What strategies do they use to negotiate the aging process? What age related issues have you observed older family and friends experience in their everyday lives? What role do social structures play in the lived experiences of older individuals?

The Algorithmic Rise of the Alt-Right

JESSIE DANIELS

(2018)

On a late summer evening in 2017, members of the far-right descended on Charlottesville, Virginia, with tiki torches held up in defense of confederate general Robert E. Lee's statue in what was dubbed a "Unite the Right" rally, which had been organized mostly online. The next day, August 13, White nationalists rallied again and violently clashed with counter protestors. One drove his car into a multiracial crowd, killing one and seriously injuring 19 others. As it has turned out, the events in Charlottesville were a watershed moment in the algorithmic rise of White nationalism in the U.S.

White nationalism has gone "from being a conversation you could hold in a bathroom, to the front parlor," according to William H. Regnery II. A multimillionaire, Regnery has spent a significant sum of his inherited wealth pushing his "race realist" agenda via a publishing house and the National Policy Institute, a think-tank. When his protégé and grantee, Richard Spencer, coined the new term "alt-right" in 2008, few took notice. Back then, Jared Taylor, publisher of the White nationalist site American Renaissance, said he thought of his own efforts as "just making a racket," but now he sees himself as part of an ascendant social movement, with Spencer in a lead role. He, along with Jason Kessler, helped organize the rally in Charlottesville.

"I think Tuesday was the most important day in the White nationalist movement," Derek Black told a *New York Times* reporter. Black, a former White nationalist, was referring to the Tuesday following the Charlottesville rally, when the current occupant of the White House repeated White nationalist talking points defending the statues of America's founding slaveholders. In that New York Times interview, Black went on to describe his shock, ". . .Tuesday just took my breath away. I was sitting in a coffee shop and I thought the news from this was done when I read that he had come back and he said there were good people in the White nationalist rally and he salvaged their message." It's certainly not the first time that a sitting president has openly heralded White supremacy from the oval office, but it is the first time that the ideology of White supremacy from both extreme and mainstream sources has been spread through the algorithms of search engines and social media platforms.

There are two strands of conventional wisdom unfolding in popular accounts of the rise of the alt-right. One says that what's really happening can be attributed to a crisis in White identity: the alt-right is simply a manifestation of the angry White male who has status anxiety about his declining social power. Others contend that the alt-right is an unfortunate eddy in the vast ocean of Internet culture. Related to this is the idea that polarization, exacerbated by filter bubbles, has facilitated the spread of Internet memes and fake news promulgated by the alt-right. While the first explanation tends to ignore the influence of the Internet, the second dismisses the importance of White nationalism. I contend that we have to understand both at the same time.

For the better part of 20 years, I have been working with emerging technology and studying White supremacy in various forms of media. In the 1990s, I examined hundreds of printed newsletters from extremist groups and found that many of their talking points resonated with mainstream popular culture and politicians, like Pat Buchanan and Bill Clinton. After that, I left academia for a while and worked in the tech industry, where I produced online coverage of events like the 2000 presidential recount. When I returned to academic research, I did a follow up study tracking how some of the groups I'd studied in print had—or had not—made it on to the Internet. I spent time at places like Stormfront, the White nationalist portal launched in the mid-1990s, and found that some groups had gained a much more nefarious presence than in their print-only days. And, I interviewed young people about how they made sense of White supremacy they encountered online. About the time I finished my second book in 2008, social media platforms and their algorithms began to change the way White nationalists used the Internet. Now I look at the current ascendance of the alt-right from a dual vantage point, informed both from my research into White supremacy and my experience in the tech industry.

The rise of the alt-right is both a continuation of a centuries-old dimension of racism in the U.S. and part of an emerging media ecosystem powered by algorithms. White supremacy has been a feature of the political landscape in the U.S. since the start; vigilante White supremacist movements have been a constant since just after the confederacy lost its battle to continue slavery. The ideology of the contemporary alt-right is entirely consistent with earlier manifestations of extremist White supremacy, with only slightly modifications in style and emphasis. This incarnation is much less steeped in Christian symbolism (few crosses, burning or otherwise), yet trades heavily in antisemitism. Even the Islamophobia among the alt-right has more to do with the racialization of people who follow Islam and the long history of connecting Whiteness to citizenship in the U.S. than it does with beliefs about Christendom. Movement members aim to establish a White ethnostate, consistent with every other extremist, White nationalist movement and more than a few mainstream politicians.

This iteration is newly enabled by algorithms, which do several things. Algorithms deliver search results for those who seek confirmation for racist notions and connect newcomers to like-minded racists, as when Dylan Roof searched for "black on white crime" and Google provided racist websites and a community of others to confirm and grow his hatred. Algorithms speed up the spread of White supremacist ideology, as when memes like "Pepe the Frog" travel from 4chan or Reddit to mainstream news sites. And algorithms, aided by cable news networks, amplify and systematically move White supremacist talking points into the mainstream of political discourse. Like always, White nationalists are being "innovation opportunists," finding openings in the latest technologies to spread their message. To understand how all this works, it's necessary to think about several things at once: how race is embedded in the Internet at the same time it is ignored, how White supremacy operates now, and the ways these interact.

Building Race into the "Race-Less" Internet

The rise of the alt-right would not be possible without the infrastructure built by the tech industry, and yet, the industry likes to imagine itself as creating a "race-less" Internet. In a 1997 ad from a now-defunct telecom company, the Internet was touted as a "place where we can communicate mind-to-mind, where there is no race, no gender, no infirmities . . . only minds." Then narration poses the question, "Is this utopia?" as the word is typed out. "No, the Internet." In many ways, the ad reflected what was then a rather obscure document, written by John Perry Barlow in 1996. Barlow, a recently deceased co-founder of the Electronic Frontier Foundation, wrote *A Declaration of the Independence of Cyberspace,* a manifesto-style manuscript in which he conceives of the Internet as a "place," much like the imaginary American frontier in a Hollywood western, that should remain free from control by "governments of the industrial world," those "weary giants of flesh and steel." He ends with a grand hope for building "a civilization of the Mind in Cyberspace. May it be more humane and fair than the world your governments have made before."

While the giddy notion of a "mind-to-mind" utopia online may seem quaint by the standards of today's "don't-read-the-comments" Internet, Barlow's view remains, more than 20 years later, foundational in Silicon Valley. And it informs thinking in the tech industry when it comes to the alt-right. When several tech companies kicked alt-right users off their platforms after Charlottesville, they were met with a vigorous backlash from many in the industry. Matthew Prince, CEO and co-founder of Cloudflare, who reluctantly banned virulently racist site, *The Daily Stormer,* from his service, fretted about the decision. "As an internet user, I think it's pretty dangerous if my moral, political or economic whims play some role in deciding who can and cannot be online," he said. The Electronic Frontier Foundation issued a statement that read, in part, "we believe that no one—not the government and not private commercial enterprises—should decide who gets to speak and who doesn't," closely echoing Barlow's manifesto.

Even as the dominant discourse about technology followed the "race-less" imaginary of the sales pitch and the ideology, robust critiques that centered alternative, Afrofuturist visions emerged from scholars such as Alondra Nelson. Critical writing about the Internet has followed, demonstrating the myriad ways race is built into digital technologies. The DOS commands of "master" disk and "slave" disk prompt, Anna Everett points out, reinscribe the master/slave narrative into the level of code. Recent concerns about digital surveillance technologies draw much from pre-digital technologies developed to control enslaved peoples, Simone Browne has explained. Racial categories are coded into drop-down menus and the visual culture of nearly every platform, Lisa Nakamura observes. The nearly ubiquitous white hand-pointer acts as a kind of avatar that, in turn, becomes "attached" to depictions of White people in advertisements, the default "universal" Internet user at the keyboard that becomes part of the collective imagination, Michele White notes. Ideas about race are inextricably linked with the development of tech products, such as "Blackbird" (a web browser) or "Ms. Dewey" (a search tool), André Brock and Miriam Sweeney have written. The $13 billion digital video gaming industry has race coded into its interfaces and has enabled the alt-right, Kishonna Gray observes. The algorithms of search engines and their autocomplete features often suggest racism to users and direct them to White supremacist sites, Safiya Noble documents. And it goes on. Yet despite all this evidence that race is coded into these platforms, the ideology of color-blindness in technology—both in the industry and in popular understandings of technology—serves a key mechanism enabling White nationalists to exploit technological innovations. By ignoring race in the design process and eschewing discussion of it after products are launched, the tech industry has left an opening for White nationalists—and they are always looking for opportunities to push their ideology.

White Nationalists as Innovation Opportunists

The filmmaker D.W. Griffith is recognized as a cinematic visionary who helped launch an art form and an industry. His signature film, *Birth of a Nation* (1915), is also widely regarded as "disgustingly racist." Indeed, White supremacists seized upon it (and emerging film technology) when it was released. At the film's premiere, members of the Klan paraded outside the theatre, celebrating its depiction of their group's rise as a sign of southern White society's recovery from the humiliation of defeat in the Civil War. When Griffith screened the film at the White House for Woodrow Wilson, who is quoted in the film, the president declared *Birth of a Nation* "history writ with lightning." Capitalizing on this new technology, the KKK created film companies and produced their own feature films with titles like *The Toll of Justice* (1923) and *The Traitor Within* (1924), screening them at outdoor events, churches, and schools. By the middle of the 1920s, the Klan had an estimated five million members. This growth was aided by White supremacists' recognition of the opportunity to use the new technology of motion pictures to spread their message.

Almost a century later, another generation saw that same potential in digital technologies. "I believe that the internet will begin a chain reaction of racial enlightenment that will shake the world by the speed of its intellectual conquest," wrote former KKK Grand Wizard David Duke on his website in 1998. Duke's newsletter, the NAAWP (National Association for the Advancement of White People), was part of my earlier study, and he was one who made the transition from the print-only era to the digital era. Duke joined forces with Don Black, another former KKK Grand Wizard, who shared a belief in new technologies for "racial enlightenment." Together, they helped the movement ditch Klan robes as the *costume de rigueur* of White supremacy and trade them for high-speed modems.

Don Black created Stormfront in 1996. The site hosted a podcast created by Duke and pushed to more than 300,000 registered users at the site. Don Black's son recalled in a recent interview that they were a family of early adopters, always looking for the next technological innovations that they could exploit for the White nationalist movement:

> "Pioneering white nationalism on the web was my dad's goal. That was what drove him from the early '90s, from beginning of the web. We had the latest computers, we were the first people in the neighborhood to have broadband because we had to keep Stormfront running, and so technology and

connecting people on the website, long before social media."

Part of what I observed in the shift of the White supremacist movement from print to digital is that they were very good, prescient even, at understanding how to exploit emerging technologies to further their ideological goals.

A few years after he launched Stormfront, Don Black created another, possibly even more pernicious site. In 1999, he registered the domain name martinlutherking.org, and set up a site that appears to be a tribute to Dr. King. But it is what I call a "cloaked site," a sort of precursor to today's "fake news." Cloaked sites are a form of propaganda, intentionally disguising authorship in order to conceal a political agenda. I originally discovered this one through a student's online search during a class; I easily figured out the source by scrolling all the way to the bottom of the page where it clearly says "Hosted by Stormfront." But such sites can be deceptive: the URL is misleading and most of us, around 85%, never scroll all the way to the bottom of a page (all confirmed in interviews I did with young people while they surfed the web). So we see that White nationalists, as early adopters, are constantly looking for the vulnerabilities in new technologies as spots into which their ideology can be inserted. In the mid-1990s, it was domain name registration. The fact that a site with clunky design can be deceptive is due in large part to the web address. One young participant in my study said, "it says, martin luther king dot org, so that means they must be dedicated to that." To him, the "dot org" suffix on the domain name indicated that a non-profit group "dedicated to Dr. King" was behind the URL.

White supremacists like Don Black understood that the paradigm shift in media distribution from the old broadcast model of "one-to-many" to Internet's "many-to-many" model was an opening. The kind of propaganda at the site about Dr. King works well in this "many-to-many" sharing environment in which there are no gatekeepers. The goal in this instance is to call into question the hard won moral, cultural, and political victories of the civil rights movement by undermining Dr. King's personal reputation. Other cloaked sites suggest that slavery "wasn't that bad." This strategy, shifting the range of the acceptable ideas to discuss, is known as moving the "Overton window." White nationalists of the alt-right are using the "race-less" approach of platforms and the technological innovation of algorithms to push the Overton window.

The anything-goes approach to racist speech on platforms like Twitter, 4chan, and Reddit means that White nationalists now have many places beyond Stormfront to congregate online. These platforms have been adept in spreading White nationalist symbols and ideas, themselves accelerated and amplified by algorithms. Take "Pepe the Frog," an innocuous cartoon character that so thoroughly changed meaning that, in September 2016, the Anti-Defamation League added the character to its database of online hate symbols. This transformation began on 4chan, moved to Twitter, and, by August 2016, it had made it into a speech by presidential candidate Hillary Clinton.

"Turning Pepe into a white nationalist icon was one of our original goals," an anonymous White supremacist on Twitter told a reporter for the Daily Beast in 2016. The move to remake Pepe began on /r9k/, a 4chan board where a wide variety of users, including hackers, tech guys (and they were mostly guys), libertarians, and White supremacists who migrated from Stormfront gathered online. The content at 4chan is eclectic, or, as one writer put it, "a jumble of content, hosting anything from pictures of cute kittens to wildly disturbing images and language." "It's also one of the most popular websites ever, with 20 million unique visitors a month," according to founder Christopher "Moot" Poole. "We basically mixed Pepe in with Nazi propaganda, etc. We built that association [on 4chan]," a White nationalist who goes by @JaredTSwift said. Once a journalist mentioned the connection on Twitter, White nationalists counted it as a victory—and it was: the mention of the 4chan meme by a "normie" on Twitter was a prank with a big attention payoff.

"In a sense, we've managed to push white nationalism into a very mainstream position," @JaredTSwift said. "Now, we've pushed the Overton window," referring to the range of ideas tolerated in public discourse. Twitter is the key platform for shaping that discourse. "People have adopted our rhetoric, sometimes without even realizing it. We're setting up for a massive cultural shift," @JaredTSwift said. Among White supremacists, the thinking goes: if today we can get "normies" talking about Pepe the Frog, then tomorrow we can get them to ask the other questions on our agenda: "Are Jews people?" or "What about black on white crime?" And, when they have a sitting President who will re-tweet accounts that use #whitegenocide hashtags and defend them after a deadly rally, it is fair to say that White supremacists are succeeding at using media and technology to take their message mainstream.

Networked White Rage

CNN commentator Van Jones dubbed the 2016 election a "Whitelash," a very real political backlash by White voters. Across all income levels, White voters (including 53% of White women) preferred the candidate who had retweeted #whitegenocide over the one warning against the alt-right. For many, the uprising of the Black Lives Matter movement coupled with the putative insult of a Black man in the White House were such a threat to personal and national identity that it provoked what Carol Anderson identifies as *White Rage*.

In the span of U.S. racial history, the first election of President Barack Obama was heralded as a high point for so-called American "race relations." His second term was the apotheosis of this symbolic progress. Some even suggested we were now "post-racial." But the post-Obama era proves the lie that we were ever post-racial, and it may, when we have the clarity of hindsight, mark the end of an era. If one charts a course from the Civil Rights movement, taking 1954 (*Brown v. Board of Education*) as a rough starting point and the rise of the Black Lives Matter movement and the close of Obama's second term as the end point, we might see this as a five-decades-long "second reconstruction" culminating in the 2016 presidential election.

Taking the long view makes the rise of the alt-right look less like a unique eruption and more like a continuation of our national story of systemic racism. Historian Rayford Logan made the persuasive argument that retrenchment and the brutal reassertion of White supremacy through Jim Crow laws and the systematic violence of lynching was the White response to "too much" progress by those just a generation from slavery. He called this period, 1877–1920, the "nadir of American race relations." And the rise of the alt-right may signal the start of a second nadir, itself a reaction to progress of Black Americans. The difference this time is that the "Whitelash"

is algorithmically amplified, sped up, and circulated through networks to other White ethno-nationalist movements around the world, ignored all the while by a tech industry that "doesn't see race" in the tools it creates.

Media, Technology, and White Nationalism

Today, there is a new technological and media paradigm emerging and no one is sure what we will call it. Some refer to it as "the outrage industry," and others refer to "the mediated construction of reality." With great respect for these contributions, neither term quite captures the scope of what we are witnessing, especially when it comes to the alt-right. We are certainly no longer in the era of "one-to-many" broadcast distribution, but the power of algorithms and cable news networks to amplify social media conversations suggests that we are no longer in a "peer-to-peer" model either. And very little of our scholarship has caught up in trying to explain the role that "dark money" plays in driving all of this. For example, Rebekah Mercer (daughter of hedge-fund billionaire and libertarian Robert Mercer) has been called the "First Lady of the Alt-Right" for her $10-million underwriting of Breitbart News, helmed for most of its existence by former White House Senior Advisor Steve Bannon, who called it the "platform of the alt-right." White nationalists have clearly sighted this emerging media paradigm and are seizing—and being provided with millions to help them take hold of—opportunities to exploit these innovations with alacrity. For their part, the tech industry has done shockingly little to stop White nationalists, blinded by their unwillingness to see how the platforms they build are suited for speeding us along to the next genocide.

The second nadir, if that's what this is, is disorienting because of the swirl of competing articulations of racism across a distracting media ecosystem. Yet, the view that circulates in popular understandings of the alt-right and of tech culture by mostly White liberal writers, scholars, and journalists is one in which racism is a "bug" rather than a "feature" of the system. They report with alarm that there's racism on the Internet (or, in the last election), as if this is a revelation, or they "journey" into the heart of the racist right, as if it isn't everywhere in plain sight. Or, they write with a kind of shock mixed with reassurance that alt-right proponents live next door, have gone to college, gotten a proper haircut, look like a hipster, or, sometimes, put on a suit and tie. Our understanding of the algorithmic rise of the alt-right must do better than these quick, hot takes.

If we're to stop the next Charlottesville or the next Emanuel AME Church massacre, we have to recognize that the algorithms of search engines and social media platforms facilitated these hate crimes.

To grasp the 21st century world around us involves parsing different inflections of contemporary racism: the overt and ideologically committed White nationalists co-mingle with the tech industry, run by boy-kings steeped in cyberlibertarian notions of freedom, racelessness, and an ethos in which the only evil is restricting the flow of information on the Internet (and, thereby, their profits) in the wake of Charleston and Charlottesville, it is becoming harder and harder to sell the idea of an Internet "where there is no race, only minds." Yet, here we are, locked in this iron cage.

REFERENCES

Christopher Bail. 2016. *Terrified: How Anti-Muslim Fringe Organizations Became Mainstream. Princeton,* NJ: Princeton University Press,

Yokai Benkler, et al. 2017. "Study: Breitbart-Led Right-Wing Media System Altered Broader Media Agenda." *Columbia Journalism Review* (March 3).

Alice Marwick and Rebecca Lewis. 2017. "Media manipulation and disinformation online," Data & Society Research Institute.

David Neiwert. 2017. *Alt-America: The Rise of the Radical Right in the Age of Trump.* Brooklyn, NY: Verso Books.

Safiya U. Nobel. 2018. *Algorithms of Oppression: How Search Engines Reinforce Racism.* New York: New York University Press.

Samuel C. Woolley and Phillip K. Howard. 2016. "Political Communication, Computational Propaganda, and Autonomous Agents," *International Journal of Communication* 10: 4882–4890.

THINKING ABOUT THE READING

What makes the "Alt-Right" different and similar to white supremist groups of the past and present? What role has technology (algorithms, search engines, and social media) played in the rise of the Alt-Right? What are "innovation opportunists?" Do the gatekeepers of the technology industry have a responsibility to monitor the content shared on the Internet and restrict content that might contribute to violence and hate? What other institutions (political, legal, etc.) should be involved in this type of discussion?

CHAPTER 14

The Architects of Change

Reconstructing Society

Throughout this book, you've seen examples of how society is socially constructed and how these social constructions, in turn, affect the lives of individuals. It's hard not to feel a little helpless when discussing the control that culture, massive bureaucratic organizations, social institutions, systems of social stratification, and population trends have over our individual lives. However, social change is as much a part of society as social stability. Whether at the personal, cultural, or institutional level, change is the preeminent feature of modern societies. Social change occurs in many ways and on many levels (e.g., through population shifts and immigration, as illustrated in the previous chapter). Sociologists are also interested in specific, goal-based social movements. Who participates in social movements? What motivates this participation? How successful are they? Social movements range from neighborhood organizers seeking better funding for schools to large-scale religious groups seeking to influence law and politics regarding issues such as abortion, same-sex marriage, and immigration. Social movements come in all shapes and sizes. The readings in this final chapter provide three examples of different forms of social movements.

In the reading, "Challenging Power: Toxic Waste Protests and the Politicization of White, Working-Class Women," Celene Krauss examines the process by which women with very traditional ideas about government and family became the leading activists in the toxic waste movement. She shows that these women were not motivated by the ideology of environmental movements, but rather by direct health threats to their children.

As revealed in Jessie Daniels's work on the Alt-Right, racism and racial tensions are palpable in U.S. society right now. In "Black Lives Matter: Toward a Modern Practice of Mass Struggle," Russell Rickford tells us about a fairly new social movement that began with a Twitter hashtag in 2013, the Black Lives Matter movement. This movement originated on social media in response to the acquittal of the man who murdered Trayvon Martin and has focused on issues like racist violence, police misconduct, and social inequalities. Founded by three Black women organizers, the movement has carried over from social media to the streets while embracing a form of confrontational politics. This movement can be traced back to the concept of white supremacy and the need for an intersectional analysis and approach to social justice that Abby Ferber discusses in the next selection of this section, "Racism in America: To be Continued . . ."

The final reading in this section, "An Intersectional Queer Liberation Movement" by Joseph Nicholas DeFilippis provides a comparative analysis of two LGBTQ social movements. He finds that the underlying values and agenda of the Queer Liberation Movement and the mainstream Gay Rights Movement are fairly different, with the former emphasizing an intersectional and multi-issue political and social organizing approach that departs from the single-issue identity politics approach of the latter. While both approaches seek social justice in their own way, we see a fundamental difference between a transformative approach and a reform approach.

Something to Consider as You Read

As you read these selections, consider the connection between people's ideas, beliefs, and goals and the motivation to become involved in social change. Participation in a social movement takes time and resources. What do you care enough about to contribute your time and money? In thinking about the near future, which groups do you think are "worked up" enough about something to give a lot of time and energy in trying to create social change? If these groups prevail, what do you think the future will look like?

Challenging Power

Toxic Waste Protests and the Politicization of White, Working-Class Women

CELENE KRAUSS

(1998)

Over the past two decades, toxic waste disposal has been a central focus of women's grassroots environmental activism. Women of diverse racial, ethnic, and class backgrounds have assumed the leadership of community environmental struggles around toxic waste issues (Krauss 1993). Out of their experience of protest, these women have constructed ideologies of environmental justice that reveal broader issues of inequality underlying environmental hazards (Bullard 1990, 1994). Environmental justice does not exist as an abstract concept prior to these women's activism. It grows out of the concrete, immediate, everyday experience of struggles around issues of survival. As women become involved in toxic waste issues, they go through a politicizing process that is mediated by their experiences of class, race, and ethnicity (Krauss 1993).

Among the earliest community activists in toxic waste protests were white, working-class women. This [article] examines the process by which these women became politicized through grassroots protest activities in the 1980s, which led to their analyses of environmental justice, and in many instances to their leadership in regional and national toxic waste coalitions. These women would seem unlikely candidates for becoming involved in political protest. They came out of a culture that shares a strong belief in the existing political system, and in which traditional women's roles center around the private arena of family. Although financial necessity may have led them into the workplace, the primary roles from which they derived meaning, identity, and satisfaction are those of mothering and taking care of family. Yet, as we shall see, the threat that toxic wastes posed to family health and community survival disrupted the taken-for-granted fabric of their lives, politicizing women who had never viewed themselves as activists. . . .

This [article] shows how white, working-class women's involvement in toxic waste issues has wider implications for social change . . . These women . . . fought to close down toxic waste dump sites, to prevent the siting of hazardous waste incinerators, to oppose companies' waste-disposal policies, to push for recycling projects, and so on. Their voices show us . . . that their single-issue community protests led them through a process of politicization and their broader analysis of inequities of class and gender in the public arena and in the family. Propelled into the public arena in defense of their children, they ultimately challenged government, corporations, experts, husbands, and their own insecurities as working-class women. Their analysis of environmental justice and inequality led them to form coalitions with labor and people of color around environmental issues. These women's traditional beliefs about motherhood, family, and democracy served a crucial function in this politicizing process. While they framed their analyses in terms of traditional constructions of gender and the state, they actively reinterpreted these constructions into an oppositional ideology, which became a resource of resistance and a source of power in the public arena.

Subjective Dimensions of Grassroots Activism

In most sociological analysis of social movements, the subjective dimension of protest has often been ignored or viewed as private and individualistic. . . . [Contemporary theories] show us how experience is not merely a personal, individualistic concept: it is social. People's experiences reflect where they fit into the social hierarchy. . . . Thus, white, working-class women interpret their experience of toxic waste problems within the context of their particular cultural history, arriving at a critique that reflects broader issues of class and gender. . . .

. . . This article focuses on the subjective process by which white, working-class women involved in toxic waste protests construct an oppositional consciousness out of their everyday lives, experiences, and identities. As these women became involved in the public arena, they confronted a world of power normally hidden from them. This forced them to re-examine their assumptions about private and public power and to develop a broad reconceptualization of gender, family, and government.

The experience of protest is central to this process and can reshape traditional beliefs and values (see Thompson 1963). My analysis reveals the contradictory ways in which traditional culture mediates white, working-class women's subjective experience and interpretation of structural inequality. Their protests are framed in terms of dominant ideologies of motherhood, family, and a deep faith in the democratic system. Their experience also reveals how dominant ideologies are appropriated and reconstructed as an instrument of their politicization and a legitimating ideology used to justify resistance. For example, as the political economy of growth displaces environmental problems into their communities, threatening the survival of children and family and creating everyday crises, government toxic waste policies are seen to violate their traditional belief that a democratic government will protect their families. Ideologies of motherhood and democracy become political resources which these women use to initiate and justify their resistance, their increasing politicization, and their fight for a genuine democracy.

Methodological Considerations

My analysis is based on the oral and written voices of white, working-class women involved in toxic waste protests. Sources include individual interviews, as well as conference presentations, pamphlets, books, and other written materials that have emerged from this movement. Interviews were conducted with a snowball sample of twenty white, working-class women who were leaders in grassroots protest activities against toxic waste landfills and incinerators during the 1980s. These women ranged in age from twenty-five to forty; all but one had young children at the time of their protest. They were drawn from a cross section of the country, representing urban, suburban, and rural areas. None of them had been politically active before the protest; many of them, however, have continued to be active in subsequent

community movements, often becoming leaders in state-wide and national coalitions around environmental and social justice issues. I established contact with these women through networking at activist conferences. Open-ended interviews were conducted between May 1989, and December 1991, and lasted from two to four hours. The interview was designed to generate a history of these women's activist experiences, information about changes in political beliefs, and insights into their perceptions of their roles as women, mothers, and wives.

Interviews were also conducted with Lois Gibbs and four other organizers for the Citizens Clearinghouse for Hazardous Wastes (CCHW). CCHW is a nation-wide organization created by Gibbs, who is best known for her successful campaign to relocate families in Love Canal, New York. Over the past two decades, this organization has functioned as a key resource for community groups fighting around toxic waste issues in the United States. Its leadership and staff are composed primarily of women, and the organization played a key role in shaping the ideology of working-class women's environmental activism in the 1980s. . . .

The Process of Politicization

Women identify the toxic waste movement as a women's movement, composed primarily of mothers. As one woman who fought against an incinerator in Arizona and subsequently worked on other anti-incinerator campaigns throughout the state stressed: "Women are the backbone of the grassroots groups, they are the ones who stick with it, the ones who won't back off." Because mothers are traditionally responsible for the health of their children, they are more likely than others within their communities to begin to make the link between toxic waste and their children's ill health. And in communities around the United States, it was women who began to uncover numerous toxin-related health problems: multiple miscarriages, birth defects, cancer, neurological symptoms, and so on. Given the placement of toxic waste facilities in working-class and low-income communities and communities of color, it is not surprising that women from these groups have played a particularly important role in fighting against environmental hazards.

White, working-class women's involvement in toxic waste issues is complicated by the political reality that they, like most people, are excluded from the policy-making process. For the most part, corporate and governmental disposal policies with far-reaching social and political consequences are made without the knowledge of community residents. People may unknowingly live near (or even on top of) a toxic waste dump, or they may assume that the facility is well regulated by the government. Consequently, residents are often faced with a number of problems of seemingly indeterminate origin, and the information withheld from them may make them unwitting contributors to the ill health of their children.

The discovery of a toxic waste problem and the threat it poses to family sets in motion a process of critical questioning about the relationship between women's private work as mothers and the public arena of politics. The narratives of the women involved in toxic waste protests focus on political transformation, on the process of "becoming" an activist. Prior to their discovery of the link between their family's health and toxic waste, few of these women had been politically active. They saw their primary work in terms of the "private" sphere of motherhood and family. But the realization that toxic waste issues threatened their families thrust them into the public arena in defense of this private sphere. According to Penny Newman:

> We woke up one day to discover that our families were being damaged by toxic contamination, a situation in which we had little, if any, input. It wasn't a situation in which we chose to become involved, rather we did it because we had to . . . it was a matter of our survival. (Newman 1991, 8)

Lois Gibbs offered a similar account of her involvement in Love Canal:

> When my mother asked me what I wanted to do when I grew up, I said I wanted to have six children and be a homemaker. . . . I moved into Love Canal and I bought the American Dream: a house, two children, a husband, and HBO. And then something happened to me and that was Love Canal. I got involved because my son Michael

had epilepsy . . . and my daughter Melissa developed a rare blood disease and almost died because of something someone else did. . . . I never thought of myself as an activist or an organizer. I was a housewife, a mother, but all of a sudden it was my family, my children, and my neighbors . . .

It was through their role as mothers that many of these women began to suspect a connection between the invisible hazard posed by toxic wastes and their children's ill health, and this was their first step toward political activism. At Love Canal, for example, Lois Gibbs's fight to expose toxic waste hazards was triggered by the link she made between her son's seizures and the toxic waste dump site. After reading about toxic hazards in a local newspaper, she thought about her son and then surveyed her neighbors to find that they had similar health problems. In Woburn, Massachusetts, Ann Anderson found that other neighborhood children were, like her son, being treated for leukemia, and she began to wonder if this was an unusually high incidence of the disease. In Denver, mothers comparing stories at Tupperware parties were led to question the unusually large number of sick and dying children in their community. These women's practical activity as mothers and their extended networks of family and community led them to make the connection between toxic waste and sick children—a discovery process rooted in what Sara Ruddick (1989) has called the everyday practice of mothering, in which, through their informal networks, mothers compare notes and experiences, developing a shared body of personal, empirical knowledge.

Upon making the link between their family's ill health and toxic wastes, the women's first response was to go to the government, a response that reflects a deeply held faith in democracy embedded in their working-class culture. They assumed that the government would protect the health and welfare of their children. Gibbs reports:

> I grew up in a blue-collar community, I was very patriotic, into democracy . . . I believed in government. . . . I believed that if you had a complaint, you went to the right person in government. If there was a way to solve the problem, they would be glad to do it.

An Alabama activist who fought to prevent the siting of an incinerator describes a similar response:

> We just started educating ourselves and gathering information about the problems of incineration. We didn't think our elected officials knew. Surely, if they knew that there was already a toxic waste dump in our county, they would stop it.

In case after case, however, these women described facing a government that was indifferent, if not antagonistic, to their concerns. At Love Canal, local officials claimed that the toxic waste pollution was insignificant, the equivalent of smoking just three cigarettes a day. In South Brunswick, New Jersey, governmental officials argued that living with pollution was the price of a better way of life. In Jacksonville, Arkansas, women were told that the dangers associated with dioxin emitted from a hazardous waste incinerator were exaggerated, no worse than "eating two or three tablespoons of peanut butter over a thirty-year period." Also in Arkansas, a woman who linked her ill health to a fire at a military site that produced Agent Orange was told by doctors that she was going through a "change of life." In Stringfellow, California, eight hundred thousand gallons of toxic chemical waste pumped into the community [water supply] flowed directly behind the elementary school and into the playground. Children played in contaminated puddles yet officials withheld information from their parents because "they didn't want to panic the public."

Government's dismissal of their concerns about the health of their families and communities challenged these white, working-class women's democratic assumptions and opened a window on a world of power whose working they had not before questioned. Government explanations starkly contradicted the personal, empirical evidence which the women discovered as mothers, the everyday knowledge that their children and their neighbors' children were ill. Indeed, a recurring theme in the narratives of these women is the transformation of their beliefs about government. Their politicization is rooted in a deep sense of violation, hurt, and betrayal from finding out their government will not protect their families. Echoes of this disillusionment are heard from women throughout the country. In the CCHW publication *Empowering Women* (1989, 31) one activist noted:

> All our lives we are taught to believe certain things about ourselves as women, about democracy and justice, and about people in positions of authority. Once we become involved with toxic waste problems, we need to confront some [of] our old beliefs and change the way we view things.

Lois Gibbs summed up this feeling when she stated:

> There is something about discovering that democracy isn't democracy as we know it. When you lose faith in your government, it's like finding out your mother was fooling around on your father. I was very upset. It almost broke my heart because I really believed in the system. I still believe in the system, only now I believe that democracy is of the people and by the people, that people have to move it, it ain't gonna move by itself.

These women's loss of faith in "democracy" as they had understood it led them to develop a more autonomous and critical stance. Their investigation shifted to a political critique of the undemocratic nature of government itself, making the link between government inaction and corporate power, and discovering that government places corporate interests and profit ahead of the health needs of families and communities. At Love Canal, residents found that local government's refusal to acknowledge the scope of the toxic waste danger was related to plans of Hooker Chemical, the polluting industry, for a multi-million dollar downtown development project. In Woburn, Massachusetts, government officials feared that awareness of the health hazard posed by a dump would limit their plans for real estate development. In communities throughout the United States, women came to see that government policies supported waste companies' preference of incineration over recycling because incineration was more profitable.

Ultimately, their involvement in toxic waste protests led these women to develop a perspective on environmental justice rooted in issues of class and a critique of the corporate state. They argued that government's claims—to be democratic, to act on behalf of the public interest, to hold the family sacrosanct—are false. One woman who fought an incinerator in Arizona recalled:

> I believed in government. When I heard EPA, I thought, "Ooh, that was so big." Now I wouldn't believe them if they said it was sunny outside. I have a list of the revolving door of the EPA. Most of them come from Browning Ferris or Waste Management, the companies that plan landfills and incinerators.

As one activist in Alabama related:

> I was politically naive. I was real surprised because I live in an area that's like the Bible belt of the South. Now I think the God of the United States is really economic development, and that has got to change.

Another activist emphasized:

> We take on government and polluters. . . . We are up against the largest corporations in the United States. They have lots of money to lobby, pay off, bribe, cajole, and influence. They threaten us. Yet we challenge them with the only things we have—people and the truth. We learn that our government is not out to protect our rights. To protect our families we are now forced to picket, protest and shout. (Zeff, 1989, 31)

In the process of protest, these women were also forced to examine their assumptions about the family as a private haven, separate from the public arena, which would however be protected by the policies and actions of government should the need arise. The issue of toxic waste shows the many ways in which government allows this haven to be invaded by polluted water, hazardous chemicals, and other conditions that threaten the everyday life of the family. Ultimately, these women arrived at a concept of environmental injustice rooted in the inequities of power that displace the costs of toxic waste unequally onto their communities. The result

was a critical political stance that contributed to the militancy of their activism. Highly traditional values of democracy and motherhood remained central to their lives: they justified their resistance as mothers protecting their children and working to make the promise of democracy real. Women's politicization around toxic waste protests led them to transform their traditional beliefs into resources of opposition which enabled them to enter the public arena and challenge its legitimacy, breaking down the public/private distinction.

Appropriating Power in the Public Arena

Toxic waste issues and their threat to family and community prompted white, working-class women to redefine their roles as mothers. Their work of mothering came to extend beyond taking care of the children, husband, and housework; they saw the necessity of preserving the family by entering the public arena. In so doing, they discovered and overcame a more subtle process of intimidation, which limited their participation in the public sphere.

As these women became involved in toxic waste issues, they came into conflict with a public world where policy makers are traditionally white, male, and middle class. The Citizen's Clearinghouse for Hazardous Waste, in the summary of its 1989 conference on women and organizing, noted:

> Seventy to eighty percent of local leaders are women. They are women leaders in a community run by men. Because of this, many of the obstacles that these women face as leaders stem from the conflicts between their traditional female role in the community and their new role as leader: conflicts with male officials and authorities who have not yet adjusted to these persistent, vocal, head-strong women challenging the system. . . . Women are frequently ignored by male politicians, male government officials and male corporate spokesmen.

Entering the public arena meant overcoming internal and external barriers to participation, shaped by gender and class. White, working-class women's reconstructed definition of motherhood became a resource for this process, and their narratives reveal several aspects of this transformation.

For these women, entering the public arena around toxic waste issues was often extremely stressful. Many of them were initially shy and intimidated, as simple actions such as speaking at a meeting opened up wider issues about authority, and experiences of gender and class combined to heighten their sense of inadequacy. Many of these women describe, for example, that their high-school education left them feeling ill-equipped to challenge "experts," whose legitimacy, in which they had traditionally believed, was based on advanced degrees and specialized knowledge.

One woman who fought to stop the siting of an incinerator in her community in Arizona recalled: "I used to cry if I had to speak at a PTA meeting. I was so frightened." An activist in Alabama described her experience in fighting the siting of an incinerator in her community:

> I was a woman . . . an assistant Sunday School teacher. . . . In the South, women are taught not to be aggressive, we're supposed to be hospitable and charitable and friendly. We don't protest, we don't challenge authority. So it was kind of difficult for me to get involved. I was afraid to speak. And all of a sudden everything became controversial. . . . I think a lot of it had to do with not knowing what I was. . . . The more I began to know, the better I was . . . the more empowered.

Male officials further exacerbated this intimidation by ignoring the women, by criticizing them for being overemotional, and by delegitimizing their authority by labeling them "hysterical housewives"— a label used widely, regardless of the professional status of the woman. In so doing, they revealed an antipathy to emotionality, a quality valued in the private sphere of family and motherhood but scorned in the public arena as irrational and inappropriate to "objective" discourse.

On several levels, the debate around toxic waste issues was framed by policy makers in such a way as to exclude women's participation, values, and expression. Women's concerns about their children were trivialized by being placed against a claim that the wider community benefits from growth and progress. Information was withheld from them. Discourse was framed as rational, technical, and scientific, using the testimony of "experts" to discredit the everyday empirical knowledge of the women. Even such details as seating arrangements reflected traditional power relations and reinforced the women's internalization of those relations.

These objective and subjective barriers to participation derived from a traditional definition of women's roles based on the separation of the public and private arenas. Yet it is out of these women's political redefinition of the traditional role of mother that they found the resources to overcome these constraints, ultimately becoming self-confident and assertive. They used the resources of their own experience to alter the power relations they had discovered in the public arena.

The traditional role of mother, of protector of the family and community, served to empower these activists on a number of levels. From the beginning, their view of this role provided the motivation for women to take risks in defense of their families and overcome their fears of participating in the public sphere. A woman who fought the siting of an incinerator in Arkansas described this power:

> I was afraid to hurt anyone's feelings or step on anyone's toes. But I'm protective and aggressive, especially where my children are concerned. That's what brought it out of me. A mother protecting my kids. It appalled me that money could be more important than the health of my children.

A mother in New Jersey described overcoming her fear in dealing with male governmental officials at public hearings, "When I look at a male government official, I remember that he was once a little boy, born of a woman like me, and then I feel more powerful." In talking about Love Canal, Lois Gibbs showed the power of motherhood to carry women into activities alien to their experience:

> When it came to Love Canal, we never thought about ourselves as protestors. We carried signs, we barricaded, we blocked

the gates, we were arrested. We thought of it as parents protecting our children. In retrospect, of course, we were protesting. I think if it had occurred to us we wouldn't have done it.

In these ways, they appropriated the power they felt in the private arena as a source of empowerment in the public sphere. "We're insecure challenging the authority of trained experts," notes Gibbs, "but we also have a title of authority, 'mother.'"

Working-class women's experiences as organizers of family life served as a further source of empowerment. Lois Gibbs noted that women organized at Love Canal by constantly analyzing how they would handle a situation in the family, and then translating that analysis into political action. For example, Gibbs explained:

If our child wanted a pair of jeans, who would they go to? Well they would go to their father since their father had the money—that meant we should go to Governor Carey.

Gibbs drew on her own experience to develop organizing conferences that helped working-class women learn to translate their skills as family organizers into the political arena.

I decided as a housewife and mother much of what I learned to keep the household running smoothly were skills that translated very well into this new thing called organizing. I also decided that this training in running a home was one of the key reasons why so many of the best leaders in the toxic movement—in fact, the overwhelming majority—are women, and specifically women who are housewives and mothers. (Zeff 1989, 177)

Of her work with the CCHW, Gibbs stated:

In our own organization we're drawing out these experiences for women. So we say, what do you mean you're not an organizer? Are you a homemaker—then God damn it you can organize and you don't know it. So,

for example, when we say you need to plan long-term and short-term goals, women may say, I don't know how to do that. . . . We say, what do you mean you don't know how to do that? Let's talk about something in the household—you plan meals for five, seven, fourteen days—you think about what you want for today and what you're going to eat on Sunday—that is short-term and long-term goals.

Movement language like "plug up the toilet," the expression for waste reduction, helped women to reinterpret toxic waste issues in the framework of their everyday experience. "If one does not produce the mess in the first place, one will not have to clean it up later," may sound like a maternal warning, but the expression's use in the toxic waste context implies a radical economic critique, calling for a change in the production processes of industry itself.

As women came to understand that government is not an objective, neutral mediator for the public good, they discovered that "logic" and "objectivity" are tools used by the government to obscure its bias in favor of industry, and motherhood became a strategy to counter public power by framing the terms of the debate. The labels of "hysterical housewives" or "emotional women," used by policy makers to delegitimize the women's authority, became a language of critique and empowerment, one which exposed the limits of the public arena's ability to address the importance of family, health, and community. These labels were appropriated as the women saw that their emotionalism, a valued trait in the private sphere, could be transformed into a powerful weapon in the public arena.

What's really so bad about showing your feelings? Emotions and intellect are not conflicting traits. In fact, emotions may well be the quality that makes women so effective in the movement. . . . They help us speak the truth.

Finally, through toxic waste protests, women discovered the power they wield as mothers to bring moral issues to the public, exposing the contradictions of a society that purports to value motherhood and family, yet creates social policies that undermine these values:

We bring the authority of mother—who can condemn mothers? . . . It is a tool we have. Our crying brings the moral issues to the table. And when the public sees our children it brings a concrete, moral dimension to our experience. . . . They are not an abstract statistic.

White, working-class women's stories of their involvement in grassroots toxic waste protests reveal their transformations of initial shyness and intimidation into the self-confidence to challenge the existing system. In reconceptualizing their traditional roles as mothers, these women discovered a new strength. As one activist from Arizona says of herself, "Now I like myself better. I am more assertive and aggressive." These women's role in the private world of family ultimately became a source of personal strength, empirical knowledge, and political strategy in the public sphere. It was a resource of political critique and empowerment which the women appropriated and used as they struggled to protect their families.

Overcoming Obstacles to Participation: Gender Conflicts in the Family

In order to succeed in their fights against toxic wastes in their homes and communities, these women confronted and overcame obstacles not only in the public sphere, but also within the family itself, as their entry into the public arena disrupted both the power relationships and the highly traditional gender roles within the family. Divorce and separation were the manifestations of the crises these disruptions induced. All of the women I interviewed had been married when they first became active in the toxic waste movement. By the time of my interviews with them, more than half were divorced.

A central theme of these women's narratives is the tension created in their marriages by participation in toxic waste protests. This aspect of struggle, so particular to women's lives, is an especially hidden dimension of white, working-class women's activism. Noted one activist from New York:

People are always talking to us about forming coalitions, but look at all we must deal

with beyond the specific issue, the flack that comes with it, the insecurity of your husband that you have outgrown him. Or how do you deal with your children's anger, when they say you love the fight more than me. In a blue-collar community that is very important.

For the most part, white, working-class women's acceptance of a traditional gendered division of labor has also led them to take for granted the power relations within the family. Penny Newman, who was the West Coast Director of CCHW, reflected on the beginnings of her community involvement:

I had been married just a couple of years. My husband is a fireman. They have very strict ideas of what family life is in which the woman does not work, you stay at home. . . . I was so insecure, so shy, that when I finally got to join an organization, a woman's club, . . . it would take me two weeks to build up the courage to ask my husband to watch the kids that night. I would really plan out my life a month ahead of time just to build in these little hints that there is a meeting coming up in two weeks, will you be available. Now, if he didn't want to do it, or had other plans, I didn't go to the meeting. (Zeff 1989, 183)

Involvement in toxic waste issues created a conflict between these traditional assumptions and women's concerns about protecting their children, and this conflict made visible the power relations within the family. The CCHW publication *Empowering Women* (1989, 33) noted that:

Women's involvement in grassroots activism may change their views about the world and their relations with their husbands. Some husbands are actively supportive. Some take no stand: "Go ahead and do what you want. Just make sure you have dinner on the table and my shirts washed." Others forbid time away from the family.

Many of these women struggled to develop coping strategies to defuse conflict and accommodate traditional gender-based power relations in the family. The strategies included involving husbands in protest activities and minimizing their own leadership roles. As Lois Gibbs commented: "If you bring a spouse in, if you can make them part of your growth, then the marriage is more likely to survive, but that is real hard to do sometimes." Will Collette, a former director at CCHW, relates the ways in which he has observed women avoiding acknowledged leadership roles. He described this encounter with women involved in a toxic waste protest in New York:

I was sitting around a kitchen table with several women who were leading a protest. And they were complaining about how Lou and Joe did not do their homework and weren't able to handle reports and so on. I asked them why they were officers and the women were doing all the work. They said, "That's what the guys like, it keeps them in and gives us a little peace at home."

In a similar vein, Collette recalled working with an activist from Texas to plan a large public hearing. Upon arriving at the meeting, he discovered that she was sitting in the back, while he was placed on the dais along with the male leadership, which had had no part in the planning process.

As the women became more active in the public arena, traditional assumptions about gender roles created further conflict in their marriages. Women who became visible community leaders experienced the greatest tension. In some cases, the husbands were held responsible for their wives' activities, since they were supposed to be able to "control" their wives. For example, a woman who fought against an incinerator in Arkansas related:

When the mayor saw my husband, he wanted to know why he couldn't keep his pretty little wife's mouth shut. As I became more active and more outspoken, our marriage became rockier. My husband asked me to tone it down, which I didn't do.

In other cases, women's morals were often called into question by husbands or other community members. Collette relates the experience of an activist in North Dakota who was rumored to be having an affair. The basis for the rumor, as Collette describes, was that "an uppity woman has got to be

promiscuous if she dares to organize. In this case, she was at a late-night meeting in another town, and she slept over, so of course she had to have had sex."

Toxic waste issues thus set the stage for tremendous conflict between these women and their husbands. Men saw their roles as providers threatened: the homes they had bought may have become valueless; their jobs may have been at risk; they were asked by their wives to take on housework and child care. Meanwhile, their wives' public activities increasingly challenged traditional views of gender roles. For the women, their husbands' negative response to their entry into the public sphere contradicted an assumption in the family that both husband and wife were equally concerned with the well-being of the children. In talking about Love Canal, Gibbs explained:

The husband in a blue-collar community is saying, get your ass home and cook me dinner, it's either me or the issue, make your choice. The woman says: How can I make a choice, you're telling me choose between the health of my children and your fucking dinner, how do I deal with that?

When women were asked to choose between their children and their husbands' needs, they began to see the ways in which the children had to be their primary concern.

At times this conflict resulted in more equal power relations within the marriages, a direction that CCHW tried to encourage by organizing family stress workshops. By and large, however, the families of activist women did not tolerate this stress well. Furthermore, as the women began openly to contest traditional power relations in the family, many found that their marriages could not withstand the challenges. As one activist from Arkansas described:

I thought [my husband] didn't care enough about our children to continue to expose them to this danger. I begged him to move. He wouldn't. So I moved my kids out of town to live with my mom.

All twenty women interviewed for this article were active leaders around toxic waste issues in their communities, but only two described the importance of their husband's continuing support. One white woman who formed an interracial coalition in

Alabama credited her husband's support in sustaining her resolve:

> I've had death threats. I was scared my husband would lose his job, afraid that somebody's going to kill me. If it weren't for my husband's support, I don't think I could get through all this.

In contrast, most of these activists described the ongoing conflict within their marriages, which often resulted in their abandoning their traditional role in the family, a process filled with inner turmoil. One woman described that turmoil as follows:

> I had doubts about what I was doing, especially when my marriage was getting real rocky. I thought of getting out of [the protest]. I sat down and talked to God many, many times. I asked him to lead me in the right direction because I knew my marriage was failing and I found it hard leaving my kids when I had to go to meetings. I had to struggle to feel that I was doing the right thing. I said a prayer and went on.

Reflecting on the strength she felt as a mother, which empowered her to challenge her government and leave her marriage, she continued:

> It's an amazing ordeal. You always know you would protect your children. But it's amazing to find out how far you will go to protect your own kids.

The disruption of the traditional family often reflected positive changes in women's empowerment. Women grew through the protest; they became stronger and more self-confident. In some cases they found new marriages with men who respected them as strong individuals. Children also came to see their mothers as outspoken and confident.

Thus, for these women, the particularistic issue of toxic waste made visible oppression not only in the public sphere, but also in the family itself. As the traditional organization of family life was disrupted, inequities in underlying power relations were revealed. In order to succeed in fighting a toxic waste issue, these women had also to engage in another level of struggle as they reconceptualized

their traditional role in family life in order to carry out their responsibilities as mothers.

Conclusion

The narratives of white, working-class women involved in toxic waste protests in the 1980s reveal the ways in which their subjective, particular experiences led them to analyses that extended beyond the particularistic issue to wider questions of power. Their broader environmental critique grew out of the concrete, immediate, everyday experience of struggling around survival issues. In the process of environmental protest, these women became engaged with specific governmental and corporate institutions and they were forced to reflect on the contradictions of their family life. To win a policy issue, they had to go through a process of developing an oppositional or critical consciousness which informed the direction of their actions and challenged the power of traditional policy makers. The contradiction between a government that claimed to act on behalf of the family and the actual environmental policies and actions of that government were unmasked. The inequities of power between white, working-class women and middle-class, male public officials were made visible. The reproduction within the family of traditional power relationships was also revealed. In the process of protest these women uncovered and confronted a world of political power shaped by gender and class. This enabled them to act politically around environmental issues, and in some measure to challenge the social relationships of power, inside and outside the home.

Ideologies of motherhood played a central role in the politicizing of white, working-class women around toxic waste issues. Their resistance grew out of an acceptance of a sexual division of labor that assigns to women responsibility for "sustaining the lives of their children and, in a broader sense, their families, including husband, relatives, elders and community.". . .

The analysis of white, working-class women's politicization through toxic waste protests reveals the contradictory role played by dominant ideologies about mothering and democracy in the shaping of these women's oppositional consciousness. The analysis these women developed was not a rejection of these ideologies. Rather, it was a reinterpretation, which became a source of power in the public arena. Their beliefs provided the initial impetus for involvement in toxic waste protests, and became a rich source of empowerment as they appropriated and reshaped traditional ideologies and meanings into an ideology of resistance. . . .

REFERENCES

Bullard, Robert D. 1990. *Dumping in Dixie: Race, Class and Environmental Quality*. Boulder, CO: Westview Press.

Bullard, Robert D. 1994. *Communities of Color and Environmental Justice*. San Francisco: Sierra Club Books.

Citizen's Clearing House for Hazardous Wastes. 1989. *Empowering Women*. Washington, DC: Citizen's Clearinghouse for Hazardous Wastes.

Krauss, Celene. 1993. "Women and Toxic Waste Protests: Race, Class and Gender as Resources of Resistance." *Qualitative Sociology* 16(3): 247–262.

Newman, Penny. 1991. "Women and the Environment in the United States of America." Paper presented at the Conference of Women and the Environment, Bangladore, India.

Ruddick, Sara. 1989. *Maternal Thinking: Towards a Politics of Peace*. New York: Ballantine Books.

Thompson, E. P. 1963. *The Making of the English Working Class*. New York: Pantheon Books.

Zeff, Robin Lee. 1989. "Not in My Backyard/Not in Anyone's Backyard: A Folklorist Examination of the American Grassroots Movement for Environmental Justice." Ph.D. dissertation, Indiana University.

THINKING ABOUT THE READING

Krauss describes how ordinary women became mobilized to construct a movement for social change when they felt their children's health was being threatened. Did their traditional beliefs about motherhood and family help or hinder their involvement in this protest movement? What effect did their participation have on their own families? Why do the women Krauss interviewed identify the toxic waste movement as a women's movement? Why don't men seem to be equally concerned about these health issues? How did the relative powerlessness of their working-class status shape the women's perspective on environmental justice?

Black Lives Matter

Toward a Modern Practice of Mass Struggle

RUSSELL RICKFORD

(2016)

Born as a Twitter hashtag, Black Lives Matter has evolved into a potent alternative to the political paralysis and isolation that racial justice proponents have faced since the election of Obama. In just over two years, the young movement has reinvigorated confrontation politics, giving voice to a popular and righteous rage, establishing a new touchstone of grassroots resistance, and ending the acquiescence that has crippled progressive forces in the age of Obama. The upsurge, which has centered on the crucial, galvanizing issue of police misconduct, also shows signs of addressing larger questions of social inequity. With continued momentum, Black Lives Matter may help reverse the counteroffensive against workers and people of color that has defined the long aftermath of the 1960s and 1970s liberation struggles.[1] To surpass the relatively ephemeral accomplishments of precursors such as Occupy Wall Street, however, the emerging movement must draw on and modernize the creative traditions of popular insurgency. It must become a sustained, truly mass struggle, confronting ferocious backlash and overcoming multiple challenges while developing its considerable strengths.

Black Lives Matter began, quite modestly, as #BlackLivesMatter. The hashtag was created in 2013 by Patrice Cullors, Alicia Garza, and Opal Tometi—Califomia and New York-based organizers active in incarceration, immigration, and domestic labor campaigns—after the acquittal of George Zimmerman for the murder in Florida of seventeen-year-old Trayvon Martin. The slogan's deeper significance as the rallying cry for an incipient movement crystallized in 2014 during the Ferguson, Missouri, uprisings against police brutality. In the words of activists, the hashtag leapt from social media "into the streets." Black Lives Matter, which Garza has called "a love note" to black communities, now serves as shorthand for diverse organizing efforts—both sporadic and sustained—across the country. The most recognizable expression of widespread black outrage against police aggression and racist violence, the phrase has engendered a spirited, if decentralized, movement.

Birth of a Contemporary Human Rights Movement

The variety of local campaigns associated with Black Lives Matter confounds attempts to portray the movement in fine detail. Still, the contours of a modern human rights struggle are discernible. Black Lives Matter is youthful, though it has reenergized older activists who are eager to connect with a new generation of organizers. It arises from an organic black protest tradition, while drawing impassioned participants of all colors. Its leadership departs sharply from the model of the singular, charismatic clergyman or politician. Founded by black women, two of whom are queer, the movement has galvanized an array of grassroots activists in multiple communities. Few are full-time organizers, though many have had encounters with racialized policing or otherwise are personally affected by mass incarceration. Many are also feminist, LGBTQ, working-class or low-income, social media savvy, and streetwise. Like other members of the movement, they are waging an unpretentious, democratic, militant crusade, determined to remain autonomous both from the American political establishment and from old guard leaders, such as Jesse Jackson and Al Sharpton, seen as more invested in punditry than in popular struggie.[2]

> [Members of Black Lives Matter are] . . . determine to remain autonomous from both the American political establishment and from old guard leaders, such as Jesse Jackson and Al Sharpton.

It is this commitment to independence and militancy that has shaped the tactics of the movement. Demanding accountability for racist violence and an immediate end to the murder of black people at the hands of the state, Black Lives Matter activists have used a host of disruptive techniques to advance their cause. Their mainstay has been occupation—of highways, intersections, sporting events, retail stores, malls, campaign events, police stations, and municipal buildings. They have organized "die-ins," marches, and rallies in multiple cities, viewing creative disturbance as a means of dramatizing routine attacks on black life.[3] Tellingly, the mantra of such demonstrations has evolved from "Hands up, don't shoot!" to the more emphatic "Shut it down!" Whether the movement categorically rejects—or simply mistrusts—electoral politics remains unclear. What is evident is that most Black Lives Matter adherents recognize the inherent shortcomings of appeals to politicians, the courts, and other "acceptable" channels of redress, and have wholeheartedly embraced the arena of the street.

Political Tendencies within the Movement

This bold strategy has by no means stopped or even slowed the crescendo of violence. The achievements of Black Lives Matter are nevertheless striking. First, the movement has remained largely unfettered by "respectability politics," the belief that subjugated groups can win support for their cause simply by adhering to conventional standards of decorum. As exponents of Black Lives Matter are keenly aware, rituals of propriety will not dignify dark skin that society as a whole detests and degrades. Movement participants have refused to engage in victim blaming. They have resisted dead-end narratives that emphasize "black-on-black crime" or that prescribe cultural rehabilitation while eschewing righteous dissent. (Such perspectives reinforce the racist premise that black pathology—not white supremacy—is chiefly responsible for the state's systematic assault on black people.)

. . . [R]ituals of propriety will not dignify dark skin that society as a whole detests and degrades.

They have amassed concrete victories, too. Scattered instances of police officers being charged and disciplined for misconduct suggest that popular outcry can help force concessions from even the most repressive system.[4] The movement's real success, however, lies in popularizing radical discourse and providing a vibrant model of democratic participation. As the movement's founders have written,

When we say Black Lives Matter, we are broadening the conversation around state violence to include all of the ways in which Black people are intentionally left powerless at the hands of the state. We are talking about the ways in which Black lives are deprived of our basic human rights and dignity . . . How Black women bearing the burden of a relentless assault on our children and our families is state violence. How Black queer and trans folks bear a unique burden from a hetero patriarchal society that disposes of us like garbage and simultaneously fetishizes us and profits off of us, and that is state violence.[5]

Such rhetoric suggests that far-reaching change—not the mere amelioration of police abuse—is the objective.

Black Lives Matter's elements of spontaneity and self-organization reflect a grassroots surge rather than a measured and conciliatory airing of grievances. Although by no means consistent or complete, its attempts to center those closer to the margins—women, queer people, and various non-elites—through the production of blogs, reports, missives, and by simply invoking the names of unsung victims of police violence ("Say Her Name," as a related campaign is dubbed), signal an ethos of inclusiveness and a desire for a fundamental rearrangement of power relations.

. . . [D]etermination to preserve black life in the face of white supremacist violence has always been a radical principle . . .

Similar traits have defined past social movements. One thinks immediately of the uncompromising spirit of the civil rights–Black Power era, and particularly of the militancy of the Student Nonviolent Coordinating Committee (SNCC). Like Black Lives Matter participants, SNCC's young members also belonged to a generation radicalized by a shocking, highly publicized murder—the 1955 killing of Emmett Till by southern racists. Other historical analogies may be drawn. The street insurrectionists (labeled "rioters") of the 1960s in some ways antici-pated modern activists who face militarized police in urban centers.

In the current generation of protests, one detects resonances of Black Power's insistence on self-definition and human rights rather than on mere social inclusion. Of course, determination to preserve black life in the face of white supremacist violence has always been a radical principle, from the anti-lynching crusades of Ida B. Wells around the turn of the twentieth century, to the Negro Silent Protest Parade of 1917, to the protests surrounding the Scottsboro Boys case of the 1930s, to the 1951 *We Charge Genocide* petition by the Civil Rights Congress, to the exertions of the Deacons for Defense and the Black Panthers at the peak of the postwar movement. What animated these struggles—and those of countless leftist and labor causes—was their insurgent nature and the uncompromising character of their rank and file participants, traits that Black Lives Matter exemplifies.[6]

The Struggle for Racial Justice in the Age of Obama

That said, calling "the movement for black lives" (a broad designation encompassing the many formations informally linked to Black Lives Matter) a "new civil rights movement" may obscure how dramatically the social landscape has shifted in recent decades. If Obama's presence in the White House symbolizes acceptance by many Americans of the ideal of a multiracial society, the modern era also has witnessed the construction of a mass incarceration regime that viciously targets black communities. Dominant conceptions of "race relations" posit interpersonal relations, or the visibility of black elites, as critical indexes of progress. Such measures obscure both the persistence of systemic racism and the extent to which racialized practices have fueled the explosive growth of the carceral state. Enforcing racial hierarchy has been a central task of policing since the days of slave patrols. Today, however, the criminal justice system performs social control tasks—the regulation of black bodies, the harnessing of black surplus labor in the name of corporate profit—once fulfilled by Jim Crow segregation and other overt forms of discrimination.[7]

Enforcing racial hierarchy has been a central task of policing since the days of slave patrols.

Ironically, the sheer scope and intrusiveness of the modern carceral state provide distinct opportunities for organizers. By confronting racist patterns of policing, Black Lives Matter is addressing a reality that touches the lives of a wide segment of people of color. Structural racism in the post-segregation era generally has lacked unambiguous symbols of apartheid around which a popular movement could cohere. Yet mass incarceration and the techniques of racialized policing on which it depends—"broken windows," stop-and-frisk, "predictive policing," and other extreme forms of surveillance—have exposed the refurbished, but no less ruthless, framework of white supremacy. In poorer black and brown communities, recognition that cops serve primarily to monitor and subjugate rather than "to serve and protect" has fostered both deep resentment and radical, oppositional consciousness.[8]

. . . "[B]roken windows,"stop-and-frisk "predictive policing," and other extreme forms of surveillance—have exposed the refurbished . . . framework of white supremacy.

It has also created the potential for multiracial, class-conscious movements. However, despite the emergence of Black Lives Matter offshoots such as "Native Lives Matter," no national alliance of people of color has coalesced on the issue of police violence. More extensive collaboration with Latinos and undocumented populations—both groups that have participated in Black Lives Matter protests—would signal a major victory for the movement. For the moment, the relative diversity of many Black Lives Matter formations has yet to engender a consciously multiracial political surge from below, as in the "rainbow radicalism" that marked some phases of Black Power organizing during the 1960s and 1970s. Lingering interethnic tensions and divisions, as well as the burdens of daily economic survival, continue to militate against the rebirth of such an expansive "rights" consciousness and ethic of solidarity. The existing movement has drawn the backing of white leftists and certain student organizations. Yet confrontations between Black Lives Matter proponents and presidential hopeful Bernie Sanders, in which activists interrupted campaign events to demand more robust engagement with questions of structural racism, have elicited deep hostility from some of the candidate's supporters. Thankfully, such interventions have revived debate about the dynamics of race and class (and the role of white privilege) in American progressive politics.[9]

> ... [C]onfrontations between Black Lives Matter proponents and presidential hopeful Bernie Sanders ... have elicited deep hostility.

The relationship of Black Lives Matter to white working-class and poor people, who also face elevated rates of police abuse, remains unclear. The false universality of the assertion that "All Lives Matter" appeals to many white workers, especially those inclined to dismiss black claims in the name of a fictive post-racial ideal. However, racially diverse groups of workers, including active members of the Fight for $15 minimum wage campaign, have joined Black Lives Matter protests. (Collaboration between the movements has remained informal and fairly sporadic.) And although labor as a whole is split on the issue, some unions with large memberships of people of color have urged the AFL-CIO to withdraw its support for police unions, which often serve as mechanisms for suppressing civilian challenges to, and oversight of, law enforcement. The Service Employees International Union (SEIU) has issued statements of support for Black Lives Matter, but has yet to grant the movement the vigorous backing it has offered the Fight for $15 struggle. Complicating the relationship between labor and the movement for black lives is the reality that the livelihood of some workers (e.g., prison guards) depends on the carceral state. Ultimately, Black Lives Mtter may help intensify the growing pressure on the contemporary labor movement to revive its social justice roots. As a whole, however, Black Lives Matter activists have largely neglected to engage progressive trade unionism or to identify labor as a major ally.[10]

Internal Divergences and External Threats

Even as it contemplates external alliances, Black Lives Matter is grappling with its own internal tensions. The movement has avoided ties to mainstream electoral politics, which has long been a barren realm for the pursuit of genuinely progressive visions of transformation. Upon learning of their formal endorsement by the Democratic Party last fall, Black Lives Matter organizers promptly repudiated the statement of support and reaffirmed their commitment to autonomy. Yet elements within the movement (thus far not organized as distinct cliques) clearly wish to converse with, rather than merely confront, elites such as Hillary Clinton. A robust skepticism toward—rather than a strategic or ideological aversion to—electoral politics appears to characterize much of the movement. (This is an area of real potential conflict in the future.) Although many Black Lives Matter exponents see exerting mass pressure as their sole imperative, others have begun to formulate specific policy demands. Time will tell whether this impulse leads to substantive reform or merely to a conservative transition "from protest to politics."[11]

Some organizers wish to transcend reformism altogether and pursue a revolutionary path. Leftists within and beyond Black Lives Matter have urged the movement to confront its ideological contradictions (including relatively ambiguous stances on electoral politics and the principle of class struggle), disavowing any trace of collaboration with the ruling class and identifying capitalism itself—and not merely white supremacy—as the enemy. Leaders of the movement have displayed signs of a race-class analysis that acknowledges the inseparability of economic justice and black liberation. (A Black Lives Matter website identifies both black poverty and "genocide" as forms of state violence.)[12] However, the movement has yet to articulate a clear analysis of the economic underpinnings of white supremacy. Until it does so, it is unlikely to develop a specific agenda of social redistribution with which to bolster its promising rhetoric of systemic change.

Questions of gender and sexuality appear to have generated the most significant fissures within Black Lives Matter. Although black women have been on the forefront of the movement, some supporters continue to frame the struggle in terms of a putatively masculine prerogative of self-defense. The corporate media, for its part, consistently presents police brutality and extrajudicial killing as crises primarily for black men. By organizing vigils, rallies, and other events in the name of murdered women and girls, campaigns such as "Say Her Name" have fought the erasure or marginalization of the stories of black women, who face stunning rates of police assault and incarceration.

LGBTQ activists have used similar tactics to battle marginalization, even as they toil on the frontlines of struggle. Queer participants staged a constructive intervention during the Movement for Black Lives National Convening in Cleveland last summer, taking to the stage during one session to decry what they saw as elements of transphobia and heterosexism within the larger movement.[13] Willingness to reassess patriarchal and heteronormative leadership, it seems, will be a major test of Black Lives Matter's long-term viability.

> *By organizing vigils, rallies, and other events in the name of murdered women and girls, campaigns such as "Say Her Name" have fought the . . . marginalization . . . of black women.*

The competing political tendencies within Black Lives Matter have yet to become full-fledged factions. External opposition remains by far the greatest threat to the movement. The very phrase "black lives matter" has elicited tremendous anger and scorn in some quarters. (GOP candidates such as Ted Cruz have rallied their political base simply by reveling in the backlash.) Protesters in Ferguson, Baltimore, and elsewhere have been labeled "looters" and "thugs." (The latter term appears to be the racial code word of the moment.) Conditioned to accept the premise of black criminality, a large portion of white America instinctively reads black demands as cases of cynical, special pleading. Many Americans continue to practice the art of evasion, embracing expressions such as "All Lives Matter," "Police Lives Matter," and most bizarrely, "Southern Lives Matter" (a response to criticism of the display of Confederate flags). Even avowed opponents of anti-black violence have condemned militant resistance, choosing instead to issue "calls for healing and injunctions against anger."[14]

Like "All Lives Matter," such appeals seek to deflect, discredit, or suppress black protest.

Police themselves have been the most forceful agents of the Black Lives Matter backlash. The anti-racist movement is facing the kind of intense state repression that crushed Occupy Wall Street. Police spokespeople and apologists have encouraged the demonization of the struggle and have propagated the absurd claim that Black Lives Matter actually provokes assaults on cops. Meanwhile, the apparatuses of state violence have mobilized for a disgracefully one-sided war. Urban police forces have repeatedly confronted unarmed protesters with military-grade weaponry, a symptom of despotism that Americans seem to tolerate only because the most visible targets of such deployments are black. Anticipating further unrest, some law enforcement agencies have amassed a fearsome arsenal, including acoustic cannons, weaponized drones, and the foul smelling "skunk spray" used by the Israeli military in the subjugation of Palestinians. It is not surprising to learn that U.S. police and military forces view Black Lives Matter protesters as enemy combatants, subject them to extensive surveillance, and discuss their conquest in precisely the terms of a colonial occupation.[15]

These acts of coercion show no signs of cowing the resistance. Black Lives Matter, though still young, has entered a decisive phase. Whether it can expand its popular base will depend on its capacity to strengthen links to other embattled groups and grassroots movements, explicitly address the spate of violence against transgender people of color, and develop a firm ideological foundation while retaining its resiliency and élan. If it can do so, the movement may well pose a deeper challenge to existing social and political arrangements, prefiguring a more humane future and forging a theory and practice of mass struggle for our time.

NOTES

1. See Naomi Klein, *The Shock Doctrine: The Rise of Disaster Capitalism* (New York: Picador, 2007).

2. Jamilah King, "#blacklivesmatter: How Three Friends Turned a Spontaneous Facebook Post into a Global Phenomenon," *The California Sunday Magazine,* January 3, 2015, available at https://stories.californiasunday.com/2015-03-01/black-lives-matter/; Brit Bennett, "Ta-Nehisi Coates and a Generation Waking Up," *New Yorker,* July 15, 2015, available at http://www.newyorker.com/culture/culturalcomment/ta-nehisi-coates-and-a-generationwaking-up; Glen Ford, "Tamir Rice and the Meaning of 'No Justice—No Peace,'" *Block Agenda Report,* June 17, 2015, available at http://www.blackagendareport.com/tamir_rice_no_justice_no_peace; Khury Petersen-Smith, "Black

Lives Matter: A New Movement Takes Shape," *International Socialist Review,* Spring 2015, available at http://isreview.org/issue/96/black-lives-matter; "Rev. Sekou on Today's Civil Rights Leaders: 'I Take My Orders from 23-Year-Old Queer Women,'" *Yes! Magazine,* July 22, 2015, available at http://www.yesmagazine.org/peace-justice/black-lives-matter-sfavorite-minister-reverend-sekou-young-queer; Alicia Garza, "A Love Note to Our Folks," *N+I Magazine,* January 20, 2015, available at https://nplusonemag.com/onlin-only/online-only/a-love-note-to-our-folks/; Steven W. Thrasher, "'We're Winning': Jesse Jackson on Martin Luther King, Obama and #blacklivesmatter," *The Guardian,* August 16, 2015, available at http://www.theguardian.com/usnews/2015/aug/16/jesse-jackson-martin-lutherking-obama-and-blacklivesmatter.

3. Nina Shapiro, "Marissa Johnson Part of a New, Disruptive Generation of Activists," *Seattle Times,* August 15, 2015, available at http://www.seattletimes.com/seattle-news/marissa-johnson-a-generation-of-activists-who-believe-indisruption/; Bree Newsom, "When Oppression Is the Status Quo, Disruption Is a Moral Duty," *The Root,* August 7, 2015, available at http://www.theroot.com/articles/culture/2015/08/when_oppression_is_the_status_quo_disruption_is_a_moral_duty.2.html.

4. Ken Klippenstein and Paul Gottinger, "6 Police Officers across the US Were Charged with Murder This Week, Proving Strength of Protests," *U.S. Uncut,* August 20, 2015, available at http://usuncut.com/news/sixindictments-of-killer-cops-this-week-provesblacklivesmatter-is-working/.

5. "About the Black Lives Matter Network," available at http://blacklivesmatter.com/about/.

6. Clayborne Carson, *In Struggle: SNCC and the Black Awakening of the 1960s* (Cambridge: Harvard University Press, 1981); Gerald Home, *Fire This Time: The Walls Uprising and the 1960s* (Charlottesville; University Press of Virginia, 1995); Peniel E. Joseph, *Waiting til the Midnight Hour: A Narrative History of Black Power in America* (New York: Holt, 2006); Paula J. Giddings, *Ida: A Sword among Lions* (New York: HarperCollins, 2008);

Manning Marable, *Race, Reform, and Rebellion: The Second Reconstruction and Beyond in Black America, 1945-2006,* 3rd ed. (Jackson: University of Mississippi Press, 2007); Roderick Bush, *The End of White World Supremacy: Black Internationalism and the Problem of the Color Line* {Philadelphia: Temple University Press, 2009); Robin D. G. Kelley, *Freedom Dreams: The Black Radical Imagination* (Boston: Beacon Press, 2002).

7. Michelle Alexander, *The New Jim Crow: Mass Incarceration in the Age of Colorblindness* (New York: The New Press, 2010). For more recent scholarship, see the March 2015 issue of *Journal of American History* (Vol. 102, no. 1). \

8. Edward J. Escobar, "The Unintended Consequences of the Carceral State: Chicana/o Political Mobilization in Post–World War II America," *Journal of American History* 102 (2015): 174–84.

9. Sam Frizell, "Sanders and O'Malley Stumble during Black Lives Matter Protest," *Time,* July 18, 2015, available at http://time.com/3963692/bernie-sanders-martin-omalley-black-livesmatter/. For more on "rainbow radicalism," see Jeffrey O. G. Ogbar, *Black Power: Radical Politics and African American Identity* (Baltimore: Johns Hopkins University Press, 2004), 159–90.

10. "The #FightFor15 and the Black Lives Matter Movement March Together," #Fight for 15, available at http://fightfor15.org/laborday/main/the-fightfor15-and-the-black-lives-matter-movement-march-together/; Evan McMorris-Santoro and Jacob Fischler, "Unions Split, Take Sides After Ferguson," *BuzzFeed News,* August 22, 2014, available at http://www.buzzfeed.com/article/evanmcsan/organized-labor-ferguson; "Justice For Eric Garner," 1199SEIU, available at http://www.ll99seiu.org/justiceforgarner#sthash. PtVUi50a. dpbs; "Denouncing Police Unions: A Letter to the AFL-CIO," UAW Local 2865, available at https://docs.google.com/document/d/IQCWE4Tx0ti-vse9tbUBi-cL7v410-mOj2QC8Yk7HMcEM/edit? pli=I; Shawn Gude, "The Bad Kind of Unionism," *Jacobin Magazine,* Winter 2014, available at https://www.jacobinmag.com/2014/01/the-badkind-of-unionism/; Robert Korstad and

Nelson Lichtenstein, "Opportunities Found and Lost: Labor, Radicals, and the Early Civil Rights Movement," *Journal of American History* 75 (1988): 786–811; David Roediger, *The Wages of Whiteness: Race and the Making of the American Working Class* (London: Verso, 1991); Lois Weiner, "A Labor Movement That Takes Sides," *Jacobin,* September?, 2015, available at https://www.jacobinmag.com/2015/09/black-lives-matter-labor-day-dyett-strike/.

11. Amanda Terkel, "Black Lives Matter Disavows Democratic Party's Show of Support," *Huffington Post,* last updated August 31, 2015, available at http://www.huffingtonpost.com/entry/black-lives-matter dnc_55e48104e4b0c818f6188cab; "Black Lives Matter Infighting Leads to Splinter Group with Comprehensive Policy Agenda," *Your Black World,* August 21, 2015, available at http://yourblackworld.net/2015/08/21/black lives-matter-infighting-leads-to-splinter-groupwith-comprehensive-policy-agenda/: Bayard Rustin, "From Protest to Politics: The Future of the Civil Rights Movement," *Commentary,* February 1965, 25–31.

12. Bruce A. Dixon, "Where's the #BlackLives Matter Critique of the Black Misleadership Class, or Obama or Hillary?" *Black Agenda Report,* August 6, 2015, available at http://blackagendareport.comlnode/4624; Carmen Berkeley, "An Open Letter to the Black Community From 100 Black Youth," *Huffington Post,* July 15, 2013, available at http://www.huffingtonpost.com/carmen-berkley/an-open-letter-to-the-bla_b_3596688.htmll; Matt Peppe, "The Baltimore Uprising and the U.S. Government's Record on Human Rights," *Global Research,* May 6, 2014, available at http://www.globalresearch.ca/the-baltimoreuprising-and-the-u-s-governments-record-on-human-rights/5447509; Barbara Ransby, "The Class Politics of Black Lives Matter," *Dissent,* Fall 2015, available at https://www.dissentmagazine.org/article/class-politics-black-lives-matter; "About the Black Lives Matter Network," available at http://blacklivesmatter.com/about/.

13. Kali Nicole Gross, "African American Women, Mass Incarceration, and the Politics of Protection," *Journal of American History* 102 (2015): 25–33; Priscilla Ward, "My Anger Is Justified: Why Black Women's Rage Is Necessary for Change," *forharriet,* August 16, 2015, available at http://www.forharriet.com/2015/08/my-anger-is-justifiedwhy-black-womens.html? m=l; Josh Kruger, "#SayHerName Protest Exposes Tension among Philly Activists," *Philadelphia Citypaper,* July 27, 2015, available at http://citypaper.net philly-sayhernnme-protest-exposes-fissures-in-activist-community-calls-for-feminism--and-intersectionality/; Amanda Teuscher, "The Inclusive Strength of #BlackLivesMatter," *The American Prospect,* August 2, 2015, available at http://prospect.org/article/inclusive-strength-blacklivesmatter; Alicia Garza, "A Herstory of the #BlackLivesMatter Movement," *The Feminist Wire,* October 7, 2014, available at http://www.thefeministwire.com/2014/10/blacklivesmatter-2/; Danielle C. Belton, "'The 5 Biggest Challenges Facing #BlackLivesMatter," *The Root.com,* August 12, 2015, available at http://www.theroot.corn/articles/culture/2015/08/the_5_biggest_challenges_facing_blacklivesmatter.html.

14. David Weigel and Katie Zezima, "Cruz Leads a GOP Backlash to 'Black Lives Matter' Rhetoric," *Washington Post,* September 1, 2015, available at http://www.washingtonpost.com/news/post-politics/wp/2015/09/01/cruz-leads-a-gop-backlash-to-black-lives-matter-rhetoric/; Philip Holloway, "Police Lives Matter," *CNN.com,* September 4, 2015, available at http://www.cnn.com/2015/08/31/opinions/holloway-police-lives-matter/; Ayo Coly, "Healing Is Not Grieving: We Must Not 'Move Forward' In the Wake of Massacre," *Truthout,* July 3, 2015, available at http://www.truth-outorg/opinion/item/31693-healing-isnot-grieving-we-must-not-move-forward-in-the-wake-of-massacresupremacists-withoutborders.html? smid=nytcore-iphone-share&smprod=nytcore-iphone&_r=0.

15. Rania Khalek Rights, "St. Louis Police Bought Israeli Skunk Spray after Ferguson Uprising," *Electronicintifada.net,* August 13, 2015, available at https://electronicintifada.net/blogs/rania-khalek/st-louis-police-bought-israeli-skunk-spray-after-ferguson-uprising? utm_source=twitterfeed&utm_medium"twitter; Lee Fang, "Acoustic Cannon Sales to Police Surge after Black Lives Matter

Protests," *The Intercept,* August 14, 2015, available at https://firstlook.org/theintercept/2015/08/14/afterferguson-baltimore/; Jay Syrmopoulos, "New Released Documents Reveal U.S. Military Labeled All Ferguson Protesters as 'Enemy Forces,'" *The Free Thought Project.com,* April 18, 2015, available at http://thefreethoughtproject.com/released-documents-reveal-u-smilitary-labeled-ferguson-protestors-enemyforces/#JWHBwl087vuzUiPQ.01; Matt Agorist, "No Longer a Conspiracy Theory: First State Legalizes Weaponized Drones for Cops," *The Free Thought Project.com,* August 26, 2015, available at http://thefreethoughtproject.com/longer-conspiracy-theory-state-legalizes-weaponized-drones-cops/; Paddy O'Halloran, "'They Will Not Take the Street': Ferguson and Colonial Histories," *Counterpunch.org,* August 20, 2015, available at http://www.connterpunch.org/2015/08/20/they-will-not-take-thestreet-ferguson-and-colonial-histories/.

THINKING ABOUT THE READING

What is unique about the Black Lives Matter (BLM) movement compared to previous and other contemporary social movements? What are its guiding principles? What kinds of techniques does the movement use in their work? What are some of the challenges of the movement? After reading Rickford's article, has your understanding of the BLM movement shifted in any way? What does this article add to your understanding of effective methods of protest and ways to measure success for social movements?

Racism in America

To Be Continued. . .

BY ABBY FERBER

(2018)

R ace seems to be constantly in the news these days. I am going to focus the August 2017 march on Charlottesville in order to examine larger issues about hate speech, white supremacy and intersectionality and masculinity.

Hate Speech

What is hate speech? Is it legal? In the United States, any form of speech, even speech that people would define as hate speech, is legal. The first amendment to the constitution provides the basis for this: "Congress shall make no law respecting an establishment of religion, or prohibiting the free exercise thereof; or abridging the freedom of speech, or of the press; or the right of the people peaceably to assemble, and to petition the government for a redress of grievances." The courts have determined that no matter how despicable or hateful, speech is speech. Speech includes a range of expressions, including religious symbols on someone's desk, religious clothing or garb, body movements, art work, etc.

In the U.S. people have the right to express views that others would define as hateful. This only applies to public entities, government employees, any company or organization receiving public funds, etc. This explains why many public universities have faced challenges in recent years when student groups invite speakers who spout hate speech. Universities can choose not to invite such speakers; however, student clubs operate independently so that the University cannot limit the speech of such speakers, even if they represent the antithesis of the University's values. Numerous protests have taken place around the nation when speakers such as Milo Yiannopoulos are invited to speak. How do you think universities in these situations should respond? One clever tactic was taken by the University of Colorado Boulder: there the university invited Laverne Cox [one of the stars of *Orange Is the New Black* and the first openly transgender person to receive an Emmy nomination] to speak on campus.

Privately owned businesses and spaces *may* institute rules that limit free speech however. The only caveat is that the rules may not discriminate; they must apply to everyone, not just one group.

This is not the case in many other nations, however, where legal restrictions have been put on speech. For example, in 16 nations it is illegal and considered hate speech to deny the history of the Nazi Holocaust. Do you agree with this law? It is equally important to consider that in other cases, restrictions on speech may be seen as hateful: In at least half of the 16 states that comprise Germany, 16 ban teachers from wearing headscarves; France became the first European country to ban the full-face Islamic veil in public places (2011) and Austria followed in 2017. France's next step was to ban women's full-body swimsuits, known by some as "burkinis" (2016). Prime Minister Manuel Valls called the swimsuits "the affirmation of political Islam in the public space".

Hate Groups

Hate speech seems to be increasing in public spaces in the U.S. Only some of this is due to members of hate groups. According to the Southern Poverty Law Center there are currently 917 hate groups operating in the U.S. They define hate groups as groups having beliefs or practices that attack or malign an entire group of people. The majority, but not all of the groups they define as hate groups, are white supremacist groups such as neo-Nazis, Ku Klux Klan, neo-Confederates, skinheads, etc.

The march in Charlottesville on Friday, Aug. 11 was convened by white supremacist hate groups who opposed a plan to remove a statue of

Confederate General Robert E. Lee from a city park. The march had been pre-arranged and was considered a demonstration of free speech rights. Previous protests had taken place in May when the decision to remove the statue was first made. August 11 drew a large number of white, male protesters, under the banner of "Unite the Right," marching military style, carrying lit tiki torches, and chanting anti-Semitic and racist chants. A significant number of counter protesters were there. Law enforcement had little control when violence ensued, the Governor declared a state of emergency, and one young woman counter-protesting was killed by a pro-march driver who intentionally drove into the crowd, wounding many.

The march did indeed unite the right, attracting members of a variety of white supremacist hate groups. Despite their many differences they joined together, along with the (not so) new "Alt-right" (white supremacists who perform under a new, less threatening name, and aim to attract young members). The ideology that united these groups is white supremacy—the belief that whites are inherently and biologically superior and all other racial groups are inferior. Why were the marchers using anti-Semitic chants in defense of confederate monuments? Because anti-Semitism is a key feature of the white supremacist worldview: Jews are seen as the masterminds behind a conspiracy to eliminate the white race, and it is the responsibility of white men to stand up and protect their rightful place in power. That was what these men were there to do, and they were joined by many white men that were not associated with any of these groups. The message of the protest drew in large numbers of white males not formally tied to any white supremacist organizations yet embraced the message of the march. White supremacist ideology has become more accessible over the years with the growth of white supremacist websites and forums. No longer must one sneak out of their house donning a white robe, worried about who might see them. The web provides the security of anonymity while also allowing for greater participation. It also allows people to simply read and embrace the ideology. In fact, most of those responsible for hate crimes in the U.S., including acts of domestic terrorism, have no affiliation with a specific hate group. Additionally, like the latest massacre in Las Vegas, domestic terrorists have all been men. The long trail of marchers in Charlottesville was also a parade of men. Why? And why is this seldom even acknowledged? It is time we embrace an intersectional approach and acknowledge the gendered nature of white supremacy.

Intersectionality

Intersectional theories argue that race, gender, class, and significant social identities are interconnected, and cannot be fully understood on their own. No one possesses just a single identity. I am a white, heterosexual, middle-aged, upper middle-class woman. All of these identities shape my life. And when others see me, they see a white woman, not just a white person. (Ironically, white supremacists don't see me as white because they consider Jews to be a separate race. This is a perfect example of how these identities are socially constructed).

Scholars and activists of color have engaged in intersectional theorizing and practice throughout our history, although it was Kimberle Crenshaw who coined the term, and it began to be more widely employed starting in the 1980s and has grown ever since. Intersectional scholarship grew out of the activism and scholarship of women of color arguing that their lives are simultaneously shaped by their race and their gender. Intersectional theorizing is more often employed by gender scholars than race scholars. When it comes to studying the white supremacist movement, it has made little headway. The notion that whiteness and maleness are not racialized and gendered identities is still reinforced. Yet it is essential to look at white men as benefitting from both white and male privilege to understand what is going on.

The limited research that exists on gender and the organized white supremacist movement tends to focus on women in the movement. Research examines the history of women in the Ku Klux Klan, the roles of women in various groups, their motivations for joining, motivations for increased membership of women in the movement at various points, etc. Ideologically, there has always been a very strong emphasis upon white women as the reproducers of the race. According to their writing and websites, women in the movement are responsible for the bearing and rearing of children, fulfilling their duty to reproduce the white race, and also educating and socializing their children to the racist beliefs of the movement.

Men, on the other hand, are the primary recruits and on-line audience for White Supremacist groups. Over and over again articles, blog posts, comments, etc. declare that men are the saviours of the race. They are often attacked as not masculine enough and then encouraged to proclaim their real manhood through the movement and its ideology. They are implored to "rescue" white women from men of color, so that they will instead produce white babies. Whites are declared to be the civilized race, and white men are depicted as having built this nation. It is their duty to protect it from endless attacks.

Large numbers of white men were attracted to the march because of a shared sense that white people are losing control of the county, and losing out. They see themselves as victims. Masculinity in the U.S. is very narrowly defined—real men are supposed to be tough, powerful, and in control (not so far off from white supremacist ideology). Since the legal successes of the Civil Rights, women's liberation, LGBT, and disability rights movements, in conjunction with the relatively recent vicious vilification of immigrants and Muslims, the Black Lives Matter movement, and fear of becoming a minority in the U.S. have all intensified the fears of white men who look at the world as a zero-sum game.

Despite *feeling* victimized, white men continue to rule. They overwhelmingly fill the top seats of power in the government, finance and business worlds. White men *feel* powerless because they *have* been losing ground—economically. All but the wealthy white elites are worse off today financially than they were in the past. The wealth gap between the very wealthy and everyone else has increased dramatically since the 1980s. Due to technological advances, the outsourcing of manufacturing jobs, and the growth of low paying, unstable service sector jobs, many young white men recognize that they will not do as well economically as their fathers.

The crash in the housing and financial markets during The Great Recession contributed further to declining wealth accumulation. The recession damaged the net worth of all families, across race. Given the lower assets of African American and Hispanic families prior to the recession, however, these groups suffered the most and were more likely to lose their homes. Most remarkable is the fact that the economic recovery did not comparably benefit all families. Instead, the recovery actually widened both the class and racial wealth gap.

During the first two years of recovery, 100% of gains went to the wealthiest 7% of people, who saw their net worth, as a group, grow from $19.8 trillion to $25.4 trillion (a rise of 28%). For the remaining 93%, their combined net worth decreased 4 percent, from $15.4 trillion to $14.8 trillion. In terms of race, just after the recession, the wealth of white households was eight times that of black households, and increased to thirteen times the amount of wealth by 2013. What this means is that whites have suffered economic losses, due to the dramatic increase between the very wealthiest families and everyone else; at the same time they have fared much better than African American and Hispanic families, who still have not fully recovered. But this reality is not talked about. Instead, undocumented immigrants, terrorism by Muslim extremists, and working women are blamed.

Right wing media (including their tremendous growth via social media) have been providing endless confirmations of these myths. Now, the Presidency of Donald Trump has invited white men from across a wide spectrum to seek to "reclaim" power. Trump continuously asserts white supremacist assumptions through his statements and actions that support the belief that our country is under attack and must be defended, whether from immigrants from the South, Muslims, globalization, liberated women, gays and lesbians, or transgender people. Much of the racism that was covert in the past is now overt and front stage. We must abandon the myth that white supremacist beliefs are limited to members of hate groups.

The ideology of white supremacy has always served to benefit the very wealthy whites of this nation. Rather than looking up for the source of their loss, many white men follow the fingers which point the blame on every other group instead. And the number of people pointing in the wrong direction are growing louder and louder.

Post-Charlottesville pleas that Americans come together and "heal" are the constant refrain after every major racial conflict. However, there can be no real healing until the foundational problems like the wealth gap are reversed. The term white supremacist does not describe a handful of specific groups; it describes our nation.

REFERENCES

Blee, Kathleen M. 2008. *Women of the Klan: Racism and Gender in the 1920s*. Berkeley: University of California Press.

Ferber, Abby. 2016. *"White Supremacy and Gender." The Wiley Blackwell Encyclopedia of Gender and Sexuality Studies, First Edition*. Edited by Nancy A. Naples. John Wiley & Sons, Ltd.

Ferber, Abby L., ed. 2004. *Home-Grown Hate: Gender and the White Supremacist Movement*. New York: Routledge.

Ferber, Abby L. 1998. *White Man Falling: Race, Gender, and White Supremacy*. Lanham: Rowman & Littlefield. http://www.pewresearch.org/fact-tank/2014/12/12/racial-wealth-gaps-great-recession/

THINKING ABOUT THE READING

What does Ferber's discussion of white supremacy and hate groups contribute to your understanding of racism and recent events like the march in Charlottesville and the Emanuel AME Church massacre? Should there be more legal restrictions on hate speech to protect the public and vulnerable groups? What does Ferber and an earlier reading on the Alt-Right tell us about the use of technology in white supremacy groups? What does is tell us about the importance of intersectional theorizing and practice?

An Intersectional Queer Liberation Movement

JOSEPH NICHOLAS DEFILIPPIS

(2018)

From 2000–2009, I worked as one of the co-founders and executive director of a small organization in New York called Queers for Economic Justice (QEJ). During this period, QEJ worked closely with a number of other small, grassroots, radical queer groups, locally and across the country. Working with them was logical, because these queer liberation groups each had values, goals, constituents, and strategies that were similar to those of QEJ. These values, goals, constituents, and strategies were, however, markedly different from those of the national LGBTQ organizations and statewide equality groups that dominate the mainstream gay-rights movement (referred to here as the GRM). It was clear to me from the beginning that there were two very different types of organizations operating alongside each other in the movement.

Over the years, I witnessed many disagreements (about priorities and strategies) between the queer liberation groups and the larger GRM organizations, leading to ongoing tensions between the two different kinds of organizations. When I later began graduate studies in sociology and social work, I decided to focus my research on these queer liberation organizations, studying different aspects of their work, including those tensions with the GRM. In this essay I show how these queer liberation organizations share values and targets that comprise a significant social movement that is distinct from the GRM.

The Mainstream Gay Rights Movement

Over the past two decades, the GRM has had tremendous success moving forward its agenda. The work of the GRM organizations has principally involved advocacy and legislative lobbying, and litigation in state and federal courts; these efforts have been framed in the context of "equality" for LGBTQ people. These equality groups—ranging from national organizations such as the Human Rights Campaign to statewide equality groups at the local level—have pursued equality primarily by increasing LGBTQ people's access to institutions previously restricted to them (i.e., marriage, military service, etc.), and legal remedies for discrimination (i.e., hate crimes legislation, and employment non-discrimination).

Conceptually, the focus on LGBTQ equality has rested on a default understanding of LGBTQ people as united under an umbrella of homophobic discrimination. The GRM has employed a laser-sharp focus on combatting homophobic discrimination, making it not merely its primary goal, but its solitary goal. However, this conception ignores the impacts of racism, classism, xenophobia, transphobia, and other intersectional experiences that complicate the notion of monolithic "gayness" (Cohen, 1999; Vaid, 2012). In focusing exclusively on combatting homophobia, the GRM have excluded LGBTQ people of color, low-income LGBTQ people, and transgender people. Nevertheless, the GRM has been largely successful at characterizing themselves in the public eye as *the* organizations representing the interests of *the* LGBTQ community.

An Alternate Movement

While GRM organizations have pursued their equality-based agenda, grassroots LGBTQ groups have actively organized around intersectional, multi-issue interests. Structuring their work around core principles of intersectionality and centering the interests of the most marginal among queer communities, these queer liberation organizations explicitly center the leadership and membership of queers who are people of color (POC), transgender, poor and/or immigrant. These organizations employ both a redistribution (economics-based) and recognition (identity-based) politic in their activism. While referring to themselves as LGBTQ organizations, queer liberation organizations also position LGBTQ concerns as inextricably linked with concerns related to identities including race, class, gender, national status, and institutions like the immigration and the criminal/prison legal systems. In this way, they expand notions of who constitutes "the LGBTQ community" and consequently shift the conversation about that community's most pressing interests.

In this essay I highlight the underlying values and shared agenda of seven queer liberation organizations: Affinity Community Services in Chicago; allgo in Austin; Audre Lorde Project (ALP) in New York; National Queer Asian Pacific Islander Alliance (NQAPIA) in New York; Queers for Economic Justice (QEJ) in New York (now closed); Southerners on New Ground (SONG) in Atlanta; and Sylvia Rivera Law Project (SRLP) in New York. For each group, I conducted interviews with staff and analyzed mission statements and promotional videos.

I argue that they not only differ from the equality-based framework of the GRM but also constitute their own Queer Liberation Movement (QLM) distinct in its own right from the mainstream movement. The QLM offers a model of queer activism that is ultimately broader, more intersectional, and more justice-centered than the mainstream movement.

Gamson's Framework of Three Targets

To understand how the QLM groups are outside of the GRM but aligned with each other, I use the ideas of influential social movement scholar William Gamson. Gamson (1975) presented a framework useful for understanding what he called "the nature of a challenging group" (p. 14), or any organization concerned principally with challenging a political, social, or economic system.

He suggested that challenging groups organize their efforts around three distinct, though often related, targets: targets of influence, of mobilization, and of benefits. These characteristics of challenging groups can differentiate the QLM from the GRM, while also illustrating points of alignment among the Queer Liberation Organizations (QLO).

A challenging group's *targets of influence* are the set of individuals, policies, or institutions they identify as problematic and seek to influence in order to achieve their desired social change. In some cases, the targets of influence are individuals (e.g., an elected official), while in others, they may be significantly

broader (e.g., the public education system). The *targets of mobilization*, are those people whom the challenging group needs to activate in order to impact the targets of influence, i.e., the constituency. Finally, *the targets of benefits* are the people most likely to benefit from the changed condition, once the target of influence has shifted its conduct. In short, they are the people who are helped if the challenging group is successful in its efforts.

Targets of the Mainstream Gay Rights Movement

In the context of Gamson's three targets, the GRM organizations' primary targets of influence are elected officials and the judicial system. The GRM attempts to influence elected officials through lobbying efforts, and they target the judicial system in the form of litigation. The GRM has attempted to influence these targets by focusing on single-issue policy concerns such as the exclusion of LGBTQ people from existing legal and social structures; consequently, their agenda has focused primarily on gaining inclusion into those structures. Specifically, GRMs have focused on access to family protections (e.g., marriage and adoption), inclusion of sexual orientation in hate crime and civil rights/anti-discrimination laws (e.g., employment protection and access to the military), and support for youth, specifically in the context of the education system (e.g., safe schools, Gay-Straight Alliances, etc.). The majority of GRM resources have been spent on those issues.

Gamson (1975) has suggested that the targets of mobilization and the targets of benefits are sometimes closely aligned. This stands to reason; after all, the people most likely to benefit directly are also often those most likely to be motivated to take part in activism towards that change. In the context of the mainstream gay rights movement, this has certainly been the case. The GRM has structured its work around the pursuit of equality for gay and lesbian people. Based on an understanding of homophobia as the prime cause of inequality between LGBTQ and straight people, the movement has effectively argued that homophobia can be remedied through the inclusion of LGBTQ people in institutions and laws formerly closed to them. Given that all LGBTQ people must navigate homophobia, which is a central barrier to equality, the GRM assumes its agenda is in the best interest of all LGBTQ people. Consequently, the GRM's stated constituency is all LGBTQ people. In practice, however, the constituency is predominantly the White, middle-class gay and lesbian citizens who are most motivated by an equality rhetoric that centers homophobia so prominently among "the community's" interests. Similarly, the beneficiaries of the GRM are rhetorically all LGBTQ people, but in practice consist of mostly White, middle-class gays and lesbians who most directly stand to benefit from the narrow range of policy and legal interests advanced by the movement.

Queer Liberation Movement: Three Shared Principles

The QLM groups approach their work from an entirely different orientation. These organizations share an intersectional analysis in their activist commitments and seek to center the interests of the most marginal among queer people with an emphasis on "trickle-up" social justice and transformation rather than reform.

Intersectionality

An intersectional analysis is a corrective to decades of a White, middle-class "gay rights" single-issue agenda and makes clear that homophobia alone is an incomplete explanation for the multiple marginalizations experienced by queer POC, poor queer people, queer people who are immigrants or incarcerated, trans people, and more. According to the intersectional perspective that guides QLM organizations it is impossible to understand any one form of oppression without understanding how it is impacted by other forms of oppression. People have both advantages and disadvantages due to their locations in multiple systems (capitalism, racism, sexism, heterosexism), and could receive privilege from their position in one system (e.g., racism), but be disadvantaged because of their position in another overlapping system (e.g., homophobia).

In their origin stories, most QLOs describe their founders' frustration with other organizations' lack of an intersectional approach in their work. These organizations were born out of a desire to create a place that centers the intersections of their communities' identities. For example, in my interview with Ben de Guzman, former NQAPIA Co-Director, he explained, "All of those (GRM) groups are predominantly White. Their perspectives don't appropriately include communities of color perspectives . . . We look at ourselves as providing a more intersectional analysis and lifting up queer POC and immigrants." These queer liberation groups bring theorizing about intersectionality into practice, in why they do their work, who does the work, and how they do the work. And by operating from a shared value of intersectionality, they have developed a very different platform from the GRM's focus on White, affluent gays and lesbians.

Trickle-Up Social Justice

A focus on intersectionality has led the QLM organizations, both independently and in their collaborative work, to additional shared principles. The GRM has frequently been accused of inaccurately assuming that policies which help middle-class White people will "trickle down" and also benefit LGBTQ people of color or poor people. The QLM groups do the reverse. They choose their priorities by engaging in what Dean Spade, co-founder of the Sylvia Rivera Law Project, has called "Trickle Up Social Justice." Informed by bell hooks's concept of organizing from margin-to-center, this approach stresses that until the needs of the most vulnerable members of a community are addressed, progress toward other goals simply reinforces the dominance of those people most advantaged. Put differently, as long as organizing priorities remain targeted on the interests of White affluent gays and lesbians, "victories" will benefit those people over queers of color or poor queer people—and often at their expense. The reverse, however, is not true. When the interests of the most marginal are centered, justice will "trickle up"—the benefits of activism will be shared even by those who hold positions of greater privilege. Organizing in this way, by identifying first the interests of the most vulnerable among queer communities, the QLM organizations employ a version of trickle-up social justice, in which benefit is conferred first to those in most need of it.

Transformation, Not Reform

Because of the QLM's intersectional analysis and margin-to-center orientation, they view many social institutions as broken and in need of complete overhauls. They seek not access and reform but, rather, transformation and redistribution. By contrast, the GRM does not, overall, question the fairness of the institutions into which it has sought equal access. It does not seek to overhaul or dismantle institutions such as marriage or the military; rather, it merely seeks LGBTQ admission.

While QLM groups do often advocate for access into the systems they target, this is usually a short-term goal. Almost all the interview participants explain that their concerns extend far beyond merely gaining access for LGBTQ people to social institutions. In their views, access to a system that treats people poorly is no victory. The queer liberation groups are critical of the larger systems in which they are working, whether it is capitalism, immigration policies, or the criminal legal system. For these groups, the context for any of their specific day-to-day work is their larger vision of social justice, best articulated in the Sylvia Rivera Law Project's mission statement: "We can't just work to reform the system. The system itself is the problem." In the following sections, I describe the QLM's agenda and examine how the QLM has focused its efforts on the complete transformation of specific institutions.

Queer Liberation Organizations: Three Shared Targets

Those three shared values among the QLM organizations (intersectionality, trickle-up social justice, and broad social transformation) come together to constitute the foundation of an activism agenda that differs from the GRM in many ways. These values are instrumental in shaping how the organizations prioritize their targets of influence, mobilization, and benefit. The following chart shows a comparison of the targets of the QLM and the GRM.

Perhaps the most important difference is that all the QLM groups began with a recognition that a segment of the queer community was not being served by the agendas of mainstream organizations. Most began with an explicit commitment, for instance, to centering the interests of queer people of color. Based on the guidance of their beneficiaries, the QLM organizations tend to focus their activism efforts in three principal areas: 1) health and healthcare, social service delivery, and anti-poverty efforts; 2) immigration justice; and 3) criminal legal system. While some of the organizations may also work on additional issues, these three issues are prioritized by most of the groups in my study. I turn now to a brief examination of each of those three areas.

Health and Healthcare, Social Service Delivery, and Anti-Poverty Efforts

Despite mainstream public imagination, which depicts the LGBTQ community as White, affluent, and stylish, poverty rates are higher among queer communities than in the general population, compared along lines of race, gender, and sexual orientation (DeFilippis, 2016, Gates, 2014). Like their heterosexual peers, queer POC generally earn lower incomes than White men and women. Transgender people have much higher unemployment rates, poverty rates, and homelessness rates than the general population. LGBTQ individuals and families often lack health care and are more likely than their heterosexual counterparts to be without health insurance (Redman, 2010). LGBTQ people of color are even more likely to have their healthcare needs gone unmet (Kreheley, 2009). The high rates of joblessness and poverty among transgender populations means that they are particularly likely to live with a lack of health care or health insurance (Transgender Law Center, 2013).

In response to these issues of poverty and lack of access to social services and healthcare, the QLM groups often focus their work on influencing government programs that provide public benefits and health services. Six QLM organizations work explicitly on issues such as poverty, welfare, homelessness, healthcare, Medicaid, and HIV, and four have devoted substantial resources towards influencing public policies about public benefits and healthcare systems. Other QLM groups target other health and human services providers, and/or try to influence the GRM groups (to get them to focus on healthcare and social services).

Table 14.1

Comparison of Primary Targets		
	Queer Liberation Movement	**Mainstream Gay Rights Movement**
Primary Targets of Influence	Community members, elected officials, and social justice organizations positioned to transform: • The Criminal Legal Systems • Healthcare Systems • The Immigration System • Social Services and Welfare	Elected officials and courts that are well positioned to affect policies relevant to: • Anti-Discrimination Laws • Hate Crime Legislation • Marriage • Military • Youth/Education
Primary Targets of Mobilization	• LGBTQ Immigrants • Low-Income LGBTQ People • LGBTQ People of Color • Transgender People	• All LGBTQ People* • White, middle class, cisgender citizens*
Primary Targets of Benefits	• LGBTQ Immigrants • Low-Income LGBTQ People • LGBTQ People of Color • Transgender People • All LGBTQ People	• All LGBTQ People* • White, middle-class, cisgender citizens*

*There is disagreement about these claims. GRM leaders maintain they mobilize and benefit all LGBTQ people, while critics have long argued that they primarily mobilize and benefit White middle-class, cisgender citizens.

To this end, QLM organizations have employed a variety of strategies to effect change in those systems they have named as antagonistic. For instance, until it closed in 2014, Queers for Economic Justice (QEJ) targeted New York City's Department of Homeless Services, successfully influencing their policies. According to Kenyon Farrow, former QEJ executive director:

> [QEJ focused on] organizing and advocacy in the shelter systems and with the welfare system . . . [Staff] spent two years leading a successful campaign to get the City to change its policy around transgender homeless shelter residents, and now people can self-select which shelters they want to be in. This was a real victory. And staff worked for three years to get the city's shelter system to allow domestic partners access to the shelters for homeless families. And we won. Before that, you needed to be married. So, the shelter project has accomplished a lot.

By focusing their work on the shelter system in this way, QEJ prioritized the needs of people at the bottom of the economic ladder and made the shelter system their target of influence.

Similarly, three New York–based queer liberation organizations (ALP, QEJ, and SRLP) collaborated to influence the NYC welfare system, striving to eliminate barriers to TANF (Temporary Assistance for Needy Families) for transgender people by targeting the Human Resource Administration (HRA). Guided by beneficiaries, themselves affected by these systems, these organizations also targeted Medicaid and other healthcare systems, around discrimination against transgender people in healthcare. SRLP filed a class action lawsuit and worked with ALP to organize a related grassroots organizing campaign, against New York State Medicaid policy that denied health care to transgender people. They have also worked together to change NYC's birth certificate policy, which required transgender people who need healthcare to have surgery, although many could not afford it or did not want it.

On its website, the queer POC organization allgo claims that oppression and inadequate health care results in queer POC succumbing to preventable or treatable illness and disease. As a result, allgo has selected non-queer-specific health providers in Texas as a primary target of influence. For example, they worked with Austin's health department on a project for Black women of childbearing age, helping them develop a plan for the inclusion of queer POC. In addition, allgo has always focused on HIV (including offering HIV/AIDS prevention trainings, and providing safer sex education and supplies to community members), and its recent work has expanded to include other sexual health issues and reproductive justice. It also runs an extensive wellness program, offering breast care education and information (and access to free mammograms and breast exams once a year), and wellness workshops/discussions and support programs, with a focus on queer men of color. By making the connections between HIV rates among communities of color and queer people (and also recognizing that these are not mutually exclusive categories), and by making connections between healthcare, HIV, and reproductive justice, allgo demonstrates an example of work grounded in an intersectional analysis.

Similarly, Affinity works in Chicago on health and wellness issues facing Black LGBTQ people. Their work started in part as a response to the disparate health outcomes they see among Black queer women. Executive director Kim L. Hunt explains that Affinity views health broadly, with their work ranging from overall physical well-being, to reproductive health and STIs, to physical safety (hate crimes and intimate partner violence), to mental health issues (such as depression and suicide prevention). Hunt states that Affinity does this work "on a range of things because we are approaching this from an intersectional lens rather than an LGBTQ-silo lens. And because of that we also work with a lot of organizations that are outside of the LGBTQ community." She explains that Affinity often finds it more useful to partner with non-LGBTQ racial and economic justice organizations than with the gay equality groups:

> Because the larger LGBTQ organizations are not ready to examine race and poverty, our members are really more anxious to work with organizations who are tackling those

issues. They may not have the LGBTQ component down, but that might be something we bring to those movements that makes them more inclusive.

It is significant that Affinity, like other QLM groups, would sooner work with progressive non-queer organizations than with the GRM. Many of the QLM activists explained to me that this was because progressive POC organizations or economic justice groups were more willing to expand their work to include LGBTQ people than the gay and lesbian equality groups were to address racial justice or poverty.

These examples illustrate how the QLM groups employ their values of intersectionality and centering the interests of their beneficiaries as they work on poverty and healthcare. However, as they do this work they also enact the value of social transformation rather than simply reform. Many of the organizations ground their anti-poverty work not merely in the context of bringing greater opportunity to queer people but to questioning capitalism itself. For instance, QEJ's Kenyon Farrow states, "I don't think it is possible to be politically or legally equal under capitalism." And SRLP founder Dean Spade, while insisting that activists focus on the actual material conditions of people's lives, claims that hardships in the community "are being exploited and increased by neoliberal austerity measures." By connecting their day-to-day work to a larger critique of capitalism and neoliberalism, the queer liberation groups work toward a larger vision of social change than mere reform.

Immigration Justice

An intersectional analysis must go beyond race, class, and gender to incorporate issues such as nationality and migration (Mehrotra, 2010). Aligned with this value, QLM groups explicitly target the U.S. immigration system and its effects at the intersections of citizenship status, race, gender, sexual orientation, and class. At least 904,000 LGBTQ immigrants live in the United States, almost a third of whose documentation status is precarious (Gates, 2013). Immigration laws in the United States are largely centered around two concepts: "merit" and the reunification of the "family," which is most often defined in nuclear and heteronormative terms. Consequently, the advocacy of the mainstream immigrant movement often emphasizes heteronormative relationships (marriage and biological family) and conceptions of normality (e.g., hard-working immigrants) to gain basic citizenship rights. At the same time, the mainstream GRM has focused its (minimal) immigration efforts on seeking protection and citizenship status exclusively for those immigrants who are partners of U.S. citizens.

As a result, most LGBTQ immigrants have been marginalized within both the immigrant rights movement (because of the hetero-normative nature of immigration policies), and the mainstream GRM (because of its focus on romantic couples or refugees). These queer immigrants lack support as they contend with homophobia and transphobia within their communities of origin, and xenophobia and racism within the LGBTQ movement. This coupled with restrictions upon immigrants' access to public benefits has contributed to heightened poverty within LGBTQ immigrant communities, and therefore LGBTQ immigrant communities are left to fend for themselves. At this time, most LGBTQ organizations do not assist queer immigrants who are already in the country and struggling to make a living. LGBTQ immigrants face economic hardship, food insecurity, and lack of healthcare (Gates, 2013).

Given this context and the queer liberation organizations' values of intersectional activism and organizing for social transformation rather than single-issue policy reform, these groups have selected three primary targets of influence around immigration justice: 1) the mainstream immigration rights movement; 2) the mainstream gay rights movement and LGBTQ communities in general; and ultimately 3) U.S. immigration policy broadly.

Mainstream Immigration Rights Movement

Many queer liberation organizations in particular have structured at least part of their work around challenging the mainstream immigration rights movement. Part of this commitment has grown from these organizations' own analysis of the shifting demographics in their local (queer) communities. In the South, for instance, increased immigration has highlighted the compounded marginalization experienced by queer immigrants, who due to intersections of heterosexism, transphobia, and xenophobia, often enjoy even less of a social safety net than their heterosexual peers. In response, SONG is not merely targeting the government to gain more access for LGBTQ immigrants; they are also targeting the immigrant rights movement, attempting to complicate the analyses of groups within this movement. SONG and other queer liberation organizations work in active partnership with existing immigrant rights coalitions. Some of SONG's immigration-related work has focused specifically on the issues facing LGBTQ people, such as their 2014 protests against Immigration and Customs Enforcement's (ICE) treatment of transgender detainees in immigration detention. However, the majority of SONG's immigration efforts are not specifically LGBTQ-focused. Examples of this include their campaigns in 2015, organizing against North Carolina's HB318 (a bill which prohibited local officials from using their cities as "Sanctuary Zones" for immigrants) and participating in protests against plans to provide ICE agents with increased access to jails. SONG has continued to focus on non-LGBTQ-specific immigration work, such as their 2016 protests outside of the Etowah Detention Center in Gadsden, Alabama, and their organizing work, that same year, against Georgia's anti-immigrant "felony driving law."

By working in sustained partnership with non-queer immigrant justice groups, SONG and other QLM groups make the immigrant rights movement more inclusive of queer people, while pushing it to expand its analysis. ALP, for instance, has sought to radicalize the existing immigrant justice movement along the dimensions of gender and sexuality. According to ALP's former Executive Director Cara Page,

> The understanding of how queer and trans POC are centrally located inside of immigrant justice has really elevated to a different level, especially in the global south . . . it's a movement we've always been inside of but we are now radicalizing . . . We are transforming that movement by bringing that queer and trans lens. By looking at gender violence, and sexuality, and politicalizing what that means in terms of body, and sovereignty, and state. And taking the immigrant justice movement to another level.

By targeting the immigrant justice movement, and bringing a queer analysis to it, groups like ALP and SONG broaden the work of that movement, while simultaneously expanding the definition of what constitutes a "gay issue."

Mainstream LGBTQ Communities and Organizations

In 2007, QEJ organized the drafting of a vision statement, outlining the political priorities of LGBTQ immigrants, which was signed by 50 organizations (DasGupta, 2012). Their concerns were varied, including the policing of the border, the HIV ban, the process of applying for asylum, the guest worker program, the provisions for harboring asylum-seeking immigrants, an end of immigrant detentions, eliminating the high-income requirements for immigrant sponsors, broader definitions of family (beyond marriage) and kinship patterns for sponsorship. The aforementioned issue of bi-national couples (the primary immigration focus of the national gay rights organizations for over two decades) was included but was not centralized as a high priority.

While 50 LGBTQ groups signed on (most small, local organizations, including community centers closely connected to the needs of community members), most of the national LGBTQ organizations did not. Indeed, they often claimed that the vision statement was "too broad" and not sufficiently focused on LGBTQ-specific issues (DasGupta, 2012). QLM organizations work inside and alongside the GRM to influence the conversation about immigration policy. They push the GRM to expand its work beyond the issue of American citizens' right to keep their foreign-born partner in the country. Ben de Guzman, former Co-Director of the National Queer Asian Pacific Islander Alliance (NQAPIA), argues

> We really spent a lot of time engaging [GRM groups] to make sure that the LGBTQ movement knew that immigration was not just about bi-national couples, that there are all these other ways in which LGBTQ folks who have immigrants in their families or who are immigrants themselves are affected and have a stake.

Now that the legalization of same-sex marriage has made moot this issue of bi-national couples, the GRM has very little on its immigration agenda. However, the QLM continues to push the GRM to recognize the needs of LGBTQ immigrants. For instance, NQAPIA organizes community forums on LGBTQ immigrants' rights, publishes documents about undocumented LGBTQ Asian American and Pacific Islander (AAPI) immigrants, provides legal analysis of the impact of immigration reform legislation on AAPI LGBTQ communities, organizes Asian American communities to support LGBTQ rights, and provides trainings for queer AAPI activists.

US Immigration Policy

Although NQAPIA and many other queer liberation organizations focus on the needs of LGBTQ immigrants, their work is not limited merely to LGBTQ access to the immigration system; it is situated in a larger vision of comprehensive immigration transformation. Their ongoing immigrants' rights campaign advocates for, among other things, legalization of undocumented immigrants, expanded visa programs for students and workers (both low-wage and professional), and legal protections to guard against racial profiling, detentions, and deportations. These are not merely "gay issues"—they are issues of concern to all immigrants.

NQAPIA incorporates these larger issues in much of its programming, such as when it works with mainstream, ethnic, and LGBTQ media (via press conferences, op-eds, etc.) to promote immigrants' rights and discuss comprehensive immigration reform. For example, in 2016 NQAPIA members engaged in advocacy and public education about two significant immigrant programs initiated by the Obama administration: The Deferred Action for Childhood Arrivals (DACA) and Deferred Action for Parental Accountability (DAPA) programs.

SONG, QEJ, and ALP take these larger issues around immigration one step further, arguing for a wholesale transformation in how immigration and citizenship are conceptualized in the United States, and addressing how immigration and citizenship debates are laden with raced and classed implications. SONG's Helm-Hernandez articulates their commitment in this way:

> We see (comprehensive immigration reform) as a step in our longer goal to actually

transform the idea of citizenship, to talk about indigenous sovereignty and the role of indigenous communities in defining that conversation. We push back on the White nativist movement that assumes that only White people have claim to the US, only White people have claim to legitimate citizenship in this country . . . Our people have demanded citizenship as one of the main ways to honor the reality that most undocumented communities are reduced only to labor. This assumption that we're disposable, and as long as you can stand up and work and produce, then you can be here. In the shadows, but you can be here. And as long as you don't become a person with disabilities, as long as you're not queers, as long as all of these other things, because then it's thank you for your labor and good day.

This analysis makes connections between immigration policy with issues of race, labor, capitalism, disability, and sexuality. This is typical of the intersectional analysis that unites the QLM and distinguishes it from the GRM.

Between 2006–2008, ALP and QEJ each issued various policy papers about immigration, using an intersectional lens to address numerous aspects of immigration policy. ALP and QEJ each argued that guest worker programs result in the exploitation of temporary workers while simultaneously undercutting the U.S. labor movement. Such an analysis explicitly draws connections between immigration policy and economic policy, and situates all workers (LGBTQ people and heterosexual cisgender people, citizen and noncitizen) in solidarity with each other.

QLOs take an approach to USA immigration policy that avoids single-issue analysis and, instead, looks for solutions that address the complexities of immigration policy. They work to influence the entire immigration system and expand the current parameters of the immigration debate set by the GRM, the immigrant rights movement, and immigration opponents. The following excerpts from a speech given by Trishala Deb, ALP's former Immigration Rights Program Coordinator, illustrates these multi-faceted targets:

We are in a critical moment within the broader struggle for the rights of migrants in the United States and in the world. I am

speaking of the mounting costs of a very small sector of wealthy people accumulating unimaginable resources off the backs of the majority of the world. Every year, over 175 million people migrate around the world in search of a sustainable existence . . . We must accept that the transnational economy that some people benefit from is completely dependent on the suppression of economic autonomy throughout the global south.

Here Deb identifies the criminal legal system, ICE, and the military as linked. She challenges her audience to make these structural connections too, and to expand the focus of their work to address all of these systems. Her assessment is meant to serve as a call to action.

We can build local coalitions and national strategies which will consolidate our collective understanding and power to say to anyone in Washington: we will not go through another mass registration program which results in the loss of the most vulnerable among us, we will not accept . . . another guest worker policy, we will not consent to billions of our money spent to incarcerate entire families, including children, on top of the trillions of dollars in profit being used to kill our families abroad . . . We will not consent to surveillance drones used on our southern borders, the way they are used to patrol the wall in Palestine; we are not temporary, disposable, or alien.

These QLM organizations are consistent in their selection of antagonists (the GRM, the mainstream immigration movement, and the US immigration system as a whole). Similarly, they share targets of benefits and mobilization—immigrants generally, and in some cases queer immigrants more specifically.

Criminal Legal System

Queer POC, youth, and transgender people are particularly targeted by law enforcement, and regularly face police brutality (Center for American Progress & Movement Advancement Project, 2016).

LGBTQ people of color face distinct obstacles accessing legal counsel, getting pre-trial release, and receiving a fair sentence. Once on trial, LGBTQ people's sexual orientation or gender identity is often used to bias juries (Center for American Progress & Movement Advancement Project, 2016). They are more likely to suffer violence and sexual assault in prison and to be placed in solitary confinement. Indeed, they face problems with the criminal legal system as a whole. It has "a toxic effect on queer communities at every conceivable level: the marginalization and subsequent criminalization of queer youth; bias in the judicial system; trauma during incarceration in prisons and jails; and in disproportionate sentencing, particularly death penalty cases" (Cammett, 2009, p. 11).

Transgender people are particularly impacted. The rate of incarceration for transgender people is three times as high as the rate of the general population (Grant, Mottet, & Tanis). Once in prison, transgender people continue to be targeted. They are subject to excessive punishment and overuse of segregation, and must contend with transphobic healthcare, including denial of hormones and discrimination in even routine medical. They are housed in men's or women's prisons based on their assigned sex, regardless of how they may identify. Once there, they face rampant physical and sexual abuse (Jenness, Maxson, Matsuda, & Sumner, 2007).

The GRM has largely ignored these issues. Instead, its work on the criminal legal system has focused on expanding hate crime legislation, a priority supported by many of its White, middle-class constituents, but one which has been widely criticized by communities of color for lacking an intersectional analysis about the racist and classist nature of the criminal legal system. The QLM, on the other hand, has taken those issues seriously, and many of the groups have made criminal justice work a central part of their work.

Part of the QLM's work responds to the surveillance and harassment of low-income neighborhoods and communities of color by police. They work to challenge police targeting of their communities. Dean Spade, founding director of SRLP, highlights the ways in which criminalization in the lives of poor people is "highly ritualized, highly gendered; both in terms of who gets arrested and what the police think looks unusual and which neighborhoods they spend time patrolling." Cara Page, of ALP, expands on this

point, pointing to her organization's participation in coalition work on police reform, characterized by efforts to resist "a right-wing agenda that further marginalized our communities and policed our bodies." She explains that ALP and their coalition allies have been "struggling with city government on *where* policing is, and how the increase of policing is certainly connected to the racial and economic injustices of our communities." These quotes reflect an intersectional understanding of queer people's lives and their interactions with the criminal legal system. In the analysis put forward by these organizations, sexual orientation and gender identity are factors in the policing of these organizations' communities, but so too are race and class.

In addition to working on the issue of police surveillance and targeting, QLM organizations focus on how LGBTQ people are treated when they are incarcerated. Several organizations engage in advocacy work that targets policies within prisons. Some also provide direct services to incarcerated or formerly incarcerated people. For instance, allgo has provided trainings for staff in the juvenile justice system, explaining how to better serve LGBTQ people, with a particular focus on trans-sensitivity and education. In addition, they have also worked to change policies for LGBTQ people in Texas jails— both the adult and juvenile prison systems. By not limiting their work to improving services for people within the prisons (by simultaneously working to change larger policies that guide the prison system as a whole), allgo illustrates the commitment shared by the larger QLM to not settle for mere access to existing (and problematic) institutions, but to also fight for broader transformation.

Given the structural limitations inhibiting mobilization of many people who stand to benefit most from their efforts (incarcerated and criminalized people), QLM groups often mobilize other populations, including those most likely to be targeted by the police, family members of incarcerated people, and/or in neighborhoods that are most heavily surveilled by the police. However, QLM groups also find ways to incorporate the incarcerated people most directly impacted by the criminal legal system. For instance, Reina Gossett described how SRLP works with a Prison Advisory Committee comprised of 70 people incarcerated in NY state who "really help SRLP decide what to advocate for, what to press for, what issues are the most important facing people who are currently incarcerated." Gossett explained this is because

> We believe that the people who are navigating these issues are the experts on these issues and are really powerful and capable of changing these issues . . . people who are currently incarcerated are going to know what are the most pressing issues to advocate for and organize around when it comes to the prison system. And often those are the very people, whether they are incarcerated or whether they are low income; the very people who are navigating an issue are historically pushed out of social movements.

This commitment to centering the people at the bottom, and recognizing their expertise and ability to guide the movement, is another marked difference between the QLM and the GRM, which is predominantly led by White, middle-class, college-educated people.

An important unifying feature of the QLM's work on the criminal legal system is their resistance to expanding the prison industrial complex. Kenyon Farrow articulates this as a point of distinction between the QLM and the GRM: "You have [GRM organizations] advocating for stronger hate crime legislation at the same time that we see other social movements, and communities of color, in particular, really rejecting the use of criminalization as a strategy for solving a whole range of problems." Across organizations, these activists believe that queer communities experience more violence at the hands of the criminal legal system than they do from homophobic strangers on the street. Consequently, they argue that hate crime legislation helps to strengthen a system that should instead be disempowered, if not completely abolished.

While the GRM targets the criminal legal system for the creation of more laws (hate crime legislation), the QLM has, instead, targeted other entities as sites in which to create safety, while simultaneously targeting the criminal legal system to decrease its power. According to QEJ's Kenyon Farrow, the QLM is "moving to stop prisons or policing strategies." In fact, prison abolition lurks in the background of much of the queer liberation organizations' work. Although the day-to-day work of some QLM

organizations involves providing direct legal services for individual prisoners, class action suits, or sensitivity training for prison staff, their long-term goals appear to be creating safety outside of the criminal legal system while also pursuing prison abolition. This commitment is shared among queer liberation organizations and is perhaps best articulated by Reina Gossett, formerly of SRLP: "A lot of my energy goes into a movement to abolish the prison industrial complex."

In addition, some of the QLM groups are working to build alternatives to the current criminal system. For example, the "Safe Neighborhood Campaign" (a project of ALP's "Safe Outside the System" Collective) challenges hate and police violence by using community-based strategies rather than relying on the police. This campaign builds numerous safe spaces in Brooklyn that publicly identify as willing to open their doors to community members fleeing from violence, and whose staff have been trained on homophobia, transphobia, and how to prevent violence without relying on law enforcement. ALP's Cara Page says, ". . . our strategy is about saying, yes, there are hate crimes, so what are we doing inside of our communities with allies, with families, with other queer and trans POC?" In ALP's approach to criminal justice, the targets of mobilization are community members themselves. ALP is working to transform relationships in local communities, and build safety by training neighbors to take care of each other, rather than to fear each other. Page adds:

> Instead of assuming that the state or criminal system or military is defining safety and will save us from each other, we are looking (at our neighbors) eye to eye, in the words of Audre Lorde, and asking of ourselves and each other "Who am I willing to be for your safety? Who are you willing to be for mine?"

Conclusion

This strategy of building alternatives to, rather than seeking access into, problematic institutions illustrates how the QLM rejects the GRM's reformist equality-based approach, seeking instead to transform society in pursuit of justice. The seven organizations included in this study are hardly alone. They work in partnership with numerous other similar groups across the country, who I argue are also part of the QLM.

This existence of the QLM is significant because, as Lisa Duggan (2004) has documented, the GRM has successfully depicted LGBT people as mainstream, and itself as the centrist movement that represents them. However, the QLM shows this to be false. There is a large undervalued constituency pursing a much queerer set of politics. While there have always been radical outlier organizations in the GRM, my research shows that there is now a level of coherence and connection among the QLM organizations, indicating that the possibilities for queer liberation (rather than gay equality) may be stronger than is usually recognized. This post-marriage moment raises important questions about the future of LGBTQ activism. The queer liberation movement presents new possibilities for intersectional, multi-issue political and social organizing extending well beyond single-issue identity politics.

REFERENCES

Badgett, M.V.L., Durso, L.E., & Schneebaum, A. (2013). *New patterns of poverty in the lesbian, gay, and bisexual community.* University of California Los Angeles School of Law, Williams Institute.

Cammett, A. (2009). *Queer lockdown: Coming to terms with the ongoing criminalization of LGBTQ communities.* The University of Nevada Las Vegas, William S. Boyd School of Law.

Center for American Progress and Movement Advancement Project (2016). *Unjust: How the broken criminal justice system fails LGBTQ people of color.*

Cohen, C. (1999). What is this movement doing to my politics? *Social text, No. 61, Out front: Lesbians, gays, and the struggle for workplace rights,* 111–118.

Cohen, C.J. (1997). Punks, bulldaggers, and welfare queens: The radical potential of queer politics? *GLQ: A Journal of Lesbian and Gay Studies, 3*(4), 437–465.

DasGupta, D. (2012). Queering immigration: Perspectives on cross-movement organizing. *A New Queer Agenda: The Scholar and The Feminist Online. 10*(1–2).

DeFilippis, J. N. (2016). "What about the rest of us?" An overview of LGBTQ poverty issues and a call to action. *Journal of Progressive Human Services, 27*(3), 143–174.

DeFilippis, J.N. & Anderson-Nathe, B. (2017). Embodying margin to center: Intersectional activism among queer liberation organizations. In M. Brettschneider, S. Burgess, & C. Keating (Eds.), *LGBTQ politics: A critical reader. A new collection of essays.* NYU Press.

Duggan, L. (2004). *The twilight of equality?* Boston, MA: Beacon Press.

Gamson, W. A. (1975). *The strategy of social protest.* Homewood, IL: Dorsey Press.

Gates, G.J. (2013). *LGBTQ Adult immigrants in the United States.* University of California Los Angeles School of Law The Williams Institute. Retrieved from http://williamsinstitute.law.ucla.edu/wp-content/uploads/LGBTQImmigrants-Gates-Mar-2013.pdf

Gates, G.J. (2014). *Food insecurity and SNAP (food stamps) participation in LGBTQ communities.* University of California Los Angeles School of Law The Williams Institute. Retrieved from http://williamsinstitute.law.ucla.edu/wp-content/uploads/Food-Insecurity-in-LGBTQ-Communities.pdf

Grant, J.M., Mottet, L.A., & Tanis, J. (2011). *Injustice at every turn: A report of the national transgender discrimination survey.* The National Gay and Lesbian Task Force. Retrieved from http://www.thetaskforce.org/downloads/reports/reports/ntds_full.pdf

Hooks, B. (2000). *Feminist theory: From margin to center.* Chicago, IL: Pluto Press.

Jenness, V., Maxson, C. L., Matsuda, K. N., & Sumner, J. M. (2007). *Violence in California correctional facilities: An empirical examination of sexual assault.* National PREA Resource Center. Retrieved from http://www.prearesourcecenter.org/sites/default/files/library/55-preapresentationpreareportucijennessetal.pdf

Kreheley, J. (2009). *How to close the LGBTQ health disparities gap: Disparities by race and ethnicity.* Center for American Progress.

Mehrotra, G. (2010). Toward a continuum of intersectionality theorizing for feminist social work scholarship. *Affilia, 25*(4), 417–430.

Mogul, J. L., Ritchie, A. J., & Whitlock, K. (2011). *Queer (in)justice: The criminalization of LGBTQ people in the united states.* Boston, MA: Beacon Press.

Redman, L.F. (2010). Outing the invisible poor: Why economic justice and access to health care is an LGBTQ issue. *Georgetown Journal on Poverty Law & Policy, 17,* 451–459.

Transgender Law Center. (2013). *Recommendations for transgender health care.* Retrieved from http://www.transgenderlaw.org/resources/tlchealth.htm

Vaid, U. (2012). *Irresistible revolution: Confronting race, class and the assumptions of LGBTQ politics.* New York, NY: Magnus Books.

THINKING ABOUT THE READING

How does the Queer Liberation Movement (QLM) differ from the mainstream Gay Rights Movement (GRM) in terms of values, agendas, and targets? What are the strengths and shortcomings of these two approaches? Do you think one is more effective than the other? How does the discussion of these two types of social movements compare to the previous readings in this section on Citizens Clearinghouse for Hazardous Wastes and the Black Lives Matter movement? What kind of social movements have you participated in and how do they compare to the ones you have read about in this section?

Credits

Chapter 1

From *The Sociological Imagination, Fourth Anniversary Edition* by C. Wright Mills. Copyright © 2000 by Oxford University Press, Inc. Reprinted by permission of Oxford University Press, USA.

"The My Lai Massacre: A Military Crime of Obedience" in *Crimes of Obedience* by Herbert Kelman and V. Lee Hamilton. Copyright © 1989 by Yale University Press. Reprinted by permission of Yale University Press.

McIntyre, Lisa. "Hernando Washington" in *The Practical Skeptic: Readings in Sociology, Fifth Edition*. Copyright © 2011 by McGraw Hill Higher Education. Reprinted with permission.

Chapter 2

"The (Mis)Education of Monica and Karen" by Laura Hamilton and Elizabeth A. Armstrong. *Contexts*, Fall 2012. Reprinted with permission from The American Sociological Association.

Culture of Fear by Barry Glassner. Copyright © 1999 by Barry Glassner. Reprinted by permission of Basic Books, a member of Perseus Books Group.

"The Social Context of Hoarding Behavior: Building a Foundation for Sociological Study," Megan Shaeffer in *Sociology Compass*, Vol. 11, Issue 4, April 2017. Reprinted with permission from John Wiley & Sons, Inc.

Chapter 3

Reprinted by permission of Waveland Press, Inc. from Earl Babbie, *Observing Ourselves: Essays in Social Research*. Long Grove, IL: Waveland Press, Inc. Copyright © 1986, reissued 1998. All rights reserved.

Jenness, Valerie. 2010. "From Policy to Prisoners to People: A 'Soft Mixed Methods' Approach to Studying Transgender Prisoners." *Journal of Contemporary Ethnography*, 35(5), 517–553. Reprinted with permission from SAGE Publications, Inc.

"Scientific Thinking" from *Critical Thinking: Tools for Evaluating Research* by Peter Nardi. Copyright © 2017 by The Regents of the University of California. Reprinted with permission from the University of California Press.

Chapter 4

From "Body Ritual among the Nacirema" by Horace Miner. *American Anthropologist*, 58(3), June 1956.

On the Fireline: Living and Dying with Wildland Firefighters by Matthew Desmond. Copyright © 2007. Reprinted with permission from The University of Chicago Press.

Hanser, Amy. "From Hippie to Hip-Hop: Street Vending in Vancouver, BC," in *Food Trucks, Cultural Identity, and Social Justice: From Loncheras to Lobsta Love,* edited by Julian Agyeman, Caitlin Matthews, and Hannah Sobel. Copyright © 2017. Massachusetts Institute of Technology, by permission of The MIT Press.

Chapter 5

"Life as a Maid's Daughter: An Exploration of the Everyday Boundaries of Race, Class, and Gender" by Mary Romero in *Feminisms in the Academy,* edited by Mary Romero, Abigail J. Stewart, and Domna Stanton. Copyright © 1995. Used by permission of The University of Michigan Press.

"Tiger Girls on the Soccer Field" by Hilary Levey Friedman. *Contexts,* Fall 2013. Reprinted with permission from The American Sociological Association.

"Working the Code: Girls, Gender and Inner-City Violence," by Nikki Jones in *Australian and New Zealand Journal of Criminology*, Vol. 41, Issue 1, April 2008. Reprinted by permission of the author.

Chapter 6

Excerpts from *The Presentation of Self in Everyday Life* by Erving Goffman. Copyright © 1959 by Erving Goffman. Used by permission of Doubleday, an imprint of the Knopf Doubleday Publishing Group, a division of Random House LLC, and Penguin Books Ltd. All rights reserved.

Stein, Arlene. (2017). "Performing Trans Masculinity Online," in D. M. Newman, J. O'Brien, & M. Robertson (Eds.), *Sociology, Exploring the Architecture of Everyday Life: Readings* (11th ed., pp. 131–134). Thousand Oaks, CA: Sage.

"Public identities: Managing race in public spaces," in *Blue-Chip Black: Race, Class, and Status in the New Black Middle Class* by Karyn R. Lacy. Copyright © 2007 by the University of California Press. Reprinted with permission.

Chapter 7

"The Radical Idea of Marrying for Love" from *Marriage, a History: From Obedience to Intimacy, Or How Love Conquered Marriage* by Stephanie Coontz. Copyright © 2005 by the S. J. Coontz Company. Used by permission of Viking Penguin, a division of Penguin Group (USA), Inc.

"Gay parenthood and the end of paternity as we knew it," in *Unhitched: Love, Marriage, and Family Values from West Hollywood to Western China* by Judith Stacey. Copyright © 2011 by New York University. Reprinted by permission of New York University Press.

"Life & Love Outside the Citizenship Binary: The Lived Experiences of Mixed Status Couples in the United States," in *Living Together, Living Apart: Mixed Status Families and U.S. Immigration Policy*, edited by April Schueths and Jodie Lawston. Copyright © 2015 by the University of Washington Press. Reprinted with permission.

Chapter 8

Snead-Greene, Cheryle D. and Royster, Michael D. "Imprisoned Black Women in Popular Media," in *Caged Women: Incarceration, Representation, & Media,* edited by Shirley A. Jackson and Laurie L. Gordy. Copyright © 2018 Routledge. Reprinted with permission.

"Overcoming the Obscene in Evangelical Sex Websites" from *Christians under Covers: Evangelicals and Sexual Pleasure on the Internet,* by Kelsy Burke. Copyright © 2016 by The Regents of the University of California. Reprinted with permission from the University of California Press.

Gailey, Jeannine A. (2012). "Fat Shame to Fat Pride: Fat Women's Sexual and Dating Experiences." *Fat Studies,* 1, 114–127. Reprinted with permission from Taylor & Francis.

Chapter 9

"Cool Stores, Bad Jobs" by Yasemin Besen-Cassino. *Contexts,* Spring 2013. Reprinted with permission from The American Sociological Association.

"Separate and Unequal Justice" is excerpted from Chapter 1 of *Crook County: Racism and Injustice in America's Largest Criminal Court,* by Gonzalez Van Cleve, Nicole. Copyright © 2017 by Nicole Martorano Van Cleve. All rights reserved. Used with permission of Stanford University Press, www.sup.org.

Gwynne Dyer, "Anybody's Son Will Do" from *War: The New Edition.* Original Copyright © 1985 Gwynne Dyer. Revised Edition Copyright © 2004 Gwynne Dyer. Second Revised Edition Copyright © Gwynne Dyer. Used by permission of The Susijn Agency Ltd., and Vintage Canada, a division of Penguin Random House Canada Limited.

Chapter 10

"Branded with Infamy: Inscriptions of Poverty and Class in America" by Vivyan C. Adair. *Signs,* Vol. 27, Issue 2. Copyright © 2002 The University of Chicago. Reprinted with permission.

Streib, Jessi. (2015). "Marrying across Class Lines." *Contexts,* 14(2), 40–45. Reprinted with permission from The American Sociological Association.

Winddance Twine, France and Alfrey, Lauren. (2017). "Becoming a Geek Girl: Race, Inequality and the Social Geography of Childhood." In D. M. Newman, J. O'Brien, & M. Robertson (Eds.), *Sociology, Exploring the Architecture of Everyday Life: Readings* (11th ed., pp. 240–254). Thousand Oaks, CA: Sage.

Chapter 11

From "Optional Ethnicities" by Mary Waters from *Origins and Destinies: Immigration, Race and Ethnicity in America, First Edition,* edited by Pedraza and Rumbaut. Copyright © 1996 by South-Western, a part of Cengage Learning, Inc. Reproduced by permission. www.cengage.com/permissions

From "Black Women and a New Definition of Womanhood," in *Black Working Wives: Pioneers of the American Family Revolution* by Bart Landry. Copyright © 2000 by the Regents of the University California. Reprinted by permission of the University of California Press.

Miller, Shaeleya. (2018). "Racial Exclusion in Queer Student Organizations." In D. M. Newman, J. O'Brien, & M. Robertson (Eds.), *Sociology, Exploring the Architecture of Everyday Life: Readings* (11th ed., pp. 273–248). Thousand Oaks, CA: Sage.

Chapter 12

Excerpts from *Still a Man's World: Men Who Do "Women's Work"* by Christine L. Williams. Copyright © 1995 by the Regents of the University California. Reprinted by permission of the University of California Press.

Rios, Victor and Sarabia, Rachel. "Synthesized Masculinities: The Mechanics of Manhood among Delinquent Boys" in *Exploring Masculinities: Identity, Inequality, Continuity, and Change.* Edited by C.J. Pascoe and Tristan Bridges. Copyright © 2016 by Oxford University Press. Reprinted by permission of Oxford University Press, USA.

"Parents' Construction of Teen Sexuality: Sex Panics, Contradictory Discourses, and Social Inequality" by Sinikka Elliott in *Symbolic Interaction*, 33(2), 191–212, Spring 2010. Reprinted with permission from John Wiley & Sons.

Chapter 13

"Love and Gold" by Arlie Russell Hochschild from *Global Woman: Nannies, Maids and Sex Workers in the New Economy*, edited by Barbara Ehrrenreich and Arlie Russell Hochschild. Copyright © 2002 by Barbara Ehrenreich and Arlie Russell Hochschild. Reprinted by permission of Henry Holt and Company.

"Embodied Experiences of Older Lesbians" by Kathleen F. Slevin in *Age Matters: Realigning Feminist Thinking*, edited by Toni M. Calasanti and Katheleen F. Slevin. Copyright © 2006 by Taylor & Francis Group, LLC. Reprinted with permission.

Daniels, Jessie. "The Algorithmic Rise of the Alt-Right," *Contexts*, Winter 2018. Reprinted with permission from The American Sociological Association.

Chapter 14

From *Community Activism and Feminist Politics: Organizing across Race, Class, and Gender* by Nancy A. Naples. Copyright © 1998 by Routledge. Reproduced by permission of Routledge/Taylor & Francis Books, Inc.

Rickford, Russell. (2016). "Black Lives Matter: Toward a Modern Practice of Mass Struggle." *New Labor Forum*, 25(1), 34–42. Reprinted with permission from the Murphy Institute and the City University of New York.

Ferber, Abby. (2018). "Racism in America: To Be Continued . . ." In D. M. Newman, J. O'Brien, & M. Robertson (Eds.), *Sociology, Exploring the Architecture of Everyday Life: Readings* (11th ed., pp. 361–364). Thousand Oaks, CA: Sage.

DeFilippis, Joseph Nicholas. (2018). "An Intersectional Queer Liberation Movement for 'Trickle-Up' Social Justice." In D. M. Newman, J. O'Brien, & M. Robertson (Eds.), *Sociology, Exploring the Architecture of Everyday Life: Readings* (11th ed., pp. 365–377). Thousand Oaks, CA: Sage.